BUSINESS MATH

PRACTICAL APPLICATIONS

Cheryl Cleaves
Margie Hobbs
Paul Dudenhefer

State Technical Institute of Memphis

PRENTICE HALL CAREER & TECHNOLOGY
Englewood Cliffs, New Jersey   07632

Library of Congress Cataloging-in-Publication Data

CLEAVES, CHERYL S.,
 Business math : practical applications / Cheryl Cleaves, Margie
Hobbs, Paul Dudenhefer. — 3rd ed.
  p.   cm.
 Includes index.
 ISBN 0-13-105735-9
 1. Business mathematics.   I. Hobbs, Margie J.,
 II. Dudenhefer, Paul.   III. Title
 HF5691.C53 1993b   92-24686
 650′.01′513—dc20   CIP

Editorial/production supervision: *Barbara Marttine*
Interior design and page layout: *Andy Zutis*
Cover design: *Marianne Frasco*
Photo research: *Page Poore and Tobi Zausner*
Photo editor: *Lori Morris-Nantz*
Prepress buyer: *Ilene Levy*
Manufacturing buyer: *Ed O'Dougherty*
Acquisitions editor: *Frank Burrows*
Supplements editor: *Cindy Harford*
Editorial assistant: *Scott Montgomery*
Development editor: *Linda Bedell*

Cover photograph: Reginald Wickham

Chapter opening photograph credits:

Chapter 1	Reginald Wickham	Chapter 11	Diebold
Chapter 2	Michael Salas/The Image Bank	Chapter 12	Courtesy of Steelcase Inc.
Chapter 3	Richard Hutchings/Photo Researchers	Chapter 13	Laima Druskis
Chapter 4	Laima Druskis	Chapter 14	Brett Froomer/The Image Bank
Chapter 5	Reginald Wickham	Chapter 15	Reginald Wickham
Chapter 6	Reginald Wickham	Chapter 16	Reginald Wickham
Chapter 9	Ken Karp	Chapter 17	Reginald Wickham
Chapter 10	Murray Alcosser/The Image Bank	Chapter 18	Anne Rippy/The Image Bank

All material from USA TODAY
Reprinted with permission, copyright 1991 and 1992, USA TODAY.

Printed in the United States of America
10 9 8 7 6 5 4 3

ISBN   0-13-105735-9

Prentice-Hall International (UK) Limited, *London*
Prentice-Hall of Australia Pty. Limited, *Sydney*
Prentice-Hall Canada, Inc., *Toronto*
Prentice-Hall Hispanoamericana, S.A., *Mexico*
Prentice-Hall of India Private Limited, *New Delhi*
Prentice-Hall of Japan, Inc., *Tokyo*
Simon & Schuster Asia Pte. Ltd., *Singapore*
Editora Prentice-Hall do Brasil, Ltda., *Rio de Janeiro*

PREFACE

To the Student

In almost any career you pursue, the business math you learn in this book will serve you well and help you get ahead. Anyone can learn to deal with a certain amount of math, even those who have avoided the formal study of mathematics. We have given much thought to the best way to teach business math. If you will follow the course of the book as we have laid it out, making use of the special features we have put in the text, you will get the most out of this book and out of this course. The following features are meant to help you learn business math procedures.

LEARNING OBJECTIVES. Each section begins with a statement of learning objectives, which lay out for you what you should look for and learn in that section. If you read and think about these before you begin the section, you will know what to look for as you go through the section.

KEY TERMS DEFINED. Part of learning business math is learning the basic vocabulary of business. This vocabulary is introduced in the text, and in the margin the terms are repeated with definitions. Each key term appears in **boldface** in a second color in the index. The terms in the margin offer you a good opportunity to review for a test.

SELF-CHECKS. These short quizzes appear at the end of each section throughout the chapter; they are a signal to you to check yourself to make sure that you understand what you have just read or worked out before you go on to the next topic. The solutions are at the end of each chapter, so you can get immediate feedback on whether you have understood the material.

STEP-BY-STEP BOXES. These boxes appear throughout the text to help to introduce a new procedure. To make these procedures as clear as possible, we break them down for you into step-by-step instructions. Each box is then followed by an example.

CALCULATOR SOLUTION BOXES. The use of a calculator is basic in all types of math, and especially business math. In most chapters we have a calculator solution box that deals with a key procedure from that chapter. The box shows how to analyze the procedure and set up a problem for a calculator solution; it then shows the keystrokes involved in the solution.

TIPS AND TRAPS BOXES. These boxes point up helpful hints or pitfalls involved in business math procedures. Often, looking at the wrong and right way of doing something can save you from a costly or time-consuming error down the line. We do not always have to learn from our own mistakes—sometimes we can learn from other people's experience and not make the same mistakes ourselves.

REAL-WORLD APPLICATION BOXES. Just when you were wondering what all this has to do with the real world, along comes a Real-World Application box to tell you! These boxes present a problem from the business world and show how the procedures learned in the chapter are used to solve the problem. Examples include banking, apartment rental, excise taxes and the hotel business, buying property and paying taxes on it, figuring tips for food service, and many more. The boxes also contain extra exercises if you want to pursue the subject further and try your skills.

SUMMARY CHART. Each chapter ends with a handy summary in the form of a chart. This chart summarizes the step-by-step boxes from that chapter, with new examples. The chart also contains the page numbers where each topic is covered in the chapter, so you can go back and check it if you have questions. This chart is an excellent tool to use to review a chapter.

END OF CHAPTER EXERCISES. These exercises review all the procedures and topics covered in the chapter. These exercises may be assigned by your instructor as homework, or you may want to work them on your own for extra practice. The answers to odd-numbered exercises are at the end of the book.

TRIAL TEST. Take this to test yourself before you face the real one in class. Again, answers to odd-numbered exercises appear at the end of the book; your professor has the worked-out solutions to the entire test.

BUSINESS MATH IN ACTION. These problems incorporate and are based on USA TODAY SNAPSHOTS, the graphics used on a daily basis on the first page of every section of USA TODAY. The graphics, which display statistical information of interest to business and consumers, demonstrate how widespread math applications are in business and the world around you. In addition to providing a "real world" problem solving opportunity, they are intended to increase your awareness of the relevance of mathematics to your everyday life and to demonstrate the ways in which you will regularly use the math concepts you are learning.

If you use all the features in this book, you will be learning business math in a most efficient and effective way. But we also have some supplements besides the text that will help you even more.

CALCULATOR. The use of a calculator is basic in all types of math, especially business math. Instructions for using a calculator are on the back inside cover of your book. Calculator solutions to examples appear throughout the book.

STUDENT SOLUTIONS MANUAL WITH REVIEW PROBLEMS. This manual can be purchased at your bookstore. It will give you extra "learning insurance" to help you master this course. The manual contains worked-out solutions to the odd-numbered exercises in the section reviews, and a trial test from each chapter of the text. (Answers to these exercises appear in the back of your text, but here in the manual you can study the full worked-out solutions and a complete glossary.)

How to Study Business Math. Your professor has free copies of this booklet, which goes over the various learning techniques you can use in class and in preparation for class to make learning business math much more efficient.

Student Tutorial Software. This unique learning program helps you to master business math concepts. It includes pretests that allow you to solve problems and compare their answers with the correct solution. Upon completion of the pretest, you can enter a problem solution module for additional practice or you can take another test. All problems in the problem solution module have detailed, step-by-step solutions available. The program is user friendly and designed for you to use independently for self-review of any unit.

Business Math Quick Reference Tables. Annual percentage rate, simple interest, compound interest, percent value tables and more—all bound into a free-standing manual to facilitate your homework preparation and in-class testing. Free in quantity to adopters.

Stock Market and Investment Practice Set. This practice set gives basic information on how to make decisions about investing money. As part of the stocks and bonds sections, you pick stocks and bonds to "buy" and follow their progress over a month, at which point you "sell" them and calculate the amount of profit or loss.

To the Instructor

We have tried to provide a text that your students will enjoy using and that you will find easy and helpful to teach from. In addition to the text, we have provided a complete supplements package to make your teaching life easier.

The most important supplement is the Annotated Instructor's Edition, which contains the complete student text with worked-out solutions to all exercises as well as teaching aids in the margins and lecture notes with points to stress in the front of the book. The rest of the supplements are described in full in the Annotated Instructor's Edition; for your convenience a short list is given here:

• **Annotated Instructor's Edition** • Test Item File and Computerized Test Item File • Testing Resource Library • Transparency Acetates • Video Tapes • Classroom Presentation Software • Lotus 1-2-3®/Twin® Templates for Selected Exercises • Solutions to all Problems on Disk (ASCII format) • Lecture Outlines on Disk with Accompanying Hard Copy • Student Solutions Manual with Review Problems • Student Tutorial Software • How to Study Math Booklet • Stock Market and Investment Practice Set • Business Math Quick Reference Tables

Acknowledgments

Comments and suggestions from a broad cross-section of business math instructors are always crucial in a project of this size, and we thank our reviewers for their interest and help. They were invaluable in pointing out any inaccuracies or errors that were overlooked and in making valuable suggestions in various stages of the manuscript.

Camille Anthony, Bay State Junior College

Bernadette Antkoviak, Harrisburg Area Community College

Kanta K. Idnani, Phillips College

Barbara Jackson, Skagit Valley College

Frederick Janke, Tompkins-Cortland Community College

Fay Armstrong, Houston Community
College
Corine Baker, S. Seattle Community
College
Jerome Baness, Illinois Valley
Community College
Rex Bishop, Charles County
Community College
Elizabeth Bliss, Trident Technical
College
Marg Y. Blyth, Detroit College of
Business
James Carey, Onondaga Community
College
Charles Cheetham, County College of
Morris
Janet Ciccarelli, Herkimer County
Community College
Dick Clark, Portland Community
College
Rita Cross, Northland Community
College
John Cuniffe, Northland Pioneer
College
James F. Dowis, Des Moines Area
Community College
Norm Dreisen, Essex Community
College
William L. Drezdzon, Oakton
Community College
Nell Edmundson, Miami Dade
Community College
Margaret Ferguson, Houston
Community College
Clark Ford, Middle Tennessee State
University
Joseph F. Galio, Cuyahoga Community
College District
Frank Goulard, Portland Community
College
Cecil Green, Riverside Community
College
Stephen Griffin, Tarrant County Junior
College
Jackie Hedgpeth, Antelope Valley
College
Joseph Hinsburg, Pima County
Community College

John Johnson, Seattle Central
Community College
Carolyn Karnes, Macomb Community
College
Kenneth Ketelhohn, Milwaukee Area
Technical College
Ed Laughbaum, Columbus State
Community College
S. Lee, Heald Business College
Nolan Lickey, Westark Community
College
Jane Loprest, Bucks County
Community College
D. Maas, Lansing Community College
Lynn Mack, Piedmont Technical
College
Robert Malena, Community College of
Allegheny County, South Campus
Paul Martin, Aims Community College
Roberta Miller, Indian River
Community College
Linda Mogren, DeKalb Technical
Institute
Mary Pretti, State Technical Institute
at Memphis
Dave Randall, Oakland Community
College
Joan Ryan, Lane Community College
Lona P. Scala, Roberts-Walsh Business
School
Gerald W. Shields, Austin Community
College
Beverly Sisk, Gwinnett Technical
Institute
Debiruth Stanford, DeVry Institute of
Technology
Herbert Stein, Merritt College
Alice Steljes, Illinois Valley Community
College
Louise Stevens, Golden West College
Kitty Tabers, Oakton Community
College
Keith Wilson, Oklahoma City
Community College
Chuck Wiseman, Oakland Community
College

We also want to thank Roberta Lewis, who contributed to the Stocks
and Bonds chapter of the text; Lynn Mack, who helped write the Annotated
Instructor's Edition margin notes; and Shirley Lawrence, and Diane L.
Powell who contributed Real World Application boxes and wrote the lecture
outlines for the Annotated Instructor's Edition.

Accuracy is always a concern in mathematics, and we were fortunate to
have the help of several colleagues who worked with us to produce the level
of accuracy needed in a college textbook. The reviewers mentioned were of
course our first source of corrections and queries. We also had the help
of Elizabeth Bliss of Trident Technical College, Deanne Ingram, and James
Page of ATI Training Center, Dallas, Texas, who checked every example,
exercise, trial test, and work-out solution in the text, the Student Solutions
Manual, and the Annotated Instructor's Edition.

The manuscripts of the text and the Test Item File were also class
tested by Kathleen Murphrey of San Antonio College and Mike Armstrong of

Highline Community College so that any remaining errors found in the class setting could be corrected.

The production of a book would not come together without the help and input of many individuals. Although the list of persons who worked on this edition is extensive, we would like to single out a few key persons. We acknowledge first Barbara Marttine, the production editor, who did an excellent job of keeping us on schedule and ensuring that the text would meet her high standards; and acquisitions editors Jim Boyd, who guided this edition through the months of its preparations, and Frank Burrows, who took over the project and saw it through to its final publication. We thank Linda Beddell, the developmental editor, for her contributions; William Thomas, the copy editor, in helping us maintain consistency; Robert A. Brechner of Miami Dade Community College who wrote Chapter 10, Charles Chatham of County College at Morris who provided the solutions for that chapter, and John E. Falls and Daniel Kraska who wrote the Challenge Problems. We also thank Cindy Harford, the supplements editor; Andy Zutis, who provided the book design and the page layout; Marianne Frasco, cover director; and Scott Montgomery, editorial assistant.

We appreciate the contribution of those who provided technical information on business procedures and forms. We also acknowledge the reviewers and users of past editions, who made comments and sugggestions for improvement and helped make this book successful. We also thank Betty Wilson and John Edmonds for their assistance.

Finally, we express our deepest gratitude to our families: Charles Cleaves; Allen and Holly Hobbs; Gaynell, Paul, Paulette, David, and Diane Dudenhefer. Their support and encouragement were vital to the completion of this project.

Cheryl Cleaves
Margie Hobbs
Paul Dudenhefer

Basic Calculations

Much of our world—especially the business part of our world—runs on numbers and calculations. We go to the store that advertises the sale, take out a CD at the bank with the highest interest rates, apply for mortgages at the bank with the best terms, and grumble about lower take-home pay when social security withholding goes up.

This course will prepare you to enter the business world with the mathematical survival tools needed to blaze a successful career path. The chapters on business topics build on your knowledge of basic mathematics, so it is important to begin the course with a review of the basic mathematics skills that you will need in the chapters to come.

In most businesses, arithmetic computations are done on a calculator or computer. Even so, every businessperson needs a thorough understanding of basic mathematics in order to make the best use of a calculator. *A machine will only do what you tell it to do. Pressing a wrong key or performing the wrong operations on a calculator will result in a rapid but incorrect answer.* If you understand the mathematics and know how to make reasonable estimates, you can catch and correct these errors.

Calculating With Whole Numbers

LEARNING OBJECTIVES

1. Read and round whole numbers.
2. Add and subtract whole numbers.
3. Multiply and divide whole numbers.

We begin our review with *whole numbers* (numbers without fractions or decimals). Most business calculations involving whole numbers involve one or more of four basic *mathematical operations:* addition, subtraction, multiplication, and division.

Reading Whole Numbers

place-value system: a system in which a digit has a value according to its place, or position, in a number.

Reading numbers is easier when you understand the **place-value system** that is part of our decimal number system. The chart in Figure 1-1 shows that system applied to the number 381,345,287,369,021.

To apply this chart to any number, just follow the steps in the following Step-by-Step box. (You'll find these boxes, and examples illustrating their use, throughout this text.)

STEP BY STEP

Reading a Whole Number

Step 1. Beginning at the right end of the number, use commas to separate the number into groups of 3 digits.

Step 2. Name the groups (*units, thousands, millions,* and so on).

Step 3. Starting at the left end of the number, read the numerals in each group and indicate the group name.
   a. If a group has all zeros, it does not have to be read.
   b. The group name *units* does not have to be read.
   c. Do *not* use the word "and" at any time.

Trillions			Billions			Millions			Thousands			Units		
Hundred trillions (100,000,000,000,000)	Ten trillions (10,000,000,000,000)	Trillions (1,000,000,000,000)	Hundred billions (100,000,000,000)	Ten billions (10,000,000,000)	Billions (1,000,000,000)	Hundred millions (100,000,000)	Ten millions (10,000,000)	Millions (1,000,000)	Hundred thousands (100,000)	Ten thousands (10,000)	Thousands (1,000)	Hundreds (100)	Tens (10)	Ones (1)
3	8	1	3	4	5	2	8	7	3	6	9	0	2	1

Figure 1-1   Place-Value Chart for Whole Numbers

EXAMPLE 1

Read the number 3007047203.

3,007,047,203	Start at the right end of the number and use commas to separate the number into groups of 3 digits.
billions, millions, thousands, units	Name the groups from left to right.
three billion, seven million, forty-seven thousand, two hundred three.	Read the numbers and the name for each group of digits.

Rounding Numbers

Very specific numbers are not always necessary or desirable. For example, the board of directors does not want to know to a penny what was spent on office supplies (though the accounting staff should know). Less detailed **rounded** numbers are the solution. In general, you should round a number to a specified place or to the first digit from the left in a number, following these rules:

round, rounding: a way to find an estimated or approximate answer.

STEP BY STEP

Rounding a Whole Number to a Specified Place or Digit

Step 1. Find the digit in the place to which you are rounding.

Step 2. Look at the next digit to the right.

　　a. If this digit is less than 5, replace it and any other digits to the right with zeros.

　　b. If this digit is 5 or more, add 1 to the digit in the place to which you are rounding, and replace all digits to the right of the place to which you are rounding with zeros.

EXAMPLE 2

Round 2,748 to the nearest hundred and to the first digit.

Rounding to the nearest hundred

2,748	The digit in the hundreds place is 7.
2,748	The digit to the right of 7 is 4, so step 2a applies.
2,700	Replace all digits to the right of the 7 with zeros.

Rounding to the first digit

2,748	The digit to the right of the first digit is 7, so step 2b applies.
3,000	Add 1 to 2 and replace all digits to the right of the 3 with zeros.

How much is a ton of money?
A ton of $1 bills: $980,000
A ton of half-dollars: $36,288
A ton of dimes: $36,288
A ton of pennies: $2,917

Source: USA TODAY research, Treasury Dept.
By Aaron Hightower, USA TODAY

addends: numbers being added.

sum, or **total:** answer or result in addition.

In an addition problem, the numbers being added are called **addends.** The answer, or result of the addition, is called the **sum,** or **total.**

$$
\begin{array}{r}
2 \\
3 \\
+\ 4 \\
\hline
9
\end{array}
$$

2, 3, +4 ← addends

9 ← sum or total

STEP BY STEP

To Add Whole Numbers

Step 1. Arrange the numbers in columns.

Step 2. Begin by finding the sum of the digits in the units column, and write the sum directly below the units column.

Step 3. If the sum is more than 9, record the units digit and *carry* the tens digit to the next column to the left.

Step 4. Continue this process until you have added all columns.

EXAMPLE 3

Add 452 + 83 + 3,256.

$$
\begin{array}{r}
{\scriptstyle 11} \\
452 \\
83 \\
3,256 \\
\hline
3,791
\end{array}
$$

You can check your total by adding the numbers twice, once from the top of the list to the bottom and once from the bottom to the top.

nonzero digit: a digit that is not zero.

In many situations, it is helpful to estimate the answer to a problem *before* finding the exact answer if only so you can tell when you've erred in using your calculator.

A quick and often-used way to estimate a sum is to round each addend to **one nonzero digit** and add the rounded addends. In the previous example, convert 452 to 500, 83 to 100, 3,256 to 3,000 and the answer should be approximately 3,600. You can use the same approch of rounding to estimate in other mathematical operations.

EXAMPLE 4

$$
\begin{array}{r}
{\scriptstyle 22} \\
885 \\
569 \\
343 \\
231 \\
+\ 562 \\
\hline
2,590
\end{array}
\quad
\begin{array}{l}
\text{rounds to} \\
\text{rounds to} \\
\text{rounds to} \\
\text{rounds to} \\
\text{rounds to}
\end{array}
\quad
\begin{array}{r}
900 \\
600 \\
300 \\
200 \\
+\ 600 \\
\hline
2,600
\end{array}
$$

Note that in this case, the total, 2,590, rounds to 2,600.

Subtracting Whole Numbers

In a subtraction problem, the number being subtracted (the amount being taken away) is called the **subtrahend.** The number from which the subtrahend is being taken (the original amount) is the **minuend.** The answer or

4

result (the amount of the original quantity that remains) is called the **difference.**

STEP BY STEP

To Subtract Whole Numbers

Step 1. Arrange the numbers in columns.

Step 2. Begin by finding the difference of the digits in the units column and write the difference directly below the units column.

Step 3. If the digit in the minuend is less than the digit in the subtrahend, *borrow* "1," which represents a group of 10, from the digit to the left and add ten to the units digit.

Step 4. Continue this process until you have subtracted all columns.

subtrahend: the amount being subtracted.

minuend: the original amount from which something is subtracted.

difference: the answer or result of subtraction.

EXAMPLE 5

Subtract 27 from 64.

$$
\begin{array}{r}
64 \\
-\ 27 \\
\end{array}
$$

Arrange the numbers so that the digits in the ones place line up.

$$
\begin{array}{r}
{}^{5\ 14} \\
6\!\!\!/\,4\!\!\!/ \\
-\ 27 \\
\hline
37 \\
\end{array}
$$

7 is larger than 4, so you must borrow one 10 from the tens place (thus 6 becomes 5), and add 10 ones to the ones place. Subtract ones; then subtract tens.

Check:

$$
\begin{array}{r}
37 \\
+\ 27 \\
\hline
64 \\
\end{array}
$$

The sum of the subtrahend and difference equals the minuend. The difference is correct.

Multiplying Whole Numbers

Multiplication and division work together much the same way that addition and subtraction do. Multiplication gives us a way of understanding how the parts fit together to make a whole and division explains how the whole can be broken up or divided into parts. Multiplication and division are also the bases of many of the important calculations made in the business world.

A multiplication problem has three elements. The **multiplicand** is the number being multiplied. The **multiplier** is the number used to multiply. The **product** is the result of multiplying the multiplicand by the multiplier.

To perform multiplication, arrange the multiplicand above the multiplier and follow these rules.

multiplicand: the number that is being multiplied; the first number in a multiplication problem.

multiplier: the number that is used to multiply by; the second number in a multiplication problem.

product: the answer, or result, in multiplication.

STEP BY STEP

Multiplying Whole Numbers by Two or More Digits

Step 1. Write the problem so that the ones, tens, hundreds, and all following places of the multiplicand and multiplier line up.

Step 2. Write the first number of each partial product directly below the corresponding number in the multiplier.

EXAMPLE 6

```
        127    ←—— multiplicand
  ×      53    ←—— multiplier
        381    ←—— first partial product    3 × 127 = 381
      6 35     ←—— second partial product   5 × 127 = 635
      6,731    ←—— product
```

The 1 in 381 lines up with the 3 in 53.

The 5 in 635 lines up with the 5 in 53.

TIPS & TRAPS

When you multiply numbers that contain two or more digits, it is crucial to *place the partial products* properly. A common mistake in multiplying is to forget to indent the partial products. *Always* write the digit on the right of each partial product directly below the corresponding digit in the multiplier.

```
        265                                              265
  ×      23                                        ×      23
        795    We get the second partial product, 530, by    795
        530    multiplying 2 × 265. Therefore, the 0 in     5 30
      1,325    530 should be directly below the 2 in 23.     6,095
  WRONG                                                 CORRECT
```

You can check the product by multiplying the numbers twice or by multiplying the numbers in reverse order.

Zeros, used correctly, are a part of some of the most helpful shortcuts in multiplying and dividing numbers. Used incorrectly, they can give you your worst headaches. You must pay careful attention to the position of zeros in partial products. When one of the numbers being multiplied is 10, 100, or 1,000, you can use a shortcut to find the product.

STEP BY STEP

Multiplying When a Number Ends in Zero

Step 1. Separate the zeros at the end of each number.

Step 2. Multiply the nonzero numbers.

Step 3. Attach to the end of the product the total number of zeros separated out in step 1.

EXAMPLE 7

Multiply 20,700 by 860.

```
      207 | 00      Three zeros are        Separate 3 zeros at the end of
  ×    86 | 0       separated here.        20,700 and 860. Line up the first
                                           nonzero numbers to the left of the
    1 242 |                                zeros. Find the product of the
   16 56  |                                nonzero numbers.
   17,802 | 000     Three zeros are        Reattach the zeros that were sepa-
                    reattached here.       rated in the first step.
```

20,700 × 860 = 17,802,000

If the multiplier has a zero in the middle (such as 102, 507, or 1,306, for example), you can use another shortcut to multiplication.

Instead of writing a partial product consisting only of zeros, write a partial product of zero directly below the zero in the multiplier and then write the digit on the right of the next partial product on the same line, directly below the appropriate digit in the multiplier.

EXAMPLE 8

Multiply 144 by 203.

$$
\begin{array}{r}
144 \\
\times\ 203 \\
\hline
432 \\
28\ 80 \\
\hline
29{,}232
\end{array}
$$

The partial product 0 lines up with the 0 in 203.
The 8 in the partial product of 2×144 lines up with the 2 of 203.

Dividing Whole Numbers

A division problem consists of a **dividend** (the number being divided), a **divisor** (the number doing the dividing), and a **quotient** (the number of times the divisor goes into the dividend). (If a divisor does not divide a dividend into equal parts, the answer will include both a quotient and a **remainder**.) To perform division, follow these rules:

dividend: number being divided.

divisor: number doing the dividing.

quotient: the answer, or result, of division.

remainder: the amount left over if division does not come out even.

STEP BY STEP

Dividing Whole Numbers

Step 1. Divide the divisor into the first group of digits in the dividend that is larger than or equal to the divisor and place the partial quotient over the last digit in that group.

Step 2. Multiply the partial quotient by the divisor and subtract.

Step 3. Make sure the difference is smaller than the divisor before continuing.

Step 4. Bring down the next digit.

Step 5. Repeat steps 1 through 4 until all digits of the dividend have been used.

EXAMPLE 9

Find the quotient of 78 divided by 5. Check the answer.

$$
\begin{array}{r}
15\ \text{R}3 \\
5\overline{)78} \\
\underline{5} \\
28 \\
\underline{25} \\
3
\end{array}
$$

When you check the answer to a division problem with a remainder, you multiply the divisor times the quotient and then add the remainder. The dividend should equal the divisor times the quotient plus the remainder.

Check:

$$
\begin{array}{rr}
15 & 75 \\
\times\ 5 & +\ 3 \\
\hline
75 & 78
\end{array}
$$

The answer is correct.

Be very careful in lining up the numbers in a division problem and in entering zeros in the quotient.

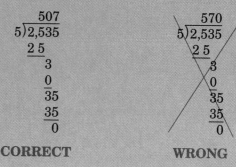

CORRECT   WRONG

You will find Self-Check questions throughout each chapter. These questions give you a chance to review the material you have just read and see how well you have understood the chapter so far. After you have done the exercises, check your answers against the solutions provided at the end of the chapter.

  Self-Check 1.1

1. Read the number 4,204,049,201.

2. Round 3,645 to the nearest hundred, and round 3,645 to the first digit.

3. Add the following numbers and check the sum.

$$\begin{array}{r} 328 \\ 583 \\ + \ 726 \end{array}$$

4. Subtract 36 from 55 and check your answer.

5. Multiply 6,823 by 634.

6. Multiply 730 by 60.

7. Multiply 904 by 24.

8. Divide 96 by 6.

 1.2

Calculating with Fractions

LEARNING OBJECTIVES

1. Identify types of fractions and make equivalent fractions.
2. Add and subtract fractions and mixed numbers.
3. Multiply and divide fractions and mixed numbers.

Fractions, in their many forms, are used in the business world every day: "All Winter Coats $\frac{1}{3}$ Off!" "Four Out of Five Doctors Recommend. . . ." "$\frac{1}{3}$ the Calories of Butter." "Half-Price Sale Today!" In this section we will explore different types of fractions and how to add, subtract, multiply and divide them. Let's first review the meanings of some important terms before we begin to work with fractions.

Numerator: The top term in a fraction. This is the *dividend,* or number *being divided.*

Denominator: The bottom term in a fraction. This is the *divisor,* or the number that *divides into* the numerator.

Fraction line: The horizontal line separating the numerator and denominator; $\frac{2}{4}$ means $2 \div 4$.

$$2 \longleftarrow \text{numerator}$$
$$- \longleftarrow \text{fraction line}$$
$$4 \longleftarrow \text{denominator}$$

Proper fraction: A fraction with numerator smaller than its denominator. A proper fraction has a value less than 1.

$$\frac{3}{4}, \quad \frac{1}{2}, \quad \frac{9}{10}, \quad \frac{4}{7}$$

Improper fraction: A fraction with numerator equal to or greater than its denominator. An improper fraction has a value equal to or greater than 1.

$$\frac{7}{7}, \quad \frac{8}{3}, \quad \frac{10}{2}, \quad \frac{15}{13}$$

Mixed number: A number composed of both a whole number and a fraction.

$$3\frac{7}{8}, \quad 1\frac{2}{5}$$

Converting Fractions

Since fractions have so many different forms, it is often necessary to convert or change a fraction to a different type of fraction before you can solve a problem.

STEP BY STEP

Changing Improper Fractions to Whole or Mixed Numbers

Step 1. Divide the numerator of the improper fraction by the denominator.

Step 2. a. If there is no remainder, the quotient is the *whole number* equivalent of the improper fraction.

b. If there is a remainder, the improper fraction is a mixed number. The fraction in the mixed number is the remainder of the division written over the original denominator.

EXAMPLE 10

Change $\frac{139}{8}$ to a whole or mixed number.

$$\begin{array}{r} 17 \text{ R3, or } 17\frac{3}{8} \\ 8\overline{)139} \\ \underline{8} \\ 59 \\ \underline{56} \\ 3 \end{array}$$

Divide 139 by 8. The quotient is 17 R3, which equals $17\frac{3}{8}$.

$$\frac{139}{8} = 17\frac{3}{8}$$

---

numerator: the top term of a fraction or the number being divided.

denominator: the bottom term of a fraction, or the number that divides into the numerator.

fraction line: the horizontal line separating the numerator and denominator of a fraction; the division symbol.

proper fraction: a fraction with a numerator smaller than its denominator.

improper fraction: a fraction with a numerator equal to or larger than its denominator.

mixed number: a number composed of both a whole number and a fraction.

Sometimes you need to convert a mixed number to an improper fraction. The denominator of the improper fraction is always the same as the denominator of the fractional part of the mixed number.

STEP BY STEP

Changing Mixed Numbers to Improper Fractions

Step 1. Multiply the denominator by the whole number.

Step 2. Add the result from step 1 to the numerator.

Step 3. Write the result from step 2 over the original denominator.

EXAMPLE 11

Change $2\frac{3}{4}$ to an improper fraction.

$$2\frac{3}{4} = \frac{(4 \times 2) + 3}{4} = \frac{11}{4}$$

Reducing Fractions to Lowest Terms

Sometimes the objective of converting a fraction is to express it "in its lowest terms." If you multiply or divide both the numerator and the denominator of a fraction by the same number, the value of the fraction remains the same. A fraction is said to be in lowest terms when there is no number (other than 1) that can divide evenly into both the numerator and the denominator.

STEP BY STEP

Reducing a Fraction to Lowest Terms

Step 1. Inspect the numerator and denominator to find any whole number that can divide evenly into both numbers.

Step 2. Divide both the numerator and denominator by that number, and inspect the new fraction to find any other number that can divide evenly into both parts of the fraction.

Step 3. Repeat steps 1 and 2 until there are no more numbers that will divide evenly into both numerator and denominator.

EXAMPLE 12

Reduce $\frac{30}{36}$ to lowest terms.

$$\frac{30}{36} = \frac{30 \div 2}{36 \div 2} = \frac{15}{18}$$

Both the numerator and denominator can be divided evenly by 2.

$$\frac{15}{18} = \frac{15 \div 3}{18 \div 3} = \frac{5}{6}$$

Both the numerator and denominator of the new fraction can be divided evenly by 3.

$$\frac{30}{36} = \frac{5}{6}$$

No more numbers can divide evenly into both the numerator and denominator. The fraction is now in lowest terms.

The fastest way to reduce a fraction to lowest terms is to divide the numerator and denominator by the **greatest common divisor (GCD)**, which is the greatest number that divides evenly into both parts of a fraction. Let's look at a helpful shortcut to finding the GCD.

greatest common divisor (GCD): the greatest or largest number that will divide into a group of two or more numbers.

STEP BY STEP

A Shortcut for Finding the Greatest Common Divisor of Two Numbers

Step 1. Divide the larger number by the smaller number.

Step 2. Divide the remainder from step 1 into the divisor from step 1.

Step 3. Divide the remainder from step 2 into the divisor from step 2.

Step 4. Continue this division process until the division has no remainder. The divisor that produced no remainder is the greatest common divisor.

EXAMPLE 13

Use the GCD shortcut to write $\frac{168}{198}$ in lowest terms.

$$168\overline{)198} \quad \text{1 R30}$$

Divide the larger number by the smaller number.

$$30\overline{)168} \quad \text{5 R18}$$

Divide the original divisor by the remainder of the first division.

$$18\overline{)30} \quad \text{1 R12}$$

Divide the divisor of each previous division by the remainder of that division.

$$12\overline{)18} \quad \text{1 R6}$$

$$6\overline{)12} \quad \text{2}$$

The divisor that does not yield a remainder is the greatest common divisor.

$$\frac{168}{198} = \frac{168 \div 6}{198 \div 6} = \frac{28}{33}$$

Divide the numerator and denominator by the GCD to reduce the fraction to lowest terms.

Rewriting Fractions in Higher Terms

Just as you can reduce a fraction to lowest terms by dividing the numerator and denominator by the same number, you rewrite a fraction in *higher* terms by *multiplying* the numerator and denominator by the same number. This is important in addition and subtraction of fractions, as you shall see later in this chapter. You write a fraction as a new fraction with a greater denominator by multiplying both the numerator and denominator by the number that gives the new denominator.

STEP BY STEP

Changing a Fraction to a New Fraction with a Greater Denominator

Step 1. Divide the *new* denominator by the *old* denominator. The result of this division tells you by what number you must multiply the old denominator to get the new denominator.

Step 2. Multiply *both* the numerator and denominator by the number you found in Step 1. This gives you the new fraction.

EXAMPLE 14

Rewrite $\dfrac{5}{8}$ as a fraction with a denominator of 72.

$\dfrac{5}{8} = \dfrac{?}{72}$ 　　State the problem clearly.

$8)\overline{72}$ with quotient 9 　　Divide the new denominator (72) by the old denominator (8) to find the number by which the numerator and denominator must be multiplied. That number is 9.

$\dfrac{5}{8} = \dfrac{5 \times 9}{8 \times 9} = \dfrac{45}{72}$ 　　Multiply the numerator and denominator by 9 to get the new fraction with a denominator of 72.

Adding Fractions

If you are adding several fractions with the same denominator, you add the numerators to find the numerator of the sum and then write that number over the original denominator. You then reduce the sum to lowest terms. Then convert improper fractions to whole or mixed numbers.

EXAMPLE 15

Find the sum of $\dfrac{1}{4} + \dfrac{3}{4} + \dfrac{4}{4}$.

$\dfrac{1}{4} + \dfrac{3}{4} + \dfrac{4}{4} = \dfrac{8}{4}$ 　　The sum of the numerators is the numerator of the sum. The original denominator is the denominator of the sum.

$\dfrac{8}{4} = 2$ 　　Convert the improper fraction to a whole number.

Before you can add fractions with different denominators, however, you should find their **least common denominator (LCD)**—the smallest number that can be divided evenly by each original denominator.

least common denominator (LCD): the least or smallest number into which each of two or more denominators divides evenly.

STEP BY STEP

Finding the Least Common Denominator of Two or More Fractions

Step 1. Write the denominators in a horizontal row and divide each one by the smallest prime number that can divide evenly into any of the numbers. A **prime number** is a whole number larger than 1 that is divisible only by itself and 1. The first ten prime numbers are 2, 3, 5, 7, 11, 13, 17, 19, 23, and 29.

Step 2. Write a new row of numbers using the quotients of the division in step 1 and bringing down any numbers that are not divisible by the first prime number.

Step 3. Continue this process until the only number in the row is 1.

Step 4. Multiply all the prime numbers along the left side to find the lowest common denominator.

prime number: a wh... ber larger than 1 that ble only by itself and ...

EXAMPLE 16

Find the least common denominator of $\frac{5}{6}$, $\frac{5}{8}$, and $\frac{1}{12}$.

$$
\begin{array}{r|rrr}
2 & 6 & 8 & 12 \\
2 & 3 & 4 & 6 \\
2 & 3 & 2 & 3 \\
3 & 3 & 1 & 3 \\
\hline
 & 1 & 1 & 1
\end{array}
$$

Find the LCD: Write the denominators in a row and divide by 2, which is the smallest prime number.

Repeat the division with 2. 2 does not divide evenly into 3, so we bring the 3 down to the next line.

$2 \times 2 \times 2 \times 3 = 24$

The LCD equals the product of all the prime numbers on the left.

The LCD is 24.

Now that you know how to find a common denominator, we can consider the rules for adding fractions with different denominators:

STEP BY STEP

Adding Fractions with Different Denominators

Step 1. Find the least common denominator.

Step 2. Change each fraction to an equivalent fraction having the least common denominator.

Step 3. Add the numerators.

Step 4. The least common denominator becomes the denominator of the sum.

Step 5. Reduce the fraction to lowest terms. Change any improper fractions to whole or mixed numbers.

EXAMPLE 17

Find the sum of $\frac{5}{6}$, $\frac{5}{8}$, and $\frac{1}{12}$. We saw in Example 16 that the least common denominator for these fractions is 24.

$$\frac{5 \times 4}{6 \times 4} + \frac{5 \times 3}{8 \times 3} + \frac{1 \times 2}{12 \times 2} = \frac{20}{24} + \frac{15}{24} + \frac{2}{24} = \frac{20 + 15 + 2}{24} = \frac{37}{24} = 1\frac{13}{24}$$

Adding mixed numbers is like adding fractions except that you first add the fractions together and then add to that total the result of adding the whole numbers.

EXAMPLE 18

Add $3\dfrac{2}{5} + 10\dfrac{3}{10} + 4\dfrac{4}{15}$.

{1}	{2}	{3}
Find the LCD.	Change the fractions to equivalent fractions with the LCD as denominator.	Add whole numbers and the fractions.

{1}

Find the LCD.

$$\begin{array}{r} 2)\overline{5\quad 10\quad 15} \\ 3)\overline{5\quad\ \ 5\quad 15} \\ 5)\overline{5\quad\ \ 5\quad\ \ 5} \\ \overline{1\quad\ \ 1\quad\ \ 1} \end{array}$$

LCD =
$2 \times 3 \times 5 = 30$

{2}

$\dfrac{2}{5} = \dfrac{?}{30}$ $5)\overline{30}\,^{6}$ $\dfrac{2}{5} = \dfrac{2 \times 6}{5 \times 6} + \dfrac{12}{30}$

$\dfrac{3}{10} = \dfrac{?}{30}$ $10)\overline{30}\,^{3}$ $\dfrac{3}{10} = \dfrac{3 \times 3}{10 \times 3} = \dfrac{9}{30}$

$\dfrac{4}{15} = \dfrac{?}{30}$ $15)\overline{30}\,^{2}$ $\dfrac{4}{15} = \dfrac{4 \times 2}{15 \times 2} = \dfrac{8}{30}$

{3}

$3\dfrac{2}{5} = 3\dfrac{12}{30}$

$10\dfrac{3}{10} = 10\dfrac{9}{30}$

$+\ 4\dfrac{4}{15} = 4\dfrac{8}{30}$

$\overline{\qquad\qquad 17\dfrac{29}{30}}$

Subtracting Fractions

You subtract fractions much the same way you add them.

STEP BY STEP

Subtracting Fractions

Step 1. If the fractions have different denominators, find the LCD.

Step 2. Change each fraction to an equivalent fraction with the LCD as the denominator.

Step 3. Subtract the fractions and the whole numbers. Reduce the answer to lowest terms.

EXAMPLE 19

Subtract $\dfrac{5}{12} - \dfrac{4}{15}$

{1}	{2}	{3}
Find the LCD.	Change the fractions to equivalent fractions that have the LCD as denominator.	Subtract. Reduce the answer to lowest terms.

{1}

Find the LCD.

$$\begin{array}{r} 2)\overline{12\quad 15} \\ 2)\overline{\ \ 6\quad 15} \\ 3)\overline{\ \ 3\quad 15} \\ 5)\overline{\ \ 1\quad\ \ 5} \\ \overline{\ \ 1\quad\ \ 1} \end{array}$$

$2 \times 2 \times 3 \times 5 = 60$

{2}

$\dfrac{5}{12} = \dfrac{5 \times 5}{12 \times 5} = \dfrac{25}{60}$

$\dfrac{4}{15} = \dfrac{4 \times 4}{15 \times 4} = \dfrac{16}{60}$

{3}

$\dfrac{25}{60} - \dfrac{16}{60} = \dfrac{9}{60} = \dfrac{3}{20}$

You subtract mixed numbers in much the same way that you add mixed numbers.

STEP BY STEP

Subtraction of Mixed Numbers

Step 1. If the fractions have different denominators, find the LCD and change the fractions to equivalent forms with the LCD as denominator.

Step 2. If necessary, borrow 1 from the whole number in the minuend; subtract 1 from the whole number and add 1, in the form of the LCD over the LCD, to the fraction.

Step 3. Subtract the fractions and the whole numbers and then reduce the fraction to lowest terms.

Students and the media
College students spend an average 20 hours a week listening to the radio and watching TV—more than they spend in class.

Activity	Hours spent per week
Listening to the radio	11
Watching broadcast TV	6
Watching cable TV	3
Going to class	12-15

Source: Decisions Center Inc.; national survey of 2,100 full and part-time students

"Students and the Media"
By Shelley Arps, USA TODAY

EXAMPLE 20

Subtract $10\frac{1}{3} - 7\frac{3}{5}$.

$$10\frac{1}{3} = 10\frac{5}{15}$$
$$-\ \ 7\frac{3}{5} = \ \ 7\frac{9}{15}$$

$$10\frac{5}{15} = \ \ 9\frac{20}{15}$$
$$-\ \ 7\frac{9}{15} = \ \ 7\frac{9}{15}$$
$$2\frac{11}{15}$$

Convert both fractions to equivalent fractions with denominators of 15. We cannot subtract $\frac{9}{15}$ from $\frac{5}{15}$, so we borrow 1 from 10, write the 1 as $\frac{15}{15}$, and add it to $\frac{5}{15}$.

Rewrite the problem to show the borrowing, and then subtract the whole numbers and the fractions. The fraction is already in lowest terms, so you do not have to reduce it.

Multiplying Fractions

When you multiply and divide fractions, you do *not* use common denominators.

STEP BY STEP

Multiplying Fractions

Step 1. Multiply the numerators to find the numerator of the product.

Step 2. Multiply the denominators to find the denominator of the product.

Step 3. Reduce the answer to lowest terms.

EXAMPLE 21

Multiply $\frac{3}{5} \times \frac{5}{7}$.

$$\frac{3}{5} \times \frac{5}{7} = \frac{15}{35} = \frac{3}{7}$$

When you multiply fractions, you save time by reducing fractions *before* you multiply them. In a multiplication problem, if *any* numerator and *any* denominator can be divided by the same number, you can reduce the fractions before you multiply them. You can then multiply the reduced numbers faster and with greater accuracy than you could multiply the larger numbers.

To multiply mixed numbers, change the mixed numbers to fractions.

STEP BY STEP

Multiplying Mixed Numbers

Step 1. Change the mixed numbers to improper fractions.

Step 2. Multiply the numerators and the denominators.

Step 3. Reduce the answer to lowest terms.

EXAMPLE 22

Multiply $2\frac{1}{3} \times 3\frac{3}{4}$.

$$2\frac{1}{3} \times 3\frac{3}{4} = \frac{(3 \times 2) + 1}{3} \times \frac{(4 \times 3) + 3}{4} =$$ Change the mixed numbers to improper fractions.

$$\frac{7}{\cancel{3}_1} \times \frac{\cancel{15}^5}{4} = \frac{35}{4}$$ Reduce 3 and 15 to 1 and 5. Multiply the numerators and denominators.

$$\frac{35}{4} = 8\frac{3}{4}$$ Change the answer to a mixed number.

Dividing Fractions

Division of fractions is very similar to multiplication of fractions. Multiplication and division work together for fractions just as they do for whole numbers.

Before we discuss the division of fractions, we need to look at **reciprocals.** Two numbers are reciprocals if their product is 1. Thus, $\frac{2}{3}$ and $\frac{3}{2}$ are reciprocals ($\frac{2}{3} \times \frac{3}{2} = 1$) and $\frac{7}{8}$ and $\frac{8}{7}$ are reciprocals ($\frac{7}{8} \times \frac{8}{7} = 1$). To write the reciprocal of a fraction, interchange the numerator and denominator. The reciprocal of any whole number is a fraction with that number as the denominator and a numerator of 1. For example, the reciprocal of 2 is $\frac{1}{2}$.

reciprocals: two numbers that give a product of 1 when multiplied by each other. $\frac{7}{8}$ and $\frac{8}{7}$ are reciprocals.

STEP BY STEP

Using Reciprocals to Divide Fractions

Step 1. Change whole and mixed numbers to improper fractions.

Step 2. Find the reciprocal of the divisor.

Step 3. *Multiply* the dividend by the *reciprocal* of the divisor.

Step 4. Express the answer as a fraction, whole number or mixed number.

EXAMPLE 23

Find the quotient of $\dfrac{3}{4} \div \dfrac{1}{6}$.

$\dfrac{3}{4} \div \dfrac{1}{6} = \dfrac{3}{4} \times \dfrac{6}{1}$

Multiply the dividend by the reciprocal of the divisor. The reciprocal of $\dfrac{1}{6}$ is $\dfrac{6}{1}$.

$\dfrac{3}{\overset{}{\underset{2}{4}}} \times \dfrac{\overset{3}{6}}{1} = \dfrac{9}{2}$

Reduce 6 and 4 to 3 and 2.

$\dfrac{9}{2} = 4\dfrac{1}{2}$

Express the answer as a mixed number.

EXAMPLE 24

Find the quotient of $5\dfrac{1}{2} \div 7\dfrac{1}{3}$.

$5\dfrac{1}{2} \div 7\dfrac{1}{3} = \dfrac{(2 \times 5) + 1}{2} \div \dfrac{(3 \times 7) + 1}{3} = \dfrac{11}{2} \div \dfrac{22}{3}$

Change the mixed numbers to improper fractions.

$\dfrac{11}{2} \div \dfrac{22}{3} = \dfrac{\overset{1}{11}}{2} \times \dfrac{3}{\underset{2}{22}} = \dfrac{3}{4}$

Multiply the dividend by the reciprocal of the divisor. Reduce 11 and 22 to 1 and 2 before multiplying.

 Self-Check 1.2

9. Convert $\dfrac{388}{16}$ to a whole or mixed number.

10. Change $6\dfrac{2}{3}$ to an improper fraction.

11. Reduce to lowest terms: $\dfrac{48}{78}$.

12. Convert $\dfrac{3}{8}$ to an equivalent fraction with a denominator of 152.

13. $\dfrac{1}{9} + \dfrac{2}{9} + \dfrac{3}{9}$

14. $\dfrac{3}{5} + \dfrac{7}{8} + \dfrac{2}{10}$

15. $4\dfrac{5}{6} + 7\dfrac{1}{2}$

16. $\dfrac{8}{9} - \dfrac{2}{9}$

17. $\dfrac{3}{4} - \dfrac{5}{7}$

18. $9\dfrac{1}{2} - 6\dfrac{2}{3}$

19. $\dfrac{5}{7} \times \dfrac{1}{6}$

20. $5\dfrac{3}{4} \times 3\dfrac{8}{9}$

21. Find the reciprocals of:

   a. $\dfrac{3}{5}$ **b.** 9 **c.** $3\dfrac{3}{8}$

22. $\dfrac{5}{8} \div \dfrac{3}{4}$

23. $5\dfrac{1}{4} \div 2\dfrac{2}{3}$

1.3

Calculating with Decimals

LEARNING OBJECTIVES

1. Read and round decimals.
2. Add and subtract decimals.
3. Multiply and divide decimals.
4. Convert between decimals and fractions.

Decimal numbers, like fractions, give us a way of writing amounts that are less than one, or part of a whole. We use decimals in some form or another every day—even our money system is based on decimals. Calculators utilize decimals, and decimals are the basis of percent, interest, and markup and markdown calculations.

decimal fraction: a fraction with a denominator of 10, 100, 1,000, and the like.

Reading and Rounding Decimals

A **decimal fraction** is a fraction with a denominator of 10, 100, 1,000, 10,000, 100,000 (or any power of 10). Examples of decimal fractions are numbers such as $\frac{3}{10}$ or $\frac{288}{100}$. You can write these fractions in decimal form, 0.3, or 2.88, by extending the place-value chart in Figure 1-1, as Figure 1-2 shows.

Thousands	Hundreds	Tens	Ones	Decimal point	Tenths	Hundredths	Thousandths	Ten-thousandths	Hundred-thousandths	Millionths
2	3	1	5	.	6	2	7	4	3	2

Figure 1-2   Place-Value Chart for Decimals

When you read a decimal you read a decimal as you would read a whole number, but you also say the name of the place value of the last digit in the number. You read 0.209 as "two hundred nine thousandths."

When a decimal is attached to a whole number, insert the word "and" between the units place and the decimal. That is, 2.12 is "two *and* twelve hundredths."

You round decimals for the same reasons and in a way similar to that for rounding whole numbers.

STEP BY STEP

Rounding a Decimal to a Specified Place or Digit

Step 1. Find the digit in the place to which you are rounding.

Step 2. Look at the next digit to the right.
     a. If the digit is less than 5, drop it and any other digits to the right.
     b. If the digit is 5 or more, add 1 to the place to which you are rounding and drop all digits to the right of that place.

EXAMPLE 25

Round 17.3754 to the nearest hundredth.

17.3754	The digit in the hundredths place is 7.
17.3754	The digit to the right of 7 is 5, so we add 1 to 7 and drop all digits to the right of the
17.38	8.

17.3754 rounded to the nearest hundredth is 17.38.

EXAMPLE 26

Round $193.48 to the nearest dollar.

$193.48	Rounding to the nearest dollar also means rounding to the nearest whole number.
$193.48	The digit in the ones place is 3.
$193	The digit to the right of 3 is 4, so we drop the 4 and all digits to the right of the decimal point.

$193.48 rounded to the nearest dollar is $193.

EXAMPLE 27

Round $17.375 to the nearest cent.

$17.375	Since one cent is one hundredth of a dollar, rounding to the nearest cent means rounding to the nearest hundredth. The digit in the hundredths place is 7.
$17.375	The digit to the right of 7 is 5, so we round the 7 to 8 and drop all digits to the right
$17.38	of 8.

$17.375 rounded to the nearest cent is $17.38.

Adding and subtracting decimals is very similar to adding and subtracting whole numbers.

STEP BY STEP

Adding or Subtracting Decimal Numbers

Step 1. Arrange the numbers so that the decimals are in the same vertical line, adding zeros after the decimal numbers in subtraction problems, if needed, to make the decimal parts of the subtrahend and minuend of equal length.

Step 2. Add or subtract as indicated.

Step 3. Place the decimal in the answer in the same vertical line with other decimals.

EXAMPLE 28

Add $32 + 2.55 + 8.85 + 0.625$.

```
  32
   2.55
   8.85
   0.625
 44.025
```

A decimal point is understood to follow the 32.

All decimal points are lined up with one another. Add the numbers as you would add whole numbers.

TIPS & TRAPS

A common mistake in adding decimals is not to align the decimal points.

```
  15    ←— not lined up        15        All digits and
 4.28       correctly         4.28       decimals points are
 3.04                         3.04       lined up correctly.
0.7 35  ←— not lined up       0.735
1.4 82      correctly        23.055
WRONG                        CORRECT
```

EXAMPLE 29

Subtract $26.3 - 15.84$.

```
     5 12 10
   2 6.3 0
 - 1 5.8 4
   1 0.4 6
```

Write the numbers so that the decimal points line up. Subtract the numbers, borrowing as you would in whole-number subtraction.

Multiplying Decimals

When you multiply and divide fractions, you do not find a common denominator. Likewise, when you multiply decimals, it is not necessary to line up the decimal points. It is important, however, to keep track of the number of decimal places in the numbers being multiplied.

STEP BY STEP

Multiplying Decimals

Step 1. First multiply the numbers, ignoring the decimal points.

Step 2. Count and add the number of digits to the right of the decimal points in the numbers being multiplied.

Step 3. Start at the *right* end of the product and count *back* as many places to the left as the *total* number of places you found in step 2.

Step 4. If there are more digits to the right of the decimal points than there are places in the product, insert zeros in front of the product.

EXAMPLE 30

Multiply 3.5×3.

$$
\begin{array}{r}
3.5 \\
\times\ 3 \\
\hline
10.5
\end{array}
$$

There is 1 digit to the right of the decimal point.
The product has 1 digit to the right of the decimal pont.

EXAMPLE 31

Multiply 2.35×0.015

$$
\begin{array}{r}
2.35 \\
\times\ 0.015 \\
\hline
1175 \\
235\ \ \\
\hline
0.03525
\end{array}
$$

There are 2 digits to the right of the decimal point.

There are 3 digits to the right of the decimal point.

There are 5 places to the right of the decimal point in the product.

Note that the zero to the left of the decimal product in Example 31 is not necessary, but it helps to point out the decimal. Because of this, we always use the zero to the left of the decimal point.

TIPS & TRAPS

A common mistake is to drop unnecessary zeros *before* placing the decimal point in the product.

$$
\begin{array}{r}
2.5 \\
\times\ 0.14 \\
\hline
100 \\
25\ \ \\
\hline
0.0350
\end{array}
\qquad
\begin{array}{r}
2.5 \\
\times\ 0.14 \\
\hline
100 \\
25\ \ \\
\hline
0.350
\end{array}
$$

There is 1 digit to the right of the decimal point.
There are 2 digits to the right of the decimal point.
Count 3 places to the left of the last digit in the product.

WRONG   **CORRECT**

In the division of decimals, you must pay careful attention to lining up digits and decimal points and follow the same procedures you used in the division of whole numbers.

STEP BY STEP

Dividing a Decimal by a Whole Number

Step 1. Place the decimal point in the quotient directly above the decimal point in the dividend.

Step 2. Divide as you would divide whole numbers.

If the division does not come out even, you can carry it out as far as you want by adding more zeros to the dividend. If you are planning to round an answer to a specific place, you carry the division out to one place *beyond* the specified place and then round the answer.

EXAMPLE 32

Divide 5.95 ÷ 17.

```
      0.35
17)5.95
    5 1
    ̅ ̅ ̅ ̅
     85
     85
     ̅ ̅
```

EXAMPLE 33

Find the quotient of 37.4 ÷ 24 to the nearest hundredth.

```
     1.558    rounds to 1.56
24)37.400
   24
   ̅ ̅ ̅
   13 4
   12 0
   ̅ ̅ ̅ ̅
    1 40
    1 20
    ̅ ̅ ̅ ̅
      200
      192
      ̅ ̅ ̅
        8
```

We are rounding the answer to the nearest hundredth, so we carry the division out to the thousandths place and then round.

TIPS & TRAPS

A common mistake is to add zeros to the dividend without inserting a decimal first. Divide: 12 ÷ 8.

```
    1 5
8)12 0        ⟵  The zero was
  8              added, but the
  ̅ ̅              decimal point
  4 0            was left out.
  4 0
```
WRONG

```
    1.5
8)12.0        ⟵  The zero and decimal
  8              point are placed cor-
  ̅ ̅              rectly in the dividend,
  4 0            and the decimal
  4 0            point in the quotient
  ̅ ̅ ̅            is in the correct place.
```
CORRECT

STEP BY STEP

Dividing a Decimal by a Decimal

Step 1. Change the divisor into a whole number by moving the decimal point to the right.

Step 2. Move the decimal point in the dividend the *same number* of places as it was moved in the divisor.

Step 3. Place the decimal point in the quotient directly above the *new* decimal point in the dividend.

Step 4. Divide as you would divide whole numbers.

EXAMPLE 34

Find the quotient of 59.9 ÷ 0.39 to the nearest hundredth.

$$0.39 \overline{)59.9} \longrightarrow 39 \overline{)5{,}990}$$

Move both decimal points 2 places to the right.

$$
\begin{array}{r}
153.589 \quad \text{rounds to } 153.59 \\
39\overline{)5{,}990.000} \\
3\,9 \\
\hline
2\,09 \\
1\,95 \\
\hline
140 \\
117 \\
\hline
23\,0 \\
19\,5 \\
\hline
3\,50 \\
3\,12 \\
\hline
380 \\
351 \\
\hline
\end{array}
$$

Divide, carrying the division out to the thousandths place. Round the answer.

Converting Between Decimals and Fractions

Sometimes you need to change or convert a number from decimal form into fractional form. Remember, decimals are another way of writing fractions with denominators of 10, 100, 1,000, 10,000, and so on.

STEP BY STEP

Converting a Decimal to a Fraction

Step 1. Write the decimal number, without the decimal point, as the numerator.

Step 2. The denominator is 1 followed by as many zeros as there are places to the right of the decimal point.

Step 3. Reduce the resulting fraction to lowest terms.

EXAMPLE 35

Change 0.38 to a fraction.

$$\frac{38}{100}$$

The decimal number, without the decimal point, is the numerator of the fraction. There are 2 places to the right of the decimal point, so the denominator has 2 zeros after the 1.

$$\frac{38}{100} = \frac{19}{50}$$

Reduce the fraction to lowest terms.

To convert a fraction to a decimal, remember that fractions indicate division. Therefore, you can rewrite the fraction as a division problem. When you divide a decimal, you can continue adding zeros to the *right* of the decimal point without changing the value of the number. This lets you carry out a division as far as you want to.

STEP BY STEP

Converting a Fraction to a Decimal

Step 1. Write the numerator as a number with a decimal point and a zero after it.

Step 2. Divide the numerator by the denominator, taking the division out as many places as necessary to complete the division. Continue adding zeros to the right of the decimal point.

EXAMPLE 36

Change $\frac{1}{4}$ to a decimal number.

$$\begin{array}{r} 0.25 \\ 4\overline{)1.00} \\ \underline{8} \\ 20 \\ \underline{20} \end{array}$$

Divide the numerator by the denominator, adding as many zeros to the right of the decimal point as you need to complete the division.

$$\frac{1}{4} = 0.25$$

When the division comes out even (that is, there is no remainder), we say that the division terminates, and the quotient is called a **terminating decimal.** If, however, the division *never* comes out even (there is always a remainder), we call the number a **nonterminating** or **repeating decimal.** If so, either write the answer as a mixed decimal or round it.

terminating decimal: the quotient of a division of a fraction that comes out even, with no remainder.

nonterminating or repeating, decimal: the quotient of a division that does not come out even, no matter how many decimal places it is carried to.

EXAMPLE 37

Change $\frac{2}{3}$ to a decimal number.

$$\begin{array}{r} 0.66\frac{2}{3} \quad \text{or } 0.67 \text{ (rounded)} \\ 3\overline{)2.00} \\ \underline{1\,8} \\ 20 \\ \underline{18} \\ 2 \end{array}$$

24. Write the word names of each decimal.
    a. 0.582   **b.** 1.0009

25. Round $493.91 to the nearest dollar.

26. Add 6.005 + 0.03 + 924 + 3.9.

27. Subtract 407.96 − 298.39.

28. 19.7
   $\underline{\times\ \ 4}$

29. 0.0321 × 10
   Round to the nearest hundredth

30. 123.72 ÷ 12

31. $35\overline{)589.06}$

32. $0.35\overline{)0.0084}$

33. Convert 0.68 to a fraction.

Convert the following fractions to decimals. Round to the nearest hundredth.

34. $\dfrac{1}{15}$

35. $\dfrac{3}{7}$

**General Tips
for Using
the Calculator**

In the business world most calculations are made using a calculator. The three types of calculators that are commonly used in business are the basic handheld, the scientific or business handheld, and the desktop calculator. Each type calculator has similarities, but also some major differences. In this text we will focus on the basic, scientific, or business handheld calculator.

To add, subtract, multiply, or divide using a handheld calculator, use the +, −, ×, or ÷ operation key. The numbers and operation keys are entered as they appear from left to right. The last number in the sequence may be followed by either the operation key or the equal key.

In the display window, the sum will accumulate each time the addition operation key is pressed.

$$\boxed{\text{AC}}\ 452\ \boxed{+}\ 83\ \boxed{+}\ 3{,}256\ \boxed{=}\ \Rightarrow\ 3791.$$

In subtraction it is important to enter the minuend (first or top number) first.

$$\boxed{\text{AC}}\ 64\ \boxed{-}\ 27\ \boxed{=}\ \Rightarrow\ 37.$$
$$\boxed{\text{AC}}\ 20700\ \boxed{\times}\ 860\ \boxed{=}\ \Rightarrow\ 17802000.$$

Be sure to enter the dividend (number being divided) first.

$$\boxed{\text{AC}}\ 57384\ \boxed{\div}\ 26\ \boxed{=}\ \Rightarrow\ 2207.076923$$

To find the whole number value of the remainder while the full calculator answer is displayed, subtract the digits that are to the left of the decimal point. Then multiply by the divisor. The number in the display will be the remainder or will be a value that rounds to the remainder when rounded to the nearest whole number. 2207.076923 (already in display) − 2207 × 26 = ⇒ 1.999998. The quotient is 2207 R 2.

Some scientific and business calculators have a special key for making calculations with fractions. On these calculators, numbers can be entered as fractions and results can be displayed either in fraction or decimal form (or mixed number form for improper fractions). The key is generally labeled $\boxed{a^{b/c}}$. The numerator and denominator are separated with a special symbol. The fraction $\frac{2}{3}$ appears as $2\lrcorner 3$. The mixed number $3\frac{1}{5}$ appears as $3\lrcorner 1\lrcorner 5$.

To reduce the fraction, enter the numerator, press the fraction key, then enter the denominator. To display the fraction in lowest terms press the equal key.

$$\boxed{AC}\ 30\ \boxed{a^{b/c}}\ 36\ \boxed{=}\ \Rightarrow\ 5\lrcorner 6$$

To display the decimal equivalent (see Section 1.3) press the fraction key following the equal key.

$$5\lrcorner 6\ \text{(already in display)}\ \boxed{a^{b/c}}\ \Rightarrow\ 0.833333333$$

When entering decimal numbers in a calculation, press the decimal key when it appears in the number. Ending zeros on the *right* of the decimal point do not have to be entered. Beginning zeros on the *left* of the decimal point do not have to be entered.

$$\boxed{AC}\ 32\ \boxed{+}\ 2.55\ \boxed{+}\ 8.85\ \boxed{+}\ .625\ \boxed{=}\ \Rightarrow\ 44.025$$

Summary, Section 1.1

Topic	Page	What to Remember	Examples
Reading whole numbers	2	Use commas to separate the number into groups of 3 digits and name the groups (units, thousands, millions, and so on). Read the number from left to right, naming the numerals in each group and the group name. If a group has all zeros, it does not have to be read. Do not read the group name units or use the word *and* in reading a number.	574 is read "five hundred seventy-four." 3,804,321 is read "three million, eight hundred four thousand, three hundred twenty-one."
Rounding numbers	3	Find the digit in the place to which you are rounding. Look at the digit to the right. If it is less than 5, replace it and any other digits to the right with zeros. If the digit is 5 or more, add 1 to the digit to which you are rounding, and replace all the digits to the right with zeros.	4,860 rounded to the nearest hundred is 4,900. 7,439 rounded to the nearest thousand is 7,000. 4,095 rounded to the first digit is 4,000.

Topic	Page	What to Remember	Examples
Adding in columns	4	When adding numbers with more than one digit, find the sum of the numbers in the units column, and write it directly below the units column. If the sum is more than 9, write the number of units in the sum in the units column, and carry the number of tens in the sum over into the tens column. Continue until all columns are added.	$$\begin{array}{r} 1 \\ 364 \\ +\ 473 \\ \hline 837 \end{array}$$
Subtracting	5	When subtracting a large digit from a smaller one, borrow from the column to the left of the column you are subtracting, adding 10 to the column on the right and subtracting 1 from the digit in the left column.	$$\begin{array}{r} {}^{4}\ {}^{14} \\ 7\ 5\ 4 \\ -\ 3\ 2\ 9 \\ \hline 4\ 2\ 5 \end{array}$$
Multiplying	5	Multiply each digit in the multiplicand by each digit of the multiplier, placing the partial products directly below the corresponding digit in the multiplier. Then add the partial products.	$$\begin{array}{r} 543 \\ \times\ 32 \\ \hline 1\ 086 \\ 16\ 29 \\ \hline 17,376 \end{array}$$
Dividing	7	Divide the dividend by the divisor, placing numbers in the quotient above the corresponding digits in the dividend, multiplying the quotient digit by the divisor, and subtracting the product from the partial dividend.	$$\begin{array}{r} 287\ \text{R1} \\ 3\overline{)862} \\ \underline{6} \\ 26 \\ \underline{24} \\ 22 \\ \underline{21} \\ 1 \end{array}$$

Summary, Section 1.2

Topic	Page	What to Remember	Examples
Types of fractions	9	Proper fraction: Numerator is smaller than denominator.	$\dfrac{5}{8},\ \dfrac{55}{73},\ \dfrac{356}{893}$
		Improper fraction: Numerator is equal to or larger than denominator.	$\dfrac{8}{8},\ \dfrac{36}{19},\ \dfrac{488}{301}$
		Mixed number: A number made up of a whole number and a fraction.	$5\dfrac{2}{9},\ 33\dfrac{1}{3},\ 45\dfrac{54}{73}$

Topic	Page	What to Remember	Examples
Changing an improper fraction to a whole or mixed number	9	Divide the numerator by the denominator. If there is no remainder, then the improper fraction is equivalent to a whole number. If there is a remainder, write it over the original denominator to find the fraction in the mixed number.	$\dfrac{150}{3} \rightarrow 3\overline{)150} \rightarrow 50$ $\dfrac{152}{3} \rightarrow 3\overline{)152}^{\,50\frac{2}{3}}$ $\phantom{3\overline{)152}} \dfrac{150}{2}$
Changing a mixed number to an improper fraction	10	Multiply the whole number by the denominator of the fraction and add the product to the original numerator of the fraction. This is the new numerator. The new denominator is the same as the original denominator in the fraction.	$5\dfrac{5}{8} = \dfrac{(5 \times 8) + 5}{8} = \dfrac{45}{8}$
Reducing a fraction to lowest terms	10	See if the numerator and denominator can both be divided evenly by the same number. Divide and see if the new numerator and denominator can both be divided by some number. Continue until there are no more numbers that can divide both terms.	$\dfrac{12}{36} = \dfrac{12 \div 2}{36 \div 2} = \dfrac{6}{18}$ $= \dfrac{6 \div 2}{18 \div 2} = \dfrac{3}{9}$ $= \dfrac{3 \div 3}{9 \div 3} = \dfrac{1}{3}$
GCD shortcut	11	To find the GCD of two numbers, divide the larger number by the smaller number. Divide the remainder of the first division into the divisor from the first division. Divide the remainder of the second division into the divisor from the second division. Continue dividing until the answer to the division has no remainder. The last divisor that produced no remainder is the GCD.	Find the GCD of 27 and 36. $\begin{array}{r} 1\text{ R9} \\ 27\overline{)36} \\ \underline{27} \\ 9 \end{array} \quad \begin{array}{r} 3 \\ 9\overline{)27} \\ \underline{27} \end{array}$ The GCD is 9.
Changing a fraction to a new fraction with a greater denominator	12	Divide the *new* denominator by the *old* denominator. Multiply the quotient times the numerator and denominator of the old fraction to find the new fraction.	Write $\dfrac{3}{4}$ as an equivalent fraction with denominator of 20. $\begin{array}{r} 5 \\ 4\overline{)20} \end{array} \quad \dfrac{3 \times 5}{4 \times 5} = \dfrac{15}{20}$
Adding fractions with like denominators	12	The sum of the numerators is the numerator of the sum. The denominator is the same denominator as in the fractions being added. Write the new fraction in lowest terms.	$\dfrac{3}{5} + \dfrac{7}{5} + \dfrac{5}{5} = \dfrac{15}{5} = 3$
Prime numbers	13	A prime number is a whole number greater than 1 that is divisible only by itself and 1.	The first ten prime numbers are 2, 3, 5, 7, 11, 13, 17, 19, 23, and 29.

Topic	Page	What to Remember	Examples
Finding the LCD of two or more fractions	12	Write the denominators in a horizontal row and divide each one by the smallest prime number that can divide evenly into any of the numbers. Write a new row of numbers using the quotients of the division in the first step, bringing down any numbers that are not divisible by this prime number. Continue this process until the only number in the row is 1. Multiply all the prime numbers to find the least common denominator of the factors.	Find the least common denominator of $\frac{5}{6}$, $\frac{6}{15}$, and $\frac{7}{20}$. $\begin{array}{r}2)\overline{6 \quad 15 \quad 20}\\ 2)\overline{3 \quad 15 \quad 10}\\ 3)\overline{3 \quad 15 \quad 5}\\ 5)\overline{1 \quad 5 \quad 5}\\ \overline{1 \quad 1 \quad 1}\end{array}$ LCD = $2 \times 2 \times 3 \times 5 = 60$
Adding fractions with unlike denominators	13	Find the LCD of all the fractions and change each fraction to an equivalent fraction with that denominator. The sum of the numerators is the numerator of the sum. The LCD is the denominator of the sum. Reduce to lowest terms. Change improper fractions to whole or mixed numbers.	Add $\frac{5}{6} + \frac{6}{15} + \frac{7}{20}$. Per preceding example, LCD = 60. $\frac{5 \times 10}{6 \times 10} = \frac{50}{60}$ $\frac{6 \times 4}{15 \times 4} = \frac{24}{60}$ $\frac{7 \times 3}{20 \times 3} = \frac{21}{60}$ $\frac{5}{6} + \frac{6}{15} + \frac{7}{20} = \frac{50}{60} + \frac{24}{60} + \frac{21}{60}$ $= \frac{95}{60} = \frac{19}{12} = 1\frac{7}{12}$
Subtracting fractions	14	Find the LCD if necessary and change the fractions to equivalent fractions with that denominator. Subtract the numerators and reduce the difference to lowest terms.	$\frac{7}{8} - \frac{1}{3} = \frac{21}{24} - \frac{8}{24} = \frac{13}{24}$
Borrowing in the subtraction of mixed numbers	15	Find the LCD if necessary and change the fractions to equivalent fractions with that denominator. If necessary, borrow a 1 from the whole number in the minuend and add it to the fraction in the minuend. Subtract the fractions and reduce the difference to lowest terms.	$24\frac{1}{2} = 24\frac{2}{4} = 23\frac{6}{4}$ $-\ 11\frac{3}{4} = 11\frac{3}{4} = 11\frac{3}{4}$ $\overline{12\frac{3}{4}}$
Multiplying fractions	15	Multiply the numerators to find the numerator of the product. Multiply the denominators to find the denominator of the product. Write the answer in lowest terms.	$\frac{3}{2} \times \frac{12}{17} = \frac{36}{34} = 1\frac{2}{34} = 1\frac{1}{17}$ or $\frac{3}{\underset{1}{2}} \times \frac{\overset{6}{12}}{17} = \frac{18}{17} = 1\frac{1}{17}$
Multiplying mixed numbers	16	Change the mixed numbers to improper fractions. Multiply the numerators and denominators. Reduce the product fraction to lowest terms.	$3\frac{3}{4} \times 3\frac{2}{3} = \frac{15}{4} \times \frac{11}{3} = \frac{165}{12} = \frac{55}{4} = 13\frac{3}{4}$ or $\frac{\overset{5}{15}}{4} \times \frac{11}{\underset{1}{3}} = \frac{55}{4} = 13\frac{3}{4}$

Topic	Page	What to Remember	Examples
Finding the reciprocal of a number	16	Write the number as a fraction. If the number is a whole number, write it as a fraction with a denominator of 1. Turn the fraction upside down: Let the numerator become the denominator and the denominator become the numerator.	The reciprocal of 6 is $\frac{1}{6}$. The reciprocal of $\frac{2}{3}$ is $\frac{3}{2}$. The reciprocal of $1\frac{1}{2}$ is $\frac{2}{3}$.
Using reciprocals to divide fractions	16	Find the reciprocal of the divisor. If the dividend or divisor is a mixed number, change it to an improper fraction. *Multiply* the dividend by the *reciprocal* of the divisor. Write the answer in lowest terms.	To divide $\frac{55}{68}$ by $\frac{11}{17}$, multiply $\frac{55}{68} \times \frac{17}{11}$. $$\overset{5}{\underset{4}{\frac{55}{68}}} \times \overset{1}{\underset{1}{\frac{17}{11}}} = \frac{5}{4} = 1\frac{1}{4}$$

Summary, Section 1.3

Topic	Page	What to Remember	Examples
Reading decimals	18	Ignore the decimal point and read the number as an ordinary whole number. Name the place value of the last digit.	0.3869 is read "three thousand, eight-hundred sixty-nine ten-thousandths."
Rounding a decimal to a specified place or digit	19	Find the digit to which you are rounding. Look at the next digit to the right. If the digit is less than 5, drop it and any other digits to the right. If the digit is 5 or more, add 1 to the place to which you are rounding, and drop all digits to the right.	37.357 rounded to the nearest tenth is 37.4. 3.4819 rounded to the first digit is 3.
Adding decimal numbers	20	Write the numbers in a column with the decimal points lined up. A decimal point is understood to follow the final digit in the whole number. Add the numbers as you add whole numbers. Place the decimal point in the answer under the decimal points in the addends.	$$\begin{array}{r} 32.68 \\ 3.31 \\ +\ \ 49 \\ \hline 84.99 \end{array}$$
Subtracting decimal numbers	20	Write the minuend and subtrahend so that the decimal points line up. If the minuend has fewer digits than the subtrahend, add as many zeros as you need to the right of the decimal so that every digit in the subtrahend has a digit above it in the minuend. Subtract as you subtract whole numbers. Place the decimal point in the answer under the decimal points of the subtrahend and minuend.	$$\begin{array}{r} 568.91 \\ -\ 376.75 \\ \hline 192.16 \end{array}$$ $$\begin{array}{r} 24.70 \\ -18.25 \\ \hline 6.45 \end{array}$$

Topic	Page	What to Remember	Examples
Multiplying decimals	20	Multiply the numbers, ignoring the decimal points. Write the decimal point so that the product of the decimal numbers has the number of decimal places that multiplicand and multiplier have together.	$\begin{array}{r}36.48\\ \times\ 2.52\\ \hline 72\ 96\\ 18\ 24\ 0\\ 72\ 96\\ \hline 91.92\ 96\end{array}$ 2 decimal places $\big\}$ 4 places 2 decimal places $\big\}$ total
Dividing a decimal by a whole number	22	Place the decimal point in the quotient directly above the decimal point in the dividend. Divide as you would with whole numbers.	$\begin{array}{r}1.3\\ 45\overline{)58.5}\\ 45\\ \hline 13\ 5\\ 13\ 5\end{array}$
Dividing any number by a decimal	23	Multiply the divisor and dividend by 10,100, or 1000 as needed to make the divisor a whole number. Do this by moving the decimal points in the divisor and dividend the same number of places to the right.	$3.5\overline{)0.770}$ is changed to $35\overline{)7.70}$. $\begin{array}{r}0.22\\ 35\overline{)7.70}\\ 7\ 0\\ \hline 70\\ 70\end{array}$
Changing a decimal into a fraction	23	Write the decimal number without the decimal point as the numerator. The denominator is 1 followed by as many zeros as there are places to the right of the decimal point. Reduce the fraction to lowest terms.	$0.584 = \dfrac{584}{1,000} = \dfrac{73}{125}$
Changing a fraction into a decimal number	24	Divide the numerator by the denominator. Add zeros to the right of the decimal point, carrying the division out as far as necessary to complete the division.	$\dfrac{57}{76} = \begin{array}{r}0.75\\ 76\overline{)57.00}\\ 53\ 2\\ \hline 3\ 80\\ 3\ 80\end{array}$
Changing a mixed number into a decimal number	24	Change the fraction to a decimal and add it to the whole number part.	$3\dfrac{3}{5} = 3 + \begin{array}{r}0.6\\ 5\overline{)3.0}\\ 3\ 0\end{array} = 3.6$

Self-Check Solutions, Section 1.1

1. Four billion, two hundred four million, forty-nine thousand, two hundred one

2. 3,600; 4,000

3.
$$\begin{array}{r}^{11}\\ 3\!\!\!/28\\ 583\\ +\ 726\\ \hline 1,637\end{array}$$

4.
$$\begin{array}{r}^{415}\\ 5\!\!\!/5\\ -\ 36\\ \hline 19\end{array}\qquad \begin{array}{r}36\\ +\ 19\\ \hline 55\end{array}$$

5.

	6,823			634
	× 634			× 6,823
(6823 × 4) =	27 292	(634 × 3) =		1 902
(6823 × 3) =	204 69	(634 × 2) =		12 68
(6823 × 6) =	4 093 8	(634 × 8) =		507 2
	4,325,782	(634 × 6) =		3 804
				4,325,782

6.

$$\begin{array}{c|c} 73 & 0 \\ \times\ 6 & 0 \\ \hline 438 & 00 \end{array}$$

$730 \times 60 = 43{,}800$

7.

	904
	× 24
(904 × 4) =	3 616
(904 × 2) =	18 08
	21,696

8.

$$\begin{array}{r} 16 \\ 6\overline{)96} \\ \underline{6} \\ 36 \\ \underline{36} \\ 0 \end{array}$$

Self-Check Solutions, Section 1.2

9.
$$\begin{array}{r} 24 \quad \text{R4} \quad \text{or} \quad 24\frac{4}{16} = 24\frac{1}{4} \\ 16\overline{)388} \\ \underline{32} \\ 68 \\ \underline{64} \\ 4 \end{array}$$

10. $6\frac{2}{3} = \dfrac{(3 \times 6) + 2}{3} = \dfrac{20}{3}$

11. $\dfrac{48}{78} = \dfrac{48 \div 6}{78 \div 6} = \dfrac{8}{13}$

12. $\dfrac{3}{8} = \dfrac{?}{152}$

$$\begin{array}{r} 19 \\ 8\overline{)152} \end{array}$$

$\dfrac{3}{8} = \dfrac{3 \times 19}{8 \times 19} = \dfrac{57}{152}$

13. $\dfrac{1}{9} + \dfrac{2}{9} + \dfrac{3}{9} = \dfrac{6}{9} = \dfrac{2}{3}$

14.
$$\dfrac{3}{5} = \dfrac{24}{40}$$
$$\dfrac{7}{8} = \dfrac{35}{40}$$
$$+\ \dfrac{2}{10} = \dfrac{8}{40}$$
$$\dfrac{67}{40} = 1\dfrac{27}{40}$$

15.
$$4\dfrac{5}{6} = 4\dfrac{5}{6}$$
$$+\ 7\dfrac{1}{2} = 7\dfrac{3}{6}$$
$$11\dfrac{8}{6} = 11\dfrac{4}{3} = 12\dfrac{1}{3}$$

16. $\dfrac{8}{9} - \dfrac{2}{9} = \dfrac{6}{9} = \dfrac{2}{3}$

17.
$$\dfrac{3}{4} = \dfrac{21}{28}$$
$$-\ \dfrac{5}{7} = \dfrac{20}{28}$$
$$\dfrac{1}{28}$$

18.

$$9\frac{1}{2} = 9\frac{3}{6} = 8\frac{9}{6}$$
$$-\ 6\frac{2}{3} = 6\frac{4}{6} = 6\frac{4}{6}$$
$$\overline{\qquad\qquad\qquad\quad 2\frac{5}{6}}$$

19. $\dfrac{5}{7} \times \dfrac{1}{6} = \dfrac{5}{42}$

20. $5\dfrac{3}{4} \times 3\dfrac{8}{9} = \dfrac{(4 \times 5) + 3}{4} \times \dfrac{(9 \times 3) + 8}{9}$

$$= \dfrac{23}{4} \times \dfrac{35}{9} = \dfrac{805}{36} = 22\dfrac{13}{36}$$

21. a. $\dfrac{5}{3}$ **b.** $\dfrac{1}{9}$ **c.** $3\dfrac{3}{8} = \dfrac{27}{8}$, so the reciprocal is $\dfrac{8}{27}$

22. $\dfrac{5}{8} \div \dfrac{3}{4} = \dfrac{5}{\overset{}{\underset{2}{8}}} \times \dfrac{\overset{1}{4}}{3} = \dfrac{5}{6}$

23. $5\dfrac{1}{4} \div 2\dfrac{2}{3} = \dfrac{21}{4} \div \dfrac{8}{3} = \dfrac{21}{4} \times \dfrac{3}{8} = \dfrac{63}{32} = 1\dfrac{31}{32}$

Self-Check Solutions, Section 1.3

24. a. Five hundred eighty-two thousandths
   b. One and nine ten-thousandths

25. $494

26.
```
    6.005
    0.03
    924
 +    3.9
 ─────────
  933.935
```

27.
```
    407.96
 −  298.39
 ─────────
    109.57
```

28.
```
   19.7
 ×    4
 ──────
   78.8
```

29. $0.0321 \times 10 = 0.321$

30.
```
        10.31
  12)123.72
     12
     ──
     03
      0
     ──
     3 7
     3 6
     ───
       12
       12
```

31.
```
         16.830, or 16.83
  35)589.060
     35
     ───
     239
     210
     ───
      29 0
      28 0
      ────
       1 06
       1 05
       ────
          10
```

32.
```
         0.024  or  0.02
  0.35)0.00 840
       70
       ───
       140
       140
```

33. $0.68 = \dfrac{68}{100} = \dfrac{17}{25}$

34. $\begin{array}{r} 0.066 \\ 15\overline{)1.000} \\ \underline{90} \\ 100 \\ \underline{90} \\ 10 \end{array}$ or 0.07

35. $\begin{array}{r} 0.428 \\ 7\overline{)3.000} \\ \underline{2\ 8} \\ 20 \\ \underline{14} \\ 60 \\ \underline{56} \\ 4 \end{array}$ or 0.43

End of Chapter Problems

Show how these numbers are read by writing the word name of each number.

1. 4,209

2. 97,168

3. 301,000,009

4. 5,200,000

Round to the indicated place.

5. 378 (nearest hundred)

6. 8,248 (nearest hundred)

7. 9,374 (nearest thousand)

8. 348,218 (nearest ten thousand)

9. 834 (nearest ten)

10. 29,712 (nearest thousand)

11. 29,712 (nearest ten thousand)

12. 275,398,484 (nearest million)

13. 27,500,000,078 (nearest billion)

14. 897,284,017 (nearest ten million)

Round to the first digit.

15. 3,784,809   **16.** 2,063,948   **17.** 5,178

18. 17,295,183,109   **19.** 10,097,437   **20.** 5,475

21. 396   **22.** 18,924   **23.** 685,294

24. 7,098,764

Section 1.1, Objective 2

Add. Check each sum.

25.	**26.**	**27.**	**28.**	**29.**	**30.**
6	1	6	7	4	8
3	9	9	2	5	8
4	5	4	7	6	1
+ 7	8	9	7	1	2
	+ 2	6	7	3	4
		+ 1	+ 8	+ 9	+ 9

Add. Check each sum.

31.	**32.**
8,152	9,892
3,363	7,433
4,529	4,090
8,327	5,282
+ 6,416	+ 1,987

Write in columns and add.

33. 47 + 385 + 87 + 439 + 874

34. 32,948 + 6,804 + 15,695 + 415 + 7,739

Add.

35.		**36.**		**37.**		**38.**	
	734		683		1,661		44,349
	643		252		9,342		71,486
	688		867		2,994		67,565
	656		867		5,778		57,971
	928		325		1,770	+	48,699
	197		274		5,445		
	785		835		1,770		
	527		713		2,656		
	337		118		3,874		
+	278	+	627	+	8,724		

Estimate by rounding each number to the first digit. Then find the exact sum.

39.   74,374
           82,849
           72,494
       +   89,219

40.   374
           847
           521
           873
       +   482

41.   3,748
           9,409
           3,577
       +   4,601

Estimate by rounding each number to the nearest hundred. Then find the exact answer.

42.		**43.**	
	3,470		747
	843		854
	3,872		324
+	574	+	687

44.   4,274
       643
   1,274
+   97

Solve.

45. Mary Luciana bought 48 pencils, 96 pens, 36 diskettes, and 50 bottles of correction fluid. How many items did she buy?

46. Jorge Englade has 57 baseball cards from 1978, 43 cards from 1979, 104 cards from 1980, 210 cards from 1983, and 309 cards from 1987. How many cards does he have in all?

47. Linda Cagle collects dolls. She has 12 antique dolls, 135 Barbie dolls, 35 Shirley Temple dolls, and 287 other dolls. How many dolls are there in all?

48. A furniture-manufacturing plant had the following labor-hours in one week: Monday, 483; Tuesday, 472; Wednesday, 497; Thursday, 486; Friday, 464; Saturday, 146; Sunday, 87. Find the total labor-hours worked during the week.

49. A student had the following test scores: 92, 87, 96, 85, 72, 84, 57, 98. What is the student's total number of points?

Subtract. Check your answer.

50.	51.	52.	53.
75,184	937,452	2,090,684	3,000,000
− 65,428	− 395,773	− 224,943	− 291,438

54.	55.	56.	57.
19,000,000	7,007,000	9,010,000	29,007,400
− 14,284,394	− 3,018,094	− 3,687,429	− 18,457,396

Estimate by rounding each number to the first digit. Then find the exact answer.

58.   9,748
      − 5,676

59.   370,408
      − 187,506

60.   83,748,194
      − 27,209,104

Estimate by rounding each number to the nearest thousand. Then subtract to get an exact answer.

61.   12,748
      − 5,438

62.   84,378
      − 28,746

63.   109,849
      −   35,464

Solve.

64. Sam Andrews has 42 packages of hamburger buns on hand but expects to use 130 packages. How many must he order?

65. Frieda Salla had 148 tickets to sell for a baseball show. If she has sold 75 tickets, how many does she still have to sell?

66. An inventory shows 596 fan belts on hand. If the normal in-stock count is 840, how many should be ordered?

Multiply. Check each product.

67.	5,931	68.	5,565	69.	1,987	70.	78,626	71.	708
	× 835		× 839		× 394		× 87		× 59

72.	2,105	73.	70,803	74.	2,174	75.	1,700	76.	3,987
	× 64		× 98		× 308		× 507		× 1,033

Multiply.

77. 33 × 500 **78.** 283 × 3,000 **79.** 160 × 300 **80.** 405 × 400

81. 50 × 600 **82.** 25 × 10,000 **83.** 7,870 × 6,000 **84.** 974 × 7,000

85. 270 × 600 **86.** 560 × 9,000

Estimate by rounding each number to the first digit. Then find the exact answer.

87. 7,489
× 34

88. 378
× 72

Estimate by rounding each number to the nearest hundred. Then find the exact answer.

89. 3,128
× 478

90. 378
× 546

Solve.

91. An office has 15 printers. The supply coordinator is expected to keep 8 ribbons for each printer. How many ribbons should be kept on hand?

92. A florist has 152 orders for 12 red roses. How many roses are required to fill the orders?

93. A day-care center has 28 children. If each child eats one piece of fruit each day, how many pieces of fruit are required for a week (5 days)?

Divide.

94. $7\overline{)315}$ **95.** $5\overline{)213}$

96. $9\overline{)216}$ **97.** $6\overline{)314}$

Divide.

98. $1{,}232 \div 16$

99. $4{,}020 \div 12$

100. $1{,}247 \div 23$ **101.** $3{,}362 \div 32$

Estimate each quotient. Then find the exact quotient.

102. $85\overline{)748{,}431}$ **103.** $346\overline{)174{,}891}$

Solve.

104. A parts dealer has 2,988 washers. The washers are packaged with 12 in each package. How many packages can be made?

105. A stack of countertops measures 238 inches. If each countertop is 2 inches thick, how many are in the stack?

106. If 127 employees earn $1,524 in one hour, what is the average hourly wage per employee?

107. Sequoia Brown has 15 New Zealand coins, 32 Canadian coins, 18 British coins, and 12 Australian coins in her British Commonwealth collection. How many coins does she have in this collection?

108. Jessica Lisker mailed 62 birthday cards, 6 get-well cards, 2 sympathy cards, and 5 graduation cards to the customers on her sales route. How many cards did she mail?

109. John Chang ordered 48 paperback novels for his bookstore. When he received the shipment, he learned that 11 were on back order. How many novels did he receive?

110. Baker's Department Store sold 23 pairs of ladies' patent leather pumps. If the store's original inventory was 43 pairs of the shoes, how many pairs remain in inventory?

111. An oral communication textbook contains 3 pages of review at the end of each of its 16 chapters. What is the total number of pages devoted to reivew?

112. A sales clerk earns $5 an hour. If she works 32 hours a week, how much does she earn in a week?

113. Juan Mendez must fill a school order for 77 dozen pencils. Since a dozen is 12, how many pencils are needed for the order?

114. Galina makes $320 a week. If she works 40 hours a week, what is her hourly pay rate?

115. A garage has five cars to tune. If each car has 8 cylinders, and each cylinder requires one spark plug, how many spark plugs are needed to tune the cars?

116. Holding-tank deodorant for travel trailer and marine use is sold in packages containing six 8-ounce bottles. How many ounces are in each package of six bottles?

Change to whole or mixed numbers.

117. $\dfrac{124}{6}$
118. $\dfrac{52}{15}$

119. $\dfrac{84}{12}$
120. $\dfrac{83}{4}$

121. $\dfrac{17}{2}$
122. $\dfrac{77}{11}$

123. $\dfrac{62}{5}$
124. $\dfrac{19}{10}$

125. $\dfrac{372}{25}$
126. $\dfrac{904}{9}$

Change to improper fractions.

127. $5\dfrac{5}{6}$
128. $7\dfrac{3}{8}$

129. $4\dfrac{1}{3}$
130. $10\dfrac{1}{5}$

131. $33\dfrac{1}{3}$
132. $66\dfrac{2}{3}$

Reduce each fraction to lowest terms. Try to use the greatest common divisor.

133. $\dfrac{25}{40}$
134. $\dfrac{18}{20}$

135. $\dfrac{15}{18}$
136. $\dfrac{20}{30}$

137. $\dfrac{21}{24}$
138. $\dfrac{30}{48}$

139. $\dfrac{21}{56}$
140. $\dfrac{27}{36}$

141. $\dfrac{48}{64}$ **142.** $\dfrac{16}{48}$

143. $\dfrac{24}{60}$ **144.** $\dfrac{18}{63}$

Reduce to lowest terms.

145. $\dfrac{56}{72}$ **146.** $\dfrac{54}{84}$

147. $\dfrac{120}{144}$ **148.** $\dfrac{78}{104}$

149. $\dfrac{75}{125}$ **150.** $\dfrac{78}{96}$

151. $\dfrac{32}{48}$ **152.** $\dfrac{220}{242}$

153. $\dfrac{65}{120}$ **154.** $\dfrac{30}{140}$

Rewrite as a fraction with the indicated denominator.

155. $\dfrac{3}{4} = \dfrac{}{72}$ **156.** $\dfrac{7}{9} = \dfrac{}{81}$

157. $\dfrac{5}{6} = \dfrac{}{12}$ **158.** $\dfrac{5}{8} = \dfrac{}{32}$

159. $\dfrac{2}{3} = \dfrac{}{15}$ **160.** $\dfrac{4}{7} = \dfrac{}{49}$

161. $\dfrac{9}{11} = \dfrac{}{77}$ **162.** $\dfrac{3}{14} = \dfrac{}{56}$

163. $\dfrac{9}{11} = \dfrac{}{143}$ **164.** $\dfrac{4}{15} = \dfrac{}{105}$

165. A company employed 105 people. If 15 of the employees left the company in a 3-month period, what fractional part of the employees left?

166. If 8 students in a class of 30 earned grades of A, what fractional part of the class earned A's?

Section 1.2, Objective 2

Find the least common denominator for these fractions.

167. $\dfrac{1}{4}, \dfrac{1}{12}, \dfrac{11}{16}$ **168.** $\dfrac{7}{8}, \dfrac{1}{14}, \dfrac{13}{16}$

169. $\frac{2}{3}, \frac{1}{5}, \frac{1}{7}, \frac{10}{12}$

170. $\frac{1}{8}, \frac{5}{9}, \frac{7}{12}, \frac{9}{17}$

171. $\frac{5}{72}, \frac{7}{48}, \frac{7}{36}, \frac{5}{42}$

Add.

172. $\frac{3}{4} + \frac{4}{5}$

173. $\frac{7}{8} + \frac{1}{2}$

174. $\frac{2}{5} + \frac{2}{3}$

175. $\frac{3}{4} + \frac{7}{8}$

176. $\frac{5}{6} + \frac{17}{18}$

177. $\frac{1}{4} + \frac{11}{12} + \frac{7}{16}$

178. $\dfrac{1}{6} + \dfrac{7}{8} + \dfrac{5}{12}$

179. $\dfrac{7}{9} + \dfrac{13}{16} + \dfrac{2}{3}$

180. $\dfrac{5}{6} + \dfrac{1}{12} + \dfrac{4}{9}$

181. $\dfrac{3}{4} + \dfrac{7}{15} + \dfrac{5}{6} + \dfrac{3}{5} + \dfrac{3}{20}$

182. $7\dfrac{1}{2} + 4\dfrac{3}{8}$

183. $11\dfrac{5}{6} + 8\dfrac{2}{3}$

184. $15\dfrac{1}{2} + 9\dfrac{3}{4}$

185. $7\dfrac{2}{3} + 3\dfrac{5}{6} + 4\dfrac{1}{2}$

186. $8\frac{7}{10} + 9\frac{1}{5} + 5\frac{1}{2}$

187. $3\frac{1}{4} + 2\frac{1}{3} + 3\frac{5}{6}$

188. $\begin{aligned} 73\frac{1}{2} \\ + \ 18\frac{1}{3} \\ \hline \end{aligned}$

189. $\begin{aligned} 36\frac{2}{3} \\ + \ 28\frac{1}{2} \\ \hline \end{aligned}$

190. $\begin{aligned} 96\frac{5}{6} \\ + \ 57\frac{4}{7} \\ \hline \end{aligned}$

191. $\begin{aligned} 20\frac{7}{12} \\ 27\ \frac{5}{8} \\ + \ 7\ \frac{5}{6} \\ \hline \end{aligned}$

192. $\begin{aligned} 54\frac{1}{2} \\ 37\frac{2}{3} \\ + \ 15\frac{5}{6} \\ \hline \end{aligned}$

193. $\begin{aligned} 11\frac{2}{3} \\ 68\frac{1}{5} \\ + \ 57\frac{5}{8} \\ \hline \end{aligned}$

194. Two types of fabric are needed for curtains. The lining requires $12\frac{3}{8}$ yards and the curtain fabric needed is $16\frac{5}{8}$ yards. How many yards of fabric are needed?

195. Three pieces of lumber measure $5\frac{3}{8}$ feet, $7\frac{1}{2}$ feet, and $9\frac{3}{4}$ feet. What is the total length of the lumber?

Subtract.

196. $\dfrac{5}{12} - \dfrac{1}{4}$

197. $\dfrac{2}{3} - \dfrac{1}{6}$

198. $\dfrac{1}{2} - \dfrac{1}{3}$

199. $\dfrac{6}{7} - \dfrac{5}{14}$

200. $\dfrac{13}{16} - \dfrac{2}{3}$

201. $\dfrac{11}{15} - \dfrac{1}{6}$

$$\frac{22}{30} - \frac{5}{30} = \frac{17}{30}$$

Subtract. *Remember:* Fractions must have a *common denominator*. Borrow when necessary. Reduce the answer to lowest terms.

202. $7\dfrac{4}{5} - 4\dfrac{1}{2}$

203. $4\dfrac{1}{2} - 3\dfrac{6}{7}$

204. $4\dfrac{5}{6} - 3\dfrac{1}{3}$

205. $8\dfrac{2}{3} - 2\dfrac{1}{2}$

206. $4\dfrac{5}{12} - 1\dfrac{1}{3}$

207. $3\dfrac{1}{2} - 1\dfrac{1}{4}$

208. $7\frac{5}{9}$

   $-\,5\frac{1}{2}$

209. $564\frac{5}{9}$

   $-\,317\frac{5}{6}$

210. $232\frac{2}{15}$

   $-\,189\frac{2}{5}$

211. $83\frac{1}{9}$

   $-\,46\frac{1}{3}$

212. $9\frac{3}{7}$

   $-\,7\frac{3}{5}$

213. $106\frac{1}{4}$

   $-\,37\frac{9}{24}$

214. $38\frac{1}{2}$

   $-\,26\frac{1}{3}$

215. $182\frac{9}{12}$

   $-\,90\frac{5}{6}$

216. $317\frac{3}{4}$

   $-\,196\frac{2}{3}$

Solve.

217. A board $3\frac{5}{8}$ feet long must be sawed from a 6-foot board. How long is the remaining piece?

218. Cindy Vaughn worked the following hours during a week: $7\frac{3}{4}$, $5\frac{1}{2}$, $6\frac{1}{4}$, $9\frac{1}{4}$, and $8\frac{3}{4}$. Louise Vaughn worked 40 hours. Who worked the most hours? How many more?

Section 1.2, Objective 3

Multiply.

219. $\dfrac{1}{4} \times \dfrac{7}{8}$ **220.** $\dfrac{9}{10} \times \dfrac{3}{4}$

221. $\dfrac{5}{6} \times \dfrac{1}{3}$ **222.** $\dfrac{1}{8} \times \dfrac{7}{8}$

223. $\dfrac{3}{5} \times \dfrac{3}{4}$ **224.** $\dfrac{1}{2} \times \dfrac{1}{2}$

Multiply and change answers that are improper fractions to mixed numbers.

225. $5 \times \dfrac{2}{3}$ **226.** $\dfrac{3}{7} \times 8$

227. $\dfrac{7}{8} \times 3$ **228.** $6 \times \dfrac{4}{5}$

Multiply and reduce to lowest terms. Reduce before multiplying whenever possible.

229. $\dfrac{5}{6} \times \dfrac{2}{3}$ **230.** $\dfrac{3}{4} \times \dfrac{4}{5}$

231. $\dfrac{3}{4} \times \dfrac{8}{9} \times \dfrac{7}{12}$ **232.** $\dfrac{2}{5} \times \dfrac{5}{6} \times \dfrac{7}{8}$

233. $\dfrac{9}{10} \times \dfrac{8}{5} \times \dfrac{7}{15}$

234. $\dfrac{9}{10} \times \dfrac{2}{5} \times \dfrac{5}{9} \times \dfrac{3}{7}$

235. $\dfrac{5}{9} \times \dfrac{8}{21} \times \dfrac{9}{10} \times \dfrac{6}{7}$

236. $\dfrac{15}{25} \times \dfrac{13}{20} \times \dfrac{14}{30}$

237. $\dfrac{1}{8} \times \dfrac{3}{5} \times \dfrac{40}{41}$

Multiply.

238. $3\dfrac{1}{3} \times 4\dfrac{1}{4}$

239. $4\dfrac{1}{5} \times 8\dfrac{5}{6}$

240. $6\dfrac{2}{9} \times 4\dfrac{1}{2}$

241. $7\dfrac{5}{8} \times 9\dfrac{5}{6}$

242. $8\dfrac{2}{5} \times 9\dfrac{4}{9}$

243. $9\dfrac{1}{6} \times 10\dfrac{2}{7}$

244. $10\dfrac{1}{2} \times 1\dfrac{5}{7}$

Solve.

245. Suzanna Kale received $\frac{3}{4}$ of a regular day's pay as a tribute to her birthday. If she regularly earns \$64 a day, how much birthday pay did she receive?

246. A recipe for pecan pralines calls for the following.

$\dfrac{3}{4}$ cup brown sugar $\dfrac{1}{4}$ teaspoon vanilla

$\frac{3}{4}$ cup white sugar

2 tablespoons margarine

$\frac{1}{2}$ cup evaporated milk

1 cup pecans

Helen Brewer is making treats for her second-grade class, so she must make $2\frac{1}{2}$ times as many pralines as this recipe yields. How much of each ingredient is needed?

247. The price of computers has fallen by $\frac{2}{5}$. If the original price of a computer was \$10,275, by how much has the price fallen?

248. After a family reunion, $10\frac{2}{3}$ cakes were left. If Janie Womble took $\frac{3}{8}$ of these cakes, how many did she take?

Find the reciprocal of each of the following numbers.

249. $\frac{5}{8}$

250. $\frac{2}{3}$

251. $\frac{1}{4}$

252. 8

253. $3\frac{1}{4}$

254. $2\frac{3}{8}$

255. $1\frac{3}{5}$

256. $2\frac{5}{9}$

Perform each division and reduce the answer to lowest terms.

257. $\frac{3}{4} \div \frac{1}{4}$

258. $\frac{5}{6} \div \frac{1}{8}$

259. $\frac{15}{36} \div \frac{7}{8}$

260. $\frac{3}{8} \div 3$

261. $\frac{3}{10} \div 6$

262. $15 \div \frac{3}{4}$

263. $7\dfrac{1}{2} \div 2$

264. $7\dfrac{1}{2} \div 1\dfrac{2}{3}$

265. $3\dfrac{1}{7} \div 5\dfrac{1}{2}$

266. $6\dfrac{4}{5} \div 8\dfrac{5}{6}$

Solve.

267. A board 244 inches long is cut into pieces that are each $7\frac{5}{8}$ inches. How many pieces can be cut?

268. A stack of $1\frac{5}{9}$-inch plywood measures 91 inches. How many pieces of plywood are in the stack?

269. If city sales tax is $5\frac{1}{2}\%$ and state sales tax is $2\frac{1}{4}\%$, what is the total sales tax rate on purchases made in the city?

270. Mary Morales has three lengths of $\frac{3}{4}$-inch PVC pipe: $1\frac{1}{5}$ feet, $2\frac{3}{4}$ feet, and $1\frac{1}{2}$ feet. What is the total length of pipe?

271. Frank Soo placed a piece of $\frac{5}{8}$-inch plywood and a piece of $\frac{3}{4}$-inch plywood on top of one another to create a spacer between two 2 × 4's, but the spacer was $\frac{1}{8}$ inch too thick. How thick should the spacer be?

272. Robert Washington must trim $2\frac{3}{16}$ feet from a board 8 feet long. How long will the board be after it is cut?

273. Certain financial aid students must pass $\frac{2}{3}$ of their courses each term in order to continue their aid. If a student is taking 18 hours, how many hours must be passed?

274. Wallboard measuring $\frac{5}{8}$ inch thick is in a stack $62\frac{1}{2}$ inches high. How many sheets of wallboard are in the stack?

275. Sol's Hardware and Appliance Store is selling electric clothes dryers for $\frac{1}{3}$ off the regular price of $288. What is the sale price of the dyer?

276. A recipe for French toast that serves six calls for $\frac{3}{4}$ cup granulated sugar, 1 cup evaporated milk, $\frac{1}{3}$ teaspoon vanilla, and 12 thick slices of French bread. How much of each ingredient is needed to serve only three?

277. Chair rail molding 144 inches long must be cut into pieces of $35\frac{1}{2}$ inches each. How many pieces can be cut from the molding?

278. A farmer wants to stock several ponds with 500 catfish fingerlings. If the farmer expects to lose $\frac{1}{6}$ of the fingerlings, would ordering 560 be enough to expect 500 to survive?

Section 1.3, Objective 1

Write the words used to read these decimals.

279. 0.5   **280.** 0.27

281. 0.108   **282.** 0.013

283. 0.00275   **284.** 0.120704

Write the word name of each decimal.

285. 17.8   **286.** 3.04

287. 128.23

288. 3,000.003

289. 500.0007

290. 184.271

291. $0.08\frac{1}{3}$

292. $0.016\frac{2}{3}$

293. $0.83\frac{1}{3}$

294. $5.37\frac{1}{2}$

Round to the indicated place.

295. 0.1345 (nearest thousandth)

296. 384.72 (nearest tenth)

297. 384.73 (nearest ten)

298. 1,745.376 (nearest hundredth)

299. 1,745.376 (nearest hundred)

300. 32.57 (nearest whole number)

301. $175.24 (nearest dollar)

302. $5.333 (nearest cent)

Section 1.3, Objective 2

Add.

303. 0.3 + 0.05 + 0.266 + 0.63

304. 31.005 + 5.36 + 0.708 + 4.16

305. 78.87 + 54 + 32.9569 + 0.0043

306. 9.004 + 0.07 + 723 + 8.7

Solve.

307. A shopper purchased a cake pan for $8.95, a bath mat for $9.59, and a bottle of shampoo for $2.39. Find the total cost of the purchases.

308. Robert McNab ordered 18.3 square meters of carpet for his halls, 123.5 square meters of carpet for bedrooms, 28.7 square meters of carpet for the family room, and 12.9 square meters of carpet for the play room. Find the total number of square meters of carpet he ordered.

Subtract.

309. 500.05 − 123.31

310. 815.01 − 335.6

311. 125.35 − 67.8975

312. 404.04 − 135.8716

313. 423 − 287.4

314. 807.38 − 529.79

315. 482.073 − 62.97

316. 5,003.02 − 689.93

317.   486.57
      − 160.83

318.   1,423.97
       − 802.89

319.   21.0357
       − 18.7289

320.   5.8376
       − 2.9608

321.   0.02135
       − 0.019876

322.   6.213502
       − 3.098107

Solve.

323. Four tires that retailed for $486.95 are on sale for $397.99. By how much are the tires reduced?

324. If two lengths of metal sheeting measuring 12.5 inches and 15.36 inches are cut from a roll of metal measuring 96 inches, how much remains on the roll?

325. Leon Treadwell's checkbook had a balance of $196.82 before he wrote checks for $21.75 and $82.46. What was his balance after he wrote the checks?

326. Janet Morris weighed 149.3 pounds before she began a weight-loss program. After 8 weeks she weighed 129.7 pounds. How much did she lose?

Multiply.

327. 27.63   **328.**   384   **329.**   6.42   **330.**   0.0015
　　 × 7　　　　　　 × 3.51　　　　 × 7.8　　　　　 × 6.003

331.   75.84   **332.** 73.41   **333.** 27.58 × 10   **334.** 1.394 × 100
　　 × 0.28　　　　 × 15

335. 0.19874 × 1000   **336.** 54 × 100   **337.** 27.3 × 1000

338. 38.17 × 10,000   **339.** 1,745.4 × 10   **340.** 0.1754 × 1,000,000

341. 37 × 10,000   **342.** 0.004 × 10

Solve.

343. Find the cost of 1,000 gallons of paint if 1 gallon costs $12.85.

344. Ernie Jones worked 37.5 hours at the rate of $5.97 per hour. Calculate his earnings.

Divide. Round to the nearest hundredth if division does not terminate.

345. 1.65 ÷ 11   **346.** 0.105 ÷ 15   **347.** $25\overline{)54.68}$

348. $27\overline{)365.04}$ **349.** $34\overline{)291.48}$ **350.** $74\overline{)85.486}$

351. $2.8\overline{)94.546}$ **352.** $0.041\overline{)8.897}$

353. $296.36 \div 0.19$ **354.** $0.0056\overline{)0.4576}$

355. $0.68\overline{)41,285}$ **356.** $923.19 \div 0.541$

357. $85.72 \div 10$　　　　**358.** $4.139 \div 100$　　　　**359.** $19.874 \div 1000$

360. $39 \div 10$　　　　**361.** $0.18 \div 100$　　　　**362.** $274.85 \div 10,000$

363. $3,749,298 \div 100,000$　　　　**364.** $574 \div 10,000$　　　　**365.** $0.178 \div 10$

366. $3,741.29 \div 100$

Solve.

367. If 100 gallons of gasoline costs $98.90, what is the cost per gallon?

368. If Dynamo Sugar costs $2.87 for 80 ounces, what is the cost per ounce?

Section 1.3, Objective 4

Change to a fraction in lowest terms.

369. 0.75　　　　**370.** 0.6　　　　**371.** 0.64

372. 3.075　　　　**373.** 5.5　　　　**374.** 17.05

Change to decimals. Divide to hundredths and make a fraction of the remainder.

375. $\dfrac{3}{5}$　　　　**376.** $\dfrac{2}{7}$　　　　**377.** $\dfrac{1}{8}$

378. $\dfrac{5}{6}$　　　　**379.** $\dfrac{4}{9}$　　　　**380.** $\dfrac{3}{11}$

Perform the indicated operations.

381. $2\dfrac{3}{4} + 5.83$　　　　**382.** $3.9 \div 1\dfrac{1}{5}$

383. $5\dfrac{1}{7} \times 4.2$

384. $12.8 \div 3\dfrac{1}{3}$

385. $\dfrac{1}{2} \times 0.278$ **386.** $325\dfrac{1}{4} \times 0.13$ **387.** $37\dfrac{4}{5} \div 3.78$

388. $\dfrac{3.7}{1\dfrac{1}{2}}$

Additional Problems

1. Phil McPearson is planning to build a fence around his backyard. The sides of his yard measure 34.6 feet, 117.37 feet, 31.7 feet and 119.61 feet. How many feet of fencing are required to surround his yard?

2. Steven Rancey ordered 14.2 square yards of carpet for his bedroom, 6.2 square yards for the hall, 49.6 square yards for the living room, and 19.2 square yards for the dining room. Find the total number of square yards of carpet Steven ordered.

3. The auto parts store has a special on fuel filters. Normally, the price of one filter is $2.38, but with this sale you can purchase two fuel filters for only $4.00. How much are you saving if you purchase two fuel filters at the sale price instead of two filters at the regular price?

4. Marcia Carter weighed 146.32 pounds before she began a weight-loss program. After eight weeks she weighed 119.6 pounds. How much did she lose?

5. Last weekend, Greg Sanders rode his bike a total of 63.84 miles in a two-day race. If Greg rode 29.72 miles on Saturday, how many miles did he ride on Sunday?

6. The art department has a budget of $189.72 to purchase art supplies. After purchasing 32 paintbrushes for $1.89 each, six jars of paint remover for $0.97 each, and four cans of red paint for $3.09 each, how much money was left in the budget?

7. The Croissant Bakery is open five days a week and uses 46.73 pounds of flour per day in its recipes. Donuts usually require about 15.3 pounds of flour a day. How much flour is left each day after baking the donuts?

8. Sondra Roberts's car gets approximately 27 miles per gallon of fuel. If one gallon of fuel costs $1.11, how much does it cost her to drive 115 miles?

Challenge Problem

Comparative Budgeting

Terry Kelly has recorded the following financial information for 1993. She now wants to prepare a budget for 1994 to use as a guide.

INCOME:

Gross income	32,720
Interest income	141
Dividend income	364
Total	33,225

EXPENSES:

Living	15,898
Home maintenance	825
Auto maintenance & repair	195
Insurance premiums (medical, auto, home, life)	1,578
Taxes (sales, income, FICA, real property, personal property)	10,630
Medical (not covered by insurance)	450
Planning investment	2,000
Unspent income	1,649
Total	33,225

Terry is scheduled to receive a salary increase of $1636 in 1994. She expects the dividend income to increase by $\frac{1}{4}$ and the interest income to double. She hopes her living expenses will increase no more than $1,000 and to decrease maintenance on her home and auto by $\frac{2}{5}$. Her accountant estimates her taxes will increase by approximately $500. Her insurance premiums will increase by $200. No change in uncovered medical expenses is expected. Kelly will increase her planned investment by $500.

Make the needed adjustments to prepare Kelly's budget for 1994. Adjust the unspent income category so that the total expenses equals total income.

Section 1.1

Perform the indicated operations.

1. $483 + 291 + 468$

2. $8{,}042 - 3{,}587$

3. 523×86

4. 870×90

5. $32\overline{)25{,}120}$

6. $48\overline{)5{,}040}$

7. $558 \div 9$

8. $8\overline{)409}$

Write the following numbers in words.

9. 503

10. 12,056,039

Round the following to the indicated place.

11. 84,321 (nearest hundred)

12. 58,967 (nearest thousand)

13. 80,235 (first digit)

14. 587,213 (first digit)

Estimate the following by rounding to hundreds.

15. $863 + 983 + 271$

16. $987 - 346$

Estimate the following by rounding to the first digit.

17. 892×46

18. $53\overline{)4{,}021}$

19. An inventory clerk counted the following items: 438 rings, 72 watches, and 643 pen and pencil sets. How many items were counted?

20. A warehouse is 31 feet high. Boxes that are each 2 feet high are to be stacked in the warehouse. How many boxes may be stacked one on top of the other in this warehouse? $24 \times 31 = 744$

Section 1.2

Perform the indicated operation. Reduce all answers to lowest terms.

1. $\dfrac{5}{6} - \dfrac{4}{6}$

2. $\dfrac{5}{8} + \dfrac{9}{10}$

3. $\dfrac{5}{8} \times \dfrac{7}{10}$

4. $\dfrac{5}{6} \div \dfrac{3}{4}$

5. $10\dfrac{1}{2} \div 5\dfrac{3}{4}$

6. $56 \times 32\dfrac{6}{7}$

7. $98\dfrac{2}{3} - 53\dfrac{4}{5}$

8. $2\dfrac{1}{2} + 3\dfrac{1}{3}$

9. $6\dfrac{4}{7} \times 5\dfrac{1}{4}$

10. $35\dfrac{3}{4} + 57\dfrac{5}{6} + 38\dfrac{5}{9}$

11. $5\dfrac{3}{4} - 2\dfrac{7}{8}$

12. $\dfrac{4}{7} \times \dfrac{10}{11}$

13. $257 + 53\frac{5}{6}$

14. $\frac{4}{5} - \frac{1}{3}$

15. $137 - 89\frac{4}{5}$

16. $\frac{24}{35} \times \frac{5}{32}$

17. $324\frac{3}{4} - 115$

Solve.

18. Dale Burton ordered $\frac{3}{4}$ truckload of merchandise. If approximately $\frac{1}{3}$ of the $\frac{3}{4}$ truckload of merchandise has been unloaded, how much remains to be unloaded?

19. A chicken grower orders 860 baby chicks but expects to lose $\frac{1}{8}$ of them. How many does the grower expect to lose?

20. A company that employs 580 people expects to lay off 87 workers. What fractional part of the workers are expected to be laid off?

Section 1.3

1. Round 30.5375 to the first digit.

2. Write the word name of 24.1307.

Perform the indicated operation.

3. 39.17 − 15.078   **4.** 27.418 × 100   **5.** 0.387 + 3.17 + 17 + 204.3

6. 28.34 ÷ 50 (nearest hundredth)   **7.**   324   **8.** 0.138 ÷ 10
                                                 × 1.38

9. 128 − 38.18   **10.**   17.75   **11.** 2,347 + 0.178 + 3.5 + 28.341
                                    × 0.325

12. 91.25 ÷ 12.5   **13.** 317.24 − 138   **14.** 374.17 ÷ 100   **15.** $2\frac{5}{8} - 1.015$

16. Change $\frac{5}{7}$ to a decimal (nearest hundredth).

17. Change 0.34 to a fraction reduced to lowest terms.

18. What is the cost of $5\frac{1}{2}$ dozen doughnuts if they cost $2.49 a dozen?

19. A patient's chart showed a temperature reading of 101.23 degrees Fahrenheit at 3 P.M. and 99.47 degrees Fahrenheit at 10 P.M. What was the drop in temperature?

How we spend our paychecks

For every $100 we spend:

Housing costs (rent, utilities, furniture) — $41.36

Transportation[1] — $17.80

Food and beverages — $17.71

Medical care — $6.39

Clothing — $6.07

Entertainment — $4.32

Other goods and services — $6.35

1 – Gasoline, cars, airline tickets

Source: Department of Labor

By Marty Baumann, USA TODAY

QUESTIONS

1. Total the amounts to verify that the sum equals $100 as shown.

2. Ann White has a monthly paycheck of $1500. According to the given statistics, how much should she budget in each category.

3. Niyi Adashepi has a weekly paycheck of $375. According to the given statistics, how much should he budget in each category.

2

Bank Records

When it's time to pay the bills, whether personal or business-related, most Americans turn to a checkbook. The specific forms, policies, and procedures for checking accounts may vary from bank to bank, but once you know the reasoning behind these banking procedures, it is easy enough to understand the minor variations that occur. For business purposes and for personal use, it is important to use banking forms correctly, to keep accurate records, and to track financial transactions carefully.

Using Checking Account Forms

LEARNING OBJECTIVES

1. Complete a bank deposit slip.
2. Write a bank check.
3. Fill out a check stub.
4. Use a check register.
5. Endorse a check.

Deposit Slip

As a general rule, you must deposit money into a checking account before you can withdraw it by writing a check. A **deposit slip** is filled out when money (either checks or cash) is to be added to an account. Figure 2-1 shows a sample deposit slip. Deposit slips are available to the person opening an account along with a set of preprinted checks. The bank's account number and the customer's account number are written at the bottom of the slip in magnetic ink.

A deposit slip has a place for the date and for listing the checks and cash to be deposited. Cash and checks are listed separately, and each individual check is listed. The deposits are then added and the sum is written in the place marked "Total." If the depositor wishes to receive a portion of the deposit, this amount is entered in the place marked "Less Cash Received" and subtracted from the total. The difference is entered in the place marked "Net Deposit." Other notations and reminders vary from bank to bank.

deposit slip: a blank form provided by the bank; it is used to record cash or checks that are being deposited into an account.

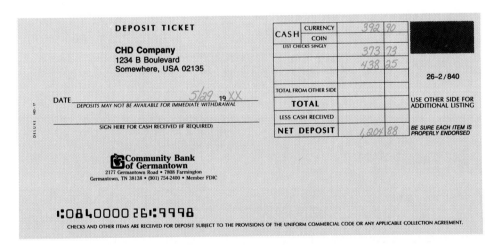

Figure 2-1 A Deposit Slip

Making Out A Bank Check

The main form used in a checking account is a **check**, a piece of paper ordering the bank to pay someone an amount of money from a particular account. Figure 2-2 shows the basic features of a check.

When a checking account is opened, those persons authorized to write checks on the account must sign a signature card, which is kept on record at the bank. Whenever there is a question about a signature or whether or not a person is authorized to write checks on an account, the bank refers to the signature card to resolve the question.

check: a piece of paper ordering the bank to pay someone an amount of money from a particular account.

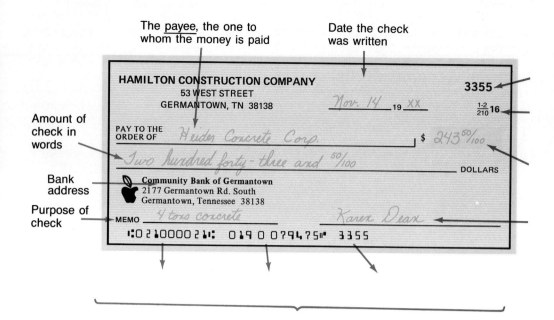

Figure 2-2 A Sample Check

payee: the person or company to whom a check is made out—the one who gets the money.

payor: the person or company issuing a check; also called the *maker*.

EXAMPLE 1

Write a check dated April 8, 19XX, to Disk-O-Mania in the amount of $84.97, for computer diskettes.

Enter the date, 4/8/XX.

Write the name of the payee, Disk-O-Mania.

Enter the amount of the check in numbers.

Enter the amount of the check in words. Note the fraction $\frac{97}{100}$ showing cents, or hundredths of dollars.

Write the purpose of the check on the memo line.

Sign your name.

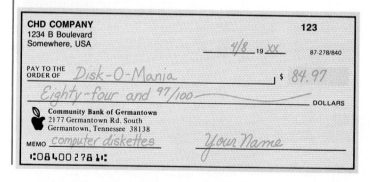

Filling out a Check Stub

check stub: a blank form attached to a check and used to record all checks, deposits, and other transactions, and to keep a running balance.

Most businesses and individuals who have checking accounts use either a check stub or a check register to record all the checks they write and all the deposits they make. Check stubs are provided by the bank, usually in a bound book with the perforated check attached to its stub.

A **check stub** has a place to list the check number (if it is not preprinted), the date, the amount of the check, the person to whom the check is made, and what the check is written for. There is also a place to record the balance forward (the balance after the last check was written), the amount deposited since that time, the amount of the check, and the new balance.

When filling out the check stub, you add any deposits and subtract the amount of the check to get the new balance. It's a good idea to fill out the check stub *before* writing the check so that you won't forget to do it.

EXAMPLE 2

Complete the stub for check number 150, written on April 8, 19XX, to Disk-O-Mania in the amount of $84.97 for computer diskettes. The amount brought forward is $8,324.09. Deposits of $325, $694.30, and $82.53 were made after the previous check was written.

The check number, 150, is preprinted in this case.

Enter the date, 4/8/XX.

Enter the amount, $84.97.

Enter the payee, Disk-O-Mania.

Enter the purpose, computer diskettes.

Enter the balance, $8,324.09

Total and enter the deposits, $1,101.83

Find the new total, $9,425.92

Enter the amount of the check, $84.97

123	Date 4/8 19 XX
Amount $84.97	
To Disk-O-Mania	
For computer diskettes	

Balance Forward	8,324	09
Deposits	1,101	83
Total	9,425	92
Amount This Check	84	97
Balance	9,340	95

Subtract the amount of the check to find the new balance, $9,340.95.

Using a Check Register

Like check stubs, a **check register** allows you to maintain a record of all checks you have written and deposits you have made. The check register is a bound set of forms supplied by the bank and kept with the checks. The check register provides space to enter the check number, date, description of transaction (payee and purpose of check), and amount of each check, the date and amount of each deposit, and the balance after each transaction. Registers also have a column where you can enter the amount of any check fee (some banks charge a fee for each check written), and a √ column used to balance a checking account periodically (see Section 2.2). Figure 2-3 shows a sample check register page.

check register: a bound set of blank forms supplied by a bank and kept with the checks; it is used to record all checks, deposits, interest and other transactions and to keep a running balance.

Figure 2-3   A Check Register

NUMBER	DATE	DESCRIPTION OF TRANSACTION	AMOUNT OF CHECK	√	FEE	AMOUNT OF DEPOSIT	BALANCE $ 6,843 00
		RECORD ALL CHARGES OR CREDITS THAT AFFECT YOUR ACCOUNT	$		$	$	
543	8/9	Golden Wheat Dist.	685 56				6,157 44
544	8/9	Consolidated Berry Farms	89 78				6,067 66
	8/9	Cash withdrawal	250 00				5,817 66
	8/10	Deposit				1,525 61	7,343 27

Endorsing a Check

Before a check can be cashed, it must be **endorsed.** That is, the payee must sign the check on the back. There are several different types of check

endorse: signing or stamping the back of a check by the payee.

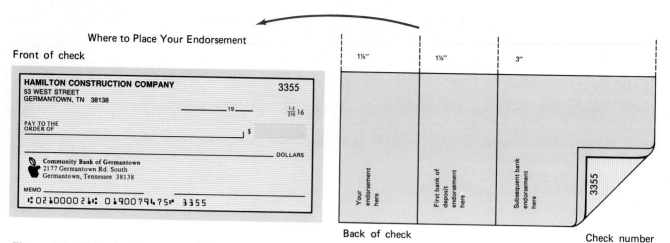

Front of check

Where to Place Your Endorsement

Figure 2-4 Rules for Placement of Check Endorsements

endorsements. The simplest type, which you would use if you wanted to cash a check made payable to you, is your signature on the back of the check. If you want to deposit the check instead, sign your name and write under it "for deposit only" and your checking account number. This is called a **restricted endorsement,** since it says that the money can only be deposited in your account, not paid out. There are other types of restricted endorsements that businesses use to safeguard the process of paying out money; in general, these involve an exact identification of the person to whom money can be paid.

In 1988 the Federal Reserve Board issued regulations concerning the way that endorsements can be placed on checks. As Figure 2-4 shows, the endorsement must be placed within $1\frac{1}{2}$ inches from the left edge of the check. The rest of the back of the check is reserved for bank endorsements. Many check-printing companies now mark this space and provide lines for endorsements.

restricted endorsement: occurs when the payee signs a check on the back and adds "for deposit only" and the account number so that the check can *only* be deposited to that account; it cannot be cashed.

Self-Check

Enter the following transactions in the bank records for Park's Oriental Grocery Store with the account number 63-1579-5. On April 29, 19XX, with an account balance brought forward of $7,869.40 Mr. Man Park added $858.63 in cash and two checks in the amounts of $157.38 and $32.49. Later that day, he wrote a check in the amount of $155.30 to Green Harvest for fresh vegetables.

1. Fill out the deposit slip for April 29, 19XX.

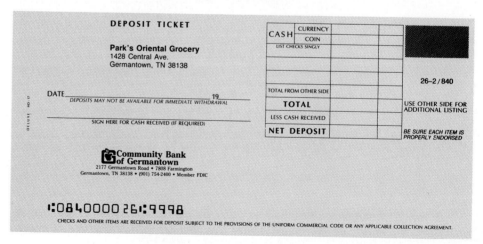

2. Write a check dated April 29, 19XX, to Green Harvest in the amount of $155.30 for fresh vegetables. Fill out the check stub for this check.

456	Date _____ 19 ___
Amount _____	
To _____	
For _____	
Balance Forward	
Deposits	
Total	
Amount This Check	
Balance	

Park's Oriental Grocery   456
1428 Central Ave.
Germantown, TN 38138   _____ 19 ___   87-278/840

PAY TO THE
ORDER OF _____ | $

_____ DOLLARS

Community Bank of Germantown
2177 Germantown Rd. South
Germantown, Tennessee 38138

MEMO _____   _____

⑈08400278⑈

3. Enter all the transactions described in the check register. Show the new balance brought forward for Park's Oriental Grocery Store.

		RECORD ALL CHARGES OR CREDITS THAT AFFECT YOUR ACCOUNT						BALANCE	
NUMBER	DATE	DESCRIPTION OF TRANSACTION	AMOUNT OF CHECK	✓	FEE	AMOUNT OF DEPOSIT	$		
			$		$	$			

2.2

Reconciling a Checking Account

LEARNING OBJECTIVES

1. Read a bank statement.
2. Reconcile the bank statement with the checkbook.

Each month, banks send statements to their checking account customers to enable account holders to reconcile any differences between that statement and the customer's own check stubs or check register. (To make things simple, we will refer to a customer's check stubs or check register as the *checkbook*.)

Reading a Bank Statement

The primary tool for reconciling an account is the monthly **bank statement,** a listing of all transactions that took place in the customer's account during the past month. It includes all checks cashed, all deposits made, all service charges, and the like. A sample bank statement is shown in Figure 2-5.

Most bank statements have a section explaining the various letter codes and symbols contained in the statement. One of the first steps to take when

bank statement: monthly statement sent by the bank to an account holder listing all transactions in the account for that month.

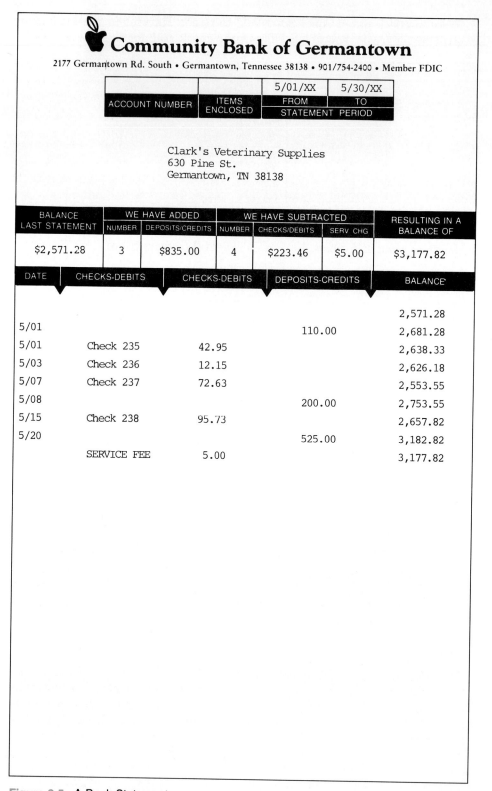

Community Bank of Germantown

2177 Germantown Rd. South • Germantown, Tennessee 38138 • 901/754-2400 • Member FDIC

ACCOUNT NUMBER	ITEMS ENCLOSED	5/01/XX FROM	5/30/XX TO
		STATEMENT PERIOD	

Clark's Veterinary Supplies
630 Pine St.
Germantown, TN 38138

BALANCE LAST STATEMENT	WE HAVE ADDED		WE HAVE SUBTRACTED			RESULTING IN A BALANCE OF
	NUMBER	DEPOSITS/CREDITS	NUMBER	CHECKS/DEBITS	SERV CHG	
$2,571.28	3	$835.00	4	$223.46	$5.00	$3,177.82

DATE	CHECKS-DEBITS		CHECKS-DEBITS	DEPOSITS-CREDITS	BALANCE
					2,571.28
5/01				110.00	2,681.28
5/01	Check 235	42.95			2,638.33
5/03	Check 236	12.15			2,626.18
5/07	Check 237	72.63			2,553.55
5/08				200.00	2,753.55
5/15	Check 238	95.73			2,657.82
5/20				525.00	3,182.82
	SERVICE FEE	5.00			3,177.82

Figure 2-5 A Bank Statement

you receive a bank statement is to check this explanatory section for any terms that you do not understand in the statement.

One of the items that may appear on a bank statement is a **service charge.** This is a fee the bank charges for maintaining the checking account; it may be a standard monthly fee or a charge for each check.

Another type of bank charge appearing on their bank account statement

service charge: a fee the bank charges for operating a checking account.

is for checks that "bounce" (are not backed by sufficient funds). If someone writes you a check but does not have enough money in their bank account to cover it, their bank will return the check to you through your bank and may charge your bank account a **returned check fee** for handling it. If *you* write such a check, your bank will charge you a **nonsufficient funds (NSF) fee.**

In addition, bank statements reflect any use of an **automatic teller machine (ATM).** If you withdraw cash or make a deposit using an ATM, you should make a record of it in your checkbook immediately. Otherwise, it's all too easy to overdraw your account.

Finally, many banks allow customers to pay bills automatically with automatic transfers. For example, loan payments, credit-card payments, and other bills can be routinely paid by the bank on a certain day of the month. These transfers also appear on the bank statement.

What does *not* appear on the bank statement is any check you wrote or deposit you made after the statement is printed, too late for it to reach the bank in time to be included in this month's statement. For this reason and others, your bank statement and your checkbook may not agree initially.

Reconciling the Bank Statement and the Checkbook

The first thing to do when you receive a bank statement is to go over it and check its contents against your checkbook. You can check off all the checks and deposits listed on the statement by using the √ column we showed earlier in the check register (Figure 2-3) or by marking the check stub.

As just noted, you will probably find that some **outstanding checks** recorded in your checkbook are not listed on the bank statement. Similarly, you may also have **deposits in transit** in your records that do not appear on your bank statement. Both outstanding checks and deposits in transit occur because these transactions did not clear the bank in time to appear on that month's statement.

TIPS & TRAPS

When you are reconciling the bank statement with the checkbook in actual practice, it is helpful to mark in your checkbook the checks and deposits that have cleared the bank and are included with the statement. After you have made this notation, you can quickly see that the *unmarked* checks and deposits have *not* been included in the bank statement. These should be used as outstanding checks and deposits. When checks have cleared the bank, they should be arranged in numerical sequence and placed in a safe storage place in case they are needed at a later date as proof of payment.

A *returned check* is a check that is made out to you and deposited in your account but is not honored by the maker's bank, usually because there is not enough money in the maker's account to pay it. In such cases, the bank deducts the amount of the check (along with a fee in many instances) from your account. Thus, returned checks can also cause your checkbook and the bank statement not to be in agreement.

When the bank statement and the checkbook do not initially agree, you need to take steps to reconcile the two. The process of making the bank statement agree with the checkbook balance is called *reconciling a bank statement,* or **bank reconciliation.**

returned check fee: a fee charged to your account when someone writes you a check without the funds to cover it and you deposit it in your account. When *you* write a check without the funds to cover it, you are charged an *NSF* fee.

nonsufficient funds (NSF) fee: a fee charged to your account when you write a check and do not have enough money in your account to cover it.

automatic teller machine (ATM): a computerized banking service offered by many banks; the account holder can perform many banking functions using a bank card and bank computer, without the help of a bank teller.

outstanding checks: checks that do not reach the bank in time to appear on the monthly statement.

deposits in transit: deposits made by mail or during or after regular banking hours that do not clear the bank in time to appear on the monthly bank statement. Also called *outstanding deposits.*

bank reconciliation: a process in which the bank statement and the account holder's checkbook are brought into agreement.

adjusted bank statement balance: consists of the balance on the bank statement plus any outstanding deposits minus any outstanding checks.

adjusted checkbook balance: consists of the checkbook balance minus any service fees and minus any returned items.

STEP BY STEP

Reconciling a Bank Statement

Step 1. Add the amount of deposits in transit to the ending bank statement balance.

Step 2. Subtract the amount of outstanding checks from the sum of the bank statement balance plus the deposits in transit.

Step 3. Add to the checkbook balance the amount of any deposits appearing on the bank statement but not in the checkbook.

Step 4. Subtract any charges appearing on the bank statement from the checkbook balance resulting from step 3.

Step 5. Compare the amounts in Steps 2 and 4.

These steps can be boiled down to two rules:

- **Adjusted bank statement balance** = ending balance on statement + outstanding deposits − outstanding checks
- **Adjusted checkbook balance** = checkbook balance + unrecorded deposits − service fees − returned checks

A reconciliation form is usually printed on the back of the bank statement. The form leads you through the reconciliation process. Use the reconciliation form and statement to reconcile the bank statement and check register.

EXAMPLE 3

Use the bank statement and check register in Figure 2-6 and prepare a bank reconciliation.

The adjusted statement balance and the adjusted checkbook balance are the same, so the statement and check register are reconciled. This adjusted balance should be indicated in the check register.

Calculator Solution

Calculators are very helpful in reconciling bank records. The work in Example 3 can be done on a calculator in the following steps.

To Find the Adjusted Statement Balance:

$\boxed{\text{AC}}$ 2973.24 $\boxed{+}$ 243.27 $\boxed{+}$ 175   Begin with the statement balance; add the outstanding deposits.

$\boxed{-}$ 142.53 $\boxed{-}$ 12.75 $\boxed{-}$ 297.38   Subtract the outstanding checks.

$\boxed{-}$ 93.51 $\boxed{=}$ ⇒2845.34

To Find the Adjusted Checkbook Balance:

$\boxed{\text{AC}}$ 2891.30 $\boxed{-}$ 3.21 $\boxed{-}$ 42.75   Begin with the checkbook balance; subtract the service fees and returned items.

$\boxed{=}$ ⇒2845.34

Front of Bank Statement

🍎 **Community Bank of Germantown**

2177 Germantown Rd. South • Germantown, Tennessee 38138 • 901/754-2400 • Member FDIC

ACCOUNT NUMBER	ITEMS ENCLOSED	FROM	TO
	1	9/1/XX	9/28/XX
		STATEMENT	PERIOD

JOHN HAMILTON
1234 SOUTH ST.
GERMANTOWN, TN 38138

BALANCE LAST STATEMENT	WE HAVE ADDED		WE HAVE SUBTRACTED			RESULTING IN A BALANCE OF
	NUMBER	DEPOSITS/CREDITS	NUMBER	CHECKS/DEBITS	SERV CHG	
$2,772.86	2	$942.18	17	$741.80	$3.21	$2,973.24

DATE	CHECKS-DEBITS	CHECKS-DEBITS	DEPOSITS-CREDITS	BALANCE
9/1	12.18	6.24		2,754.44
9/3	28.76	42.75 (returned item)		2,682.93
9/7	146.17			2,536.76
9/10	43.68	17.32		2,475.76
9/15	62.19		500.00	2,913.57
9/17	12.88	32.16		2,868.53
9/20	68.00			2,800.53
9/23	42.37	12.96		2,745.20
9/23	36.01			2,709.19
9/24			400.00	3,109.19
9/25	178.13			2,931.06
9/27			42.18	2,973.24

Account Holder's Check Register

RECORD ALL CHARGES OR CREDITS THAT AFFECT YOUR ACCOUNT

NUMBER	DATE	DESCRIPTION OF TRANSACTION	AMOUNT OF CHECK	√	FEE	AMOUNT OF DEPOSIT	BALANCE 2346 39
1094	9/23	Andy's Shoe Shop	42 37	√			2304 02
1095	9/23	Lucky's Super Market	12 96	√			2791 16
1096	9/23	Lou's Fabric Store	36 01	√			2755 15
1097	9/24	Lifetime I. Co.	142 53				2612 62
Dep	9/24	Payroll Salary		√		400 00	3012 62
1098	9/25	Modern Hardware Inc.	12 75				2999 87
1099	9/25	Luca's Tire Store	178 13	√			2821 74
Dep	9/27	From Sale of Trailer				243 27	3065 01
Dep	9/27	Southern Telephone (Ref)		√		42 18	3107 19
1100	9/27	Lucky's Super Market	297 38				2809 81
Dep	9/29	From Lucille Young				175 00	2984 81
1101	9/30	Shoreline Gas Company	93 51				2891 30
	9/30	Adjusted Balance					2845 34

REMEMBER TO RECORD AUTOMATIC PAYMENTS / DEPOSITS ON DATE AUTHORIZED.

Back of Bank Statement

$ 2,973 24	BALANCE AS SHOWN ON BANK STATEMENT		BALANCE AS SHOWN IN YOUR CHECKBOOK	$ 2,891 30
418 27	ADD DEPOSITS NOT SHOWN ON STATEMENT		SUBTRACT AMOUNT OF SERVICE CHARGE	3 21
3,391 51	NEW TOTAL		NEW TOTAL	2888 09
546 17	*SUBTRACT TOTAL OF OUTSTANDING CHECKS	SHOULD ↔ EQUAL	ADJUSTMENTS IF ANY	42 75
2845 34	YOUR ADJUSTED STATEMENT BALANCE		YOUR ADJUSTED CHECKBOOK BALANCE	2845 34

* OUTSTANDING CHECKS

CHECK NUMBER	DATE	AMOUNT
1097	9/24	$ 142 53
1098	9/25	12 75
1100	9/27	297 38
1101	9/30	93 51
	TOTAL........	$

Figure 2-6 Bank Reconciliation Example

The federal government set up the Federal Deposit Insurance Corporation to guarantee bank deposits against bank failure. To pay for this insurance, banks are charged an FDIC insurance fee.

All costs of FDIC insurance were assumed by most banks prior to 1991.

In 1991, this insurance increased significantly due to the failure of several banks. As a result, many banks began the practice of passing on all or part of the cost of FDIC insurance to customers. The cost of the insurance to the financial institution was raised from 12 cents to 23 cents per $100. This increase of 11 cents per $100 dollars is the same as 0.11% or 0.0011. Some banks passed the increase along to customers, while other banks passed the entire cost of the insurance to customers.

REAL WORLD APPLICATION

How Long Can They Hold Your Money?

As of September 1, 1988, there are limits on how long banks can "hold" deposits. (By "hold," we mean the time the bank takes to process a check—the amount of time between when you deposit cash or a check and when the money is recorded by the bank as being in your account.) A number of things affect this time period, as you can see from the chart below. One of the most important is whether the check being deposited is from a local bank or a bank in another city or state.

No one likes to have checks bounce, and we all try to avoid having an overdrawn account. This chart shows one more reason why it is a good idea not to overdraw your account—the bank can take twice as long to hold deposits in accounts that are frequently overdrawn. That means that you may have to wait 7 to 11 working days before you can use the money from a check you deposit.

Application Questions

1. You live in one city and work in another and your employer's bank is not the same bank or in the same town as your bank. You deposit your paycheck for $493.70 on Thursday morning, July 3. According to your checkbook, your balance before you make this deposit is $281.50. You have a doctor's bill for $500 that was due July 1. When will it be safe to write the check?

2. You deposit a check in an ATM on Friday afternoon, January 5, in another town from where you bank. The ATM is not in the bank where you have an account, but it accepts cards and deposits from other banks in the same state. When you get your bank statement at the end of the month, you are dismayed to see that a check you wrote bounced because the January 5 deposit did not clear the bank until January 15. Why did it take so long?

How Long Can They Hold Your Money?

The number of business days that banks, savings and loan associations, and credit unions can hold deposits, as of September 1, 1988.

Deposits	Days	Deposits	Days
AT TELLER WINDOWS		**INTO A NEW ACCOUNT**	
Cash	1	Cash	1
Checks:		Checks	Institutions may set policy
Up to $100	1		
Remainder over $100	3 local*; 7 nonlocal	Government and cashiers' checks:	
		Up to $5,000	1
Government checks	1	Remainder over $5,000	9
Cashier's check	1	**FOR FREQUENTLY OVERDRAWN ACCOUNTS**	
Electronic transfer	1		
AT ATM BEFORE NOON†		Checks	7 local: 11 nonlocal
Cash	2		
Check	3 local; 7 nonlocal		
Government check (U.S.)	1		
Government check (state, local)	2		
Cashier's check, certified check	2		

*Local means drawn on banks in the same city.

†For deposits after noon, add a day; deposits made at automatic teller machines maintained by banks where depositor has no account may be held 7 days.

Source: American Bankers Association

The charges are handled differently by different banks. Here is how you calculate the monthly FDIC insurance assessment for a bank account when only the 0.11% increase is paid by the customer.

1. Multiply average monthly balance by 0.0011.
2. Divide the result from step 1 by the number of days in a year (365).
3. Multiply the result from step 2 by the number of days in the month.

EXAMPLE 4

Find the monthly FDIC insurance assessment for a bank account that has an average daily balance of $2,065.84 for the month of May, which has 31 days.

$2065.84 \times 0.0011 = 2.272424$
$2.272424 \div 365 = 0.0062258$
$0.0062258 \times 31 = 0.192998$ or $0.19   (rounded)

 Self-Check

4. A bank statement shows a balance of $12.32. The service charge for this statement period was $2.95. The checkbook showed deposits of $300.00, $100, and $250.00 that did not appear on the statement. Outstanding checks were in the amount of $36.52, $205.16, $18.92, $25.93, and $200.00. The checkbook balance was $178.74. Reconcile the bank statement with the checkbook balance.

$	BALANCE AS SHOWN ON BANK STATEMENT		BALANCE AS SHOWN IN YOUR CHECKBOOK	$
	ADD DEPOSITS NOT SHOWN ON STATEMENT		SUBTRACT AMOUNT OF SERVICE CHARGE	
	NEW TOTAL		NEW TOTAL	
	*SUBTRACT TOTAL OF OUTSTANDING CHECKS		ADJUSTMENTS IF ANY	
	YOUR ADJUSTED STATEMENT BALANCE	SHOULD ⟷ EQUAL	YOUR ADJUSTED CHECKBOOK BALANCE	

* OUTSTANDING CHECKS

CHECK NUMBER	DATE	AMOUNT	
		$	
		TOTAL........	$

Summary

Topic	Page	What to Remember	Examples
Deposit slip	67	A deposit slip is a form that tells the bank which account should receive money (cash or checks) that is being deposited. Imprinted deposit slips are provided with the checks for an account and, like the checks, they carry the name of the account holder. For every deposit, a deposit slip must be filled out to describe each check and all the cash being deposited.	
Imprinted check	67	A check is a piece of paper ordering the bank to pay someone an amount of money from a particular account. An imprinted check carries the name of the account holder, who must fill in the name of the person or company to whom the money is to be paid.	
Check stub	68	A check stub is a form that comes with most business checking accounts and provides spaces to record information about every check that is written. It also has spaces to record deposit and balance information.	
Check register	69	A check register is a bound set of forms on which the account holder records every transaction made in an account. The register indicates the current balance brought forward and lists all checks, withdrawals, deposits and other charges.	

Topic	Page	What to Remember	Examples

Bank statement — 71

A bank statement is a monthly record that most banks send to each account holder. The statement shows all deposits, withdrawals, and service charges and summarizes all other activity in the account.

The account holder must compare the bank statement with his or her check register to make sure both records are complete and accurate and to reconcile the bank statement.

Community Bank of Germantown
2177 Germantown Rd. South • Germantown, Tennessee 38138 • 901/754-2400 • Member FDIC

ACCOUNT NUMBER	ITEMS ENCLOSED	5/01/XX FROM	5/30/XX TO
		STATEMENT PERIOD	

Clark's Veterinary Supplies
630 Pine St.
Germantown, TN 38138

BALANCE LAST STATEMENT	WE HAVE ADDED		WE HAVE SUBTRACTED			RESULTING IN A BALANCE OF
	NUMBER	DEPOSITS/CREDITS	NUMBER	CHECKS/DEBITS	SERV. CHG	
$2,571.28	3	$835.00	4	$223.46	$5.00	$3,177.82

DATE	CHECKS-DEBITS		CHECKS-DEBITS	DEPOSITS-CREDITS	BALANCE
					2,571.28
5/01				110.00	2,681.28
5/01	Check 235	42.95			2,638.33
5/03	Check 236	12.15			2,626.18
5/07	Check 237	72.63			2,553.55
5/08				200.00	2,753.55
5/15	Check 238	95.73			2,657.82
5/20				525.00	3,182.82
	SERVICE FEE	5.00			3,177.82

Bank reconciliation — 73

Bank reconciliation is the process of comparing the transactions recorded in the check register with those listed on the bank statement.

Adjusted statement balance = balance on statement + outstanding deposits − outstanding checks.

Adjusted checkbook balance = checkbook balance − service fees − returned items.

$ 316 56	BALANCE AS SHOWN ON BANK STATEMENT	BALANCE AS SHOWN IN YOUR CHECKBOOK	$ 842 87
2 000 00	ADD DEPOSITS NOT SHOWN ON STATEMENT	SUBTRACT AMOUNT OF SERVICE CHARGE	14 00
2316 56	NEW TOTAL	NEW TOTAL	828 87
1487 69	*SUBTRACT TOTAL OF OUTSTANDING CHECKS	ADJUSTMENTS IF ANY	
828 87	YOUR ADJUSTED STATEMENT BALANCE	YOUR ADJUSTED CHECKBOOK BALANCE	828 87

SHOULD EQUAL

* OUTSTANDING CHECKS

CHECK NUMBER	DATE	AMOUNT
3105	8/15	$ 17 83
3106	8/15	19 27
3112	8/16	126 83
3114	8/17	42 00
3117	8/18	16 17
ATM	8/20	50 00
ATM	8/21	80 00
3118	8/22	325 14
3119	8/23	683 32
3120	8/24	127 13
	TOTAL	1487 69 $

1.

DEPOSIT TICKET		
Park's Oriental Grocery		
1428 Central Ave.		
Germantown, TN 38138		

CASH	CURRENCY	8 58	63
	COIN		
LIST CHECKS SINGLY		1 57	38
		3 2	49

DATE _____4/29_____ 19 XX

DEPOSITS MAY NOT BE AVAILABLE FOR IMMEDIATE WITHDRAWAL

_____ SIGN HERE FOR CASH RECEIVED (IF REQUIRED) _____

26-2/840

TOTAL FROM OTHER SIDE		
TOTAL		
LESS CASH RECEIVED		
NET DEPOSIT	1,0 4 8	50

USE OTHER SIDE FOR ADDITIONAL LISTING

BE SURE EACH ITEM IS PROPERLY ENDORSED

Community Bank of Germantown
2177 Germantown Road • 7808 Farmington
Germantown, TN 38138 • (901) 754-2400 • Member FDIC

⑈08⑈0000 26⑈:9998

CHECKS AND OTHER ITEMS ARE RECEIVED FOR DEPOSIT SUBJECT TO THE PROVISIONS OF THE UNIFORM COMMERCIAL CODE OR ANY APPLICABLE COLLECTION AGREEMENT.

2.

717	Date 4/29 19 XX
Amount $155.30	
To Green Harvest	
For fresh vegetables	

Balance	7,869	40
Deposits	1,048	50
Total	8,917	90
Amount This Check	155	30
Balance	8,762	60

Park's Oriental Grocery — **456**
1428 Central Ave.
Germantown, TN 38138

April 29 19 XX   87-278/840

PAY TO THE ORDER OF _____Green Harvest_____ $ 155.30

One hundred and fifty- five and 30/100 _____ DOLLARS

Community Bank of Germantown
2177 Germantown Rd. South
Germantown, Tennessee 38138

MEMO fresh vegetables   Man Park

⑈08⑈00 278⑈: 63 1579 5⑈ 456

3.

RECORD ALL CHARGES OR CREDITS THAT AFFECT YOUR ACCOUNT							
NUMBER	DATE	DESCRIPTION OF TRANSACTION	AMOUNT OF CHECK	✓	FEE	AMOUNT OF DEPOSIT	BALANCE
							7869 40
	4/29	Deposit				1048 50	8917 90
456	4/29	Green Harvest	155 30				8762 60

4.

$ 12	32	BALANCE AS SHOWN ON BANK STATEMENT			BALANCE AS SHOWN IN YOUR CHECKBOOK	$ 178	74
650	00	ADD DEPOSITS NOT SHOWN ON STATEMENT			SUBTRACT AMOUNT OF SERVICE CHARGE	2	95
662	32	NEW TOTAL			NEW TOTAL	175	79
486	53	*SUBTRACT TOTAL OF OUTSTANDING CHECKS			ADJUSTMENTS IF ANY		
175	79	YOUR ADJUSTED STATEMENT BALANCE	SHOULD ⟷ EQUAL		YOUR ADJUSTED CHECKBOOK BALANCE	175	79

* OUTSTANDING CHECKS

CHECK NUMBER	DATE	AMOUNT	
		$ 36	52
		205	16
		18	92
		25	93
		200	00
		TOTAL...... 486	53	$

End of Chapter Problems

1. Write a check dated June 13, 19XX, to Byron Johnson in the amount of $296.83 for a washing machine.

KRA, INC.   **456**
2596 Jason Blvd.
Kansas City, KS 00000   _____ 19 ____   87-278/840

PAY TO THE
ORDER OF _____| $ _____

_____ DOLLARS

 Community Bank of Germantown
 2177 Germantown Rd. South
 Germantown, Tennessee 38138

MEMO _____ _____

⑆08400278⑈

2. Write a check dated August 18, 19XX, to Valley Electric Co-op in the amount of $189.32 for utilities.

Fileclip, Co.   **789**
10003 Lapolma Av.
Radcliff, NH 00000   _____ 19 ____   87-278/840

PAY TO THE
ORDER OF _____| $ _____

_____ DOLLARS

 Community Bank of Germantown
 2177 Germantown Rd. South
 Germantown, Tennessee 38138

MEMO _____ _____

⑆08400278⑈

3. Complete a deposit slip to add checks in the amounts of $136.00 and $278.96 and $480 cash on May 8, 19XX.

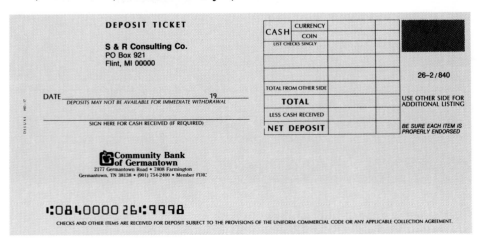

4. Complete a deposit slip on November 11, 19XX, to show the deposit of $100 in cash, checks in the amounts of $87.83, $42.97, and $106.32, with a $472.13 total from the other side of the deposit slip. Your account number is 8021346.

DEPOSIT TICKET

T. J. Jackson Enterprises
3232 Faxon Ave.
Cordora, ME 00000

DATE_____ 19_____

DEPOSITS MAY NOT BE AVAILABLE FOR IMMEDIATE WITHDRAWAL

_____
SIGN HERE FOR CASH RECEIVED (IF REQUIRED)

Community Bank of Germantown
2177 Germantown Road • 7808 Farmington
Germantown, TN 38138 • (901) 754-2400 • Member FDIC

⑈0840000 26⑈9998

CHECKS AND OTHER ITEMS ARE RECEIVED FOR DEPOSIT SUBJECT TO THE PROVISIONS OF THE UNIFORM COMMERCIAL CODE OR ANY APPLICABLE COLLECTION AGREEMENT.

CASH	CURRENCY	
	COIN	
LIST CHECKS SINGLY		

26-2/840

TOTAL FROM OTHER SIDE	
TOTAL	
LESS CASH RECEIVED	
NET DEPOSIT	

USE OTHER SIDE FOR ADDITIONAL LISTING

BE SURE EACH ITEM IS PROPERLY ENDORSED

786		
	Date_____19____	
Amount_____		
To_____		
For_____		
Balance Forward		
Deposits		
Total		
Amount This Check		
Balance		

5. Complete the stub for check 786, written on May 10, 19XX, to Jacqueline Voss Office Supplies in the amount of $28.97 for office supplies. The amount brought forward is $4,307.21.

6. Complete the stub for check 1021, written on September 30, 19XX, to Louis Jenkins Plumbing Service for plumbing repairs. The amount brought forward is $1,021.03 and the amount of the check is $65. Deposits of $146.00 and $297.83 were made before the check was written.

1021		
	Date_____19 XX	
Amount_____		
To_____		
For_____		
Balance Forward		
Deposits		
Total		
Amount This Check		
Balance		

7. Enter the following information and transactions in the check register for Happy Center Day Care. On July 10, 19XX, with an account balance of $983.47, check 1213 was written to Linens Inc. for $220.00 for laundry services, and check 1214 was written to Bugs Away for $65.00 for extermination services. On July 11, $80 was withdrawn from an automatic teller machine, and on July 12, checks in the amount of $123.86, $123.86, and $67.52 were deposited. Show the balance after these transactions.

		RECORD ALL CHARGES OR CREDITS THAT AFFECT YOUR ACCOUNT					BALANCE	
NUMBER	DATE	DESCRIPTION OF TRANSACTION	AMOUNT OF CHECK	√	FEE	AMOUNT OF DEPOSIT	$	
			$		$	$		

8. Fill out a deposit slip to show a check for $524.75 and $75.00 cash deposited on April 7, 19XX, to the CHD Company account.

```
                    DEPOSIT TICKET                    CASH |        | CURRENCY |   |   |
                                                            |        | COIN     |   |   |
                    CHD Company                              | LIST CHECKS SINGLY |   |   |
                    1234 B Boulevard                         |        |          |   |   |
                    Somewhere, USA 02135                     |        |          |   |   |
                                                            |        |          |   |   |
                                                                                      26-2/840
    DATE_____19___    TOTAL FROM OTHER SIDE |   |
          DEPOSITS MAY NOT BE AVAILABLE FOR IMMEDIATE WITHDRAWAL   TOTAL         |   |   USE OTHER SIDE FOR
                                                             LESS CASH RECEIVED |   |   ADDITIONAL LISTING
          SIGN HERE FOR CASH RECEIVED (IF REQUIRED)          NET DEPOSIT        |   |   BE SURE EACH ITEM IS
                                                                                      PROPERLY ENDORSED
              Community Bank
              of Germantown
         2177 Germantown Road • 7808 Farmington
       Germantown, TN 38138 • (901) 754-2400 • Member FDIC

    ⑆084000026⑈9998

    CHECKS AND OTHER ITEMS ARE RECEIVED FOR DEPOSIT SUBJECT TO THE PROVISIONS OF THE UNIFORM COMMERCIAL CODE OR ANY APPLICABLE COLLECTION AGREEMENT.
```

9. Write a check dated June 12, 19XX, to Alpine Industries in the amount of $85.50 for building supplies.

```
    Barter Home Repair                                              8212
    302 Cannon Dr.
    Germantown, TN 38138
                                                    _____ 19 ____    87-278/840

    PAY TO THE
    ORDER OF _____|  $
    _____ DOLLARS

         Community Bank of Germantown
         2177 Germantown Rd. South
         Germantown, Tennessee  38138

    MEMO _____    _____
    ⑆084002781⑆
```

10. Fill out the check stub for a check payable to Turner Wallcoverings for wallpaper installation in the amount of $145. The amount brought forward is $37.43. A cash deposit of $200 was made May 3.

11. Enter the following information and transactions in the check register for Sloan's Tree Service. On May 3, 19XX, with an account balance of $876.54, check 234 was written to Organic Materials for $175 for fertilizer and check 235 was written to Klean Kuts in the amount of $524.82 for a chain saw. On May 5, checks in the amount of $147.63 and $324.76 were deposited. Show the balance after these transactions.

```
    110                          Date _____ 19 ___
    Amount _____
    To _____
    For _____

    Balance Forward    |          |
    Deposits           |          |
    Total              |          |
    Amount This Check  |          |
    Balance            |          |
```

		RECORD ALL CHARGES OR CREDITS THAT AFFECT YOUR ACCOUNT					BALANCE	
NUMBER	DATE	DESCRIPTION OF TRANSACTION	AMOUNT OF CHECK	✓	FEE	AMOUNT OF DEPOSIT		

12. Answer the following questions about White Landscape Service's bank statement.
- **a.** How many deposits were made during the month?
- **b.** What amount of service charge was paid?
- **c.** What was the amount of the largest check written?
- **d.** How many checks appear on the bank statement?
- **e.** Give the balance at the beginning of the statement period.
- **f.** Give the balance at the end of the statement period.
- **g.** What is the amount of check 718?
- **h.** On what date did check 717 clear the bank?

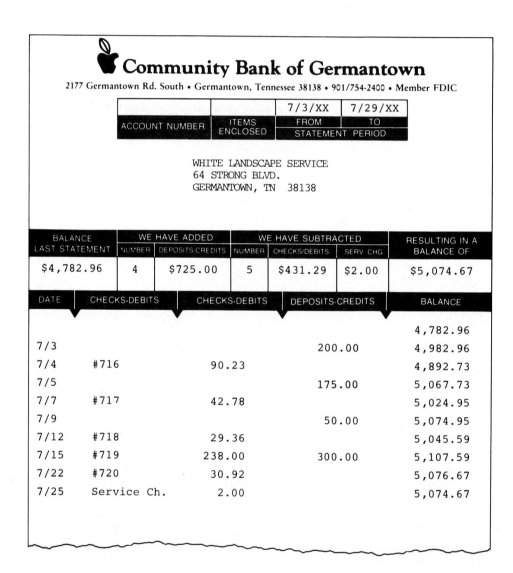

Community Bank of Germantown

2177 Germantown Rd. South • Germantown, Tennessee 38138 • 901/754-2400 • Member FDIC

ACCOUNT NUMBER	ITEMS ENCLOSED	7/3/XX FROM	7/29/XX TO
		STATEMENT PERIOD	

WHITE LANDSCAPE SERVICE
64 STRONG BLVD.
GERMANTOWN, TN 38138

BALANCE LAST STATEMENT	WE HAVE ADDED		WE HAVE SUBTRACTED			RESULTING IN A BALANCE OF
	NUMBER	DEPOSITS·CREDITS	NUMBER	CHECKS/DEBITS	SERV CHG	
$4,782.96	4	$725.00	5	$431.29	$2.00	$5,074.67

DATE	CHECKS-DEBITS	CHECKS-DEBITS	DEPOSITS-CREDITS	BALANCE
				4,782.96
7/3			200.00	4,982.96
7/4	#716	90.23		4,892.73
7/5			175.00	5,067.73
7/7	#717	42.78		5,024.95
7/9			50.00	5,074.95
7/12	#718	29.36		5,045.59
7/15	#719	238.00	300.00	5,107.59
7/22	#720	30.92		5,076.67
7/25	Service Ch.	2.00		5,074.67

13. Use the blank reconciliation form to reconcile the accompanying checkbook register and statement. Checks and deposits that have cleared the bank but are not shown on the pages of the check register are listed on a previous page of the check register.

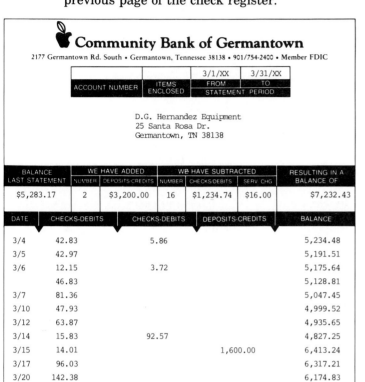

Community Bank of Germantown

2177 Germantown Rd. South • Germantown, Tennessee 38138 • 901/754-2400 • Member FDIC

ACCOUNT NUMBER	ITEMS ENCLOSED	3/1/XX FROM	3/31/XX TO
		STATEMENT PERIOD	

D.G. Hernandez Equipment
25 Santa Rosa Dr.
Germantown, TN 38138

BALANCE LAST STATEMENT	WE HAVE ADDED NUMBER	DEPOSITS-CREDITS	WE HAVE SUBTRACTED NUMBER	CHECKS/DEBITS	SERV. CHG	RESULTING IN A BALANCE OF
$5,283.17	2	$3,200.00	16	$1,234.74	$16.00	$7,232.43

DATE	CHECKS-DEBITS	CHECKS-DEBITS	DEPOSITS-CREDITS	BALANCE
3/4	42.83	5.86		5,234.48
3/5	42.97			5,191.51
3/6	12.15	3.72		5,175.64
	46.83			5,128.81
3/7	81.36			5,047.45
3/10	47.93			4,999.52
3/12	63.87			4,935.65
3/14	15.83	92.57		4,827.25
3/15	14.01		1,600.00	6,413.24
3/17	96.03			6,317.21
3/20	142.38			6,174.83
3/25	487.93			5,686.90
3/29	38.47			5,648.43
3/31	Service Charge	16.00	1,600.00	7,232.43

RECORD ALL CHARGES OR CREDITS THAT AFFECT YOUR ACCOUNT

NUMBER	DATE	DESCRIPTION OF TRANSACTION	AMOUNT OF CHECK	√	FEE	AMOUNT OF DEPOSIT	BALANCE 6413 24
783	3/16		96 03	√			6317 21
784	3/16		58 17				6259 04
785	3/16		73 27				6185 87
786	3/18		142 38	√			6043 49
787	3/20		487 93	√			5555 56
788	3/25		38 47	√			5517 09
789	3/27		72 83				5444 26
790	3/28		146 17				5298 09
791	3/29		152 03				5146 06
Dep.	3/31	salary		√		1600 00	6746 06
792	3/31		182 13				6563 93
793	3/31		16 18				6547 75
		adjusted balance					6531 65

REMEMBER TO RECORD AUTOMATIC PAYMENTS / DEPOSITS ON DATE AUTHORIZED.

$	BALANCE AS SHOWN ON BANK STATEMENT		BALANCE AS SHOWN IN YOUR CHECKBOOK	$
	ADD DEPOSITS NOT SHOWN ON STATEMENT		SUBTRACT AMOUNT OF SERVICE CHARGE	
	NEW TOTAL		NEW TOTAL	
	*SUBTRACT TOTAL OF OUTSTANDING CHECKS		ADJUSTMENTS IF ANY	
	YOUR ADJUSTED STATEMENT BALANCE	SHOULD EQUAL	YOUR ADJUSTED CHECKBOOK BALANCE	

* OUTSTANDING CHECKS

CHECK NUMBER	DATE	AMOUNT
		$
	TOTAL..........	$

14. The July bank statement for A and H Iron Works shows a balance of $37.94 and a service charge of $8.00. The checkbook register showed deposits of $650 and $375.56 that did not appear on the statement. Outstanding checks were in the amounts of $217.45, $57.82, $17.45, and $58.62. The checkbook balance was $720.16. Reconcile the bank statement with the checkbook balance.

$		BALANCE AS SHOWN ON BANK STATEMENT			BALANCE AS SHOWN IN YOUR CHECKBOOK	$	
		ADD DEPOSITS NOT SHOWN ON STATEMENT			SUBTRACT AMOUNT OF SERVICE CHARGE		
		NEW TOTAL			NEW TOTAL		
		*SUBTRACT TOTAL OF OUTSTANDING CHECKS			ADJUSTMENTS IF ANY		
		YOUR ADJUSTED STATEMENT BALANCE	SHOULD ◄──► EQUAL		YOUR ADJUSTED CHECKBOOK BALANCE		

* OUTSTANDING CHECKS

CHECK NUMBER	DATE	AMOUNT	
	TOTAL..............	$	

15. The September bank statement for Dixon Fence Company shows a balance of $275.25 and a service charge of $7.50. The checkbook register showed deposits of $120.43 and $625.56 that did not appear on the statement. Outstanding checks were in the amounts of $144.24, $154.48, $24.17, and $18.22. A $100 ATM withdrawal did not appear on the statement. The checkbook balance was $587.63. Reconcile the bank statement with the checkbook balance.

$		BALANCE AS SHOWN ON BANK STATEMENT			BALANCE AS SHOWN IN YOUR CHECKBOOK	$	
		ADD DEPOSITS NOT SHOWN ON STATEMENT			SUBTRACT AMOUNT OF SERVICE CHARGE		
		NEW TOTAL			NEW TOTAL		
		*SUBTRACT TOTAL OF OUTSTANDING CHECKS			ADJUSTMENTS IF ANY		
		YOUR ADJUSTED STATEMENT BALANCE	SHOULD ⟷ EQUAL		YOUR ADJUSTED CHECKBOOK BALANCE		

* OUTSTANDING CHECKS

CHECK NUMBER	DATE	AMOUNT	
	TOTAL............		$

16. The adjusted balance of the Taylor Flowers check register and bank statement are not equal. The bank statement shows a balance of $135.42 and a service charge of $8.00. The checkbook register shows deposits of $112.88 and $235.45 that did not appear on the statement. The checkbook register shows outstanding checks in the amounts of $17.42 and $67.90 and two cleared checks recorded as $145.69 and $18.22. The two cleared checks were written for $145.96 and $18.22. The checkbook balance was $406.70. Reconcile the bank statement with the checkbook balance.

$		BALANCE AS SHOWN ON BANK STATEMENT		BALANCE AS SHOWN IN YOUR CHECKBOOK	$	
		ADD DEPOSITS NOT SHOWN ON STATEMENT		SUBTRACT AMOUNT OF SERVICE CHARGE		
		NEW TOTAL		NEW TOTAL		
		*SUBTRACT TOTAL OF OUTSTANDING CHECKS		ADJUSTMENTS IF ANY		
		YOUR ADJUSTED STATEMENT BALANCE	SHOULD ⟷ EQUAL	YOUR ADJUSTED CHECKBOOK BALANCE		

* OUTSTANDING CHECKS

CHECK NUMBER	DATE	AMOUNT	
		TOTAL..................	$

17. The adjusted balances of the Randazzo's Market check register and bank statement are not equal. The bank statement shows a balance of $1,102.35 and a service charge of $6.50. The checkbook register shows a deposit of $265.49 that did not appear on the statement. The checkbook register shows outstanding checks in the amounts of $617.23 and $456.60 and two cleared checks recorded as $45.71 and $348.70. The two cleared checks were written for $45.71 and $384.70. The checkbook balance was $336.51. Reconcile the Randazzo's Market's bank statement with the checkbook balance.

$		BALANCE AS SHOWN ON BANK STATEMENT			BALANCE AS SHOWN IN YOUR CHECKBOOK	$	
		ADD DEPOSITS NOT SHOWN ON STATEMENT			SUBTRACT AMOUNT OF SERVICE CHARGE		
		NEW TOTAL			NEW TOTAL		
		*SUBTRACT TOTAL OF OUTSTANDING CHECKS			ADJUSTMENTS IF ANY		
		YOUR ADJUSTED STATEMENT BALANCE	SHOULD ⟷ EQUAL		YOUR ADJUSTED CHECKBOOK BALANCE		

* OUTSTANDING CHECKS

CHECK NUMBER	DATE	AMOUNT		
		TOTAL..............	$	

18. Answer the following questions about the bank statement for Henry Fusco Quick Shop.
   a. How many deposits were made during the month?
   b. What amount of service charge was paid?
   c. What was the amount of the smallest check written?
   d. How many checks appear on the bank statement?
   e. Give the balance at the beginning of the statement period.
   f. Give the balance at the end of the statement period.
   g. What is the amount of check 375?
   h. On what date did check 377 clear the bank?

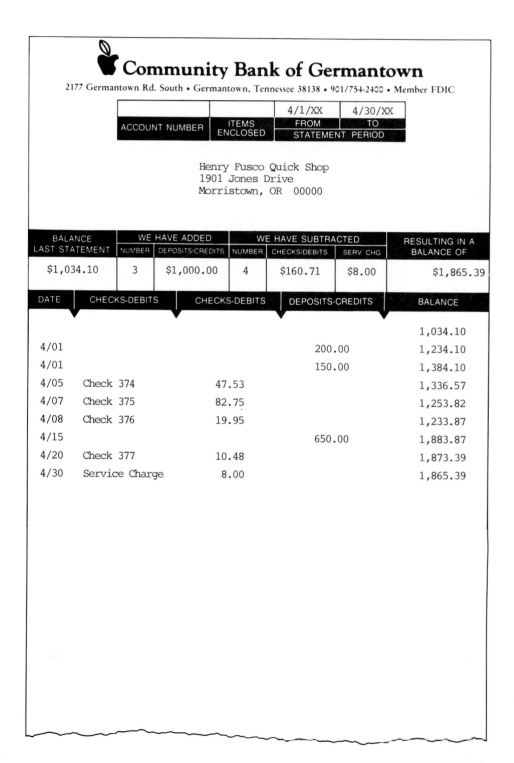

Community Bank of Germantown

2177 Germantown Rd. South • Germantown, Tennessee 38138 • 901/754-2400 • Member FDIC

ACCOUNT NUMBER	ITEMS ENCLOSED	4/1/XX FROM	4/30/XX TO
		STATEMENT PERIOD	

Henry Fusco Quick Shop
1901 Jones Drive
Morristown, OR 00000

BALANCE LAST STATEMENT	WE HAVE ADDED		WE HAVE SUBTRACTED			RESULTING IN A BALANCE OF
	NUMBER	DEPOSITS/CREDITS	NUMBER	CHECKS/DEBITS	SERV CHG	
$1,034.10	3	$1,000.00	4	$160.71	$8.00	$1,865.39

DATE	CHECKS-DEBITS	CHECKS-DEBITS	DEPOSITS-CREDITS	BALANCE
				1,034.10
4/01			200.00	1,234.10
4/01			150.00	1,384.10
4/05	Check 374	47.53		1,336.57
4/07	Check 375	82.75		1,253.82
4/08	Check 376	19.95		1,233.87
4/15			650.00	1,883.87
4/20	Check 377	10.48		1,873.39
4/30	Service Charge	8.00		1,865.39

19. Answer the following questions about the bank statement for Zucker's Apparel.
   a. How many deposits were made during the month?
   b. What amount of service charge was paid?
   c. How much were the total deposits?
   d. How many checks appear on the bank statement?
   e. Give the balance at the beginning of the statement period.
   f. Give the balance at the end of the statement period.
   g. What is the amount of check 453?
   h. On what date did check 457 clear the bank?

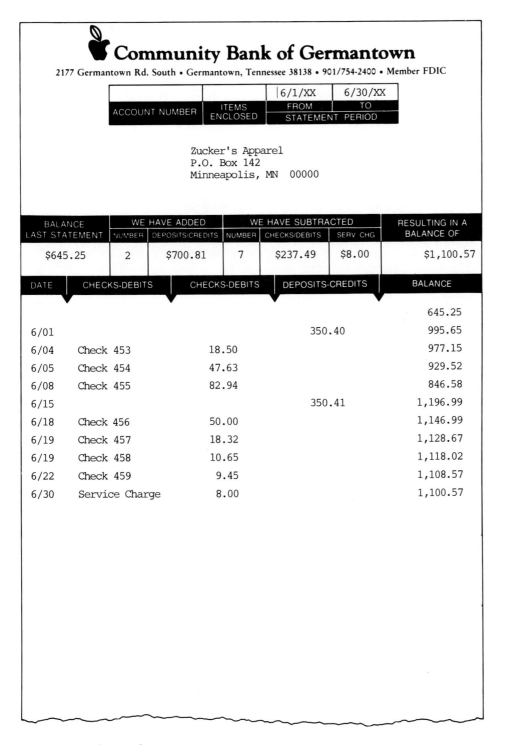

Community Bank of Germantown

2177 Germantown Rd. South • Germantown, Tennessee 38138 • 901/754-2400 • Member FDIC

ACCOUNT NUMBER	ITEMS ENCLOSED	6/1/XX FROM	6/30/XX TO
		STATEMENT PERIOD	

Zucker's Apparel
P.O. Box 142
Minneapolis, MN 00000

BALANCE LAST STATEMENT	WE HAVE ADDED NUMBER	DEPOSITS/CREDITS	WE HAVE SUBTRACTED NUMBER	CHECKS/DEBITS	SERV CHG	RESULTING IN A BALANCE OF
$645.25	2	$700.81	7	$237.49	$8.00	$1,100.57

DATE	CHECKS-DEBITS	CHECKS-DEBITS	DEPOSITS-CREDITS	BALANCE
				645.25
6/01			350.40	995.65
6/04	Check 453	18.50		977.15
6/05	Check 454	47.63		929.52
6/08	Check 455	82.94		846.58
6/15			350.41	1,196.99
6/18	Check 456	50.00		1,146.99
6/19	Check 457	18.32		1,128.67
6/19	Check 458	10.65		1,118.02
6/22	Check 459	9.45		1,108.57
6/30	Service Charge	8.00		1,100.57

Challenge Problem

Projecting Net Worth

Terry Kelly (whom we met in Chapter 1) talked with her investment counselor. She was advised to calculate her current net worth and to project her 1994 net worth to determine if her 1994 budget would accomplish her objective of increasing her net worth. She listed the following assets and liabilities for 1993. To calculate her net worth she found the difference between total assets and total liabilities.

ASSETS:

Checking Account	2,099
Savings Account	2,821
Auto	10,500
Home and Furnishings	65,000
Stocks and Bonds	4,017
Other Personal Property	3,200
Total assets	

LIABILITIES:

Car Loan	8,752
Home mortgage	54,879
Personal loan	1,791
Total liabilities	

Terry's home appreciated (increased) in value by 1/25 while her car depreciated (decreased) in value by 1/8. Her car loan will decrease by $2,100 while her home mortgage balance decreased by $887. Kelly plans to pay her personal loan in full by the end of 1994. Of her $2,000 planned investment, she will place $1,000 in savings and $1,000 in stocks and bonds. She also plans to reinvest the interest income of $141 (in savings) and the dividend income of $364 (in stocks and bonds) earned in 1993. She projects her checking account balance will be $1,500 at year-end for 1994.

Calculate Terry's total assets and total liabilities for 1993. Then calculate her net worth for 1993. Use the information given to project Terry's assets and liabilities for 1994. Then project her 1994 net worth. How much does Terry expect her net worth to increase (or decrease) from 1993 to 1994?

Trial Test

1. Fill out the check stub provided. The balance brought forward is $2,301.42, deposits were made for $200 on May 12 and $83.17 on May 20, and check 195 was written on May 25 to Lon Associates for $152.50 for supplies.

2. Answer the following questions about Dan Wilson's bank statement.
   a. What is the balance at the beginning of the statement period?

   b. How many checks cleared the bank during the statement period?

   c. What was the service charge for the statement period?
   d. Check 272 was written for what amount?
   e. On what date did check 275 clear the account?
   f. What was the total of the deposits?
   g. What was the balance at the end of the statement period?
   h. What was the total amount for all checks written during the period?

	Date _____ 19 ___
Amount	
To	
For	
Balance Forward	
Deposits	
Total	
Amount This Check	
Balance	

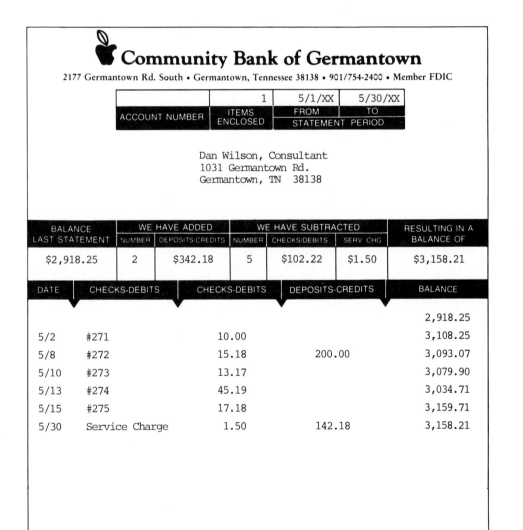

Community Bank of Germantown
2177 Germantown Rd. South • Germantown, Tennessee 38138 • 901/754-2400 • Member FDIC

ACCOUNT NUMBER	ITEMS ENCLOSED	FROM	TO
	1	5/1/XX	5/30/XX
		STATEMENT PERIOD	

Dan Wilson, Consultant
1031 Germantown Rd.
Germantown, TN 38138

BALANCE LAST STATEMENT	WE HAVE ADDED		WE HAVE SUBTRACTED			RESULTING IN A BALANCE OF
	NUMBER	DEPOSITS/CREDITS	NUMBER	CHECKS/DEBITS	SERV CHG	
$2,918.25	2	$342.18	5	$102.22	$1.50	$3,158.21

DATE	CHECKS-DEBITS	CHECKS-DEBITS	DEPOSITS-CREDITS	BALANCE
				2,918.25
5/2	#271	10.00		3,108.25
5/8	#272	15.18	200.00	3,093.07
5/10	#273	13.17		3,079.90
5/13	#274	45.19		3,034.71
5/15	#275	17.18		3,159.71
5/30	Service Charge	1.50	142.18	3,158.21

3. Reconcile the checkbook balance of $1,817.93 with the bank statement balance of $860.21. A service fee of $15.00 and one returned item of $213.83 were charged against the account. Outstanding deposits were in the amounts of $800.00 and $412.13. Outstanding checks were written for $243.17, $167.18, $13.97, $42.12, and $16.80. Find each of the following.

a. Bank statement balance	**e.** Checkbook balance
b. Outstanding deposits	**f.** Service fee
c. Outstanding checks	**g.** Returned items
d. Adjusted bank statement balance	**h.** Adjusted checkbook balance

$		BALANCE AS SHOWN ON BANK STATEMENT		BALANCE AS SHOWN IN YOUR CHECKBOOK	$	
		ADD DEPOSITS NOT SHOWN ON STATEMENT		SUBTRACT AMOUNT OF SERVICE CHARGE		
		NEW TOTAL		NEW TOTAL		
		*SUBTRACT TOTAL OF OUTSTANDING CHECKS		ADJUSTMENTS IF ANY RETURNED ITEM		
		YOUR ADJUSTED STATEMENT BALANCE	SHOULD ↔ EQUAL	YOUR ADJUSTED CHECKBOOK BALANCE		

* OUTSTANDING CHECKS

CHECK NUMBER	DATE	AMOUNT	
		$	
	TOTAL..........	$	

A look at statistics that shape your finances

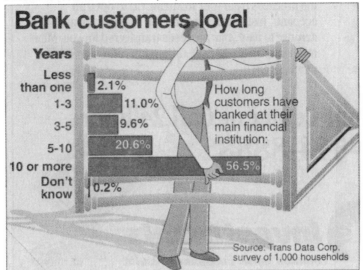

Bank customers loyal

Years

Less than one	2.1%
1-3	11.0%
3-5	9.6%
5-10	20.6%
10 or more	56.5%
Don't know	0.2%

How long customers have banked at their main financial institution:

Source: Trans Data Corp. survey of 1,000 households

By Julie Stacey, USA TODAY

QUESTIONS

1. What percent of bank customers keep their account at a bank for less than 5 years?

2. What percent of bank customers have banked at their present financial institution for 5 or more years?

3. What are some reasons for changing banks?

4. What details must be considered to move an account from one bank to another?

3

Using Equations to Solve Problems

equation: a symbolic statement that the numbers and symbols on each side of the equal sign have the same value.

unknown: the quantity in a problem or an equation that is not given or known; usually represented by a letter in an equation.

Solving many business problems—be it determining an employee's wages, or inventory levels, or profits—involves answering the question "How much?" Often, the simplest way to find the answer is to convert the question into an *equation*. An **equation** is really just mathematical shorthand for a question, in which you substitute an equal sign for the verb in the sentence, use letters to represent any **unknown** quantity, and connect the elements involved with mathematical symbols such as $+$, $-$, $\times$, and $\div$. *Solving an equation* means finding the missing or unknown amount. To solve an equation, you isolate the unknown on one side of the equation with numbers and mathematical symbols all on the other side.

For example, take the question "How much profit did a company make when it had receipts of $50,000 and expenses of $20,000?" In equation form, we could abbreviate profits as P and write the question as

$$P = \$50,000 - \$20,000$$

Here we can subtract to find that $P = \$30,000$.

In this chapter we will first consider how to solve an equation that has already been set up before turning to the somewhat more complicated process of converting a question into a mathematical equation in order to solve a word problem.

3.1 Solving Equations

Suppose 15 of the 25 people who work at Pandora Carton Manufacturers work on the day shift. How many people work there in the evening? You know that 15 people work there during the day, that 25 people work there in all, and that some unknown quantity work there in the evening. Assign the letter N to the unknown number of night-shift workers. The information from the problem can then be written in words as "the night-shift workers plus the day-shift workers equal 25" and in symbols: $N + 15 = 25$.

You can solve many equations if you follow a few steps:

STEP BY STEP

Solving a Simple Equation

Step 1. Do the opposite of the operation that is used in the equation. Addition and subtraction are opposite operations; so are multiplication and division. If a number is added, you subtract the number; if a number is multiplied, you divide the number, and so on.

Step 2. Do the same on *both* sides of the equation.

EXAMPLE 1

Solve the equation $N + 15 = 25$. (A number increased by 15 is 25.)

$$\begin{array}{rr} N + 15 = & 25 \\ -15 & -15 \\ \hline N \quad = & 10 \end{array}$$

$$N = 10$$

In this equation, 15 is added, so you do the opposite: You subtract 15 from both sides of the equation. This leaves you with $N = 10$.

Check:

$$N + 15 = 25$$
$$10 + 15 \stackrel{?}{=} 25$$
$$25 = 25$$

To check, put the answer into the original equation in place of the letter and see if both sides of the equation represent the same number.

The following examples show these two steps applied to equations involving a number of different operations.

EXAMPLE 2

Find the value of A if $A - 5 = 8$. (A number decreased by 5 is 8.)

$$\begin{array}{rr} A - 5 = & 8 \\ +5 & +5 \\ \hline A \quad = & 13 \end{array}$$

The equation shows 5 is subtracted, so you do the opposite: You add 5 to both sides of the equation.

Check:

$$A - 5 = 8$$
$$13 - 5 \stackrel{?}{=} 8$$
$$8 = 8$$

To check, substitute the number for the letter in the equation and see if both sides yield the same number.

Beginning with the next example, certain mathematical conventions for representing multiplication and division will be used in the equation. You will need to become familiar with the conventions, or customary notation, used in writing equations.

TIPS &TRAPS

Customary Notation Used in Writing Equations

$$2A = 2 \times A \qquad\qquad \frac{A}{B} = A \div B$$

$$2A = 2 \cdot A$$

$$AB = A \times B \qquad 3(A + B) = 3A + 3B = 3 \times A + 3 \times B$$

$$A = 1 \times A$$

$$3(7) = 3 \times 7$$

EXAMPLE 3

Solve the equation $2A = 18$. (A number multiplied by 2 is 18.)

$2A = 18$
$\dfrac{2A}{2} = \dfrac{18}{2}$
$A = 9$

The equation shows multiplication by 2; so you do the opposite: You divide both sides of the equation by 2.

Check:
$2A = 18$
$2(9) \stackrel{?}{=} 18$
$18 = 18$

To check, substitute the number for the letter in the equation and see if both sides are equal.

EXAMPLE 4

Find the value of A if $\dfrac{A}{4} = 5$. (A number divided by 4 is 5.)

$\dfrac{A}{4} = 5$
$4\left(\dfrac{A}{4}\right) = 5(4)$
$A = 20$

The equation shows division by 4, so you do the opposite: You multiply both sides of the equation by 4.

Check:

$\dfrac{A}{4} = 5$
$\dfrac{20}{4} \stackrel{?}{=} 5$
$5 = 5$

To check, substitute the number for the letter in the equation and see if both sides are equal.

Solving for Multiple Operations

Not all equations used in the business world are this direct. Many require several more solution steps. When you solve an equation, be sure to follow these rules concerning the order in which you do the steps.

STEP BY STEP

Steps for Solving an Equation Involving More Than One Operation

Step 1. Remove values that are added or subtracted by applying the opposite operations to both sides.

Step 2. Next, remove any value involving multiplication or division with the unknown by applying the opposite operation to both sides.

EXAMPLE 5

Find A if $2A + 1 = 15$. (Two times a number increased by 1 is 15.)

The equation uses both addition and multiplication; handle addition first and then multiplication.

$$
\begin{array}{rcr}
2A + 1 = & & 15 \\
-1 & & -1 \\
\hline
2A & = & 14
\end{array}
$$

The equation shows addition of 1, so do the opposite: Subtract 1 from both sides of the equation.

$$
\begin{aligned}
2A &= 14 \\
\frac{2A}{2} &= \frac{14}{2} \\
A &= 7
\end{aligned}
$$

The equation shows multiplication by 2, so do the opposite: Divide both sides of the equation by 2.

Check:
$$
\begin{aligned}
2A + 1 &= 15 \\
2(7) + 1 &\overset{?}{=} 15 \\
14 + 1 &\overset{?}{=} 15 \\
15 &= 15
\end{aligned}
$$

To check, you substitute the number for the letter in the equation and see if both sides are equal.

EXAMPLE 6

Solve the equation $\dfrac{A}{5} - 3 = 1$.

(A number divided by 5 and decreased by 3 is 1.)

The equation uses both subtraction and division; you handle subtraction first and then division.

$$
\begin{array}{rcr}
\dfrac{A}{5} - 3 = & & 1 \\
+3 & & +3 \\
\hline
\dfrac{A}{5} & = & 4
\end{array}
$$

The equation shows subtraction of 3, so do the opposite: Add 3 to both sides of the equation.

$$
\dfrac{A}{5} = 4
$$

$$
5\left(\dfrac{A}{5}\right) = 4(5)
$$

$$
A = 20
$$

The equation shows division by 5, so multiply both sides by 5.

Check:
$$
\dfrac{A}{5} - 3 = 1
$$

$$
\dfrac{20}{5} - 3 \overset{?}{=} 1
$$

$$
4 - 3 \overset{?}{=} 1
$$

$$
1 = 1
$$

To check, substitute the number for the letter in the equation and see if both sides are equal.

The next example shows what to do when parentheses are involved in an equation.

STEP BY STEP

Solving Equations Containing Parentheses

Step 1. Remove parentheses by multiplying the number just before the parentheses times each quantity inside the parentheses.

Step 2. Next, do additions and subtractions.

Step 3. Then, do multiplications and divisions.

EXAMPLE 7

Solve the equation $5(A + 3) = 25$.

$5(A + 3) = 25$
$5A + 15 = 25$

The parentheses must be removed first, so you perform the operation that will do that—multiplication. (You are *not* doing the opposite of what is shown in the equation, and you do *not* do it on both sides of the equation, just where the parentheses occur.)

$$
\begin{array}{rcr}
5A + 15 &=& 25 \\
-15 && -15 \\
\hline
5A &=& 10
\end{array}
$$

Now the equation shows addition of 15, so you do the opposite: Subtract 15 from both sides of the equation.

$$
\frac{5A}{5} = \frac{10}{5}
$$
$$
A = 2
$$

The equation shows multiplication, so do the opposite: Divide both sides of the equation by 5.

TIPS & TRAPS

Parentheses in an equation should grab your attention, because they say DO ME FIRST; you need to perform the operations to remove the parentheses before you do anything else in the equation. Trying to deal with an equation *without* removing parentheses can lead to wrong answers, as shown here.

Find X if $5(X - 2) = 45$.

$5(X - 2) = 45$

$$
\begin{array}{rcr}
5X - 10 &=& 45 \\
+10 && +10 \\
\hline
5X &=& 55
\end{array}
$$

$$
\frac{5X}{5} = \frac{55}{5}
$$

$$
X = 11
$$

CORRECT

$$
\begin{array}{rcr}
5(X - 2) &=& 45 \\
+2 && +2 \\
\hline
5X &=& 47
\end{array}
$$

$$
\frac{5X}{5} = \frac{47}{5}
$$

$$
X = 9\frac{2}{5}
$$

WRONG

Check:

$5(A + 3) = 25$

$5(2 + 3) \stackrel{?}{=} 25$

$10 + 15 \stackrel{?}{=} 25$

$25 = 25$

To check, substitute the number for the letter in the equation and see if both sides are equal.

Equations with Multiple Use of the Unknown

Some problems involve the use of the unknown more than once in an equation.

STEP BY STEP

Combining Unknowns in an Equation

Step 1. Combine the unknowns by adding or subtracting the numbers in front of the letters. If no number is written in front of a letter, it is understood to be a 1. Thus, $X = 1X$.

Step 2. Next, do additions and subtractions.

Step 3. Then, do multiplications and divisions.

EXAMPLE 8

Find A if $A + 3A - 2 = 14$.

$A + 3A - 2 = 14$

First, combine the unknowns. Remember that A is the same as $1A$, so $A + 3A = 4A$.

$$\begin{array}{rcr} 4A - 2 = & & 14 \\ + 2 & + & 2 \\ \hline 4A \quad = & & 16 \end{array}$$

The equation uses both subtraction and multiplication; handle subtraction first. Do this by *adding* 2 to both sides of the equation.

$$\frac{4A}{4} = \frac{16}{4}$$

$$A = 4$$

The equation shows multiplication by 4, so do the opposite: Divide both sides of the equation by 4.

Check:

$A + 3A - 2 = 14$

$4 + 3(4) - 2 \stackrel{?}{=} 14$

$4 + 12 - 2 \stackrel{?}{=} 14$

$16 - 2 \stackrel{?}{=} 14$

$14 = 14$

To check, substitute the number for the letter in the equation and see if both sides are the same.

 Self-Check

Identify the operation illustrated in each equation.

1. $P + I = A$ **2.** $R = \dfrac{M}{N}$ **3.** $AS = T$ **4.** $S = R - T$

Find the value of N.

5. $N + 3 = 12$ **6.** $N - 5 = 44$ **7.** $4N = 36$ **8.** $\dfrac{N}{7} = 3$

9. $3N + 5 = 17$ **10.** $\dfrac{N}{3} - 1 = 10$ **11.** $2(N + 6) = 18$ **12.** $N - 9 + 3N = 19$

3.2 Converting Word Problems into Equations

LEARNING OBJECTIVE

1. Use the key word approach to analyze and solve word problems and check the answers.

When you first read a word problem, you must ask: What are we supposed to find? What facts are given? What facts are implied?

To solve a word problem, you should use a systematic approach in writing an equation to answer the question. The following steps should be useful.

STEP BY STEP

Writing Equations

Step 1. Separate the known from the unknown quantities.

Step 2. Decide what quantities are equal to each other.

Step 3. Choose a symbol for the unknown quantity.

Step 4. Set up an equation with mathematical operations and symbols to describe the conditions of the problem. It is generally preferred to place unknown quantities on the left.

Certain key words in a problem give you clues as to whether a certain quantity is added to, subtracted from, or multiplied or divided by another quantity. For example, if a word problem tells you that Carol's salary in 1993 *exceeds* her 1982 salary by $2,500, you know that you should *add* $2,500 to her 1982 salary to find her 1993 salary. Many times, when you see the word *of* in a problem, you can assume that the problem involves multiplication. Table 3-1 summarizes important key words and what they generally mean when they are used in a word problem. This list should help you analyze the information in word problems and write the information in symbols.

Table 3-1 Key Words and What They Generally Mean in Word Problems

Addition	Subtraction	Multiplication	Division	Equality
The sum of	Less than	Times	Divide(s)	Equals
Plus/total	Decreased by	Multiplied by	Divided by	Is/was/are
Increased by	Subtracted from	Of	Divided into	Is equal to
More/more than	Difference between	The product of	Half of (divided by two)	The result is
Added to	Diminished by	Twice (two times)	Third ($\frac{1}{3}$ times)	What is left
Exceeds	Take away	Double (two times)	Per	What remains
Expands	Reduced by	Triple (three times)		The same as
Greater than	Less/minus	Half ($\frac{1}{2}$ times)		Gives/giving
Gain/profit	Loss			Makes
Longer	Lower			Leaves
Older	Shrinks			
Heavier	Smaller than			
Wider	Younger			
Taller	Slower			

EXAMPLE 9

Full-time employees at Eddie's Fast Eatery differ from part-time employees in number of hours worked. If part-timers work 6 hours per day and the difference is 4 hours per day (with full-timers working more), how long do full-timers work? The word *difference* in the problem tells you to use subtraction to find the unknown number.

Unknown	Facts	Plan	Solution
Number of full time hours = n	Other number = 6 Difference = 4	If 6 is subtracted from a number, the result is 4. $n - 6 = 4$	$\begin{array}{rcr} n - 6 = & & 4 \\ + 6 & & + 6 \\ \hline n = & & 10 \end{array}$

Check
$10 - 6 \overset{?}{=} 4$
$4 = 4$

The number of full-time hours is 10.

EXAMPLE 10

Wanda plans to save $\frac{1}{10}$ of her salary each week. If her weekly salary is $350, find the amount she will save each week.

The word *of* in the problem tells you to use multiplication to find the unknown number.

Unknown	Facts	Plan	Solution
Amount to be saved = S	Total salary = $350 Portion to be saved = $\frac{1}{10}$	$\frac{1}{10}$ of salary will be saved. $\frac{1}{10}(350) = S$	$S = \frac{1}{\underset{1}{10}} \cdot \frac{\overset{35}{350}}{1}$ $S = 35$

Check
$\frac{1}{10}(350) \overset{?}{=} 35$
$35 = 35$

Wanda will save $35 a week.

TIPS & TRAPS

It's a good idea to read a word problem several times. With each reading a different aspect of the problem is analyzed.

1. Read for a general understanding of the problem.

2. Read to determine what you want to find.

3. Read to locate the given and implied facts.

4. Read to relate the known and unknown facts (write the equation).

5. After solving the equation, read to see if the solution satisfies the conditions of the problem.

EXAMPLE 11

At Alexander's Cafe last Wednesday, there were twice as many requests for seats in the nonsmoking section as there were requests for seats in the smok-

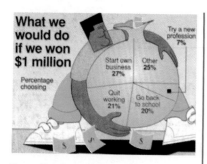
ing section. If a total 342 customers came through the cafe that day, how many were smokers? How many were nonsmokers?

Study the key words: In "twice as many" requests for the nonsmoking section, the word *twice* indicates that you should let S equal the number of smokers and let $2S$ equal the number of nonsmokers. The expression "a total of 342 customers" tells us that the *sum* of the number of smokers and the number of nonsmokers will equal the number of customers.

Unknown	Facts	Plan	Solution
Number of smokers = S Number of non-smokers = $2S$	Total number of customers = 342	Number of smokers + number of nonsmokers = total number of customers. Combine terms. Divide both sides of the equation by 3. Multiply 114 by 2 to find $2S$.	$S + 2S = 342$ $3S = 342$ $S = 114$ $2S = 228$

There were 114 smokers and 228 nonsmokers.

Check
Does $114 + 2(114)$ $= 342?$ $342 = 342$

EXAMPLE 12

Juana supervises six times as many data entry clerks as Millie. There are ten fewer clerks working for Millie than working for Juana. How many people are working for each supervisor?

Study the key words: In "six times as many," the words *six times* indicate that you should let M equal the number of clerks working for Millie and let $6M$ equal the number of clerks working for Juana. The expression "ten fewer clerks" tells us that the *difference between $6M$ and M* is ten.

Unknown	Facts	Plan	Solution
Number of Millie's employees = M Number of Juana's employees = $6M$ (six times as many)	The difference between the number of clerks working for Juana and the number working for Millie is 10.	Subtract the number of Millie's clerks from the number of Juana's clerks and get a difference of 10. Combine terms. Divide both sides of the equation by 5. Multiply 2 by 6 to find $6M$.	$6M - M = 10$ $5M = 10$ $M = 2$ $6M = 12$

Millie supervises 2 clerks; Jauna supervises 12 clerks.

Check
Does $6(2) - 2 = 10?$ $12 - 2 \overset{?}{=} 10$ $10 = 10$

Many problems give a *total* number of two types of items. You want to know the number of each of the two types of items. The next example illustrates this type of problem.

How to Solve Another Tricky Word Problem

Many problems encountered daily can be solved by using proportions. Most problems that involve a relationship between two sets of numbers can be solved by this technique, but you must be careful to be consistent in setting up the equation.

Proportions contain two equal ratios (fractions) used to compare two quantities; for example, using 2 ounces out of a 4-gallon bottle of cleaning fluid is proportional to using 4 ounces out of an 8-gallon bottle. Expressed as a proportion, this example would be

$$\frac{2 \text{ oz}}{4 \text{ gal}} = \frac{4 \text{ oz}}{8 \text{ gal}}$$

If one of the four numbers in the proportion is missing, you can find it by using cross-multiplication:

$$\frac{3}{x} \times \frac{7}{5}$$

$$7 \cdot x = 3 \cdot 5$$

$$7x = 15$$

$$\frac{7x}{7} = \frac{15}{7}$$

$$x = 2\frac{1}{7}$$

In solving a word problem by this method, it is helpful to write in words the units being compared. There are usually three known values and two different units. Write a comparison of the two units and solve the problem.

Example: Your car gets 23 miles to a gallon of gas. How far can you go on 16 gallons of gas?

$$\frac{\text{miles}}{\text{gallons}} \longrightarrow \frac{23 \text{ miles}}{1 \text{ gal}} = \frac{x \text{ miles}}{16 \text{ gals}}$$

$$1x = 23 \cdot 16$$

$$1x = 368$$

$$x = 368 \text{ miles on 16 gallons}$$

Example: The label on a container of weed killer gives directions for mixing 3 ounces to 2 gallons of water. If your sprayer holds 5 gallons, how many ounces of the weed killer must you use?

$$\frac{\text{ounces}}{\text{gallons}} \longrightarrow \frac{3 \text{ oz}}{2 \text{ gal}} = \frac{x \text{ oz}}{5 \text{ gal}}$$

$$2x = 15$$

$$x = 7\frac{1}{2} \text{ ounces}$$

Application Questions

1. A scale drawing of an office building is not labeled, but indicates $\frac{1}{4}'' = 5'$. On the drawing, one wall measures 2 inches. How long is the wall?

2. A recipe uses 3 cups of flour to $1\frac{1}{4}$ cups of milk. If you have 2 cups of flour, how much milk should you use?

3. For 32 hours of work, you are paid $241.60. How much would you receive for 37 hours?

EXAMPLE 13

The Cheerful card shop spent a total of $950 ordering 600 cards from Wit's End Co., whose humorous cards cost $1.75 each and whose nature cards cost $1.50 each. How many of each style card did the card shop order? How much did it spend on each type of card?

Study the problem: You know the total cost ($950) and the total number of cards ordered (600). You also know how much each type of card costs. The number of humorous cards added to the number of nature cards totals 600. The amount of money spent on both types of cards totals $950. In this type of problem, you may use the most expensive item as the variable, H, or the number of humorous cards. Then, the nature cards can be represented as $600 - H$, the total number of cards minus the humorous cards.

Unknown	Facts	Plan	Solution
Number of humorous cards = H	Total number of cards = 600	The sum of the costs of both types of cards equals the total sale.	$1.75H + 1.50(600 - H) = 950$
Number of nature cards = $600 - H$	Cost of humorous cards = $\$1.75H$	Remove the parentheses	$1.75H + 900 - 1.50H = 950$
	Cost of nature cards = $\$1.50(600 - H)$	Combine terms.	
	Total sale = $\$950$	Subtract 900 from both sides of the equation.	$0.25H + 900 = 950$ $0.25H = 50$
		Divide both sides of the equation by 0.25.	$H = 200$
		Subtract 200 from 600 to find $600 - H$.	$600 - H = 400$ $600 - 200 = 400$

200 humorous cards were bought and
400 nature cards were bought.

Check
Does $1.75(200) + 1.5(600 - 200) = 950$? $350 + 900 - 300 \overset{?}{=} 950$ $950 = 950$

  Self-Check 3.2

13. The difference in hours between full-timers and the part-timers who work 5 hours a day is 4 hours. How long do full-timers work?

14. Manny plans to save $\frac{1}{12}$ of his salary each week. If his weekly salary is $372, find the amount he will save each week.

15. Last week at the Sunshine Valley Rock Festival, Joel sold three times as many tie-dyed T-shirts as silk-screened shirts. He sold 176 shirts altogether. How many tie-dyed shirts did he sell?

16. Elaine sold three times as many magazine subscriptions as Ron did. Ron sold 16 fewer subscriptions than Elaine did. How many subscriptions did each sell?

17. Will ordered two times as many boxes of ballpoint pens as boxes of felt-tip pens. Ballpoint pens cost $3.50 per box, and felt-tip pens cost $4.50. If Will's order of pens totaled $46, how many boxes of each type of pen did he buy?

18. A real-estate salesperson bought promotional calendars and date books to give to her customers at the end of the year. The calendars cost $0.75 each and the date books cost $0.50 each. She ordered a total of 500 promotional items and spent $300. How many of each item did she order?

Summary

Topic	Page	What to Remember	Examples
Solving an equation	99	Do the *opposite* of the operation that is shown in the equation, and do it on *both sides* of the equation:	
		If the equation shows addition, subtract the same number from both sides of the equation.	$A + 11 = 19$. Find the value of A. $A + 11 = 19$ $\underline{ - 11 \quad -11}$ $A = 8$

Chapter 3   Using Equations to Solve Problems

Topic	Page	What to Remember	Examples
Solving an equation	99	If the equation shows subtraction, add the same number to both sides of the equation.	$A - 7 = 12$. Find the value of A. $\begin{aligned} A - 7 &= 12 \\ +7 \quad &\quad +7 \\ \hline A &= 19 \end{aligned}$
		If the equation show multiplication, divide both sides of the equation by the same number.	$4A = 36$. Find the value of A. $\dfrac{4A}{4} = \dfrac{36}{4}$ $A = 9$
		If the equation shows division, multiply both sides of the equation by the same number.	$\dfrac{A}{7} = 6$. Find the value of A. $\dfrac{A}{7} \times 7 = 6 \times 7$ $A = 42$
Equations with more than one operation	101	Do the additions and subtractions first; then do the multiplications and divisions.	$\begin{aligned} 4A + 4 &= 20 \\ 4A + 4 &= 20 \\ -4 \quad &\quad -4 \\ \hline 4A &= 16 \end{aligned}$ Find the value of A. Undo addition first. $\dfrac{4A}{4} = \dfrac{16}{4}$ Then undo division. $A = 4$
Removing parentheses	102	Remove parentheses by multiplying everything within the parentheses by the number to the left of the parentheses.	$\begin{aligned} 3(A + 4) &= 27 \\ 3A + 12 &= 27 \\ -12 \quad &\quad -12 \\ \hline 3A &= 15 \end{aligned}$ $\dfrac{3A}{3} = \dfrac{15}{3}$ $A = 5$
Combining unknowns	103	Combine all possible variables before taking other steps to solve the equation.	$A - 5 + 5A = 25$ $\begin{aligned} 6A - 5 &= 25 \\ +5 \quad &\quad +5 \\ \hline 6A &= 30 \end{aligned}$ $\dfrac{6A}{6} = \dfrac{30}{6}$ $A = 5$
Using key words	104	Use key words in a problem to convert the facts of a word problem to mathematical symbols.	See Table 3-1 for key words.
Difference problems	105	The word *difference* in the problem tells you to use subtraction to write the equation.	The difference in cost per unit between plastic playing cards and $3 paper cards is $12. How much do the plastic cards cost?

Unknown	Facts	Solution
Cost of plastic cards = n	Other number = 3 Difference = 12 $n - 3 = 12$	$\begin{aligned} n - 3 &= 12 \\ +3 \quad &\quad +3 \\ \hline n &= 15 \end{aligned}$

Topic	Page	What to Remember	Examples

Finding a part   105

Of in the problem usually tells you to use multiplication to find the unknown number.

Gabriella spends $\frac{2}{5}$ of her workday typing. If she works 40 hours a week, how many hours does she type each week?

Unknown	Facts	Solution
Number of hours typing = T	Total hours at work = 40	$T = \frac{2}{5} \times 40$
	Part of day spent typing = $\frac{2}{5}$	$T = 16$ hours

Finding parts of a whole   106

Twice as many tells you that one part of the whole is two times the size of the other part, and *total* tells you to add the two parts.

There are twice as many students in the daytime aerobics class as there are in the night class. If there are 48 students total, how many students are in each class?

Unknown	Facts	Solution
Number of night students = S	Total number of students = 48	$S + 2S = 48$
Number of day students = $2S$		$3S = 48$
		$\dfrac{3S}{3} = \dfrac{48}{3}$
		$S = 16$
		$2S = 32$

Finding parts, given a total   107

The total minus one part equals the other part.

Charles sold 20 sets of baseball cards for a total of $525. Fleer sets sell for $30 and Tops sets sell for $25. How many sets of each type were sold?

Unknown	Facts	Solution
Number of Fleer sets sold = F	Total number of sets sold = 20	$30F + 25(20 - F) = 525$
Number of Tops sets sold = $20 - F$	Value of Fleer sets = $30F$	$30F + 500 - 25F = 525$
		$5F + 500 = 525$
	Value of Tops sets = $25(20 - F)$	$5F = 525 - 500$
		$5F = 25$
	Total value = $525	$F = 5$ (Fleer sets)
	$30F + 25(20 - F) = 525$	$20 - F = 15$ (Tops sets)

Self-Check Solutions

1. Addition   **2.** Division   **3.** Multiplication   **4.** Subtraction

5.
$$\begin{array}{rcr} N + 3 &=& 12 \\ -\ 3 && -\ 3 \\ \hline N &=& 9 \end{array}$$

6.
$$\begin{array}{rcr} N - 5 &=& 44 \\ +\ 5 && +\ 5 \\ \hline N &=& 49 \end{array}$$

7.
$$\begin{array}{rcl} 4N &=& 36 \\ \dfrac{4N}{4} &=& \dfrac{36}{4} \\ N &=& 9 \end{array}$$

8.
$$\frac{N}{7} = 3$$
$$7\left(\frac{N}{7}\right) = 3(7)$$
$$N = 21$$

9.
$$\begin{array}{rcr} 3N + 5 &=& 17 \\ -\ 5 && -\ 5 \\ \hline 3N &=& 12 \end{array}$$
$$\frac{3N}{3} = \frac{12}{3}$$
$$N = 4$$

10.
$$\frac{N}{3} - 1 = 10$$
$$\underline{\quad +1 \quad + 1}$$
$$\frac{N}{3} = 11$$

$$3\left(\frac{N}{3}\right) = 11(3)$$
$$N = 33$$

11.
$$2(N + 6) = 18$$
$$2N + 12 = 18$$
$$\underline{\quad -12 \quad -12}$$
$$2N = 6$$

$$\frac{2N}{2} = \frac{6}{2}$$
$$N = 3$$

12.
$$N - 9 + 3N = 19$$
$$4N - 9 = 19$$
$$\underline{\quad +9 \quad +9}$$
$$4N = 28$$

$$\frac{4N}{4} = \frac{28}{4}$$
$$N = 7$$

13.

Unknown	Facts	Plan	Solution
Number of full time hours = N	Part time hours worked = 5 Difference = 4	If 5 is subtracted from a number, the result is 4. Add 5 to both sides.	$N - 5 = 4$ $\underline{\quad +5 \quad +5}$ $N = 9$

The number of full-time hours is 9.

Check
$9 - 5 \overset{?}{=} 4$ $4 = 4$

14.

Unknown	Facts	Plan	Solution
Amount to be saved = S	Total salary = $372 Portion to be saved = $\frac{1}{12}$	$\frac{1}{12}$ of salary will be saved. Multiply.	$\frac{1}{12}(372) = S$ $\frac{1}{12} \cdot \frac{372}{1} = S$ $31 = S$

Manny will save $31 each week.

Check
$\frac{1}{12} \cdot \frac{372}{1} \overset{?}{=} 31$ $31 = 31$

15.

Unknown	Facts	Plan	Solution
Number of silk-screen shirts sold = N	Total number of shirts sold = 176	Number of silk-screen shirts sold + number of tie-dyed shirts sold = 176. Combine terms. Divide both sides of the equation by 4.	$N + 3N = 176$ $4N = 176$ $\frac{4N}{4} = \frac{176}{4}$ $N = 44$
Number of tie-dyed shirts sold = $3N$ (three times as many)		Find the number of tie-dyed shirts by multiplying 44 by 3.	$3N = 132$

There were 44 silk-screen and 132 tie-dyed shirts sold.

Check
Does $44 + 3(44) \overset{?}{=} 176$ $44 + 132 \overset{?}{=} 176$ $176 = 176$

16.

Unknown	Facts	Plan	Solution
Number of subscriptions sold by Ron = M Number of subscriptions sold by Elaine = $3M$ (three times as many)	The difference between the number of Elaine's and Ron's subscriptions = 16.	Subtract the number of Ron's from the number of Elaine's and get a difference of 16. Combine terms. Divide both sides by 2. Multiply 8 by 3.	$3M - M = 16$ $2M = 16$ $\dfrac{2M}{2} = \dfrac{16}{2}$ $M = 8$ $3M = 24$

Ron sold 8 magazine subscriptions and Elaine sold 24.

Check

$3(8) - 8 \overset{?}{=} 16$
$24 - 8 \overset{?}{=} 16$
$16 = 16$

17.

Unknown	Facts	Plan	Solution
Number of boxes of felt-tip pens = N Number of boxes of ballpoint pens = $2N$	Total value of felt-tip pens = $\$4.50N$ Total value of ballpoint pens = $\$3.50 \times 2N$ Total order = $\$46$	Total value of felt-tip pens plust total value of ballpoint pens = total order. Multiply. Combine the numbers. Divide both sides of the equation by 11.50 Multiply 4 by 2.	$4.50N + (3.50 \times 2N) = 46$ $4.50N + 7.00N = 46$ $11.50N = 46$ $\dfrac{11.50N}{11.50} = \dfrac{46}{11.50}$ $N = 4$ $2N = 8$

Will ordered 4 boxes of felt-tip pens and 8 boxes of ballpoint pens.

Check

$4.50(4) + (3.50 \times 8) \overset{?}{=} 46$
$18 + 28 \overset{?}{=} 46$
$46 = 46$

18.

Unknown	Facts	Plan	Solution
Number of calendars = C Number of datebooks = $500 - C$	Total number of calendars and datebooks = 500 Cost of calendars = $\$0.75C$ Cost of datebooks = $\$0.50(500 - C)$ Total order = $\$300$	The cost of calendars plust the cost of the datebooks = the total order. Remove parentheses. Combine terms. Subtract 250 from both sides. Divide both sides by 0.25. Subtract 200 from 500.	$0.75C + 0.50(500 - C) = 300$ $0.75C + 250 - 0.50C = 300$ $0.25C + 250 = 300$ $-250 \quad -250$ $\overline{0.25C \quad 50}$ $\dfrac{0.25C}{0.25} = \dfrac{50}{0.25}$ $C = 200$ $500 - C = 300$

200 calendars and 300 datebooks were ordered.

Check

$0.75(200) + 0.50(500 - 200) \overset{?}{=} 300$
$150 + 0.50(300) \overset{?}{=} 300$
$300 = 300$

End of Chapter Problems

Identify the operation or operations illustrated in the following equations.

1. $M - N = P$ **2.** $AB = R$ **3.** $D = \dfrac{P}{Q}$

4. $F = G + H$ **5.** $C = AM - J$

6. $\dfrac{A}{P} + R = S$

Find the value of the variable.

7. $N - 5 = 12$ **8.** $N + 8 = 20$

9. $5N = 35$ **10.** $3N = 27$

11. $\dfrac{A}{6} = 2$ **12.** $\dfrac{A}{2} = 3$

13. $2N + 4 = 12$ **14.** $3N - 5 = 10$

15. $\dfrac{A}{3} + 4 = 12$ **16.** $2(X - 3) = 8$

17. $4X - X = 21$ **18.** $3X - 4 + 2X = 11$

19. Ace Motors sold a total of 15 cars and trucks during one promotion sale. Six of the vehicles sold were trucks. What is the number of cars that were sold?

Unknown	Facts	Solution
		Check

20. Edna's Book Carousel ordered several cookbooks but when the shipment was received, there was a difference of 6 books. Only 12 had been received. What is the number of books that was ordered?

Unknown	Facts	Solution
		Check

21. The Queen of Diamonds Card Shop ordered an equal number of twelve different cards. If a total of sixty cards were ordered, how many of each type of card was ordered?

Unknown	Facts	Solution
		Check

22. The Stork Club is a chain of baby clothing stores. The owner of the chain divided a number of Easter bonnets by the seven stores in the chain. If each store got nine bonnets, what was the number of bonnets distributed by the owner of the chain?

Unknown	Facts	Solution
		Check

23. An electrician pays $\frac{2}{5}$ of the money he earns for supplies. If he earned $240 for a certain job, how much did he spend on supplies?

Unknown	Facts	Plan	Solution

	Check

24. Liz Bliss spends 18 hours on a project and estimates that she has completed $\frac{1}{3}$ of the project. How many hours does she expect the project to take?

Unknown	Facts	Plan	Solution

	Check

25. An inventory clerk is expected to have 2,000 fan belts in stock. If the current count is 1,584 fan belts, how many more should be ordered?

Unknown	Facts	Plan	Solution

	Check

26. A personal computer costs $4,000, and a printer costs $1,500. What is the total cost of the equipment?

Unknown	Facts	Plan	Solution

			Check

27. Carrie McConnel spends $\frac{1}{6}$ of her weekly earnings on groceries. How much does she spend on groceries if her weekly earnings are $345?

Unknown	Facts	Plan	Solution

			Check

28. A purse that sells for $68.99 is reduced by $25.50. What is the price of the purse after the reduction?

Unknown	Facts	Plan	Solution

			Check

29. Shaquita Davis earns $350 for working 40 hours. How much does she make for each hour of work?

Unknown	Facts	Plan	Solution

			Check

30. Wilson's Auto, Inc., has 37 employees and a weekly payroll of $10,878. If each employee makes the same amount, how much does each make?

Unknown	Facts	Plan	Solution
			Check

31. Molly McWherter earns $7.36 per hour. How much would she make for 37 hours of work?

Unknown	Facts	Plan	Solution
			Check

32. An imprint machine makes 1,897 imprints per hour. How many imprints can be made in 12 hours?

Unknown	Facts	Plan	Solution
			Check

33. Wallpaper costs $12.97 per roll and a kitchen requires 9 rolls. What is the cost of the wallpaper needed to paper the kitchen?

Unknown	Facts	Plan	Solution
			Check

34. Mack Construction Co. was billed for plasterboard installation. If the job required 3,582 square feet of plasterboard and cost $2,435.76, what was the cost per square foot?

Unknown	Facts	Plan	Solution

			Check

35. Allen Brent purchased 250 pounds of tomatoes, 400 pounds of potatoes, 50 pounds of broccoli, and 130 pounds of birdseed for his chain stores. If all items are placed on the same shipment, what is the total weight of the shipment?

Unknown	Facts	Plan	Solution

			Check

36. Harks Manufacturer is negotiating a waste-removal contract. A study indicates that, in general, 304 pounds of waste are produced on Monday, 450 pounds are produced on Tuesday, 483 pounds are produced on Wednesday, 387 pounds are produced on Thursday, and 293 pounds are produced on Friday. The plant is closed on Saturday and Sunday. How many pounds of waste are produced per week?

Unknown	Facts	Plan	Solution

			Check

Chapter 3   Using Equations to Solve Problems

37. Cecil Hastings was overstocked with men's shirts and reduced the price from $18.99 to $15.97. How much was each shirt reduced?

Unknown	Facts	Plan	Solution

	Check

38. Cecil (Problem 37) counted 216 shirts to be reduced. What was the total amount of reduction for 216 shirts?

Unknown	Facts	Plan	Solution

	Check

39. The wholesale cost of an executive desk is $375, and the wholesale cost of a secretarial desk is $300. Allen Furniture Company filled an order for 40 desks, costing a total of $12,825. How many desks of each type were ordered?

Unknown	Facts	Plan	Solution

	Check

40. A computer store sold 144 cases of two grades of computer paper. Microperforated paper cost $15.97 per case, and standard perforated paper cost $9.75 per case. If the store had paper sales totaling $1,715, how many cases of each type were sold? What was the dollar value of each type sold?

Unknown	Facts	Plan	Solution

	Check

41. Bright Ideas purchased 1,000 light bulbs. Headlight bulbs cost $13.95 each, and taillight bulbs cost $7.55 each. If Bright Ideas spent $9,342 on headlight stock, how many headlights and how many taillights did it get? What was the dollar value of the headlights ordered? What was the dollar value of the taillights ordered?

Unknown	Facts	Plan	Solution

	Check

Additional Problems

1. A nurse received a bachelor's degree and so will be given a pay raise equal to one-third of his current monthly salary. If the new monthly salary will be $2,652, how much is the raise?

Unknown	Facts	Plan	Solution

Check

2. Three second-grade students, Jerry, Lisa, and Gloria, collected a total of 164 aluminum cans. Jerry collected 73 cans, and Lisa collected 15 more than Gloria. How many cans did Lisa and Gloria each collect?

Unknown	Facts	Plan	Solution

Check

3. A chemical plant needs to transfer 219 gallons of hazardous material stored in four large drums to its main office. Regulations require the plant's truck to carry only small drums. If one large drum holds three times as much as a small drum, how many gallons will each small drum hold?

Unknown	Facts	Plan	Solution

	Check

4. A news stand sells twice as many weekly papers on Monday as it does the rest of the week. If the news stand sold 486 papers for the week, how many were sold on Monday?

Unknown	Facts	Plan	Solution

	Check

5. During a marathon weekend sale of new automobiles, Anfernee Exum sold four times as many vehicles as another salesperson. Together, both salespersons sold 10 vehicles. How many vehicles did Mr. Exum sell?

Unknown	Facts	Plan	Solution

	Check

6. Diamond Builders Supply sold 52 boxes of self-stick floor tile for a total of $3,350. If standard self-stick floor tile sells for $50 a box and deluxe self-stick floor tile sells for $75 a box, how many boxes of each tile were sold?

Unknown	Facts	Plan	Solution

	Check

7. Mary Munn's salary is larger than her husband's salary by $2,600. If their combined income is $50,200, how much does Mrs. Munn earn?

Unknown	Facts	Plan	Solution

Check

8. Washington's Hardware ordered 200 circuit breakers for $1,056.25. If the 15-amp circuit breakers cost $4.50 each and the 20-amp breakers cost $5.75 each, how many of each breaker were ordered?

Unknown	Facts	Plan	Solution

Check

9. Bart earns $0.50 an hour more than his brother Art. Fargo, their manager, earns $1.50 an hour more than Art. If all three together earn a total of $17.00 per hour, how much does each earn per hour?

Unknown	Facts	Plan	Solution

	Check

10. Raoul Ruiz spends on the average $\frac{1}{6}$ of each work day in administrative tasks. If he spends $1\frac{1}{2}$ hours a day in administrative tasks, how much time does he spend a day in tasks?

Unknown	Facts	Plan	Solution

	Check

Challenge Problem

Mixing the Right Formula

Solve for W in the formula $P = 2L + 2W$. In what regard is this formula used? What do each of the letters W, P, and L represent? Explain some of the advantages that are gained from using algebraic formulas to solve questions.

Trial Test

Identify the operation illustrated in the following formulas.

1. $P + I = A$

2. $S - M = C$

3. $F = PA$

4. $R = \dfrac{P}{B}$

Solve.

5. $N + 7 = 18$

6. $5N = 45$

7. $\dfrac{A}{3} = 6$

8. $B - 8 = 7$

9. $3A - 5 = 10$

10. $5A + 8 = 33$

11. $2(N + 1) = 14$

12. $5A + A = 30$

13. The sum of a number and 12 is 38. Find the number.

Unknown	Facts	Plan	Solution
			Check

14. The product of a number and 6 is 42. What is the number?

Unknown	Facts	Plan	Solution
			Check

15. An employee who was earning $249 weekly received a raise of $36. How much is the new salary?

Unknown	Facts	Plan	Solution
			Check

16. An inventory clerk is expected to keep 600 filters on hand. A physical count shows there are 298 filters in stock. How many filters should be ordered?

Unknown	Facts	Plan	Solution
			Check

17. A container of oil holds 585 gallons. How many containers each holding 4.5 gallons will be needed if all the oil is to be transferred to the smaller containers?

Unknown	Facts	Plan	Solution

	Check

18. The buyer for a specialty gift store purchased an equal number of two types of designer telephones for a total cost of $7,200. The top-quality phones cost $120 each, and the plastic phones cost $80 each. How many of each type of phone were purchased and what was the total dollar value of each type?

Unknown	Facts	Plan	Solution

	Check

19. A five-and-ten store sold plastic cups for $3.50 each and ceramic cups for $4 each. If 400 cups were sold for a total of $1,458, how many cups of each type were sold? What was the dollar value of each type of cup sold?

Unknown	Facts	Plan	Solution

	Check

20. An appliance dealer sold 9 more washing machines than dryers. Washing machines sell for $480 and dryers sell for $350. If total dollar sales were $21,750, how many of each appliance were sold? What was the dollar value of washing machines sold and the dollar value of dryers sold?

Unknown	Facts	Plan	Solution

	Check

BUSINESS MATH IN ACTION

Calculating alcohol

How much of each beverage one has to drink to consume 2.4 gallons of pure alcohol — the annual USA average:

54 gallons

19 gallons

6 gallons

Distilled spirits   Wine   Beer

Source: National Institute on Alcohol Abuse and Alcoholism

By Web Bryant, USA TODAY

QUESTIONS

1. Write equations to find the number of gallons of the nonalcholic liquid in 54 gallons of beer, in 19 gallons of wine, and in 6 gallons of distilled spirits. Solve each equation.

2. One gallon of liquid contains 128 ounces. How many ounces of pure alcohol are in 6 gallons of distilled spirits? How many ounces of pure alcohol are in 1 gallon of distilled spirits?

3. How many times as much beer is required to yield the same alcohol content as 6 gallons of bourbon?

4. In which drink is there more alcohol content, a 12-ounce can of beer or a 1-ounce shot of bourbon? Explain your answer.

Percents

Percents are one of the most important arithmetic processes used in business. Percents give us a special way of writing fractions that lets us compare parts with wholes and with one another. Because percents are used throughout the business world, it is essential to gain a thorough understanding of this mathematical concept, which is used throughout this text.

The word **percent** means *hundredths,* or *per hundred,* or *over* 100 (in a fraction). That is, 44 percent equals 44 hundredths, or 44 per hundred, or $\frac{44}{100}$. Remember, $\frac{44}{100}$ can be written as 0.44. If you find that 44 percent of the students in the class watch a certain television program, you are saying that the number of students who watch that show divided by the total number of students can be expressed as the fraction $\frac{44}{100}$ or as the decimal 0.44. It does not mean that there are exactly 100 students in the class; there could be 50 in the class, 22 of whom watch the program ($\frac{22}{50} = \frac{44}{100}$). Rather, it means that the fraction showing the number of watchers divided by the total number of students can be converted to a fraction with a numerator of 44 and denominator of 100. If you find that 22% of the students in another class watch the show, you are saying that the number of students who watch that show divided by the total number of students can be expressed as the fraction $\frac{22}{100}$ or as the decimal 0.22. Again, it does not mean that 22 students in the second class watch the show in question; there could be 50 in the class, 11 of whom watch the program ($\frac{11}{50} = \frac{22}{100}$). Instead, the number of students who watch the show divided by the total number of students can be expressed as a fraction with numerator of 22 and denominator of 100. Thus, percents allow you to compare the popularity of the show in the two classes, even though the classes have different total numbers of students.

percent: a hundredth of a whole amount; a fraction with a denominator of 100. *Percent means per hundred.*

The symbol for *percent* is %. You can write 35 percent symbolically as 35%, or as the common fraction $\frac{35}{100}$, or as the decimal fraction 0.35.

$$35 \text{ percent } = 35 \text{ hundredths} = 35\% = \frac{35}{100} = 0.35$$

Just as there are mixed fractions and decimals, so there are mixed percents. Examples of mixed percents would include such numbers as $25\frac{1}{7}\%$ or $66\frac{2}{9}\%$.

4.1 Converting Decimals and Fractions to Percents

LEARNING OBJECTIVES

1. Convert decimals to percents.
2. Convert fractions to percents.

The businessperson must be able to handle percents in whatever form they appear, even if they are written as fractions or as decimals. A person who cannot convert fractions and decimals to their percent equivalents will have difficulty managing a business.

In this section we will examine how to write both fractions and decimals as percents.

Converting Decimals to Percents

We know that hundredths and percent have the same meaning. That is, 0.01 (1 hundredth) = 1%.

Also,

$$0.02 = 2\%$$
$$0.03 = 3\%$$
$$\vdots$$
$$0.10 = 10\%$$
$$0.11 = 11\%$$
$$\vdots$$

You can convert a decimal into a percent by multiplying the decimal by 100% and adding a percent sign:

$$0.11 \times 100\% = 11\%$$

STEP BY STEP

Converting a Decimal to a Percent

Multiply the decimal by 100% (move the decimal point two places to the right). The answer will keep the percent sign.

EXAMPLE 1

Convert the following decimals to percents.

$0.27 \times 100\% = 0.27.\% = 27\%$ Multiply 0.27 by 100% (move the decimal point two places to the right). Write a % sign after the number.

$0.875 \times 100\% = 0.87.5\% = 87.5\%$ Multiply 0.875 by 100% (move the decimal point two places to the right). Write a % sign after the number.

$1.73 \times 100\% = 1.73.\% = 173\%$ Multiply 1.73 by 100% (move the decimal point two places to right). Write a % sign after the number.

$0.004 \times 100\% = 0.00.4\% = 0.4\%$ Multiply 0.004 by 100% (move the decimal point two places to the right). Write a % sign after the number.

As you can see, the procedure is the same regardless of the number of decimal places in the number and regardless of whether the number is more than, equal to, or less than 1.

Converting Fractions to Percents

The numerator of a fraction with a denominator of 100 is the percent. However, fractions that do not have a denominator of 100 can be changed to a percent by first changing the fraction to a decimal equivalent and then multiplying it by 100%.

STEP BY STEP

Converting a Fraction to a Percent

Step 1. Write the fraction as a decimal by dividing the numerator by the denominator.

Step 2. Multiply by 100% (move the decimal point two places to the right), and write the % sign.

EXAMPLE 2

Convert the following fractions to percents.

$\dfrac{67}{100} \times 100\% = 0.67 \times 100\% = 0.67.\% = 67\%$

$\dfrac{1}{4}$ $4\overline{)1.00}$ with quotient 0.25 $0.25 \times 100\% = 0.25.\% = 25\%$
$\phantom{4\overline{)1.}}\underline{8}$
$\phantom{4\overline{)1.}}20$
$\phantom{4\overline{)1.}}\underline{20}$

$3\dfrac{1}{2}$ $2\overline{)1.0}$ with quotient 0.5 $3 + 0.5 = 3.5;\ 3.5 \times 100\% = 3.50.\% = 350\%$
$\phantom{2\overline{)1.}}\underline{1\,0}$

$$\frac{7}{4} \qquad 4\overline{)7.00} \qquad 1.75 \times 100\% = 1.75.\% = 175\%$$

$$\begin{array}{r} 1.75 \\ 4\overline{)7.00} \\ \underline{4} \\ 3\ 0 \\ \underline{2\ 8} \\ 20 \\ \underline{20} \end{array}$$

$$\frac{2}{3} \qquad 3\overline{)2.000} \qquad 0.666 \text{ rounds to } 0.67. \qquad 0.67 \times 100\% = 0.67.\% = 67\%$$

$$\begin{array}{r} 0.666 \\ 3\overline{)2.000} \\ \underline{1\ 8} \\ 20 \\ \underline{18} \\ 2 \end{array}$$

 Self-Check 4.1

1. Change the following decimals to percents.
   a. 0.39   **b.** 0.693   **c.** 2.92   **d.** 0.0007

2. Change the following fractions to percents.
   a. $\dfrac{39}{100}$ **b.** $5\dfrac{1}{4}$ **c.** $\dfrac{9}{4}$

4.2 Converting Percents to Decimals and Fractions

LEARNING OBJECTIVES

1. Convert percents to decimals.
2. Convert mixed percents to decimals.
3. Convert percents to fractions.

Many types of business dealings call for converting percents to decimals or fractions. A sign tells you that all the shoes on the table are 25% off the marked price, but the shoes have different prices and the sign does not tell you the actual amount of money subtracted from the price of each pair of shoes. Similar situations are common in business. Normally, percents tell you only about the relationship between two things, and they cannot be used in percent form for doing calculations. PERCENTS MUST BE WRITTEN IN DECIMAL or FRACTIONAL EQUIVALENTS BEFORE THEY CAN BE USED IN CALCULATIONS involving multiplication or division: You must convert 25% to a decimal, 0.25, or to a fraction, $\frac{1}{4}$, before you can use the information to solve a problem. In this section, we will show you how to make these changes.

Converting Percents to Decimals

To write percents as decimals, you reverse the procedure for converting decimals to percents. That is, you divide by 100 and drop the percent (%) sign. Remember, to divide a decimal number by 100, you move the decimal point two places to the *left*.

Converting a Percent to a Decimal

Divide the percent by 100% (move the decimal point two places to the left, and drop the % sign from the number.)

EXAMPLE 3

Change the following percents to decimals.

$37\% = 37\% \div 100\% = .37. = 0.37$

$26.5\% = 26.5\% \div 100\% = .26.5 = 0.265$

$127\% = 127\% \div 100\% = 1.27. = 1.27$

$7\% = 7\% \div 100\% = .07. = 0.07$

$0.9\% = 0.9\% \div 100\% = .00.9 = 0.009$

Converting Mixed Percents to Decimals

When you change a mixed percent to a decimal, you first write the fractional part as a decimal. If the fraction converts to a terminating decimal (that is, the division of the numerator by the denominator comes out even), you convert the fraction to its equivalent decimal before you change the percent to a decimal.

$$3\frac{1}{2}\% = 3.5\% = 3.5\% \div 100\% = 0.035.$$

If the fraction converts to a repeating decimal, you convert the fraction to a decimal and round to some appropriate decimal place, usually hundredths. Then you change the percent to a decimal number.

$$2\frac{1}{3}\% = 2.33\% = 2.33\% \div 100\% = 0.0233.$$

The basic procedure is the same, whether the percent is more than 100%, less than 1%, or a mixed-number percent.

STEP BY STEP

Converting a Mixed or Fractional Percent to a Decimal

Step 1. Change the fraction to a decimal by dividing the numerator by the denominator. If the division does not terminate, round to the desired place.

Step 2. Write the whole number part and the fraction part together as a mixed decimal number.

Step 3. Divide by 100% (move the decimal point two places to the left, and drop the % sign.)

EXAMPLE 4

Change the following mixed or fractional percents to decimal numbers.

$$27\frac{1}{2}\% = 27\% + 0.5\% = 27.5\% = 27.5\% \div 100\% = 0.27.5 = 0.275 \qquad 2\overline{\smash)1.0}^{\,0.5} \\ \underline{1\ 0}$$

$$\frac{1}{4}\% = 0.25\% = 0.25\% \div 100\% = 0.00.25 = 0.0025 \qquad 4\overline{\smash)1.00}^{\,0.25} \\ \underline{8} \\ 20 \\ \underline{20}$$

$$167\frac{1}{3}\% = 167\% + 0.33\% = 167.33\% = 167.33\% \div 100\% \qquad 3\overline{\smash)1.000}^{\,0.33\overline{3},\ or\ 0.33} \\ \underline{9} \\ 10 \\ \underline{9} \\ 10$$
$$= 1.67.33$$
$$= 1.6733$$

Converting Percents to Fractions

To write percents as fractions, you divide by 100% which causes you to drop the percent sign. To do this, you use the procedure for dividing fractions. You use the same procedure whether the percent is more than 100%, less than 1%, or a mixed-number percent.

STEP BY STEP

Changing a Percent to a Fraction

Step 1. Divide the percent by 100% by writing the percent in the numerator of the fraction with the denominator of 100% or by multiplying the number by $\frac{1}{100}\%$.

Step 2. Reduce the fraction to lowest terms, writing it as a mixed number if it is more than 1.

EXAMPLE 5

Change the following percents to fractions or mixed fractions.

$$175\% = \frac{175\%}{100\%} = 1\frac{75}{100} = 1\frac{3}{4} \qquad 66\frac{2}{3}\% = \frac{66\frac{2}{3}\%}{100\%} = \frac{200}{3} \div \frac{100}{1} = \frac{200}{3} \times \frac{1}{100} = \frac{2}{3}$$

TIPS & TRAPS

In converting decimals, percents, and fractions from one form to another, it is helpful to know certain equivalent forms. It is especially helpful to know:

$$\frac{1}{3} = 0.33\overline{3} = 0.33 \text{ (rounded)} = 0.33\frac{1}{3} = 33\frac{1}{3}\%$$

$$\frac{2}{3} = 0.66\overline{6} = 0.67 \text{ (rounded)} = 0.66\frac{2}{3} = 66\frac{2}{3}\%$$

Self Check 4.2

3. Change the following percents to decimals.

   a. $15\frac{1}{2}\%$ **b.** $\frac{1}{8}\%$ **c.** $125\frac{1}{3}\%$ **d.** $\frac{3}{7}\%$

Convert the following percents to fractions.

4. a. 45%   **b.** 180%

5. a. $\frac{3}{4}\%$ **b.** $33\frac{1}{3}\%$

 4.3

LEARNING OBJECTIVES

1. Solve percentage problems for the portion.
2. Solve percentage problems for the base.
3. Solve percentage problems for the rate.

Many problems in business are solved by using percents, and many of the business problems that involve percents are solved by using the formula

$$\text{Portion} = \text{rate} \times \text{base}$$

or

$$P = R \times B$$

in which the **base** (B) is the original number or entire quantity, the **portion** (P) is the part of the base, and the **rate** (R) is a percent that tells us how the base and the portion are related. In the statement "50 is 20% of 250," 250 is the base (the entire quantity), 50 is the portion, and 20% is the rate.

   You may often need to use the percentage formula in a different form. You can *rearrange* the basic percentage formula, $P = R \times B$, to solve for R or B by dividing both sides of the formula by either R or B.

   To solve the percentage formula for rate (R), divide both sides of the formula by base (B):

$$P = R \times B, \quad \frac{P}{B} = \frac{R \times \overset{1}{\cancel{B}}}{\cancel{B}_{1}}, \quad \frac{P}{B} = R, \quad \text{or} \quad R = \frac{P}{B}$$

   To solve the percentage formula for base (B), divide both sides of the formula by rate (R):

$$P = R \times B, \quad \frac{P}{R} = \frac{\overset{1}{\cancel{R}} \times B}{\cancel{R}_{1}}, \quad \frac{P}{R} = B, \quad \text{or} \quad B = \frac{P}{R}$$

   Figure 4-1 shows an easy way to remember how to find any one of the three terms in the percentage formula. Simply put your finger over the missing term and look at the diagram to see the relationship between the other two terms. The diagram tells you whether to multiply or divide the numbers you know.

base: an original number, entire amount, or whole quantity.

portion: a part of a whole amount.

rate: a percent indicating how the portion (or part) relates to the base (or whole).

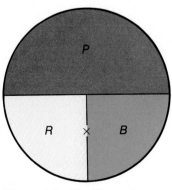

Figure 4-1 The Percentage Formula Diagram

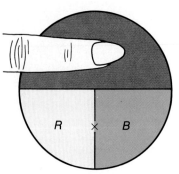

Figure 4-2 Using the Percentage Formula Diagram to Solve for Portion

Solving for Portion

Figure 4-2 shows the percentage formula diagram when solving for portion. Put your finger over the P and note that the diagram shows $R \times B$. Remember, whenever you substitute a known amount for rate, you must change the amount of the rate from percent form to decimal form or to fractional form.

STEP BY STEP

The Percentage Formula: Solving for Portion

Step 1. Express rate in decimal or fractional form.

Step 2. Portion = rate × base

or

$$P = R \times B$$

Base is the original number or quantity.
Rate is a percent expressed in decimal or fractional form.
Portion is the number that is a part of the base.

EXAMPLE 6

Find P if $R = 6\%$ and $B = \$20$.

$P = R \times B$	The portion is unknown.
$P = 6\% = 0.06. = 0.06$	The rate is 6%. Change the percent to a decimal before using it to solve the problem.
$P = R \times B = 0.06 \times \$20$ $\quad = \$1.20$	Substitute the known amounts into the formula and find the value of P.

TIPS & TRAPS

It is important to change the rate (percent) to a decimal or a fraction *before* you make any calculations. Look at what happens in Example 6 if you do not change the rate to a decimal number.

$$P = 6\% \times \$20 = \$120$$
WRONG

You must express the percent as a decimal, as we did in Example 6, to find the correct answer:

$$P = 0.06 \times \$20 = \$1.20$$
CORRECT

Solving for Base

Figure 4-3 shows the percentage formula diagram for solving for base. Put your finger over the B and note that the diagram shows $\dfrac{P}{R}$.

STEP BY STEP

The Percentage Formula: Solving for Base

Step 1. Express rate in decimal or fractional form.

Step 2. Base $= \dfrac{\text{portion}}{\text{rate}}$, or $B = \dfrac{P}{R}$

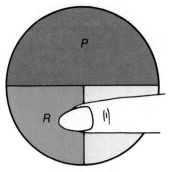

Figure 4-3 Using the Percentage Formula Diagram to Solve for Base

EXAMPLE 7

Find B if $P = 42$ and $R = 33\frac{1}{3}\%$.

$B = \dfrac{P}{R}$

The base, or entire quantity, is unknown.

$R = 33\frac{1}{3}\% = \dfrac{1}{3}$

The rate, $33\frac{1}{3}\%$, must be changed to a fraction or decimal before it can be used in the formula. ($33\frac{1}{3}\%$ gives a nonterminating decimal.)

$B = \dfrac{P}{R} = \dfrac{42}{\frac{1}{3}}$

Substitute the known amounts in the formula and find the value of B.

$42 \div \dfrac{1}{3} = \dfrac{42}{1} \times \dfrac{3}{1} = 126$

In Example 7, we can change the percent to a decimal and solve the problem in one continuous calculator sequence. Note: slight error due to rounding.

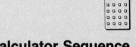

$\boxed{\text{AC}}$ 1 $\boxed{\div}$ 3 $\boxed{=}$ $\boxed{\text{M}^+}$ $\boxed{\text{CE/C}}$ 42 $\boxed{\div}$ $\boxed{\text{MRC}}$ $\boxed{=}$ $\Rightarrow$ 126.001

Calculator Sequence

REAL WORLD APPLICATION

If you own a business that occupies space in a shopping center or mall, your lease may require you to pay a percent of the common area maintenance (CAM). This fee pays for parking lot maintenance, grounds contracts, garbage collection, taxes, sign maintenance, and other expenses that are part of the operating expenses of such a project. The amount each business pays depends on the size of the building. Each percent is based on the square footage per building or space and the total square footage of the mall or shopping center.

If your building is 8,640 square feet and the shopping center has a total of 69,590 square feet, then you occupy 12.42% of the space and must pay 12.42% of the CAM.

$$\frac{8,640}{69,590} = 0.1242 = 12.42\%$$

The total common area maintenance is $9,519.34; your share of the CAM is 12.42% of this total, or $1,182.30.

$$12.42\% \times \$9,519.34 = 0.1242 \times \$9,519.34$$
$$= \$1,182.30$$

Application Questions

1. If your business occupies 1,400 square feet in a mall containing 88,260 square feet, what percent of the mall do you occupy? If the total common area maintenance is $15,621.88, what is your share of the expense?

2. A lease requires the owner of a business occupying 2,000 square feet of a 78,900-square-foot shopping center to pay a percent of the yearly taxes based on space occupied. If the taxes for the year are $18,789, how much must the owner pay?

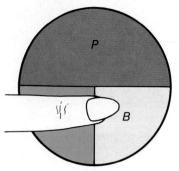

Figure 4-4 Using the Percentage Formula Diagram to Solve for Rate

Solving For Rate

Figure 4-4 shows the percentage formula diagram for solving for rate. Put your finger over the R and note that the diagram shows $\frac{P}{B}$. Using the formula $R = \frac{P}{B}$ to solve for a missing rate results in the decimal or fractional equivalent of the rate, which must be written in percent form. Multiply the decimal times 100% by moving the decimal point two places to the right and writing a % sign after the number to convert the rate to a percent.

STEP BY STEP

The Percentage Formula: Solving for Rate

Step 1. Rate = $\dfrac{\text{portion}}{\text{base}}$,   or $R = \dfrac{P}{B}$

Step 2. Convert R to a percent.

EXAMPLE 8

Find R if $P = 20$ and $B = 200$.

$R = \dfrac{P}{B}$ The rate, or percent, is unknown.

$R = \dfrac{20}{200} = 0.1$ Substitute the known values into the formula and do the arithmetic.

$R = 0.1 = 0.10.\% = 10\%$ The answer is a decimal and must be changed to percent form.

 Self-Check 4.3

6. Find P if $R = 25\%$ and $B = 300$.

7. Find B if $P = 36$ and $R = 66\frac{2}{3}\%$.

8. Find R if $P = 70$ and $B = 280$.

4.4

Solving Percentage Problems

LEARNING OBJECTIVES

1. Solve applied problems for the portion.
2. Solve applied problems for the base.
3. Solve applied problems for the rate.
4. Find the percent of increase or decrease in applied problems.

The percentage formula in its different forms has many applications in the business world. In the chapters to come, we will use percentages to calculate sales and property taxes, trade and cash discounts, markup, markdown, and turnover and other business calculations. Percentages are also used in working with interest, depreciation and overhead, and income taxes. Before you can apply percentages in these business settings, however, you must understand how to analyze and solve a percentage problem.

Very few percentage problems that you encounter in business tell you the values of P, R, and B directly. Percentage problems are usually written in words that must be analyzed before you can tell which form of the percentage formula you should use or which term of the formula corresponds to which number in the problem. In this section, we analyze and solve some typical problems using the percentage formula.

STEP BY STEP

Solving a Percentage Problem

Step 1. Examine the words carefully to identify each term correctly.
    a. Rate is always expressed as a percent.
    b. The number that immediately follows the word *of* is usually the base or entire quantity.
    c. The number that is not a percent and does not follow the word *of* is usually the portion.

Step 2. Always change the rate, which is expressed as a percent, to a decimal or fraction before you solve the equation.

Step 3. When you solve for rate, change the answer, which will be in the form of a decimal or fraction to a percent.

Solving for Portion

EXAMPLE 9

During a special 1-day sale, 20% of the customers making purchases in the morning used store coupons. If 600 customers made purchases that morning, how many customers used coupons?

First, identify the terms. The rate is the percent, and the base is the total number *of* customers, 600.

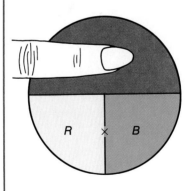

$P = ?$, so $P = R \times B$	The portion is the unknown to be solved for.
$R = 20\% = .20. = 0.20$ or 0.2	The rate is 20%. Change the percent to a decimal before using it to solve the problem.
$B = 600$	The base is 600. Note that 600 is the total number of customers that made purchases that morning.
$P = R \times B = 0.2 \times 600 = 120$	Substitute the known amounts and do the arithmetic.
Does $P = R \times B$? $120 = 0.2 \times 600$ $120 = 120$	Check your answer by substituting all the known amounts into the equation and doing the arithmetic.

REAL WORLD APPLICATION

If you have considered renting or buying a home, you may want to think about the following rule of thumb used in many real estate offices: Your rent or house payment should not be more than about 25% of your monthly gross pay.

If your gross pay is $1,000 a month, then your rent payment should not be more than $250 month.

$$\$1,000 \times 25\% = \$1,000 \times 0.25 = \$250$$

Example: You are interested in renting an apartment for $325 a month. Your monthly gross pay is $1,050. Should you be able to afford this payment, based on this rule of thumb?

$$\frac{\$325}{\$1,050} = 0.3095 = 31\%$$

Since $325 is about 31% of your monthly salary, you may find this apartment too expensive.

Application Questions

1. In looking for an apartment, you see an advertisement for an apartment that rents for $405 a month. If your monthly salary is $1,625, is this apartment affordable for you?

2. If your gross pay is $1,250 a month, what is the approximate rent you should be able to pay?

3. If your house payment is $375 a month and your monthly gross pay is $1,115, what percent of your pay is your house payment?

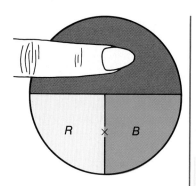

EXAMPLE 10

If $66\frac{2}{3}\%$ of the 900 employees in a company choose a particular health insurance plan, how many people from that company are enrolled in the plan?

First, identify the terms. The rate is the percent, and the base is the number that follows the word *of*.

$P = ?$, so $P = R \times B$

The portion is the unknown to be solved for.

$R = 66\frac{2}{3}\% = \dfrac{2}{3}$

The rate is $66\frac{2}{3}\%$. Change the percent to a fraction before using it to solve the problem.

$B = 900$

The base is 900. Note that 900 is the number that immediately follows the word *of*.

$P = R \times B$

Substitute the known values into the formula and do the arithmetic.

$$= \frac{2}{3} \times \frac{\overset{300}{900}}{1} = 600$$

Does $P = R \times B$?

$600 = \dfrac{2}{3} \times 900$

$600 = 600$

Check your answer by substituting all the known amounts into the equation and doing the arithmetic.

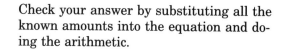

Solving for Base

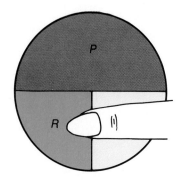

EXAMPLE 11

Stan sets aside 25% of his weekly income for rent. If he sets aside $50 each week, what is his weekly income?

The following key words may help you recognize the rate, base, or portion more quickly:

Rate is always written as a percent.

Base is called total amount, original amount, entire amount, and so on; it usually follows the word *of*. Sometimes there is no number with the word that follows *of*, but that word appears in another sentence with an amount. This amount is the base.

Portion is called part, partial amount, percentage, amount of increase or decrease, amount of change, and so on. It is often associated with the word *is*.

Identify the terms: The rate is the number written as a percent. The portion is given, $50. Notice that the unknown quantity, weekly income, follows the word *of*. This is a clue that you are looking for the base.

$P = \$50$	The portion is $50.
$R = 25\% = .25. = 0.25$	The rate is 25%. Change the percent to a decimal before doing the arithmetic.
$B = ?$, so $B = \dfrac{P}{R}$	The base is the unknown to be solved for.
$B = \dfrac{\$50}{0.25} = \$200$	Substitute the known values into the formula and do the arithmetic.

EXAMPLE 12

Thirty percent of Hill Community College's graduates continued their education at 4-year colleges. If 60 people continued their education, how many Hill Community College graduates were there?

Identify the terms: You might not recognize the rate immediately because it is written in words, thirty percent. The base is the total number of graduates, so 60 is the portion of the graduates who continue their education.

$P = 60$	The portion of the base is 60.
$R = 30\% = .30. = 0.30$ or 0.3	The rate is 30%. Express the percent as a decimal.
$B = ?$	
$B = \dfrac{P}{R}$	The base is the unknown to be solved for.
$B = \dfrac{60}{0.3} = 200$	Substitute the known values into the formula and do the arithmetic.

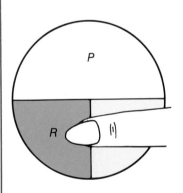

Solving for Rate

EXAMPLE 13

If 20 automobiles were sold from a lot that had 50 automobiles on sale, what percent of the sale cars were purchased?

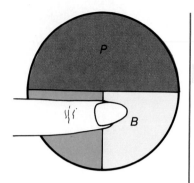

When you identify the terms in a percent problem, look for the rate, or the number written as a percent, first. In this problem, you can see that the rate is unknown.

$P = 20$	The portion is 20.
$B = 50$	The base is 50.
$R = ?$, so $R = \dfrac{P}{B}$	The rate is the unknown to be solved for.
$R = \dfrac{20}{50} = 0.40. = 40\%$	Substitute the known values into the formula and do the arithmetic. The solution for the rate is a decimal number, 0.4, which must be written as a percent.

Finding Percent of Increase or Decrease

Change is often expressed in terms of a percent difference between two amounts. An announcement that transit fares will increase by 10% on January 1 means that the base is the original, lower fare; the portion is the amount of change; and the rate is 10%.

STEP BY STEP

> **Finding Percent of Increase or Decrease**
>
> **Step 1.** Find the difference between the original amount and the increased or decreased amount. The difference is the portion.
>
> **Step 2.** Divide the portion by the original amount using the following version of the percentage formula:
>
> $$R = \frac{P}{B}$$
>
> **Step 3.** Rewrite the decimal or fraction as a percent.

EXAMPLE 14

Ellis was earning $375 per week until he received a raise. Now he earns $397.50 per week. What percent of increase did he receive?

$\begin{array}{r} \$397.50 \\ -\ \ 375.00 \\ \hline \$\ 22.50 \end{array}$	Find the difference between the old and new amounts. The difference, $22.50, is the portion.
$P = \$22.50$	The portion is $22.50.
$R = ?$, so $R = \dfrac{P}{B}$	The rate (percent of increase) is the unknown to be solved for.
$B = \$375$	The base is $375, the original salary.
$R = \dfrac{\$22.50}{\$375} = 0.06 = 6\%$	Substitute the known values into the formula and do the arithmetic. Rewrite the decimal, 0.06, as a percent, 6%.

EXAMPLE 15

A computer printer cost $980 last year. Now the same printer costs $882. What was the percent of decrease in price from last year?

$980	Subtract the new (lower) price from the
-882	original (higher) price. The difference, $98,
$\overline{\$\ 98}$	is the portion.

$P = \$98$ The portion is $98.

$R = ?$, so $R = \dfrac{P}{B}$ The rate (percent of decrease) is the unknown to be solved for.

$B = \$980$ The base is $980, the original cost.

$R = \dfrac{98}{980} = 0.1 = 10\%$ Substitute the known value into the formula and do the arithmetic. Rewrite the decimal, 0.1, as a percent, 10%.

 Self-Check 4.4

9. Find 40% of 160.

10. What number is $33\frac{1}{3}\%$ of 150?

11. What number is 154% of 30?

12. Jenny sold 80% of the tie-dyed T-shirts she took to the Green Valley Music Festival. If she sold 42 shirts, how many shirts did she bring?

13. Ali gave correct answers to 23 of the 25 questions on the driving test. What percent of the questions did he get correct?

14. Mathilda just started a new job where she earns $450 per week. At her previous job, she earned $400 per week. What was her percent raise when she began her new job?

15. The number of sixth-grade students at Spring Valley Elementary School fell from 78 in 1989 to 68 in 1990. What was the percent of decrease in sixth-grade students?

Summary

Topic	Page	What to Remember	Examples
Changing a decimal to a percent	132	Multiply the decimal by 100 by moving the decimal point two places to the right and add a % sign.	$0.15 = 15\%$
Changing a fraction with a denominator of 100 to a percent	133	Write the numerator with a % sign after it.	$\dfrac{37}{100} = 37\%$
Changing any fraction to a percent	133	Divide the numerator by the denominator. Move the decimal point two places to the right and write the % sign.	$\dfrac{3}{5} = 0.60 = 60\%$
Changing a percent to a decimal	134	Move the decimal point two places to the left and drop the % sign from the number.	$48\% = 0.48$ $157\% = 1.57$

Topic	Page	What to Remember	Examples
Changing a percent that contains a fraction to a decimal	135	Divide the numerator of the fraction by the denominator. Write the whole-number part and fractional part as a decimal number. Move the decimal point two places to the left and drop the % sign.	$33\frac{1}{3}\% = 33.33\% = 0.3333$ or $33\frac{1}{3}\% = 0.33\frac{1}{3}$
Changing a percent to a fraction	136	Write the percent as a fraction with 100 in the denominator. Write the fraction in lowest terms.	$75\% = 0.75 = \dfrac{75}{100} = \dfrac{3}{4}$
Solving for portion	138	$P = R \times B$. Always remember to change the rate from percent form to decimal or fractional form before you do the arithmetic.	$B = 20$ and $R = 15\%$. Find P. $P = R \times B = 0.15 \times 20 = 3$
Solving for base	138	$B = \dfrac{P}{R}$. Always remember to change the rate from percent form to decimal or fractional form before you do the arithmetic.	$P = 36$ and $R = 9\%$. Find B. $B = \dfrac{P}{R} = \dfrac{36}{0.09} = 400$
Solving for rate	140	$R = \dfrac{P}{B}$. Remember to convert the answer from decimal form to percent form.	$P = 4$ and $B = 5$. Find R. $R = \dfrac{P}{B} = \dfrac{4}{5} = 0.80 = 80\%$
Solving an applied percentage problem	140	Identify each term. Rate is always written as a percent and must be rewritten as a decimal or fraction. The number after the word *of* is usually the base, or entire quantity. The number that is not a percent and does not follow the word *of* is usually the percentage. If you are solving for rate, remember to change the answer from decimal form to percent form.	What number is 30% of 150? $R = 30\% = 0.3,\ B = 150$ $P = R \times B = 0.3 \times 150 = 45$

Self-Check Solutions

1. a. $0.39 \times 100\% = 0.39.$; 39%   **b.** $0.693 \times 100\% = 0.69.3$; 69.3%
   c. $2.92 \times 100\% = 2.92.$; 292%   **d.** $0.0007 \times 100\% = 0.00.07$; 0.07%

2. a. $\dfrac{39}{100} = 39\%$

   b. $5\frac{1}{4} = \dfrac{21}{4}$; $4)\overline{21.00}$ $\dfrac{5.25}{}$; $5.25 \times 100\% = 5.25.$; 525%

$$\begin{array}{r} 5.25 \\ 4)\overline{21.00} \\ \underline{20} \\ 1\,0 \\ \underline{8} \\ 20 \end{array}$$

c. $\dfrac{9}{4}$; $4\overline{)9.00}$; $2.25 \times 100\% = 2.25.$; 225%

$$\begin{array}{r} 2.25 \\ 4\overline{)9.00} \\ \underline{8} \\ 1\,0 \\ \underline{8} \\ 20 \\ \underline{20} \end{array}$$

3. a. $15\dfrac{1}{2}\% = 15.5\% = 15.5\% \div 100\% = 0.155$

b. $\dfrac{1}{8}\% = 0.125\% = 0.125\% \div 100\% = 0.00125$

$$\begin{array}{r} 0.125 \\ 8\overline{)1.000} \\ \underline{8} \\ 20 \\ \underline{16} \\ 40 \\ \underline{40} \end{array}$$

c. $125\dfrac{1}{3}\% = 125.\overline{3}\% = 125.\overline{3}\% \div 100\% = 1.253$ (rounded)

d. $\dfrac{3}{7}\% = 0.428\% \div 100\% = 0.004$ (rounded)

$$\begin{array}{r} 0.\overline{4285714} \\ 7\overline{)3.0000000} \\ \underline{2\,8} \\ 20 \\ \underline{14} \\ 60 \\ \underline{56} \\ 40 \\ \underline{35} \\ 50 \\ \underline{49} \\ 10 \\ \underline{7} \\ 30 \\ \underline{28} \\ 2 \end{array}$$

4. a. $45\% = \dfrac{45\%}{100\%} = \dfrac{9}{20}$ **b.** $180\% = \dfrac{180\%}{100\%} = \dfrac{18}{10} = \dfrac{9}{5} = 1\dfrac{4}{5}$

5. a. $\dfrac{3}{4}\% = \dfrac{3}{4}\% \times \dfrac{1}{100\%} = \dfrac{3}{400}$ **b.** $33\dfrac{1}{3}\% = 33\dfrac{1}{3} \times \dfrac{1}{100\%} = \dfrac{\overset{1}{\cancel{100}}}{3} \times \dfrac{1}{\underset{1}{\cancel{100}}} = \dfrac{1}{3}$

6. $R = 25\% = .25. = 0.25$; $B = 300$

$P = R \times B$

$P = 0.25 \times 300$

$\quad = 75$

7. $P = 36$; $R = 66\dfrac{2}{3}\% = \dfrac{2}{3}$

$B = \dfrac{P}{R}$

$B = \dfrac{36}{\frac{2}{3}}$, or $36 \div \dfrac{2}{3}$

$\quad = \dfrac{\overset{18}{\cancel{36}}}{1} \times \dfrac{3}{\underset{1}{\cancel{2}}}$

$\quad = 54$

8. $P = 70; B = 280$

$$R = \frac{P}{B} = \frac{70}{280} = 0.25$$

$$= 25\%$$

9. $R = 40\% = 0.40; B = 160$
$P = R \times B = 0.4 \times 160 = 64$

10. $R = 33\frac{1}{3}\% = \frac{1}{3}$

$B = 150$

$$P = R \times B = \frac{1}{\cancel{3}_1} \times \frac{\overset{50}{\cancel{150}}}{1} = 50$$

11. $R = 154\% = 1.54; B = 30$
$P = R \times B = 1.54 \times 30 = 46.2,$
which rounds to 46

12. $R = 80\% = 0.80$ or $0.8; P = 42$

$$B = \frac{P}{R}$$

$$B = \frac{42}{0.8}$$

$$= 52.5, \text{ or approximately 53 shirts}$$

13. $P = 23; B = 25$

$$R = \frac{P}{B}$$

$$R = \frac{23}{25} = 0.92 = 92\%$$

14. $450 - 400 = \$50$ (increase)

$P = \$50; B = 400$ (original salary)

$$R = \frac{P}{B}$$

$$R = \frac{50}{400} = 0.125 = 12.5\%$$

15. $78 - 68 = 10$ (decrease)

$P = 10; B = 78$ (original count)

$$R = \frac{P}{B}$$

$$R = \frac{10}{78} = 0.128 \quad \text{(rounded)}$$

$$= 12.8\%$$

End of Chapter Problems

Change the following decimals to percents.

1. 0.23   **2.** 0.675

3. 0.82   **4.** 2.63

5. 0.03   **6.** 0.007

7. 0.34   **8.** 3.741

9. 0.601   **10.** 0.0004

11. 1   **12.** 0.6

13. 3

Convert the following fractions or mixed numbers to percents.

14. $\dfrac{17}{100}$ **15.** $\dfrac{99}{100}$ **16.** $\dfrac{6}{100}$

17. $\dfrac{20}{100}$ **18.** $\dfrac{52}{100}$

19. $\dfrac{13}{20}$

20. $\dfrac{1}{10}$

21. $3\dfrac{2}{5}$

22. $\dfrac{5}{4}$

23. $7\dfrac{1}{2}$

Change each decimal or whole number to a percent.

24. 0.37

25. 0.811

26. 0.2

27. 2.54

28. 4

Change each fraction or mixed number to a percent. Round to the nearest hundredth percent if necessary.

29. $\dfrac{39}{100}$

30. $\dfrac{2}{5}$

31. $\dfrac{1}{3}$

32. $1\dfrac{5}{8}$

33. $\dfrac{3}{100}$

Section 4.2

Change the following percents to decimals.

34. 98%

35. 84.6%

36. 256%

37. 52%

38. 91.7%

39. 3%

40. 0.5%

41. 0.02%

42. 6%

43. 9%

Convert each percent to a whole number, mixed number, or fraction, reduced to lowest terms.

44. 10%

45. 20%

46. 6%

47. 170%

48. 89%

49. 361%

50. 250%

Write each percent as a decimal.

51. 36%

52. 274%

53. 6%

54. 30%

55. 0.4%

Convert each percent to a whole number, mixed number, or fraction, reduced to lowest terms.

56. 45%

57. 25%

58. 225%

59. 300%

60. $12\frac{1}{2}\%$

Fill in the missing blanks.

	Percent	Fraction	Decimal
61.	$33\frac{1}{3}\%$	(a)	(b)

	Percent	Fraction	Decimal
62.	(a)	$\frac{2}{5}$	(b)
63.	(a)	(b)	0.125
64.	50%	(a)	(b)
65.	(a)	(b)	0.8
66.	$87\frac{1}{2}\%$	(a)	(b)
67.	(a)	$\frac{5}{8}$	(b)

Find P, R, or B using the basic percentage formula or one of its forms.

68. $B = 300$, $R = 27\%$ **69.** $B = \$1,900$, $R = 106\%$

70. $B = 1,000$, $R = 2\frac{1}{2}\%$

71. $B = \$500$, $R = 7.25\%$

72. $P = 25$, $B = 100$ **73.** $P = 170$, $B = 85$

74. $P = 2$, $B = 6$ **75.** $P = 18$, $B = 300$

76. $P = \$600$, $R = 5\%$ **77.** $P = 26$, $R = 6\frac{1}{2}\%$

78. $P = \$15.50$, $R = 7.75\%$ **79.** $P = 6$, $R = 120\%$

Round numbers to the nearest hundredth and percents to the nearest whole-number percent.

80. $B = 36$, $R = 42\%$ **81.** $P = 68$, $B = 85$

82. $P = \$835$, $R = 3.2\%$ **83.** $R = 72\%$, $B = 16$

84. $R = 136\%$, $B = 834$ **85.** $P = 397$, $B = 200$

86. $P = 52$, $R = 17\%$ **87.** $P = 512$, $B = 128$

88. $P = 125$, $B = 50$ **89.** $B = 892$, $R = 63\%$

90. $B = 643$, $R = 8\%$ **91.** $P = 803$, $B = 4,015$

Use the percentage formula or a variation to solve the following problems.

92. Find 30% of 80.   **93.** Find 150% of 20.

94. 30% of 27 equals what number? **95.** What number is 70% of 300?

96. 90% of what number is 27? **97.** 82% of what number is 94.3?

98. $33\frac{1}{3}\%$ of what number is 60? **99.** 112 is 14% of what number?

100. 97 is what percent of 100? **101.** What percent of 54 is 36?

102. 51.52 is what percent of 2,576?

103. What percent of 180 is 60?

104. 42 is what percent of 21? **105.** 27 is what percent of 9?

106. Eighty percent of one store's customers paid with credit cards. Forty customers came in that day. How many customers paid for their purchases with credit cards?

107. If a picture frame costs $30 and the tax on the frame is 6% of the cost, how much is the tax on the picture frame?

108. Seventy percent of the town's population voted in an election. If 1,589 people voted, what is the population of the town?

109. Five percent of a batch of fuses were found to faulty during an inspection. If 27 fuses were faulty, how many fuses were inspected?

110. Thirty-seven of the 50 shareholders attended the meeting. What percent of the shareholders attended the meeting?

111. In Memphis the sales tax is $7\frac{3}{4}\%$. How much tax is paid on a purchase of $20.60? (Round to the nearest cent.)

112. A business math student answered 60 questions correctly on a 75-question test. What percent of the questions were answered correctly?

113. A football stadium has a capacity of 53,983. If 47,892 fans attended a game, what percent of the seats were filled?

114. A large university campus has 197 restrooms. If 38 of these are designed to accommodate diasabled persons, what percent can accommodate the disabled?

115. The United Way expects to raise $63 million in the current drive. The chairperson projects that 60% of the funds will be raised in the first 12 weeks. How many dollars are expected to be raised in the first 12 weeks?

116. The financial officer for an accounting firm allows $3,400 for supplies in the annual budget. After 3 months, $898.32 has been spent on supplies. Is this figure within 25% of the annual budget?

117. An accountant who is currently earning $42,380 annually expects a 6.5% raise. What is the amount of the expected raise?

118. A single-family property increased in value from $85,900 to $94,060. What was the percent of the increase?

119. The price of a personal computer fell from $3,400 to $2,890. Find the percent of decrease.

120. Larry Gates's salary increased from $14,804 to $16,062.34. What was the percent raise?

121. Karl Atkins is a member of a union that contracted to take a temporary wage decrease of 6%. If Karl was earning $7.50 per hour, how much was his wage cut? What is his new hourly rate?

Additional Problems

1. At the Evans Formal Wear department store, all suits are reduced 20% from the retail price. If Charles Stewart purchased a suit that originally retailed for $258.30, how much did he save?

2. A soccer stadium in Manchester, England, has a capacity of 78,753 seats. If 67,388 seats were filled, what percent of the stadium seats were vacant? Round to the nearest tenth of a percent.

3. Joe Passarelli earns $8.67 per hour working for Dracken International. If Joe earns a merit raise of 12%, how much will he earn per hour?

4. Last year the Glee Toy Store grossed $894,412.67 on a new product. This year the same product grossed only $612,897.12. What percent did the product's gross earnings fall? Round to the nearest tenth of a percent.

5. Heidi Hager buys $\frac{1}{4}$ pound of Jaw Breakers at $3.76 per pound. What was the total cost of the Jaw Breakers?

6. An ice cream truck began its daily route with 95 gallons of ice cream. The truck driver sold 78% of the ice cream. How many gallons of ice cream were sold?

7. A stock holder sold her shares and made a profit of $1,466. If this is a profit of 23%, how much were the shares worth when she originally purchased them?

8. A family wrote three checks for their automobile note, house note, and insurance for a total sum of $889.43. If 25% was spent for the automobile note and 40% was spent for the house note, what percent was spent on insurance?

9. The Drammelonnie Department Store sold 30% of its shirts in stock. If the department store sold 267 shirts, how many shirts did the store have in stock?

10. If a finance company repossessed 16% of the 550 cars it financed, how many cars did it repossess?

Challenge Problem

Mainframes Selling Like Hotcakes

Brian Sangean has been offered a job in which he will be paid strictly on a commission basis. He will receive a 2% commission on all sales of computer hardware he closes. Brian's goal for a gross yearly salary is $30,000. How much computer hardware must Brian sell in order to meet his target salary?

Trial Test

Change each percent to a decimal.

1. 24%

2. 68.7%

3. 9%

4. 20%

5. $27\frac{1}{2}\%$

6. 276%

7. 0.5%

8. $156\frac{2}{3}\%$

9. $\frac{1}{8}\%$

10. 0.04%

Convert each decimal to a percent.

11. 0.24

12. 0.925

13. 0.6

14. 3.64

15. $0.37\frac{1}{2}$

Convert each percent to a fraction or mixed number.

16. 35%

17. $87\frac{1}{2}\%$

18. $\frac{1}{4}\%$

19. $33\frac{1}{3}\%$

20. 375%

Change each fraction or mixed number to a percent.

21. $\frac{21}{100}$ **22.** $\frac{1}{5}$

23. $\frac{3}{8}$ **24.** 1

25. $\frac{7}{9}$

Solve.

26. Find 30% of $240.   **27.** Find 1% of 26.

28. What number is $33\frac{1}{3}\%$ of 96?   **29.** 25% of 452 equals what number?

30. What number is 10% of 478?   **31.** 50 is what percent of 20?

32. What percent of 8 is 7?   **33.** 100% of 32 is how much?

34. 120% of $36 is how much?   **35.** 0.3% of what number is 6.39?

36. What number is $\frac{1}{2}\%$ of 500?   **37.** 22% of what number is 24.86?

38. Find the interest on a loan of $500 if the simple interest is $10\frac{3}{4}\%$ of the amount borrowed.

39. What is the sales tax on an item that costs $42 if the tax rate is 6%?

40. If 100% of 22 rooms are full, how many rooms are full?

41. Twelve employees at a meat packing plant were sick on Monday. If the plant employs 360 people, what percent of the employees were sick on Monday?

42. A department store had 15% turnover in personnel last year. If the store employs 600 people, how many employees were replaced last year?

43. One hundred seventeen of the 150 students in a class received passing grades. What percent of the class passed?

44. The Dawson family left a 15% tip for a restaurant check. If the check totaled $19.47, find the amount of the tip. What was the total cost of the meal, including the tip?

45. In a class of 29 students, 3 are color-blind. Find the percent of the class that is color-blind. Round to the nearest whole percent.

46. The Corner Gas Station sold 52,600 gallons of gasoline. Of this amount, 19,400 gallons were premium unleaded. What percent of the gas sold was premium unleaded? Round to the nearest whole percent.

47. If a 40-question test has 24 questions that are multiple choice, what percent of the questions are multiple choice?

48. A certain make and model of automobile was projected to have a 3% rate of defective autos. If the number of defective automobiles was projected to be 1,698, how many automobiles were to be produced?

49. A family's income increased by $2,300, which was a 15% increase. What was the family's original income?

50. Of the 52 questions on this trial test, 15 are word problems. What percent of the problems are word problems? (Round to the nearest whole number percent.)

51. Karen Denny, a management trainee, earns $21,560. When she completes the training program, she will earn $24,794. What percent increase does she expect?

52. Alan Wise paid $24,840 for a new van. Because he found he was unable to make the payments, he had to sell the van. A buyer agreed to pay him $19,623.60 for the van. What was his rate of loss?

How past years stack up

The number of players who filed for salary arbitration, the number of cases that went to a hearing and the results of those since the process started in 1974:

Year	Players filed	Settled before arbitration	Released before case	Entered process	Player won	Team won
1974	53	24	0	29	13	16
1975	38	23	0	15	6	9
1978	16	7	0	9·	2	7
1979	40	24	2	14	8	6
1980	65	39	0	26	15	11
1981	96	74	1	21	11	10
1982	103	80	1	22	8	14
1983	88	57	1	30	13	17
1984	80	70	0	10	4	6
1985	98	85	0	13	6	7
1986	159	124	0	35	15	20
1987	109	83	0	26	10	16
1988	111	92[1]	0	18	7	11
1989	136	123[2]	0	12	7	5
1990	162	138	0	24	14	10
1991	157	140	0	17	6	11

There was no arbitration in 1976-77 because of players' negotiations concerning the reserve system.

1-Includes one player vetoed by club; 2-Includes one player who withdrew.

Source: USA TODAY research

QUESTIONS

1. Calculate the percent of players who filed for salary arbitration but settled before arbitration for the years 1975, 1980, 1985, 1990.

2. Was a player who filed for salary arbitration more likely to settle before arbitration in 1975 or in 1985. Explain your answer.

3. Of the players who entered the arbitration process, calculate the percent of players who won in 1975,

1980, 1985, and 1990. Do these percents indicate a trend? Explain your answer.

Although the rates fluctuate each year, there is a trend favoring players that has increased from 40% in 1975 to 58.3% in 1990.

4. In the five-year period from 1986 through 1990, which year had the largest percent of increase in the number of players who filed for arbitration from the previous year?

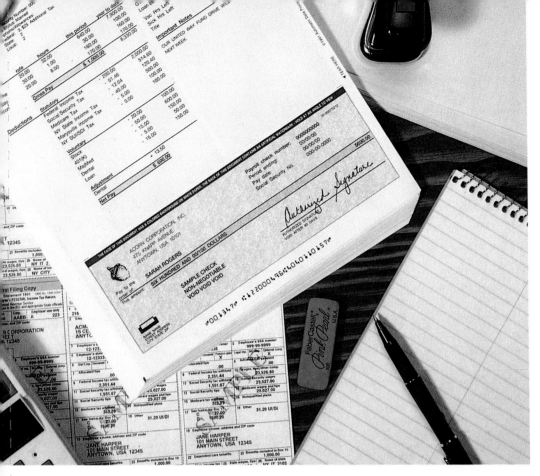

Payroll

Pay is constantly on the minds of employees and employers alike. If you have worked and received a paycheck, you know that a large part is taken out of your paycheck before you ever see it. Your employer *withholds* (deducts) taxes, union dues, medical insurance payments, and so on. Thus there is a difference between **gross earnings (gross pay)**, the amount earned before deductions, and **net earnings (net pay)**—*take-home pay*—the amount in the paycheck.

    This chapter considers payroll issues from the point of view of the employee and the employer. Employers have the option of paying their people in salary or in wages and of making payments monthly or weekly. Employers also have a responsibility to withhold taxes and pay them to the government.

gross earnings (gross pay): total amount of earnings before any deductions are made.

net earnings (net pay): amount of pay left after deductions are made (also called *take-home pay*).

Calculating Gross pay

LEARNING OBJECTIVES

1. Find the gross pay of salaried personnel.
2. Find the gross pay of workers paid hourly wages.
3. Determine piecework wages.
4. Determine commission payments.

Employees can be paid a yearly salary or an hourly wage, and some employees are paid solely or partially by a commission. Companies differ in how often they pay employees, which determines how many paychecks an employee receives in a year. If employees are paid *weekly*, they receive 52 paychecks a year; if they are paid **biweekly** (every other week), they receive 26 paychecks a year. **Semimonthly** (twice a month) paychecks are issued 24 times a year, and *monthly* paychecks come 12 times a year. This section shows what all these possibilities mean to the person who is collecting the paycheck.

biweekly: every other week, 26 pay periods per year.

semimonthly: twice a month, 24 pay periods in a year.

Finding the Gross Pay of Salaried Personnel

salary: an amount of money paid to an employee for work done.

Salary is usually stated as a certain amount of money paid each year. Salaried employees are paid the agreed-upon salary whether they work fewer or more than the usual number of hours. To find the amount of a salaried employee's paycheck before deductions, divide the amount of the salary by the number of paychecks the employee will receive in the course of a year.

EXAMPLE 1

If Mary Ward earns a salary of $30,000 a year and is paid biweekly, how much is her paycheck before taxes are taken out? If Mary were paid semimonthly, how much would her paycheck be before taxes?

$30,000 ÷ 26 = $1,153.85   Biweekly paychecks are issued 26 times a year, so divide Mary's salary by 26.

$30,000 ÷ 24 = $1,250   Semimonthly paychecks are issued 24 times a year, so divide Mary's salary by 24.

Finding the Gross Pay of Workers Paid Hourly Wages

hourly rate (hourly wage): rate of pay for each hour worked.

overtime rate: rate of pay for hours worked beyond 40 hours in a week (sometimes given for work on holidays). It must be at least 1.5 times the regular pay rate.

Some jobs pay according to the number of hours an employee has worked since the last paycheck. The **hourly rate**, or **hourly wage**, is the amount of money paid for each hour the employee works. The Fair Labor Standards Act of 1938 set a standard work week of 40 hours. An hourly employee's pay is made up of a regular hourly rate and an **overtime rate**. When such employees work 40 hours in a week, they get the regular rate. When they work more than 40 hours they are paid the regular rate for the 40 hours and the overtime rate for the hours over 40 worked. The overtime rate is often called time and a half. By law it must be at least 1.5 (one and one-half) times the regular rate.

To figure how much an hourly employee has earned since the last paycheck, you multiply the number of hours worked (up to 40 hours) times the hourly rate of pay. If the employee has worked overtime, you use the following method to figure gross earnings.

STEP BY STEP

Calculating Gross Earnings with Overtime

Step 1. Multiply 40 hours times the regular rate of pay.

Step 2. Multiply the number of overtime hours worked times the regular rate times 1.5.

Step 3. Add the two amounts from steps 1 and 2 for the total pay.

EXAMPLE 2

Marcia Scott, whose regular rate of pay is $7.25 per hour, worked 46 hours last week. Find her gross pay for last week.

$40 \times \$7.25 = \$290$ Find the amount earned for 40 hours of work at the regular rate of pay.

$6 \times \$7.25 \times 1.5 = \$65.25$ Find the overtime earnings by multiplying the number of overtime hours times the regular rate times 1.5. Round to the nearest cent.

$\$290 + \$65.25 = \$355.25$ Add the regular-rate earnings and the overtime-rate earnings to find Marcia's total gross earnings.

Determining Piecework Wages

Some employers motivate employees to produce more by paying according to the amount of acceptable work done. Such **piecework rates** are typically offered in production or manufacturing jobs. Garment makers and some other types of factory workers, agricultural workers, and employees who perform repetitive tasks such as stuffing envelopes or packaging parts may be paid by this method. The gross earnings of such workers are calculated by multiplying the number of items produced by the pay per item.

piecework rate: pay rate based on the amount of acceptable work done.

EXAMPLE 3

A shirt manufacturer pays a worker $0.12 for each acceptable shirt completed under the prescribed job description. If the worker had the following work record, find the gross earnings for the week: Monday, 250 shirts; Tuesday, 300 shirts; Wednesday, 178 shirts; Thursday, 326 shirts; Friday, 296 shirts.

$250 + 300 + 178 + 326 + 296 = 1,350$ shirts   Find the total number of shirts made.

$1,350 \times \$0.12 = \$162$ Multiply the number of shirts by the piece rate to find the gross pay.

differential piece rate: pay rate based on the number of items produced; increases as the items produced per time period increase (also called *escalating piece rate*).

Sometimes employees earn wages at a **differential piece rate**, also called an *escalating piece rate*. As the number of items produced by the worker increases, so does the pay per item. This method of paying wages offers employees an even greater incentive to complete more pieces of work in a given period of time.

EXAMPLE 4

Last week, Jorge Sanchez assembled 317 microchip boards. Find Jorge's gross earnings if the manufacturer pays at the following differential piece rate:

Microchip boards	Rate per board
1–100	$1.32
101–300	$1.42
301 and over	$1.58

First 100 items: $1.32 \times 100 = \$132.00$ Find how many boards were
Next 200 items: $1.42 \times 200 = \$284.00$ completed at each pay rate,
Last 17 items: $1.58 \times 17 = \underline{\$26.86}$ multiply the number of boards
                                      $\$442.86$ by the rate, and add the amounts.

Determining Commission Payments

commission: earnings based on a percent of total sales.

straight commission: salary based entirely on a percent of total sales.

salary plus commission: a certain basic salary that is earned in addition to a commission on sales.

Many salespeople earn a **commission** based on a percent of their total sales. Those whose entire salary is a percent of total sales are said to work on **straight commission**. Those who receive a basic sum in addition to a commission on sales are said to work on a **salary plus commission** basis.

A commission can be an amount of money earned per article sold, a percent of the value of each article sold, or an amount or percent over a specified quota. In the latter case, salespeople must sell a specified number of items before they start earning commission.

EXAMPLE 5

A restaurant-supplies salesperson receives 5% of his total sales as commission. His sales totaled $5,000 during a given week. Find his gross earnings.
    Use the percentage formula, $P = R \times B$.

$P = 0.05 \times \$5,000 = \$250$ Change the rate of 5% to a decimal and multiply it times the base of $5,000.

EXAMPLE 6

Ms. Jones is paid by the salary-plus-commission method. She receives $150 weekly in salary and 3% of all sales over $2,000. If she sold $6,000 worth of goods, find her gross earnings.

$\$6,000 - \$2,000 = \$4,000$ Find the amount on which commission is paid.

$P = R \times B$
  $= 0.03 \times 4,000$
  $= \$120$ (commission)
               Change the rate of 3% to a decimal. Multiply the rate times the base of $4,000. Ms. Jones' commission is $120.

$\$120 + \$150 = \$270$ Add the commission and salary to find gross earnings.

 Self-Check 5.1

1. If Melvin Smith earns a salary of $19,000 a year and is paid weekly, how much is his weekly paycheck before taxes are taken out?

2. Doris Ilardis worked 47 hours one week. Her regular pay was $7.60 per hour. Find her gross earnings for the week.

3. Louisa Adamson, whose regular rate of pay is $8.25 per hour, worked 44 hours last week. Find her gross pay for last week.

4. A belt manufacturer pays a worker $0.75 for each buckle attached under the prescribed job description. If Franklin had the following work record, find the gross earnings for the week: Monday, 32 buckles, Tuesday, 34 buckles, Wednesday, 38 buckles, Thursday, 35 buckles, Friday, 30 buckles.

5. Last week, Melissa packaged 180 boxes of Holiday Cheese Assortment. Find her gross earnings if she is paid at the following differential piece rate:

Cheese packages	Rate per package
1–100	$1.32
101–300	$1.42
301 and over	$1.58

6. A paper mill sales representative receives 6% of his total sales as commission. His sales last week totaled $5,000. Find his gross earnings.

7. Ms. Ferris is paid by the salary-plus-commission method. She receives $175 weekly in salary and 4% of all sales over $2,000. If she sold $6,000 in merchandise, find her gross earnings.

5.2

Determining Payroll Deductions

LEARNING OBJECTIVES

1. Find federal withholding tax by the table method.
2. Find federal withholding tax by the percentage method.
3. Find Social Security and Medicare tax.
4. Figure net earnings.
5. Calculate the employer's taxes.

As anyone who has ever drawn a paycheck knows, many deductions stand between gross and net pay. Deductions include federal, state, and local taxes, FICA (Social Security) taxes, union dues, medical insurance, credit union payments, and a host of others. By law, employers are responsible for withholding and paying their employees' taxes. In fact, the bookkeeping involved in payroll provides a major source of employment for many people in the business world.

The largest deduction from an employee's paycheck usually comes in the form of *income tax*, which is the same as **federal withholding tax (FWT)**. The amount of tax withheld is based on three things: the employee's gross earnings, the employee's marital status, and number of withholding exemptions the person can claim. A **withholding allowance**, also called an **exemption**, is an amount of gross earnings that is not subject to tax. Each employee is permitted one personal withholding allowance, one for a spouse if the spouse does not work, and one for each dependent (such as a child or elderly parent who lives with the taxpayer but does not work). Employees all fill out W-4 forms showing how many withholding allowances or exemptions they claim. The employer uses this information to figure how much to deduct

federal withholding tax (FWT): a federal tax based on income, marital status, and exemptions that is paid by all persons earning a certain amount of money in the United States. An estimated amount is usually withheld from a person's paycheck.

withholding allowance (exemption): an allowance that reduces the amount of federal withholding tax owed or withheld. One allowance each is permitted for the taxpayer, the taxpayer's spouse, and each of the taxpayer's children, elderly, and other dependents.

------------- Cut here and give the certificate to your employer. Keep the top portion for your records. -------------

Form **W-4** Department of the Treasury Internal Revenue Service	**Employee's Withholding Allowance Certificate** ► **For Privacy Act and Paperwork Reduction Act Notice, see reverse.**	OMB No. 1545-0010

1 Type or print your first name and middle initial	Last name	**2** Your social security number
Steven A. Katz		128-82-5556

Home address (number and street or rural route)	**3** Marital Status	☒ Single ☐ Married
1312 Loch Ave.		☐ Married, but withhold at higher Single rate.
City or town, state, and ZIP code		**Note:** If married, but legally separated, or spouse is a nonresident alien, check the Single box.
Johntown, NJ 07781		

4 Total number of allowances you are claiming (from line G above or from the Worksheets on back if they apply) . . . **4** | 1

5 Additional amount, if any, you want deducted from each pay . . . . **5** $

6 I claim exemption from withholding and I certify that I meet **ALL** of the following conditions for exemption:
- Last year I had a right to a refund of **ALL** Federal income tax withheld because I had **NO** tax liability; **AND**
- This year I expect a refund of **ALL** Federal income tax withheld because I expect to have **NO** tax liability; **AND**
- This year if my income exceeds $500 and includes nonwage income, another person cannot claim me as a dependent.

If you meet all of the above conditions, enter the year effective and "EXEMPT" here . . . ► **6** | 19

7 Are you a full-time student? (**Note:** Full-time students are not automatically exempt.) . . . . **7** ☐ Yes ☒ No

Under penalties of perjury, I certify that I am entitled to the number of withholding allowances claimed on this certificate or entitled to claim exempt status.

Employee's signature ► Steven A. Katz   Date ► October 18 , 19XX

8 Employer's name and address (**Employer:** Complete 8 and 10 only if sending to IRS)	**9** Office code (optional)	**10** Employer identification number
Herbert Fare Hospital		203-146

Figure 5-1 A W-4 Form

from each employee's paycheck for withholding tax. Figure 5-1 shows a sample W-4 form.

There are two ways to figure the amount of withholding tax for an employee, by the table method or by the percentage method.

Finding Federal Withholding Tax by the Table Method

The table method uses one of a number of tables provided in a pamphlet (Circular E) published by the Internal Revenue Service and called *The Employer's Tax Guide* (Revised February 1992). Tables 5-1 and 5-2 show portions of these tables: Table 5-1 is for Single Persons—Semimonthly Payroll Period and Table 5-2 (on page 168) is for Married Persons—Weekly Payroll Period. To use these tables, you must know the person's salary, whether it is a weekly or semimonthly salary, whether the person is single or married, and how many withholding allowances are claimed.

STEP BY STEP

Using a Tax Table

Step 1. Read down the columns at the left that are labeled "At least" and "But less than" until you come to the range that includes the person's salary. In Table 5-1, if the salary is $750, you would find the range that says "At least 740/But less than 760."

Step 2. Look across the table until you find the correct number of withholding allowances.

Step 3. The number shown where the column and row intersect is the amount of tax that the person owes either weekly or semimonthly, depending on which table you use.

EXAMPLE 7

Toni Liss has a gross semimonthly income of $840, is single, and claims three withholding allowances. Find the amount of withholding tax to be deducted from her gross earnings by using Table 5-1. The amount $840 is seen in *both* the "At least" and "But less than" columns. Since $840 is not in the range "At least $820 but less than $840," choose the withholding given in the row "At least $840 but less than $860" under the column for three withholding allowances. The withholding tax is $69.

EXAMPLE 8

Bill Johnson is married, has a gross weekly salary of $515, and claims two withholding allowances. Find the amount of withholding tax to be deducted from his gross salary. Look in the first two columns of Table 5-2 to find the range for $515. Then move across to the column for two withholding allowances. The amount of withholding tax is $47.

Table 5-1

SINGLE Persons—SEMIMONTHLY Payroll Period
(For Wages Paid After February 1992)

And the wages are—		And the number of withholding allowances claimed is—										
At least	But less than	0	1	2	3	4	5	6	7	8	9	10
		The amount of income tax to be withheld shall be—										
$780	$800	$103	$89	$74	$60	$46	$31	$17	$3	$0	$0	$0
800	820	106	92	77	63	49	34	20	6	0	0	0
820	840	109	95	80	66	52	37	23	9	0	0	0
840	860	112	98	83	69	55	40	26	12	0	0	0
860	880	115	101	86	72	58	43	29	15	0	0	0
880	900	118	104	89	75	61	46	32	18	3	0	0
900	920	121	107	92	78	64	49	35	21	6	0	0
920	940	124	110	95	81	67	52	38	24	9	0	0
940	960	127	113	98	84	70	55	41	27	12	0	0
960	980	133	116	101	87	73	58	44	30	15	1	0
980	1,000	139	119	104	90	76	61	47	33	18	4	0
1,000	1,020	144	122	107	93	79	64	50	36	21	7	0
1,020	1,040	150	125	110	96	82	67	53	39	24	10	0
1,040	1,060	155	129	113	99	85	70	56	42	27	13	0
1,060	1,080	161	134	116	102	88	73	59	45	30	16	1
1,080	1,100	167	140	119	105	91	76	62	48	33	19	4
1,100	1,120	172	145	122	108	94	79	65	51	36	22	7
1,120	1,140	178	151	125	111	97	82	68	54	39	25	10
1,140	1,160	183	157	130	114	100	85	71	57	42	28	13
1,160	1,180	189	162	135	117	103	88	74	60	45	31	16
1,180	1,200	195	168	141	120	106	91	77	63	48	34	19
1,200	1,220	200	173	147	123	109	94	80	66	51	37	22
1,220	1,240	206	179	152	126	112	97	83	69	54	40	25
1,240	1,260	211	185	158	131	115	100	86	72	57	43	28
1,260	1,280	217	190	163	137	118	103	89	75	60	46	31
1,280	1,300	223	196	169	142	121	106	92	78	63	49	34
1,300	1,320	228	201	175	148	124	109	95	81	66	52	37
1,320	1,340	234	207	180	153	127	112	98	84	69	55	40
1,340	1,360	239	213	186	159	132	115	101	87	72	58	43
1,360	1,380	245	218	191	165	138	118	104	90	75	61	46
1,380	1,400	251	224	197	170	143	121	107	93	78	64	49
1,400	1,420	256	229	203	176	149	124	110	96	81	67	52
1,420	1,440	262	235	208	181	155	128	113	99	84	70	55
1,440	1,460	267	241	214	187	160	133	116	102	87	73	58
1,460	1,480	273	246	219	193	166	139	119	105	90	76	61
1,480	1,500	279	252	225	198	171	144	122	108	93	79	64
1,500	1,520	284	257	231	204	177	150	125	111	96	82	67
1,520	1,540	290	263	236	209	183	156	129	114	99	85	70
1,540	1,560	295	269	242	215	188	161	134	117	102	88	73
1,560	1,580	301	274	247	221	194	167	140	120	105	91	76
1,580	1,600	307	280	253	226	199	172	146	123	108	94	79
1,600	1,620	312	285	259	232	205	178	151	126	111	97	82
1,620	1,640	318	291	264	237	211	184	157	130	114	100	85
1,640	1,660	323	297	270	243	216	189	162	136	117	103	88
1,660	1,680	329	302	275	249	222	195	168	141	120	106	91
1,680	1,700	335	308	281	254	227	200	174	147	123	109	94
1,700	1,720	340	313	287	260	233	206	179	152	126	112	97
1,720	1,740	346	319	292	265	239	212	185	158	131	115	100
1,740	1,760	351	325	298	271	244	217	190	164	137	118	103
1,760	1,780	357	330	303	277	250	223	196	169	142	121	106
1,780	1,800	363	336	309	282	255	228	202	175	148	124	109
1,800	1,820	368	341	315	288	261	234	207	180	154	127	112
1,820	1,840	374	347	320	293	267	240	213	186	159	132	115
1,840	1,860	379	353	326	299	272	245	218	192	165	138	118
1,860	1,880	385	358	331	305	278	251	224	197	170	144	121
1,880	1,900	391	364	337	310	283	256	230	203	176	149	124
1,900	1,920	396	369	343	316	289	262	235	208	182	155	128
1,920	1,940	402	375	348	321	295	268	241	214	187	160	134
1,940	1,960	407	381	354	327	300	273	246	220	193	166	139
1,960	1,980	413	386	359	333	306	279	252	225	198	172	145
1,980	2,000	419	392	365	338	311	284	258	231	204	177	150
2,000	2,020	425	397	371	344	317	290	263	236	210	183	156
2,020	2,040	431	403	376	349	323	296	269	242	215	188	162
2,040	2,060	438	409	382	355	328	301	274	248	221	194	167
2,060	2,080	444	414	387	361	334	307	280	253	226	200	173

$2,080 and over   Use Table 3(a) for a **SINGLE person** on page 26. Also see the instructions on page 24.

Page 37

Table 5-2

MARRIED Persons—WEEKLY Payroll Period
(For Wages Paid After February 1992)

And the wages are—		And the number of withholding allowances claimed is—										
At least	But less than	0	1	2	3	4	5	6	7	8	9	10
		The amount of income tax to be withheld shall be—										
$0	$120	$0	$0	$0	$0	$0	$0	$0	$0	$0	$0	$0
120	125	1	0	0	0	0	0	0	0	0	0	0
125	130	2	0	0	0	0	0	0	0	0	0	0
130	135	3	0	0	0	0	0	0	0	0	0	0
135	140	3	0	0	0	0	0	0	0	0	0	0
140	145	4	0	0	0	0	0	0	0	0	0	0
145	150	5	0	0	0	0	0	0	0	0	0	0
150	155	6	0	0	0	0	0	0	0	0	0	0
155	160	6	0	0	0	0	0	0	0	0	0	0
160	165	7	0	0	0	0	0	0	0	0	0	0
165	170	8	1	0	0	0	0	0	0	0	0	0
170	175	9	2	0	0	0	0	0	0	0	0	0
175	180	9	3	0	0	0	0	0	0	0	0	0
180	185	10	3	0	0	0	0	0	0	0	0	0
185	190	11	4	0	0	0	0	0	0	0	0	0
190	195	12	5	0	0	0	0	0	0	0	0	0
195	200	12	6	0	0	0	0	0	0	0	0	0
200	210	13	7	0	0	0	0	0	0	0	0	0
210	220	15	8	2	0	0	0	0	0	0	0	0
220	230	16	10	3	0	0	0	0	0	0	0	0
230	240	18	11	5	0	0	0	0	0	0	0	0
240	250	19	13	6	0	0	0	0	0	0	0	0
250	260	21	14	8	1	0	0	0	0	0	0	0
260	270	22	16	9	3	0	0	0	0	0	0	0
270	280	24	17	11	4	0	0	0	0	0	0	0
280	290	25	19	12	6	0	0	0	0	0	0	0
290	300	27	20	14	7	0	0	0	0	0	0	0
300	310	28	22	15	9	2	0	0	0	0	0	0
310	320	30	23	17	10	3	0	0	0	0	0	0
320	330	31	25	18	12	5	0	0	0	0	0	0
330	340	33	26	20	13	6	0	0	0	0	0	0
340	350	34	28	21	15	8	1	0	0	0	0	0
350	360	36	29	23	16	9	3	0	0	0	0	0
360	370	37	31	24	18	11	4	0	0	0	0	0
370	380	39	32	26	19	12	6	0	0	0	0	0
380	390	40	34	27	21	14	7	1	0	0	0	0
390	400	42	35	29	22	15	9	2	0	0	0	0
400	410	43	37	30	24	17	10	4	0	0	0	0
410	420	45	38	32	25	18	12	5	0	0	0	0
420	430	46	40	33	27	20	13	7	0	0	0	0
430	440	48	41	35	28	21	15	8	2	0	0	0
440	450	49	43	36	30	23	16	10	3	0	0	0
450	460	51	44	38	31	24	18	11	5	0	0	0
460	470	52	46	39	33	26	19	13	6	0	0	0
470	480	54	47	41	34	27	21	14	8	1	0	0
480	490	55	49	42	36	29	22	16	9	2	0	0
490	500	57	50	44	37	30	24	17	11	4	0	0
500	510	58	52	45	39	32	25	19	12	5	0	0
510	520	60	53	47	40	33	27	20	14	7	0	0
520	530	61	55	48	42	35	28	22	15	8	2	0
530	540	63	56	50	43	36	30	23	17	10	3	0
540	550	64	58	51	45	38	31	25	18	11	5	0
550	560	66	59	53	46	39	33	26	20	13	6	0
560	570	67	61	54	48	41	34	28	21	14	8	1
570	580	69	62	56	49	42	36	29	23	16	9	3
580	590	70	64	57	51	44	37	31	24	17	11	4
590	600	72	65	59	52	45	39	32	26	19	12	6
600	610	73	67	60	54	47	40	34	27	20	14	7
610	620	75	68	62	55	48	42	35	29	22	15	9
620	630	76	70	63	57	50	43	37	30	23	17	10
630	640	78	71	65	58	51	45	38	32	25	18	12
640	650	79	73	66	60	53	46	40	33	26	20	13
650	660	81	74	68	61	54	48	41	35	28	21	15
660	670	82	76	69	63	56	49	43	36	29	23	16
670	680	84	77	71	64	57	51	44	38	31	24	18
680	690	85	79	72	66	59	52	46	39	32	26	19
690	700	87	80	74	67	60	54	47	41	34	27	21
700	710	88	82	75	69	62	55	49	42	35	29	22
710	720	90	83	77	70	63	57	50	44	37	30	24
720	730	91	85	78	72	65	58	52	45	38	32	25

Page 30

Finding Federal Withholding Tax by the Percentage Method

Many companies calculate withholding tax and prepare payrolls by computer. Computerized payrolls generally do not depend on tax tables; instead they use percentage calculations. The federal government publishes Form Y, which shows the percentage of the income that should be withheld from the salary of an individual in a certain income bracket. You cannot use a simple percentage calculation to find the amount of tax owed because the tax rate increases as the income increases.

We show two tables here that are issued by the federal government for calculating income tax. Table 5-3, Income Tax Withholding—Percentage Method, shows how much to subtract from gross pay for each withholding allowance claimed. After this is done, you turn to Table 5-4, Tables for Percentage Method of Withholding, which shows the amount of tax to be withheld.

STEP BY STEP

Calculating Tax by the Percentage Method

Step 1. Use Table 5-3. Multiply the number of withholding allowances times the amount shown in the right column, depending on whether wages are weekly, semimonthly, and so on.

Step 2. Subtract the product found in step 1 from gross pay; the result is the taxable income.

Step 3. Use Table 5-4 and the taxable income figured in step 2. Follow the directions in the table to calculate the correct amount of tax to be withhold.

Table 5-3

Percentage Method Income Tax Withholding Table

Payroll Period	One with-holding allowance
Weekly	$44.23
Biweekly.	88.46
Semimonthly	95.83
Monthly	191.67
Quarterly.	575.00
Semiannually	1,150.00
Annually	2,300.00
Daily or miscellaneous (each day of the payroll period)	8.85

44.23
x 3
132.69

Table 5-4

Tables for Percentage Method of Withholding
(For Wages Paid After February 1992)

TABLE 1—If the Payroll Period With Respect to an Employee is Weekly

(a) SINGLE person—including head of household:

If the amount of wages (after subtracting withholding allowances) is:	The amount of income tax to be withheld shall be:
Not over $47	0

Over—	But not over —		of excess over—
$47	—$438	15%	—$47
$438	—$913	$58.65 plus 28%	—$438
$913	. . . .	$191.65 plus 31%	—$913

(b) MARRIED person—

If the amount of wages (after subtracting withholding allowances) is:	The amount of income tax to be withheld shall be:
Not over $115	0

Over—	But not over—		of excess over—
$115	—$760	15%	—$115
$760	—$1,513	$96.75 plus 28%	—$760
$1,513	. . . .	$307.59 plus 31%	—$1,513

TABLE 2—If the Payroll Period With Respect to an Employee is Biweekly

(a) SINGLE person—including head of household:

If the amount of wages (after subtracting withholding allowances) is:	The amount of income tax to be withheld shall be:
Not over $94	0

Over—	But not over —		of excess over—
$94	—$875	15%	—$94
$875	—$1,825	$117.15 plus 28%	—$875
$1,825	. . . .	$383.15 plus 31%	—$1,825

(b) MARRIED person—

If the amount of wages (after subtracting withholding allowances) is:	The amount of income tax to be withheld shall be:
Not over $231	0

Over—	But not over—		of excess over—
$231	—$1,519	15%	—$231
$1,519	—$3,027	$193.20 plus 28%	—$1,519
$3,027	. . . .	$615.44 plus 31%	—$3,027

TABLE 3—If the Payroll Period With Respect to an Employee is Semimonthly

(a) SINGLE person—including head of household:

If the amount of wages (after subtracting withholding allowances) is:	The amount of income tax to be withheld shall be:
Not over $102	

Over—	But not over —		of excess over—
$102	—$948	15%	—$102
$948	—$1,977	$126.90 plus 28%	—$948
$1,977	. . . .	$415.02 plus 31%	—$1,977

(b) MARRIED person—

If the amount of wages (after subtracting withholding allowances) is:	The amount of income tax to be withheld shall be:
Not over $250	0

Over—	But not over—		of excess over—
$250	—$1,646	15%	—$250
$1,646	—$3,279	$209.40 plus 28%	—$1,646
$3,279	. . . .	$666.64 plus 31%	—$3,279

TABLE 4—If the Payroll Period With Respect to an Employee is Monthly

(a) SINGLE person—including head of household:

If the amount of wages (after subtracting withholding allowances) is:	The amount of income tax to be withheld shall be:
Not over $204	0

Over—	But not over —		of excess over—
$204	—$1,896	15%	—$204
$1,896	—$3,954	$253.80 plus 28%	—$1,896
$3,954	. . . .	$830.04 plus 31%	—$3,954

(b) MARRIED person—

If the amount of wages (after subtracting withholding allowances) is:	The amount of income tax to be withheld shall be:
Not over $500	0

Over—	But not over—		of excess over—
$500	—$3,292	15%	—$500
$3,292	—$6,558	$418.80 plus 28%	—$3,292
$6,558	. . . .	$1,333.28 plus 31%	—$6,558

EXAMPLE 9

Find the tax on Yaz Elliot's semimonthly gross earnings of $1,150. He is single and claims two withholding allowances.

2 × $95.83 = $191.66	Use Table 5-3. Multiply the number of withholding allowances claimed times the amount of a withholding allowance for a semimonthly payroll period.
$1,150 − $191.66 = $958.34	Subtract the withholding allowance from gross income to find taxable income.
$958.34 is in the $948 to $1,977 bracket	Turn to Table 5-4 and find taxable income range in the left column for a semimonthly employee.

The schedule in Table 5-4 tells us that the tax in that bracket is $126.90 + 28% of income in excess of $948.

$958.34 − $948 = $10.34	Subtract $948 from the taxable income in order to find the amount of income in excess of $948.
$10.34 × 0.28 = $2.90	Find 28% of the amount of income in excess of $948.
$126.90 + $2.90 = $129.80	Add $2.90 to $126.90 to find the amount of tax to be withheld.

$129.80 is the amount of tax to be withheld.

When the amount of tax is calculated by the percentage method, the result may differ slightly from the result obtained in the tax table, but the amounts will be close enough to be acceptable.

Social Security and Medicare Tax

FICA (Federal Insurance Contributions Act) tax (Social Security (SS) tax): a federal tax that goes into a fund that pays monthly benefits to retired and disabled workers.

The second-largest amount withheld from an employee's paycheck is usually the deduction for FICA tax. **FICA (Federal Insurance Contributions Act) tax** is also referred to as **Social Security (SS) tax.** It comes from an emergency measure passed by Congress during the depression of the 1930s. The money from this tax goes into a fund that pays monthly benefits to retired and disabled workers. Prior to 1991, funds collected under the Social Security tax act were used for both Social Security and Medicare benefits. Beginning in 1991, funds were collected separately for these two programs.

The amount of tax and the amount of salary that is taxed change periodically as the Congress passes new legislation. In a recent year, the FICA tax rate was 6.2% (0.062) of the first $55,500 gross earnings. This means that after a person has earned $55,500 in a year, no FICA tax will be withheld on any additional money he or she earns. A person who earns $55,500 in a year pays exactly the same FICA tax as a person who earns $100,000. In this same year, the wage base for Medicare was $130,200 and the rate was 1.45% (0.0145).

Medicare tax: a federal tax used to provide health-care benefits to retired and disabled workers.

Employers also pay a share of FICA and **Medicare tax:** The employer contributes the same amount as the employee contributes to an employee's Social Security account. Employers can figure FICA and Medicare tax for employees and themselves by using a FICA and Medicare table, part of which is shown in Tables 5-5 and 5-6, or by using the percentage method, multiplying the salary times 6.2% and 1.45%, respectively.

These are tax tables somewhat like the federal income tax tables discussed earlier in the chapter, in that they also have "Wages at least" and

Table 5-5

gross × 6.290 = gross py

6.2% Social Security Employee Tax Table for 1992

Note: *Wages subject to social security are generally also subject to the Medicare tax. See page 51.*

Wages at least	But less than	Tax to be withheld	Wages at least	But less than	Tax to be withheld	Wages at least	But less than	Tax to be withheld	Wages at least	But less than	Tax to be withheld
58.63	58.80	3.64	69.92	70.09	4.34	81.21	81.38	5.04	92.50	92.67	5.74
58.80	58.96	3.65	70.09	70.25	4.35	81.38	81.54	5.05	92.67	92.83	5.75
58.96	59.12	3.66	70.25	70.41	4.36	81.54	81.70	5.06	92.83	92.99	5.76
59.12	59.28	3.67	70.41	70.57	4.37	81.70	81.86	5.07	92.99	93.15	5.77
59.28	59.44	3.68	70.57	70.73	4.38	81.86	82.02	5.08	93.15	93.31	5.78
59.44	59.60	3.69	70.73	70.89	4.39	82.02	82.18	5.09	93.31	93.47	5.79
59.60	59.76	3.70	70.89	71.05	4.40	82.18	82.34	5.10	93.47	93.63	5.80
59.76	59.92	3.71	71.05	71.21	4.41	82.34	82.50	5.11	93.63	93.80	5.81
59.92	60.09	3.72	71.21	71.38	4.42	82.50	82.67	5.12	93.80	93.96	5.82
60.09	60.25	3.73	71.38	71.54	4.43	82.67	82.83	5.13	93.96	94.12	5.83
60.25	60.41	3.74	71.54	71.70	4.44	82.83	82.99	5.14	94.12	94.28	5.84
60.41	60.57	3.75	71.70	71.86	4.45	82.99	83.15	5.15	94.28	94.44	5.85
60.57	60.73	3.76	71.86	72.02	4.46	83.15	83.31	5.16	94.44	94.60	5.86
60.73	60.89	3.77	72.02	72.18	4.47	83.31	83.47	5.17	94.60	94.76	5.87
60.89	61.05	3.78	72.18	72.34	4.48	83.47	83.63	5.18	94.76	94.92	5.88
61.05	61.21	3.79	72.34	72.50	4.49	83.63	83.80	5.19	94.92	95.09	5.89
61.21	61.38	3.80	72.50	72.67	4.50	83.80	83.96	5.20	95.09	95.25	5.90
61.38	61.54	3.81	72.67	72.83	4.51	83.96	84.12	5.21	95.25	95.41	5.91
61.54	61.70	3.82	72.83	72.99	4.52	84.12	84.28	5.22	95.41	95.57	5.92
61.70	61.86	3.83	72.99	73.15	4.53	84.28	84.44	5.23	95.57	95.73	5.93
61.86	62.02	3.84	73.15	73.31	4.54	84.44	84.60	5.24	95.73	95.89	5.94
62.02	62.18	3.85	73.31	73.47	4.55	84.60	84.76	5.25	95.89	96.05	5.95
62.18	62.34	3.86	73.47	73.63	4.56	84.76	84.92	5.26	96.05	96.21	5.96
62.34	62.50	3.87	73.63	73.80	4.57	84.92	85.09	5.27	96.21	96.38	5.97
62.50	62.67	3.88	73.80	73.96	4.58	85.09	85.25	5.28	96.38	96.54	5.98
62.67	62.83	3.89	73.96	74.12	4.59	85.25	85.41	5.29	96.54	96.70	5.99
62.83	62.99	3.90	74.12	74.28	4.60	85.41	85.57	5.30	96.70	96.86	6.00
62.99	63.15	3.91	74.28	74.44	4.61	85.57	85.73	5.31	96.86	97.02	6.01
63.15	63.31	3.92	74.44	74.60	4.62	85.73	85.89	5.32	97.02	97.18	6.02
63.31	63.47	3.93	74.60	74.76	4.63	85.89	86.05	5.33	97.18	97.34	6.03
63.47	63.63	3.94	74.76	74.92	4.64	86.05	86.21	5.34	97.34	97.50	6.04
63.63	63.80	3.95	74.92	75.09	4.65	86.21	86.38	5.35	97.50	97.67	6.05
63.80	63.96	3.96	75.09	75.25	4.66	86.38	86.54	5.36	97.67	97.83	6.06
63.96	64.12	3.97	75.25	75.41	4.67	86.54	86.70	5.37	97.83	97.99	6.07
64.12	64.28	3.98	75.41	75.57	4.68	86.70	86.86	5.38	97.99	98.15	6.08
64.28	64.44	3.99	75.57	75.73	4.69	86.86	87.02	5.39	98.15	98.31	6.09
64.44	64.60	4.00	75.73	75.89	4.70	87.02	87.18	5.40	98.31	98.47	6.10
64.60	64.76	4.01	75.89	76.05	4.71	87.18	87.34	5.41	98.47	98.63	6.11
64.76	64.92	4.02	76.05	76.21	4.72	87.34	87.50	5.42	98.63	98.80	6.12
64.92	65.09	4.03	76.21	76.38	4.73	87.50	87.67	5.43	98.80	98.96	6.13
65.09	65.25	4.04	76.38	76.54	4.74	87.67	87.83	5.44	98.96	99.12	6.14
65.25	65.41	4.05	76.54	76.70	4.75	87.83	87.99	5.45	99.12	99.28	6.15
65.41	65.57	4.06	76.70	76.86	4.76	87.99	88.15	5.46	99.28	99.44	6.16
65.57	65.73	4.07	76.86	77.02	4.77	88.15	88.31	5.47	99.44	99.60	6.17
65.73	65.89	4.08	77.02	77.18	4.78	88.31	88.47	5.48	99.60	99.76	6.18
65.89	66.05	4.09	77.18	77.34	4.79	88.47	88.63	5.49	99.76	99.92	6.19
66.05	66.21	4.10	77.34	77.50	4.80	88.63	88.80	5.50	99.92	100.00	6.20
66.21	66.38	4.11	77.50	77.67	4.81	88.80	88.96	5.51			
66.38	66.54	4.12	77.67	77.83	4.82	88.96	89.12	5.52			
66.54	66.70	4.13	77.83	77.99	4.83	89.12	89.28	5.53			
66.70	66.86	4.14	77.99	78.15	4.84	89.28	89.44	5.54			
66.86	67.02	4.15	78.15	78.31	4.85	89.44	89.60	5.55			
67.02	67.18	4.16	78.31	78.47	4.86	89.60	89.76	5.56			
67.18	67.34	4.17	78.47	78.63	4.87	89.76	89.92	5.57			
67.34	67.50	4.18	78.63	78.80	4.88	89.92	90.09	5.58			
67.50	67.67	4.19	78.80	78.96	4.89	90.09	90.25	5.59			
67.67	67.83	4.20	78.96	79.12	4.90	90.25	90.41	5.60			
67.83	67.99	4.21	79.12	79.28	4.91	90.41	90.57	5.61			
67.99	68.15	4.22	79.28	79.44	4.92	90.57	90.73	5.62			
68.15	68.31	4.23	79.44	79.60	4.93	90.73	90.89	5.63			
68.31	68.47	4.24	79.60	79.76	4.94	90.89	91.05	5.64			
68.47	68.63	4.25	79.76	79.92	4.95	91.05	91.21	5.65			
68.63	68.80	4.26	79.92	80.09	4.96	91.21	91.38	5.66			
68.80	68.96	4.27	80.09	80.25	4.97	91.38	91.54	5.67			
68.96	69.12	4.28	80.25	80.41	4.98	91.54	91.70	5.68			
69.12	69.28	4.29	80.41	80.57	4.99	91.70	91.86	5.69			
69.28	69.44	4.30	80.57	80.73	5.00	91.86	92.02	5.70			
69.44	69.60	4.31	80.73	80.89	5.01	92.02	92.18	5.71			
69.60	69.76	4.32	80.89	81.05	5.02	92.18	92.34	5.72			
69.76	69.92	4.33	81.05	81.21	5.03	92.34	92.50	5.73			

Wages	Taxes
100	$6.20
200	12.40
300	18.60
400	24.80
500	31.00
600	37.20
700	43.40
800	49.60
900	55.80
1,000	62.00

"But less than" columns. Look at Table 5-5 to determine the Social Security tax. If the gross weekly earnings are more than $100, you have to look at the lower-right side of the chart. Here you find gross weekly earnings in amounts up to $1,000. If the gross earnings are $675, you take the amount for $600 given in the lower-right corner, $37.20, and then you look up the rest of the *gross* earnings figure, $75, and find that the tax on that is $4.65. Add the two tax amounts together to find the total FICA tax owed: $37.20 + $4.65 = $41.85.

Look at Table 5-6 on page 172 to determine the Medicare tax. If the gross earnings are $675, you take the amount given for $600 in the lower right hand corner, $8.70. Then you look up the rest of the gross earnings figure, $75.00 and find that the tax on that amount is $1.09. Add the two amounts together to find the total Medicare tax owed: $8.70 + $1.09 = $9.79

Table 5-6

1.45% Medicare Tax Table for 1992

Wages at least	But less than	Tax to be withheld	Wages at least	But less than	Tax to be withheld	Wages at least	But less than	Tax to be withheld	Wages at least	But less than	Tax to be withheld
$0.00	$0.35	$0.00	28.63	29.32	.42	57.59	58.28	.84	86.56	87.25	1.26
.35	1.04	.01	29.32	30.00	.43	58.28	58.97	.85	87.25	87.94	1.27
1.04	1.73	.02	30.00	30.69	.44	58.97	59.66	.86	87.94	88.63	1.28
1.73	2.42	.03	30.69	31.38	.45	59.66	60.35	.87	88.63	89.32	1.29
2.42	3.11	.04	31.38	32.07	.46	60.35	61.04	.88	89.32	90.00	1.30
3.11	3.80	.05	32.07	32.76	.47	61.04	61.73	.89	90.00	90.69	1.31
3.80	4.49	.06	32.76	33.45	.48	61.73	62.42	.90	90.69	91.38	1.32
4.49	5.18	.07	33.45	34.14	.49	62.42	63.11	.91	91.38	92.07	1.33
5.18	5.87	.08	34.14	34.83	.50	63.11	63.80	.92	92.07	92.76	1.34
5.87	6.56	.09	34.83	35.52	.51	63.80	64.49	.93	92.76	93.45	1.35
6.56	7.25	.10	35.52	36.21	.52	64.49	65.18	.94	93.45	94.14	1.36
7.25	7.94	.11	36.21	36.90	.53	65.18	65.87	.95	94.14	94.83	1.37
7.94	8.63	.12	36.90	37.59	.54	65.87	66.56	.96	94.83	95.52	1.38
8.63	9.32	.13	37.59	38.28	.55	66.56	67.25	.97	95.52	96.21	1.39
9.32	10.00	.14	38.28	38.97	.56	67.25	67.94	.98	96.21	96.90	1.40
10.00	10.69	.15	38.97	39.66	.57	67.94	68.63	.99	96.90	97.59	1.41
10.69	11.38	.16	39.66	40.35	.58	68.63	69.32	1.00	97.59	98.28	1.42
11.38	12.07	.17	40.35	41.04	.59	69.32	70.00	1.01	98.28	98.97	1.43
12.07	12.76	.18	41.04	41.73	.60	70.00	70.69	1.02	98.97	99.66	1.44
12.76	13.45	.19	41.73	42.42	.61	70.69	71.38	1.03	99.66	100.00	1.45
13.45	14.14	.20	42.42	43.11	.62	71.38	72.07	1.04			
14.14	14.83	.21	43.11	43.80	.63	72.07	72.76	1.05			
14.83	15.52	.22	43.80	44.49	.64	72.76	73.45	1.06			
15.52	16.21	.23	44.49	45.18	.65	73.45	74.14	1.07			
16.21	16.90	.24	45.18	45.87	.66	74.14	74.83	1.08			
16.90	17.59	.25	45.87	46.56	.67	74.83	75.52	1.09			
17.59	18.28	.26	46.56	47.25	.68	75.52	76.21	1.10			
18.28	18.97	.27	47.25	47.94	.69	76.21	76.90	1.11			
18.97	19.66	.28	47.94	48.63	.70	76.90	77.59	1.12			
19.66	20.35	.29	48.63	49.32	.71	77.59	78.28	1.13	Wages	Taxes	
20.35	21.04	.30	49.32	50.00	.72	78.28	78.97	1.14	100	$1.45	
21.04	21.73	.31	50.00	50.69	.73	78.97	79.66	1.15	200	2.90	
21.73	22.42	.32	50.69	51.38	.74	79.66	80.35	1.16	300	4.35	
22.42	23.11	.33	51.38	52.07	.75	80.35	81.04	1.17	400	5.80	
23.11	23.80	.34	52.07	52.76	.76	81.04	81.73	1.18	500	7.25	
23.80	24.49	.35	52.76	53.45	.77	81.73	82.42	1.19	600	8.70	
24.49	25.18	.36	53.45	54.14	.78	82.42	83.11	1.20	700	10.15	
25.18	25.87	.37	54.14	54.83	.79	83.11	83.80	1.21	800	11.60	
25.87	26.56	.38	54.83	55.52	.80	83.80	84.49	1.22	900	13.05	
26.56	27.25	.39	55.52	56.21	.81	84.49	85.18	1.23	1,000	14.50	
27.25	27.94	.40	56.21	56.90	.82	85.18	85.87	1.24			
27.94	28.63	.41	56.90	57.59	.83	85.87	86.56	1.25			

Always "round" figures @ the end

EXAMPLE 10

An employee has a gross weekly income of $267. Use Tables 5-5 and 5-6 to find how much FICA and Medicare tax should be withheld.

$267 = $200 + $67

Social Security tax on $200 = $12.40

Look in Table 5-5 to find the amount of tax to be withheld on $200 and on $67.

Social Security tax on $67 = $ 4.15   Add the two amounts.
$12.40 + $4.15   = $16.55   Total FICA tax to be withheld.

Medicare tax on $200 = $2.90
Medicare tax on $67   = 0.97
Total Medicare tax   = $3.87
  to be withheld

EXAMPLE 11

Lisa Perez, vice-president of marketing for Golden Sun Enterprises, earns $57,200 annually, or $1100 per week. Find the amount of FICA and Medicare taxes that should be withheld for the 51st week.

At the end of the 51st week, Lisa will have earned a total gross salary of $56,100. Since FICA tax is withheld on only the first $55,500, she does not pay FICA on $600 of her 51st week's earnings. We subtract $600 from her weekly gross of $1100 to find that she pays FICA on only $500 of her earnings that week.

$500 \times 0.062 = \$31.00$

Multiply her taxable income by the 6.2% tax rate to find how much FICA tax should be withheld in the 51st week. No additional FICA tax would be withheld for the year.

Since Medicare tax is paid on a tax base of $130,200, Lisa Perez must pay the Medicare tax on the full week's salary of $1100.
$\$1100 \times 0.0145 = \$15.95$

Figuring Net Earnings

In addition to federal taxes, a number of other deductions may be made from an employee's paycheck. Often state and local income taxes must also be withheld by the employer. Other deductions are made at the employee's request, such as insurance or union dues. When all these deductions have been made, the amount left is called *net earnings*, or *take-home* pay.

EXAMPLE 12

Hillary Sinclair's gross weekly earnings are $276. She is married and claims two withholding allowances. Five percent of her gross earnings is deducted for her retirement fund and $5.83 is deducted for insurance. Find her net earnings.

gross PY × 5% = I. R. A.

Income tax withholding:
$11.00

In Table 5-2, find the amount of income tax to be withheld.

FICA tax withholding:
$276 \times 0.062 = \$17.11$

Find the FICA tax by the percentage method: 6.2% of $276 = $276 × 0.062

Medicare tax withholding:
$276 \times 0.0145 = \$4.00$

Retirement fund withholding:
$0.05 \times \$276 = \$13.80$

Use the formula $P = R \times B$. Multiply rate (5% = 0.05) by base (gross pay of $276).

Add all deductions:
Total deductions
= income tax + FICA tax + Medicare + insurance + retirement fund
= $11.00   + $17.11   + $4.00   + $5.83   + $13.80   = $51.74

Gross earnings − total deductions = net earnings
$276   − $51.74   = $224.26

Calculating the Employer's Taxes

The major taxes paid by employers are the employer's share of the FICA tax, which we have already discussed, and federal and state unemployment taxes. Federal and state unemployment taxes do not affect the paycheck of the employee. They are paid entirely by the employer. **Federal unemployment tax (FUTA)** is currently 6.2% of the first $7,000 earned by an employee in a year *minus* any amount that the employer has paid in **state unemployment tax (SUTA)**, whose limit is 5.4% of the first $7,000. SUTA varies from state to state and also depends on the employment record of the company in question. A company with a good employment record is one that does not fire employees frequently, a practice that places heavier demands on

federal unemployment tax (FUTA): a federal tax that is paid by the employer for each employee.

state unemployment tax (SUTA): a state tax that is paid by the employer.

REAL WORLD APPLICATION

How to Read Your Pay Stub

With all the various ways of being paid and figuring gross earnings, not to mention the many deductions that are made and the ways of figuring net earnings, some people may feel that they need a separate course in how to figure out their pay stubs! The accompanying figure shows a sample pay stub and explains the various categories of payments and deductions contained on it. Your pay stub may not look exactly like this, but it will probably contain many of these entries, so it pays to get the hang of how to read it. Companies can make mistakes, and in this case they'll be making a mistake with your money!

Application Questions

1. What is the gross pay for this pay period?

2. Find the total amount deducted from the check. What percent of the gross pay is the total deducted?

3. Based on the amount of federal withholding tax listed on the pay stub, use Table 5-2 to find the number of withholding allowances claimed.

4. What amount will appear on the paycheck that goes with this pay stub?

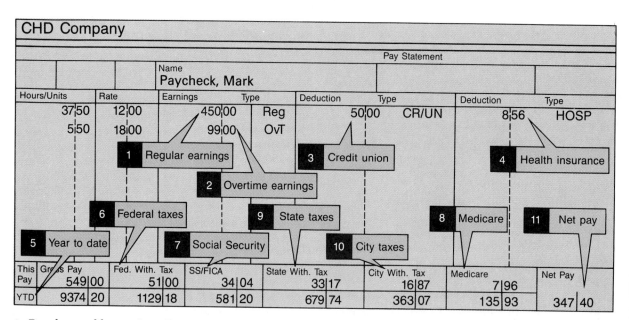

1. Regular weekly earnings ($450.00)

2. Overtime earnings ($99.00): $12.00 × 1.5 = $18.00 an hour for hours over 37.5 per week. 5.5 hrs. × $18 = $99.00

3. Credit union ($50.00): Here's a $50 automatic deduction for a contribution to a credit union savings plan.

4. Health insurance ($8.56): Other insurance premiums that could be deducted automatically include life and dental insurance.

5. YTD ($9374.20): Year-to-date running totals let you know how much you've been paid so far this year.

6. Federal withholding tax ($51.00): If you are paid weekly, multiply this number by 52 to estimate how much you will pay in federal taxes by year's end.

7. Social Security/FICA ($34.04): Contact the Social Se-

curity Administration to make sure your account is being and has been properly credited.

8. Medicare ($7.96): 1991 was the first year this category was used.

9. State withholding tax ($33.17): The amount of state tax varies from state to state.

10. City withholding taxes ($16.87): Many cities do not require a city income tax.

11. Net pay ($347.40): This is the amount you take home for this particular week.

the state's unemployment benefit funds. An employer with a good employ-ment record might pay less than 5.4% SUTA. To calculate FUTA, an em-ployer pays the SUTA and subtracts that amount from the 6.2% owed to the federal government for the FUTA.

EXAMPLE 13

Melanie McFarren earned $15,300 last year. If the state unemployment tax (SUTA) is 5.4% of the first $7,000 earned in a year, how much SUTA must Melanie's employer pay for her?

$P = R \times B$
$= 5.4\% \times \$7,000$
$= 0.054 \times \$7,000 = \$378$

Use the percentage formula. The base is $7,000 because SUTA is paid only on the first $7,000 earned in a given year.

EXAMPLE 14

Find the amount of federal unemployment tax (FUTA) the company must pay for Melanie (Example 13). Remember, the FUTA rate is 6.2% of the first $7,000 earned in a year minus the amount that has been paid for the SUTA.

$P = R \times B$
$= 6.2\% \times \$7,000$
$= 0.062 \times \$7,000 = \$434$

Use the percentage formula. The base is $7,000 because SUTA and FUTA are paid only on the first $7,000 earned in a given year. This is the *total amount* of unemploy-ment tax to be paid to *both* SUTA and FUTA.

FUTA = total unemployment
tax − SUTA
$= \$434 − \$378 = \$56$

Subtract the SUTA amount (calculated in Example 13) from the total amount to find the FUTA amount due.

Self-Check 5.2

8. B. J. Mullin is married, has a gross weekly salary of $486, and claims three withholding allowances. Use the table method to find the amount of withholding tax to be deducted from his weekly salary.

9. Maddy Waxman has a gross weekly income of $380, is single, and claims one withholding allowance. Find the amount of withholding tax to be de-ducted from her weekly paycheck using the percentage method.

10. Erica Echison earns a gross weekly income of $270. Use Table 5-5 to find how much FICA tax should be withheld.

11. Doug Bloch earns $55,900 annually, or $1,075 per week. Find the amount of FICA tax and Medicare tax that should be withheld from his check dur-ing the 52nd week.

12. Misty Diehl's gross weekly earnings are $415. Three percent of her gross earnings is deducted for her retirement fund and $4.79 is deducted for in-surance. Find the net earnings if Misty is married and claims two with-holding allowances.

13. Shirley Cable earned $20,418 last year. If the SUTA is 5.4% of the first $7,000 earned in a year, how much SUTA must Shirley's employer pay for her?

14. How much FUTA must Shirley's company pay for her?

Summary

Topic	Page	What to Remember	Examples
Salary	162	A salaried employee's paycheck equals the annual salary divided by the number of paychecks issued during the year.	If Barbara earns $23,500 per year, how much is her weekly gross pay? $\frac{\$23,500}{52} = \$451.92$
Hourly pay	162	Hourly employees are paid an hourly rate for the number of hours worked since the last paycheck.	Aldo earns $6.25 per hour. He worked 38 hours this week. What is his gross pay? $38 \times \$6.25 = \$237.50$
Overtime pay	163	Multiply 40 hours times the regular rate, and multiply the number of overtime hours times 1.5 times the regular pay rate. Add the two numbers.	Belinda worked 44 hours one week. Her regular pay was $7.75 per hour. Find her gross earnings. $40 \times \$7.75 = \$310$ $4 \times \$7.75 \times 1.5 = \$46.50$ $\$310 + \$46.50 = \$356.50$
Piecework pay	163	Piecework pay is based on the amount of acceptable work completed.	Willy, who earns $0.30 for each widget he twists, twisted 1,224 widgets last week. Find his gross earnings. $1,224 \times \$0.30 = \$367.20$
Differential, or escalating, piece rate	163	The amount of pay per item increases as the number of items produced increases.	Nadine does piecework for a jeweler and earns $0.25 per piece for finishing 1 to 25 pins, $0.50 per piece for 26 to 50 pins, and $0.75 per piece for pins over 50. Yesterday she finished 70 pins. How much did she earn? $(25 \times \$.25) + (25 \times \$.50) + (20 \times \$.75) = \$33.75$
Straight commission	164	A person's salary is based on a percent of his or her total sales.	Bart earns a 4% commission on the appliances he sells. His sales last week totaled $8,000. Find his gross earnings. $0.04 \times \$8,000 = \$320$
Salary plus commission	164	A person receives a basic salary plus a percent of his or her sales.	Elaine earns $250 weekly plus 2% of all sales over $1,500. Last week she made $9,500 worth of sales. Find her gross earnings. $\$9,500 - \$1,500 = \$8,000$ Commission = $0.02 \times \$8,000 = \$160$ $\$250 + \$160 = \$410$
Federal withholding tax (table method)	166	Find the correct table (single or married) in Circular E to determine the amount of federal tax to be withheld. Then locate the amount in the column with the correct number of withholding allowance.	Archy is married, has a gross weekly salary of $480, and claims two withholding allowances. Find his withholding tax. Look in the first two columns of Table 5-2 to find the range for $480. The amount of federal tax to be withheld is $42.
Federal withholding tax (percentage method)	168	Many companies with computerized payrolls use the percentage method of calculating federal withholding tax. The percentages vary according to payroll period and whether a person is married or single and are given in Circular E.	Find the federal tax on Ruth's monthly income of $1,438. She is single and claims 2 exemptions. 2 exemptions $\times$ $191.67 = $383.34 $\$1,438 - \$383.34 = \$1,054.66$ $1,054.66 is in the $204 to $1,896 bracket (Table 5-4), so the amount of withholding tax is 15% of the amount over $204. $\$1,054.66 - \$204 = \$850.66$ $\$850.66 \times \$0.15 = \$127.60$
FICA withholding (table method)	170	Find the correct salary range in the FICA withholding table to find the amount of FICA tax to be withheld for a given salary.	Wes earns $46,280 per year. If he earns $890 each week, what is his weekly FICA withholding? Look in the lower-right-hand box of the table and find the taxes for $800. This amount is $49.60. Next, locate the wages range containing $90. The amount of tax for $90 is $5.58. The total FICA for the week is $\$49.60 + \$5.58 = \$55.18$.

176

Topic	Page	What to Remember	Examples
FICA with-holding (per-centage method)	172	The FICA tax rate used in this text is 6.2 percent (0.062) of the first $55,500 gross earnings. The employer pays the same amount of FICA tax for each employee as the employee pays.	Calculate the FICA for Wes using the percentage method, $890 × 0.062 = $55.18.
Medicare withholding (table method)	172	Find the correct range in the Medicare withholding table to find the amount of Medicare tax to be withheld for a given salary.	Find Wes's Medicare tax for his weekly salary of $890. Look in the lower-right box of the table and find the tax for $800. This amount is $11.60. Next, locate the wages range containing $90. The amount of tax for $90 is $1.31. The total Medicare tax for the week is $11.60 + $1.31 = $12.91
Medicare withholding (percentage method)	173	The Medicare tax rate used in this text is 1.45% (0.0145) of the first $130,200 gross earnings. The employer pays the same amount of Medicare tax for each employee as each employee pays.	Calculate the Medicare tax for Wes using the percentage method. $890 × 0.0145 = $12.905 which rounds to $12.91.
Other deductions	173	An employer may withhold insurance payments, union dues, and state and local taxes from an employee's paycheck.	Beth's gross weekly earnings are $388. Four percent of her gross earnings is deducted for her retirement fund and $7.48 is deducted for insurance. Find her net earnings if Beth is married and claims three withholding allowances. Income tax withholding from Table 5-2 = $21. FICA tax withholding by the percentage method: $388 × 0.062 = $24.06. Medicare withholding by the percentage method: $388 × 0.0145 = $5.63. Retirement fund withholding: 0.04 × $388 = $15.52. Add all deductions: Income tax + FICA tax + Medicare + insurance + retirement fund = $21 + $24.06 + $5.63 + $7.48 + $15.52 = $73.69 Net earnings = $314.31
SUTA (state unemploy-ment tax)	175	The SUTA varies from state to state, but this text uses 5.4% of the first $7,000 earned by an employee in a year.	Joe earned $19,800 last year. If the SUTA is 5.4% of the first $7,000 earned in a year, how much SUTA must Joe's employer pay for him? 5.4% × $7,000 = 0.054 × $7,000 = $378
FUTA (fed-eral unem-ployment tax)	175	The FUTA is currently 6.2% of the first $7,000 earned by an employee in a year *minus* any SUTA that the employer has paid, with a limit of 5.4%.	How much FUTA must Joe's company pay for him? 6.2% × $7,000 = 0.062 × $7,000 = $434 (*total* unemployment tax) $434 − $378 = $56 FUTA owed

Self-Check Solutions

1. $19,000 ÷ 52 = $365.38

2.
$$40 × $7.60 = $304 \quad \text{(regular-rate pay)}$$
$$7 × $7.60 × 1.5 = + $ 79.80 \text{ (overtime pay)}$$
$$\overline{$383.80} \text{ (gross earnings)}$$

3.
$$40 × $8.25 = $330$$
$$4 × $8.25 × 1.5 = + $ 49.50$$
$$\overline{$379.50}$$

4. Total buckles = 32 + 34 + 38 + 35 + 30 = 169
   Gross earnings = 169 × $0.75 = $126.75

5. First 100 boxes: $1.32 × 100 = $132
   Last 80 boxes: $1.42 × 80 = + $113.60
   $245.60 (gross earnings)

6. $P = RB$
   = 0.06 × $5,000
   = $300 (gross earnings)

7. $6,000 − $2,000 = $4,000 (amount on which commission is paid)
   $P = RB$
   = 0.04 × $4000
   = $160
   $160 + $175 = $335 (gross earnings)

8. Find the table for married persons. Move down the *at least* column to the amount $480. Then move across to the column marked 3 at the top. The amount is $36.

9. Using Table 5-3 for a weekly salary of a single person with one withholding allowance, we see that the amount is $44.23. We subtract $44.23 from gross pay, $380, and get $335.77; this is the taxable income. Look next at Table 5-4: the tax is 15% of the excess amount over $47 so you subtract $47 from $335.77 and get $288.77, and multiply that times 15%: $288.77 × 0.15 = $43.32.

10. $270 − $200 = $70. Look in the box in the lower-right corner of Table 5-5. Find $200 under *wages* and read $12.40 in the *taxes* column. Then look in the second *wages at least* column to find $69.92. $70 is in this range. The tax is $4.34. The total tax is $12.40 + $4.34 = $16.74.

11. $1,075 × 52 = $55,900
    FICA is not paid on $400 of the fifty-second week's earnings.
    $1,075 − $400 = $675
    FICA *is* paid on $675 of the earnings.
    $675 × 0.062 = $41.85 (FICA tax paid on fifty-second week's earnings)
    Medicare is paid on the entire $1,075.
    $1,075 × 0.0145 = $15.59

12. 0.03 × $415 = $12.45 (retirement deduction)
    $4.79 (insurance deduction)
    0.062 × $415 = $25.73 (Social Security deduction)
    0.0145 × $415 = $6.02 (Medicare deduction)
    $32 (withholding tax deduction)
    $80.99 (total deductions)
    Net earnings = $415 − $80.99 = $334.01

13. 5.4% × $7,000 = 0.054 × $7000
    = $378 SUTA owed

14. 6.2% × $7000 = 0.062 × $7000 = $434
    $434 − $378 = $56 FUTA owed

End of Chapter Problems

1. James Knowles has a salaried job. He earns $425 a week. One week, he worked 46 hours. Find his gross earnings for the week.

2. Ms. Chaille worked 27 hours in one week at $5.25 per hour. Find her gross earnings.

3. Mr. Stout worked 40 hours at $12 per hour. Find his gross earnings for the week.

4. Ms. Wood worked 52 hours in a week. She was paid at the hourly rate of $6.50 with time and a half for overtime. Find her gross earnings.

5. Mr. Jinkins worked a total of 58 hours in one week. Of these hours, he was paid for 8 at the regular overtime rate of 1.5 times his hourly wage and for 10 at the holiday rate of 2 times his hourly wage. Find his gross earnings for the week if his hourly pay is $14.95.

6. Mr. James is paid 1.5 times his regular pay for all hours worked in a week exceeding 40. He worked 52 hours and earns $8.50 per hour. Calculate his gross pay.

7. Find the gross earnings of each employee.

Employee	\	\	Hours Worked	\	\	\	\	Hourly Rate	Regular Hours	Regular Pay	Overtime Hours	Overtime Pay	Gross Pay
	M	T	W	T	F	S	S						
Allen, H.	8	9	8	7	10	4	0	$9.86	_____	_____	_____	_____	_____
Brown, J.	4	6	8	9	9	5	0	$4.97	_____	_____	_____	_____	_____
Pick, J.	8	8	8	8	8	4	0	$6.87	_____	_____	_____	_____	_____
Sayer, C.	9	10	8	9	11	9	0	$5.82	_____	_____	_____	_____	_____
Lovet, L.	8	8	8	8	0	0	0	$7.15	_____	_____	_____	_____	_____

8. Complete the following payroll records for employees who earn time and a half for more than 40 hours on Monday through Friday and on Saturday and double time for any work on Sunday.

Employee	M	T	W	T	F	S	S	Regular Hours	Hourly Rate	Regular Pay	$1\frac{1}{2}$ Over-time Pay	Double Time Pay	Gross Earnings
Mitze, A	8	8	4	3	8	2	4	——	$8.00	——	——	——	——
James, Q.	8	8	8	8	8	0	4	——	$4.70	——	——	——	——
Adams, A.	5	6	8	11	10	9	5	——	$6.75	——	——	——	——
Smith, M.	8	8	8	8	8	8	8	——	$4.55	——	——	——	——

9. For sewing buttons on shirts, employees are paid $0.08 a shirt. Marty Hughes completes an average of 500 shirts a day. Find her average gross weekly earnings for a 5-day week.

10. Employees are paid $3.50 per piece for a certain job. In a week's time, Scott Marvel produced a total of 78 pieces. Find his gross earnings for the week.

Widgets International pays widget twisters at the following escalating piece rate for properly twisted widgets.

Items per week	Piece rate
1–150	$1.85
151–300	$1.95
301 and over	$2.08

Find the gross weekly earnings for employees who twisted the following number of widgets in a week.

11. 117 widgets

12. 158 widgets

13. 257 widgets

14. 325 widgets

15. Patsy Hilliard is paid 5% commission on sales of $18,200. Find her gross salary.

16. Cheryl Hart, a computer salesperson is paid 1% commission for all sales. If she needs a monthly income of $1,500, find the monthly sales volume she must meet.

17. Tara Shaw sells produce and earns 5% commission on $8,000 in produce sales. Find his gross pay on this sale.

18. Find the gross pay of Minda Waller, a yarn company sales representative, who earns 5% of her total sales of $6,000.

19. Find the gross pay of Jerome Ware who is a salesperson who receives a 10% commission on $8,000 in sales.

20. Shirley Ward is a salesperson and is paid a salary of $200 plus 3% of all sales. Find her gross income if new sales are $8,000.

21. Kenya Maris is a real estate salesperson and receives a 6% commission on the sale of a piece of property for $130,000. Find his gross pay for this sale.

22. Debra Young sells $250,000 in equipment. At a 7% straight commission, calculate the gross earnings.

23. Vincent Ores is paid a salary of $400 plus 8% of sales. Calculate the gross income if new sales are $9,890.

24. Darrell Bright earns $150 plus 7% commission on all sales over $2,000. What are the gross earnings if sales for a week are $3,276?
$3,276 − $2,000 = $1,276 (sales on which commission is paid)

25. Find the gross earnings if Juanita Wilson earns $275 plus 2% of all sales over $3,000 and the sales for a week are $5,982.

$5,982 − $3,000 = $2,982 (sales on which commission is paid)

26. Dieter Tillman is paid $2,000 plus 5% of the total sales volume. If the salesperson sold $3,000 in merchandise, find the gross earnings.

Section 5.2

Use Table 5-2 (weekly payroll period) to find the amount of withholding tax for the gross earnings of the following married persons with the indicated number of withholding allowances.

27. $225, 4 exemptions

28. $238.50, 2 exemptions

29. $475, 0 exemptions

30. $295, 3 exemptions

31. $395, 3 exemptions 22

Use Tables 5-3 and 5-4 and the percentage method to find the amount of federal income tax to be withheld from the gross earnings of the following married persons who are paid weekly and have the indicated number of withholding allowances.

32. $273.96, 5 exemptions

33. $620, 8 exemptions

34. $875, 2 exemptions

35. $1,020, 3 exemptions

In Exercises 36 to 40, refer to Tables 5-5 and 5-6 to determine the amount of FICA tax and Medicare tax to be deducted from the gross weekly earnings.

36. $73

37. $89

38. $187

39. $368

40. $87.98

Use the percentage method to find the FICA and Medicare taxes for the following:

41. Weekly gross income of $157

42. Monthly gross income of $3,500

43. Yearly gross income of $24,000

44. Semimonthly gross income of $426

45. Yearly gross income of $18,225

46. Yearly gross income of $61,300

Complete the following payroll register. All employees are married and paid weekly and the number in parentheses is the number of withholding allowances that each person claims.

Employee & Withholding Allowances	Gross Earnings	With-holding tax	FICA	Medicare	Other Deductions	Total Deductions	Net Earnings
47. Abrams (3)	$145.00	_____	____	_____	$21.94	_____	_____
48. Cowgill (0)	$139.25	_____	____	_____	$15.21	_____	_____
49. Mason (4)	$165.00	_____	____	_____	$ 0	_____	_____
50. Sachs (2)	$476.28	_____	____	_____	$19.38	_____	_____

51. Deductions for Irene Gamble are as follows: withholding tax $47; FICA tax $27.83, retirement, $24.95, insurance, $8.45. Find the total deductions.

52. Vince Brimaldi earned $32,876 last year. If the state unemployment tax is 5.4% of the first $7,000 earned in a year, how much SUTA must Vince's employer pay for him if the employer pays at the 5.4% rate?

Additional Problems

1. LaShonda Landri works 47 hours in one week and earns $7.55 an hour with time and a half for overtime. Find her gross weekly pay.

2. Luella Elmo has a gross biweekly income of $1,250, is married, and claims two withholding allowances. Use the percentage method (Tables 5-3 and 5-4) to find the amount of withholding tax to be deducted from her gross earnings.

3. Greg Paszel has gross weekly earnings of $575. Four percent of his gross earnings is deducted for retirement and $8.65 is deducted for insurance. Find the total deductions if Mr. Paszel is single and claims one withholding allowance. (Use Tables 5-3, 5-4, 5-5, and 5-6.)

4. Paul Heiden is married and claims two withholding exemptions. If he earns $576.52 a week, what is his net weekly pay after FICA, Medicare tax, and federal withholding tax are deducted? For convenience, use Tables 5-2, 5-5, and 5-6.

5. Ida Pacino earns 6% commission on all sales she makes. Find her commission if she sells $9,650 in the pay period.

6. Juan Ferrier earns $275 a week plus 3% commission on all merchandise sales over $1,200. If he sells $6,700 in merchandise one week, how much are his gross earnings?

7. Yvonne Arceneaux packages shrimp to be quick frozen. She is paid $1.00 per package on all packages up to 150, $1.25 for packages from 151 to 300, and $1.50 for all packages over 300. Find her gross pay if she finished 315 packages in one pay period.

8. Henry Heil is a food server earning $2.75 an hour plus a 15% gratuity automatically added to all food checks. If Mr. Heil works 30 hours one week and sold $2,150 in food, how much should his gross earnings be for the week?

9. How much SUTA tax must Best Toys pay for Sheila Alford who earns $986 per week if the SUTA tax rate is 5.4% of the wages?

10. How much FUTA tax must Best Toys pay for Sheila Alford in Problem 9 if the FUTA tax rate is 6.2% of the first $7,000 minus the SUTA tax?

Challenge Problem

Complete the following time card for Janice Anderson. She earns time-and-a-half overtime when she works more than 8 hours on a weekday or Saturday. She earns double time on Sundays and holidays.

WEEKLY TIME CARD
CHD Company

Name	Janice Anderson			SS#	000-00-0000	

Pay for period ending

DATE	IN	OUT	IN	OUT	Total Regular Hours	Total Overtime Hours
M 8/4	7:00	11:00	11:30	7:30		
Tu 8/5	8:00	12:00	12:30	4:30		
W 8/6	8:00	12:00	12:30	4:30		
Th 8/7	7:00	11:00	12:30	5:30		
F 8/8	8:00	12:00	12:30	4:30		
Sa 8/9	7:00	12:00				
Su 8/10						

	HOURS	RATE	PAY
Regular			
Overtime (1.5×)			
Overtime (2×)			
Total			

Calculate Janice's net pay if she is single and claims 1 exemption. She pays Social Security and Medicare tax on the full amount.

Use Table 5–4.

Trial Test

1. Cheryl Douglas works 43 hours in a week for a salary of $354 per week. What are Cheryl's gross weekly earnings?

2. June Jackson earns $5.83 an hour. Find her gross earnings if she worked 46 hours (time and a half for overtime).

3. Willy Bell checks wrappers on cans in a cannery. He receives $0.07 for each case of cans. If he checks 750 cases on an average day, find his gross weekly salary. (A work week is 5 days.)

4. Stacey Ellis is paid on the following escalating piece rate: 1–100, $1.58; 101–250, $1.72; 251–up, $1.94. Find her gross earnings for completing 475 pieces.

5. Dorothy Ford, who sells restaurant supplies, works on 3% commission. If her sales for a week are $4,200, find her gross earnings.

6. Carlo Mason works on 5% commission. If he sells $7,500 in merchandise, find his gross earnings.

7. Find the gross earnings of Sallie Johnson who receives a 9% commission and whose sales totaled $5,800.

8. Use the percentage method to find the FICA tax (at 6.2%) and the Medicare tax (at 1.45%) for Anna Jones whose gross earnings are $213.86. Round to the nearest cent.

9. Use Tables 5-5 and 5-6 to find the FICA and Medicare tax for Michele Cottrell whose gross earnings are $361.25.

10. How much income tax should be withheld for Terry McLean, a married employee who earns $286 weekly and has two exemptions? (Use Table 5-2.)

11. Use Table 5-2 to find the income tax paid by Charlotte Jordan who is married with four exemptions, if her weekly gross earnings are $276.

12. Jo Ann Maxwell has gross earnings of $157. She has a 3% retirement deduction and pays $21 for insurance. What is the total of these deductions?

13. If LaQuita White had net earnings of $177.58 and total deductions of $43.69, find her gross earnings.

14. Rita Rainey has a gross income of $258.21 and total deductions of $31.17. Find the net earnings.

Complete the weekly register for married employees. The number of each person's exemptions is listed after each name. Round to the nearest cent.

Employee (Exemptions)	Gross Earnings	FICA	Medicare	Withholding Tax	Other Deductions	Net Earnings
15. Jackson (0)	$235.00	_____	_____	_____	$25.12	_____
16. Love (1)	173.80	_____	_____	_____	12.87	_____
17. Chow (2)	292.17	_____	_____	_____	0	_____
18. Ferrante (3)	77.15	_____	_____	_____	4.88	_____
19. Towns (4)	210.13	_____	_____	_____	0	_____

15.

16.

17.

18.

19.

20. How much SUTA tax must Anaston, Inc. pay to the state for a part-time employee who earns $5,290? The SUTA tax rate is 5.4% of the wages.

21. How much SUTA tax must University Dry Cleaners pay to the state for an employee who earns $38,200?

22. How much FUTA tax must J & K, Ltd. pay to the state for the employee in Problem 21? The FUTA tax rate is 6.2% of the first $7,000 minus the SUTA tax.

23. How much SUTA tax does the employee in Problem 21 pay?

A look at statistics that shape the nation

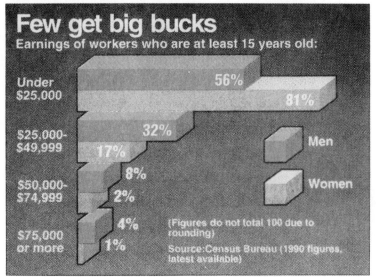

Few get big bucks

Earnings of workers who are at least 15 years old:

Under $25,000 — 56% / 81%

$25,000-$49,999 — 32% / 17%

$50,000-$74,999 — 8% / 2%

$75,000 or more — 4% / 1%

Men

Women

(Figures do not total 100 due to rounding)

Source: Census Bureau (1990 figures, latest available)

By Marty Baumann, USA TODAY

QUESTIONS

1. What percent of the workers who are at least 15 years old earn $50,000 or more?

2. In a representative sample of 1000 persons, 750 men and 250 women, how many men and women on the average would be expected in each of the following categories? Round to the nearest whole person.

3. Do the categories for men total 750? Do the categories for women total 250? Explain why or why not.

6

Trade and Cash Discounts

discount: an amount of money that is deducted from an original price.

A **discount** is an amount of money that is deducted or subtracted from an original price. In business, manufacturers and distributors give discounts as incentives for a sale or as a convenient way of pricing merchandise to retail merchants. Two common types of discounts used in business are *trade* and *cash discounts*.

6.1

Understanding Single Trade Discounts

LEARNING OBJECTIVES

1. Calculate trade discounts using the formula method.
2. Calculate trade discounts using the complements method.

Most products go from the manufacturer to the consumer by way of the wholesale merchant (wholesaler) and the retail merchant (retailer).

Manufacturer
↓
Wholesaler
↓
Retailer
↓
Consumer

Manufacturers often describe each of their products in a book or catalog that is made available to wholesalers or retailers. In such catalogs, manufacturers suggest a price at which each product should be sold to the consumer. This price is called the **suggested retail price,** the **catalog price,** or, most commonly, the **list price.**

When a manufacturer sells an item, the manufacturer deducts a certain amount from the list price of the article. The amount deducted is called the **trade discount.** The retailer pays the **net price,** which is the difference between the list price and the trade discount.

The trade discount is not usually stated in the published catalog. Instead, the wholesaler or retailer calculates it from the list price and the **discount rate.** The discount rate is the *percent* of the list price that the manufacturer allows the purchaser to deduct from the list price.

The manufacturer makes available lists of discount rates for all articles in the catalog. The discount rates vary considerably depending on such factors as the customer class, the season, the condition of the economy, whether a product is being discontinued, and the manufacturer's efforts to encourage larger purchases. Each time the discount rate changes, the manufacturer updates the listing. Each new discount rate refers to the original list price in the catalog.

When only one discount rate is quoted on the list price for an item, this discount rate is known as a **single discount rate.**

suggested retail price (catalog price or list price): the price at which a product should be sold to the consumer; this price is usually listed in a manufacturer's catalog.

trade discount: the amount deducted by the manufacturer from the list price of an article.

net price: the amount paid by the retailer for an article; this amount is the difference in the list price and the trade discount of the article.

discount rate: the percent of the list price that the manufacturer allows the retailer to deduct from the list price.

single discount rate: a term used to indicate that only one discount rate is applied to the list price.

trade discount: the result of multiplying the list price by the single discount rate.

net price: the result of subtracting the trade discount from the list price.

Calculating Trade Discounts—The Formula Method

To find the trade discount for an item when the list price and a single discount rate are given, use the following formula.

STEP BY STEP

Calculating the Amount of the Trade Discount

Trade discount = list price × single discount rate

Note that this formula is in fact a version of the basic percentage formula,

Portion (part) = rate (percent) × base (whole)   or $P = R \times B$

and you use it the same way you used the percentage formula in Chapter 4.

Once you have found the amount of the trade discount for an item, you can calculate the *net price* of the item.

STEP BY STEP

Calculating the Net Price of a Discounted Item

Net price = list price − trade discount

EXAMPLE 1

The list price of a refrigerator is $600. Your local appliance store can buy the refrigerator at the list price less 20%. Find the trade discount and the net price of the refrigerator.

Trade discount = list price × single discount rate

$600 × 20% = $600 × 0.20   Change the percent discount to a decimal
           = $120   and multiply the list price times the decimal.

Net price = list price − trade discount

$600 − $120 = $480   Subtract the trade discount from the list price to find the net price.

Calculating Trade Discounts—The Complements Method

There is another method for calculating the net price when you know the list price and the single discount rate. This method is often used when you do not need to know the actual amount of the trade discount, only the net price.

The method uses the complements of percents. The **complement** of a percent is the difference between that percent and 100%. For example, the complement of 35% is 65%, since 100% − 35% = 65%. The complement of 20% is 80% because 100% − 20% = 80%.

If the single discount rate is the percentage of the list price that the retailer *does not* pay, then 100% minus the single discount rate, which equals the complement of the discount rate, is the portion of the list price the retailer *does* pay.

complement: the difference between 100% and the percent of discount.

STEP BY STEP

Using Complements to Find the Net Price

Step 1. Find the complement by subtracting the single discount rate from 100%.

Step 2. Multiply the complement (in decimal form) by the list price to get the net price:

Net price = list price × (100% − single discount rate)

EXAMPLE 2

A stationery supply store buys 300 pens at $0.30 each, 200 legal pads at $0.60 each, and 100 boxes of paper clips at $0.90 each. The discount rate for the order is 12%. Find the net price of the order.

300 × $0.30 = $ 90   Find the list price of the pens.

200 × $0.60 = $120   Find the list price of the legal pads.

100 × $0.90 = $ 90   Find the list price of the paper clips.
            $300   Add to find the total list price.

Net price = list price × (100% − single discount rate)

$300 × (100% − 12%)   Subtract the discount rate from 100% to
     = $300 × 88%   find the complement.

     = $300 × 0.88   Multiply the total list price times the decimal
     = $264   equivalent of the complement to find the net price.

Self-Check 6.1

1. Use the method of Example 1 to complete Invoice 2501. Use the method of Example 2 to check that your net price is correct.

Quantity	Description	Unit Price	Invoice No. 2501 October 15, 19— Total Price
15	Notebooks	$1.50	_____
10	Looseleaf paper	$0.89	_____
30	Ballpoint pens	$0.79	_____
		Total list price	_____
		40% trade discount	_____
		Net price	_____

 6.2

Calculating Trade Discount Series

LEARNING OBJECTIVES

1. Use the net decimal equivalent to find the net price.
2. Find the amount of discount using the single-discount equivalent.

Sometimes a manufacturer wants to promote a particular item or encourage additional business from a retailer. Also, customers may be entitled to additional discounts as a result of buying large quantities. In such cases, the manufacturer may offer additional discounts that are deducted one after another from the list price. Such discounts are called a **trade discount series.** For example, a discount series would be written as $400 (list price) with a discount of 20/10/5 (discount rates). That is, a discount of 20% is allowed off the list price, a discount of 10% is allowed off the amount that was left after the first discount, and a discount of 5% is allowed off the amount that was left after the second discount. It *does not* mean a total discount of 35% is allowed.

trade discount series: trade discounts that are deducted successively from the list price by the manufacturer to promote a particular item or encourage additional business from a retailer.

One way to calculate the net price is to make a series of calculations:

$400 × 0.20 = $80 $400 − $80 = $320   The first discount is taken on the list price of $400, which then leaves $320.

$320 × 0.10 = $32 $320 − $32 = $288   The second discount is taken on $320, which leaves $288.

$288 × 0.05 = $14.40 $288 − $14.40 = $273.60   The third discount is taken on $288, which leaves the net price of $273.60.

Thus, the net price of a $400 order with a discount of 20/10/5 is $273.60. Always remember: In a trade discount series you *never* add the discount rates together; a discount series of 20/10/5 does *not* equal a single discount of 35%.

As you can see, it is very time consuming to figure a trade discount series this way. The business world uses a faster way of calculating the net price of a purchase after a series discount has been taken.

net decimal equivalent: the decimal that results from multiplying the complement of each discount rate in a series discount.

To calculate the net price directly, find the complement of each discount rate, write these complements as equivalent decimals, and multiply the decimals. The result is called the **net decimal equivalent.** Then multiply the list price times the net decimal equivalent to get the net price.

STEP BY STEP

Finding Net Price with the Net Decimal Equivalent

Step 1. Find the complement of each discount rate and write it as an equivalent decimal.

Step 2. Multiply the decimals in step 1. The product is the net decimal equivalent.

Step 3. Multiply the list price times the net decimal equivalent. The product is the net price.

EXAMPLE 3

Find the net price of an order with a list price of $600 and a trade discount series of 15/10/5. (*Remember:* To find the complement, you subtract the discount rate from 100%.)

$100\% - 15\% = 85\% = 0.85$ Find the complement of each discount rate
$100\% - 10\% = 90\% = 0.90$ and write it as an equivalent decimal.
$100\% - 5\% = 95\% = 0.95$

$0.85 \times 0.90 \times 0.95 = 0.72675$ Multiply the decimals times each other to find the net decimal equivalent.

Net price = list price × net decimal equivalent

$\$600 \times 0.72675 = \$436.05$ Multiply the list price times the net decimal equivalent to find the net price. Round to the nearest cent.

TIPS & TRAPS

We have said that the series discount rate of 20/10/5 is *not* equivalent to the single discount rate of 35% (which is the *sum* of 20%, 10%, and 5%). Let's look at what happens if you combine the series discount rates incorrectly, and then show the correct way.

Example: Find the net price of an article listed at $100 with a discount of 20/10/5.

~~Net price = list price × (100% − single discount rate)~~
~~$100 × (100% − 35%) = $100 × 0.65 = $65~~

WRONG

Net decimal equivalent = 0.8 × 0.9 × 0.95 = 0.684
Net price = list price × net decimal equivalent
$100 × 0.684 = $68.40

CORRECT

A common business application of this method is to compare prices and terms offered by competing manufacturers selling the same or similar items. The following example shows this application using a calculator.

One manufacturer lists a desk at $700 with a discount of 20/10/10. Another manufacturer lists the same desk at $650 with a discount of 10/10/10. Which is the better deal?

In calculating both net prices, use the formula

Calculator Solution

Net price = list price × net decimal equivalent

Find the compliment of each discount rate mentally.

Find the net price of the first desk in one continuous series of calculations:

Net price = $\boxed{AC}$ 700 $\boxed{\times}$ .8 $\boxed{\times}$ .9 $\boxed{\times}$ .9 $\boxed{=}$ ⇒ 453.60

Find the net price of the second desk in another series of calculations:

Net price = $\boxed{AC}$ 650 $\boxed{\times}$ .9 $\boxed{\times}$ .9 $\boxed{\times}$ .9 $\boxed{=}$ ⇒ 473.85

The better deal is the desk listed at $700 with a discount of 20/10/10 because the net price of this desk is $20.25 less than the other desk.

Finding the Amount of Discount Using the Single-Discount Equivalent

You know how much you have to pay for an item (the net decimal equivalent × list price), but what if you want to know how much you have *saved* by using a discount series? You can calculate the savings the long way, by finding the net price and then subtracting the net price from the list price. Or, you can apply the complements method to do the same thing in fewer steps by finding the **single discount equivalent**—the complement of the percent form of the net decimal equivalent.

single discount equivalent: a percent that is the complement of the percent form of the net decimal equivalent.

STEP BY STEP

Finding the Amount of Discount with the Single Discount Equivalent

Single discount equivalent = 100% − net decimal equivalent (in percent form) or 1 − net decimal (in decimal form)
Amount of discount = List price × Single discount (in decimal form)

EXAMPLE 4

Use the single discount equivalent to calculate the amount of the discount on a $1,500 fax machine with a discount series of 30/20/10.

100% − 30% = 70% = 0.7	Find the complement of each discount rate
100% − 20% = 80% = 0.8	and write it as an equivalent decimal.
100% − 10% = 90% = 0.9	
0.7(0.8)(0.9) = 0.504	Multiply the decimals times each other to find the net decimal equivalent.
1.000 − 0.504 = 0.496	Subtract the net decimal equivalent from 1 to find the single discount equivalent.

Thus, the single discount equivalent for the trade discount series 30/20/10 is 0.496 or 49.6%.

$1,500 × 0.496 = $744   Multiply the list price times the single-discount equivalent to find the amount of the discount.

 Self-Check 6.2

2. Find the net price of an order with a list price of $800 and a trade discount series of 12/10/8. Use the net decimal equivalent.

3. Use the single discount equivalent to calculate the amount of the discount on a $2,200 purchase with a discount series of 25/15/10.

4. One distributor lists a dot-matrix printer at $460 with a discount of 15/12/5. Another distributor lists the same printer at $380 with a discount of 10/10/50. Which is the better deal?

6.3

Determining Cash Discounts

LEARNING OBJECTIVES

1. Discount by using the ordinary dating method.
2. Calculate end of month discounts.
3. Determine receipt of goods discounts.
4. Determine partial payments.
5. Determine freight terms.

cash discount: a reduction of the amount due on an invoice allowed by manufacturers and distributors to encourage prompt payment of a bill.

Many manufacturers and wholesalers allow customers to take a **cash discount,** a reduction of the amount due on an invoice to encourage prompt payment of the bill. The cash discount is a specified percentage of the price of the goods. Customers who pay their bills within a certain amount of time receive a cash discount. Many companies use computerized billing systems that compute the exact amount of a cash discount and show it on the invoice, so that the customer does not need to figure the discount and resulting net price. But the customer must still determine when the bill must be paid to receive the discount.

Bills are often due within 30 days from the date of the invoice. To figure out the exact day of the month the payment is due, you have to know how many days are in a month, 30 or 31 (or 28 in the case of February). There are two ways to help remember which months have 30 days and which have 31. The first method shown in Figure 6-1, is called the *knuckle method*. Each knuckle represents a month with 31 days and each space between knuckles represents a month with 30 days (except February, which has 28 days unless it is a leap year, when it has 29). Another way to remember which months have 30 days and which have 31 is the following rhyme:

The knuckle months (Jan., March, May, July, Aug., Oct., and Dec.) have 31 days. The other months have 30 or fewer days.

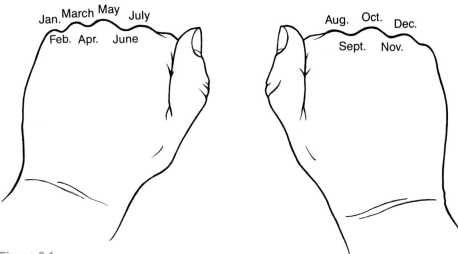

Figure 6.1

Thirty days hath September
April, June, and November;
February has 28 alone,
All the rest have 31;
Excepting leap year—that's the time
When February's days are 29.

With this in mind, let's look at one of the most common credit terms and dating methods.

Discounting by the Ordinary Dating Method

Many firms offer credit terms 2/10, n/30 (read as "two ten, net thirty"). The 2/10 means a 2% discount may be taken if the bill is paid within 10 days of the invoice date. The n/30 means the net amount of the bill is due if the bill is paid after 11 days but within 30 days of the date on the invoice. After the 30th day, the bill is overdue, and the buyer may have to pay interest charges.

For example, if an invoice is dated January 4 with credit terms of 2/10, n/30 and is paid on or before January 14, then a 2% discount is allowed. The net amount of the bill is due if it is paid on January 15 or any day up to and including February 3. If the bill is paid on February 4 or any day after February 4, it is subject to interest charges.

STEP BY STEP

Finding the Amount of the Cash Discount

Multiply the net amount by the percent (in decimal form) in the sales terms.

To find the amount of the cash discount, multiply the net amount on the invoice by the percent stated in the sales terms. To find the discounted amount (the amount to be paid), subtract the cash discount from the net amount on the invoice. Another way to find the amount due is to multiply the net amount times the complement of the discount rate, as you did for trade discounts in the first part of this chapter.

STEP BY STEP

Finding the Discounted Amount to be Paid

Subtract the cash discount from the net amount

or

multiply the net amount by the complement of the discount rate.

EXAMPLE 5

Find the discount date and the due date for an invoice dated July 27 with terms 2/10, n/30.

July is a "knuckle" month, so it has 31 days. To find the number of days from July 27 to the end of the month, subtract.

31	days in July
− 27	date on invoice
4	days remaining in July

Next, subtract the 4 from the number of days in the discount.

10	days in the discount period
− 4	days in July
6th	day in August, the last day to pay and claim a discount

The same procedure is used to determine the due date for the invoice. There are 4 days remaining in July, so subtract to find the number of days in August before the bill is due.

30	days in the period to pay the bill
− 4	days in July
26th	day in August, the last day to pay the bill before it is past due

Another common credit term is 2/10, 1/15, n/30. These terms are read "two ten, one fifteen, net thirty." A 2% discount is allowed if the bill is paid within 10 days after the invoice date, a 1% discount is allowed if the bill is paid during the 11th through 15th days, and the net amount is due if the bill is paid during the 16th through 30th days after the invoice date.

For example, a bill dated September 2 with sales terms 2/10, 1/15, n/30 receives a 2% discount if paid on or before September 12. A 1% discount is allowed if the bill is paid on September 13 or any day up to and including September 17. The net amount of the bill is due if it is paid on September 18 or any day up to and including October 2. If the bill is paid on October 3 or any day after October 3, it is subject to interest charges.

EXAMPLE 6

Sycamore Enterprises received a $1,248 bill for computer supplies, dated September 2, with sales terms 2/10, 1/15, n/30. A 5% penalty is charged for payment after 30 days. Find the amount due if the bill is paid (a) on or before September 12; (b) on or between September 13 and September 17; (c) on or between September 18 and October 2; and (d) on or after October 3.

(a) If the bill is paid on or before September 12 (within 10 days), the 2% discount applies:

$$\text{Discount} = \$1{,}248 \times 2\% = \$1{,}248 \times 0.02 = \$24.96$$

Amount due = $1,248 − $24.96 = $1,223.04

(b) If the bill is paid on or between September 13 and September 17 (within 15 days), the 1% discount applies:

$$\text{Discount} = \$1{,}248 \times 1\% = \$1{,}248 \times 0.01 = \$12.48$$

Amount due = $1,248 − $12.48 = $1,235.52

(c) If the bill is paid on or between September 18 and October 2 (within 30 days), the net amount of $1,248 is due.

(d) If the bill is paid on or after October 3, a 5% penalty is added:

$$\text{Amount of penalty} = \$1{,}248 \times 5\% = \$1{,}248 \times 0.05 = \$62.40$$

$$\text{Amount due} = \$1{,}248 + \$62.40 = \$1{,}310.40$$

Calculating End of Month (EOM) Discounts

Sometimes the sales terms read 2/10 EOM, where EOM stands for **end of month.** These terms mean that a 2% discount is allowed if the bill is paid during the first 10 days of the month *after* the month in the date of the invoice. Thus, if a bill is dated November 19, a 2% discount is allowed as long as the bill is paid on or before December 10.

end-of-month (EOM) discount: sales terms that allow a percent discount if the bill is paid during a specified period after the first day of the month after the month of the invoice.

EXAMPLE 7

Newman, Inc., received a bill for janitorial services dated September 17 for $5,000 with terms 2/10 EOM. The invoice was paid on October 9. How much did Newman, Inc., pay?

Since the bill was paid within the first 10 days of the month after the month on the invoice, a 2% discount was allowed. The complement of 2% is 98%.

Amount due = $5,000 × 98% = $5,000 × 0.98 = $4,900

The amount due on October 9 is $4,900.

An exception to this rule occurs when the invoice is dated *on or after the 26th of the month.* When this happens, the discount is allowed if the bill is paid during the first ten days of the *second month after* the month in the date on the invoice. Thus, if an invoice is dated May 28 with terms 2/10 EOM, a 2% discount is allowed as long as the bill is paid on or before July 10. This exception allows retailers adequate time to pay the invoice.

EXAMPLE 8

Archie's Shoes received a $200 bill for copying services dated April 27. The terms on the invoice were 3/10 EOM. The firm paid the bill on June 2. How much did it pay?

Since the bill was paid within the first 10 days of the second month after the month on the invoice, a 3% discount was allowed. The complement of 3% is 97%.

Amount due = $200 × 97% = $200 × 0.97 = $194

receipt of goods (ROG) discount: sales terms in which the discount is determined from the day the goods are received instead of the invoice date.

Sometimes credit terms hinge on the day the *goods are received* instead of the invoice date. In such cases, the terms may be written 1/10 *ROG*, where ROG stands for **receipt of goods.** These terms mean that a 1% discount is allowed on the bill if it is paid within 10 days of the receipt of goods.

That is, if an invoice is dated September 6 but the goods do not arrive until the 14th and the sales terms are 2/15 ROG, then a 2% discount is allowed if the bill is paid on any date up to and including September 29. If no net period is given in the sales terms, it is understood to be 30 days from the receipt of goods.

EXAMPLE 9

An invoice for $400 is dated November 9 and has sales terms 2/10 ROG. The machine parts arrive November 13. (a) If the bill is paid on November 21, what is the amount due? (b) If the bill is paid on December 2, what is the amount due?

(a) Since the bill is being paid within 10 days of the receipt of goods, a 2% discount is allowed. The complement of 2% is 98%.

Amount due = $400 × 98% = $400 × 0.98 = $392

(b) No discount is allowed, since the bill is not being paid within 10 days of the receipt of goods. Thus, $400 is due.

TIPS & TRAPS

It is important to be able to distinguish types of payment terms as they appear on an invoice. For example, an invoice for $200 is dated September 28 but the merchandise arrives on October 15. The sales terms are 2/10 ROG, but the account manager thinks this means the bill can be paid within 10 days of the second month after the month in the date of the invoice (EOM) and pays the bill with a 2% discount on November 5. Does the discount apply? No, since the bill should have been paid within 10 days of the receipt of the goods. That date is the 25th of October.

Making Partial Payments

A company sometimes cannot pay the full amount due in time to take advantage of discount credit terms. Most sellers allow buyers to make partial payments and take advantage of the discount terms if the partial payment is made within the time specified in the credit terms. When this happens, the discount terms apply only to the partial payment, or the portion of the entire bill that is actually paid. The remaining balance of the bill is expected to be paid within the time specified by the credit terms. Some sellers penalize buyers for payments made after the date specified in the terms. This penalty is usually a percent of the unpaid balance.

To find how much the bill is reduced by a partial payment, divide the parital payment by the complement of the discount rate in decimal form to find out how much credit exists toward paying the total bill.

Finding the Amount of Outstanding Balance after a Partial Payment

Step 1. Find the complement of the discount rate.

Step 2. Divide the partial payment by the complement of the discount rate.

Step 3. Subtract this amount from the total bill to get the outstanding balance.

EXAMPLE 10

The Semmes Corporation received an $875 invoice for cardboard cartons with terms of 3/10, n/30. The firm could not pay the entire bill within 10 days but sent a check for $500. What amount was credited to Semmes's account?

$$\frac{\text{Partial payment}}{1 - 0.03} = \frac{\$500}{0.97}$$

Divide the amount of the partial payment by the complement of the discount rate to find the amount credited to the bill.

$$= \$515.46$$

$$\$875 - \$515.46 = \$359.54$$

Subtract the amount of credit from the total invoice to find the outstanding balance.

TIPS & TRAPS

Remember to find the *complement* of the discount rate and then divide the partial payment by this complement. Students sometimes just multiply the discount rate times the partial payment, which is wrong.

From Example 10,

$\$500 \times 0.03 = \$15$
$\$500 + \$15 = \$515$
$\$875 - \$515 = \$360$

WRONG

From Example 10,

$$\frac{\$500}{0.97} = \$515.46$$

$\$875 - \$515.46 = \$359.54$

CORRECT

Determining Freight Terms

Manufacturers rely on a wide variety of carriers (truck, rail, ship, plane, and the like) to distribute their goods. The terms of freight shipment are indicated on a document called a **bill of lading** that is attached to each shipment. This document includes a description of the merchandise, the number of pieces, weight, name of consignee, destination, and method of payment of freight charges. Freight payment terms are usually specified on the *manufacturer's price list* so that purchasers clearly understand who is responsible for freight charges and under what circumstances. The cost of shipping may be paid by the buyer or seller. If the freight is paid by the buyer, the bill of lading is marked **FOB** ("free on board" at the) **shipping point** and *freight collect*. For example, CCC Industries located in Tulsa purchased parts from Rawhide in Chicago. Rawhide ships FOB Chicago, so CCC Industries must

bill of lading: a document included on each shipment of goods that shows important information about the shipment, such as content, distribution, and freight charges.

FOB shipping point: stands for free on board at the shipping point, and means that the buyer of the goods pays freight costs.

pay the freight from Chicago to Tulsa. The freight company then collects freight charges from CCC upon delivery of the goods.

   If the freight is paid by the seller, the bill of lading may be marked **FOB destination** and *freight one paid*. If Rawhide paid the freight in the preceding example, the term FOB Tulsa could also have been used. Many manufacturers pay shipping charges for shipments above some minimum dollar value. Some shipments of very small items may be marked *prepay and add*. That is, the seller pays the shipping charge and adds it to the invoice, so the buyer pays the shipping charge to the seller rather than to the freight company. Cash discounts do *not* apply to freight or shipping charges. When cash discounts are calculated on such invoices, the shipping charges are subtracted from the total *before* the net price is calculated. The shipping charges are then added back to the net price to get the total amount to be paid to the seller.

FOB destination: stands for free on board at the destination, and means that the seller of the goods pays freight costs.

EXAMPLE 11

Calculate the cash discount and net amount paid for an $800 order of business forms with sales terms of 3/10, 1/15, n/30 if the cost of shipping was $40 (which is included in the $800). The invoice was dated June 13, marked *freight prepay and add*, and paid June 24.

Cost of merchandise = Total invoice − shipping fee = $800 − $40 = $760	Apply the discount rate to *only* the cost of the merchandise.
Cash discount = $760 × 0.01 = $7.60 Net amount = $800 − $7.60 = $792.40	The bill was paid within 15 days, so the 1% discount applies. Discount is taken from total bill.

Self-Check 6.3

5. Ms. Alvarez received an invoice dated March 9, with terms 2/10, n/30, amounting to $540. She paid the bill on March 12. How much was the cash discount? How much did Ms. Alvarez pay?

6. How much would have to be paid on an invoice for $450 with terms 4/10, 1/15, n/30 if the bill is paid (a) 7 days after the invoice date; (b) 15 days after the invoice date; (c) 25 days after the invoice date?

7. Maddy's Muffins received a bill for $648, dated April 6, with sales terms 2/10, 1/15, n/30. A 3% penalty is charged for payment after 30 days. Find the amount due if the bill is paid (a) on or before April 16; (b) on or between April 17 and April 21; (c) on or between April 22 and May 6; (d) on or after May 7.

8. Ed Rosicky received a bill for $800 dated July 5th, with sales terms of 2/10 EOM. He paid the bill on August 8th. How much did Ed pay?

9. An invoice for $900 is dated October 15 and has sales terms 2/10 ROG. The merchandise arrives October 21. (a) If the bill is paid on October 27, what is the amount due? (b) If the bill is paid on November 3, what is the amount due?

10. Delois Johnson could not pay the entire amount of a bill for $730 within the discount period, so she made a payment of $400. If the terms of the transaction were 3/10, n/30, find the amount credited to the account and find the outstanding balance due within 30 days of the invoice date.

11. Lucy's Bicycle Shop received a shipment of bicycles from Wish Company. The bill of lading was marked FOB destination. Who paid the freight?

REAL WORLD APPLICATION

Trade Discounts

An important part of owning a business is the purchasing of equipment and supplies to run the office. Before paying an invoice, all items must be checked and amounts refigured before writing the check for payment. At this time the terms of the invoice can be applied.

Application Questions

Using the information on the invoice below, fill in the extended amount for each line, the merchandise total,

the tax amount, and the total invoice amount. Locate the terms of the invoice and find how much you would write a check for to pay Harper on each of the following dates:

March 5, 1989
March 12, 1989
March 25, 1989

INVOICE DATE	TERMS	DATE OF ORDER	ORDERED BY	PHONE NO.	REMIT TO ▶	HARPER General Accounting Office
02/27/XX	2/10, 1/15, n/30	02/27/XX		803-000-4488		

LINE NO.	MANUFACTURER PRODUCT NUMBER	QTY. ORD.	QTY. B.O.	QTY. SHP.	U/M	DESCRIPTION	UNIT PRICE		EXTENDED AMOUNT
001	REMYY370/02253	3	0	3	EA	TONER, F/ROYAL TA210 COP I	11.90		
002	Sk 1230M402	5	0	3	EA	CORRECTABLE FILM RIBBON	10.95		
003	JRLM01023	10	0	10	EA	COVER-UP CORRECTION TAPE	9.90		
004	rTu123456	9	0	9	EA	PAPER, BOND, WHITE, 8½ x 11	58.23		

DATE REC'D. _____	01460900001			5.00		0.00	TOTAL INVOICE AMOUNT ▶	
	OUR ORDER NO.	MDSE. TOTAL	TAX RATE	TAX AMOUNT		FREIGHT AMOUNT		

Summary

Topic	Page	What to Remember	Examples
Finding the amount of a single trade discount	191	Trade discount = list price × single discount rate	The list price is $76 and the trade discount is 25%. Find the amount of trade discount. $$\$76 \times 25\% = \$76 \times 0.25$$ $$= \$19$$
Finding the net price	191	Net price = list price − trade discount	Net price = $76 − $19 = $57
Finding net price using the complement of the single discount rate.	192	Use the *complement* of the decimal form of the discount rate. Net price = list price × (100% − single discount rate)	The list price is $480 and the trade discount is 15%. Find the net price. Net price $$= \$480 \times (1.00 - 0.15)$$ $$= \$480 \times 0.85 = \$408$$

Topic	Page	What to Remember	Examples
Finding net price of an item with a series discount	194	Multiply the complements of the decimal form of each discount to find the net decimal equivalent. Net price = list price × net decimal equivalent	The list price is $960, and the discount series is 10/5/2. Find the net price. $(1.00 - 0.1) \times (1.00 - 0.05) \times (1.00 - 0.02) =$ $(0.9) \times (0.95) \times (0.98) = 0.8379$ $0.8379 \times \$960 = \$804.38$
Finding the amount of discount with the single discount equivalent	195	Multiply the complements of the decimal forms of each discount to find the net decimal equivalent. Subtract the net decimal equivalent from 1 to find the decimal form of the single discount equivalent. Multiply the list price by the single discount equivalent to find the amount of discount.	The list price is $2,800 and the discount series is 25/15/10. Find the amount of discount. $(1.00 - 0.25) \times (1.00 - 0.15) \times (1.00 - 0.1)$ $= (0.75) \times (0.85) \times (0.9) = 0.57375$ $1 - 0.57375 = 0.42625$ Amount of discount = $\$2,800 \times 0.42625 = \$1,193.50$
Calculating due dates	196	Count from the *next day after* the date of the invoice, *or* add the number of days to the invoice date. If the invoice date and due date are in different months, subtract the number of days remaining in the first month from the total number of days to the due date. The number is the due date in the second month. Use the knuckle method to determine how many days are in each month: each knuckle represents a 31-day month, and each space between knuckles represents a 28-, 29-, or 30-day month.	By what date must an invoice dated July 10 be paid if it is due in 10 days? July 10 + 10 days = July 20. By what date must an invoice dated May 15 be paid if it is due in 30 days? May 31 − May 15 = 16 days remaining in the first month; 30 − 16 = 14. The due date is June 14.
Ordinary dating method discount	197	Sales terms of 2/10, n/30, mean the buyer takes a 2% discount within 10 days of the invoice date but must pay the net amount after 10 days and within 30 days of the invoice date.	What are the discount date and the due date of a $2,500 invoice dated July 17 with terms 2/10, n/30? How much money would be due on each date? *Discount date:* July 17 + 10 days = July 27 Amount due on or before discount date $= \$2,500 \times (1.00 - 0.02) = \$2,500 \times 0.98 = \$2,450$ *Due date:* July 31 − July 17 = 14 days remaining in the first month 30 − 14 = 16, so the net amount, $2,500, is due on or before August 16.
End of month (EOM) discount	199	Sales terms 2/10 EOM mean that a 2% discount is allowed if the bill is paid during the first 10 days of the month *after* the month in the invoice date. See exception on page 199	To take the discount, by what date would Smith, Inc., have to pay an $880 bill dated November 5 with terms 2/10 EOM? How much would the firm pay? Discount date = December 10 Amount due on or before December 10 $= \$880 \times (1.00 - 0.02) = \$880 \times 0.98 = \$862.40$
Receipt of goods (ROG) discount	200	Sales terms 1/10 ROG mean that a 1% discount is allowed on the bill if it is paid within 10 days of the receipt of the goods.	How much would have to be paid on an invoice for $500 with terms 1/10 ROG if the merchandise arrives April 2 and is paid on April 8? $\$500 \times (1.00 - 0.01)$ $\$500 \times 0.99 = \$495$ amount paid

Topic	Page	What to Remember	Examples
Partial payments	200	Discount terms may be applied to partial payments made within the time specified. To find the amount of outstanding balance after a partial payment has been made with a discount: Divide the partial payment by the complement of the discount rate; then subtract this amount from the total bill.	Estrada's Restaurant purchased carpet for $1,568 with sales terms of 3/10, n/30 and paid $1,000 on the bill within the 10 days specified. How much was credited to Estrada's account and what balance remained? $1,000 \div 0.97 = $1,030.93$ credited to account $1,568 - $1,030.93 = 537.07 balance due
Freight terms: FOB shipping point	201	FOB shipping point means the buyer pays freight costs.	A shipment is sent from a manufacturer in Boston to a wholesaler in Dallas and is marked FOB destination. Who pays the freight cost? The manufacturer pays.
FOB destination		FOB destination means the seller pays freight costs.	

Self-Check Solutions

1.

	Total Price
	$22.50
	8.90
	23.70
Total list price	55.10
40% trade discount	−22.04
	$33.06

Complements method
$$1 - 0.4 = 0.6$$
$$\$55.10 \times 0.6 = \$33.06$$

2. $100\% - 12\% = 88\%$, and $88\% = 0.88$
$100\% - 10\% = 90\%$, and $90\% = 0.9$
$100\% - 8\% = 92\%$, and $92\% = 0.92$

$$0.88(0.9)(0.92) = 0.72864$$
$$\$800 \times 0.72864 = \$582.91 \quad \text{net price}$$

3. $100\% - 25\% = 75\%$, and $75\% = 0.75$
$100\% - 15\% = 85\%$, and $85\% = 0.85$
$100\% - 10\% = 90\%$, and $90\% = 0.9$

$$0.75(0.85)(0.9) = 0.57375$$
$$1 - 0.57375 = 0.42625 \quad \text{single discount equivalent}$$
$$\$2,200 \times 0.42625 = \$937.75 \quad \text{trade discount}$$

4. $100\% - 15\% = 85\%$, and $85\% = 0.85$
$100\% - 12\% = 88\%$, and $88\% = 0.88$
$100\% - 5\% = 95\%$, and $95\% = 0.95$

$$\$460 \times 0.85(0.88)(0.95) = 326.876 = \$326.88 \quad \text{net price}$$

$100\% - 10\% = 90\%$, and $90\% = 0.9$
$100\% - 10\% = 90\%$, and $90\% = 0.9$
$100\% - 50\% = 50\%$, and $50\% = 0.5$

$$\$380 \times 0.9(0.9)(0.5) = \$153.90 \quad \text{net price}$$

The $380 printer is a better deal.

5. $\$540(0.02) = \$10.80$ cash discount
   $\$540 - \$10.80 = \$529.20$ amount to pay

6. a. $\$450(0.04) = \$18$ cash discount
    $\$450 - \$18 = \$432$ amount to pay
 b. $\$450(0.01) = \$4.50$ cash discount
    $\$450 - \$4.50 = \$445.50$ amount to pay
 c. $\$450$ due (no discount)

7. a. $\$648(0.02) = \$12.96$ cash discount
   $\$648 - \$12.96 = \$635.04$ amount due
 b. $\$648(0.01) = \$6.48$ cash discount
   $\$648 - \$6.48 = \$641.52$ amount due
 c. $\$648$ due (no discount)
 d. $\$648(0.03) = \$19.44$ penalty
   $\$648 + \$19.44 = \$667.44$ due

8. $\$800(0.02) = \$16$ cash discount
  $\$800 - \$16 = \$784$ amount paid

9. a. $\$900(0.02) = \$18$ cash discount
   $\$900 - \$18 = \$882$ amount due
 b. $\$900$ due (no discount)

10. $\$400 \div 0.97 = \$412.37$ amount credited
  $\$730 - \$412.37 = \$317.63$ outstanding balance due

11. Wish Company paid the freight.

End of Chapter Problems

Section 6.1

Complete the following table. Round all answers to the nearest cent.

List Price	Single Discount Rate	Trade Discount
1. $300	15%	_____
2. $48	10%	_____
3. $127.50	20%	_____
4. $100	12%	_____
5. $37.85	20%	_____
6. $425	15%	_____

7. Find the trade discount on a conference table listed at $1,025 less 10% (single discount rate).

8. The list price for velvet by Harris Fabrics is $6.25 per yard less 6%. What is the trade discount? Round to the nearest cent.

9. Find the trade discount on a suit listed at $165 less 12%.

10. Rocha Bros. offered a $12\frac{1}{2}\%$ discount on a tractor listed at $10,851. What was the trade discount? Round to the nearest cent.

11. Find the trade discount on an order of 30 lamps listed at $35 each less 9%.

12. The list price on skirts is $22, and the list price on corduroy jumpers is $37. If Petitt's Clothing Store orders 30 skirts and 40 jumpers at a discount rate of 11%, what is the trade discount on the purchase?

13. A stationery shop bought 10 boxes of writing paper that were listed at $1 each and 200 greeting cards listed at $0.50 each. If the single discount rate for the purchase is 15%, find the trade discount.

Complete the following table. Round all answers to the nearest cent.

	List Price	Trade Discount	Net Price
14.	$1,480	$301	_____
15.	$21	$3	_____
16.	$24.62	$5.93	_____
17.	$6.85	$0.72	_____
18.	$0.89	$0.12	_____
19.	$378.61	$42.58	_____

20. The list price of carpeting from Marie's Mill Outlet is $19 per square yard. The trade discount is $2.50 per square yard. What is the net price per square yard?

Complete the following table.

	List Price	Single Discount Rate	Trade Discount	Net Price
21.	$25	5%	_____	_____
22.	$1,263	12%	_____	_____
23.	$0.89	2%	_____	_____
24.	$27.50	3%	_____	_____
25.	$2,100	17%	_____	_____

Complete the following table.

	List Price	Single Discount Rate	Complement	Net Price
26.	$15.97	4%	_____	_____
27.	$421	5%	_____	_____
28.	$138.54	6%	_____	_____
29.	$721.18	3%	_____	_____
30.	$16.97	11%	_____	_____

Section 6.2

Complete the following table.

	List Price	Discount Rates	Decimal Equivalents of Complements	Net Decimal Equivalent	Net Price
31.	$200	20/10	_____	_____	_____
32.	$50	10/7/5	_____	_____	_____
33.	$1,500	20/15/10	_____	_____	_____
34.	$35	20/15/5	_____	_____	_____
35.	$400	15/5	_____	_____	_____

36. Discount rates of 10% and 5% were allowed on ladies' scarves listed at $4. What was the net price of each scarf?

37. Find the net price of an item listed at $800 with a series discount of 25/10/5.

38. A trade discount series of 10/5/5 is offered on a typewriter, which is listed at $800. Also, a trade discount series of 5/10/5 is offered on a desk chair listed at $250. Find the total net price for the typewriter and the chair. Round to the nearest cent.

39. Five desks are listed at $400 each, with a trade discount of 20/10/10. Also, ten bookcases are listed at $200 each, discounted 10/20/10. Find the total net price for the desks and bookcases.

Complete the following table.

	Net Decimal Equivalent	Net Decimal Equivalent in Percent Form	Single Discount Equivalent in Percent Form
40.	0.765	_____	_____
41.	0.82	_____	_____
42.	0.6835	_____	_____
43.	0.6502	_____	_____
44.	0.7434	_____	_____

Find the *single discount equivalent* for the following discount series.

45. 20/10

46. 30/20/5

47. 10%, 5%, 2%

48. 10/5

49. 20/15

50. A television set is listed at $400 less 20%. The same set is listed by another manufacturer for $425 less 21%. Which is the better deal?

51. A hutch is listed at $650 with a trade discount of $65. The same hutch is listed by another manufacturer for $595 with a trade discount of $25. Which is the better deal?

52. One manufacturer lists an aquarium for $58.95 with a trade discount of $5.90. Another manufacturer lists the same aquarium for $60 with a trade discount of $9.45. Which is the better deal?

53. One manufacturer lists a table at $200 less 12%. Another manufacturer lists the same table at $190 less 11%. Which is the better deal?

54. One manufacturer lists picture frames at $20 each, discounted 10/5/10. Another manufacturer lists the same picture frames at $19 with a series discount of 10/10/10. Which is the better deal?

55. A trunk is listed at $250 discounted 10/10/5. The same trunk is listed by another manufacturer for $260 discounted 10/10/10. Which is the better deal?

Section 6.3

56. Mr. Matthews received a bill dated March 1 with sales terms 3/10, n/30. What percent discount will he receive if he pays the bill on March 5?

57. Ms. Wagner received a bill dated September 3 with sales terms 2/10, n/30. Did she receive a discount if she paid the bill on September 15?

58. An invoice dated February 13 had sales terms 2/10, n/30. The bill was paid February 19. Was a cash discount allowed?

59. Mr. Carruth received an invoice for $300 dated March 3 with sales terms 1/10, n/30. He paid the bill on March 6. What was his cash discount?

60. Find the cash discount on an invoice for $270 dated April 17 with terms 2/10, n/30 if the bill was paid April 22.

61. Find the cash discount on an invoice for $50 dated May 3 with terms 1/15, n/30 if the bill was paid May 14.

62. Mr. Collings received an invoice dated June 5 for $70 with terms 2/10, n/30. He paid the bill on June 9. What was his cash discount and how much did he pay?

63. Mrs. Randle received an invoice dated July 3 for $165 with terms 2/10, n/30. She paid the bill on July 7. How much did she pay?

64. How much would have to be paid on an invoice for $350 with terms 2/10, 1/15, n/30, if the bill is paid (a) 7 days after the invoice date; (b) 15 days after the invoice date; (c) 25 days after the invoice date?

65. How much would have to be paid on an invoice for $28 with terms 3/10 EOM if the bill dated June 8 is paid (a) July 2; (b) July 20?

66. Mr. Baldwin received an invoice for $650 dated January 26. The sales terms in the invoice were 2/10 EOM. He paid the bill on March 4. How much did Mr. Baldwin pay?

67. How much would have to be paid on an invoice for $328 with terms 2/10 ROG if the merchandise invoice is dated January 3, the merchandise arrives January 8, and the invoice is paid (a) January 11; (b) January 15; (c) January 25?

68. Find the cash discount and net amount paid on an invoice dated August 19 if it is paid on August 25 and has terms 3/10, 1/15, n/30. The amount of the invoice is $826.

69. Leona Horne purchased a recliner for $624 with sales terms of 2/15, n/30. If she made a partial payment of $200 within 15 days, how much was credited to her account and what was her outstanding balance after the credit?

Additional Problems

1. Find the net decimal equivalent and the single discount equivalent for the series 15/10/5.

2. Emilio Suarez received an invoice for $850 dated April 9 with sales terms 3/15 ROG. The merchandise arrived April 13. If the invoice was paid on April 22, what was the amount due?

3. Marie DeBouchel received a bill for $1,725 on May 26. The sales terms on the invoice were 3/10 EOM. If she paid the bill on June 4, how much did she pay?

4. Frank DeShazo received an invoice for $625 dated July 9 with sales terms 3/10, n/30. If he paid the bill on July 13, what was his cash discount?

5. One office supply distributor lists a pen-and-pencil set for $25 less 10/20 and another lists the same set for $27 less 10/10/5. Which is the better deal?

6. A retailer can purchase a laptop computer for $2,300 less a 35% trade discount. How much is the discount?

7. Mose White purchased store supplies for $123 with sales terms 10/5/5. What was the net price if Mr. White took advantage of the entire discount series?

8. Ms. Ford received an invoice dated October 1 with sales terms 3/10, 2/15, n/30. What percent discount will she receive if she pays the invoice on November 5?

9. Campbell Sales purchased merchandise worth $745 and made a partial payment of $300 on day 13. If the sales terms were 2/15, n/30, how much was credited to the account? What was the outstanding balance?

10. Elmer Wilson purchased roll vinyl floor covering for $1,150 with sales terms of 3/15, n/30. He paid $800 on the bill within 15 days. How much was credited to his account? What was his outstanding balance after the payment?

Challenge Problem

When are Terms of Purchase, Terms of Endearment?

Swift's Dairy Mart receives a shipment of refrigeration units totaling $2,386.50 including a shipping charge of $32. Swift's returns $350 worth of the units. Terms of the purchase are 2/10, n/30. If Swift's takes advantage of the discount, what is the net amount payable?

Trial Test

1. The list price of a refrigerator is $550. The retailer can buy the refrigerator at the list price minus 20%. Find the trade discount.

2. The list price of a television is $560. The trade discount is $27.50. What is the net price?

3. A retailer can buy a lamp that is listed at $36.55 for 20% less than the list price. How much does the retailer have to pay for the lamp?

4. A manufacturer lists a dress at $39.75 with a trade discount of $3.60. Another manufacturer lists the same dress at $42 with a trade discount of $6.75. Which is the better deal?

5. One manufacturer lists a chair for $250 less 20%. Another manufacturer lists the same chair at $240 less 10%. Which manufacturer is offering the better deal?

6. Find the net price if a discount series of 20/10/5 is deducted from $70.

7. Find the net decimal equivalent of the series 20/10/5.

8. Find the single discount equivalent for the discount series 20/20/10.

9. What do the initials ROG represent?

10. A retailer buys 20 boxes of stationery at $4 each and 400 greeting cards at $0.50 each. The discount rate for the order is 15%. Find the trade discount.

11. A retailer buys 30 electric frying pans listed at $40 each for 10% less than the list price. How much does the retailer have to pay for the frying pans?

12. What is the complement of 15%?

13. What do the initials EOM represent?

14. Ms. Ryan received a bill dated September 1 with sales terms 3/10, 1/15, n/30. What percent discount will she receive if she pays the bill on September 6?

15. Mr. Williams received an invoice for $200 dated March 6 with sales terms 1/10, n/30. He paid the bill on March 9. What was his cash discount?

16. Mrs. Montgomery received a bill for $300 dated April 7. The sales terms on the invoice were 2/10 EOM. If she paid the bill on May 2, how much did Mrs. Montgomery pay?

17. An invoice for $400 dated December 7 has sales terms 2/10 ROG. The merchandise arrived December 11. If the bill is paid on December 18, what is the amount due?

18. If the bill in Problem 17 is paid on January 2, what is the amount due?

19. A trade discount series of 10% and 20% is offered on 20 dartboards that are listed at $14 each. Also, a trade discount series of 20% and 10% is offered on 10 bowling balls that are listed at $40 each. Find the total net price for the dartboards and bowling balls.

20. Zing Manufacturing lists artificial flower arrangements at $30 less 10% and 10%. Another manufacturer lists the same flower arrangements at $31 less 10%, 10%, and 5%. Which is the better deal?

21. The Dean Specialty Company purchased monogrammed items worth $895 and made a partial payment of $600 on day 12. If the sales terms were 3/15, n/30, how much was credited to the account? What was the outstanding balance?

Summer savings on European travel

The latest cuts in first-class and business airfares to Europe are not apt to extend to vacationers, experts say. But that doesn't mean that there aren't plenty of bargains.

"Every week we do new ($100-$300 off) specials. It's that crazy," says David Thomas of TWA Getaway Vacations.

A sampler of summer deals:

▶ **Airlines.** If you can find a seat, many advance-purchase, midweek restricted fares are good deals. Example: Cincinnati-Paris round trip on Delta, $598.

▶ **Hotels.** Sheraton's "Freedom of Europe" promotion cuts 50% off rates in nine cities, starting at $86 per room. "Summer Spectacular" rates at 37 Inter-Continental and Forum hotels are 36%-65% less, as low as $119 per room.

▶ **Tours.** British Airways, reviving the '80s idea of a quick trip abroad, offers "London on the Town" — airfare, three nights lodging and breakfasts, $883-$1,062.

Crossing the Atlantic

The European Travel Commission predicts more than 7 million U.S. travelers will visit Europe this year — making 1992 second only to 1990's record high of 7.5 million. In past years:

	Millions
1985	6.4
1986	5.1
1987	6.1
1988	6.5
1989	6.9
1990	7.5
1991	6.4

Copyright 1992, USA TODAY. Reprinted with permission.

QUESTIONS

1. A major airline gives a corporate discount of 35% off regular coach fare. If the "super saver" fare for a flight from Cincinnati to Paris is $598 and the regular coach fare is $889, which deal should Briggs, Inc., use?

2. Charles Temple, president of Briggs, Inc., will stay at the Paris Sheraton and is eligible for a 40% discount. He is scheduled to stay 5 nights in the hotel. The rack rate (non discounted rate) for this hotel room is $329 per night. If local and hotel tax is 15% of the discounted bill, how much should Temple expect to pay for his hotel stay?

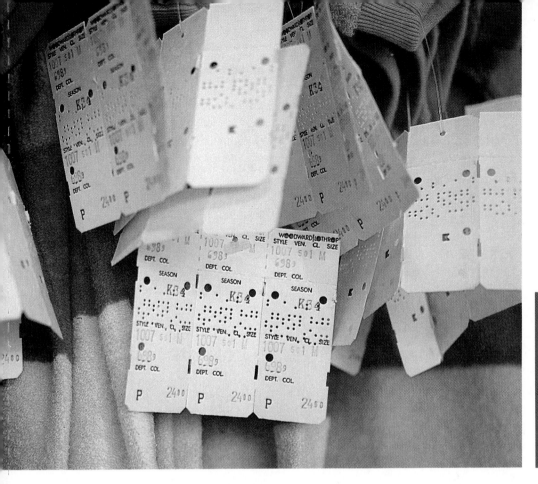

Markup and Markdown

Any successful business must keep prices low enough to attract customers, yet high enough to pay expenses and make a profit. In business, purchases are made at several different levels. A retailer usually purchases from a distributor. A distributor or wholesaler usually purchases from a manufacturer. A manufacturer purchases raw materials to make the product. A businessperson bases pricing decisions on a number of different factors. Let's look at some of these factors before examining the mathematics of the business of buying and selling.

Selling price   The price of merchandise being sold.

Cost   The price paid for merchandise.

Markup   The difference between the cost and selling price. It usually must be enough to pay expenses and make a profit. Markup is sometimes called *gross profit* or *margin*.

Operating expenses   The cost of running a business operation, including such expenses as wages, salaries, rent, utilities, advertising, and insurance.

Gross profit   The difference between the selling price and cost when the selling price exceeds the cost of the item.

Gross loss   The difference between the selling price and cost when the cost exceeds the selling price of the item.

Net profit   The difference between the gross profit and the operating expenses when the gross profit exceeds the operating expenses.

Net loss   The difference between the gross profit or gross loss and the operating expenses when the operating expenses exceed the gross profit or gross loss.

Markdown   The amount that merchandise has been reduced.

Reduced price   The price to which merchandise is reduced.

7.1

Markup

LEARNING OBJECTIVES

1. Find the cost, markup, selling price, or percent of markup when the markup is based on the cost.

2. Find the cost, markup, selling price, or percent of markup when the markup is based on the selling price.

3. Compare markup based on the cost with markup based on the selling price.

Markup can be calculated as a percentage of either the cost or the selling price of an item. Most manufacturers calculate markup as a percentage of *cost,* since they typically keep their records in terms of cost. Some wholesalers and a few retailers also use this method. Most retailers, however, use the *selling price* as a base in computing markup, since they keep most of their records in terms of selling price.

Three basic formulas describe the relationship between cost, markup, and selling price, regardless of whether the markup is based on cost or selling price.

STEP BY STEP

Finding Selling Price, Cost, and Markup

1. To find selling price, we use this formula:

   Selling price = cost + markup, $S = C + M$

2. To find cost, we use a variation of the formula:

   Cost = selling price − markup, $C = S - M$

3. To find markup, we use another variation:

   Markup = selling price − cost, $M = S - C$

You can use these formulas to find the value of any one of the three elements if you know the values of the other two. Markup can be either a dollar amount or a percent. When it is expressed as a percent, it is expressed as a percent of cost or selling price.

Most markup problems give you two out of the three elements and ask you to find the third. To organize the information you have and determine what you need to find out, draw up a table with cost (C) and markup (M) on top and selling price (S) on the bottom, like this:

100%	C	$
%	M	$
%	S	$

To complete the table, place percents on the left and dollar amounts on the right.

Notice that when markup is based on cost, cost is always 100%, as noted in the table. The rest of the numbers, both percents and dollars, can be filled in according to the problem, as shown in the first example.

EXAMPLE 1

The Mad Hatter's Shoppe buys hats from Carroll Millinery for $3 each and sells them for $5 each. Find the amount of markup and the percent of markup based on cost.

First, use a table to set up the problem.

100%	C	$3
	M	
	S	$5

Remember, when doing a markup based on cost, the cost is always 100%. Fill in the other two amounts you know from the problem: cost = $3 and selling price = $5.

Since M is what you don't know, you need to use the formula $M = S - C$. Amount of markup = selling price − cost. The amount of markup is $2. Next, use the percentage formula to find the *percent* of markup. As you saw in Chapter 4, the percentage formula may be written $P = R \times B$, $R = \dfrac{P}{B}$, or $B = \dfrac{P}{R}$. When finding markup based on cost, use the cost as the *base*, the amount of markup as the *portion,* and the percent of markup as the *rate.* The percentage formula diagram is shown here in the margin.

Use the form $R = \dfrac{P}{B}$ of the percentage formula to find the percent of markup based on the cost.

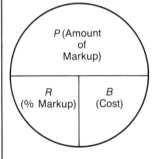

$$R = \frac{P}{B} = \frac{M}{C} = \frac{2}{3}$$

Divide the amount of markup (portion) by the cost (the base) to find the percent of markup (the rate).

$$= 0.6666, \text{ or } 67\% \text{ (rounded)} \quad \text{The rate of markup based on cost is } 67\%$$

Look back at the table: Cost plus markup equals selling price for both percents and dollar amounts.

100%	C	$3
67%	M	$2
167%	S	$5

Check:
$167\% \times 3 = 1.67 \times 3$ Cost ($3) is still the **base.**
$= \$5 \text{(rounded)}$ The answer is correct.

In most instances you may know the cost and the markup percent based on cost and need to find the amount of markup and the selling price. You can compute these amounts more easily if you use the table format.

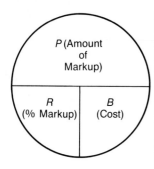

EXAMPLE 2

A boutique pays $5 a pair for handmade earrings and sells them at a 50% markup based on cost. Find the amount of markup and the selling price of the earrings.

Selling price = cost + amount of markup

$$
\begin{array}{rll}
100\% & C & \$5 \text{ (base)} \\
(\text{rate}) + \underline{50\%} & \underline{M} & \text{(portion)} \\
150\% & S &
\end{array}
$$

The markup is based on cost, so we know the cost is the base, or 100%. We add the cost percent (100) and the markup percent (50) to find the selling price percent.

Use the percentage formula $P = R \times B$ to find the amount of markup:

$$
\begin{aligned}
P &= 0.50 \times 5 \\
&= 2.50
\end{aligned}
$$

Multiply the markup percent (rate) times the cost (base) to find the amount of markup.

Now we can add the cost and markup and complete the table:

$$
\begin{array}{rll}
100\% & C & \$5 \\
+ 50\% & M & \$2.50 \\
\hline
150\% & S & \$7.50
\end{array}
$$

The selling price is $7.50.

Check:
$150\% \times 5 = 1.5 \times 5 = \$7.50$ The answer is correct.

To enhance sales, sometimes items are marked down from the selling price. Before making this decision, you would want to know how much the item costs. When researching the cost through invoices is impractical, you can calculate the cost and amount of markup by using the selling price and a standard markup percent.

EXAMPLE 3

A camera sells for $20. The markup is 50% of the cost. Find the cost of the camera and the amount of markup.

Selling price = cost + amount of markup

$$
\begin{array}{rlll}
100\% & C & & \\
+ 50\% & M & & \\
\hline
150\% & S & \$20 &
\end{array}
$$

The markup is based on cost, so we know the cost is the base, or 100%. We add the cost percent (100) and the markup percent (50) to find the selling price percent.

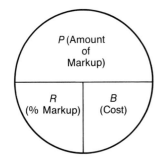

In this example, you must use 150% and $20 to find the cost (base). Thus, 150% of the cost equals $20. Since you are looking for the base, you use the formula $B = \dfrac{P}{R}$.

$$
B = \frac{P}{R} = \frac{20}{1.5} = \$13.33, \text{ rounded to the nearest cent}
$$

Thus, the cost is $13.33. To find the amount of markup, subtract: $20 - 13.33 = \$6.67$. Complete the table as a check:

$$
\begin{array}{rll}
100\% & C & \$13.33 \\
+ 50\% & M & \$ 6.67 \\
\hline
150\% & S & \$20.00
\end{array}
$$

Check:
$150\% \times 13.33 = 1.5 \times 13.33 = \$20$ (rounded)

As noted earlier, most retailers base markup on the selling price because this method works best with their other records. Just as when the markup is based on *cost,* the *cost* is the *base* and represents 100%, so when the markup is based on *selling price,* the *selling price* is the *base* and represents 100%.

EXAMPLE 4

A calculator costs $5 and sells for $10. Find the percent of markup based on the selling price.

Amount of markup = selling price − cost

	C	$ 5
+	M	
100%	S	$10

The markup is based on selling price, so you know the selling price is the base, or 100%.

$10
−$ 5
$ 5

Subtract the cost from the selling price to find the amount of markup.

The amount of markup, $5, is the portion, and the selling price, $10, is the base. Use the formula $R = \dfrac{P}{B}$ to find the rate:

$$R = \frac{P}{B} = \frac{5}{10} = 0.5 = 50\%$$

The percent of markup based on selling price is 50%.

Complete the table as a check of your work. To complete the table, you still need the percent that represents the cost.

50%	C	$ 5
+ 50%	M	$ 5
100%	S	$10

Subtract the markup percent from the selling price percent to find the cost percent (100% − 50% = 50%), completing the table.

Check:
50% × 10 = 0.5 × 10 = $5   The answer is correct.

In some instances you may have records indicating the amount of markup and the percent of markup without including either the cost or the selling price. While the cost and selling price can be calculated from the markup and percent of markup, it is not likely that this situation will occur often.

EXAMPLE 5

Find the cost and selling price if a textbook is marked up $5 with a 20% markup based on the selling price. (If the selling price percent is 100% and the markup is 20%, then the cost percent equals 100% − 20%, or 80%.)

Selling price = cost + amount of markup

80%	C	
20%	M	$ 5
100%	S	

The markup is based on selling price, so the selling price is the base, or 100%.

Use the formula $B = \dfrac{P}{R}$ to find the base or selling price. The portion is $5 and the rate is 20%, or 0.2.

$$B = \frac{P}{R} = \frac{\$5}{0.2} = \$25 \quad \text{The base or selling price is } \$25.$$

80%	C	$20	Complete the table.
20%	M	$ 5	$25 − $5 = $20.
100%	S	$25	

Check:
80% × 25 = 0.8 × 25 = $20   The answer is correct.

EXAMPLE 6

Find the markup and cost of a box of pencils that sells for $2.99 and is marked up 25% of the selling price.

Selling price = cost + amount of markup

75%	C		The markup is based on selling price, so
25%	M		the selling price is the base, or 100%.
100%	S	$2.99	

Since you are looking for the markup, or portion, use the basic formula $P = RB$. The selling price, or base, is $2.99, and the rate is 25%.

$P = RB$
$= 0.25(2.99)$
$= \$0.75$ (round to the nearest cent)

Multiply the rate times the base (selling price) to find the portion (markup).

75%	C	$2.24	Complete the table.
25%	M	$0.75	$2.99 − $0.75 = $2.24
100%	S	$2.99	

Check:
75% × 2.99 = 0.75 × 2.99
= $2.24 (rounded)   The answer is correct.

EXAMPLE 7

Find the selling price and amount of markup for a pair of jeans that costs the retailer $28 and is marked up 30% of the selling price.

100% − 30% = 70%   Selling price percent minus markup percent equals cost percent.

Selling price = cost + amount of markup

70%	C	$28	Markup is based on selling price, so the
30%	M		selling price is the base, or 100%.
100%	S		

You do not know the markup, so you cannot use the amount of markup to find the selling price. You do know the cost is $28, which is 70% of the selling price. Use the formula $B = \dfrac{P}{R}$ to find the selling price, or base.

$B = \dfrac{P}{R} = \dfrac{\$28}{0.7} = \$40$

Divide the portion (cost) by the rate to find the base (selling price).

70%	C	$28	($40 − $28 = $12)
30%	M	$12	
100%	S	$40	

Check:
30% × 40 = 0.3 × 40 = $12   The answer is correct.

All problems of this type are solved in basically the same way. The important thing to remember is that when the markup percent is based on the selling price, the selling price is the base and represents 100%; when the markup percent is based on the cost, the cost is the base and represents 100%. You can then use the percentage formula or one of its variations, substitute in the two known values, and solve for the third value.

Comparing Markup Based on the Cost with Markup Based on the Selling Price

If you go into a store and are told that the markup percent is 25%, you don't know whether that means markup based on cost or on selling price. What's the difference? Let's use a new computer as an example. The store pays $600 for it and sells it for $800. Here is the difference in percent of markup:

$$\frac{\$200 \text{ markup}}{\$800 \text{ selling price}} = 25\% \text{ markup based on selling price}$$

$$\frac{\$200 \text{ markup}}{\$600 \text{ cost}} = 33\frac{1}{3}\% \text{ markup based on cost}$$

There may be times when you need to switch from a markup based on cost to a markup based on selling price, or vice versa. Here is how to do it.

STEP BY STEP

Converting from Markup Percent Based on Selling Price to Markup Percent Based on Cost

Step 1. Find the percent of markup based on selling price.

Step 2. Use the following formula:

$$\frac{\text{Markup percent based on selling price (decimal form)}}{1 - \text{markup percent based on selling price (decimal form)}}$$

$$= \text{markup percent (decimal form) based on cost}$$

EXAMPLE 8

A desk is marked up 50% based on selling price. What is the equivalent percent based on the cost?

50% = 0.5   Convert the percent to a decimal and put it in the formula.

$$\frac{\text{Markup percent based on selling price}}{1 - \text{markup percent of selling price}} = \text{markup percent based on cost}$$

$$\frac{0.5}{1 - 0.5} = \frac{0.5}{0.5} = 1, \text{ or } 100\% \qquad \text{The markup based on cost is } 100\%.$$

Basic calculator using memory:

$$\boxed{AC} \ 1 \ \boxed{-} \ .5 \ \boxed{=} \ \boxed{M+} \ \boxed{C} \ .5 \ \boxed{\div} \ \boxed{MR} \ \boxed{=}$$
Display 1.

Calculator Solution

Scientific calculator using parenthesis:

$$\boxed{AC} \ .5 \ \boxed{\div} \ \boxed{(} \ 1 \ \boxed{-} \ .5 \ \boxed{)} \ \boxed{=}$$
Display   1.

STEP BY STEP

Converting from Markup Percent Based on Cost to Markup Percent Based on Selling Price

Step 1. Find the percent of markup based on cost.

Step 2. Use the following formula:

$$\frac{\text{Markup percent based on cost (decimal form)}}{1 + \text{markup percent based on cost (decimal form)}}$$

$$= \text{markup percent (decimal form) based on selling price}$$

EXAMPLE 9

A VCR is marked up 40% based on cost. What is the markup percent based on selling price?

40% = 0.4   Convert the percent to a decimal and use the formula.

$$\frac{\text{Markup percent based on cost}}{1 + \text{markup percent based on cost}} = \text{markup percent based on selling price}$$

$$\frac{0.4}{1 + 0.4} = \frac{0.4}{1.4}$$

= 0.2857, or 28.57%   The markup based on selling price is 28.57%.

Self-Check 7.1

1. Bottoms Up buys mugs for $2 each and sells them for $6 each. Find the amount of markup and the percent of markup based on the cost.

2. It's a Cinch pays $4 each for handmade belts and sells them at a 60% markup based on cost. Find the amount of markup and the selling price of the belts.

3. A compact disc player sells for $300. The markup is 40% of the cost. Find the cost of the CD player and the markup.

4. A compact disc costs $4 and sells for $12. Find the percent of markup based on the selling price.

5. Find the cost and selling price if a hard hat is marked up $5 with a 40% markup based on the selling price.

6. Find the markup and cost of a magazine that sells for $3.50 and is marked up 50% of the selling price.

7. Find the selling price and amount of markup if a box of photocopier paper costs $40 and is marked up 60% of the selling price.

8. A chair is marked up 60% based on selling price. What is the percent of markup based on cost?

9. A lamp is marked up 120% based on cost. What is the percent of markup based on the selling price?

7.2

Markdown

LEARNING OBJECTIVE

1. Calculate markdown.

Merchants often have to reduce the price of merchandise from the price at which it was originally marked. There are many reasons for this. Sometimes merchandise is marked too high to begin with. Sometimes it gets worn or dirty or goes out of style. Flowers, fruits, vegetables, and baked goods that have been around a day or two must be sold for less than fresh items. Competition from other stores may also require that a retailer lower prices.

Calculating Markdowns

No matter what the reason for the reduction in price, you can determine the amount of markdown by subtracting the sale price from the original selling price. You can then figure the percent of markdown by using a variation of the percentage formula, $R = \dfrac{P}{B}$.

STEP BY STEP

Calculating Amount of Markdown and Percent of Markdown

Step 1. Amount of markdown can be found with this formula:

Amount of markdown = original selling price − sale price

Step 2. Percent of markdown can then be found with the percentage formula:

$R = \dfrac{P}{B}$, where R = percent of markdown, B = original selling price, and P = amount of markdown

EXAMPLE 10

A lamp originally sold for $36 and was marked down to sell for $30. Find the *amount of markdown* and the *markdown percent* (to the nearest hundredth).

Markdown = original selling price − sale price

= $36 − $30 = $6 The amount of markdown was $6.

To find the markdown percent, use $36 (original price) as the base (B) and $6 (amount of markdown) as the portion (P). Use the formula $R = \dfrac{P}{B}$.

$R = \dfrac{P}{B}$ 　　　　　Divide the amount of markdown by the original selling price and change the decimal to a percent.

$= \dfrac{\text{amount of markdown}}{\text{original selling price}}$

$= \dfrac{\$6}{\$36} = 0.1667 = 16.67\%$ 　(rounded)

The lamp was marked down 16.67%.

If you know the original price of an item and the markdown percent, you can determine the amount of markdown and subtract this amount from the original price to get the sale price.

$$\text{Sale price} = \text{original selling price} - \text{markdown}$$

EXAMPLE 11

A wallet was originally priced at \$12 and was reduced by 25%. Find the amount of markdown and the sale price.

Use the percentage formula $P = RB$ to find the amount of markdown. The original price is the base.

$P = 25\% \times \$12 = 0.25 \times \$12$ The original price, \$12, is the base, and the rate is 25%.

   $= \$3$ The amount of markdown is \$3.

To find the sale price, use the markdown formula:

Sale price = original selling price − markdown

  $\$12 - \$3 = \$9$

The sale price is \$9.

 Self-Check 7.2

10. A typewriter originally sold for \$480 and was marked down to sell for \$420. Find the amount of markdown and the markdown percent.

11. A calculator that was originally priced at \$78 was reduced by 15%. Find the amount of markdown and the sale price (reduced price).

7.3 Markup and Markdown in the Marketplace

LEARNING OBJECTIVES

1. Calculate a series of markdowns and markups.
2. Calculate markup for perishable or seasonal items.

Prices are in a continuous state of flux in the business world. Markups are made to cover increased costs. Markdowns are made to move merchandise more rapidly or to move dated or perishable merchandise.

Calculating a Series of Markdowns and Markups

Every business expects to mark down the price of seasonal and slow-moving merchandise. Sometimes prices are marked down several times or marked up between markdowns before the merchandise is sold. The percent of each markdown is based on the *previous selling price*.

EXAMPLE 12

Belinda's China Shop paid a wholesale price of $600 for a set of imported china. Belinda marked up the china 50% on the selling price on August 8. On October 1, she marked the china down 25% for a special 10-day promotion. On October 11, she marked the china up 15%. The china was again marked down 30% for a preholiday sale. Because it still had not sold, it was marked down an additional 10% after the holidays. What was the final selling price of the china?

Original selling price

Selling price = cost + markup	Find the original selling price.
$C = \$600$, $M = 0.5S$	Markup was 50% of the selling price.
	$(50\% \times S = 0.5S)$

$$S = 600 + 0.5S$$
$$1.0S = 600 + 0.5S$$
$$\underline{-0.5S = \quad -0.5S}$$
$$0.5S = 600$$

Subtract $0.5S$ from each side of the equation.

$$\frac{0.5S}{0.5} = \frac{600}{0.5}$$

Divide each side of the equation by 0.5.

The original selling price was $1,200.

$$S = \frac{600}{0.5} = \$1,200$$

25% markdown on October 1

100% (original selling price) − 25% (markdown) = 75% (new selling price)

$1,200 × 75% = $1,200 × 0.75   The selling price from October 1 through
= **$900**   October 10 is 75% of the original price.

15% markup on October 11

100% (previous selling price) + 15% (markup) = 115% (new selling price)

$900 × 115% = $900 × 1.15   The selling price on October 11 is 115% of
= $1,035   the previous price (October 1 to 10).

30% markdown for preholiday sale

100% (previous selling price) − 30% (markdown) = 70% (new selling price)

1,035 × 70% = 1,035 × 0.70   The selling price for the preholiday sale is
= **$724.50**   70% of the previous (October 11) price.

Final markdown

100% − 10% = 90%   The china was finally
724.50 × 90% = 724.50 × 0.90 = $652.05.   priced at $652.05.

Calculating Markup and Markdown for Perishable or Seasonal Items

Most businesses anticipate that some seasonal merchandise will have to be marked down from the original selling price. Stores that sell perishable or strictly seasonal items (fresh fruits, vegetables, swimsuits, or coats, for example) usually anticipate from past experience how much merchandise will have to be marked down or thrown out due to spoilage. For example, most retail stores mark down holiday items to 50% of the original price the day after the holiday. Thus merchants set the original markup of such an item to obtain the desired profit level based on the projected number of items sold at "full price" (the original selling price).

EXAMPLE 13

Green's Grocery specializes in fresh fruits and vegetables. A portion of most merchandise must be reduced for quick sale, and some must be thrown out because of spoilage. Hardy Green, the owner, must mark the selling price of

---

REAL WORLD APPLICATION

Sale Prices

From 9.00 AM until noon Saturday
TAKE AN ADDITIONAL 25% OFF
Already Reduced Prices

No. _Donna's_
STYLE _#2684_
SIZE _Medium_
PRICE _$48.00_

During "off times" of the season or slow times of day, some department stores offer an extra incentive for shoppers as shown in the headlines above. How do you determine if you can afford the items advertised?

If a shirt is originally priced $48, a 20% discount gives a sale price of $38.40.

$P = RB$ The original price, $48, is the base; the rate is 20%.

$= 20\% \times \$48$

$= \$9.60$ The amount of markdown is $9.60.

Sale price = original price − markdown

$= \$48.00 - \$9.60$

$= \$38.40$

The additional 25% is taken off the sale price, which gives a final sale price of $28.80.

$P = RB$ The sale price, $38.40, is the base. The rate is the additional 25%.

$= 25\% \times \$38.40$

$= \$9.60$ The amount of markdown is $9.60.

Final sale price = sale price − markdown

$= \$38.40 - \$9.60$

$= \$28.80$

Your answer will not be the same if you add 20% and 25% and then find the sale price.

$P = RB$

$P = 45\% \times \$48$

$P = \$21.60$

Sale price = $48 − $21.60

$= \$26.40$ NOT THE SALE PRICE!

Application Questions

1. What is the final sale price of an item originally priced $110, if it is marked down 20% and an additional 10% is to be taken from this reduced price?

2. During a bonus sale at a local department store, you are given an additional 20% discount off the following already discounted ticketed items:

No. _Donna's_
STYLE _#7162_
SIZE _8_
PRICE _$31.99_

No. _Donna's_
STYLE _#237_
SIZE _−_
PRICE _$10.99_

No. _Donna's_
STYLE _#3762_
SIZE _8_
PRICE _$15.99_

What is your final total price to be paid?

3. From a sale rack marked 25% off, you select the following items:

Item	Original price
dress	$85
blouse	$25
slacks	$30
sweater	$40

Because you are shopping during an anniversary sale, you are given an additional 10% off. What is the total amount you have spent?

incoming produce high enough to make the desired amount of profit while taking expected markdowns and spoilage into account. Hardy receives 400 pounds of bananas, for which he pays $0.15 per pound. On the average, 8% of the bananas will spoil. Find the selling price per pound to obtain a 175% markup on cost.

$400 × 0.15 = $60	Figure the cost of the bananas to Hardy.
$60 × 1.75 = $105	Figure the dollar amount of markup.
$S = C + M$	Figure the total selling price.
= $60 + $105 = $165	Hardy must receive $165 for the bananas he expects to sell.
100% − 8% = 92%	If 8% of the bananas are likely to spoil, he
400 × 0.92 = 368	can expect to sell 92%. Find how many pounds he can expect to sell. He can expect to sell 368 pounds of bananas.

Find the selling price per pound.

$$\frac{\text{Total selling price}}{\text{Number of pounds expected to sell}} = \frac{\$165}{368} = \$0.448 \text{ or } \$0.45$$

Hardy must sell the bananas for $0.45 per pound to receive the profit he desires. If he sells more than 92% of the bananas, he will receive additional profit.

Self-Check 7.3

12. The Splash Shop paid a wholesale price of $24 each for Le Paris swimsuits. On May 5 it marked up the suits 50% of this cost. On June 15, the swimsuits were marked down 15% for a 2-day sale, and on June 17 they were marked up again by 10%. On August 30, the shop sold all remaining swimsuits for 40% off. What was the final selling price of a Le Paris swimsuit?

13. Farmer Brown's fruit stand sells fresh fruits and vegetables. Becky Brown, the manager, must mark the selling price of incoming produce high enough to make the desired amount of profit while taking expected markdowns and spoilage into account. Becky paid $0.35 per pound for 300 pounds of grapes. On the average, 12% of the grapes will spoil. Find the selling price per pound needed to obtain a 175% markup on cost.

Summary

Topic	Page	What to Remember	Examples
Markup based on cost	218	Selling price (S) = cost (C) + markup (M) Cost is the base, or 100%.	The next three examples show how to work with markup based on cost.
Finding markup	218	Markup amount = $S − C$	$C = \$2$, $S = \$4$. Find the markup amount and percent. $M = S − C = \$4 − \$2 = \$2$ The markup amount is $2. $\frac{\$2}{\$2} = 1 = 100\%$ The markup percent is 100%.

Topic	Page	What to Remember	Examples
Finding markup amount and selling price	219	The markup is based on cost, so C is the base, or 100%. Multiply the markup percent (rate) times the cost (base) to find the markup amount (portion).	$C = \$1.50$, $M = 40\%$. Find the markup amount and the selling price. Markup amount $= 0.40(1.50) = \$0.60$ $S = C +$ markup amount $\quad = \$1.50 + \$0.60 = \$2.10$ The markup amount is \$0.60 and the selling price is \$2.10. *Check:* $S = C +$ markup amount $\$2.10 = \$1.50 + \$0.60$
Finding the cost and the amount of markup	220	The markup is based on cost, so C is the base, or 100%, S is the portion, and the markup percent is the rate. Add the markup percent to the cost percent to find the selling price percent.	$S = C +$ markup amount $S = \$45$; M percent $= 60\% = 0.6$. Find the cost and the markup amount and percent. Cost = selling price divided by the selling price percent: $C = \dfrac{S}{S\%} = \dfrac{45}{1.6} = \$28.13$ The cost is \$28.13. Markup amount $= S - C = \$45 - \$28.13 = \$16.87$ *Check:* $S = C + M$ $\$28.13 + \$16.87 = \$45$
Markup based on selling price	221	Selling price $(S) =$ cost $(C) +$ markup amount (M) Selling price is the base, or 100%.	The next four examples show how to work with markup based on selling price.
Finding the markup percent based on selling price	221	S is the base, or 100%, the markup amount is the portion, and the percent of markup is the rate.	$S = \$80$, $C = \$60$. Find the markup percent. Markup amount $= S - C = \$80 - \$60 = \$20$ $R = \dfrac{P}{B} = \dfrac{20}{80} = 0.25 = 25\%$ *Check:* $S = C + M$ $\$80 = \$60 + \$20$
Finding cost and selling price	221	S is the base, or 100%, the markup amount is the portion, and the percent of markup is the rate.	Markup amount $= \$50$, markup percent $= 25\%$ $= 0.25$. Find the cost and selling price. $B = \dfrac{P}{R} = \dfrac{50}{0.25} = \$200$ The selling price is \$200. $C = S - M$ $\quad = \$200 - \$50 = \$150$ The cost is \$150. *Check:* $S = C + M$ $\$200 = \$150 + \$50$
Finding markup and cost	222	The selling price is the base, the markup amount is the portion, and the markup percent is the rate.	$S = \$12.80$ and markup percent $= 20\% = 0.2$. Use $P = RB$ to find the markup, or portion. $P = RB = 0.2 \times 12.8 = 2.56$ The markup amount is \$2.56. $C = S - M = \$12.80 - \$2.56 = \$10.24$ *Check:* $S = C + M$ $12.80 = \$10.24 + \$2.56$.

Topic	Page	What to Remember	Examples
Finding selling price and amount of markup	222	S is the base, or 100%, the cost is the portion of the selling price, and the markup percent is the rate.	$C = \$6.00$, markup percent $= 70\% = 0.7$ of the selling price. Cost $= 30\% = 0.3$ $0.3S = \$6.00$ $\dfrac{0.3S}{0.3} = \dfrac{6}{0.3}$ $S = \$20$ $M = S - C$ $\$20 - \$6 = \$14$ The markup amount is \$14.
Markdown	225	Markdown = original price − sale price and Sale price = original price − markdown $\dfrac{\text{Markdown amount}}{\text{original price}}$ $\qquad$ = markdown percent $\qquad\qquad$ (decimal form)	The next three examples show how to solve problems involving markdown.
Finding the markdown amount and percent	225	The original price is the base, or 100%, the markdown amount is the portion, and the markdown percent is the rate. Use $R = \dfrac{P}{B}$ to find the markdown percent. Markdown percent (decimal form) $\qquad = \dfrac{\text{markdown amount}}{\text{original price}}$	Original price $= \$4.50$, sale price $= \$3$. Find the markdown amount and percent. Markdown = original price − sale price $= \$4.50 - \$3.00 = \$1.50$ The markdown amount is \$1.50. $\dfrac{1.50}{4.50} = 33\%$ (rounded) The markdown percent is 33%.
Finding the amount of markdown and the sale price	226	The original price is the base, the markdown amount is the portion, and the markdown percent is the rate. Use the formula $P = RB$.	Original price $= \$780$, markdown percent $= 20\% = 0.2$. Find the amount of markdown and the sale price Markdown amount $\qquad$ = markdown percent × original price $\qquad = 0.2 \times \$780 = \$156$ The markdown amount is \$156. Sale price = original price − markdown $\qquad = \$780 - \$156 = \$624$ The sale price is \$624.
Calculating a series of markdowns and markups	226	Each markup or markdown is taken on the previous selling price. Multiply the previous selling price by the decimal complement of the markdown percent to find the new price after a markdown. Multiply the previous price by 1 plus the decimal form of the markup percent to find the new price after a markup.	Cost $= \$7$. Marked up 70% on cost, then marked down 20%, marked down an additional 10%, then marked up 20%, and marked down a final 25%. What was the final price? $7 \times 1.7 = \$11.90$ $11.90 \times 0.8 = 9.52$ $9.52 \times 0.9 = 8.57$ $8.57 \times 1.2 = 10.28$ $10.28 \times 0.75 = 7.71$. The final price was \$7.71.
Setting the price of perishable items	227	Figure the total cost, the amount of markup needed, and the total selling price. Figure how much of the item is likely to be sold and divide that amount into the total selling price.	400 lemons cost \$25, and 25% are expected to rot before being sold. A 75% markup on cost is needed. Total selling price: $\$25 \times 1.75 = \$43.75$ Number expected to sell $= 400 \times 0.75 = 300$ Selling price per lemon $= \dfrac{\$43.75}{300} = \$0.15$ The lemons should be sold at \$0.15 each.

Self-Check Solutions

1.

100%	C	\$2
200%	M	\$4
300%	S	\$6

$\text{Markup} = S - C = \$6 - \$2 = \$4$

$$\left(\begin{array}{l}\text{Percent of markup}\\\text{based on cost}\end{array}\right) = \frac{P\ (\text{markup})}{B\ (\text{cost})} = \frac{\$4}{\$2} = 2 = 200\%$$

2.

100%	C	\$4.00
60%	M	\$2.40
160%	S	\$6.40

$\text{Markup} = R\ (\text{percent markup}) \times B\ (\text{cost})$

$= 0.60 \times \$4 = \$2.40$

$\text{Selling price} = C + M = \$4 + \$2.40 = \$6.40$

3.

100%	C	\$214.29
40%	M	\$ 85.71
140%	S	\$300.00

$C\% + M\% = S\%$

$100\% + 40\% = 140\%$

$$\text{Cost} = \frac{P\ (\text{selling price})}{R\ (\text{percent of selling price based on cost})}$$

$$= \frac{\$300}{1.4} = \$214.29 \text{ (rounded)}$$

$\text{Markup} = S - C = \$300 - \$214.29 = \$85.71$

4.

33.33%	C	\$ 4
66.67%	M	\$ 8
100 %	S	\$12

Find amount of markup first.

$M = S - C = \$12 - \$4 = \$8$

$$\left(\begin{array}{l}\text{Percent of markup}\\\text{based on selling price}\end{array}\right) = \frac{P\ (\text{markup})}{B\ (\text{selling price})} = \frac{\$8}{\$12}$$

$$= 0.6667$$

$$= 66.67\%$$

5.

60%	C	\$ 7.50
40%	M	\$ 5.00
100%	S	\$12.50

$S\% - M\% = C\%$

$100\% - 40\% = 60\%$

$$\text{Selling price} = \frac{P\ (\text{amount of markup})}{R\ \left(\begin{array}{l}\text{percent of markup}\\\text{based on selling price}\end{array}\right)} = \frac{\$5}{0.4} = \$12.50$$

$C = S - M = \$12.50 - \$5 = \$7.50$

6.

50%	C	\$1.75
50%	M	\$1.75
100%	S	\$3.50

$S\% - M\% = C\%$

$100\% - 50\% = 50\%$

$\text{Markup} = B\ (\text{selling price}) \times R\ (\text{percent markup based on selling price})$

$= \$3.50 \times 0.5 = \$1.75$

Since the markup and cost are represented by the same percents, their dollar amounts will be equal.

7.

40%	C	$ 40
60%	M	$ 60
100%	S	$100

$S\% - M\% = C\%$

$100\% - 60\% = 40\%$

$$\text{Selling price} = \frac{P \text{ (cost)}}{R \text{ (percent of cost based on selling price)}}$$

$$= \frac{\$40}{0.4} = \$100$$

$$M = S - C = \$100 - \$40 = \$60$$

8. Markup percent based on cost

$$= \frac{\text{markup percent based on selling price}}{1 - \text{markup percent based on selling price}}$$

$$= \frac{0.60}{1 - 0.60} = \frac{0.60}{0.40} = 1.5, \text{ or } 150\%$$

9. Markup percent based on selling price

$$= \frac{\text{markup percent based on cost}}{1 + \text{markup percent based on cost}} = \frac{1.20}{1 + 1.20} = \frac{1.20}{2.20} = 0.5455, \text{ or}$$

$$54.55\%$$

10. Markdown = original selling price − sale price

$$= \$480 - \$420 = \$60$$

$$\% \text{ markdown} = \frac{P}{B} = \frac{\$60}{\$480} = 0.125 = 12.5\%$$

11. Markdown = $R \times B = 0.15 \times \$78 = \$11.70$

Sale price = original price − markdown = $\$78 - \$11.70 = \$66.30$

12. *May 5 markup:*

Markup = $R \times B = 0.5 \times \$24 = \$12$

$S = C + M = \$24 + \$12 = \$36$ (original selling price)

June 15 markdown:

Markdown = $R \times B = 0.15 \times \$36 = \$5.40$

Sale price = $\$36 - \$5.40 = \$30.60$

June 17 markup:

Markup = $R \times B = 0.10 \times \$30.60 = \$3.06$

New marked price = $\$30.60 + \$3.06 = \$33.66$

August 30 markdown:

Markdown = $R \times B = 0.40 \times \$33.66 = \$13.46$

Final sale price = $\$33.66 - \$13.46 = \$20.20$

13.

$$\text{Cost} = 300 \times \$0.35 = \$105$$

$$\text{Amount of markup} = \$105 \times 1.75 = \$183.75$$

$$\text{Total selling price} = C + M = \$105 + \$183.75 = \$288.75$$

$$\% \text{ of grapes expected to sell} = 100\% - 12\% = 88\%$$

$$\binom{\text{Pounds of grapes}}{\text{expected to sell}} = 300 \times 0.88 = 264 \text{ pounds}$$

$$\text{Selling price per pound} = \frac{\$288.75}{264} = \$1.09 \text{ per pound}$$

End of Chapter Problems

In each of the following, find the missing numbers in the table if the markup is based on the cost.

1. 100% C $50
    50% M $25
         S

2. C $4
    25% M $1
          S

3. 100% C $41
    100% M
          S

4. C $25
         M
         S $30

In each of the following, find the missing numbers in the table if the markup is based on the selling price.

5. 42% C $38
         M
    100% S

6.

	C	$86
50%	M	
	S	

7.

	C	
15%	M	$8
	S	

8. 42%

	C	$16
	M	
	S	

Solve the following problems. Be careful to notice whether markup is based on the cost or the selling price.

9. A hairdryer costs $15 and is marked up 40%. Find the markup and selling price based on the cost.

10. A hairbrush costs $3 and is marked up 40%. Find the markup and selling price based on the cost.

236 _____

11. A blender is marked up $9 and sells for $45. Find the cost and markup percent if the markup is based on the cost.

12. A package of cassette tapes costs $12 and is marked up $7.20. Find the selling price and percent of markup based on the cost.

13. A computer table sells for $198.50 and costs $158.70. Find the markup and markup percent based on the cost. Round to the nearest tenth percent.

14. Find the cost and markup on an office chair if the selling price is $75 and this item is marked up 100% of the cost.

15. If a flower arrangement is marked up $12, which is 50% of the cost, find the cost and selling price.

16. A toaster sells for $28.70 and has a markup of 50% based on the selling price. Find the amount of markup and the cost.

17. A briefcase is marked up $15.30, which is 30% of the selling price. Find the cost and selling price of the item.

18. A three-ringed binder costs $4.60 and is marked up $3.07. Find the selling price and the percent of markup based on the selling price. Round percents to the nearest hundredth.

19. A hole punch costs $40 and sells for $58.50. Find the percent of markup based on selling price and the amount of markup. Round percents to the nearest hundredth.

20. A pair of bookends sells for $15. Its cost is $10. Find the percent of markup based on the selling price.

21. A desk organizer sells for $35, which includes a markup of 60% of the selling price. Find the cost and amount of markup.

Fill in the blanks in Exercises 22 through 33. Round percents to the nearest hundredth percent. (The answers for Exercises 22 through 33 are given first. The solutions follow.)

	Cost	Markup	Selling Price	Markup Percent Based on Cost	Markup Percent Based on Selling Price
22.	$ 38	$ 20	$_____	_____	_____
23.	$___	$ 32	$ 89	_____	_____
24.	$486	_____	_____	_____	30%
25.	$ 1.56	_____	$ 2	_____	—
26.	_____	$ 5.89	_____	15%	_____
27.	_____	$ 27.38	_____	40%	_____
28.	$ 25	_____	_____	_____	48%
29.	_____	_____	$124	150%	—
30.	_____	$ 28	_____	_____	27%
31.	_____	_____	$ 18.95	_____	15%
32.	$ 16.28	$ 15.92	_____	_____	_____
33.	$ 8.99	_____	_____	21%	_____

Room has been left here for your worked out solutions to Exercises 22 through 33.

22.

23.

24.

25.

26.

27.

28.

29.

30.

31.

32.

33.

34. A fiberglass shower surround originally sold for $379.98 and was marked down to sell for $341.98. Find the amount of markdown and the markdown percent.

35. A three-speed fan originally sold for $29.88 and was reduced to sell for $25.40. Find the amount of markdown and the markdown percent.

36. An area rug originally sold for $89.99 and was reduced to sell for $65. Find the amount of markdown and the markdown percent.

37. A room air conditioner that originally sold for $509.99 was reduced to sell for $400. Find the amount of markdown and the markdown percent.

38. A portable CD player was originally priced at $249.99 and was reduced by 20%. Find the amount of markdown and the sale price (reduced price).

39. A set of rollers was originally priced at $39.99 and was reduced by 30%. Find the amount of markdown and the sale price.

40. A set of stainless cookware was originally priced at $79 and was reduced by 25%. Find the amount of markdown and the sale price.

41. A down comforter was originally priced at $280 and was reduced by 64%. Find the amount of markdown and the sale price.

42. Crystal stemware originally marked to sell for $31.25 was reduced 20% for a special promotion. The stemware was then reduced an additional 30% to turn inventory. What were the amount of markdown and the sale price for each reduction?

43. A camcorder that originally sold for $1,199 was reduced to sell for $999. It was then reduced an additional 40%. What were the amount of markdown and markdown percent for the first reduction, and what was the final selling price for the camcorder?

44. James McDonell operates a vegetable store. He purchases 800 pounds of potatoes at $0.18 per pound. If he anticipates a spoilage rate of 20% of the potatoes and wishes to make a profit of 140% of the purchase, how much must he mark the potatoes per pound?

45. Helen Jimenez received a shipment of oranges that was shipped after a severe frost, so she expects losses to be high. She paid $0.26 per pound for the 500 pounds and expects to lose 35% of the oranges. If she wishes to make 125% markup on cost, find the selling price per pound.

Additional Problems

1. Loose-leaf paper in a college bookstore is marked up 30% of its cost. Find the cost if the selling price is $2.34 per package.

2. A $5\frac{1}{4}$-inch double-sided, double-density floppy disk costs $0.90 and sells for $1.50. Find the percent of markup based on selling price.

3. A radio sells for $45, which includes a markup of 65% of the selling price. Find the cost and the amount of markup.

4. Laura Kee purchased a small refrigerator for her dorm room for $95.20, which included a markup of $27.20 based on the cost. Find the cost and percent of markup.

5. A receiving clerk is asked to price a shipment of sweatshirts by marking them up 45% of the cost. If the sweatshirts cost $20 each, how much is the markup and what is the selling price?

6. Anna White waited for a sale to buy the sweater she wanted. If the sweater is on sale for 30% off the selling price, how much will she pay for the sweater originally marked $47.50?

7. A male Siamese fighting fish was marked down 75% in a pet shop's going-out-of-business sale. If the fish was on sale for $3.50, how much was the original selling price?

8. Willie Spritzer operates a seafood market. Mr. Spritzer purchased 50 dozen live blue crabs at $5.50 a dozen. If he anticipates a loss of 12% of the live crabs and wishes to make a profit of 125% of the purchase, how much must he mark the live crabs per dozen?

9. A stopwatch originally sold for $16.50 and was reduced to sell for $11.50. Find the amount of markdown and the markdown percent. (Round percent to the nearest whole number).

10. Teddy Jeanfreau ordered 600 pounds of Red Delicious apples for the produce section of the supermarket. He paid $0.32 per pound for the apples and expected 15% of them to spoil. If the store wants to make a markup on cost of 90%, what should be the per-pound selling price?

Challenge Problem

Oh, But for Defects!

Pro Peds, a local athletic shoe manufacturer, makes a training sneaker at a cost of $8.40 per pair. A check of previous factory runs indicates that 10% of the sneakers will be defective and must be sold to Odd Tops, Inc. as irregulars for $12 per pair. If Pro Peds produces 1,000 pairs of the sneakers and desires a mark up of 100% on cost, find the selling price per pair of the regular shoes.

Trial Test

1. A calculator sells for $23.99 and cost $16.83. What is the markup?

2. A mixer sells for $109.98 and has a markup of $36.18. Find the cost.

3. A cookbook has a 34% markup on cost. If the markup is $5.27, find the cost of the cookbook.

4. A computer stand sells for $385. What is the amount of markup if it is 45% of the selling price?

5. A box of computer paper costs $16.80. Find the selling price if there is a 35% markup based on cost.

6. The reduced price of a dress is $54.99. Find the original price if a reduction of 40% is taken.

7. A daily organizer that originally sold for $86.90 was discounted 30%. What is the amount of discount?

8. What is the discount price of the organizer in Problem 7?

9. If a television cost $87.15 and was marked up $39.60, what is the selling price?

10. A refrigerator that sells for $387.99 was marked down $97. What is the sale price?

11. What was the percent of markdown for the refrigerator in Problem 10?

12. A wallet cost $16.05 to produce. The wallet sells for $25.68. What is the percent markup on cost?

13. A lamp costs $88. What is the selling price if the markup is 45% of the selling price?

14. A file cabinet originally sold for $215 but was damaged and had to be reduced. If the reduced cabinet sold for $129, what was the percent of markdown based on the original price?

15. A bookcase desk originally sold for $129.99 was marked down 25%. During the sale it was damaged and had to be reduced by 50% more. What was the final selling price of the desk?

16. Donald Byrd, the accountant for Quick Stop Shop, calculates the selling price for all produce. If 400 pounds of potatoes were purchased for $0.13 per pound and 18% of the potatoes were expected to rot before being sold, determine the price per pound that the potatoes must sell for if a profit of 120% of the purchase price is desired.

Copyright 1992, USA TODAY. Reprinted with permission.

QUESTIONS

1. Find the percent of markdown based on the original selling price for the model ST-88 tripod to the nearest whole percent.

3. Find the percent of markdown based on the original selling price for the model C280 tripod to the nearest whole percent.

2. Find the percent of markdown based on the manufacturer's suggested retail price for the model ST-88 tripod to the nearest whole percent.
Markdown percent based on manufacturer's suggested retail price:

4. Find the percent of markdown based on the manufacturer's suggested retail price for the model C280 tripod to the nearest whole percent.

8

Simple Interest and Simple Discount

interest: the price or fee for using money.

simple interest: the amount of money paid or earned on a loan or investment of a lump sum for a specified period of time.

compound interest: a procedure for calculating interest at regular intervals, covered in Chapter 9.

principal: the amount of money borrowed or invested.

rate: the percent or decimal or fractional equivalent of the percent that is charged or earned for the use of money.

time: the number of days, months, or years that money is loaned or invested.

Every business and every person at some time borrows or invests money. A person (or business) who borrows money must pay for the use of the money. A person who invests money will be paid by the person or firm who uses the money. The price paid for using money is called **interest.**

In the business world, we encounter two basic kinds of interest, *simple* and *compound.* **Simple interest** is used when a loan or investment is repaid in a lump sum. The person using the money has use of the full amount of money for the entire time of the loan or investment. **Compound interest,** which is explained in Chapter 9, most often applies to savings accounts, installment, loans and credit cards.

Both types of interest take into account three factors: the principal, the interest rate, and the time period of borrowing. **Principal** is the amount of money borrowed or invested. **Rate** is the percent of interest charged on the loan or earned on the investment each year. The rate, or percent, is always written as a decimal number or fraction when we solve simple interest problems. **Time** is the number of days, months, or years that the money is borrowed or invested. In solving problems, the time is usually written as a number of years or as a fraction of a year.

248

8.1

Using the Simple Interest Formula

LEARNING OBJECTIVES

1. Find simple interest.
2. Determine the maturity value of a loan.
3. Find time in fractional parts of a year.
4. Use variations of the simple interest formula.

Finding Simple Interest

The following formula shows how interest, principal, rate and time are related in simple interest problems and gives us a way of figuring one of these values if the other three values are known.

STEP BY STEP

Simple Interest Formula

$$\text{Interest} = \text{Principal} \times \text{Rate} \times \text{Time}$$

$$I = PRT$$

I = amount of interest, P = amount of principal, R = percent of interest or rate, and T = time of loan

Remember, in solving problems, rate must *always* be written in decimal or fraction form, and time is generally written as a number of years or a fraction of a year.

EXAMPLE 1

Find the interest paid on a loan of $1,500 for 1 year at a simple annual interest rate of 12%.

$I = PRT$	Use the simple interest formula.
I is unknown.	
$P = \$1,500$	
$R = 12\% = 0.12$	Write the rate in decimal form.
$T = 1$ year	
$I = (\$1,500)(0.12)(1) = \$180$	Substitute numbers for letters in the equation and multiply.

The interest on the loan is $180.

EXAMPLE 2

The Kanette's Salon borrowed $5,000 at $12\frac{1}{2}\%$ simple interest for 2 years to buy new hair dryers. How much interest did it pay?

$I = PRT$ Use the simple interest formula.

I is unknown.

$P = \$5000$

$R = 12\frac{1}{2}\% = 0.125$ (See Chapter 4, Example 4, if you need to review changing a mixed percent to a decimal.)

$T = 2$ years

$I = (\$5,000)(0.125)(2)$ Substitute numbers for letters and multiply.
   $= \$1,250$

Kanette's Salon will pay $1,250 interest.

Determining the Maturity Value of a Loan

maturity value: the amount of principal plus the amount of interest.

    The *total* amount of money due at the end of a loan period—the amount of the loan *and* the interest—is called the **maturity value** of the loan. A formula that can be used to find the maturity value of a loan is $MV = P(1 + rt)$, where MV is the maturity value of the loan, P is the principal, r is the rate, and t is the time expressed in years. This formula is often used when the maturity value is desired, rather than the amount of interest, because the maturity value can be found without first finding the interest.

STEP BY STEP

Finding the Maturity Value of a Loan

Maturity value = amount of principal + amount of interest

or

$$\text{Maturity value} = \text{principal } (1 + \text{rate} \times \text{time})$$
$$MV = P(1 + rt)$$

EXAMPLE 3

How much money will the Kanette's Salon (Example 2) pay at the end of 2 years?

Maturity value = principal + interest
$$= \$5,000 + \$1,250 = \$6,250$$

or

$MV = P(1 + rt)$

$MV = \$5,000(1 + 0.125 \times 2)$ Multiply in parentheses then add.

$MV = \$6,250$

Kanette's Salon will pay $6,250 at the end of the loan period.

Finding Time in Fractional Parts of a Year

    Not all loans or investments are made for a whole number of years, but time *is* figured in years unless otherwise specified. To convert months to the decimal equivalent of a year, *divide* the number of months by 12.

EXAMPLE 4

Convert 5 months and 15 months to years, expressed in decimal form.

5 months = $\dfrac{5}{12}$ year   5 months equal $\dfrac{5}{12}$ year.

$\begin{array}{r} 0.4166666 \\ 12\overline{)5.0000000} \end{array}$ year = 0.42 year   To write the fraction as a decimal, divide the number of months (the numerator) by the number of months in a year (the denominator).

5 months = 0.42 year (rounded)

15 months = $\dfrac{15}{12}$ years   15 months equal $\dfrac{15}{12}$ years.

$\begin{array}{r} 1.25 \\ 12\overline{)15.00} \end{array}$ years   To write the fraction as a decimal, divide the number of months (the numerator) by the number of months in a year (the denominator).

15 months = 1.25 years

EXAMPLE 5

To save money for a shoe-repair shop, Stan Upright invested $2,500 for 45 months at $12\frac{1}{2}\%$ interest. How much interest did he earn?

$I = PRT$ Use the simple interest formula.

I is unknown.

$P = \$2,500$

$R = 12\frac{1}{2}\% = 0.125$ Write the rate as a decimal number.

$T = 45 \text{ months} = \dfrac{45}{12}$ years   Write the time in terms of years.

$I = \$2,500(0.125)\left(\dfrac{45}{12}\right)$ Substitute numbers for letters, multiply, and round to the nearest cent.
$ = \$1,171.88$

Stan Upright earned $1,171.88 in interest.

When time is expressed in months, the calculator sequence is the same as when time is expressed in years, except that we do not enter a whole number for the time. Instead, we enter the months, divide by 12, and then press the = key. All other steps are the same. To solve the equation using a calculator without the percent key, use the decimal equivalent of $12\frac{1}{2}\%$.

$\boxed{AC}$ 2500 $\boxed{\times}$ .125 $\boxed{\times}$ 45 $\boxed{\div}$ 12 $\boxed{=}$ ⇒ 1171.875

To solve the equation using a calculator with a percent key, enter

$\boxed{AC}$ 2500 $\boxed{\times}$ 12.5 $\boxed{\%}$ $\boxed{\times}$ 45 $\boxed{\div}$ 12 ⇒ 1171.875

Calculator Solution

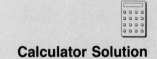

Using Variations of the Simple Interest Formula

So far in this chapter, we have used the formula $I = PRT$ to find the simple interest on a loan. However, sometimes you need to find the principal

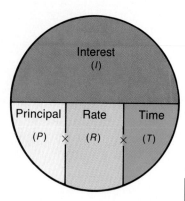

Figure 8-1 A Diagram of the Simple Interest Formula

or the rate or the time instead of the interest. You can remember the different forms of this formula with a circle diagram (see Figure 8-1) like the one used for percents. Cover the unknown term with your finger to see the correct form of the simple interest formula needed to find the missing value:

$$I = PRT \qquad P = \frac{I}{RT} \qquad R = \frac{I}{PT} \qquad T = \frac{I}{PR}$$

EXAMPLE 6

To buy new knives for his restaurant, Mr. Cooke borrowed $800 for $3\frac{1}{2}$ years and paid $348 simple interest on the loan. What rate of interest did he pay?

REAL WORLD APPLICATION

Balloon Payment Loans

Are you interested in buying a "new" used car or installing a pool? A simple interest loan with a low monthly payment sounds good, but be sure you understand what this monthly payment means.

A simple interest loan with a final "balloon payment" can be a good deal for both the consumer and the banker. For the banker, this loan reduces the rate risk, since the loan rate is actually locked in for a short period of time. For the consumer, this loan allows you to make lower monthly payments.

Example: You borrow $5,000 at 13% simple interest rate for a year.

For 12 monthly payments:

$$\$5,000 \times 13\% \times 1 = \$650 \text{ interest}$$

$$\frac{\$5,650}{12} = \$470.83 \text{ monthly payment}$$

Your banker will offer to make the loan as if it is to be extended over 5 years, or 60 monthly payments. This means a much lower monthly payment.

For 60 monthly payments:

$$\frac{\$5,650}{60} = \$94.17 \text{ monthly payment}$$

The lower monthly payment is tempting! The banker will expect you to make these lower payments for a year. You will actually make 11 payments of $94.17:

$$\$94.17 \times 11 = \$1,035.87 \text{ amount paid during the first 11 months}$$

The 12th and final payment, the *balloon payment*, is the *remainder* of the loan:

$$\$5,650 - \$1,035.87 = \$4,614.13$$

At this time you are expected to pay the balance of the loan in the balloon payment shown above. Don't panic!

Usually the loan is refinanced for another year. But beware—you may have to pay a higher interest rate for the next year.

Application Questions

1. Find the monthly payment for a $2,500 loan at 12% interest for 1 year extended over a 3-year period.

2. What is the amount of the final balloon payment for a $1,000 loan at 10% interest for 1 year, extended over 5 years?

3. a. You need a loan of $5,000 at 10% interest for 1 year. What is the amount of the monthly payment?

b. If your banker agrees to extend the monthly payments over 2 years, how much will your monthly payments be? How much will the final balloon payment be?

$$R = \frac{I}{PT}$$

R is unknown.
$I = \$348$
$P = \$800$
$T = 3.5$ years

$$R = \frac{348}{(800)(3.5)} = 0.124$$

Find the correct form of the simple interest formula on the circle diagram.

Substitute numbers for letters in the equation; then multiply, divide, and round.

$0.124 = 12.4\%$

Change the rate from decimal form to percent form by moving the decimal point two places to the right.

He paid 12.4% interest.

Multiply $P \times T$, store the result in memory, and divide I by the stored product:

Calculator Solution

$\boxed{AC}$ 800 $\boxed{\times}$ 3.5 $\boxed{=}$ $\boxed{M^+}$ $\boxed{CE/C}$ 348 $\boxed{\div}$ $\boxed{MRC}$ $\boxed{=}$ $\Rightarrow$ 0.1242857, or

Divide I by P and divide the result by T:

$\boxed{AC}$ 348 $\boxed{\div}$ 800 $\boxed{\div}$ 3.5 $\boxed{=}$ $\Rightarrow$ 0.1242857

EXAMPLE 7

Ms. Cox wanted to borrow some money to expand her egg farm. She was told she could borrow a sum of money for 18 months at 18% simple interest and pay $540 in interest charges. How much money could she borrow?

$$P = \frac{I}{RT}$$

Find the correct form of the simple interest formula on the circle diagram.

P is unknown
$I = \$540$
$R = 18\% = 0.18$
$T = 18$ months $= \dfrac{18}{12}$
$\phantom{T = 18 \text{ months}} = 1.5$ years

$$P = \frac{540}{0.18(1.5)} = \$2,000$$

Substitute numbers for letters in the equation, multiply, and divide.

The principal is $2,000.

Multiply $R \times T$, store the result in memory, and divide I by the stored product:

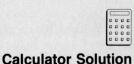

Calculator Solution

$\boxed{AC}$ .18 $\boxed{\times}$ 1.5 $\boxed{=}$ $\boxed{M^+}$ $\boxed{CE/C}$ 540 $\boxed{\div}$ $\boxed{MRC}$ $\boxed{=}$ $\Rightarrow$ 2000, or

Divide I by R and divide the result by T.

$\boxed{AC}$ 540 $\boxed{\div}$ .18 $\boxed{\div}$ 1.5 $\boxed{=}$ $\Rightarrow$ 2000

EXAMPLE 8

Lee's Tree Service borrowed $2,400 at 14% simple interest to repair its tree-topper. If it paid $840 interest, what was the duration of the loan?

$$T = \frac{I}{PR}$$

Find the correct form of the simple interest formula on the circle diagram.

T is unknown.
$I = \$840$
$P = \$2,400$
$R = 14\% = 0.14$

$$T = \frac{840}{2,400(0.14)} = 2.5 \text{ years}$$

Substitute numbers for letters in the equation, multiply, and divide.

The duration of the loan is 2.5 years.

 Self-Check 8.1

1. Find the interest paid on a loan of $2,400 for 1 year at a simple interest rate of 11%.

2. Find the interest paid on a loan of $800 at $8\frac{1}{2}\%$ simple interest for 2 years.

3. Find the total amount of money (maturity value) that the borrower will pay back on a loan of $1,400 at $12\frac{1}{2}\%$ simple interest for 3 years.

4. Convert the following to years, expressed in decimal form: 8 months, 40 months

5. Maddy Brown needed start-up money for her bakery. She borrowed $1,200 for 30 months and paid $360 simple interest on the loan. What interest rate did she pay?

6. Raul Fletes needed money to buy lawn equipment. He borrowed $500 for 7 months and paid $53.96 in interest. What was the rate of interest?

7. Linda Davis agreed to lend money to Alex Luciano at a special interest rate of 9%, on the condition that he borrow enough that he would pay her $500 in interest over a 2-year period. What was the minimum amount Alex could borrow?

8. Rob Thweatt needed money for college. He borrowed $6,000 at 12% simple interest. If he paid $360 interest, what was the duration of the loan?

 8.2

Ordinary and Exact Time

ordinary time: 30 days per month regardless of the month of the year.

ordinary interest: interest that is calculated using 360 days as the denominator of the time fraction.

exact time: the exact number of days of a loan or investment.

exact interest: interest that is calculated using 365 days (or 366 days in a leap year) as the denominator of the time fraction.

LEARNING OBJECTIVES

1. Find ordinary and exact time.
2. Find the due date.
3. Use time fractions in the interest formula.
4. Use tables to calculate simple interest.

Sometimes the time of a loan is indicated by the beginning and ending dates of the loan rather than by a specific number of months or days. In such cases, you must first determine the number of days to be counted in each month. If you count 30 days in each month, the time is **ordinary.** If you count the exact number of days in a month, the time is **exact time.** Interest is called **ordinary interest** when 360 is used for the denominator of the time fraction. Interest is called **exact interest** when 365 (or 366 in a leap year) is used for the denominator of the time fraction.

Table 8-1 The Number of Each Day of the Year (for Calculating Dates)

Days of month	Jan.	Feb.	Mar.	Apr.	May	Jun.	Jul.	Aug.	Sept.	Oct.	Nov.	Dec.
1	1	32	60	91	121	152	182	213	244	274	305	335
2	2	33	61	92	122	153	183	214	245	275	306	336
3	3	34	62	93	123	154	184	215	246	276	307	337
4	4	35	63	94	124	155	185	216	247	277	308	338
5	5	36	64	95	125	156	186	217	248	278	309	339
6	6	37	65	96	126	157	187	218	249	279	310	340
7	7	38	66	97	127	158	188	219	250	280	311	341
8	8	39	67	98	128	159	189	220	251	281	312	342
9	9	40	68	99	129	160	190	221	252	282	313	343
10	10	41	69	100	130	161	191	222	253	283	314	344
11	11	42	70	101	131	162	192	223	254	284	315	345
12	12	43	71	102	132	163	193	224	255	285	316	346
13	13	44	72	103	133	164	194	225	256	286	317	347
14	14	45	73	104	134	165	195	226	257	287	318	348
15	15	46	74	105	135	166	196	227	258	288	319	349
16	16	47	75	106	136	167	197	228	259	289	320	350
17	17	48	76	107	137	168	198	229	260	290	321	351
18	18	49	77	108	138	169	199	230	261	291	322	352
19	19	50	78	109	139	170	200	231	262	292	323	353
20	20	51	79	110	140	171	201	232	263	293	324	354
21	21	52	80	111	141	172	202	233	264	294	325	355
22	22	53	81	112	142	173	203	234	265	295	326	356
23	23	54	82	113	143	174	204	235	266	296	327	357
24	24	55	83	114	144	175	205	236	267	297	328	358
25	25	56	84	115	145	176	206	237	268	298	329	359
26	26	57	85	116	146	177	207	238	269	299	330	360
27	27	58	86	117	147	178	208	239	270	300	331	361
28	28	59	87	118	148	179	209	240	271	301	332	362
29	29	*	88	119	149	180	210	241	272	302	333	363
30	30		89	120	150	181	211	242	273	303	334	364
31	31		90		151		212	243		304		365

*See the discussion on leap year. For centennial years (those at the turn of the century), leap years occur only when the number of the year is divisible by 400. Thus, 2000 will be a leap year (2000/400 divides exactly), but 1700, 1800, and 1900 were not leap years.

Suppose you take out a loan on July 12 that is due September 12. If you use ordinary time, you consider the time to be 2 months, 2 × 30 days = 60 days. If you figure the exact time, you must add the 19 days remaining in July, the 31 days in August, and the 12 days in September, to get the total of 62 days. This calculation is much simpler if you use Table 8-1, which gives the number of each day in the year.

Finding Ordinary and Exact Time

To use Table 8-1 to find the exact time of the loan just described, note that July 12 is the 193rd day of the year and September 12 is the 255th day. Subtract 193 from 255 to find the total number of days.

$$
\begin{array}{r}
255 \\
\underline{193} \\
62 \text{ days}
\end{array}
$$

If the period of a loan includes February, count it as 30 days for ordinary time but 28 days for exact time. In leap years, February has 29 days, so the exact time is determined by counting 28 days and adding 1 to the total number of days if February 29 is within the loan period.

It is easy to remember which years are leap years: They are the years whose numbers are divisible by 4. (Remember the rule for divisibility by 4: If the last *two* digits form a number that is divisible by 4, the entire number is divisible by 4). The year 1996 is a leap year because 96 is divisible by 4; thus, 1996 is divisible by 4.

EXAMPLE 9

A loan made on September 5 is due July 5 of the *following year*. Find the ordinary time and exact time for the loan in a non-leap year and a leap year.

Ordinary time in a non-leap year or leap year

There are 10 months between September and July.
10 months × 30 days/month = 300 days

Exact time in a non-leap year

December 31 = day 365 September 5 = day 248 117 days	Look in Table 8-1 to find the exact time of the loan in the first year.
July 5 is the 186th day	Look in Table 8-1 to find the number of July 5.
117 + 186 = 303 days	Add the number of days in each year to find the exact time of the loan.

Exact time in a leap year

117 + 186 + 1 = 304 days	In a leap year, you add an extra day to get the correct answer.

Finding the Due Date

due date: the date that a loan matures or is due. It is a specific length of time from the beginning date of a loan.

Sometimes the beginning date of a loan and the number of days for which it is made are known, and the **due date** must be determined. If the beginning date and the due date are in the same year, simply add the number of days of the loan to the number of the beginning date (from Table 8-1) and find the corresponding end date. If the beginning date and due date are in different years, a two-step solution is needed.

EXAMPLE 10

Figure the due date using ordinary time and exact time for a 90-day loan made on November 15.

Ordinary time

Count 3 months from November 15 to find a due date of February 15.	In ordinary time, there are 30 days in a month, and 90 days is the same as 3 months.

Exact time

November 15 = day   319
   +   90 days
      409
	Use Table 8-1 to find the number for November 15, and add 90 days to that number.

Since there are only 365 days in an exact year, the loan is due in the second year. Subtract the number of days in an exact year (365) from the number of days of the loan to find the number of the due date in the second year.

Day   409
  − 365 days
       44

The loan is due on day 44 in the second year.

Day 44 = February 13

Find day 44 in Table 8-1.

The loan is due February 13.

Using Time Fractions

Whenever you solve an interest problem, you need to know whether the time and interest are ordinary or exact so that you can write the time fraction correctly. Remember, in interest problems time is usually expressed in terms of years. An ordinary month is always $\frac{1}{12}$ of a year. In exact time, a day is $\frac{1}{365}$ year; in ordinary time, where each month is considered to have 30 days, a day is $\frac{1}{360}$ year. There are three commonly used methods for determining the time fraction in interest problems.

1. Ordinary interest using ordinary time:

$$\frac{\text{Ordinary time (30 days per month)}}{360}$$

2. Exact interest using exact time:

$$\frac{\text{Exact time (exact days of loan)}}{365}$$

3. Ordinary interest using exact time:

$$\frac{\text{Exact time (exact days of loan)}}{360}$$

To make these fractions easy to recall, just remember that if you are calculating *ordinary interest* the *denominator* of the time fraction is 360. If you are calculating *exact interest,* the denominator is 365. Ordinary or exact *time* tells you what to put in the *numerator* of the time fraction. For ordinary time, 30 days per month is used. For exact time, the exact number of days of the loan is used.

TIPS & TRAPS

Thinking of fractions like these might help you remember how to write the time fraction for any combination of ordinary and exact interest and time.

Numerator   ordinary time: 30 days in a month
Denominator   ordinary interest: 360 days in a year

exact time: 28, 29, 30, or 31 days in a month
       exact interest: 365 days in a year

EXAMPLE 11

Use ordinary time to find the ordinary interest on a loan of $500 at 17%. The loan was made on March 15 and was due on May 15 of the same year.

$$P = 500$$
$$R = 17\% = 0.17$$
$$T = \frac{60}{360}$$
$$I = PRT = (\$500)(0.17)\left(\frac{60}{360}\right) = \$14.17 \quad \text{(to nearest cent)}$$

The interest is $14.17.

EXAMPLE 12

Find the exact interest using exact time on the loan in Example 11.

Here we are finding *exact interest,* so the denominator of the time fraction is 365. The numerator of the time fraction is the *exact* number of days from March 15 to May 15 because the problem calls for exact time.

To figure exact time: May 15 = 135
March 15 = $\underline{74}$
61 days

$$I = PRT$$
$$P = \$500$$
$$R = 0.17$$
$$T = \frac{61}{365}$$
$$I = \$(500)(0.17)\left(\frac{61}{365}\right) = \$14.21 \quad \text{(to nearest cent)}$$

The interest is $14.21.

EXAMPLE 13

Find the ordinary interest using exact time for the loan in Example 11.

Here, the denominator of the time fraction is 360 because the problem calls for ordinary interest, and the numerator is 61 since this is the exact number of days from March 15 to May 15.

$$I = PRT$$
$$P = \$500$$
$$R = 17\% = 0.17$$
$$T = \frac{61}{360}$$
$$I = \$(500)(0.17)\left(\frac{61}{360}\right) = \$14.40 \quad \text{(to nearest cent)}$$

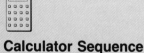

Calculator Sequence

Examples 11, 12, and 13 can be calculated and compared using a calculator:

Ex 11: [AC] 500 [×] .17 [=] [M⁺] [×] 60 [÷] 360 [=] ⇒ 14.166666

Ex 12: [AC] [MR] [×] 61 [÷] 365 [=] ⇒ 14.205479

Ex 13: [AC] [MR] [×] 61 [÷] 360 [=] ⇒ 14.402777

banker's rule: the method for calculating simple interest that uses a 360-day year (ordinary interest) and the exact time. This method yields a slightly higher amount of interest.

Note that the amount of interest varies in each case. The last method illustrated, *ordinary interest using exact time,* is most often used by bankers when lending money because it yields a slightly higher amount of interest. It is sometimes called the **banker's rule.** When bankers pay interest on savings accounts, however, they usually use a 365-day year.

The many tables available for finding ordinary and exact interest make it easy to calculate the interest on loans.

Using a Table to Calculate Simple Interest

EXAMPLE 14

Find the exact interest on a loan of $6,500 at 11.75% for 45 days.

Use Table 8-2 (on page 260) to find the interest. Move down the "Rate/Day" column to 45 days; then move across to $11\frac{3}{4}\%$. The number 1.448630 is the interest on $100 for 45 days. The interest on $6,500 is

$$\frac{\$6,500}{\$100} \times 1.448630 = 65 \times 1.448630 = \$94.16 \quad \text{(to nearest cent)}$$

To check this answer, we use the formula $I = PRT$.

Check:

$$I = PRT$$
$$= \$6,500 \times 0.1175 \times \left(\frac{45}{365}\right) = \$94.16$$

REAL WORLD APPLICATION

Cash Discounts Versus Borrowing

Borrowing money to pay cash for large purchases is sometimes profitable when a cash discount is allowed on the purchases. Joann Jimanez purchased a computer and printer for her typing service during a special promotion for $5,890, with cash terms of 3/10, n/90. She does not have the cash to pay the bill now but she will within the next 3 months and plans to use the loan to pay for the equipment. She finds a bank that will loan her the money at 13% (using ordinary interest) for 80 days. Should she take advantage of the special promotion and cash discount?

Application Questions

1. Calculate the cash discount and interest if the loan is made.

2. Calculate the savings from borrowing.

3. Discuss the points that should be considered before making a decision.

Table 8-2 Simple Interest Table (Exact Interest)

Rate Day	Interest per $100					
	$11\frac{1}{2}\%$	$11\frac{3}{4}\%$	12.00%	$12\frac{1}{4}\%$	$12\frac{1}{2}\%$	$12\frac{3}{4}\%$
1	0.031507	0.032192	0.032877	0.033562	0.034247	0.034932
2	0.063014	0.064384	0.065753	0.067123	0.068493	0.069863
3	0.094521	0.096575	0.098630	0.100685	0.102740	0.104795
4	0.126027	0.128767	0.131507	0.134247	0.136986	0.139726
5	0.157534	0.160959	0.164384	0.167808	0.171233	0.174658
6	0.189041	0.193151	0.197260	0.201370	0.205479	0.209589
7	0.220548	0.225342	0.230137	0.234932	0.239726	0.244521
8	0.252055	0.257534	0.263014	0.268493	0.273973	0.279452
9	0.283562	0.289726	0.295890	0.302055	0.308219	0.314384
10	0.315068	0.321918	0.328767	0.335616	0.342466	0.349315
11	0.346575	0.354110	0.361644	0.369178	0.376712	0.384247
12	0.378082	0.386301	0.394521	0.402740	0.410959	0.419178
13	0.409589	0.418493	0.427397	0.436301	0.445205	0.454110
14	0.441096	0.450685	0.460274	0.469863	0.479452	0.489041
15	0.472603	0.482877	0.493151	0.503425	0.513699	0.523973
16	0.504110	0.515068	0.526027	0.536986	0.547945	0.558904
17	0.535616	0.547260	0.558904	0.570548	0.582192	0.593836
18	0.567123	0.579452	0.591781	0.604110	0.616438	0.628767
19	0.598630	0.611644	0.624658	0.637671	0.650685	0.663699
20	0.630137	0.643836	0.567534	0.671233	0.684932	0.698630
21	0.661644	0.676027	0.690411	0.704795	0.719178	0.733562
22	0.693151	0.708219	0.723288	0.738356	0.753425	0.768493
23	0.724658	0.740411	0.756164	0.771918	0.787671	0.803425
24	0.756164	0.772603	0.789041	0.805479	0.821918	0.838356
25	0.787671	0.804795	0.821918	0.839041	0.856164	0.873288
26	0.819178	0.836986	0.854795	0.872603	0.890411	0.908219
27	0.850685	0.869178	0.887671	0.906164	0.924658	0.943151
28	0.882192	0.901370	0.920548	0.939726	0.958904	0.978082
29	0.913699	0.933562	0.953425	0.973288	0.993151	1.013014
30	0.945205	0.965753	0.986301	1.006849	1.027397	1.047945
31	0.976712	0.997945	1.019178	1.040411	1.061644	1.082877
32	1.008219	1.030137	1.052055	1.073973	1.095890	1.117808
33	1.039726	1.062329	1.084932	1.107534	1.130137	1.152740
34	1.071233	1.094521	1.117808	1.141096	1.164384	1.187671
35	1.102740	1.126712	1.150685	1.174658	1.198630	1.222603
36	1.134247	1.158904	1.183562	1.208219	1.232877	1.257534
37	1.165753	1.191096	1.216438	1.241781	1.267123	1.292466
38	1.197260	1.223288	1.249315	1.275342	1.301370	1.327397
39	1.228767	1.255479	1.282192	1.308904	1.385616	1.362329
40	1.260274	1.287671	1.315068	1.342466	1.369863	1.397260
41	1.291781	1.319863	1.347945	1.376027	1.404110	1.432192
42	1.323288	1.352055	1.380822	1.409589	1.438356	1.467123
43	1.354795	1.384247	1.413699	1.443151	1.472603	1.502055
44	1.386301	1.416438	1.446575	1.476712	1.506849	1.536986
45	1.417808	1.448630	1.479452	1.510274	1.541096	1.571918
46	1.449315	1.480822	1.512329	1.543836	1.575342	1.606849
47	1.480822	1.513014	1.545205	1.577397	1.609589	1.641781
48	1.512329	1.545205	1.578082	1.610959	1.643836	1.676712
49	1.543836	1.577397	1.610959	1.644521	1.678082	1.711644
50	1.575342	1.609589	1.643836	1.678082	1.712329	1.746575

9. Figure the due date using ordinary time and exact time for a loan made on October 15 for 120 days.

10. A loan made on March 10 is due September 10 of the *following year.* Find the ordinary time and exact time for the loan in a non–leap year and a leap year.

For Questions 11 to 13, use the following information: A loan for $3,000 with an interest rate of 15% was made on June 15 and was due on August 15.

11. Use ordinary time to find the ordinary interest on the loan.

12. Find the exact interest using exact time.

13. Find the ordinary interest using exact time.

For Questions 14–16, use Table 8-2.

14. Find the exact interest on a loan of $3,500 at $12\frac{1}{2}\%$ interest for 45 days.

15. Find the exact interest on a loan of $1,000 at 12% interest for 10 days.

16. Find the exact interest on a loan of $1,850 at $11\frac{1}{2}\%$ interest for 21 days.

8.3

Promissory Notes

LEARNING OBJECTIVES

   1. Calculate bank discount and proceeds on a simple discount note.

   2. Calculate bank discount and proceeds for a discounted note.

promissory note: a legal document or instrument in which the borrower promises to repay a loan.

maker: the person or company borrowing money.

When a business or individual borrows money, it is customary for the borrower to sign a legal document promising to repay the loan. The document is called a **promissory note.** The note includes all necessary information about the loan. The **maker** is the person borrowing the money. The **payee** is the person loaning the money. The **term** of the note is the length of time for which the money is borrowed; the due date, or maturity date, is the date on which the loan is due to be repaid. The rate is the percent of interest charged. The principal, or **face value,** of the note is the amount borrowed. The *maturity value* is the sum of the principal plus the interest and is the total amount due when the loan is repaid. Figure 8-2 (on page 262) shows a sample promissory note signed by Mary Fisher of Fisher's Tackle Shop.

payee: the person loaning the money.

term: the length of time for which money is borrowed or invested.

face value: the amount of money borrowed on a promissory note.

Calculating Bank Discount and Proceeds on a Simple Discount Note

bank discount: the interest or fee on a discounted note that is subtracted from the amount borrowed at the time the loan is made.

If money is borrowed from a bank, the bank often collects its fee, which is called a **bank discount,** at the time the loan is made. Thus, the maker receives the amount of the loan minus the bank discount. The sum received is called the **proceeds.** To calculate the bank discount and proceeds, use the formula $I = PRT$, as shown in the box.

proceeds: the amount that the maker of a discounted note receives; face value − discount = proceeds.

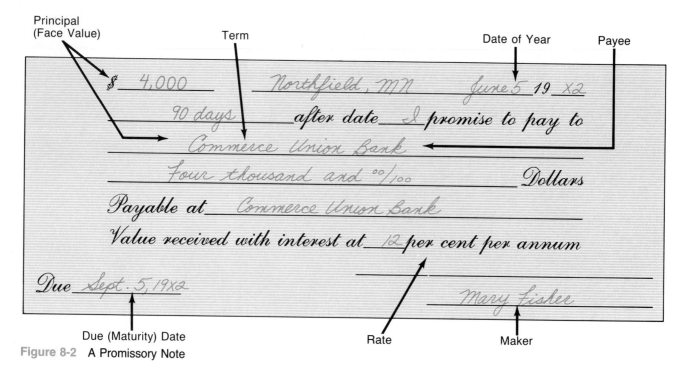

Principal (Face Value) Term Date of Year Payee

Due (Maturity) Date Rate Maker

Figure 8-2 A Promissory Note

STEP BY STEP

Calculating Bank Discount and Proceeds on a Simple Discount Note

Step 1. Calculate bank discount using $I = PRT$ (I = bank discount).

Step 2. Calculate proceeds using the following formula:

$$\text{Proceeds} = \text{face value} - \text{bank discount}$$

EXAMPLE 15

Find the bank discount and proceeds on the promissory note shown in Figure 8-2. It is a loan to Mary Fisher of $4,000 at 12% from June 5 to September 5.

$$\begin{aligned}
\text{Bank discount} &= P \times R \times T \\
&= \$4,000 \times 0.12 \times \frac{90}{360} \\
&= \$120
\end{aligned}$$

$$\begin{aligned}
\text{Proceeds} &= \$4,000 - \$120 \\
&= \$3,880
\end{aligned}$$

The bank discount is $120.

The proceeds are $3,880.

The bank discount is $120. To find the proceeds, the amount that Ms. Fisher actually receives from the bank, subtract the bank discount from the face value of the note.

undiscounted note: a promissory note for which the interest is not collected when the note is made.

The difference between the simple interest note (which is also called an **undiscounted** promissory **note**) and the simple discount note is that with the simple discount note the interest is figured on the maturity value, but the borrower has use of only the proceeds (maturity value − discount). Thus, if Bill borrows $5,000 with a discount of 18% or $900, he gets the use of only $4,100, but the bank charges interest figured on the full $5,000.

Here is a comparison of the simple interest versus simple discount notes:

	Simple Interest Note	Simple Discount Note
Face value	$5,000	$5,000
Interest	900	900
Amount available to borrower	5,000	4,100
Maturity value	5,900	5,000

Calculating Bank Discount and Proceeds for a Discounted Note

Many businesses accept simple interest and simple discount notes as payment for the sale of goods. If these businesses in turn need cash, they may sell such notes to a bank. Selling a note to a bank in return for cash is called discounting a note. The note is called a **discounted note.**

When the bank discounts a note, it gives the business owning the note the maturity value of the note minus a bank discount. The bank receives the full maturity value of the note from the maker when it comes due.

This process is handled the same way as a simple discount note. You have to find the discount period, which is the number of days the *bank* holds the note. The bank's discount is based on how long it holds the note. The following diagram shows how the discount period is figured:

discounted note: a promissory note for which the interest or fee is discounted or subtracted at the time the loan is made.

Time of note

Jul. 14 —————————————→ Sept. 12

                Discount period

Aug. 3 ——————————→ Sept. 12

There is a four-step procedure for calculating the amount of discount and proceeds for a discounted note.

STEP BY STEP

Calculating Bank Discount and Proceeds for a Discounted Note

Step 1. Calculate the maturity value of the note.

Step 2. Calculate the discount period.

Step 3. Calculate the amount of bank discount ($I = PRT$).

Step 4. Calculate the proceeds (proceeds = maturity value − bank discount).

EXAMPLE 16

Alpine Pleasures, Inc., delivers ski equipment to retailers in July but does not expect payment until mid-September, so the retailers agree to sign promissory notes for the equipment. These notes have a 10% interest rate. One promissory note held by Alpine is for $8,000, was made on July 14, and is due September 12. Alpine needs cash, so it takes the note to its bank. On August 3, the bank agrees to buy the note at a 12% discount rate. Find the proceeds for the note.

A table can help you organize the facts:

Date of Note	Principal of Note	Interest Rate	Date of Discounted Note	Bank Discount Rate	Maturity Date
July 14	$8,000	10%	Aug. 3	12%	Sept. 12

Step 1. Calculate the maturity value of the note.

September 12 = day 255
July 14   = day 195
                    60 days

First you have to calculate exact number of days from July 14 to Sept. 12. Use Table 8-1. There are 60 days.

$I = P \times R \times T$

Use the interest equation to find exact interest.

$$= \$8,000 \times 0.1 \times \frac{60}{365}$$

$= \$131.51$ (rounded)

The interest is $131.51.

Maturity value
    = principal + interest
    = $8,000 + $131.51
    = $8,131.51

To find the maturity value, add the principal and interest.
The maturity value is $8,131.51.

Step 2. Calculate the discount period.

Discount period
    = number of days from August 3 to September 12

To calculate the number of days in the discount period, you use Table 8-1 and subtract 215 from 255.

September 12 = day 255
August 3   = day 215
                    40 days

The discount period is 40 days.

Step 3. Calculate the amount of bank discount.

$I = P \times R \times T$

Bank discount

$$= \text{maturity value} \times \text{bank discount rate} \times \frac{\text{discount period}}{360 \text{ days}}$$

$$= \$8,131.51 \times 0.12 \times \frac{40}{360}$$

$= \$108.42$

The amount of bank discount is $108.42.

Step 4. Calculate the proceeds.

Proceeds = maturity value − bank discount
         = $8,131.51 − $108.42
         = $8,023.09

The proceeds are $8,023.09.

Self-Check 8.3

17. Use the simple interest formula to find the amount of interest paid on a $2,500 note for 120 days if the bank charges 16% discount.

18. Find the amount of money the borrower would actually receive in the case described in Question 17.

TIPS & TRAPS

There is such a thing as a noninterest-bearing note. This means that you borrow a certain amount and pay that same amount back later. The note itself carries no interest amount on it, and the maturity value of the note is the same as the face value or principal.

What happens if a noninterest-bearing note is discounted? Use the information from Example 16.

Step 1. Calculate the maturity value of the note.

Maturity value = $8,000

In a noninterest-bearing note, the maturity value is the same as the principal.

Step 2. Calculate the discount period.

255 days − 215 days = 40 days

The discount period is 40 days.

Step 3. Calculate the amount of bank discount.

$$\text{Bank discount} = \$8,000 \times 0.12 \times \frac{40}{360}$$
$$= \$106.67$$

The bank discount is $106.67.

Step 4. Calculate proceeds.

Proceeds = $8,000 − $106.67
        = $7,893.33

The proceeds are $7,893.33

---

19. Find the maturity value of the undiscounted promissory note shown here.

$ 3,000   Rockville, M.D   Aug. 5,   19 X1

Nine Months   after date I promise to pay to

City Bank

Three thousand and 00/100   Dollars

Payable at City Bank

Value received with interest at 16½ per cent per annum

Due May 5, 19X2

Phillip Estevez

20. Carter Manufacturing holds an interest-bearing note of $5,000 that has an interest rate of 11%. The note was made on March 18 and is due November 13. Carter sells the note to a bank on June 13 at a discount rate of 14%. Find the proceeds on the bank-discounted note.

Summary

Topic	Page	What to Remember	Example
Simple interest formula	248	Interest = principal × rate × time ($I = PRT$). Always write the rate in decimal or fractional form to solve a problem, and write time as a whole or fractional part of a year.	The simple interest formula, in various forms, is used in the examples that follow.
Solving for interest	249	Interest = principal × rate × time	Milton borrowed $1,200 for 18 months at $14\frac{1}{2}\%$ interest. How much interest did he pay? I is unknown; $P = \$1,200$; $R = 14\frac{1}{2}\% = 0.145$; $T = \dfrac{18}{12}$ years = 1.5 years $I = PRT$ $= (\$1,200)(0.145)(1.5)$ $= \$261$
Maturity value	250	Maturity value = principal + interest	What is the maturity value of Milton's loan? $\$1,200 + \$261 = \$1,461$
Solving for rate	252	$\text{Rate} = \dfrac{\text{interest}}{\text{principal} \times \text{time}}$ Remember to change the decimal value of R into a percent.	$6,000 was borrowed for $3\frac{1}{2}$ years, with $2,800 simple interest paid. What was the rate of interest? R is unknown; $I = \$2,800$; $P = \$6,000$; $T = 3.5$ years $R = \dfrac{2,800}{6,000(3.5)} = 0.133 = 13.3\%$
Solving for principal	253	$\text{Principal} = \dfrac{\text{interest}}{\text{rate} \times \text{time}}$	$675 interest charges are paid on an 18-month loan at 18% interest. Find the principal. P is unknown; $I = \$675$; $R = 18\% = 0.18$; $T = 18$ months $= \dfrac{18}{12}$ years $= 1.5$ years $P = \dfrac{\$675}{0.18(1.5)} = \$2,500$
Solving for time	253	$\text{Time} = \dfrac{\text{interest}}{\text{principal} \times \text{rate}}$	$1,500 was borrowed at 16.5% interest. $866.25 interest was paid. Find the duration (time) of the loan. $I = \$866.25$; $P = \$1,500$; $R = 16.5\% = 0.165$; T is unknown. $T = \dfrac{\$866.25}{(\$1,500)(0.165)}$ $= 3.5$ years
Finding ordinary time	254	In ordinary time, a month is considered to have 30 days.	Find the ordinary time of a loan made on October 1 and due the following May 1. October to May = 7 months 7 months × 30 days/month = 210 days
Finding exact time	254	Use Table 8-1 to find the numbers of the beginning and ending dates of the loan. If the loan spans more than one year, add the number of days of the loan in each year. In a non-leap year February has 28 days and in a leap year 29 days.	Find the exact time of a loan made on June 7 and due the following March 7 in a non-leap year. December 31 = day 365 June 7 = day 158 207 days (year 1) March 7 = + 66 days (year 2) 273 days The loan is made for 273 days in all.

Topic	Page	What to Remember	Example
Ordinary interest, ordinary time	256	$$T = \frac{\begin{array}{c}\text{number} \\ \text{of} \\ \text{days}\end{array} \times \begin{array}{c}\text{30 days} \\ \text{per} \\ \text{month}\end{array}}{360 \text{ days in an ordinary year}}$$	On May 15, Nora borrowed \$6,000 at 12.5% interest. The loan was due on November 15. Use ordinary time to find the ordinary interest due on the loan. $P = \$6,000$; $R = 12.5\% = 0.125$; $T = 6$ months $$T = \frac{6 \text{ months} \times 30 \text{ days/month}}{360}$$ $$= \frac{180}{360}$$ $$I = PRT = (6,000)(0.125)\left(\frac{180}{360}\right)$$ $$= \$375$$
Exact interest, exact time	256	$$T = \frac{\text{exact number of days}}{365 \text{ days in an exact year}}$$ Use Table 8-1	Use exact interest and exact time to find the interest due on Nora's loan. To figure exact time: November 15 = day 319; May 15 = day 135; day 319 − day 135 = 184 days $P = \$6,000$; $R = 12.5\% = 0.125$; $$T = \frac{184}{365}$$ $$I = PRT$$ $$= (6,000)(0.125)\left(\frac{184}{365}\right)$$ $$= \$378.08$$
Ordinary interest, exact time (banker's rule)	258	$$T = \frac{\text{exact number of days}}{360 \text{ days in an ordinary year}}$$ Use Table 8-1	Use ordinary interest and exact time to find the interest due on Nora's loan. To figure exact time: November 15 = day 319; May 15 = day 135 day 319 − day 135 = 184 days $$T = \frac{184 \text{ exact days}}{360 \text{ days in an ordinary year}}$$ $P = \$6,000$; $R = 12.5\% = 0.125$; $$T = \frac{184}{360}$$ $$I = PRT = (6,000)(0.125)\left(\frac{184}{360}\right)$$ $$= \$383.33$$
Proceeds of a discounted bank note	261	Discount $(I) = PRT$ Proceeds = face value $= (P) - \text{discount } (I)$	The bank charged Daniel 16.5% discount on a bank note of \$1,500 for 120 days. Find the proceeds of the note. Discount (I) is unknown; $P = \$1,500$; $R = 16.5\% = 0.165$; $T = 120 \text{ days} = \frac{120}{360} \text{ year}$ $$\text{Discount} = (1,500)(0.165)\left(\frac{120}{360}\right)$$ $$= \$82.50$$ Proceeds = \$1,500 − \$82.50 $$= \$1,417.50$$

Topic	Page	What to Remember	Example
Maturity value of an undiscounted bank note	261	Maturity value = face value + interest or Maturity value = Principal (1 + rate × time) Inside parentheses, multiply first, then add.	The bank charged Daniel 16.5% interest on an undiscounted bank note of $1,500 for 120 days. Find the maturity value of the note. I is unknown; $P = \$1,500$; $R = 16.5\% = 0.165$; $T = 120$ days $= \dfrac{120}{360}$ year $$\text{Interest} = (1,500)(0.165)\left(\dfrac{120}{360}\right)$$ $$= \$82.50$$ Maturity value $= \$1,500 + \$82.50$ $$= \$1,582.50$$

Self-Check Solutions

1. $I = PRT$
$= \$2,400 \times 0.11 \times 1$
$= \$264$

2. $I = PRT$
$= \$800 \times 0.085 \times 2$
$= \$136$

3. $I = PRT$
$= \$1,400 \times 0.125 \times 3$
$= \$525$

Maturity value $= \$1,400 + \$525 = \$1,925$

4. 8 months $= \dfrac{8}{12}$ year
$= 0.6666666$, or 0.67 year

40 months $= \dfrac{40}{12}$ years
$= 3.333333$, or 3.33 years

5. $R = \dfrac{I}{PT}$ $\quad T = 30$ months $= \dfrac{30}{12}$ years $= 2.5$ years
$= \dfrac{\$360}{\$1,200 \times 2.5}$
$= \dfrac{360}{3,000}$
$= 0.12$, or 12%

6. $R = \dfrac{I}{PT}$ $\quad T = \dfrac{7}{12}$ year
$= \dfrac{\$53.96}{\$500 \times \frac{7}{12}}$ $\quad \left(\$500 \times \dfrac{7}{12} = \$291.6667\right)$
$= 0.185$, or 18.5%

7. $P = \dfrac{I}{RT}$
$= \dfrac{\$500}{0.09 \times 2}$
$= \dfrac{\$500}{0.18}$
$= \$2,777.78$

8. $T = \dfrac{I}{PR}$
$= \dfrac{\$360}{\$6,000 \times 0.12}$
$= \dfrac{360}{720}$
$= 0.5 = \dfrac{1}{2}$ year, or 6 months

9. Ordinary time: 120 days is $\dfrac{120}{30}$, or 4 months.

4 months from October 15 is February 15.
Exact time: October 15 = day   288
$$\underline{+\;\;120}$$
$$408$$

$408 - 365 = 43$ days
The 43rd day is February 12.

10. *Non-leap year*
   Ordinary time: March 10 to March 10 is 12 months, or $12 \times$
                    30 days = 360 days.
   March 10 to September 10 is 6 months, or 6×30 days = 180 days.
   360 days + 180 days = 540 days

   Exact time: March 10 to March 10 of the following year is 1 year, or
                 365 days.
   September 10 = day 253
   March 10 = $\underline{\text{day}\;\;69}$
   184 days

   $365 + 184 = 549$ days

   Leap year
   $366 + 184 = 550$ days

11. Ordinary time = 2 months, or $2 \times 30 = 60$ days
$$I = \$3{,}000 \times 0.15 \times \frac{60}{360} = \$75$$

12. Exact time: August 15 = day 227
   June 15   = $\underline{\text{day } 166}$
   61 days
$$I = \$3{,}000 \times 0.15 \times \frac{61}{365} = \$75.21$$

13. $I = \$3{,}000 \times 0.15 \times \dfrac{61}{360} = \$76.25$

14. $I = \$3{,}500 \times 1.541096 \div 100 = \$53.94$

15. $I = \$1{,}000 \times 0.328767 \div 100 = \$3.29$

16. $I = \$1{,}850 \times 0.661644 \div 100 = \$12.24$

17. $I = \$2{,}500 \times 0.16 \times \dfrac{120}{360} = \$133.33$

18. Proceeds $= \$2{,}500 - \$133.33 = \$2{,}366.67$

19. Calculate time: December 31 = day 365
   August 5 = $\underline{\text{day } 217}$
   148 days
   May 5 = $\underline{\text{day } 125}$
   273 days
$$I = \$3{,}000 \times 0.165 \times \frac{273}{360} = \$375.38$$

20. Maturity value of note: $3,000 + $375.37 = $3,375.37

$$\text{November 13} = \text{day 317}$$
$$\text{March 18} = \underline{\text{day } 77}$$
$$240 \text{ days}$$

$$I = \$5{,}000 \times 0.11 \times \frac{240}{365} = \$361.64$$

Maturity value = $5,000 + $361.64 = $5,361.64

Bank discount:
$$\text{November 13} = \text{day 317}$$
$$\text{June 13} = \underline{\text{day 164}}$$
$$153 \text{ days}$$

$$I = \$5{,}361.64 \times 0.14 \times \frac{153}{360} = \$319.02$$

Proceeds = $5,361.64 − $319.02 = $5,042.62

End of Chapter Problems

Find the simple interest in each of the following problems. Round to the nearest cent when necessary.

Principal	Rate	Time	Interest
1. $500	12%	2 years	_____
2. $1,000	$9\frac{1}{2}$%	3 years	_____
3. $3,575	21%	3 years	_____
4. $2,975	$12\frac{1}{2}$%	2 years	_____
5. $800	18%	1 year	_____

6. Capco, Inc., borrowed $4,275 for 3 years at 15% interest. How much simple interest did the company pay? How much would have to be repaid altogether?

7. Legan Company borrowed $15,280 at $16\frac{1}{2}$% for 12 years. How much simple interest did the company pay? What was the total amount paid back?

Find the rate of simple interest in each of the following problems.

Principal	Interest	Time	Rate
8. $300	$102	2 years	_____
9. $800	$124	1 year	_____
10. $1,280	$256	2 years	_____
11. $1,000	$375	3 years	_____
12. $40,000	$64,000	10 years	_____
13. $175	$52.50	2 years	_____
14. $423	$355.32	4 years	_____

In each of the following problems, find the duration (time) of the loan using the formula for simple interest.

	Principal	Rate	Interest	Time
15.	$450	10%	$135	_____
16.	$700	18%	$252	_____
17.	$1,500	$21\frac{1}{2}\%$	$483.75	_____
18.	$2,000	$16\frac{1}{2}\%$	$825	_____
19.	$800	$15\frac{3}{4}\%$	$252	_____

20. Madewell Manufacturing paid back a loan of $7,500 at $16\frac{1}{2}\%$ with $618.75 simple interest. How long was the loan outstanding?

21. Ronald Cox received $1,440 on a loan of $12,000 at 16% simple interest. How long was the money invested?

22. Simple interest of $78.01 was paid on a loan of $269 with an interest rate of $14\frac{1}{2}\%$. What length of time was required to repay the loan?

In each of the following problems, find the principal, based on simple interest.

	Interest	Rate	Time	Principal
23.	$100	10%	2 years	_____
24.	$281.25	$12\frac{1}{2}\%$	3 years	_____
25.	$90	9%	1 year	_____
26.	$180	11.25%	2 years	_____
27.	$661.50	8.82%	5 years	_____
28.	$304.64	$13\frac{3}{5}\%$	4 years	_____

29. A loan for 3 years with an annual simple interest rate of 18% cost $486 interest. Find the principal.

30. An investor earned $1,530 interest on funds invested at $12\frac{3}{4}\%$ simple interest for 4 years. How much was invested?

Write a fraction expressing each amount of time as a part of a year (12 months = 1 year).

31. 7 months

32. 18 months

33. 16 months

34. 9 months

35. 3 months

36. Draw the circle showing the four parts of an interest problem, and write the formula for each part.

37. Robert Ellis made a car loan for $2,500 to be paid off in $3\frac{1}{2}$ years. The simple interest rate for the loan was 12%. How much interest did he pay?

38. Jill Jones bought a dining-room suite and paid for the furniture in full after 1 month, with a finance charge of $18.75. If she was charged 18% interest, how much did the suite cost?

39. Sue Jackson invested $500 at 8% for 6 months. How much interest did she receive?

40. Mark Hammer borrowed $500 for 3 months and paid $12.50 interest. What was the rate of interest?

41. Find the interest paid on a loan of $1,200 for 60 days at a simple interest rate of 6%.

42. Find the interest paid on a loan of $2,100 for 90 days at a simple interest rate of 4%.

43. Find the interest paid on a loan of $800 for 12 days at a simple interest rate of 6%.

44. Time figured using 30 days per month is called what kind of time?

45. When the exact number of days in each month is used to figure time, it is called what kind of time?

Use Table 8-1 to find the exact time from the first date to the second date for non-leap years unless leap year is indicated.

46. March 15 to July 10   **47.** April 12 to November 15

48. January 18 to October 6

49. November 12 to April 15 of the next year

50. January 5 to June 7   **51.** April 7, 1992, to August 15, 1992

52. January 12, 1991, to June 28, 1991

53. February 3, 1996, to August 12, 1996

54. January 27, 1996, to September 30, 1996

55. February 15, 1990, to June 15, 1991

If a loan is made on the given date, find the date it is due, using both ordinary time and exact time.

56. March 15 for 30 days

57. January 10 for 210 days

58. May 30 for 240 days

59. August 12 for 60 days

60. June 13 for 90 days

61. December 28 for 60 days

For each of the following problems, find (a) the ordinary interest using ordinary time, (b) the exact interest using exact time, and (c) the ordinary interest using exact time. Round answers to the nearest cent.

62. $5,000 at 17% for 90 days

63. $3,500 at 18% for 60 days

64. A loan of $4,225 at 8% made on March 5, and due on May 5 of the same year

65. A loan of $1,200 at 10% made on October 15, and due on March 20 of the following year

66. A loan of $500 at $17\frac{1}{2}$% made on February 3 and due on June 15 of the same year. (The year is not a leap year.)

Use the following note for Problems 67–73.

$ 2,000   Greenville, MS Feb 10 19XX
Six months after date I promise to pay to
First State Bank
Two Thousand and 00/100 ————— Dollars
Payable at First State Bank
Value received with interest at no per cent per annum

Due Aug. 10, 19XX   Lisa Jenkins

67. Who is the maker of the note shown here?

68. Who is the payee?

69. What is the face value of the note?

70. What is the due date?

71. If the bank charged 9%, find the discount on the note.

72. Find the proceeds of the note.

73. If the bank charged 14%, find the discount on the note. Find the proceeds of the note. Compare the proceeds at 14% interest with the proceeds at 9% (Problem 72).

Use Table 8-2.

74. Find the interest on a loan of $3,700 at $12\frac{1}{4}$% for 15 days.
Find 15 days in the table and move across to $12\frac{1}{4}$%. Find 0.503425.

75. Find the interest on a loan of $2,100 at $11\frac{1}{2}$% interest for 40 days.

76. Find the interest on a loan of $3,600 at 12.75% interest for 18 days.

77. MAK, Inc., accepted an interest-bearing note for $10,000 with 9% interest. The note was made on April 10 and was due December 6. MAK needed cash and took the note to First United Bank, which offered to buy the note at a discount rate of $12\frac{1}{2}$%. The transaction was made on July 7. How much cash did MAK receive for the note?

78. Allan Stojanovich can purchase an office desk for $1,500 with cash terms of 2/10, n/30. If he can borrow the money at 12% simple interest for 20 days, will he save money by taking advantage of the cash discount offered?

Additional Problems

1. Louis Pegano borrowed $2,000 for 8 months at $16\frac{1}{2}$% simple interest. How much interest did he pay?

2. Find the rate of interest on an investment of $2,500 made by Connie Honda for a period of 2 years if she received $612.50 in interest.

3. Find the interest paid on a $2,400 loan for four months at a simple interest rate of 6%.

4. Find the length of time Mary Romeo must invest $3,200 at 15% simple interest to earn $720 interest. What is the maturity value?

5. John White financed $800 at 10% ordinary interest on July 23 for 180 days. Use ordinary time to find the interest.

6. Catherine Trailor signed a promissory note with a face value of $2,800. The note was discounted by the bank at the rate of $18\frac{1}{2}\%$. If the term of the note was 9 months, find the proceeds.

7. If a 90-day promissory note whose face value is $4,500 is discounted at the bank at the rate of 21%, find the discount.

8. Mark Bergeron borrowed $6,000 to start a carpet cleaning business. He plans to repay the loan in 30 months. How much interest must be paid if the interest rate is 10.5% simple interest?

9. Find the exact interest on a loan of $950 at $9\frac{3}{4}\%$ if the loan was made on May 12 and repaid on October 15 of the same year.

10. The bank charged Al Chung $16\frac{1}{4}\%$ interest on an undiscounted note of $2,200 for 160 days. Find the maturity value of the note.

Challenge Problem

Second Only to a Computer Virus!

A data entry clerk at Third Federal Savings and Loan spilled coffee on a diskette, wiping out some critical loan data for several of S&L's customers. Your assignment, as chief accounting department trouble shooter, is to reconstruct the missing data from the data fragment below. Express all dollar amounts correct to the nearest cent, interest rates to one decimal place, and time to the nearest day.

Customer	Interest	Principal	Rate	Time (ordinary)
Rocky's Market	$ 7.00		10%	30 days
David's Art Gallery	85.00		12%	100 days
Fortune Hardware	208.00	5,500.00		180 days
M. Converse & Son	22.50	1,460.00		90 days
Sun Twins Jai Alai	72.00	2,560.00	13.5%	
Sun Coast Brokerage	1,711.00	28,000.00	11%	

What methods do banks use to protect themselves from the loss of vital financial data?

Rocky's Market

M. Converse & Son

David's Art Gallery

Sun Twins Jai Alai

Fortune Hardware

Sun Coast Brokerage

To protect themselves from data loss as described in this question, most financial institutions use a computerized backup system with storage either on disk or magnetic tape.

Trial Test

1. Find the simple interest on $500 invested at 14% for 3 years.

2. How much money was borrowed at 17% for 6 months if the interest was $85?

3. A loan of $3,000 was made for 210 days. If ordinary interest is $350, find the rate.

4. A loan of $5,000 at 16% requires $1,200 interest. For how long is the money borrowed?

5. Find the exact time from February 13 to November 27 in a non-leap year.

6. Find the exact time from October 12 to March 28 of the following year (a leap year).

7. Find the exact time from January 28, 1996, to July 5, 1996.

8. Find the ordinary time from April 5 to December 20.

9. Find the simple interest on a loan of $20,000 at 21% interest for 2 years.

10. Use ordinary time to find the ordinary interest on a loan of $2,800 at 10% made on March 15 for 270 days.

11. Find the interest on a loan of $469 if the simple interest rate charged is 12% for 6 months.

12. A bread machine with a cash price of $188 can be purchased with a 1-year loan at 10% simple interest. Find the total amount to be repaid.

13. An investment of $7,000 is made for 6 months at the rate of 19% simple interest. How much interest will the investor earn?

14. A copier that orginally cost $300 was purchased with a loan for 12 months at 15% simple interest. What was the *total* cost of the copier?

15. Find the ordinary interest on a loan of $850 at 15%. The loan was made January 15 and was due March 15. Use ordinary time.

16. Find the exact interest in Problem 15. Use exact time in a non-leap year. Round to the nearest cent.

17. Find the duration of a loan of $3,000 if the loan required interest of $416.25 and was at a rate of $18\frac{1}{2}\%$ simple interest.

18. Find the simple interest on a loan of $165 if the interest rate is 16% over a 3-month period.

19. Find the rate of simple interest on a $1,200 loan that requires the borrower to repay a total of $1,440 after one year.

20. Find the rate of simple interest on a $600 loan with total interest of $40.50 if the loan is paid in 6 months.

21. A promissory note has a face value of $5,000 and is discounted by the bank at the rate of $18\frac{1}{2}\%$. If the note is made for 180 days, find the discount of the note.

22. A promissory note with a face value of $3,500 is discounted by the bank at the rate of $19\frac{1}{2}\%$. The term of the note is 6 months. Find the proceeds of the note.

23. Find the ordinary interest paid on a loan of $1,600 for 90 days at a simple interest rate of 16%.

24. Jerry Brooks purchases office supplies totaling $1,890. He can take advantage of cash terms of 2/10, n/30 if he obtains a short-term loan. If he can borrow the money at $10\frac{1}{2}\%$ simple ordinary interest for 20 days, will he save money if he borrows to take advantage of the cash discount? How much will he save?

Use Table 8-2.

25. Find the interest on a loan of $25,000 at $11\frac{3}{4}\%$ for 21 days.

26. Find the interest on a loan of $1,510 at $12\frac{3}{4}\%$ interest for 27 days.

27. Find the interest on a loan of $4,300 at 11.75% interest for 32 days.

A look at statistics that shape your finances

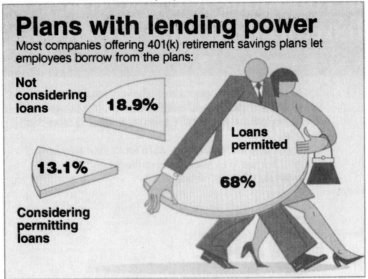

Plans with lending power

Most companies offering 401(k) retirement savings plans let employees borrow from the plans:

Not considering loans 18.9%

13.1%

Considering permitting loans

Loans permitted 68%

Source: Profit Sharing Council of America

By Marcia Staimer, USA TODAY

QUESTIONS

1. What percent of companies do not permit loans on 401(k) retirement savings plans?

2. How would you verify that all options are accounted for in the graph?

3. Check with companies in your area that offer 401(k) retirement savings plans to determine which permit loans.

9

Compound Interest and Present Value

For most loans made on a short-term basis, interest is computed by using the simple interest formula. If interest on a loan or investment is calculated more than once during the term of the loan or investment, this interest is added to the principal. This sum (principal + interest) then becomes the principal for the next calculation of interest, and interest is charged or paid on this new amount.

This process of adding interest to the principal before interest is calculated for the next period is called *compounding interest*. Compounding interest has several uses in the business world. The one with which you are probably familiar is used in a savings account, where you "earn interest on your interest."

9.1 Compound Interest and Future Value

LEARNING OBJECTIVES

1. Calculate future value (compound amount) and compound interest.
2. Use a compound interest table.
3. Compound for periods of less than a year.
4. Find the effective rate.
5. Compound interest daily.

The process of compounding interest can be repeated as many times as there are **interest periods** in the term of a loan or investment. The total amount at the end of the loan or investment term is called the **future value** or **compound amount.** The difference between the original amount of the loan or investment and the future value is the **compound interest.** Note that when we calculate compound interest, whether for a loan or investment, none of the money borrowed or invested is repaid until the *end* of the term of the loan or investment. Loans on which regular periodic payments are made are called **amortized** loans and will be discussed in Chapter 10.

The terms of a loan indicate how often and at what rate interest is compounded. To figure the interest, you use the same formula you used with simple interest, $I = P \times R \times T$. On a loan of $500 at 12% for 6 years, you first multiply $500 \times 0.12 \times 1$ (for the first year) to get the first year's interest, $60. This process is given in the following box.

interest period: the length of time during which the interest on a loan or investment is compounded.

future value: the total amount at the end of a loan or investment term (also called compound amount).

compound interest: the difference between the original amount of a loan or investment and the compound amount (or future value).

Calculating Future Value and Compound Interest

STEP BY STEP

Calculating Future Value Total and Compound Interest

Step 1. Find the interest and add it to the principal; use this sum as the base to figure next year's interest.

Step 2. Repeat this for the number of years in the loan. The final figure is the future value or compound amount.

Step 3. Find the compound interest using this formula:

Compound interest = compound amount − principal

EXAMPLE 1

A loan of $800 at 13% is made for 3 years, compounded annually. Find the compound amount and the amount of compound interest paid on the loan. Compare the compound interest with simple interest for the same period.

Find the compound amount

$800 × 0.13 = $104   Find the first year's interest.
$800 + $104 = $904   First year's interest + principal = second year's principal.

$904 × 0.13 = $117.52   Find the second year's interest.

$904 + $117.52 = $1,021.52   Second year's interest + second year's principal = third year's principal.

$1,021.52 × 0.13 = $132.80   Find the third year's interest, rounded to the nearest cent.

$1,021.52 + $132.80
    = $1,154.32   Third year's principal + third year's interest = compound amount.

Find the amount of compound interest

$1,154.32   Compound amount
− 800   Principal
$ 354.32   Compound interest

The compound interest is $354.32.

Comparing compound and simple interest
Use the simple interest formula to find the simple interest on $800 at 13% interest for 3 years.

$I = PRT$
$P = \$800; R = 13\% = 0.13; T = 3$
$I = \$800 \times 0.13 \times 3$
$\quad = \$312$

The simple interest is $312.

The compound interest is $42.32 more than the simple interest. This difference would be even greater if the interest were compounded more frequently.

TIPS & TRAPS

When compounding interest, be sure to add the interest to the *previous principal*. A common mistake is to add the interest to the *original principal*. We'll use the numbers from Example 1.

CORRECT	WRONG
$800 × 0.13 = $104	$800 × 0.13 = $104
$800 + $104 = $904	$800 + $104 = $904
$904 × 0.13 = $117.52	$904 × 0.13 = $117.52
$904 + $117.52 = $1,021.52	$800 + $117.52 = $917.52
$1,021.52 × 0.13 = $132.7976	$917.52 × 0.13 = $119.28
$1,021.52 + $132.80 = $1,154.32	$800 + $119.28 = $919.28

There is a shortcut for the method just shown. For each year of the loan, multiply the new principal times 1 + the interest rate. The product is the next year's principal. Consider Example 1 again, a loan of $800 at 13% for 3 years, compounded annually.

Year 1: $800 × 1.13 = $904

Year 2: $904 × 1.13 = $1,021.52

Year 3: $1,021.52 × 1.13 = $1,154.3176,   or $1,154.32

This shortcut eliminates the step of having to add the new interest to the old principal to find the new principal.

Using a Compound Interest Table

As you may have guessed from Example 1, compounding interest for a large number of periods is very time consuming. This task is made simpler if you use a compound interest table, as shown in Table 9-1.

The numbers in Table 9-1 show the compounded amount per dollar of principal, or the value of $1 at the end of the indicated number of years.

STEP BY STEP

Using a Compound Interest Table

Step 1. Look down the left column to find the correct number of periods or years; then look across that row to find the correct interest rate. The number listed is the compound amount for $1.

Step 2. Multiply the compound amount for $1 times the amount of the loan (principal) in dollars:

$$\text{Compound amount} = \text{amount of loan} \times \text{compound amount for \$1}$$

Table 9-1 Compound Interest Table

	Rate per Period										
Period	**1%**	**$1\frac{1}{2}$%**	**2%**	**$2\frac{1}{2}$%**	**3%**	**4%**	**5%**	**6%**	**8%**	**10%**	**12%**
1	1.01000	1.01500	1.02000	1.02500	1.03000	1.04000	1.05000	1.06000	1.08000	1.10000	1.12000
2	1.02010	1.03023	1.04040	1.05063	1.06090	1.08160	1.10250	1.12360	1.16640	1.21000	1.25440
3	1.03030	1.04568	1.06121	1.07689	1.09273	1.12486	1.15763	1.19102	1.25971	1.33100	1.40493
4	1.04060	1.06136	1.08243	1.10381	1.12551	1.16986	1.21551	1.26248	1.36049	1.46410	1.57352
5	1.05101	1.07728	1.10408	1.13141	1.15927	1.21665	1.27628	1.33823	1.46933	1.61051	1.76234
6	1.06152	1.09344	1.12616	1.15969	1.19405	1.26532	1.34010	1.41852	1.58687	1.77156	1.97382
7	1.07214	1.10984	1.14869	1.18869	1.22987	1.31593	1.40710	1.50363	1.71382	1.94872	2.21068
8	1.08286	1.12649	1.17166	1.21840	1.26677	1.36857	1.47746	1.59385	1.85093	2.14359	2.47596
9	1.09369	1.14339	1.19509	1.24886	1.30477	1.42331	1.55133	1.68948	1.99900	2.35795	2.77308
10	1.10462	1.16054	1.21899	1.28008	1.34392	1.48024	1.62889	1.79085	2.15892	2.59374	2.10585
11	1.11567	1.17795	1.24337	1.31209	1.38423	1.53945	1.71034	1.89830	2.33164	2.85312	3.47855
12	1.12683	1.19562	1.26824	1.34489	1.42576	1.60103	1.79586	2.01220	2.51817	3.18343	3.89598
13	1.13809	1.21355	1.29361	1.37851	1.46853	1.66507	1.88565	2.13293	2.71962	3.45227	4.36349
14	1.14947	1.23176	1.31948	1.41297	1.51259	1.73168	1.97993	2.26090	2.93719	3.79750	4.88711
15	1.16097	1.25023	1.34587	1.44830	1.55797	1.80094	2.07893	2.39656	3.17217	4.17725	5.47357
16	1.17258	1.26899	1.37279	1.48451	1.60471	1.87298	2.18287	2.54035	3.42594	4.59497	6.13039
17	1.18430	1.28802	1.40024	1.52162	1.65284	1.94790	2.29202	2.69277	3.70002	5.05447	6.86604
18	1.19615	1.30734	1.42825	1.55966	1.70243	2.02582	2.40662	2.85434	3.99602	5.55992	7.68997
19	1.20811	1.32695	1.45681	1.59865	1.75351	2.10685	2.52695	3.02560	4.31570	6.11591	8.61276
20	1.22019	1.34686	1.48595	1.63862	1.80611	2.19112	2.65330	3.20714	4.66096	6.72750	9.64629
21	1.23239	1.36706	1.51567	1.67958	1.86029	2.27877	2.78596	3.39956	5.03383	7.40025	10.80385
22	1.24472	1.38756	1.54598	1.72157	1.91610	2.36992	2.92526	3.60354	5.43654	8.14027	12.10031
23	1.25716	1.40838	1.57690	1.76461	1.97359	2.46472	3.07152	3.81975	5.87146	8.95430	13.55235
24	1.26973	1.42950	1.60844	1.80873	2.03279	2.56330	3.22510	4.04893	6.34118	9.84973	15.17863
25	1.28243	1.45095	1.64061	1.85394	2.09378	2.66584	3.38635	4.29187	6.84848	10.83471	17.00006
26	1.29526	1.47271	1.67342	1.90029	2.15659	2.77247	3.55567	4.54938	7.39635	11.91818	19.04007
27	1.30821	1.49480	1.70689	1.94780	2.22129	2.88337	3.73346	4.82235	7.98806	13.10999	21.32488
28	1.32129	1.51722	1.74102	1.99650	2.28793	2.99870	3.92013	5.11169	8.62711	14.42099	23.88387
29	1.33450	1.53998	1.77584	2.04641	2.35657	3.11865	4.11614	5.41839	9.31727	15.86309	26.74993
30	1.34785	1.56308	1.81136	2.09757	2.42726	3.24340	4.32194	5.74349	10.06266	17.44940	29.95992

Note: The values listed in the table have been rounded.

EXAMPLE 2

Use Table 9-1 to compute the compound interest on $500 for 6 years compounded annually at 4%.

Find period 6 in the first column of the table and move across to the 4% column. This figure is 1.26532. This means that $1 would be worth $1.26532, compounded annually.

$500 × 1.26532 = $632.66   The loan is for $500, so multiply $500 by 1.26532 to find the compound amount.

Thus, the compound amount, or future value, is $632.66.

$632.66 − $500 = $132.66   The compound amount minus the principal equals the compound interest.

Compounding for Periods of Less Than a Year

Sometimes loans or savings are compounded more than once a year. In such cases, you use the compound interest table in a three-step procedure.

STEP BY STEP

Finding Compound Interest for Periods of Less Than a Year

Step 1. Determine the number of interest periods by multiplying the number of years in the loan by the number of times compounding takes place each year.

Step 2. Find the interest rate per period by dividing the annual rate by the number of times compounding occurs per year.

Step 3. Use these two new figures to compute the compound interest, or use the table.

EXAMPLE 3

A loan of $300 at 8% is compounded *quarterly* (four times a year) for 3 years. Find the compound amount and the compound interest.

3 years × 4 periods
        = 12 periods   The loan is compounded four times a year for 3 years.

$\frac{8\%}{4} = 2\%$ Divide the annual rate of 8% by the number of periods per year to find the rate of interest for each period.

1.26824   Find 12 periods in the left-hand column of Table 9-1. Move across to the 2% column and find the compound amount per dollar of principal.

$300 × 1.26824 = $380.47   The amount of principal times the compound amount per dollar equals the total compound amount.

$380.47 is the compound amount, or future value.

$380.47

-300

$\overline{\$80.47}$

The compound amount minus principal equals the total amount of compound interest.

The compound interest on the loan is $80.47.

(If the loan were compounded annually instead of quarterly for 3 years, the compound total would be $377.91 and the compound interest would be $77.91; if the interest on the loan were simple interest, at the end of 3 years the amount of interest would be $72.)

Finding the Effective Rate

You can see from Example 3 that a loan with an interest rate of 8%, compounded quarterly, carries higher interest charges than a loan with an interest rate of 8% compounded annually or a loan with a simple interest rate of 8%. When you evaluate the interest charges on a compound interest loan, you need to know the actual or **effective rate** of interest. You find this rate by dividing the total interest for the year by the principal of the loan.

STEP BY STEP

Finding the Effective Rate of Interest

Step 1. Find the total compound interest for 1 year.

Step 2. Divide the compound interest for 1 year by the principal.

$$\text{Effective rate} = \frac{\text{total compound interest for 1 year}}{\text{principal}}$$

effective rate: the total interest for 1 year divided by the principal of a loan or investement.

EXAMPLE 4

Find the effective rate of interest for the loan of $300 at 8%, compounded quarterly, that was described in Example 3.

To find the *total interest* for the first year of the 3-year loan in Example 3, we must recalculate.

The number of periods in 1 year = 4.

Rate per period is $\dfrac{8\%}{4} = 2\%$

1.08243

Find period 4 in the left-hand column of Table 9-1. Move across to the 2% column.

$300 × 1.08243 = $324.73

The amount of principal times the compound amount per dollar equals the total compound amount.

$324.73 − $300 = $24.73

Compound amount − principal = interest. The compound interest for 1 year is $24.73.

$$\text{Effective rate} = \frac{\text{total compound interest for 1 year}}{\text{principal}}$$

$$= \frac{\$24.73}{\$300} = 0.0824, \text{ or } 8.24\%$$

Compounding Interest Daily

Some banks compound interest daily and others use continuous compounding to compute interest on savings accounts. There is no significant difference in the interest earned on money using interest compounded daily and compounded continuously. A computer is generally used in calculating interest if either daily or continuous compounding is used.

Table 9-2 is part of a table that gives interest on $100 compounded daily using 365 days as a year. Notice that this table gives the *interest* on the principal rather than the *compound amount,* as is given in Table 9-1.

EXAMPLE 5

Find the interest compounded daily on $800 at 13% for 28 days.

$800 ÷ $100 = 8	Find the number of $100. Find 28 days in the left-hand column of Table 9-2. Move across to the 13% column and find the interest for $100.
8 × $1.002070 = $8.02	Multiply the table value by 8.

Table 9-2 Daily Compounding Per $100 (365-day Basis)

	Interest per $100								
Day	**12%**	**12.25%**	**12.5%**	**12.75%**	**13%**	**13.25%**	**13.5%**	**13.75%**	**14%**
1	0.032876	0.033561	0.034246	0.034931	0.305616	0.306301	0.036986	0.037671	0.038356
2	0.065764	0.067134	0.068504	0.069875	0.071245	0.072615	0.073986	0.075356	0.076727
3	0.098662	0.100718	0.102774	0.104831	0.106887	0.108943	0.110999	0.113056	0.115112
4	0.131571	0.134314	0.137056	0.139799	0.142541	0.145284	0.148027	0.150770	0.153512
5	0.164491	0.167920	0.171350	0.174779	0.178209	0.181638	0.185068	0.188498	0.191928
6	0.197422	0.201538	0.205655	0.209772	0.213889	0.218005	0.222123	0.226240	0.230357
7	0.230364	0.235168	0.239972	0.244776	0.249581	0.254386	0.259191	0.263996	0.268802
8	0.263316	0.268808	0.274301	0.279793	0.285286	0.290780	0.296273	0.301767	0.307261
9	0.296279	0.302460	0.308641	0.314823	0.321005	0.327187	0.333369	0.339552	0.345735
10	0.329253	0.336123	0.342994	0.349864	0.356735	0.363607	0.370479	0.377351	0.384224
11	0.362238	0.369798	0.377358	0.384918	0.392479	0.400040	0.407602	0.415164	0.422727
12	0.395234	0.403483	0.411733	0.419984	0.428235	0.436487	0.444739	0.452992	0.461246
13	0.428241	0.437181	0.446121	0.455062	0.464004	0.472947	0.481890	0.490834	0.499779
14	0.461258	0.470889	0.480520	0.490153	0.499786	0.509420	0.519054	0.528690	0.538327
15	0.494287	0.504609	0.514931	0.525255	0.535580	0.545906	0.556233	0.566561	0.576889
16	0.527326	0.538340	0.549354	0.560370	0.571387	0.582405	0.593425	0.604445	0.615467
17	0.560376	0.572082	0.583789	0.595498	0.607207	0.618918	0.630631	0.642344	0.654059
18	0.593437	0.605836	0.618236	0.630637	0.643040	0.655444	0.667850	0.680257	0.692666
19	0.626509	0.639601	0.652694	0.665789	0.678885	0.691984	0.705083	0.718185	0.731288
20	0.659591	0.673377	0.687164	0.700953	0.714744	0.728536	0.742330	0.756127	0.769925
21	0.692685	0.707164	0.721646	0.736129	0.750615	0.765102	0.779591	0.794083	0.808576
22	0.725789	0.740963	0.756140	0.771318	0.786498	0.801681	0.816866	0.832053	0.847242
23	0.758905	0.774774	0.790645	0.806519	0.822395	0.838274	0.854154	0.870038	0.885923
24	0.792031	0.808595	0.825162	0.841732	0.858304	0.874879	0.891457	0.908037	0.924619
25	0.825168	0.842428	0.859692	0.876958	0.894226	0.911498	0.928773	0.946050	0.963330
26	0.858316	0.876273	0.894233	0.912195	0.930161	0.948130	0.966102	0.984078	1.002056
27	0.891475	0.910129	0.928785	0.947446	0.966109	0.984776	1.003446	1.022120	1.040796
28	0.924645	0.943996	0.963350	0.982708	1.002070	1.021435	1.040804	1.060176	1.079552
29	0.957826	0.977874	0.997927	1.017983	1.038043	1.058107	1.078175	1.098246	1.118322
30	0.991017	1.011764	1.032515	1.053270	1.074029	1.094792	1.115560	1.136331	1.157107

Self-Check 9.1

1. Thayer Farm Trust made a farmer a loan of $1,200 at 16% for 3 years, compounded annually. Find the compound amount and the amount of compound interest paid on the loan. Compare the compound interest with simple interest for the same period.

2. Use Table 9-1 to compute the compound interest charged by the First State Bank on $2,000 for 4 years compounded annually at 8%.

3. A loan of $800 for two acres of woodland is compounded quarterly at 12% for 5 years. Find the compound amount and the compound interest.

4. Find the effective rate of interest for the loan described in Problem 3.

5. Use Table 9-2 to find the interest compounded daily by Leader Financial Bank on $2,500 at $13\frac{1}{4}\%$ for 20 days.

9.2

Present Value

LEARNING OBJECTIVES

1. Calculate present value.
2. Use a present value table.

In the first part of this chapter you learned how to calculate the future value of an amount of money invested at the present time. Sometimes businesses and individuals need to know how much to invest at the present time to yield a certain amount at some specified future date. For example, a business may wish to set aside a sum of money to provide pensions for employees in years to come. Individuals may wish to set aside money now to pay for a child's college education or for a vacation. You can use the concepts of compound interest to figure the amount of money that must be set aside at present and compounded periodically to obtain a certain amount of money at some specific time in the future. The amount of money set aside now is called **present value.**

present value: the amount of money needed at present to yield, or earn, a specified amount at a future date.

Calculating Present Value

To find present value, divide the maturity value or compound amount by 1 + the interest rate expressed as a decimal. In other words, for a 6% interest rate, you would divide the maturity value by 1.06.

STEP BY STEP

Calculating Present Value for an Amount Compounded Annually

Step 1. Express the interest rate as a decimal and add it to 1.

Step 2. The sum from step 1 becomes the denominator in the following formula:

$$\text{Present value} = \frac{\text{maturity value}}{1 + \text{interest rate (as a decimal)}}$$

EXAMPLE 6

Calculate the amount of money that Read and Wright Editorial Services needs to set aside today to ensure that it will have $10,000 to buy a new desktop publishing system in 1 year if the interest rate is 8% and interest is compounded annually.

$1 + 0.08 = 1.08$ Convert the interest rate to a decimal and add to 1.

$$\frac{\$10,000}{1.08} = \$9,259.26$$ Divide the maturity value by 1.08 to get the present value.

An investment of $9,259.26 at 8% would have a value of $10,000 in 1 year.

Using a Present Value Table

If the interest in Example 6 had been compounded more than once a year, you would have to make calculations for each time the money was compounded. This would be a very time consuming process if there were a large number of compounding periods. Instead, you can use Table 9-3, which shows the present value of $1 at different interest rates for different periods. You multiply the present value of $1 from the table by the desired maturity value to find how much money must be invested in the present to give the desired future amount.

Table 9-3   Present Value Table

Period	1%	1½%	2%	2½%	3%	4%	5%	6%	8%	10%	12%
1	0.99010	0.98522	0.98039	0.97561	0.97087	0.96154	0.95238	0.94340	0.92593	0.90909	0.89286
2	0.98030	0.97066	0.96117	0.95181	0.94260	0.92456	0.90703	0.89000	0.85734	0.82645	0.79719
3	0.97059	0.95632	0.94232	0.92860	0.91514	0.88900	0.86384	0.83962	0.79383	0.75131	0.71178
4	0.96098	0.94218	0.92385	0.90595	0.88849	0.85480	0.82270	0.79209	0.73503	0.68301	0.63552
5	0.95147	0.92826	0.90573	0.88385	0.86261	0.82193	0.78353	0.74726	0.68058	0.62092	0.56743
6	0.94205	0.91454	0.88797	0.86230	0.83748	0.79031	0.74622	0.70496	0.63017	0.56447	0.50663
7	0.93272	0.90103	0.87056	0.84127	0.81309	0.75992	0.71068	0.66506	0.58349	0.51316	0.45235
8	0.92348	0.88771	0.85349	0.82075	0.78941	0.73069	0.67684	0.62741	0.54027	0.46651	0.40388
9	0.91434	0.87459	0.83676	0.80073	0.76642	0.70259	0.64461	0.59190	0.50025	0.42410	0.36061
10	0.90529	0.86167	0.82035	0.78120	0.74409	0.67556	0.61391	0.55839	0.46319	0.38554	0.32197
11	0.89632	0.84893	0.80426	0.76214	0.72242	0.64958	0.58468	0.52679	0.42888	0.35049	0.28748
12	0.88475	0.83639	0.78849	0.74356	0.70138	0.62460	0.55684	0.49697	0.39711	0.31863	0.25668
13	0.87866	0.82403	0.77303	0.72542	0.68095	0.60057	0.53032	0.46884	0.36770	0.28966	0.22917
14	0.86996	0.81185	0.75788	0.70773	0.66112	0.57748	0.50507	0.44230	0.34046	0.26333	0.20462
15	0.86135	0.79985	0.74301	0.69047	0.64186	0.55526	0.48102	0.41727	0.31524	0.23939	0.18270
16	0.85282	0.78803	0.72845	0.67362	0.62317	0.53391	0.45811	0.39365	0.29189	0.21763	0.16312
17	0.84438	0.77639	0.71416	0.65720	0.60502	0.51337	0.43630	0.37136	0.27027	0.19784	0.14564
18	0.83602	0.76491	0.70016	0.64117	0.58739	0.49363	0.41552	0.35034	0.25025	0.17986	0.13004
19	0.82774	0.75361	0.68643	0.62553	0.57029	0.47464	0.39573	0.33051	0.23171	0.16351	0.11611
20	0.81954	0.74247	0.67297	0.61027	0.55368	0.45639	0.37689	0.31180	0.21455	0.14864	0.10367
21	0.81143	0.73150	0.65978	0.59539	0.53755	0.43883	0.35894	0.29416	0.19866	0.13513	0.09256
22	0.80340	0.72069	0.64684	0.58086	0.52189	0.42196	0.34185	0.27751	0.18394	0.12285	0.08264
23	0.79544	0.71004	0.63416	0.56670	0.50669	0.40573	0.32557	0.26180	0.17032	0.11168	0.07379
24	0.78757	0.69954	0.62172	0.55288	0.49193	0.39012	0.31007	0.24698	0.15770	0.10153	0.06588
25	0.77977	0.68921	0.60953	0.53939	0.47761	0.37512	0.29530	0.23300	0.14602	0.09230	0.05882
26	0.77205	0.67902	0.59758	0.52623	0.46369	0.36069	0.28124	0.21981	0.13520	0.08391	0.05252
27	0.76440	0.66899	0.58586	0.51340	0.45019	0.34682	0.26785	0.20737	0.12519	0.07628	0.04689
28	0.75684	0.65910	0.57437	0.50088	0.43708	0.33348	0.25509	0.19563	0.11591	0.06934	0.04187
29	0.74934	0.64935	0.56311	0.48866	0.42435	0.32065	0.24295	0.18456	0.10733	0.06304	0.03738
30	0.74192	0.63976	0.55207	0.47674	0.41199	0.30832	0.23138	0.17411	0.09938	0.05731	0.00338

REAL WORLD APPLICATION

Real Estate: Is This a Good Deal?

One real estate sales technique is to encourage customers or clients to buy today, because the value of the property will probably increase during the next few years. "Buy this lot today for $30,000. In two years, I project it will sell for $32,500." Let's see if this is a wise investment.

In two years the future value is projected to be $32,500. If the interest rate is 12%, compounded annually, what amount should you invest today to have the $32,500 in 2 years?

Using Table 9-3 in the text, the factor for 12% and 2 periods is 0.79719.

Present value = $32,500 × 0.79719 = $25,908.68

By investing only $25,908.68 today at 12% for 2 years, you will have the $32,500 needed to purchase the land. You have actually paid only $25,908.68 for the lot, a savings of $4,091.32 on the $30,000 price. Of course, there are always problems with waiting to buy.

Application Questions

1. What are some of the problems with waiting to buy land?

2. What are some of the advantages of waiting?

3. Lots in a new subdivision sell for $15,600. If you invest your money today in an account earning 8% quarterly, how much will the lot actually cost you in a year assuming the price does not go up? How much do you save?

4. a. You have inherited $60,000 and plan to buy a home. If you invest the $60,000 today at 10% compounded annually, how much could you spend on the house in 1 year?
b. If you intend to spend $60,000 on a house in 1 year, how much of your inheritance should you invest today at 10% compounded annually? How much do you have left to spend on a car?

EXAMPLE 7

The Absorbant Diaper Company will need $20,000 in 10 years to buy a new diaper edging machine. How much must the firm invest at the present if it receives 10% interest compounded annually?

0.38554

The money is to be compounded for 10 periods, so we find 10 (periods) in the left column of Table 9-3 and look under the 10% column to find the present value per dollar for future value.

$20,000 × 0.38554 = $7,710.80

Multiply the present value factor times the desired future value to find the amount that must be invested in the present.

Absorbant should invest $7,710.80 today to have $20,000 in 10 years.

Self-Check 9.2

6. Compute the amount of money that should be set aside today to ensure a maturity value of $2,500 in 1 year if the interest rate is 11%, compounded annually.

7. Linda thinks she will need $2,000 in 3 years to make the down payment on a new car. How much must she invest today if she will receive 8% interest compounded annually? Use Table 9-3.

8. Use Table 9-3 to calculate the amount of money that must be invested now at 6%, compounded quarterly, to obtain $1,500 in 3 years.

Summary

Topic	Page	What to Remember	Examples
Finding compound amount without using a table	285	The interest for each year is based on the sum of the previous year's principal and interest.	Find the compound amount on $500 at 7% compounded annually for 2 years. $500 × 0.07 = $35 interest for first year $500 + $35 = $535 principal for second year $535 × 0.07 = $37.45 interest for second year $535 + $37.45 = $572.45 compound amount, or future value
Finding compound interest using a table	287	Find the number of periods in the first column of the table and move across the column for the correct percent. Multiply the principal times the number in the table to find the compound amount or future value of the loan. Subtract the present value from the future value to find the compound interest.	Use Table 9-1 to find the compound interest on $800 at 8% compounded annually for 4 years. Find period 4 in the left-hand column of the table. Move across to the 8% column and find the compound amount per dollar of principal: 1.36049. $800 × 1.36049 = $1,088.39 compound amount $1,088.39 compound amount − 800 principal $288.39 compound interest
Finding future value for periods of less than a year	288	Years × periods/year = periods of loan Interest rate per period $$= \frac{\text{annual rate}}{\text{periods per year}}$$ Find the number of periods in the loan in the first column of Table 9-1. Move across to the column for the interest rate for each period and find the compound amount per dollar of principal. Multiply the value from the table times the principal to find the future value.	Find the compound amount (future value) of $2,000 at 12% compounded semiannually for 4 years. 4 × 2 = 8 periods $$\frac{12\%}{2} = 6\% \text{ interest rate per period}$$ Find 8 periods in the left-hand column of Table 9-1 and move across to the 6% column: 1.59385. $2,000 × 1.59385 = $3,187.70 future value or compound amount
Finding the amount of compound interest	285	Amount of compound interest = compound amount or future value (use Table 9-1) − principal	Find the compound interest on $800 at 10% compounded annually for 4 years. Use the table value of 1.46410. $800 × 1.46410 = $1,171.28 compound amount or future value $1,171.28 − $800 = $371.28 compound interest
Finding the effective (actual) rate	289	Effective rate $$= \frac{\text{total interest for 1 year}}{\text{principal}}$$	Find the effective rate of interest on a loan of $3,000 at 8% compounded quarterly for 1 year. $3,000 × 1.08243 = $3,247.29 future value $3,247.29 − $3,000 = $247.29 interest for 1 year Effective rate $= \dfrac{\$247.29}{\$3,000}$ $= 0.08243$, or 8.24%

Topic	Page	What to Remember	Examples
Compounding interest daily using a table	290	Find the number of periods in the first column of Table 9-2 and move across to the column for the correct percent. Divide the principal by 100; then multiply the principal times the number in the table to find the compound daily interest for the loan or investment.	Find the interest on a $300 loan borrowed at 13% compounded daily for 21 days. Move down the left-hand column of Table 9-2 to 21 days; then move across to 13%. The table value is 0.750615. $$\frac{\$300}{100} \times 0.750615 = \$2.25$$ The interest on $300 is $2.25.
Finding present value without using a table	291	Present value = $$\frac{\text{desired future value}}{(1 + \text{decimal form of interest rate})}$$	Find the amount of money that must be invested to produce $4,000 in 1 year if the interest rate is 7% compounded annually. $$\text{Present value} = \frac{\$4,000}{1 + 0.07} = \frac{\$4,000}{1.07} = \$3,738.32$$
Finding present value using a table	292	Years × periods/year = period of investment Interest rate per period $$= \frac{\text{annual rate}}{\text{periods per year}}$$ Find the number of periods of the investment in the first column of Table 9-3. Move across to the column for the interest rate for each period and find present value per dollar of future value. Multiply the value from the table times the future value to find the present value.	Find the amount of money that must be deposited to ensure $3,000 at the end of 3 years if the investment earns 6% compounded semiannually. $3 \times 2 = 6$ periods $$\frac{6\%}{2} = 3\% \text{ rate per period}$$ Find 6 in the left-hand column of Table 9-3 and move across to the 3% column: 0.83748. $3,000 × 0.83748 = $2,512.44 The amount that must be invested now to have $3,000 in 3 years is $2,512.44

Self-Check Solutions

1.

$1,200 × 0.16 = $192.00
$1,200 + $192 = $1,392   (1st year)
$1,392 × 0.16 = $222.72
$1,392 + $222.72 = $1,614.72   (2nd year)
$1,614.72 × 0.16 = $258.36   (rounded)
$1,614.72 + $258.36 = $1,873.08   (3rd year)
                 compound amount
Compound interest = $1,873.08 − $1,200
            = $673.08

Shortcut
$1,200 × 1.16
    = $1,392
$1,392 × 1.16
    = $1,614.72
$1,614.72 × 1.16
    = $1,873.08
Simple interest
    = $1,200(0.16)(3)
    = $576

2. Find period 4 in the first column. Move across to the 8% column.
    Table value = 1.36049   (Table 9-1)
    $2,000(1.36049) = $2,720.98   compound amount
    $2,720.98 − $2,000 = $720.98   compound interest

3. 5 years × 4 quarters per year = 20 periods
    12% ÷ 4 quarters = 3% per period
    Table value = 1.80611 (Table 9.1)
    $800(1.80611) = $1,444.89   compound amount
    $1,444.89 − $800 = $644.89   compound interest

4. 1 year compounded quarterly = 4 periods at 3% per period

Table value = 1.12551 (Table 9-1)

$800(1.12551) = $900.41

$900.41 − $800 = $100.41   compound interest for 1 year

Effective rate $= \dfrac{\$100.41}{800} = 0.1255125 = 12.55\%$

5. $13\frac{1}{4}\%$ for 20 days = table value 0.728536 (Table 9-2)

$\dfrac{\$2,500}{100} = 25$

25(0.728536) = $18.21 interest

6. Present value $= \dfrac{\$2,500}{1 + 0.11} = \dfrac{\$2,500}{1.11} = \$2,252.25$

7. 3 years = 3 periods at 8%, table amount = 0.79383 (Table 9-3)

$2,000(0.79383) = $1,587.66   present amount to invest

8. 3 × 4 = 12 periods, 6% ÷ 4 = $1\frac{1}{2}\%$ per period, table amount = 0.83639 (Table 9-3)

$1,500(0.83639) = $1,254.59   amount to invest

End of Chapter Problems

1. Calculate the compound interest on a loan of $1,000 at 8% compounded annually for 2 years.

2. Calculate the compound interest on a loan of $200 at 6% compounded annually for 4 years.

3. Calculate the compound interest on a 13% loan of $1,600 for 3 years if the interest is compounded annually.

4. Consult Table 9-1 to find the interest on a loan of $10,000 for 5 years at 4%, compounded semiannually.

5. How much more interest is paid on the loan in Problem 4 than if simple interest had been used?

6. Use Table 9-1 for problems 6–13. Find the compound interest on the following loans:

Principal	Term (years)	Rate of Compound Interest	Interest	Compounded
a. $2,000	3	3%	—	Annually
b. $3,500	4	10%	—	Semiannually
c. $ 800	2	6%	—	Quarterly

7. Find the factor for compounding an amount for 25 periods at 8% per period.

8. Find the compound amount on an investment of $8,000 compounded quarterly for 7 years at 8%.

9. An investment of $1,000 is made at the beginning of each year for 2 years, compounded semiannually at 10%. Find the compound amount and the compound interest at the end of the 2 years.

10. Calculate the compound interest on a loan of $5,000 for 2 years if the interest is compounded quarterly at 12%.

11. Calculate the compound interest on a loan of $5,000 for 2 years if the interest is compounded semiannually at 12%.

12. Find the effective interest rate for the loan described in Problem 10.

13. Find the effective interest rate for the loan described in Problem 11.

14. An investment of $2000 is made at the beginning of each year for 3 years. The investment is compounded annually at 8%. Find the compound amount and the compound interest at the end of 3 years.

15. Use Table 9-2 to find the amount of interest on $100 invested for 10 days at 13% compounded daily.

16. Use Table 9-2 to find the daily interest on an investment of $5,000 invested for 30 days at $13\frac{1}{2}\%$.

17. Use Table 9-2 to find the compound interest and the compound amount on an investment of $2,000 if it is invested for 21 days at 13% compounded daily.

18. Find the interest on an investment of $1,000 for 30 days if it is invested at 12% compounded monthly. Compare this interest to the interest earned on $1,000 for 30 days at 12% compounded daily. (Use Table 9-1 and 9-2.)

19. Linda Boyd invests $2,000 at 8% compounded semiannually for 2 years and Inez Everett invests an equal amount at 8% compounded quarterly for 18 months. Use Table 9-1 to determine which investment yields the greatest interest.

20. What is the effective interest rate of each investment in Problem 19?

Section 9.2

In the following problems, find the amount of money that should be invested at the stated interest rate to yield the given amount (future value) after the indicated amount of time. Use Table 9-3.

21. $1,500 in 3 years at 10%, compounded annually

22. $2,000 in 5 years at 10%, compounded semiannually

23. $1,000 in 7 years at 8%, compounded quarterly

24. $3,500 in 12 years at 12%, compounded annually

25. $4,000 in 2 years at 12%, compounded quarterly

26. $10,000 in 7 years at 16%, compounded quarterly

27. $500 in 15 years at 8%, compounded semiannually

28. $800 in 4 years at 10%, compounded annually

29. $1,800 in 1 year at 12%, compounded monthly

30. $700 in 6 years at 8%, compounded quarterly

31. Myrna Lewis wished to have $4,000 in 4 years to tour Europe. How much must she invest today at 8% compounded quarterly to have the $4,000 in 4 years?

32. Louis Banks was offered $15,000 cash or $22,900 to be paid in 2 years for a resort cabin. If money can be invested in today's market for 12% compounded quarterly, which offer should Louis accept?

33. An art dealer offered a collector $8,000 cash for a painting. The collector could sell the painting to an individual for $11,000 to be paid in 18 months. On the current money market, investments bring 12%, compounded monthly. Which is the better deal for the collector?

34. If you were offered $700 today or $800 in 2 years, which would you accept if money can be invested at 12%, compounded monthly?

Additional Problems

1. Calculate the compound interest on a loan of $6,150 at $11\frac{1}{2}\%$ compounded annually for 3 years.

2. Maria Sanchez invested $2,000 for 2 years at 12% interest compounded semiannually. Calculate the interest she earned on her investment.

3. EZ Loan Company loaned $500 at 8% interest compounded quarterly for 1 year. Calculate how much the loan company will earn in interest.

4. Use Table 9-1 to find the compound amount on an investment of $3,000 made by Ling Lee for 5 years at 12% compounded semiannually.

5. Use Table 9-2 to find the daily interest on $2,500 invested for 21 days at 12%.

6. Mario Piazza was offered $900 now for one of his salon photographs or $1,100 in 1 year for the same photograph. Which would give Mr. Piazza a greater yield if he could invest the $900 for 1 year at 16% compounded quarterly? Use Table 9-1.

7. Horst Van Dyke wants to accumulate $5,000 for a trip to Germany in 3 years. How much must he invest today at 10% interest compounded semiannually to have the money in 3 years? Use Table 9-3.

8. A realtor has listed a log cabin on 40 acres offered by the owners for $22,000 cash or $24,000 to be paid in 2 years. If the buyer can invest the cash at 8% compounded quarterly, which would be the better offer? Use Table 9-1.

9. Use Table 9-3 to calculate how much a family should invest now at 10% compounded annually to have a $7,000 down payment on a house in 4 years.

Challenge Problem

Construction of an Interest Rate Table

Your company plans to enter several short-term financing agreements. It is your assignment to compute interest for monthly compounding at the nominal annual rate of 8%. Construct an interest rate table showing the current principal and the interest earned for each of the twelve months for one dollar compounded monthly. What is the effective rate of this financing agreement?

Trial Test

1. Calculate the compound interest on a loan of $2,000 at 7% compounded annually for 3 years.

2. Calculate the compound interest on a 14% loan of $3,000 for 4 years if interest is compounded annually.

3. Use Table 9-1 to find the interest on a loan of $5,000 for 6 years at 10% if interest is compounded semiannually.

4. Use Table 9-1 to find the compound amount on an investment of $12,000 for 7 years at 12%, compounded quarterly.

5. An investment of $1,500 is made at the beginning of each year for 2 years at 12%, compounded semiannually. Find the compound amount and the compound interest at the end of 2 years.

6. Use Table 9-1 to find the compound interest on a loan of $3,000 for 1 year at 12% if the interest is compounded quarterly.

7. Find the effective interest rate for the loan described in Problem 6.

8. Use Table 9-2 to find the daily interest on an investment of $2,000 invested at 14% for 28 days.

9. Use Tables 9-1 and 9-2 to compare the interest on an investment of $3,000 that is invested at 12% compounded monthly and daily for the month of April (30 days).

In the following problems find the amount of money that should be invested today (present value) at the stated interest rate to yield the given amount after the indicated amount of time (future value).

10. $3,400 in 4 years at 8%, compounded annually

11. $5,000 in 8 years at 8%, compounded semiannually

12. $8,000 in 12 years at 12%, compounded annually

13. $6,000 in 6 years at 12%, compounded quarterly.

14. Jamie Juarez will need $12,000 in 10 years for her daughter's college education. Her parents are willing to invest the necessary funds. How much must be invested today at 8%, compounded semiannually, to have the necessary funds for college?

15. If you were offered $600 today or $680 in 1 year, which would you accept if money can be invested at 12%, compounded monthly?

16. Derek Anderson plans to buy a house in 4 years. He will make an $8,000 down payment on the property. How much should he invest today at 6%, compounded quarterly, to have the required amount in 4 years?

17. You have $2,000 to invest and have two options. Which of the two options will yield the greatest return on your investment?
Option 1: 8% compounded quarterly for 4 years
Option 2: $8\frac{1}{4}$% compounded annually for 4 years

18. If you invest $2,000 today at 8%, compounded quarterly, how much will you have after 3 years? (Table 9-1)

19. If you invest $1,000 today at 12%, compounded daily, how much will you have after 20 days? (Table 9-2)

A look at statistics that shape your finances

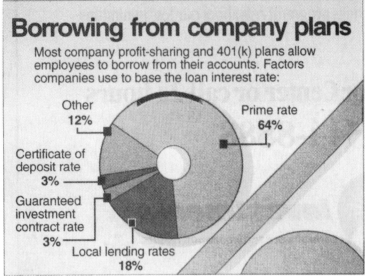

Borrowing from company plans

Most company profit-sharing and 401(k) plans allow employees to borrow from their accounts. Factors companies use to base the loan interest rate:

Other
12%

Prime rate
64%

Certificate of
deposit rate
3%

Guaranteed
investment
contract rate
3%

Local lending rates
18%

Source: Profit Sharing Council of America   By Suzy Parker, USA TODAY

QUESTIONS

1. What percent of companies base the loan interest rate on the certificate of deposit rate or the guaranteed investment contract rate?

2. Find the difference between the percent of companies that base the loan interest rate on the prime rate and the companies that base the loan interest rate on local lending rates.

3. Check with companies in your area that have employee profit sharing plans or 401(k) plans to see how they determine the loan interest rate.

10

Annuities and Sinking Funds

So far we have discussed only situations where interest was accumulated for a number of periods on one lump sum investment. Often individuals and businesses require more than one payment or investment in their financial arrangements.

When a series of equal periodic payments is put in an interest-bearing account for a specific number of periods, it is known as an **annuity.** The sum of the payments plus the interest is called the **amount of an annuity.** Pension or retirement funds, saving for a college education or vacation, a company putting away money periodically now to pay for new equipment and buildings or to retire a bond debt in the future are all examples of annuities.

In this chapter we will consider various types of annuities, their yields, and the investments necessary to obtain those yields.

10.1

The Amount of an Annuity

LEARNING OBJECTIVES

1. Calculate manually the amount of an ordinary annuity.
2. Calculate the amount of an ordinary annuity from a table.
3. Calculate manually the amount of an annuity due.
4. Calculate the amount of an annuity due from a table.

Two basic classifications of annuities are most frequently used in business: *annuities certain* and *contingent annuities*. **Annuities certain**—such as time payments on purchases, payments on a home or factory mortgage, or interest payments on bonds—have a specified number of periods. In contrast, **contingent annuities**—such as payments from life insurance policies (which are frequently payable for the lifetime of the beneficiary, an uncertain time period)—do *not* have a specific number of periods. Periods can be months, quarters, years, or any regular time period.

In addition, we can also divide both categories of annuities according to when, during a period, payment is made. In **ordinary annuities,** payment is made at the *end* of the period. In **annuities due,** payment is made at the *beginning* of the period.

annuity certain: annuity with a specified number of periods.

contingent annuity: annuity without a specified number of periods.

ordinary annuity: annuity with payment made at end of periods.

annuity due: annuity with payment made at beginning of each period.

Amount of an Ordinary Annuity Calculated Manually

The essential elements in calculating the amount of an annuity are (1) the amount of the annuity payment, (2) the number of periods for which the annuities will run, and (3) the interest rate per period. Remember, what we are looking for, the amount of an annuity, is a *future* amount of money due the investor. It is an accumulation of the annuity payments and the compound interest that accrues on those payments.

You can work annuity problems, just like compound interest problems, either manually or more conveniently by the use of a table. Business, financial, and scientific calculators often have special functions for calculating annuities.

STEP BY STEP

Calculating the Amount of an Ordinary Annuity Manually

Step 1. Find the interest on the annuity payment for the period. Note that there is no interest in the first period since an ordinary annuity's first payment is at the end of the first period.

Step 2. Add another annuity payment.

Step 3. Repeat steps 1 and 2 for the number of periods of the annuity.

EXAMPLE 1

What is the amount of an ordinary annuity of $1,000 per year for 3 years at 8% interest?

Time		Amounts	
		$1,000.00	First payment, end of first year, no interest earned.
End of year 1		$1,000.00	Value of investment before interest and second payment.
	+	$ 80.00	Earned interest ($1,000 × 0.08)
	+	$1,000.000	Second-year payment.
End of year 2		$2,080.00	Value of investment before interest and third-year payment.
	+	$ 166.40	Earned interest ($2,080 × 0.8)
	+	$1,000.00	Third-year payment.
End of year 3		$3,246.40	

Amount of an Ordinary Annuity Calculated from a Table

As you can see, the manual calculation of an ordinary annuity could become quite tedious if the number of periods was large. For example, a monthly annuity such as a savings plan, running for 5 years, would have 60 periods, and thus 60 calculations. For this reason, most business people rely on prepared tables or computers.

STEP BY STEP

Calculating the Amount of an Ordinary Annuity by Table

Step 1. Determine number of periods of the annuity (years times periods per year), and locate this value in the "period" column of Table 10-1.

Step 2. Determine the interest rate per period (annual rate divided by periods per year), and locate this rate in the "rate per period" row.

Step 3. Find the table factor at the intersection of the appropriate column and row.

Step 4. Multiply the annuity payment times the table factor.

EXAMPLE 2

Use Table 10-1 to find the amount of an ordinary annuity of $6,000 every 6 months for 5 years at 12% compounded semiannually.

5 years × 2 periods per year = 10 periods = total number of periods

$$\frac{12\% \text{ annual interest}}{2 \text{ periods per year}} = 6\% = \text{interest rate per period}$$

In Table 10-1, 10 periods at 6% gives a factor of 13.181.

$$\underset{\text{annuity payment}}{\$6,000} \times \underset{\text{table factor}}{13.181} = \underset{\text{amount of annuity}}{\$79,086}$$

Amount of an Annuity Due Calculated Manually

Because an annuity due is one in which the annuity payments are made at the beginning of each period, its amount differs from calculating the

Table 10.1 Amount of an Annuity of $1 per Period at Compound Interest

Period	Rate per Period									
	2%	3%	4%	5%	6%	7%	8%	9%	10%	12%
1	1.000	1.000	1.000	1.000	1.000	1.000	1.000	1.000	1.000	1.000
2	2.020	2.030	2.040	2.050	2.060	2.070	2.080	2.090	2.100	2.120
3	3.060	3.091	3.122	3.153	3.184	3.215	3.246	3.278	3.310	3.374
4	4.122	4.184	4.246	4.310	4.375	4.440	4.506	4.573	4.641	4.779
5	5.204	5.309	5.416	5.526	5.637	5.751	5.867	5.985	6.105	6.353
6	6.308	6.468	6.633	6.802	6.975	7.153	7.336	7.523	7.716	8.115
7	7.434	7.662	7.898	8.142	8.394	8.654	8.923	9.200	9.487	10.089
8	8.583	8.892	9.214	9.549	9.897	10.260	10.637	11.028	11.436	12.300
9	9.755	10.159	10.583	11.027	11.491	11.978	12.488	13.021	13.579	14.776
10	10.950	11.464	12.006	12.578	13.181	13.816	14.487	15.193	15.937	17.549
11	12.169	12.808	13.486	14.207	14.972	15.784	16.645	17.560	18.531	20.655
12	13.412	14.192	15.026	15.917	16.870	17.888	18.977	20.141	21.384	24.133
13	14.680	15.618	16.627	17.713	18.882	20.141	21.495	22.523	24.523	28.029
14	15.974	17.086	18.292	19.599	21.015	22.550	24.215	26.019	27.975	32.393
15	17.293	18.599	20.024	21.579	23.276	25.129	27.152	29.361	31.772	37.280
16	18.639	20.157	21.825	23.657	25.673	27.888	30.324	33.003	35.950	42.753
17	20.012	21.762	23.698	25.840	20.213	30.840	33.750	36.974	40.545	48.884
18	21.412	23.414	25.645	28.132	30.906	33.999	37.450	41.301	45.599	55.750
19	22.841	25.117	27.671	30.539	33.760	37.379	41.446	46.018	51.159	63.440
20	24.297	26.870	29.778	33.066	36.786	40.995	45.762	51.160	57.275	72.052

amount of an ordinary annuity, since the first payment is made at the *beginning* of the first period, not at the *end* as in the ordinary annuity.

STEP BY STEP

Calculating the Amount of an Annuity Due Manually

Step 1. Find the interest on the annuity payment for the period.

Step 2. Add another annuity payment.

Step 3. Repeat steps 1 and 2 for the number of periods of the annuity due.

EXAMPLE 3

What is the amount of an annuity due of $1,000 per year for 4 years at 10% interest?

Time		Amounts	
Beginning of year 1		$1,000.00	First payment
	+	$ 100.00	Earned interest for year 1 ($1,000 × 0.1)
		$1,100.00	Value of investment at end of year 1
Beginning of year 2	+	$1,000.00	Second payment
		$2,100.00	
	+	$ 210.00	Interest for year 2 ($2,100 × 0.1)
		$2,310.00	Value of investment at end of year 2

Beginning of year 3	+	$1,000.00	Third payment
		$3,310.00	
	+	$ 331.00	Interest for year 3
			($3,310 × 0.1)
		$3,641.00	Value of investment at end of
			year 3
Beginning of year 4	+	$1,000.00	Fourth payment
		$4,641.00	
	+	$ 464.10	Interest for year 4
			($4,641 × 0.1)
End of year 4		$5,105.10	

Amount of an Annuity Due Calculated from a Table

Notice, again, how time consuming the manual calculation can be, making a table desirable. To use Table 10-1 for an annuity due, through, we must take into account the fact that there will be one extra period.

STEP BY STEP

Calculating the Amount of an Annuity Due by Table

Step 1. Determine the number of periods of the annuity (years times periods per year).

Step 2. Add one period to the number found in step 1, and locate this value in the "period" column of Table 10-1.

Step 3. Determine the interest rate per period (annual rate divided by periods per year), and locate this rate in the "rate per period" row of Table 10-1.

Step 4. Find the table factor at the intersection of the appropriate column and row.

Step 5. Subtract 1.000 from the table factor to get annuity due factor.

Step 6. Multiply the annuity payment times the annuity due factor (step 5).

EXAMPLE 4

Use Table 10-1 to find the amount of an annuity due of $2,800 every 3 months for 4 years at 12% interest compounded quarterly.

4 years × 4 periods per year = 16 periods

16 periods + 1 = 17 periods = total number of periods

$$\frac{12\% \text{ annual interest}}{4 \text{ periods per year}} = 3\% = \text{interest rate per period}$$

In Table 10-1, 17 periods at 3% gives a factor of 21.762.

21.762 − 1.000 = 20.762 = annuity due factor

$2,800	×	20.762	= $ 58,133.60
annuity		annuity due	amount of
payment		factor	annuity due

Self-Check 10.1

1. Manually calculate the amount of an ordinary annuity of $3,000 per year for 2 years at 9% interest.

2. From Table 10-1, calculate the amount of an ordinary annuity of $6,500 semiannually for 7 years at 10% annual interest.

3. Manually calculate the amount of an annuity due for $12,000 per year for 3 years at 14% interest.

4. From Table 10-1, calculate the amount of an annuity due of $4,400 every 3 months for 3 years at 8% interest compounded quarterly.

 10.2

The Present Value of an Annuity

LEARNING OBJECTIVE

1. Calculate the present value of an annuity.

There are many personal and business situations in which we want to know how much money we need to invest today (one lump sum) to receive equal periodic payments of a desired amount in the future. The sum required at the beginning of the term when payouts begin is the **present value of an annuity.**

In most situations, the annuity payment in a present value type of problem starts at the end of the first period. From the previous section you will recall that this is an ordinary annuity. All the problems and examples in this section will be ordinary annuities.

present value of an annuity: the amount that must be invested now to receive equal periodic payments in the future.

Calculating the Present Value of an Annuity

To calculate the present value of an annuity, we will use Table 10-2 and a procedure similar to that for calculating the amount of an annuity.

STEP BY STEP

Calculating the Present Value of an Annuity

Step 1. Determine the number of periods of the annuity (years times periods per year), and locate this value in the "period" column of Table 10-2.

Step 2. Determine the interest rate per period (annual rate divided by periods per year), and locate this rate in the "rate per period" row.

Step 3. Find the table factor at the intersection of the appropriate column and row.

Step 4. Multiply the annuity times the table factor. This will yield the present value of the annuity.

Table 10.2 Present Value of an Annuity of $1 per Period at Compound Interest

Period	2%	3%	4%	5%	6%	7%	8%	9%	10%	12%
					Rate per Period					
1	0.980	0.971	0.962	0.952	0.943	0.935	0.926	0.917	0.909	0.893
2	1.942	1.913	1.886	1.859	1.833	1.808	1.783	1.759	1.736	1.690
3	2.884	2.829	2.775	2.723	2.673	2.624	2.577	2.531	2.487	2.402
4	3.808	3.717	3.630	3.546	3.465	3.387	3.312	3.240	3.170	3.037
5	4.713	4.580	4.452	4.329	4.212	4.100	3.993	3.890	3.791	3.605
6	5.601	5.417	5.242	5.076	4.917	4.767	4.623	4.486	4.355	4.111
7	6.472	6.230	6.002	5.786	5.582	5.389	5.206	5.033	4.868	4.564
8	7.325	7.020	6.733	6.463	6.210	5.971	5.747	5.535	5.335	4.968
9	8.162	7.786	7.435	7.108	6.802	6.515	6.247	5.995	5.759	5.328
10	8.983	8.530	8.111	7.722	7.360	7.024	6.710	6.418	6.145	5.650
11	9.787	9.253	8.760	8.306	7.887	7.499	7.139	6.805	6.495	5.938
12	10.575	9.954	9.385	8.863	8.384	7.943	7.536	7.161	6.814	6.194
13	11.348	10.635	9.986	9.394	8.853	8.358	7.904	7.487	7.103	6.424
14	12.106	11.296	10.563	9.899	9.295	8.745	8.244	7.786	7.367	6.628
15	12.849	11.939	11.118	10.380	9.712	9.108	8.559	8.061	7.606	6.811
16	13.578	12.561	11.652	10.838	10.106	9.447	8.851	8.313	7.824	6.974
17	14.292	13.166	12.166	11.274	10.477	9.763	9.122	8.544	8.022	7.102
18	14.992	13.754	12.659	11.690	10.828	10.059	9.372	8.756	8.201	7.250
19	15.678	14.324	13.134	12.085	11.158	10.336	9.604	8.950	8.365	7.366
20	16.351	14.877	13.590	12.462	11.470	10.594	9.818	9.129	8.514	7.469
25	19.523	17.413	15.622	14.094	12.783	11.654	10.675	9.823	9.077	7.843
30	22.396	19.600	17.292	15.372	13.765	12.409	11.258	10.274	9.427	8.055
40	27.355	23.115	19.793	17.159	15.046	13.332	11.925	10.757	9.779	8.244
50	31.424	25.730	21.482	18.256	15.762	13.801	12.233	10.962	9.915	8.304

EXAMPLE 5

Use Table 10-2 to find the present value of an annuity of $3,000 every 6 months for 7 years at 12% interest compounded semiannually.

7 years × 2 periods per year = 14 periods = total number of periods

$$\frac{12\% \text{ annual interest}}{2 \text{ periods per year}} = 6\% = \text{interest rate per period}$$

In Table 10-2, 14 periods at 6% gives a factor of 9.295.

$$\underset{\text{annuity payment}}{\$3,000} \times \underset{\text{table factor}}{9.295} = \underset{\text{present value of the annuity}}{\$27,885}$$

That is, by investing $27,885 now, at 12% interest compounded semiannually, you will be able to receive $3,000 every 6 months for 7 years.

Self-Check 10.2

5. What is the present value of an annuity of $680 per year for 25 years at 9% interest compounded annually?

6. Todd Simpson wants an annuity of $2,500 per year to pay for his college tuition and expenses at a local community college. How much must Todd put in the bank today at 8% annual interest in order to pay for 2 years of school?

10.3

Sinking Funds

LEARNING OBJECTIVE

1. Calculate a sinking fund payment.

Businesses often use **sinking fund** to accumulate an amount of money by the end of certain period of time to pay off a financial obligation. Some typical examples would be to retire a bond issue or to pay for equipment replacement and modernization. Essentially, what we are looking for is the payment into an ordinary annuity required to yield a known amount at a future date.

sinking fund: an annuity established at compound interest over a period of time to pay off a financial obligation.

Calculating a Sinking Fund Payment

Payments into a sinking fund are always made at the *end* of each period. These payments, along with the interest, accumulate over a period of time in order to provide the desired amount.

To calculate the series of payments required to yield a future amount, we will use Table 10-3 and the following procedure.

Table 10-3 Sinking Fund: Annuity That Amounts to $1 at Compound Interest

Period	\multicolumn{7}{c}{Rate per Period}
	1%	2%	3%	4%	6%	8%	12%
1	1.0000000	1.0000000	1.0000000	1.0000000	1.0000000	1.0000000	1.0000000
2	0.4975124	0.4950495	0.4926108	0.4901961	0.4854369	0.4807692	0.4716981
3	0.3300221	0.3267547	0.3235304	0.3203485	0.3141098	0.3080335	0.2963490
4	0.2462881	0.2426238	0.2390271	0.2354901	0.2285915	0.2219208	0.2092344
5	0.1960398	0.1921584	0.1883546	0.1846271	0.1773964	0.1704565	0.1574097
6	0.1625484	0.1585258	0.1545975	0.1507619	0.1433626	0.1363154	0.1232257
7	0.1386283	0.1345120	0.1305064	0.1266096	0.1191350	0.1120724	0.0991177
8	0.1206903	0.1165098	0.1124564	0.1085278	0.1010359	0.0940148	0.0813028
9	0.1067404	0.1025154	0.0984339	0.0944930	0.0870222	0.0800797	0.0676789
10	0.0955821	0.0913265	0.0872305	0.0832909	0.0758680	0.0690295	0.0569842
11	0.0864541	0.0821779	0.0780775	0.0741490	0.0667929	0.0600763	0.0484154
12	0.0788488	0.0745596	0.0704621	0.0675522	0.0592770	0.0526950	0.0414368
13	0.0724148	0.0681184	0.0670295	0.0601437	0.0529601	0.0465218	0.0356772
14	0.0669012	0.0626020	0.0585263	0.0546690	0.0475849	0.0412969	0.0308712
15	0.0621238	0.0578255	0.0537666	0.0499411	0.0429628	0.0368295	0.0268242
16	0.0579446	0.0536501	0.0496109	0.0458200	0.0389521	0.0329769	0.0233900
17	0.0542581	0.0499698	0.0459525	0.0421985	0.0354448	0.0296294	0.0204567
18	0.0509821	0.0467021	0.0427087	0.0389933	0.0323565	0.0267021	0.0179373
19	0.0480518	0.0437818	0.0398139	0.0361386	0.0296209	0.0241276	0.0157630
20	0.0454153	0.0411567	0.0372157	0.0335818	0.0271846	0.0218522	0.0138788
25	0.0354068	0.0312204	0.0274279	0.0240120	0.0182267	0.0136788	0.0075000
30	0.0287481	0.0246499	0.0210193	0.0178301	0.0126489	0.0088274	0.0041437
40	0.0204556	0.0165558	0.0132624	0.0105235	0.0064615	0.0038602	0.0013036
50	0.0155127	0.0118232	0.0088655	0.0065502	0.0034443	0.0017429	0.0004167

STEP BY STEP

Calculating a Sinking Fund Payment

Step 1. Determine the number of periods of the sinking fund (years times periods per year) and locate this value in the "periods" column of Table 10-3.

Step 2. Determine the interest rate per period (annual rate divided by periods per year), and locate this rate in the "rate per period" row.

Step 3. Find the table factor at the intersection of the appropriate column and row.

Step 4. Multiply the future amount desired times the table factor. This will yield the sinking fund payment required to achieve the future amount.

EXAMPLE 6

Use Table 10-3 to find the sinking fund payment required at the end of each year to accumulate $140,000 in 12 years at 8% interest compounded annually.

$$12 \text{ years} \times 1 \text{ period per year} = 12 \text{ periods} = \text{total number of periods}$$

$$\frac{8\% \text{ annual interest}}{1 \text{ period per year}} = 8\% = \text{interest rate per period}$$

In Table 10-3, 12 periods at 8% gives a factor of 0.0526950.

$$\underset{\substack{\text{future amount} \\ \text{desired}}}{\$140,000} \times \underset{\text{table factor}}{0.0526950} = \underset{\substack{\text{sinking fund} \\ \text{payment}}}{\$7,377.30}$$

That is, a sinking fund payment of $7,377.30 is required each year for 12 years at 8% to yield the desired $140,000.

Self-Check 10.3

7. What sinking fund payment would be required every 6 months to amount to $48,000, 9 years from now? The interest rate is 6% compounded semi-annually.

8. The Bamboo Furniture Company manufactures rattan patio furniture. It has just purchased a machine for $13,500 to cut and glue the pieces of wood. The machine is expected to last 5 years. If they wanted to establish a sinking fund to replace this machine, how much must be set aside each year if the interest rate is 8% compounded annually?

Summary

Topic	Page	What to Remember	Examples
Calculating the amount of an ordinary annuity manually	307	Ordinary annuity payments are made at the end of each period. Find the interest on the annuity account for the period; then add another payment. Repeat this process for the total number of periods.	Find the amount of an ordinary annuity of $2,000 per year for 2 years at 9% interest. $2,000 first payment end of year 1 +$ 180 interest ($2,000 × 0.09) +$2,000 end of year 2 $4,180 = amount of the annuity
Calculating the amount of an ordinary annuity by table	308	Determine the number of periods of the annuity and the interest rate per period. Find these values in the appropriate column and row of Table 10-1. Multiply the annuity payment times the table factor.	Use Table 10-1 to find the amount of an ordinary annuity of $5,000 semiannually for 4 years at 12%. 4 years × 2 periods per year = 8 periods $\dfrac{12\% \text{ annual interest}}{2 \text{ periods per year}} = 6\% = $ interest rate per period Table factor = 9.897 $5,000 × 9.897 = $49,485 = amount of the annuity
Calculating the amount of an annuity due manually	309	Annuity due payments are made at the beginning of each period. Find the interest on the annuity account for the period, then add another payment. Repeat this process for the total number of periods.	Find the amount of an annuity due of $3,000 for 2 years at 10% interest compounded annually. $3,000 beginning of year 1 +$ 300 interest $3,300 value end of year 1 +$3,000 payment beginning of year 2 $6,300 value beginning of year 2 +$ 630 interest $6,930 amount of the annuity
Calculating the amount of an annuity due by table	310	Determine the number of periods of the annuity and add one period. Find the interest rate per period. Find these values in the appropriate column and row of Table 10-1 and subtract 1.000. Multiply the annuity payment times the revised table factor.	Use Table 10-1 to find the amount of an annuity due of $1,500 every 3 months for 3 years at 12% compounded quarterly. 3 years × 4 periods per year = 12 periods 12 + 1 = 13 periods $\dfrac{12\% \text{ annual interest}}{4 \text{ periods per year}} = 3\% = $ interest rate per period Table factor = 15.618 15.618 − 1.000 = 14.618 $1,500 × 14.618 = $21,927 = amount of the annuity
Calculating the present value of an annuity by table	311	Determine the number of periods of the annuity and the interest rate per period. Find these values in the appropriate column and row of Table 10-2. Multiply the annuity times the table factor.	Use Table 10-2 to find the present value of an annuity of $2,500 every year for 30 years at 8% annual interest. 30 years × 1 period per year = 30 total periods $\dfrac{8\% \text{ annual interest}}{1 \text{ period per year}} = 8\% = $ interest rate per period Table factor = 11.258 $2,500 × 11.258 = $28,145 = the present value of the annuity

Topic	Page	What to Remember	Examples
Calculating the amount of a sinking fund payment by table	313	Determine the number of periods of the sinking fund and the interest rate per period. Find these values in the appropriate column and row of Table 10-3. Multiply the future amount desired times the table factor.	Use Table 10-3 to find the sinking fund payment needed at the end of every year in order to amount to $75,000 in 25 years at 6% compounded annually. 25 years × 1 period per year = 25 total periods $\dfrac{6\% \text{ annual interest}}{1 \text{ period per year}} = 6\%$ interest rate per period Table factor = 0.0182267 $75,000 × 0.0182267 = $1,367 = sinking fund payment

Self-Check Solutions

1.

		$3,000	First payment, end of first year, no interest earned.
End of year 1	+	$3,000	Value of investment before interest and second payment.
	+	$ 270	Earned interest ($3,000 × 0.09).
	+	$3,000	Second-year payment.
End of year 2		$6,270	

The amount of the ordinary annuity = $6,270.

2. 7 years × 2 periods per year = 14 periods = total number of periods

$$\frac{10\% \text{ annual interest}}{2 \text{ periods per year}} = 5\% = \text{interest rate per period}$$

In Table 10-1, 14 periods at 5% gives a factor of 19.599.

$$\underset{\text{annuity payment}}{\$6,500} \times \underset{\text{table factor}}{19.599} = \underset{\text{amount of the annuity}}{\$127,393.50}$$

3.

Beginning of year 1		$12,000.00	First-year payment.
	+	$ 1,680.00	Earned interest for year 1 ($12,000 × 0.14).
		$13,680.00	Value of investment at end of year 1.
Beginning of year 2	+	$12,000.00	Second-year payment.
		$25,680.00	
	+	$ 3,595.20	Earned interest for year 2 ($25,680 × 0.14).
		$29,275.20	Value of investment at end of year 2.
Beginning of year 3	+	$12,000.00	Third-year payment.
		$41,275.20	
	+	$ 5,778.53	Earned interest for year 3 ($41,275.20 × 0.14).
End of year 3		$47,053.73	

The amount of the annuity due = $47,053.73.

4. 3 years × 4 periods per year = 12 periods = total number of periods

12 periods + 1 = 13 periods

$$\frac{8\% \text{ annual interest}}{4 \text{ periods per year}} = 2\% = \text{interest rate per period}$$

In Table 10-1, 13 periods at 2% gives a factor of 14.680.

$$14.680 - 1.000 = 13.680 = \text{annuity due factor}$$

$4,400	×	13.680	=	$60,192
annuity payment		annuity due factor		amount of the annuity

5. 25 years × 1 period per year = 25 periods = total number of periods

$$\frac{9\% \text{ annual interest}}{1 \text{ period per year}} = 9\% = \text{interest rate per period}$$

In Table 10-2, 25 periods at 9% gives a factor of 9.823.

$680	×	9.823	=	$6,679.64
annuity payment		table factor		present value of the annuity

6. 2 years × 1 period per year = 2 periods = total number of periods

$$\frac{8\% \text{ annual interest}}{1 \text{ period per year}} = 8\% = \text{interest rate per period}$$

In Table 10-2, 2 periods at 8% gives a factor of 1.783.

$2,500	×	1.783	=	$4,457.50
annuity payment		table factor		present value of the annuity

7. 9 years × 2 periods per year = 18 periods = total number of periods

$$\frac{6\% \text{ annual interest}}{2 \text{ periods per year}} = 3\% = \text{interest rate per period}$$

In Table 10-3, 18 periods at 3% gives a factor of 0.0427087.

$48,000	× 0.0427087 =	$2,050.02
future amount desired	table factor	sinking fund payment

8. 5 years × 1 period per year = 5 periods = total number of periods

$$\frac{8\% \text{ annual interest}}{1 \text{ period per year}} = 8\% = \text{interest rate per period}$$

In Table 10-3, 5 periods at 8% gives a factor of 0.1704565.

$13,500	× 0.1704565 =	$2,301.16
future amount desired	table factor	sinking fund payment

End of Chapter Problems

Using Table 10-1, calculate the following:

	Annuity Payment	Rate	Compounded	Years	Type of Annuity	Amount of Annuity
1.	$1,400	12%	Quarterly	5	Ordinary	_____
2.	$2,900	9%	Annually	12	Ordinary	_____
3.	$125	24%	Monthly	$1\frac{1}{2}$	Annuity due	_____
4.	$10,000	20%	Semiannually	4	Ordinary	_____
5.	$800	7%	Annually	15	Annuity due	_____

6. Roni Sue deposited $1,500 at the beginning of each year for 3 years at an interest rate of 9%. Manually calculate how much this annuity will amount to at the end of the term.

7. Manually calculate how much the annuity would amount to if Roni Sue, from Problem 6, had deposited the money at the end of each year rather than at the beginning?

Use Table 10-1 for the problems that follow.

8. Barry Michael plans to deposit $2,000 at the end of every 6 months for the next 5 years to save up for a boat. If the interest rate is 12% per year, how much money will Barry have in his boat fund after 5 years?

9. Sam and Jane Crawford had a baby in 1978. At the end of that year they began putting away $900 per year at 10% interest for a college fund. When their child is 18 years old in 1996, college costs for 4 years of college are estimated to be about $10,000 per year.

   a. How much money will be in the account when the child is 18 years old?
   b. Will the Crawfords have enough saved to send their child to college? For how many years?

10. Bob Paris is 46 years old when he opens a retirement income account paying 9%. He deposits $3,000 at the beginning of each year.

a. How much will be in the account after 10 years?

b. When Bob retires at age 65, in 19 years, how much will be in the account?

11. A business deposits $4,500 at the end of each quarter in an account that earns 8% annual interest compounded quarterly. What is the value of the annuity in 5 years?

12. The Shari Joy Corporation decided to set aside $3,200 at the beginning of every 6 months to provide donation funds for a new Little League baseball field scheduled to be built in 18 months. If money is worth 12% compounded semiannually, how much will be available as a donation for the field?

Section 10.2

Using Table 10-2, calculate the following:

	Annuity Expected	Period	Rate	Years	Present Value of Annuity
13.	$1,900	Semiannually	6%	15	_____
14.	$450	Quarterly	8%	10	_____
15.	$13,500	Annually	10%	5	_____

Use Table 10-2 for the problems that follow.

16. How much must Howard Marshall invest today in order to receive $750 every 6 months for the next 7 years if interest is earned at 10% compounded semiannually?

17. Leopold Carpet Cleaners, Inc., bought a new carpet cleaning machine that is expected to last 5 years and cost $175 in maintenance per year. The company wants to open an account earning 10% annual interest that will pay the $175 maintenance per year. How much should be put in this account?

18. Ethyl Herbert wants to know how much she must deposit in her local bank today so that she would receive quarterly payments of $5,200 for 10 years at a current rate of 12% compounded quarterly.

19. Peggy Rayburn wants to know how much she must deposit today so that she will receive $2,100 every 6 months for 8 years if the deposit is compounded semiannually at 10%.

20. Kimberly Auto and Truck Leasing, Inc., is offering a lease-to-own program that requires a payment of $4,500 at the end of each year for a period of 6 years. What is the present value of the lease if the annual interest rate is 12%?

21. Robert Abraham won the grand prize of $1,000,000 in the state lottery. The prize is to be paid out in equal yearly installments of $50,000 for 20 years. Interest is 8% compounded annually. What is the amount that the state must set aside now to make the payments to the winner?

22. What is the value today of $150 payments to Michael Teems by an insurance plan every 6 months for the next 25 years if the current interest rate is 12% compounded semiannually?

Section 10.3

Using Table 10-3, calculate the following:

	Future Amount Desired	Rate	Years	Annual Sinking Fund Payment
23.	$240,000	6%	15	_____
24.	$3,000,000	8%	10	_____
25.	$50,000	12%	5	_____

Use Table 10-3 for the problems that follow.

26. How much must be set aside each 6 months by the Fabulous Toy Company to replace a $155,000 piece of equipment at the end of 8 years at 8% interest compounded semiannually?

27. Tasty Food Manufacturers, Inc., has a bond issue of $1,400,000 due in 30 years. If they wanted to establish a sinking fund to meet this obligation, how much must be set aside each year if interest rates are 6% compounded annually?

28. Lausanne Private School System needs to set aside funds for a new mainframe computer. What monthly sinking fund payment would be required to amount to $45,000, the approximate cost of the computer, in $1\frac{1}{2}$ years at 12% interest compounded monthly?

29. Zachary Alexander owns a limousine that will need to be replaced in 4 years at a cost of $65,000. How much must he put aside each year in a sinking fund at 8% annual interest to be able to afford the new limousine?

30. Goldie's Department Store has a fleet of delivery trucks that will last for 3 years of heavy use and then need to be replaced at a cost of $75,000. How much must they set aside every 3 months at 8% interest compounded quarterly to have enough money in the sinking fund to replace the trucks?

31. Danny Lawrence Properties, Inc., has a bond issue that will mature in 25 years for $1,000,000. How much must the company set aside each year at

12% interest compounded annually to meet this future obligation?

32. Tony Adams wants to save $25,000 for a new boat in 6 years. How much must be put aside in equal payments each year in an account earning 8% annual interest for Tony to be able to purchase the boat?
Total number of periods = 6 years × 1 period per year = 6 periods

Challenge Problem

Getting Ready for College

Byron Spellacy has set the goal of accumulating $30,000 for his son's college fund which will be needed 18 years in the future. How much should he deposit each year in an annuity that earns interest at 8% compounded annually? How much should he deposit each year if he waits until his son starts to school (age 6) to begin saving? Compare the two payment amounts.
Use Sinking Fund table.

Trial Test

1. Manually calculate the amount of an ordinary annuity of $9,000 per year for 2 years at 15% interest compounded annually.

2. Manually calculate the amount of an annuity due of $2,700 per year for 3 years at 11% annual interest.

3. What is the amount of an annuity due of $5,645 every 6 months for 3 years at 12% interest compounded semiannually?

4. What is the amount of an ordinary annuity of $300 every 3 months for 4 years at 8% interest compounded quarterly?

5. What is the sinking fund payment required at the end of each year to accumulate to $125,000 in 16 years at 4% interest compounded annually so that Sonia Wolff can use the money as an investment from which the interest can be used in retirement?

6. What is the present value of an annuity of $985 every 6 months for 8 years at 8% interest compounded semiannually?

7. Mike's Sport Shop deposited $3,400 at the end of each year for 12 years at 7% annual interest. How much will Mike have in the account at the end of the time period?

8. How much would the annuity amount to in Problem 7 if Mike had deposited the money at the beginning of each year instead of at the end of each year?

9. How much must be set aside each year by the Caroline Cab Company to replace four taxicabs at a cost of $90,000? The current interest rate is 6% compounded annually. The existing cabs will wear out in 3 years.

10. How much must Buddy Wilbur invest today to receive $2,800 every 6 months for the next 15 years if interest is earned at 8% compounded semiannually?

11. Edward Spencer owns a lawn maintenance business. His riding lawn-mower cost $850 and should last for 6 years. Edward wants to establish a sinking fund to buy a new mower. How much must he set aside each year at 12% annual interest to have enough money to buy the new equipment?

12. Larry and Penny want to know how much they must deposit in a retire-ment savings account today so that they will receive $1,500 every 6 months for 15 years. The retirement account is paying 10% interest com-pounded semiannually.

13. Lawrence Kenneth wants to save $2,200 at the end of each year for 11 years in an account paying 7% interest compounded annually. What will be the amount of the annuity at the end of this period of time?

14. Amanda Ashley is saving for her college expenses. She sets aside $175 at the beginning of each 3 months in an account paying 12% interest com-pounded quarterly. How much will Amanda have accumulated in the ac-count at the end of 4 years?

BUSINESS MATH IN ACTION

A look at statistics that shape your finances

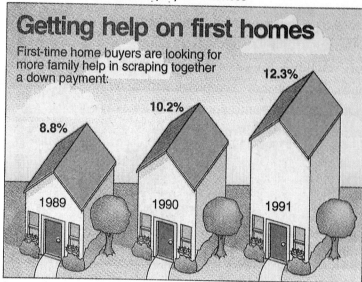

Getting help on first homes

First-time home buyers are looking for more family help in scraping together a down payment:

8.8% 1989
10.2% 1990
12.3% 1991

Source: Chicago Title & Trust

By Ron Coddington, USA TODAY

QUESTIONS

1. Tosha and Ken May are newlyweds and must save for a down payment since they can't count on any help from family. They expect to need $6,000 for a down payment and hope to buy a home in 6 years. How much should be deposited into a sinking fund each year at 8% compounded annually to achieve their goal?

2. After making 1 payment Tosha received $3,000 from an estate settlement. She and Ken now plan to buy a home after 2 more years. They decide to place

the $3,000 plus the one payment in a 2-year Certificate of Deposit which pays $8\frac{1}{2}$% compounded annually. How much will the CD be worth at maturity?

3. The Mays would like to have the rest of the down payment ready when the CD matures. How much should they invest each quarter in a sinking fund at 8% annual interest compounded quarterly?

Consumer Credit

Many individuals and businesses make purchases for which they do not pay the full amount at the time of purchase. These purchases are paid for by paying a portion of the amount owed in regular payments. This type of loan or credit, by which many of us are able to purchase equipment, supplies, and other items we need in our businesses or personal lives, is called **consumer credit.**

In the preceding chapters, we discussed the interest to be paid on loans that are paid in full on the date of maturity of the loan. But loans are often handled in other ways as well. Many times loans are made so that the maker (the borrower) pays a given amount in regular payments. This means that the borrower does not have use of the full amount of money borrowed for the full length of time it was borrowed. Instead, a certain portion of it has to be paid back with each regular payment. Loans with regular payments are called **installment loans.**

There are two kinds of installment loans. Basic installment loans are loans in which the amount borrowed plus interest is repaid in a specified number of equal payments. Examples include bank loans and loans for large purchases such as cars and appliances. **Open-end loans** are loans in which there is no fixed number of payments—the person keeps making payments until the amount is paid off, and the interest is computed on the unpaid balance at the end of each payment period. Credit card companies and retail stores most often use the open-end type of loan.

In this chapter, we will consider both types of loans, as well as the annual percentage rate at which most such loans are made.

consumer credit: a type of loan that is paid back through a number of regular payments over a period of time.

installment loan: a loan that is paid back through a specified number of payments.

open-end loan: a loan in which there is no fixed number of payments—the borrower keeps making payments until the amount is paid off, and the interest is computed on the unpaid balance at the end of each payment period.

11.1

Installment Loans

LEARNING OBJECTIVES

1. Find the total price of an installment purchase.
2. Find the amount of an installment payment.

finance charge (carrying charge): the difference between the total price and the cash price.

Should you or your business take out an installment loan? Much depends on the interest you will pay and how it is computed. Some lenders compute interest—sometimes called **finance charges** or **carrying charges**—on the average daily balance of the account. Others use the adjusted balance, which changes with each payment. In addition to accrued interest charges, installment loans often include charges for insurance, credit-report fees, or loan fees. Under the *Truth-in-Lending Law, all* these charges must be totaled and included in the determination of the interest rate.

Finding the Total Price of an Installment Purchase

cash price: the cost of an item if one had paid the full amount at the time of the sale.

total or installment price: the total amount that must be paid when the purchase is paid for over a given period of time.

down payment: a partial payment made at the time of purchase.

The **cash price** is the cost of the item if you pay the full amount at the time of the sale. The **total price** or **installment price** is the cash price of the purchase plus all other charges for paying for the purchase over a given period of time.

Total price is also the number of payments times the amount of each payment in an installment loan, plus any **down payment**. A **down payment** is a partial payment made at the time of purchase.

STEP BY STEP

> **Finding the Total (Installment) Price of a Purchase**
>
> Total price = (number of payments × amount of payment) + down payment

EXAMPLE 1

A printer was purchased on the installment plan with a $60 down payment and 12 payments of $45.58. Find the total price of the printer.

$$\text{Total price} = \left(\begin{array}{c}\text{number of}\\\text{payments}\end{array}\right) \times \left(\begin{array}{c}\text{amount of}\\\text{payment}\end{array}\right) + \text{down payment}$$

$$= \quad 12 \quad \times \quad \$45.58 \quad + \quad \$60$$

$$= \$546.96 + \$60$$

$$= \$606.96$$

Finding the Installment Payment

The amount of installment payment can be found by dividing the amount financed (installment price minus down payment) by the number of payments.

Finding the Amount of Installment Payment

Step 1. Find the amount financed:

$$\text{Amount financed} = \text{installment price} - \text{down payment}$$

Step 2. Find the amount of periodic (installment) payment:

$$\text{Installment payment} = \frac{\text{amount financed}}{\text{number of payments}}$$

EXAMPLE 2

A drafting table with built-in lighting costs $627 on the installment plan. (The finance charge is included in the installment price.) If the table is paid for in 12 equal payments with a $75 down payment, compute the amount of each monthly payment.

$$\text{Amount financed} = \text{installment price} - \text{down payment}$$

$$= \$627 - \$75 = \$552$$

$$\text{Monthly payment} = \frac{\text{amount financed}}{\text{number of payments}} = \frac{\$552}{12} = \$46$$

Sometimes the finance charge is given as a percent of the cash price. In such a case, you use the simple interest formula ($I = PRT$), with the cash price being the principal, the percent of interest charged being the rate per year, and the time being expressed in number of years.

EXAMPLE 3

Lots-of-Plots Realty can recarpet its office for $4,000 in cash or pay for it in 24 monthly installment payments with a 12% annual finance charge. Find the amount of the finance charge, the total price, and the monthly payments.

First, recall that 24 months = 2 years.

$I = PRT$	Compute the finance charge as
$= \$4,000 \times 0.12 \times 2$	simple interest
$= \$960$	The finance charge is $960.

Total price
= cash price + finance
   charge
= $4,000 + $960
= $4,960   The total price is $4,960.

$$\text{Monthly payment} = \frac{\text{amount financed}}{\text{number of monthly payments}}$$

$$= \frac{\$4,960}{24} = \$206.67 \quad \text{(rounded to the nearest cent)}$$

Self-Check 11.1

1. Find the total price of a recliner bought on the installment plan with a $100 down payment and 6 payments of $108.20.

2. Find the amount of each monthly payment on a VCR that sells for $929 on the installment plan, with 12 monthly payments and a down payment of $100.

3. Find the amount financed if a $125 down payment is made on a TV with an installment price of $579.

4. A bedroom suite has a $2,590 cash price. There is a 24% finance charge, and the suite will be paid for in 12 monthly payments. Find the amount of monthly payments.

11.2 Paying off a Loan before It Is Due: The Rule of 78

LEARNING OBJECTIVE

1. Find the finance charge refund for a loan paid back before it is due.

date of maturity: the date of the final payment on an installment loan.

refund fraction: a fraction that shows what portion of the total finance charge has not been used at the time the loan is paid off.

If an installment loan is paid in full before the **date of maturity** (the date of the last payment), some of the interest is *usually* refunded or deducted from the total value of the loan. The amount of interest refunded is calculated by multiplying the total finance charge times the **refund fraction**, a fraction that shows what portion of the total finance charge has *not* been used at the time the loan is paid off.

Finding the Finance Charge Refund

rule of 78: a method used to calculate the refund due when a loan is paid off early.

The refund fraction is the sum of the number of months remaining divided by the sum of the total number of months of the loan. Many lending institutions calculate this refund by using the **rule of 78,** which gets its name from the fact that the *sum* of the numbers 1 through 12, representing the months in a 12-month loan, is 78 $(1 + 2 + 3 + 4 + 5 + 6 + 7 + 8 + 9 + 10 + 11 + 12 = 78)$. For example, if a 12-month loan is paid off after 8 months (with 4 payments remaining), the refund fraction is

$$\frac{1 + 2 + 3 + 4}{1 + 2 + 3 + 4 + 5 + 6 + 7 + 8 + 9 + 10 + 11 + 12} = \frac{10}{78}$$

STEP BY STEP

Finding the Finance Charge Refund for a Loan Paid Back before It Is Due

Step 1. Find the refund fraction:

$$\text{Refund fraction} = \frac{\text{sum of the number of payments remaining}}{\text{sum of the total number of payments due}}$$

Step 2. Use the fraction from step 1 to find the finance charge refund:

$$\text{Finance charge refund} = \text{total finance charge} \times \text{refund fraction}$$

(This same procedure, the rule of 78, is sometimes used when refunds are made for unused portions of purchases paid for in advance, such as insurance premiums.)

EXAMPLE 4

A loan for 12 months with a finance charge of $117 is paid in full with four payments remaining. Find the amount of the finance charge (interest) refund.

Step 1. $$\frac{1 + 2 + 3 + 4}{1 + 2 + 3 + 4 + 5 + 6 + 7 + 8 + 9 + 10 + 11 + 12} = \frac{10}{78}$$

Four payments remain. Twelve payments in all were due.

Step 2. Refund = total finance charge

$$\times \frac{\text{sum of the number of payments remaining}}{\text{sum of the total number of payments due}}$$

$$\$117 \times \frac{10}{78} = \$15$$

Finding the sum of the numbers of the months is not too difficult for a short-term loan, but it is time consuming for a loan of 24 or more months. Fortunately, there is a shortcut for finding the sum of a sequence of numbers. This shortcut can be used to find the sum of the number of payments remaining, as well as the sum of the total number of payments.

STEP BY STEP

Shortcut for Finding the Sum of the Number of Payments

Sum of the number of payments

$$= \frac{\text{number of payments} \times (\text{number of payments} + 1)}{2}$$

EXAMPLE 5

A loan for 36 months, with a finance charge of $1276.50, is paid in full with 15 payments remaining. Find each part of the refund fraction. Also find the amount of finance charge to be refunded.

$$\text{Refund fraction} = \frac{\text{sum of the number of payments remaining}}{\text{sum of the total number of payments due}}$$

$$\binom{\text{Sum of the total number}}{\text{of payments remaining}} = \frac{15 + (15 + 1)}{2}$$

$$\binom{\text{Sum of the total}}{\text{of payments}}_{\text{remaining}} = \frac{36 \times (36 + 1)}{2}$$

Division can be written as the numerator (dividend) times the reciprocal of the denominator (divisor).

$$\frac{\dfrac{15 \times (15 + 1)}{2}}{\dfrac{36 \times (36 + 1)}{2}} = \frac{15 \times (15 + 1)}{\overset{}{2}_{1}} \times \frac{\overset{1}{2}}{36 \times (36 + 1)}$$

$$= \frac{15 \times (15 + 1)}{36 \times (36 + 1)} = \frac{120}{666} = \frac{20}{111}$$

Finance charge refund = finance charge × refund fraction.

$$= \$1,276.50 \times \frac{20}{111} = \$230$$

Calculator Solution

Using a calculator makes these computations go more quickly. To start, find the sum of the number of payments left to get the numerator of the refund fraction.

$$\boxed{AC}\ 15\ \boxed{+}\ 1\ \boxed{=}\ \boxed{\times}\ 15\ \boxed{\div}\ 2\ \boxed{=} \Rightarrow 120$$

Find the sum of the total number of payments due to get the denominator of the refund fraction.

$$\boxed{AC}\ 36\ \boxed{+}\ 1\ \boxed{=}\ \boxed{\times}\ 36\ \boxed{\div}\ 2\ \boxed{=} \Rightarrow 666$$

Multiply the total finance charge times the numerator of the refund fraction; then divide the result by the denominator of the refund fraction.

$$\boxed{AC}\ 1276.5\ \boxed{\times}\ 120\ \boxed{=}\ \boxed{\div}\ 666\ \boxed{=} \Rightarrow 229.9999\ \text{or}\ \$230$$

The refund fraction can be simplified so that a common fraction is used.

  m is the number of payments remaining; n is the total number of payments due.

The solution for Example 5 could have started with the step $\dfrac{15 \times (15 + 1)}{36 \times (36 + 1)}$.

 Self-Check 11.2

5. Find the refund fraction on an 18-month loan if it is paid off with 8 months remaining.

6. Ted Davis made a loan to purchase a computer. He originally agreed to pay off the loan in 18 months with a finance charge of $205. He paid the loan in full after 12 payments. How much finance charge refund should he get?

7. John Paszel made a loan for 48 months, but paid it in full after 28 months. Find the refund fraction he should use to calculate the amount of his refund.

8. If the finance charge on a loan made by Marjorie Young is $1,645 and the loan is to be paid in 48 monthly payments, find the finance charge refund if the loan is paid in full after 28 months.

11.3

Open-end Credit

LEARNING OBJECTIVES

1. Calculate interest using the unpaid balance method.
2. Calculate interest using the average daily balance method.

revolving charge accounts: open-end loans, in which borrowers keep making payments at a stated rate of interest until the loan is paid off.

Open-end loans are often called **revolving charge accounts** because, while a person or company is paying off loans that person or company may also be adding to the total loan account by making a new purchase or otherwise borrowing money on the account.

For example, you may want to use your Visa card to buy new textbooks even though you still owe for clothes bought last winter. Likewise, a business may use an open-end credit account to buy a new machine this month even though it still owes the bank for funds used to pay a major supplier 6 months ago.

Finance charges on open-end credit accounts are figured according to the *unpaid balance method* or the *average daily balance method*.

Unpaid Balance Method

When the amount owed on an account is not paid in full in any month, the company adds interest charges for the unpaid balance for that month. These interest, or finance, charges are calculated by multiplying the **unpaid balance** by the stated rate of interest:

$$\text{Interest} = \text{rate} \times \text{unpaid balance}$$

For example, if the unpaid balance on an account is \$147 and the interest rate is $1\frac{1}{2}\%$, the interest is $\$147 \times 0.015 = \$2.21$ (rounded to the nearest cent).

To figure the correct interest for the following month, you must also take into account the purchases made during the month and the payment made the month before. The activity in a revolving charge account in any one month can be summed up as follows:

unpaid balance: the amount that has not been paid off at the end of the month.

STEP BY STEP

Finding Finance Charge (Based on Unpaid Balance) and New Unpaid Balance

Step 1. Find the finance charge on the unpaid balance:

Finance charge
= unpaid balance × rate per month charged by company

Step 2. Find the new unpaid balance:

$$\begin{pmatrix}\text{previous} \\ \text{balance}\end{pmatrix} + \begin{pmatrix}\text{finance} \\ \text{charge}\end{pmatrix} + \begin{pmatrix}\text{purchases or} \\ \text{cash advances} \\ \text{during month}\end{pmatrix} - \text{payment}$$

$$= \begin{pmatrix}\text{new unpaid} \\ \text{balance}\end{pmatrix}$$

EXAMPLE 6

Strong's Boxes has an open-end credit account at a local business supply store. In September, Strong's account had an unpaid balance of \$150. During September, Strong's made purchases totaling \$356.20 and a payment of \$42.50. The supply store charges 1.7% interest per month on any unpaid balance. Find the finance charge and the unpaid balance on October 1.

Step 1. Find the finance charge on the previous unpaid balance.

$$\text{Finance charge} = \text{unpaid balance} \times \text{rate}$$

$$= \$150 \times 0.017$$

$$= \$2.55$$

Step 2. Find the unpaid balance for October 1.

$$\left(\begin{array}{c}\text{Previous} \\ \text{balance}\end{array}\right) + \left(\begin{array}{c}\text{finance} \\ \text{charge}\end{array}\right) + \left(\begin{array}{c}\text{purchases} \\ \text{during month}\end{array}\right) - \text{payment}$$

$$= \left(\begin{array}{c}\text{new unpaid} \\ \text{balance}\end{array}\right)$$

$$\$150 + \$2.55 + \$356.20 - \$42.50 = \$466.25$$

In October, Strong's made a payment of $200 and made purchases of $50. Find the finance charge and unpaid balance on November 1.

Step 1. Find the finance charge.

$$\text{Finance charge} = \text{unpaid balance} \times \text{rate}$$
$$= \$466.25 \times 0.017 = \$7.93$$

Step 2. Find the new unpaid balance.

$$\left(\begin{array}{c}\text{Previous} \\ \text{balance}\end{array}\right) + \left(\begin{array}{c}\text{finance} \\ \text{charge}\end{array}\right) + \left(\begin{array}{c}\text{purchases} \\ \text{during month}\end{array}\right) - \text{payment}$$

$$= \left(\begin{array}{c}\text{new unpaid balance} \\ \text{on November 1}\end{array}\right)$$

$$\$466.25 + \$7.93 + \$50 - \$200 = \$324.18$$

Average Daily Balance Method

average daily balance: the sum of the daily balances divided by the number of days in the billing cycle.

Rather than looking at the unpaid balance, many lenders determine the finance charge using the **average daily balance method.** In this method, the daily balances of the account are determined, and then the sum of these balances is divided by the number of days in the billing cycle. The average daily balance is then multiplied by the interest rate to find the finance charge for the month.

STEP BY STEP

Using Average Daily Balance To Find Finance Charge

Step 1. Find each daily balance:

Daily balance = previous balance + cash advances + purchases − payments

Step 2. Multiply each daily balance by the number of days it occurs to get a cumulative daily balance.

Step 3. Add together the cumulative daily balances for the billing cycle.

Step 4. Divide the total from step 3 by the number of days in the billing cycle:

$$\text{Average daily balance} = \frac{\text{sum of daily balances}}{\text{number of days in billing cycle}}$$

Step 5. Multiply the average daily balance times the interest rate per cycle to get the finance charge.

How many credit cards people have

1-3 37%
None 26%
4-6 21%
Don't know 3%
7 or more 13%

Source: Maritz Marketing Research Inc. Ameripoll, nationally representative of 1,000 adults.

By LeRoy Lottmann, USA TODAY

EXAMPLE 7

Use the following charts showing May activity in Strong's Boxes' charge account to determine the average daily balance and finance charge for the month (the bank's interest rate is 1.5% per month).

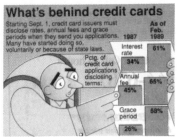

What's behind credit cards

Starting Sept. 1, credit card issuers must disclose rates, annual fees and grace periods when they send you applications. Many have started doing so, voluntarily or because of state laws.

Source: Survey by RAM Research, Frederick, Md.
By Marcia Staimer, USA TODAY

Date	Activity	Amount
May 1	Billing date	Previous balance $122.70
May 7	Payment	$ 25
May 10	Purchase (pencils)	$ 12
May 13	Purchase (envelopes)	$ 20
May 20	Cash advance	$ 50
May 23	Purchase (business forms)	$100

To figure cumulative daily balances for each day of the billing cycle, determine each change in balance and the number of days of the cycle that show the same balance. Then multiply the balance times the number of days that it holds.

For example, the balance from May 1 to May 7 is the previous month's balance of $122.70, so you calculate as follows:

$$\$122.70 \times 7 = \$858.90$$

On May 8 there is a payment of $25, which changes the balance:

$$\$122.70 - \$25 = \$97.70$$

The new balance of $97.70 holds until May 10 (3 days):

$$\$97.70 \times 3 = \$293.10$$

Continue doing this until you get to the end of the cycle. The following chart shows the results:

Date	Unpaid Balance	Number of Days	Total
May 1–May 7	$122.70	7	$ 858.90
May 8–May 10	97.70	3	293.10
May 11–May 13	109.70	3	329.10
May 14–May 20	129.70	7	907.90
May 21–May 23	179.70	3	539.10
May 24–May 31	279.70	8	2,237.60
31 days in cycle		31	$5,165.70

The average daily balance is then found by the formula:

$$\text{Average daily balance} = \frac{\text{sum of daily balances}}{\text{number of days in billing cycle}}$$

$$= \frac{\$5,165.70}{31} = \$166.64$$

The average daily balance is then multiplied by the bank's interest rate to figure the finance charge. In this example, the bank's interest rate is 1.5%:

$$\$166.64 \times 0.015 = \$2.50 \text{ finance charge for the cycle}$$

9. What is the finance charge on an unpaid balance of $275.69 if the interest rate per month is 2.3%?

10. Find the new unpaid balance on an account with an interest rate of 1.6% per month if the previous unpaid balance was $176.95 and a payment of $45 was made.

11. Suppose the charge account of Strong's Boxes at the local supply store had a 1.8% interest rate per month on the average daily balance. Find the average daily balance if Strong's had an unpaid balance on March 1 of $128.50, a payment of $20 on March 6, and a purchase of $25.60 on March 20. The billing cycle ends March 31.

12. Using Problem 11, find Strong's finance charge and unpaid balance on April 1.

11.4

Annual Percentage Rates

LEARNING OBJECTIVES

1. Use the constant ratio formula to find the annual percentage rate.
2. Use a table to find the annual percentage rate.

In 1969, the federal government passed the Truth-in-Lending Law, which requires that a lending institution tell the borrower, in writing, what the actual annual rate of interest is. This interest rate tells the borrower what the true cost of the loan is.

For example, if you borrowed $1,500 for a year and paid an interest charge of $165, you would be paying an interest rate of 11%. But if you paid the money back in 12 monthly installments of $138.75 [($1,500 + $165) ÷ 12 = $138.75], you would not have the use of the $1,500 for a full year. Instead, you would be paying it back in 12 payments of $138.75 each. Thus you are losing the use of some of the money every month, but still paying interest as if you had use of the entire amount. This means that you are really paying more than 11% interest. The true **annual percentage rate (APR)** can be calculated one of two ways, by a formula or by using a government-issued table.

annual percentage rate (APR): the actual annual rate of interest, which often differs from the stated rate because you do not have full use of the money for the whole period of the loan.

constant ratio formula: method used to find the annual percentage rate when the loan covers a short period of time.

Using the Constant Ratio Formula

You can use the **constant ratio formula** to find the annual percentage rate on any loan that is paid back in equal quarterly, monthly, or weekly installments. This formula gives a close approximation of the actual interest if the time of the loan is short. On loans made for 10 years or more, this formula will not give a fair approximation of the actual interest rate.

STEP BY STEP

Using the Constant Ratio Formula to Find the Annual Percentage Rate

Set up the constant ratio formula as follows:

Annual percentage rate

$$= \frac{2 \times \text{number of payments in 1 year} \times \text{amount of interest paid}}{\text{amount of loan} \times (\text{number of payments made on the loan} + 1)}$$

EXAMPLE 8

A loan of $6,000, borrowed for 3 years, required interest of $1,440. Find the annual percentage rate if the loan was repaid in monthly installments.

Number of payments on the loan = 3 years × 12 payments per year = 36

Annual percentage rate

$$= \frac{2 \times \text{number of payments in 1 year} \times \text{amount of interest paid}}{\text{amount of loan} \times (\text{number of payments made on the loan} + 1)}$$

$$= \frac{(2)(12)(1440)}{(6000)(36 + 1)} = 0.1556756, \text{ which rounds to 0.156, or 15.6\%}$$

Using an APR Table

While the formula provides a good approximation in many cases, the federal government issues annual percentage rate tables, which are used to find *exact* APR rates (within $\frac{1}{4}\%$, which is the federal standard). A portion of one of these tables, based on monthly payments, is shown in Table 11-1.

STEP BY STEP

Calculating APR with a Table

Step 1. Multiply the finance charge by $100 and divide by the amount financed:

$$\frac{\text{Finance charge} \times \$100}{\text{Amount financed}}$$

Step 2. Read down the left column of the table to the appropriate number of payments. Move across to find the number closest to that found in step 1. Read up that column to find the annual percentage rate at the top of the column.

EXAMPLE 9

Lewis Strang bought a motorcycle for $3,000, which was financed at $140 per month for 24 months. There was no down payment. The total finance charge was $360. Find the annual percentage rate.

$$\frac{\text{Finance charge} \times \$100}{\text{Amount financed}} = \frac{\$360 \times \$100}{\$3,000} = \$12$$

Read down the left column of the table to number 24, the number of payments to be made. Go across to find the number nearest to $12 (it is $12.14). Go up to the top of that column to find the annual percentage rate, which is 11.25%.

Table 11-1 Annual Percentage Rate Table for Monthly Payments (Finance Charge per $100 of Amount Financed)

Number of Payments	Annual percentage rate															
	10.00%	10.25%	10.50%	10.75%	11.00%	11.25%	11.50%	11.75%	12.00%	12.25%	12.50%	12.75%	13.00%	13.25%	13.50%	13.75%
1	0.83	0.85	0.87	0.90	0.92	0.94	0.96	0.98	1.00	1.02	1.04	1.06	1.08	1.10	1.12	1.15
2	1.25	1.28	1.31	1.35	1.38	1.41	1.44	1.47	1.50	1.53	1.57	1.60	1.63	1.66	1.69	1.72
3	1.67	1.71	1.76	1.80	1.84	1.88	1.92	1.96	2.01	2.05	2.09	2.13	2.17	2.22	2.26	2.30
4	2.09	2.14	2.20	2.25	2.30	2.35	2.41	2.46	2.51	2.57	2.62	2.67	2.72	2.78	2.83	2.88
5	2.51	2.58	2.64	2.70	2.77	2.83	2.89	2.96	3.02	3.08	3.15	3.21	3.27	3.34	3.40	3.46
6	2.94	3.01	3.08	3.16	3.23	3.31	3.38	3.45	3.53	3.60	3.68	3.75	3.83	3.90	3.97	4.05
7	3.36	3.45	3.53	3.62	3.70	3.78	3.87	3.95	4.04	4.12	4.21	4.29	4.38	4.47	4.55	4.64
8	3.79	3.88	3.98	4.07	4.17	4.26	4.36	4.46	4.55	4.65	4.74	4.84	4.94	5.03	5.13	5.22
9	4.21	4.32	4.43	4.53	4.64	4.75	4.85	4.96	5.07	5.17	5.28	5.39	5.49	5.60	5.71	5.82
10	4.64	4.76	4.88	4.99	5.11	5.23	5.35	5.46	5.58	5.70	5.82	5.94	6.05	6.17	6.29	6.41
11	5.07	5.20	5.33	5.45	5.58	5.71	5.84	5.97	6.10	6.23	6.36	6.49	6.62	6.75	6.88	7.01
12	5.50	5.64	5.78	5.92	6.06	6.20	6.34	6.48	6.62	6.76	6.90	7.04	7.18	7.32	7.46	7.60
13	5.93	6.08	6.23	6.38	6.53	6.68	6.84	6.99	7.14	7.29	7.44	7.59	7.75	7.90	8.05	8.20
14	6.36	6.52	6.69	6.85	7.01	7.17	7.34	7.50	7.66	7.82	7.99	8.15	8.31	8.48	8.64	8.81
15	6.80	6.97	7.14	7.32	7.49	7.66	7.84	8.01	8.19	8.36	8.53	8.71	8.88	9.06	9.23	9.41
16	7.23	7.41	7.60	7.78	7.97	8.15	8.34	8.53	8.71	8.90	9.08	9.27	9.46	9.64	9.83	10.02
17	7.67	7.86	8.06	8.25	8.45	8.65	8.84	9.04	9.24	9.44	9.63	9.83	10.03	10.23	10.44	10.63
18	8.10	8.31	8.52	8.73	8.93	9.14	9.35	9.56	9.77	9.98	10.19	10.40	10.61	10.82	11.03	11.24
19	8.54	8.76	8.98	9.20	9.42	9.64	9.86	10.08	10.30	10.52	10.74	10.96	11.18	11.41	11.63	11.85
20	8.98	9.21	9.44	9.67	9.90	10.13	10.37	10.60	10.83	11.06	11.30	11.53	11.76	12.00	12.23	12.46
21	9.42	9.66	9.90	10.15	10.39	10.63	10.88	11.12	11.36	11.61	11.85	12.10	12.34	12.59	12.84	13.08
22	9.86	10.12	10.37	10.62	10.88	11.13	11.39	11.64	11.90	12.16	12.41	12.67	12.93	13.19	13.44	13.70
23	10.30	10.57	10.84	11.10	11.37	11.63	11.90	12.17	12.44	12.71	12.97	13.24	13.51	13.78	14.05	14.32
24	10.75	11.02	11.30	11.58	11.86	12.14	12.42	12.70	12.98	13.26	13.54	13.82	14.10	14.38	14.66	14.95
25	11.19	11.48	11.77	12.06	12.35	12.64	12.93	13.22	13.52	13.81	14.10	14.40	14.69	14.98	15.28	15.57
26	11.64	11.94	12.24	12.54	12.85	13.15	13.45	13.75	14.06	14.36	14.67	14.97	15.28	15.59	15.89	16.20
27	12.09	12.40	12.71	13.03	13.34	13.66	13.97	14.29	14.60	14.92	15.24	15.56	15.87	16.19	16.51	16.83
28	12.53	12.86	13.18	13.51	13.84	14.16	14.49	14.82	15.15	15.48	15.81	16.14	16.47	16.80	17.13	17.46
29	12.98	13.32	13.66	14.00	14.33	14.67	15.01	15.35	15.70	16.04	16.38	16.72	17.07	17.41	17.75	18.10
30	13.43	13.78	14.13	14.48	14.83	15.19	15.54	15.89	16.24	16.60	16.95	17.31	17.66	18.02	18.38	18.74
31	13.89	14.25	14.61	14.97	15.33	15.70	16.06	16.43	16.79	17.16	17.53	17.90	18.27	18.63	19.00	19.38
32	14.34	14.71	15.09	15.46	15.84	16.21	16.59	16.97	17.35	17.73	18.11	18.49	18.87	19.25	19.63	20.02
33	14.79	15.18	15.57	15.95	16.34	16.73	17.12	17.51	17.90	18.29	18.69	19.08	19.47	19.87	20.26	20.66
34	15.25	15.65	16.05	16.44	16.85	17.25	17.65	18.05	18.46	18.86	19.27	19.67	20.08	20.49	20.90	21.31
35	15.70	16.11	16.53	16.94	17.35	17.77	18.18	18.60	19.01	19.43	19.85	20.27	20.69	21.11	21.53	21.95
36	16.16	16.58	17.01	17.43	17.86	18.29	18.71	19.14	19.57	20.00	20.43	20.87	21.30	21.73	22.17	22.60
37	16.62	17.06	17.49	17.93	18.37	18.81	19.25	19.69	20.13	20.58	21.02	21.46	21.91	22.36	22.81	23.25
38	17.08	17.53	17.98	18.43	18.88	19.33	19.78	20.24	20.69	21.15	21.61	22.07	22.52	22.99	23.45	23.91
39	17.54	18.00	18.46	18.93	19.39	19.86	20.32	20.79	21.26	21.73	22.20	22.67	23.14	23.61	24.09	24.56
40	18.00	18.48	18.95	19.43	19.90	20.38	20.86	21.34	21.82	22.30	22.79	23.27	23.76	24.25	24.73	25.22
41	18.47	18.95	19.44	19.93	20.42	20.91	21.40	21.89	22.39	22.88	23.38	23.88	24.38	24.88	25.38	25.88
42	18.93	19.43	19.93	20.43	20.93	21.44	21.94	22.45	22.96	23.47	23.98	24.49	25.00	25.51	26.03	26.55
43	19.40	19.91	20.42	20.94	21.45	21.97	22.49	23.01	23.53	24.05	24.57	25.10	25.62	26.15	26.68	27.21
44	19.86	20.39	20.91	21.44	21.97	22.50	23.03	23.57	24.10	24.64	25.17	25.71	26.25	26.79	27.33	27.88
45	20.33	20.87	21.41	21.95	22.49	23.03	23.58	24.12	24.67	25.22	25.77	26.32	26.88	27.43	27.99	28.55
46	20.80	21.35	21.90	22.46	23.01	23.57	24.13	24.69	25.25	25.81	26.37	26.94	27.51	28.08	28.65	29.22
47	21.27	21.83	22.40	22.79	23.53	24.10	24.68	25.25	25.82	26.40	26.98	27.56	28.14	28.72	29.31	29.89
48	21.74	22.32	22.90	23.48	24.06	24.64	25.23	25.81	26.40	26.99	27.58	28.18	28.77	29.37	29.97	30.57
49	22.21	22.80	23.39	23.99	24.58	25.18	25.78	26.38	26.98	27.59	28.19	28.80	29.41	30.02	30.63	31.24
50	22.69	23.29	23.89	24.50	25.11	25.72	26.33	26.95	27.56	28.18	28.80	29.42	30.04	30.67	31.29	31.92
51	23.16	23.78	24.40	25.02	25.64	26.26	26.89	27.52	28.15	28.78	29.41	30.05	30.68	31.32	31.96	32.60
52	23.64	24.27	24.90	25.53	26.17	26.81	27.45	28.09	28.73	29.38	30.02	30.67	31.32	31.98	32.63	33.29
53	24.11	24.76	25.40	26.05	26.70	27.35	28.00	28.66	29.32	29.98	30.64	31.30	31.97	32.63	33.30	33.97
54	24.59	25.25	25.91	26.57	27.23	27.90	28.56	29.23	29.91	30.58	31.25	31.93	32.61	33.29	33.98	34.66
55	25.07	25.74	26.41	27.09	27.77	28.44	29.13	29.81	30.50	31.18	31.87	32.56	33.26	33.95	34.65	35.35
56	25.55	26.23	26.92	27.61	28.30	28.99	29.69	30.39	31.09	31.79	32.49	33.20	33.91	34.62	35.33	36.04
57	26.03	26.73	27.43	28.13	28.84	29.54	30.25	30.97	31.68	32.39	33.11	33.83	34.56	35.28	36.01	36.74
58	26.51	27.23	27.94	28.66	29.37	30.10	30.82	31.55	32.27	33.00	33.74	34.47	35.21	35.95	36.69	37.43
59	27.00	27.72	28.45	29.18	29.91	30.65	31.39	32.13	32.87	33.61	34.36	35.11	35.86	36.62	37.37	38.13
60	27.48	28.22	28.96	29.71	30.45	31.20	31.96	32.71	33.47	34.23	44.99	35.75	36.52	37.29	38.06	38.83

Table 11-1 (continued)

Number of Payments	Annual percentage rate															
	14.00%	14.25%	14.50%	14.75%	15.00%	15.25%	15.50%	15.75%	16.00%	16.25%	16.50%	16.75%	17.00%	17.25%	17.50%	17.75%
1	1.17	1.19	1.21	1.23	1.25	1.27	1.29	1.31	1.33	1.35	1.37	1.40	1.42	1.44	1.46	1.48
2	1.75	1.78	1.82	1.85	1.88	1.91	1.94	1.97	2.00	2.04	2.07	2.10	2.13	2.16	2.17	2.22
3	2.34	2.38	2.43	2.47	2.51	2.55	2.59	2.64	2.68	2.72	2.76	2.80	2.85	2.89	2.93	2.97
4	2.93	2.99	3.04	3.09	3.14	3.20	3.25	3.30	3.36	3.41	3.46	3.51	3.57	3.62	3.67	3.73
5	3.53	3.59	3.65	3.72	3.78	3.84	3.91	3.97	4.04	4.10	4.16	4.23	4.29	4.35	4.42	4.48
6	4.12	4.20	4.27	4.35	4.42	4.49	4.57	4.64	4.72	4.79	4.87	4.94	5.02	5.01	5.17	5.24
7	4.72	4.81	4.89	4.98	5.06	5.15	5.23	5.32	5.40	5.49	5.58	5.66	5.75	5.83	5.92	6.00
8	5.32	5.42	5.51	5.61	5.71	5.80	5.90	6.00	6.09	6.19	6.29	6.38	6.48	6.58	6.67	6.77
9	5.92	6.03	6.14	6.25	6.35	6.46	6.57	6.68	6.78	6.89	7.00	7.11	7.22	7.32	7.43	7.54
10	6.53	6.65	6.77	6.88	7.00	7.12	7.24	7.36	7.48	7.60	7.72	7.84	7.96	8.08	8.19	8.31
11	7.14	7.27	7.40	7.53	7.66	7.79	7.92	8.05	8.18	8.31	8.44	8.57	8.70	8.83	8.96	9.09
12	7.74	7.89	8.03	8.17	8.31	8.45	8.59	8.74	8.88	9.02	9.16	9.30	9.45	9.59	9.73	9.87
13	8.36	8.51	8.66	8.81	8.97	9.12	9.27	9.43	9.58	9.73	9.89	10.04	10.20	10.35	10.50	10.66
14	8.97	9.13	9.30	9.46	9.63	9.79	9.96	10.12	10.29	10.45	10.67	10.78	10.95	11.11	11.28	11.45
15	9.59	9.76	9.94	10.11	10.29	10.47	10.64	10.82	11.00	11.17	11.35	11.53	11.71	11.88	12.06	12.24
16	10.20	10.39	10.58	10.77	10.95	11.14	11.33	11.52	11.71	11.90	12.09	12.28	12.46	12.65	12.84	13.03
17	10.82	11.02	11.22	11.42	11.62	11.82	12.02	12.22	12.42	12.62	12.83	13.03	13.23	13.43	13.63	13.83
18	11.45	11.66	11.87	12.08	12.29	12.50	12.72	12.93	13.14	13.35	13.57	13.78	13.99	14.21	14.42	14.64
19	12.07	12.30	12.52	12.74	12.97	13.19	13.41	13.64	13.86	14.09	14.31	14.54	14.76	14.99	15.22	15.44
20	12.70	12.93	13.17	13.41	13.64	13.88	14.11	14.35	14.59	14.82	15.06	15.30	15.54	15.77	16.01	16.25
21	13.33	13.58	13.82	14.07	14.32	14.57	14.82	15.06	15.31	15.56	15.81	16.06	16.31	16.56	16.81	17.07
22	13.96	14.22	14.48	14.74	15.00	15.26	15.52	15.78	16.04	16.30	16.57	16.83	17.09	17.36	17.62	17.88
23	14.59	14.87	15.14	15.41	15.68	15.96	16.23	16.50	16.78	17.05	17.32	17.60	17.88	18.15	18.43	18.70
24	15.23	15.51	15.80	16.08	16.37	16.65	16.94	17.22	17.51	17.80	18.09	18.37	18.66	18.95	19.24	19.53
25	15.87	16.17	16.46	16.76	17.06	17.35	17.65	17.95	18.25	18.55	18.85	19.15	19.45	19.75	20.05	20.36
26	16.51	16.82	17.13	17.44	17.75	18.06	18.37	18.68	18.99	19.30	19.62	19.93	20.24	20.56	20.87	21.19
27	17.15	17.47	17.80	18.12	18.44	18.76	19.09	19.41	19.74	20.06	20.39	20.71	21.04	21.37	21.69	22.02
28	17.80	18.13	18.47	18.80	19.14	19.47	19.81	20.15	20.48	20.82	21.16	21.50	21.84	22.18	22.52	22.86
29	18.45	18.79	19.14	19.49	19.83	20.18	20.53	20.88	21.23	21.58	21.94	22.29	22.64	22.99	23.35	23.70
30	19.10	19.45	19.81	20.17	20.54	20.90	21.26	21.62	21.99	22.35	22.72	23.08	23.45	23.81	24.18	24.55
31	19.75	20.12	20.49	20.87	21.24	21.61	21.99	22.37	22.74	23.12	23.50	23.88	24.26	24.64	25.02	25.40
32	20.40	20.79	21.17	21.56	21.95	22.33	22.72	23.11	23.50	23.89	24.28	24.68	25.07	25.46	25.86	26.25
33	21.06	21.46	21.85	22.25	22.65	23.06	23.46	23.86	24.26	24.67	25.07	25.48	25.88	26.29	26.70	27.11
34	21.72	22.13	22.54	22.95	23.37	23.78	24.19	24.61	25.03	25.44	25.86	26.28	26.70	27.12	27.54	27.97
35	22.38	22.80	23.23	23.65	24.08	24.51	24.94	25.36	25.79	26.23	26.66	27.09	27.52	27.96	28.39	28.83
36	23.04	23.48	23.92	24.35	24.80	25.24	25.68	26.12	26.57	27.01	27.46	27.90	28.35	28.80	29.25	29.70
37	23.70	24.16	24.69	25.06	25.51	25.97	26.42	26.88	27.34	27.80	28.26	28.72	29.18	29.64	30.10	30.57
38	24.37	24.84	25.30	25.77	26.24	26.70	27.17	27.64	28.11	28.59	29.06	29.53	30.01	30.49	30.96	31.44
39	25.04	25.52	26.00	26.48	26.96	27.44	27.92	28.41	28.89	29.38	29.87	30.36	30.85	31.34	31.83	32.32
40	25.71	26.20	26.70	27.19	27.69	28.18	28.68	29.18	29.68	30.18	30.68	31.18	31.68	32.19	32.69	33.20
41	26.39	26.89	27.40	27.91	28.41	28.92	29.44	29.95	30.46	30.97	31.49	32.01	32.52	33.04	33.56	34.08
42	27.06	27.58	28.10	28.62	29.15	29.67	30.19	30.72	31.25	31.78	32.31	32.84	33.37	33.90	34.44	34.97
43	27.74	28.27	28.81	29.34	29.88	30.42	30.96	31.50	32.04	32.58	33.13	33.67	34.22	34.76	35.31	35.86
44	28.42	28.97	29.52	30.07	30.62	31.17	31.72	32.28	32.83	33.39	33.95	34.51	35.07	35.63	36.19	36.78
45	29.11	29.67	30.23	30.79	31.36	31.92	32.49	33.06	33.63	34.20	34.77	35.35	35.92	36.50	37.08	37.66
46	29.79	30.36	30.94	31.52	32.10	32.68	33.26	33.84	34.43	35.01	35.60	36.19	36.78	37.37	37.96	38.56
47	30.48	31.07	31.66	32.25	32.84	33.44	34.03	34.63	35.23	35.83	36.43	37.04	37.64	38.25	38.86	39.46
48	31.17	31.77	32.37	32.98	33.59	34.20	34.81	35.42	36.03	36.65	37.27	37.88	38.50	39.13	39.75	40.37
49	31.86	32.48	33.09	33.71	34.34	34.96	35.59	36.21	36.84	37.47	38.10	38.74	39.37	40.01	40.65	41.29
50	32.55	33.18	33.82	34.45	35.09	35.73	36.37	37.01	37.65	38.30	38.94	39.59	40.24	40.89	41.55	42.20
51	33.25	33.89	34.54	35.19	35.84	36.49	37.15	37.81	38.46	39.17	39.79	40.45	41.11	41.78	42.45	43.12
52	33.95	34.61	35.27	35.93	36.60	37.27	37.94	38.61	39.28	39.96	40.63	41.31	41.99	42.67	43.36	44.04
53	34.65	35.32	36.00	36.68	37.36	38.04	38.72	39.41	40.10	40.79	41.48	42.17	42.87	43.57	44.27	44.97
54	35.35	36.04	36.73	37.42	38.12	38.82	39.52	40.22	40.92	41.63	42.33	43.04	43.75	44.47	45.18	45.90
55	36.05	36.76	37.46	38.17	38.88	39.60	40.31	41.03	41.74	42.47	43.19	43.91	44.64	45.37	46.10	46.83
56	36.76	37.48	38.20	38.92	39.65	40.38	41.11	41.84	42.57	43.31	44.05	44.79	45.53	46.27	47.02	47.77
57	37.47	38.20	38.94	39.68	40.42	41.16	41.91	42.65	43.40	44.15	44.91	45.66	46.42	47.18	47.94	47.71
58	38.18	38.93	39.68	40.43	41.19	41.95	42.71	43.47	44.23	45.00	45.77	46.54	47.32	48.09	48.87	49.65
59	38.89	39.66	40.42	41.19	41.96	42.74	43.51	44.29	45.07	45.85	46.64	47.42	48.21	49.01	49.80	50.60
60	39.61	40.39	41.17	41.95	42.74	43.53	44.32	45.11	45.91	46.71	47.51	48.31	49.12	49.92	50.73	51.55

Table 11-1 (continued)

Number of Payments	Annual percentage rate															
	18.00%	18.25%	18.50%	18.75%	19.00%	19.25%	19.50%	19.75%	20.00%	20.25%	20.50%	20.75%	21.00%	21.25%	21.50%	21.75%
1	1.50	1.52	1.54	1.56	1.58	1.60	1.62	1.65	1.67	1.69	1.71	1.73	1.75	1.77	1.79	1.81
2	2.26	2.29	2.32	2.35	2.38	2.41	2.44	2.48	2.51	2.54	2.57	2.60	2.63	2.66	2.70	2.73
3	3.01	3.06	3.10	3.14	3.18	3.23	3.27	3.31	3.35	3.39	3.44	3.48	3.52	3.56	3.60	3.65
4	3.78	3.83	3.88	3.94	3.99	4.04	4.10	4.15	4.20	4.25	4.31	4.36	4.41	4.47	4.52	4.57
5	4.54	4.61	4.67	4.74	4.80	4.86	4.93	4.99	5.06	5.12	5.18	5.25	5.31	5.37	5.44	5.50
6	5.32	5.39	5.46	5.54	5.61	5.69	5.76	5.84	5.91	5.99	6.06	6.14	6.21	6.29	6.36	6.44
7	6.09	6.18	6.26	6.35	6.43	6.52	6.60	6.69	6.78	6.86	6.95	7.04	7.12	7.21	7.29	7.38
8	6.87	6.96	7.06	7.16	7.26	7.35	7.45	7.55	7.64	7.74	7.84	7.94	8.03	8.13	8.23	8.33
9	7.65	7.76	7.87	7.97	8.08	8.19	8.30	8.41	8.52	8.63	8.73	8.84	8.95	9.06	9.17	9.28
10	8.43	8.55	8.67	8.79	8.91	9.03	9.15	9.27	9.39	9.51	9.63	9.75	9.88	10.00	10.12	10.24
11	9.22	9.35	9.49	9.62	9.75	9.88	10.01	10.14	10.28	10.41	10.54	10.67	10.80	10.94	11.07	11.20
12	10.02	10.16	10.30	10.44	10.59	10.73	10.87	11.02	11.16	11.31	11.45	11.59	11.74	11.88	12.02	12.17
13	10.81	10.97	11.12	11.28	11.43	11.59	11.74	11.90	12.05	12.21	12.36	12.52	12.67	12.83	12.99	13.14
14	11.61	11.78	11.95	12.11	12.28	12.45	12.61	12.78	12.95	13.11	13.28	13.45	13.62	13.79	13.95	14.12
15	12.42	12.59	12.77	12.95	13.13	13.31	13.49	13.67	13.85	14.03	14.21	14.39	14.57	14.75	14.93	15.11
16	13.22	13.41	13.60	13.80	13.99	14.18	14.37	14.56	14.75	14.94	15.13	15.33	15.52	15.71	15.90	16.10
17	14.04	14.24	14.44	14.64	14.85	15.05	15.25	15.46	15.66	15.86	16.07	16.27	16.48	16.68	16.89	17.09
18	14.85	15.07	15.28	15.49	15.71	15.93	16.14	16.36	16.57	16.79	17.01	17.22	17.44	17.66	17.88	18.09
19	15.67	15.90	16.12	16.35	16.58	16.81	17.03	17.26	17.49	17.72	17.95	18.18	18.41	18.64	18.87	19.10
20	16.49	16.73	16.97	17.21	17.45	17.69	17.93	18.17	18.41	18.66	18.90	19.14	19.38	19.63	19.87	20.11
21	17.32	17.57	17.82	18.07	18.33	18.58	18.83	19.09	19.34	19.60	19.85	20.11	20.36	20.62	20.87	21.13
22	18.15	18.41	18.68	18.94	19.21	19.47	19.74	20.01	20.27	20.54	20.81	21.08	21.34	21.61	21.88	22.15
23	18.98	19.26	19.54	19.81	20.09	20.37	20.65	20.93	21.21	21.49	21.77	22.05	22.33	22.61	22.90	23.18
24	19.82	20.11	20.40	20.69	20.98	21.27	21.56	21.86	22.15	22.44	22.74	23.03	23.33	23.62	23.92	24.21
25	20.66	20.96	21.27	21.57	21.87	22.18	22.48	22.79	23.10	23.40	23.71	24.02	24.32	24.63	24.94	25.25
26	21.50	21.82	22.14	22.45	22.77	23.09	23.41	23.73	24.04	24.36	24.68	25.01	25.33	25.65	25.97	26.29
27	22.35	22.68	23.01	23.44	23.67	24.00	24.33	24.67	25.00	25.33	25.67	26.00	26.34	26.67	27.01	27.34
28	23.20	23.55	23.89	24.23	24.58	24.92	25.27	25.61	25.96	26.30	26.65	27.00	27.35	27.70	28.05	28.40
29	24.06	24.41	24.27	25.13	25.49	25.84	26.20	26.56	26.92	27.28	27.64	28.00	28.37	28.73	29.09	29.46
30	24.92	25.29	25.66	26.03	26.40	26.77	27.14	27.52	27.89	28.26	28.64	29.01	29.39	29.77	30.14	30.52
31	25.78	26.16	26.55	26.93	27.32	27.70	28.09	28.47	28.86	29.25	29.64	30.03	30.42	30.81	31.20	31.59
32	26.65	27.04	27.44	27.84	28.24	28.64	29.04	29.44	29.84	30.24	30.64	31.05	31.45	31.85	32.26	32.67
33	27.52	27.93	28.34	28.75	29.16	29.57	29.99	30.40	30.82	31.23	31.65	32.07	32.49	32.91	33.33	33.75
34	28.39	28.81	29.24	29.66	30.09	30.52	30.95	31.37	31.80	32.23	32.67	33.10	33.53	33.96	34.40	34.83
35	29.27	29.71	30.14	30.58	31.02	31.47	31.91	32.35	32.79	33.24	33.68	34.13	34.58	35.03	35.47	35.92
36	30.15	30.60	31.05	31.51	31.96	32.42	32.87	33.33	33.79	34.25	34.71	35.17	35.63	36.09	36.56	37.02
37	31.03	31.50	31.97	32.43	32.90	33.37	33.84	34.32	34.79	35.26	35.74	36.21	36.69	37.16	37.64	38.12
38	31.92	32.40	32.88	33.37	33.85	34.33	34.82	35.30	35.79	36.28	36.77	37.26	37.75	38.24	38.73	39.23
39	32.81	33.31	33.80	34.30	34.80	35.30	35.80	36.30	36.80	37.30	37.81	38.31	38.82	39.32	39.83	40.34
40	33.71	34.22	34.73	35.24	35.75	36.26	36.78	37.29	37.81	38.33	38.85	39.37	39.89	40.41	40.93	41.46
41	34.61	35.13	35.66	36.18	36.71	37.24	37.77	38.30	38.83	39.36	39.89	40.43	40.96	41.50	42.04	42.58
42	35.51	36.05	36.59	37.13	37.67	38.21	38.76	39.30	39.85	40.40	40.95	41.50	42.05	42.60	43.15	43.71
43	36.42	36.97	37.52	38.08	38.63	39.19	39.75	40.31	40.87	41.44	42.00	42.57	43.13	43.70	44.27	44.84
44	37.33	37.89	38.46	39.03	39.60	40.18	40.75	41.33	41.90	42.48	43.06	43.64	44.22	44.81	45.39	45.98
45	38.24	38.82	39.41	39.99	40.58	41.17	41.75	42.35	42.94	43.53	44.13	44.72	45.32	45.92	46.52	47.12
46	39.16	39.75	40.35	40.95	41.55	42.16	42.76	43.37	43.98	44.58	45.20	45.81	46.42	47.03	47.65	48.27
47	40.08	40.69	41.30	41.92	42.54	43.15	43.77	44.40	45.02	45.64	46.27	46.90	47.53	48.16	48.79	49.42
48	41.00	41.63	42.26	42.89	43.52	44.15	44.79	45.43	46.07	46.71	47.35	47.99	48.64	49.28	49.93	50.58
49	41.93	42.57	43.22	43.86	44.51	45.16	45.81	46.46	47.12	47.77	48.43	49.09	49.75	50.41	51.08	51.74
50	42.86	43.52	44.18	44.84	45.50	46.17	46.83	47.50	48.17	48.84	49.52	50.19	50.87	51.55	52.23	52.91
51	43.79	44.47	45.14	45.82	46.50	47.18	47.86	48.55	49.23	49.92	50.61	51.30	51.99	52.69	53.38	54.08
52	44.73	45.42	46.11	46.80	47.50	48.20	48.89	49.59	50.30	51.00	51.71	52.41	53.12	53.83	54.55	55.26
53	45.67	46.38	47.08	47.79	48.50	49.22	49.93	50.65	51.37	52.09	52.81	53.53	54.26	54.98	55.71	56.44
54	46.62	47.34	48.06	48.79	49.51	50.24	50.97	51.70	52.44	53.17	53.91	54.65	55.39	56.14	56.88	57.63
55	47.57	48.30	49.04	49.78	50.52	51.27	52.02	52.76	53.52	54.27	55.02	55.78	56.54	57.30	58.08	58.82
56	48.52	49.27	50.03	50.78	51.54	52.30	53.06	53.83	54.60	55.37	56.14	56.91	57.68	58.46	59.24	60.02
57	49.47	50.24	51.01	51.79	52.56	53.34	54.12	54.90	55.68	56.47	57.25	58.04	58.84	59.63	60.43	61.22
58	50.43	51.22	52.00	52.79	53.58	54.38	55.17	55.97	56.77	57.57	58.38	59.18	59.99	60.80	61.62	62.43
59	51.39	52.20	53.00	53.80	54.61	55.42	56.23	57.05	57.87	58.68	59.51	60.33	61.15	61.98	62.81	63.64
60	52.36	53.18	54.00	54.82	55.64	56.47	57.30	58.13	58.96	59.80	60.64	61.48	62.32	63.17	64.01	64.86

Chapter 11 Consumer Credit

Self-Check 11.4

13. Use the constant ratio formula to find the annual percentage rate on a loan of $1,500 borrowed for 2 years with interest of $265. The loan is repaid in monthly payments. Round to the nearest tenth.

14. A fishing boat is purchased for $5,600 and financed for 36 months. If the total finance charge is $1,025, find the annual percentage rate using Table 11-1.

15. An air compressor costs $780 and is financed with monthly payments for 12 months. The total finance charge is $90. Find the annual percentage rate using Table 11-1.

11.5

Home Mortgages

LEARNING OBJECTIVE

1. Calculate monthly mortgage payment and total interest.

The purchase of a home is one of the most costly purchases individuals or families make in a lifetime. Most individuals must borrow money to pay for the home. Home loans are generally referred to as **mortgages** because the lending agency requires that the home be held as **collateral**. If the payments are not made as scheduled, the lending agency can take possession of the home and sell it to pay against the loan.

A home buyer may select from several types of first mortgages. A *first mortgage* is the primary mortgage on a home and is ordinarily made at the time of purchase of the home. The agency holding the first mortgage has the first right to proceeds from the sale of the home if the homeowner fails to make required payments.

One type of first mortgage is the **conventional mortgage.** Money for a conventional mortgage is usually obtained through a savings and loan institution or a bank. These loans are not insured by a government program. Two types of conventional mortgages are the **fixed-rate mortgage** and the **adjustable-rate mortgage.** The rate of interest on the loan for a fixed-rate mortgage remains the same for the entire time of the loan. Fixed-rate mortgages have several payment options. The number of years of the loan may vary, but 15- and 30-year loans are the most common. The home buyer makes the same payment (principal plus interest) for each month of the loan. Another option is the *biweekly mortgage*. The home buyer makes 26 equal payments each year rather than 12. This method builds equity more quickly than the monthly payment method.

Another option for fixed-rate loans is the *graduated payments* mortgage. The home buyer makes small payments at the beginning of the loan and larger payments at the end. Home buyers who expect their income to rise may choose this option.

The rate of interest on a loan for an adjustable-rate mortgage may escalate or de-escalate during the time of the loan. The rate of adjustable-rate

real property: land or anything permanently attached to the land, such as buildings and fences.

mortgage: the agreement that gives the tender a claim on the real property until the loan is fully paid.

collateral: real property accompanying a mortgage as security for a loan.

conventional mortgage: a loan made through a savings and loan institution or a bank that holds the property as collateral until the loan is fully repaid.

fixed-rate mortgage: a loan made for a fixed rate of interest.

adjustable rate mortgage: a loan made so that the interest rate varies, usually with the prime rate of interest.

mortgages depends upon the prime lending rate of most banks.

Several government agencies insure that first mortgage loans will be repaid. Loans with this insurance include those made under the Federal Housing Administration (FHA) and the Veterans Administration (VA). These loans may be obtained through a savings and loan institution, a bank, or a mortgage lending company and are insured by a government program.

Interest paid on home loans is an allowable deduction on personal federal income tax. For this reason, many homeowners choose to borrow money for home improvements, college education, and the like, by making a home equity loan. This type of loan is a *second mortgage* and is made against the equity in the home. In the case of a loan default, the second mortgage lender has rights to the proceeds of the sale of the home *after* the first mortgage has been paid.

Calculating the Monthly Mortgage Payment and Total Interest

amortization of a loan: the repayment of a loan in equal installments that are applied to principal and interest over a specific period of time.

The repayment of the loan in equal installments that are applied to principal and interest over a specific period of time is called the *amortization of a loan*. To calculate the monthly mortgage payment, it is customary to use an amortization chart or a business or financial calculator that has this chart programmed into the calculator. The amortization chart or schedule gives the factor that is multiplied by the dollar amount of the loan in thousands to give the total monthly payment including principal and interest. A portion of an amortization table is shown in Table 11-2.

Table 11-2 Amortization Chart (Mortgage Principal and Interest per Thousand Dollars)

Term in years	Monthly Payment for $1000							
	8%	8 1/2%	9%	9 1/2%	10%	10 1/2%	11%	11 1/2%
10	12.14	12.40	12.67	12.94	13.22	13.50	13.78	14.06
12	10.83	11.11	11.39	11.67	11.96	12.25	12.54	12.84
15	9.56	9.85	10.15	10.45	10.75	11.06	11.37	11.69
17	8.99	9.29	9.59	9.90	10.22	10.54	10.86	11.19
20	8.37	8.68	9.00	9.33	9.66	9.99	10.33	10.67
22	8.07	8.39	8.72	9.05	9.39	9.73	10.08	10.43
25	7.72	8.06	8.40	8.74	9.09	9.45	9.81	10.17
30	7.34	7.69	8.05	8.41	8.78	9.15	9.53	9.91
35	7.11	7.47	7.84	8.22	8.60	8.99	9.37	9.77

Term in years	Monthly Payment for $1000							
	12%	12 1/2%	13%	13 1/2%	14%	14 1/2%	15%	15 1/2%	16%
10	14.35	14.64	14.94	15.23	15.53	15.83	16.14	16.45	16.76
12	13.14	13.44	13.75	14.06	14.38	14.69	15.01	15.34	15.66
15	12.01	12.33	12.66	12.99	13.32	13.66	14.00	14.34	14.69
17	11.52	11.85	12.19	12.53	12.88	13.23	13.58	13.94	14.30
20	11.02	11.37	11.72	12.08	12.44	12.80	13.17	13.54	13.92
22	10.78	11.14	11.51	11.87	12.24	12.62	12.99	13.37	13.75
25	10.54	10.91	11.28	11.66	12.04	12.43	12.81	13.20	13.59
30	10.29	10.68	11.07	11.46	11.85	12.25	12.65	13.05	13.45
35	10.16	10.56	10.96	11.36	11.76	12.17	12.57	12.98	13.39

STEP BY STEP

To Calculate the Monthly Payment Using an Amortization Chart.

Step 1. Calculate the amount of the down payment.

Step 2. Calculate the amount to be financed.

Step 3. Determine how many thousands of dollars will be financed.

Step 4. Use the amortization chart to find the factor for $1,000.

Step 5. Multiply the factor times the number of thousands.

EXAMPLE 10

Lunelle Miller is purchasing a home for $87,000. Home Federal Savings and Loan has approved her loan application for a 30-year fixed-rate loan at 10%. If Lunelle agrees to pay 20% of the purchase price as a down payment, calculate the monthly payment (principal plus interest).

First, calculate the amount of the down payment.

$$\$87,000 \times 0.20 = \$17,400$$

Next, calculate the amount to be financed.

$$\$87,000 - \$17,400 = \$69,600$$

Determine how many thousands of dollars will be financed.

$$\$69,600 \div \$1,000 = 69.6$$

Use the amortization chart to find the factor for financing a loan for 30 years with a 10% interest rate. This factor is 8.78. Multiply the factor times the number of thousands.

$$\$8.78 \times 69.6 = \$611.09$$

The monthly payment of $611.09 includes the principal and interest.

To calculate the total amount of interest paid for a mortgage loan, calculate the total paid by multiplying the monthly payment by the number of months of the loan. Then subtract the amount borrowed from the total amount paid. This difference is the total interest paid.

EXAMPLE 11

Calculate the total interest paid on the loan in Example 10.

$$\text{Monthly payment} \times \text{number of years} \times 12 = \text{total paid}$$

$$\$611.09 \times 30 \times 12 = \$219,992.40$$

$$\text{Total amount paid} - \text{original amount financed} = \text{total interest}$$

$$\$219,992.40 - \$69,600 = \$150,392.40$$

The two examples show how to calculate the monthly payment and the total interest for a mortgage loan. A home buyer also needs to know that most lending companies require the borrower to pay *points* at the time the loan is made or closed. Payment of points is a one-time payment of a percent of the loan that is an additional cost of making the mortgage. One point is 1%, two points is 2%, and so on.

Other costs related to buying a home may include attorney fees, sales commissions, taxes, and insurance. Since the lending agency must be assured that the property taxes and insurance are paid on the property, the annual costs of these items are prorated each year and added for that year to the monthly payment. These funds are held in escrow until the taxes or insurance payment is due, at which time the lending agency makes the payment for the home owner.

EXAMPLE 12

If the annual insurance premium for Lunelle's home is $923 and the annual tax on the property is $950, find the adjusted monthly payment that includes principal, interest, tax, and insurance.

$$\$923 + \$950 = \$1,873$$

$$\$1,873 \div 12 = \$156.08 \quad \text{(prorated monthly taxes and insurance payment)}$$

$$\$611.09 + \$156.08 = \$767.17$$

Homeowners are often given an amortization schedule that shows the amount of principal and interest for each payment of the loan.

EXAMPLE 13

Calculate the interest and principal for the first two months of Lunelle's mortgage.

$$\text{Interest } (I) = \text{principal } (P) \times \text{rate } (R) \times \text{time } (T)$$

$$I = \$69,600 \times 0.1 \times \frac{1}{12}$$

$$I = \$580.00$$

Monthly payment (without insurance and taxes) − interest = principal

$$\$611.09 - \$580.00 = \$31.09 \quad \text{principal payment for first month}$$

To find the balance owed, subtract.

$$\$69,600 - \$31.09 = \$69,568.91$$

Calculate the interest payment for the second month.

$$I = \$69,568.91 \times 0.1 \times \frac{1}{12}$$

$$I = \$579.74$$

Monthly payment − interest = principal

$$\$611.09 - \$579.74 = \$31.35$$

Balance owed:

$$\$69,568.91 - \$31.35 = \$69,537.56$$

The first two entries of an amortization schedule for this loan follow.

Payment	Portion applied to:		
Number	Interest	Principal	Balance Owed
1	$580.00	$31.09	$69,568.91
2	$579.74	$31.35	$69,537.56

Computers are normally used to generate an amortization schedule that shows the interest and principal breakdown for each payment of the loan.

Self-Check 11.5

16. Find the down payment and mortgage amount on a home that sells for $67,000 if the down payment must be 15% of the selling price.

17. Find the monthly payment for the preceding mortgage if it is financed for 25 years at $8\frac{1}{2}\%$.

18. Find the total interest on the mortgage.

Summary

Topic	Page	What to Remember	Examples
Finding total price of an installment purchase	330	Total price = (number of payments × payment amount) + down payment	Find the total price of a computer that is paid for in 24 monthly payments of $113 if a down payment of $50 is made. $(24 \times \$113) + \$50 = \$2,712 + \$50 = \$2,762$
Finding finance charge and monthly payments	331	Finance charge = cash price × rate of interest × time Total price = cash price + finance charge Monthly payment $= \dfrac{\text{total price}}{\text{number of monthly payments}}$	Find the amount of finance charge on a computer if the cash price is $3,285 and 14% simple interest is used to calculate the total interest for 12 months. $\$3,825 \times 0.14 \times 1 = \$459.90$ Total price $= \$3,285 + \$459.90 = \$3,744.90$ Monthly payment $= \dfrac{\$3,744.90}{12} = \$312.08$
Finding the amount of monthly payments	331	Amount financed = installment price − down payment Monthly payment $= \dfrac{\text{amount financed}}{\text{number of payments}}$	A computer has an installment price of $2,187.25 when financed over 18 months. If a $100 down payment is made, find the monthly payment. $\$2,187.25 - \$100 = \$2,087.25$ $\dfrac{\$2,087.25}{18} = \$115.96$
Finding finance charge refund	332	Finance charge refund = total finance charge × refund fraction Refund fraction $= \dfrac{\text{sum of the number of payments remaining}}{\text{sum of the total number of payments due}}$ Sum of the number of payments due $= \dfrac{(\text{number of payments}) \times (\text{number of payments} + 1)}{2}$	Find the finance charge refund on a loan that has a total finance charge of $892 and was made for 24 months. The loan is paid in full with 10 months (payments) remaining. Sum of number of payments remaining $= \dfrac{10(11)}{2} = 55$ Sum of total number of payments due $= \dfrac{24(25)}{2} = 300$ Finance charge refund $= \$892 \times \dfrac{55}{300} = \$163.53$
Finding interest on a charge account	336	Interest = rate × unpaid balance Interest is usually charged on the previous month's balance, not on purchases or cash advances made during the month.	A charge account has an unpaid balance of $1,384.37 and the monthly interest rate is 1.75%. Find the interest. $0.0175 \times \$1,384.37 = \$24.23$
Finding APR with the the constant ratio formula	338	Annual percentage rate = (2 × number pay periods per year × amount interest) ÷ (loan amount × (number of payments made + 1))	Find the annual percentage rate for a loan of $13,850 that is repaid in 42 monthly installments. The interest for the loan is $2,328.20. $\text{APR} = \dfrac{2(12)(\$2,382.20)}{\$13,850(43)}$ $= 0.096 = 9.6\%$

Topic	Page	What to Remember	Examples
Finding APR using Table 11-1	339	Table value = $$\frac{\text{finance charge} \times \$100}{\text{amount financed}}$$ Find number of payments and move across to the closest value. Read up to interest rate.	Find the annual percentage rate on a loan of $500 that is repaid in 36 monthly installments. The interest for the loan is $95. $$\frac{\$95 \times \$100}{\$500} = \$19$$ Find 36 (months) in left column. Move across to 19.14 (nearest to 19). APR is at top of column, 11.75%.
Finding the down payment and mortgage amount of a mortgage	345	Multiply the percent of down payment times the total price. Subtract the down payment from the total price.	Find the down payment and mortgage amount on a $90,000 home if a 10% down payment is made. $90,000 \times 0.1 = \$9,000$ down payment $90,000 - \$9,000 = \$81,000$ mortgage amount
Finding the monthly payment using Amortizaion Chart	345	Determine how many thousands of dollars will be financed. Find the factor for $1,000 from the amortization chart and multiply it times the number of thousands.	Find the monthly payment for the preceding mortgage if it is financed for 30 years at $10\frac{1}{2}$%. $81,000 \div \$1,000 = 81$ $81 \times \$9.15 = \$741.15$
Finding the total interest on a mortgage	345	Multiply the monthly payment times the number of years times 12. From this product, subtract the amount of the mortgage.	Using the preceding mortgage, $741.15 \times 30 \times 12 - \$81,000 = \$266,814 - \$81,000$ $= \$185,814$
Completing an amortization schedule	346	Calculate the interest for the first period of the loan. Subtract the interest from the monthly payment to find the amount of principal paid. Subtract the principal from the previous balance owed to find the new balance owed.	Complete the amortization schedule for the first two payments on the preceding mortgage:

Payment Number	Portion applied to:		Balance Owed
	Interest	Principal	
1	708.75	32.40	$80,967.60
2	708.47	32.68	$80,934.92

$$\$81,000 \times 0.105 \times \frac{1}{12} = \$708.75$$

$$\$741.15 - \$708.75 = \$32.40$$

$$\$81,000 - \$32.40 = \$80,967.60$$

Repeat process for payment 2.

Self-check Solutions

1. $6 \times \$108.20 + \$100 = \$749.20$

2. $\dfrac{\$929 - \$100}{12} = \dfrac{\$829}{12} = \$69.08$

3. $\$579 - \$125 = \$454$

4. $\$2,590 \times 24\% \times 1 = \$621.60$; $$\frac{\$2,590 + \$621.60}{12} = \$267.63$$

5. $\dfrac{8(9)}{18(19)} = \dfrac{72}{342} = \dfrac{4}{19}$

6. $18 - 12 = 6$ months remaining $$\frac{6(7)}{18(19)} \times \$205 = \$25.18$$

7. $48 - 28 = 20$ months remaining

$$\frac{20(21)}{48(49)} = \frac{5}{28}$$

8. $48 - 28 = 20$ months remaining

$$\frac{20(21)}{48(49)} \times \$1,645 = \$293.75$$

9. $\$275.69 \times 0.023 = \$6.34$

10. $\$176.95 \times 0.016 = \$2.83$

$\$176.95 + \$2.83 - \$45$

$\quad = \$134.78$

11.   March 1–6 $6 \times \$128.50 = \$\ \ 771.00$

$\$128.50 - \$20 = \$108.50$

March 7–20 $14 \times 108.50 = \ \ 1,519.00$

$\$108.50 + \$25.60 = \$134.10$

March 21–31 $11 \times 134.10 = \underline{\ \ 1,475.10}$

$\overline{\$3,765.10}$

$\$3,765.10 \div 31 = \ \ \$121.45$

12. $\$121.45 \times 0.018 = \$2.19;$

$\$134.10 + \$2.19$

$\quad = \$136.29$

13. $\dfrac{2 \times 12 \times \$265}{\$1,500 \times (24 + 1)} = 17.0\%$

14. $\dfrac{\$1,025 \times \$100}{\$5,600} = \$18.30$

Move down the left column to 36. Then move across to 18.29 (nearest to $18.30). The percent at the top of this column is 11.25%, which is the rate.

15. $\dfrac{\$90 \times \$100}{\$780} = \$11.54$

Move down the left column to 12. Then move across to 11.59 (nearest to 11.54). The percent at the top of this column is 20.75%, which is the rate.

16. Down payment $= \$67,000 \times 0.15 = \$10,050$

Mortgage Amount $= \$67,000 - \$10,050 = \$56,950$

17. $\$56,950 \div \$1000 = 56.95$

Monthly Payment $= 56.95 \times \$8.06 = \$459.02$

18. $\$459.02 \times 12 \times 25 = \$137,706$

Total Interest $= \$137,706 - \$56,950 = \$80,756$

End of Chapter Problems

1. Find the finance charge on a credit card with an unpaid balance of $465 if the rate charged is 1.25%.

2. Find the new unpaid balance on an account with a previous balance of $263.50, purchases of $38.75, a payment of $35, and a finance charge of 1.5% of the unpaid balance.

3. Find the monthly rate of interest on an account with an unpaid balance of $126 and a finance charge of $2.65.

4. A television set has been purchased on the installment plan with a down payment of $120 and 6 monthly payments of $98.50. Find the total price of the television set.

5. Find the amount of each monthly payment on a water bed that is sold for $1,050 on the installment plan with a down payment of $200 and 10 monthly payments.

6. If the cash price of a refrigerator is $879 and a down payment of $150 is made, how much is to be financed?

7. What is the cash price of a chair if the total price is $679 and the finance charge is $102?

8. On August 1, the unpaid balance on a credit card was $206. During the month, purchases of $98.65 and a payment of $60 were made. Using the unpaid balance method and a finance charge of 1.5%, find the unpaid balance on September 1.

9. Use the following activity chart to find the unpaid balance on November 1. The billing cycle ended on October 31. (Use the average daily balance method.)

Date	Activity	Amount
October 1	Billing date	Previous balance $426.40
October 7	Purchase	$41.60
October 10	Payment	$70
October 15	Purchase	$31.25
October 20	Purchase	$26.80

Section 11.2

Use the rule of 78 to find the finance charge refund in each of the following.

	Finance Charge	Number of Monthly Payments	Remaining Payments	Finance Charge Refund
10.	$ 238	12	4	
11.	$1,076	18	6	
12.	$2,175	24	10	
13.	$ 476	12	5	
14.	$ 896	18	4	

Use the rule of 78 to solve the following problems.

15. The finance charge on a computer was $1,778. The loan for the computer was to be paid in 18 monthly payments. Find the finance charge refund if it is paid off in 8 months.

16. Find the refund fraction on a 48-month loan if it is paid off after 20 months.

17. Becky Whitehead has a loan with $1,115 in finance charges, which she paid in full after 8 of the 18 monthly payments. What is her finance charge refund?

18. Lanny Jacobs made a loan to purchase a computer. Find the refund due on this loan with charges of $657 if it is paid off after paying 7 of the 12 monthly payments.

19. Alice Dubois charged $455 in finance charges on a loan for 15 months. Find the finance charge refund if she pays off the loan in full after 10 payments.

20. Suppose you have borrowed money that is being repaid at $45 a month for 12 months. What is the finance charge refund after making 8 payments if the finance charge is $105?

21. Find the finance charge refund on a 15-month loan with monthly payments of $103.50 if you decide to pay off the loan at the end of the tenth month. The finance charge is $215.55.

22. You have purchased a new stereo on the installment plan. The plan calls for 12 monthly payments of $45 and a $115 finance charge. After 9 months you decide to pay off the loan. How much is the refund?

23. If you purchase a fishing boat for 18 monthly payments of $106 and an interest charge of $238, how much is the refund after 10 payments?

Section 11.3

24. Find the interest on an unpaid balance of $265 with an interest rate of $1\frac{1}{2}\%$.

25. Find the finance charge on $371 if the interest charged is 1.4% of the unpaid balance.

26. Find the new unpaid balance on an account with a previous balance of $155, purchases of $47.38, a payment of $20, and an interest charge of 1.8%.

27. A new desk for an office has a cash price of $1,500 and can be purchased on the installment plan with a 12.5% finance charge. The desk will be paid for in 12 monthly payments. Find the amount of the finance charge, the total price, and the amount of each monthly payment, if there was no down payment.

28. On June 1, the unpaid balance on a credit card was $174. During the month, purchases of $32, $14.50, and $28.75 are made. Using the unpaid balance method, find the unpaid balance on July 1 if the finance charge is 1.4% of the unpaid balance and a payment of $50 is made on June 15.

29. On January 1, the previous balance for Lynn's charge account was $569.80. On the following days, she made the purchases shown:

    January 12 $38.50   jewelry
    January 20 $44.56   clothing

On January 15, Lynn made a $50 payment. Using the average daily balance method, find the finance charge and unpaid balance on February 1 if the bank charges interest of 1.5% per month.

Section 11.4

Use the constant ratio formula to find the annual percentage rate for the following questions. Give the answers to the nearest tenth of a percent.

30. Find the annual percentage rate on a loan of $1,500 for 18 months if the loan requires $190 interest and is repaid monthly.

31. Find the annual percentage rate on a loan that is repaid weekly for 25 weeks if the amount of the loan is $300. The loan requires $20 interest.

32. Find the annual percentage rate on a loan of $3,820 if the monthly payment is $120 for 36 months.

33. Find the annual percentage rate on a loan of $700 with 12 monthly payments. The loan requires $101 interest.

34. A vacuum cleaner was purchased on the installment plan with 10 monthly payments of $10.50 each. If the cash price was $95, find the annual percentage rate.

Use Table 11-1 to find the annual percentage rate for the following.

35. A merchant charged $420 in cash for a dining-room set that could be bought for $50 down and $40.75 per month for 10 months. What is the annual percentage rate?

36. A man borrowed $500. He repaid the loan in 22 monthly payments of $26.30 each. Find the annual percentage rate.

37. An electric mixer was purchased on the installment plan for a down payment of $60 and 11 monthly payments of $11.05 each. The cash price was $170. Find the annual percentage rate.

38. A loan of $3,380 was paid back in 30 monthly payments with an interest charge of $620. Find the annual percentage rate to the nearest tenth of a percent.

39. A word processor was purchased by paying $50 down and 24 monthly payments of $65 each. The cash price was $1,400. Find the annual percentage rate to the nearest tenth of a percent.

Section 11.5

Hullett Houpt is purchasing a home for $97,000. He will finance the mortgage for 15 years and pay 11% interest on the loan. He makes a down payment that is 20% of the purchase price. Use Table 11-2 as needed.

40. Find the amount of the down payment.

41. Find the amount of the mortgage.

42. If Hullett is required to pay 2 points for making the loan, how much will the points cost?

43. Find the amount of monthly payment that includes principal and interest.

44. Find the total amount of interest Hullett will pay over the 15-year period.

45. Calculate the amount of interest Hullett would have to pay if he decided to make the loan for 30 years instead of 15 years.

46. How much interest can be saved by paying for the home in 15 years rather than 30 years?

47. Find the amount of interest and principal for the first payment of Hullett's loan.

48. Make an amortization schedule for the first three payments of the 15-year loan.

Payment Number	Portion Applied to:		Balance Owed
	Interest	Principal	
1			
2			
3			

49. Make an amortization schedule for the first three payments of the 30-year loan.

Payment Number	Portion Applied to:		Balance Owed
	Interest	Principal	
1			
2			
3			

Additional Problems

1. Selelia Taylor purchased a set of tires for $743 by putting $143 down and financing the balance at 21% simple interest for 12 months. Find the amount of the monthly payments.

2. Find the total price of a 386SX home computer system bought on the installment plan with $250 down and 12 payments of $111.33.

3. Use the rule of 78 to calculate the finance charge refund if a 24-month loan with a finance charge of $128.08 is paid off in 15 months.

4. Find the refund fraction under the rule of 78 for a 36-month loan paid off after 24 months.

5. Find the new unpaid balance on an account with a previous balance of $265.76, purchases of $52.45, a payment of $45, and an interest charge of 1.25%.

6. On October 1, the unpaid balance on a credit card account was $1,255.86. During the month, purchases of $23.75, $19.63, and $121.43 were made. A $125 payment was made on October 15, and $62.83 was credited back to the account for returned merchandise. Using the unpaid balance method, find the unpaid balance on November 1 if finance charges are 1.5%. (Treat the returned merchandise credit as if it were a payment.)

7. Use the constant ratio formula to find the annual percentage rate to the nearest tenth on a loan of $2,600 made for 18 months with interest of $819. The loan is repaid in monthly installments.

8. Use the constant ratio formula to find the annual percentage rate to the nearest tenth on a financed purchase of $2,725 if the monthly payment is $278.18 for 12 months.

9. A 6 × 6 color enlarger costs $1,295 and is financed with monthly payments for 2 years. The total finance charge is $310.80. Use Table 11-1 to find the annual percentage rate.

10. A queen-size brass bed costs $1,155 and is financed with monthly payments for 3 years. The total finance charge is $415.80. Use Table 11-1 to find the annual percentage rate.

Challenge Problem

Bob and Janice Malena need to finance $40,000 on their new home. After checking with several mortgage companies they have narrowed their choices to two options. Use Table 11-2.

Option 1: 20 year at 11%

Option 2: 25 years at 10%

If the Malenas can budget for either monthly payment, which option do you recommend? Why?

Trial Test

1. Find the finance charge on an item with a cash price of $469 if the total price is $503.

2. An item with a cash price of $578 can be purchased on the installment plan in 15 monthly payments of $46. Find the amount of finance charge.

3. A copier that originally cost $300 was sold on the installment plan at $28 per month for 12 months. Find the amount of finance charge.

4. Use Table 11-1 to find the annual percentage rate for the loan in Problem 3.

5. Use the constant ratio formula to find the actual rate of interest, to the nearest tenth of a percent, for the copier in Problem 3.

6. Use the constant ratio formula to find the actual rate of interest, to the nearest tenth of a percent, on a loan of $3,000 at 9% for 3 years if the loan had interest of $810 and was repaid monthly.

7. Find the interest on an unpaid balance of $165 if the monthly interest rate is $1\frac{3}{4}\%$.

8. Find the yearly rate of interest on a loan if the monthly rate is 2%.

9. Find the amount of interest refunded on a 15-month loan with total interest of $72 if the loan is paid in full with 6 months remaining.

10. Find the actual interest rate on a loan of $1,600 for 24 months if $200 interest is charged and the loan is repaid in monthly payments.

11. Find the actual interest rate on a loan that is repaid weekly for 26 weeks if the amount of the loan is $1,075. The interest charged is $60.

12. Office equipment was purchased on the installment plan with 12 monthly payments of $11.20 each. If the cash price was $120, find the annual percentage rate.

13. Find the new unpaid balance on an account with a previous balance of $205.60, purchases of $67.38, a payment of $40, and a finance charge of 1.75%.

14. A canoe has been purchased on the installment plan with a down payment of $75 and 10 monthly payments of $80 each. Find the total price of the canoe.

15. Find the amount of each of 12 monthly payments when the total price is $2,300 and a down payment of $400 is made.

16. How much is to be financed on a cash price of $729 if a down payment of $75 is made?

17. Find the refund fraction on a 4-year loan if it is paid off in 25 months.

18. The unpaid balance on a credit card is $288.93. During the month, purchases totaling $75.60 and one payment of $50 were made. Using the unpaid balance method and a finance rate of 1.9% per month, find the unpaid balance at the end of the cycle.

19. Use the following activity chart to find the unpaid balance based on the average daily balance and a finance rate of 1.75% per month. The billing cycle has 31 days.

Date	Activity	Amount
July 1	Billing date	Previous balance $441.05
July 4	Payment	$75
July 15	Purchase	$23.50
July 25	Purchase	$31.40

20. Ginger Katz has a home mortgage for $122,000. She plans to finance $100,000 for 15 years at $9\frac{1}{2}\%$ interest. Calculate the monthly payment and the total amount of interest. Use Table 11-2.

21. Make Ginger an amortization schedule for the first two months.

A look at statistics that shape your finances

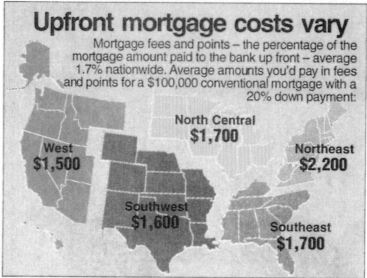

Upfront mortgage costs vary

Mortgage fees and points – the percentage of the mortgage amount paid to the bank up front – average 1.7% nationwide. Average amounts you'd pay in fees and points for a $100,000 conventional mortgage with a 20% down payment:

West $1,500

North Central $1,700

Northeast $2,200

Southwest $1,600

Southeast $1,700

Source: Federal Home Loan Mortgage Corp. By Marty Baumann, USA TODAY

QUESTIONS

1. How many points are normally paid for a mortgage of $100,000 on the West Coast?

2. How many points can you expect to pay for a mortgage of $100,000 on the Northeast coast.

3. If you buy a house in Texas, how many points should you expect to pay? Using the same number of points, how much would you pay on an $80,000 mortgage?

Depreciation

Buildings, machinery, equipment, furniture, and other items bought for the operation of a business are included among the **assets** of that business. The dollar value of each asset is used in figuring the value and profitability of the business and in figuring the taxable income for the business. The expense of running a business, including the purchase of assets, can be deducted from the company's taxable income before taxes are calculated, so it is important to have a way of keeping track of the value of assets.

Some assets have a useful life of 1 year or less, and their costs can be deducted from the business's income in the year they are purchased. The costs of items that are expected to last more than a year can be prorated and deducted over a period of years, called the **estimated life,** or **useful life,** of the item. During this time period, the asset *depreciates,* or decreases in value. At the end of an asset's estimated life, it may still have a dollar value, called the **salvage value,** or **scrap value.** The amount an asset decreases in value from its original cost is called its **depreciation.**

This chapter is concerned with determining the amount an asset has depreciated. This involves the question of how the estimated life of a piece of equipment is to be defined. In years? In miles driven, if it is a car? In items produced, if it is a machine? It also involves a question of what percentage of the original cost can be deducted each year. Some types of equipment may be used more heavily some years than others; some machines depreciate rapidly at first and slowly later; some machines may not wear out but may become outdated because a better model has been invented. All these factors must be considered in choosing the method of depreciation for a particular asset.

assets: buildings, machinery, equipment, furniture, and other items bought for the operation of a business.

estimated life (useful life): the number of years an asset is expected to be usable; for some assets the estimated life is calculated in units of production, such as miles for vehicles or units of work for some machines.

salvage value (scrap value): the estimated dollar value of an asset at the end of the asset's estimated useful life.

depreciation: the amount an asset decreases in value from its original cost.

This chapter examines six widely used depreciation methods: straight line, units of production, sum of the years' digits, declining balance, the accelerated cost recovery system (ACRS), and the modified accelerated cost recovery system (MACRS). The Internal Revenue Service regulates which methods of depreciation are allowed for income tax purposes. In general, the same depreciation method must be used throughout the useful life of any particular asset. The Internal Revenue Service (IRS) limits the use of many methods of depreciation, so you should consult the IRS or an accountant before choosing any depreciation method.

12.1

Straight-line Method of Depreciation

LEARNING OBJECTIVE

1. Calculate depreciation using the straight-line method.

straight-line depreciation: a method of depreciation in which the amount of depreciation of an asset is spread equally over the number of years of useful life of the asset.

The most commonly used method of depreciation is the **straight-line depreciation** method. It is easy to use because the depreciation is the same for each full year the equipment is used.

If you know the original cost of an asset, its estimated useful life, and its salvage value, you can find the yearly depreciation amount. In calculating depreciation, by whatever method, the cost of an asset means the *total cost*, including shipping and installation charges if the asset is a piece of equipment. The *depreciable value* is the cost minus the salvage value.

STEP BY STEP

Straight-line Depreciation Method

$$\text{Yearly depreciation} = \frac{\text{total cost of equipment} - \text{salvage value}}{\text{expected life (in years)}}$$

EXAMPLE 1

Use the straight-line method to find the yearly depreciation for a plating machine that has an expected useful life of 5 years. The plating machine cost $27,300, its shipping costs totaled $250, installation charges came to $450, and its salvage value is $1,000.

$$\text{Total cost} = \text{cost of asset} + \text{shipping} + \text{installation}$$

$$= \$27,300 + \$250 + \$450 = \$28,000$$

$$\text{Salvage value} = \$1,000$$

$$\text{Expected life} = 5 \text{ years}$$

$$\text{Yearly depreciation} = \frac{\text{total cost of equipment} - \text{salvage value}}{\text{expected life (in years)}}$$

$$= \frac{\$28,000 - \$1,000}{5} = \frac{\$27,000}{5} = \$5,400$$

The depreciation is $5,400 per year.

Table 12-1 Straight-line Depreciation Method

Year	Original Cost	Depreciation	Accumulated Depreciation	Book Value
1	$28,000	$5,400	$ 5,400	$22,600
2		$5,400	$10,800	$17,200
3		$5,400	$16,200	$11,800
4		$5,400	$21,600	$ 6,400
5		$5,400	$27,000	$ 1,000

TIPS & TRAPS

A common mistake in figuring straight-line depreciation is to divide the cost by the expected life without subtracting the salvage value of the asset. See what happens when this is done with Example 1:

$$\text{Yearly depreciation} = \frac{\text{total cost of equipment}}{\text{expected life (in years)}} = \frac{\$28,000}{5} = \$5,600$$

WRONG

$$\text{Yearly depreciation} = \frac{\text{total cost of equipment} - \text{salvage value}}{\text{expected life (in years)}}$$

$$= \frac{\$28,000 - \$1,000}{5} = \frac{\$27,000}{5} = \$5,400$$

CORRECT

Use the "equals" key to complete the calculations in the numerator before dividing by the denominator.

$$\boxed{\text{AC}}\ 27300\ \boxed{+}\ 250\ \boxed{+}\ 450\ \boxed{-}\ 1000\ \boxed{=}\ \boxed{\div}\ 5\ \boxed{=}\ \Rightarrow 5400$$

Calculator Solution

Once you have calculated the yearly depreciation, you can prepare a depreciation schedule. Using the figures from Example 1, Table 12-1 shows the original cost, the amount of depreciation taken each year, and the changing book value of the equipment. **Book value** is the original cost minus the *accumulated depreciation,* which is the total amount of depreciation taken as of a certain time. Every year the depreciation amount is subtracted from the previous year's book value to decrease the book value.

book value: the original cost of an asset minus the accumulated depreciation.

Self-Check 12.1

1. Use the straight-line method to find the yearly depreciation for a van that cost $18,000, has an expected useful life of 3 years, and has a salvage value of $3,000.

12.2

Units-of-Production Method of Depreciation

LEARNING OBJECTIVE

1. Calculate depreciation using the units-of-production method.

units-of-production depreciation: a method of depreciation that is based on the expected number of units produced by an asset, such as miles driven for a vehicle or labels produced for a label machine; each year's depreciation is based on the number of units of work produced by the asset during the year.

Machines and other types of equipment that are used heavily for a period of time and then left to sit idle for another period of time, sometimes months, are often depreciated using the **units-of-production depreciation** method. For example, earth-moving equipment and farm equipment are often idle during the winter months. Instead of basing depreciation on the expected lifetime of a piece of equipment in years, this method takes into account how the equipment is used, for example, how many items it has produced, how many miles it has been driven, how many hours it has operated, or how many times it has performed some particular operation.

The units-of-production method of depreciation is used for internal accounting purposes. Special written permission from the IRS is required for this method to be used on tax returns. Companies that use this method internally often adjust to a method acceptable by the IRS for tax-reporting purposes.

To use the units-of-production method, you first figure how much the equipment depreciates with each unit produced or each mile driven and then multiply that amount by the number of units produced or miles driven.

STEP BY STEP

Units-of-Production Depreciation Method

Step 1. Unit depreciation = $\dfrac{\text{total cost} - \text{salvage value}}{\text{expected life (in units produced)}}$

Step 2. Depreciation amount = unit depreciation × units produced

EXAMPLE 2

A label-making machine that costs $28,000 after shipping and installation is expected to print 50,000,000 labels during its useful life. If the salvage value of the machine is $1,000, find the unit depreciation and depreciation amount printing for 2,125,000 labels.

$$\text{Unit depreciation} = \frac{\text{total cost} - \text{salvage value}}{\text{expected life (in number of units produced)}}$$

$$= \frac{\$28,000 - \$1,000}{50,000,000}$$

$$= \$0.00054 \text{ depreciation per unit produced}$$

$2,125,000 \times \$0.00054 = \$1,147.50$ Do not round the unit depreciation.

The depreciation is $1,147.50.

Calculator Solution

$\boxed{\text{AC}}$ 28000 $\boxed{-}$ 1000 $\boxed{=}$ $\boxed{\div}$ 50,000,000 $\boxed{\times}$ 2,125,000 $\boxed{=}$ $\Rightarrow$ 1147.5

Table 12-2 Units-of-Production Depreciation Schedule

Year	Original Cost	Number of Labels Printed during Year	Annual Depreciation	Accumulated Depreciation	End-of-Year Book Value
1	$28,000	2,125,000	$1,147.50	$ 1,147.50	$26,852.50
2		11,830,000	$6,388.20	$ 7,535.70	$20,464.30
3		12,765,000	$6,893.10	$14,428.80	$13,571.20
4		12,210,000	$6,593.40	$21,022.20	$ 6,977.80
5		11,070,000	$5,977.80	$27,000.00	$ 1,000.00

The depreciation of the label maker is recorded in a depreciation schedule like the one shown in Table 12-2. Note that the table shows the number of labels made each year and that the number differs from year to year. This pattern of use is typical of equipment that is depreciated by the units-of-production method.

 Self-Check 12.2

2. A van that costs $18,000 is expected to be driven 75,000 miles during its useful life. If the salvage value of the van is $3,000, find the unit depreciation and the amount of depreciation after the van has been driven 56,000 miles.

12.3 Sum-of-the-Years'-Digits Method of Depreciation

LEARNING OBJECTIVE

1. Calculate depreciation using the sum-of-the-years'-digits method.

The straight-line depreciation method of depreciating an asset is the simplest way to depreciate it, but it is not always the best method of depreciation to use. Most equipment depreciates more during its first year of operation than during any other subsequent year. Most businesses want an immediate tax advantage and prefer to use a method that depreciates the largest amount possible during the first year or two. One such method is the **sum-of-the-years'-digits depreciation** method.

To compute depreciation by this method, first list, *in reverse order,* the number of years in the asset's expected life. For example, if a machine has an expected life of 5 years, you would list the digits

$$5, 4, 3, 2, 1$$

This list tells you how many remaining years of expected life the machine has each year. (Five years remain at the beginning of the first year, 4 years remain the second year, and so on.) Then find the sum of these digits:

$$5 + 4 + 3 + 2 + 1 = 15$$

You can find the sum of the years' digits by using the formula $\dfrac{n(n + 1)}{2}$, where n is the number of expected years for the asset. The value of this formula will be the denominator of the depreciation rate fraction.

$$\frac{5(5 + 1)}{2} = \frac{5(6)}{2} = 15$$

sum-of-the-years'-digits depreciation: a method of depreciating an asset by allowing the greatest depreciation during the first year and a decreasing amount of depreciation each year thereafter.

Next, we make fractions by placing each digit over the number 15:

$$\frac{5}{15}, \frac{4}{15}, \frac{3}{15}, \frac{2}{15}, \frac{1}{15}$$

These fractions show the *rate of depreciation* for each year. The first-year rate is $\frac{5}{15}$, the second-year rate is $\frac{4}{15}$, and so on.

To find each year's depreciation, multiply the rate of depreciation for the year times the depreciable amount (the difference between the original cost and the salvage value of the asset).

STEP BY STEP

Sum-of-the-Years'-Digits Method of Depreciation

Step 1. Find the depreciation rate fraction for the year in question.

$$\text{Depreciation rate fraction} = \frac{\text{number of useful years remaining}}{\dfrac{n(n+1)}{2}}$$

Step 2. To find the amount of depreciation in a specific year, multiply the rate of depreciation for the year times the depreciable amount (difference between the original cost and the salvage value of the asset).

Depreciation = depreciation rate fraction × (Total cost − salvage value)

EXAMPLE 3

Find the depreciation for each of 5 years of expected life of a bottle-capping machine that costs $27,300 and has a shipping cost of $250, and installation cost of $450, and a salvage value of $1,000. Make a depreciation schedule

Step 1. Depreciation rate fraction $= \dfrac{\text{number of useful years remaining}}{\dfrac{n(n+1)}{2}}$

$$= \frac{5(6)}{2} = 15$$

$$\frac{5}{15}, \frac{4}{15}, \frac{3}{15}, \frac{2}{15}, \frac{1}{15}$$

$$\text{Year} \quad 1 \quad 2 \quad 3 \quad 4 \quad 5$$

Write the depreciation rate fraction for each year.
($27,300 + $250 + $450) − $1,000
= $27,000 (Cost − salvage value)

Table 12-3   Sum-of-the-Years'-Digits Method of Depreciation

Year	Depreciation Rate Fraction	Cost Minus Salvage Value	Depreciation Amount	Accumulated Depreciation	Book Value
1	$\frac{5}{15}$	$27,000	$9,000	$ 9,000	$19,000
2	$\frac{4}{15}$	$27,000	$7,200	$16,200	$11,800
3	$\frac{3}{15}$	$27,000	$5,400	$21,600	$ 6,400
4	$\frac{2}{15}$	$27,000	$3,600	$25,200	$ 2,800
5	$\frac{1}{15}$	$27,000	$1,800	$27,000	$ 1,000

Step 2. At this point, a depreciation table helps organize information and calculations (see Table 12-3). Find the depreciation amount for each year by multiplying the depreciation rate fraction times the depreciable amount (cost of the asset minus the salvage value).

The calculator sequence for the first year's depreciation is

$$\boxed{\text{AC}} \; \boxed{\text{MC}} \; 5 \; \boxed{\div} \; 15 \; \boxed{=} \; \boxed{\times} \; 27000 \; \boxed{\text{M}^+} \; \boxed{=} \Rightarrow 8999.991$$

Different calculators will give varying numbers of decimal places. If a basic calculator is used, the answer shown will appear in the display. This answer should be rounded to 9000. If a scientific calculator is used, the display will show 9000.

Calculator Solution

The calculator sequence for subsequent calculations will be

$$\boxed{\text{AC}} \; \text{(year's depreciation rate fraction)} \; \boxed{\times} \; \boxed{\text{MR}} \; \boxed{=} \Rightarrow \text{year's depreciation}$$

TIPS & TRAPS

A common mistake is to list the smallest fraction rather than the largest fraction for the first year's depreciation rate. In Example 3, the smallest fraction is $\frac{1}{15}$ and the largest is $\frac{5}{15}$. The confusion often occurs because the smallest fraction goes with the largest year; that is, year 5 uses $\frac{1}{15}$, and year 1 uses $\frac{5}{15}$.

Let's look at how to figure the depreciation amount for year 1 from Example 3 again, showing both the wrong and correct ways to do it:

Year 1	Year 1
$\frac{1}{15} \times \$27{,}000 = \$1{,}800$	$\frac{5}{15} \times \$27{,}000 = \$9{,}000$
WRONG	**CORRECT**

An easy way to check yourself on this is to remember that, when using the sum-of-the-years'-digits method, the *first* year's depreciation should be the *largest*. This shows you that $9,000 is correct and $1,800 is wrong for the first year's depreciation amount.

Self-Check 12.3

3. Find the depreciation for each of the 3 years of expected life of a van that costs $18,000 and has a salvage value of $3,000.

12.4

Declining-balance Method of Depreciation

LEARNING OBJECTIVE

1. Calculate depreciation using the declining-balance method.

Another way to calculate depreciation so that the depreciation is large in the early years of the asset's life and becomes smaller in the later years is the **de-**

declining-balance depreciation: a method of depreciation that provides for large depreciation in the early years of the life of an asset; the beginning book value using this method is the cost of the asset, rather than the difference in the cost and the scrap value as in other depreciation methods.

double-declining-balance depreciation: a method of declining-balance depreciation in which the rate of depreciation is twice the straight-line depreciation rate.

straight-line rate: when used with the declining-balance method of depreciation, the straight-line rate is a fraction with a numerator of 1 and a denominator equal to the number of useful years of an asset. This fraction is usually expressed as a decimal equivalent when making calculations and a percent equivalent when identifying the rate of depreciation.

clining-balance method. Some assets can be depreciated at twice the straight-line rate, which is called the **double-declining-balance rate.**

First, you must determine the **straight-line rate** of depreciation. To do so, write a fraction with a numerator of 1 and a denominator equal to the number of useful years of an asset. Write the decimal or percent equivalent of this fraction. The decimal equivalent is used in making calculations. The percent equivalent is used to identify the *rate* of depreciation.

The double-declining rate is found by multiplying the straight-line rate by 2. If the decimal equivalent does not come out even, it should be expressed as a decimal number with *five* decimal places. The percent equivalent can be rounded to the nearest hundredth of a percent.

STEP BY STEP

Declining-balance and Double-declining-balance Methods of Depreciation

Step 1. Straight-line, declining-balance

$$\text{depreciation rate} = \frac{1}{\text{expected useful life (in years)}}$$

Step 2. Double-declining-balance

$$\text{depreciation rate} = \frac{1}{\text{expected useful life (in years)}} \times 2$$

EXAMPLE 4

An ice cream freezer has a useful life of 6 years. Find (a) the straight-line rate expressed as a decimal and percent and (b) the double-declining rate expressed as a decimal and percent.

a. Straight-line rate $= \dfrac{1}{\text{expected useful life}} = \dfrac{1}{6}$

$$\frac{1}{6} = 0.16666 \quad \text{(decimal equivalent)}$$

$$= 16.67\% \quad \text{(percent equivalent)}$$

b. Double-declining rate $= \dfrac{1}{\text{expected useful life}} \times 2 = \dfrac{1}{6} \times 2 = \dfrac{2}{6} = \dfrac{1}{3}$

$$\frac{1}{3} = 0.33333 \quad \text{(decimal equivalent)}$$

$$= 33.33\% \quad \text{(percent equivalent)}$$

After you find the rate of depreciation, multiply it times the beginning book value of the asset to find the depreciation for the first year. Note that the *beginning book value* is the total cost of the asset. *Do not* subtract the salvage value from the original book value to find the depreciable amount in this method. At the end of the year, subtract the year's depreciation from the beginning book value to find the *new* book value for the beginning of the next year. This process continues for the number of years the asset is to be depreciated or until the book value equals the salvage value. The ending balance for any given year *cannot* drop below the salvage value of the asset. In such cases, the year's ending value is the salvage value, and the year's depreciation is adjusted. There will then be no further depreciation in future years.

STEP BY STEP

Using the Declining-balance Method of Depreciation

Step 1. Find the declining rate. The decimal equivalent of the rate should be computed to five decimal places.

$$\frac{1}{\text{expected useful life}}$$

$$\left(\text{or } \frac{1}{\text{expected useful life}} \times 2 \quad \text{for double-declining balance}\right)$$

Step 2. Find the depreciation amount:

Book value × declining rate = depreciation amount

Step 3. Find next year's book value:

Book value − depreciation amount = next year's book value

Step 4. Repeat steps 2 and 3 for the required number of years, or until the book value is equal to or less than the salvage value. If book value calculates to be less than salvage value, it is adjusted to be the salvage value.

EXAMPLE 5

A packaging machine costing $28,000 with an expected life of 5 years and a resale value of $1,000 is depreciated by the declining-balance method at twice the straight-line rate. Determine the depreciation and the year-end book value for each of the 5 years.

Step 1. Double-declining rate $= \dfrac{1}{\text{expected useful life}} \times 2 = \dfrac{1}{5} \times 2 = \dfrac{2}{5}$

$$\frac{2}{5} = 0.4 = 40\%$$

Step 2. Initial book value × declining rate = depreciation amount (year 1)

$$\$28{,}000 \times 0.4 = \$11{,}200$$

Step 3. Initial book value − depreciation amount = book value (year 2)

$$\$28{,}000 - \$11{,}200 = \$16{,}800$$

Book value (year 2) × declining rate = depreciation amount (year 2)

$$\$16{,}800 \times 0.4 = \$6{,}720$$

Book value (year 2) − depreciation amount = book value (year 3)

$$\$16{,}800 - \$6{,}720 = \$10{,}080$$

Book value (year 3) × declining rate = depreciation amount (year 3)

$$\$10{,}080 \times 0.4 = \$4{,}032$$

Book value (year 3) − depreciation amount = book value (year 4)

$$\$10{,}080 - \$4{,}032 = \$6{,}048$$

Book value (year 4) × declining rate = depreciation amount (year 4)

$$\$6{,}048 \times 0.4 = \$2{,}419.20$$

Book value (year 4) − depreciation amount = book value (year 5)

$$\$6,048 - \$2,419.20 = \$3,628.80$$

Book value (year 5) × declining rate = depreciation amount (year 5)

$$\$3,628.80 \times 0.4 = \$1,451.52$$

Book value (year 5) − depreciation amount = book value (ending)

$$\$3,628.80 - \$1,451.52 = \$2,177.28$$

The given information and calculations are most useful if they are organized into a depreciation schedule like the one shown in Table 12-4.

Table 12-4 Double-declining Balance Method of Depreciation

Year	Start-of-Year Book Value	Declining Rate	Depreciation Amount for Year	End-of-Year Book Value	Accumulated Depreciation
1	$28,000.00	0.4	$11,200.00	$16,800.00	$11,200.00
2	$16,800.00	0.4	$ 6,720.00	$10,080.00	$17,920.00
3	$10,080.00	0.4	$ 4,032.00	$ 6,048.00	$21,952.00
4	$ 6,048.00	0.4	$ 2,419.20	$ 3,628.80	$24,371.20
5	$ 3,628.80	0.4	$ 1,451.52	$ 2,177.28	$25,822.72

TIPS & TRAPS

Be sure to use the total cost of the asset as the beginning book value when using the declining-balance method. A common error is to use cost − salvage value rather than just cost. That is, in Example 5,

~~Cost − salvage value = $28,000 − $1,000 = $27,000~~

~~Depreciation for year 1 = $27,000 × 0.4 = $10,800~~

WRONG

Cost × declining rate = depreciation for year 1

$$\$28,000 \times 0.4 = \$11,200$$

CORRECT

The error shown will cause the entire depreciation table to be incorrect, because each year's depreciation depends on the book value at the end of the previous year.

Self-Check 12.4

4. An acid disposal tank has a useful life of 3 years. Find (a) the straight-line declining rate expressed as a decimal and percent and (b) the double-declining rate expressed as a decimal and percent.

5. A van costing $18,000 with an expected life of 4 years and a resale value of $1,000 is depreciated by the declining-balance method at twice the straight-line rate. Determine the depreciation and the year-end book value for each of the 4 years.

Accelerated Cost-Recovery System

LEARNING OBJECTIVE

1. Calculate depreciation using the accelerated cost-recovery system (ACRS).

In 1981 the Internal Revenue Service enacted the **accelerated cost-recovery system (ACRS)** for the depreciation of property placed in service after 1980. This method of depreciation, which is used only in figuring depreciation for federal income tax purposes, allows businesses to write off the cost of assets more quickly than in the past. (The other methods of depreciation are used for accounting purposes.) The faster depreciation was meant to encourage businesses to invest in more assets despite an economic slowdown at the time.

Under ACRS, property was depreciated over a 3-, 5-, 10-, 15-, or 19-year recovery period, depending on the type of property. *Recovery period* is used in this system instead of estimated useful life. In most cases the recovery period allowed by ACRS was much shorter than the estimated useful life would have been. ACRS is not used for items that were placed in service after 1986; however, items in the 10-, 15-, or 19-year categories are still being depreciated if placed in service using ACRS. The IRS listed examples of types of property in each of the time categories to guide taxpayers. The following was taken from an IRS publication for items placed into service and depreciated using ACRS.

3-year property: Automobiles, tractor units for use over the road, light-duty trucks, and certain special manufacturing tools

5-year property: Most equipment, office furniture, and fixtures

10-year property: Certain real property such as public utility property, theme park structures, and mobile homes

15-year or 19-year real property: All real property placed in service before March 15, 1984, such as buildings not designated as 10-year property

accelerated cost-recovery system (ACRS): a method of depreciation of assets for tax purposes that allows businesses to write off costs of certain assets more quickly than with other methods of depreciation.

Table 12-5   Cost Recovery Percentages for ACRS

If the Recovery Year is:	Percentage for the Class of Property Is:			
	3-year	5-year	10-year	15-year
1	25	15	8	5
2	38	22	14	10
3	37	21	12	9
4		21	10	8
5		21	10	7
6			10	7
7			9	6
8			9	6
9			9	6
10			9	6
11				6
12				6
13				6
14				6
15				6

The depreciation deduction for property placed in service under the ACRS is figured by multiplying the *unadjusted basis* (original cost) by a rate that is determined by the IRS. This rate varies from year to year during the recovery period. Table 12-5 gives the rates as shown in a recent IRS publication.

EXAMPLE 6

Find the depreciation deduction for the tenth year for a piece of real property that was purchased for $128,000 and placed in service under the ACRS method of depreciation as a 15-year property.

$$\text{Depreciation amount (year 10)} = 6\% \times \text{cost}$$

$$= 0.06 \times \$128,000 = \$7,680$$

Even though properties are no longer placed in service using ACRS, many companies prepare a depreciation schedule when an item is placed in service. This enables the company to determine each year's depreciation amount from the schedule rather than making the calculation each year. Table 12-6 shows an example of a depreciation schedule for a $28,000 property set up on a 5-year depreciation schedule.

Table 12-6 Table Showing Accelerated Cost-recovery System (ACRS) of Depreciation

Year	Start-of-Year Book Value	ACRS Rate	Depreciation Amount for Year	End-of-Year Book Value	Accumulated Depreciation
1	$28,000	15	$4,200	$23,800	$ 4,200
2	$23,800	22	$6,160	$17,640	$10,360
3	$17,640	21	$5,880	$11,760	$16,240
4	$11,760	21	$5,880	$ 5,880	$22,120
5	$ 5,880	21	$5,880	$0	$28,000

 Self-Check 12.5

6. Find the depreciation deduction for the ninth year for a mobile home that was purchased for $58,000 and placed in service at mid-year under the ACRS method of depreciation as a 10-year property.

12.6

Modified Accelerated Cost-recovery System

LEARNING OBJECTIVE

1. Calculate depreciation using the modified accelerated cost-recovery system (MACRS).

modified accelerated cost-recovery system (MACRS): a method of depreciation of assets for tax purposes that is a modification of the ACRS method; it added two new classes of property, reclassified some types of property, and changed the depreciation rates in each category.

The Tax Reform Act of 1986 introduced some changes in the depreciation rates for property put in use after 1986 (but not affecting equipment in use before 1986). The following is a list of property classes with examples, taken from an IRS publication 53, that can be depreciated under the **modified accelerated cost-recover system (MACRS).**

3-Year property. This class includes tractor units for use over-the-road, any race horse over 2 years old when placed in service, and any other horse over 12 years old when placed in service.

Table 12-7 Depreciation Rates Using MACRS When Properties Are Placed in Service at Mid-Year

Recovery Year	Recovery Period					
	3-year	5-year	7-year	10-year	15-year	20-year
1	33.33	20.00	14.29	10.00	5.00	3.750
2	44.45	32.00	24.49	18.00	9.50	7.219
3	14.81	19.20	17.49	14.40	8.55	6.677
4	7.41	11.52	12.49	11.52	7.70	6.177
5		11.52	8.93	9.22	6.93	5.713
6		5.76	8.92	7.37	6.23	5.285
7			8.93	6.55	5.90	4.888
8			4.46	6.55	5.90	4.522
9				6.56	5.91	4.462
10				6.55	5.90	4.461
11				3.28	5.91	4.462
12					5.90	4.461
13					5.91	4.462
14					5.90	4.461
15					5.91	4.462
16					2.95	4.461
17						4.462
18						4.461
19						4.462
20						4.461
21						2.231

5-Year property. This class includes automobiles, taxis, buses, trucks, computers and peripheral equipment, office machinery (typewriters, calculators, copiers, etc.), and any property used in research and experimentation.

7-Year property. This class includes office furniture and fixtures (desks, file cabinets, etc.), and any property that does not have a class life and that has not been designated by law as being in any other class.

10-Year property. This class includes vessels, barges, tugs, similar water transportation equipment, any single purpose agricultural or horticultural structure, and any tree or vine bearing fruits or nuts.

15-Year property. This class includes roads, shrubbery, wharves (if depreciable), and any municipal wastewater treatment plant.

20-Year property. This class includes farm buildings and any municipal sewers.

IRS Publication 534 outlines all the options that may be used in figuring depreciation with MACRS. One option is to use a table of rates; several are provided by the IRS. MACRS rates when property is placed in service at mid-year are shown in Table 12-7. Other tables are available for properties placed in service at other times during the year.

EXAMPLE 7

Find the depreciation deduction for each year for a boiler that was purchased for $28,000 and placed in service at mid-year under the MACRS method of depreciation as a 5-year property.

$$\text{Depreciation amount (year 1)} = 20\% \times \text{cost}$$
$$= 0.20 \times \$28,000 = \$5,600$$

Table 12-8 Table Showing Modified Accelerated Cost-recovery System (MACRS) of Depreciation for a Five-Year Property Placed in Service at Mid-Year

Year	Start-of-Year Book Value	MACRS Rate	Depreciation Amount for Year	End-of-Year Book Value	Accumulated Depreciation
1	$28,000.00	20.00	$5,600.00	$22,400.00	$ 5,600.00
2	$22,400.00	32.00	$8,960.00	$13,440.00	$14,560.00
3	$13,440.00	19.20	$5,376.00	$ 8,064.00	$19,936.00
4	$ 8,064.00	11.52	$3,225.60	$ 4,838.40	$23,161.60
5	$ 4,838.40	11.52	$3,225.60	$ 1,612.80	$26,387.20
6	$ 1,612.80	5.76	$1,612.80	$ 0	$28,000.00

$$\text{Depreciation amount (year 2)} = 32\% \times \text{cost}$$
$$= 0.32 \times \$28{,}000 = \$8{,}960$$

$$\text{Depreciation amount (year 3)} = 19.2\% \times \text{cost}$$
$$= 0.192 \times \$28{,}000 = \$5{,}376$$

$$\text{Depreciation amount (year 4)} = 11.52\% \times \text{cost}$$
$$= 0.1152 \times \$28{,}000 = \$3{,}225.60$$

$$\text{Depreciation amount (year 5)} = 11.52\% \times \text{cost}$$
$$= 0.1152 \times \$28{,}000 = \$3{,}225.60$$

$$\text{Depreciation amount (year 6)} = 5.76\% \times \text{cost}$$
$$= 0.0576 \times \$28{,}000 = \$1{,}612.80$$

The sum of the depreciation amounts should equal the purchase price.

$$\$5{,}600 + \$8{,}960 + \$5{,}376 + \$3{,}225.60 + \$3{,}225.60 + \$1{,}612.80 = \$28{,}000.$$

These calculations are most useful if they are organized into a depreciation schedule like the one shown in Table 12-8.

 Self-Check 12.6

7. Find the depreciation deduction for each year for a tractor that was purchased for $18,000 and placed in service at mid-year under the MACRS method of depreciation as a 3-year property.

Summary

Topic	Page	What to Remember	Examples
Straight-line depreciation	364	Yearly depreciation $= \dfrac{\text{cost of equipment} - \text{salvage value}}{\text{expected life (in years)}}$	Make a depreciation table showing the yearly depreciation of a property that costs $3,700 and has a salvage value of $400 at the end of 3 years. Use the straight-line method of depreciation.

Year	Original Cost	Depreciation	Accumulated Depreciation	Book Value
1	$3,700	$1,100	$1,100	$2,600
2		$1,100	$2,200	$1,500
3		$1,100	$3,300	$ 400

Topic	Page	What to Remember	Examples
Units-of-production depreciation	366	Unit depreciation $= \dfrac{\text{total cost} - \text{salvage value}}{\text{expected life (units produced)}}$ Depreciation amount $= \text{unit depreciation} \times \text{units produced}$	Use units-of-production depreciation to make a depreciation table to show the yearly depreciation of a vehicle that cost $18,900 and has a resale value of $3,000 after 150,000 miles. The vehicle is driven 39,270 miles the first year, 37,960 miles the second year, 38,520 miles the third year, and 34,250 miles the fourth year. $\text{Unit depreciation} = \dfrac{\$18,900 - \$3,000}{\$150,000} = 0.106$

Year	Original Cost	Number of Miles Driven	Annual Depreciation	Accumulated Depreciation	End of-Year Book Value
1	$18,900	39,270	$4,162.62	$ 4,162.62	$14,737.38
2		37,960	$4,023.76	$ 8,186.38	$10,713.62
3		38,520	$4,083.12	$12,269.50	$ 6,630.50
4		34,250	$3,630.50	$15,900.00	$ 3,000.00

Topic	Page	What to Remember	Examples
Sum-of-the-years'-digits depreciation	367	$\dfrac{n(n+1)}{2} = $ denominator of rate fraction Depreciation rate fraction $= \dfrac{\text{number of useful years remaining}}{\dfrac{n(n+1)}{2}}$ Year's depreciation $= (\text{original cost} - \text{salvage value}) \times \text{depreciation rate fraction for year}$	Make a depreciation table showing the yearly depreciation of a property that cost $3,700 and has a salvage value of $400 at the end of 3 years. Use the sum-of-the-years'-digits method. (n = total years) $\text{Cost} - \text{salvage value}$ $= \$3,700 - \$400 = \$3,300$

Year	Depreciation Rate Fraction	Cost Minus Salvage Value	Depreciation Amount	Accumulated Depreciation	Book Value
1	$\frac{3}{6}$	$3,300	$1,650	$1,650	$2,050
2	$\frac{2}{6}$	$3,300	$1,100	$2,750	$ 950
3	$\frac{1}{6}$	$3,300	$ 550	$3,300	$ 400

Topic	Page	What to Remember	Examples
Declining balance depreciation	369	Straight-line declining balance rate $= \dfrac{1}{\text{expected life (in years)}}$ Double-declining balance rate $= \dfrac{1}{\text{expected life (in years)}} \times 2$	Use the double-declining balance method of depreciation to make a depreciation table for a property that cost $3,700 and has a salvage value of $400 after 3 years' use. Double-declining rate $= \dfrac{1}{3} \times 2 = \dfrac{2}{3} = 0.666667$

Year	Start-of-Year Book Value	Declining Rate	Depreciation for Year	End-of-Year Book Value	Accumulated Depreciation
1	$3,700	0.666667	$2,466.67	$1,233.33	$2,466.67
2	$1,233.33	0.666667	$ 822.22	$ 411.11	$3,288.89
3	$ 411.11	*	$ 11.11	$ 400.00	$3,300.00

*Remember, an asset *cannot* be depreciated below its salvage value. So the depreciation for year 3 is $411.11 − $400 = $11.11.

Topic	Page	What to Remember	Examples
ACRS depreciation for income tax purposes	373	A table published by the IRS is used to determine the percentage allowed for each year's depreciation for specified classes of property. The entire cost is used as a base for depreciating the property. This method can only be used for items placed in service using ACRS from 1981 through 1986.	Use the ACRS method of depreciation to find the 8th year depreciation for a real property that cost $83,700. The property is classed as a 15-year property for depreciation purposes. Depreciation amount (year 8) $= 6\% \times \$83,700 = 0.06 \times \$83,700 = \$5,022$
MACRS method of depreciation for income tax purposes	374	Tables published by the IRS are used to determine the percentage allowed for each year's depreciation for specified classes of property. Different tables are available for properties that are put into service at different times during the year.	Use the MACRS method of depreciation to make a depreciation table for a property that cost $3,700, was put in to serivce at mid-year, and is to be depreciated over a 3-year recovery period. The salvage value is $200.

Year	Start-of-Year Book Value	MACRS Rate	Depreciation Amount	End-of-Year Book Value	Accumulated Depreciation
1	$3,700	33.33	$1,233.21	$2,466.79	$1,233.21
2	$2,466.79	44.45	$1,644.65	$ 822.14	$2,877.86
3	$ 822.14	14.81	$ 547.97	$ 274.17	$3,425.83
4	$ 274.17	7.41	$ 274.17	$ 0*	$3,700

*Note that the entire cost of the property is depreciated under this method. The salvage value of $200 is handled in the accounting system as income when the property is sold.

Self-Check Solutions

1. Yearly depreciation $= \dfrac{\text{cost of equipment} - \text{salvage value}}{\text{expected life (in years)}}$

$$= \frac{\$18,000 - \$3,000}{3} = \frac{\$15,000}{3}$$

$$= \$5,000$$

2. Unit depreciation $= \dfrac{\$18,000 - \$3,000}{75,000} = \$0.20/\text{mile}$

Depreciation after 56,000 miles $= \$0.20 \times 56,000 = \$11,200$

3. Denominator of depreciation fraction $= 3 + 2 + 1 = 6$

Depreciation rate fraction for each year $= \dfrac{3}{6}, \dfrac{2}{6}, \dfrac{1}{6}$

Original cost $-$ salvage value $= \$18,000 - \$3,000 = \$15,000$

Depreciation amount (year 1) $= \$15,000 \times \dfrac{3}{6} = \$7,500$

(year 2) $= \$15,000 \times \dfrac{2}{6} = \$5,000$

(year 3) $= \$15,000 \times \dfrac{1}{6} = \$2,500$

4. a. $\frac{1}{3} = 33.33\%$, or 0.33333

    b. $\frac{1}{3} \times 2 = \frac{2}{3} = 66.67\%$, or 0.66666

5. Double-declining rate $= \frac{1}{4} \times 2 = \frac{2}{4} = \frac{1}{2}$, or 0.5

Year	Start-of-Year Book Value	Declining Rate	Depreciation Amount for Year	End-of-Year Book Value	Accumulated Depreciation
1	$18,000	0.5	$9,000	$9,000	$ 9,000
2	$ 9,000	0.5	$4,500	$4,500	$13,500
3	$ 4,500	0.5	$2,250	$2,250	$15,750
4	$ 2,250	0.5	$1,125	$1,125	$16,875

6. Depreciation amount (year 9) $= 9\% \times \text{cost} = 0.09 \times \$58,000 = \$5,220$

7. Depreciation amount (year 1) $= 33.33\% \times \text{cost}$
$$= 0.3333 \times \$18,000 = \$5,999.40$$
(year 2) $= 44.45\% \times \text{cost}$
$$= 0.4445 \times \$18,000 = \$8,001$$
(year 3) $= 14.81\% \times \text{cost}$
$$= 0.1481 \times \$18,000 = \$2,665.80$$
(year 4) $= 7.41\% \times \text{cost}$
$$= 0.0741 \times \$18,000 = \$1,333.80$$

End of Chapter Problems

1. A company automobile has an original cost of $14,500 and a trade-in (salvage) value of $2,500 after 5 years. Find its depreciable value.

2. A computer system was purchased for $7,500. Shipping charges were $75 and installation charges were $50. What was the total cost of the computer system?

Use straight-line depreciation to figure the yearly depreciation on the following. Round answers to the nearest cent.

	Total cost	Salvage Value	Expected Life
3.	$ 7,200	$ 300	3 years
4.	$ 6,000	$ 50	11 years
5.	$ 12,000	$ 2,500	5 years
6.	$ 50,000	$ 5,000	10 years
7.	$100,000	$10,000	20 years

8. A machine was purchased by the Wabash Company for $5,900. Its normal life expectancy is 4 years. If it can be traded in for $900 at the end of this time, determine the yearly depreciation by the straight-line method.

9. A stamping machine was purchased by Deskin Glass Company for $8,595. Freight and installation costs were $405. If it will be worth $2,000 after 7 years, find the annual depreciation using the straight-line method.

10. Station WMAT spent $5,000 for a new television camera. This camera will be replaced in 5 years. If the scrap value will be $500, determine the annual depreciation by the straight-line method.

11. A dress factory paid $14,000 for an assembly-line system. If the used equipment will be worth $2,000 at the end of 15 years, find the annual depreciation by the straight-line method.

12. The Acme Management Corporation purchased a computer for $5,400. Its life expectancy is projected to be 4 years, and the salvage value will be $800. Make a straight-line depreciation table like Table 12-1 to show each year's depreciation, the accumulated depreciation, and the year-end book value.

Year	Original Cost	Annual Depreciation	Accumulated Depreciation	Book Value

Section 12.2

13. A machine costs $2,500 and has an expected life of 25,000 hours. Find the unit depreciation for the computer if its salvage value is $400.

Find the unit and yearly depreciation for the following.

	Cost	Scrap Value	Expected Life	Hours Operated This Year
14.	$42,000	$2,000	80,000 (hours)	6,700
15.	$25,000	$2,500	90,000	7,000
16.	$ 4,340	$ 340	16,000	2,580
17.	$19,000	$1,000	45,000	8,000
18.	$2,370	$ 420	7,800	1,520

19. SERV-U Computer Service Company bought a laser printer for $15,000. The machine is expected to operate for 28,000 hours, after which its trade-in value will be $1,000. Find the unit depreciation for the printer. The first year the machine was operated 4,160 hours. Find the depreciation for the year.

20. A bottle-making machine costs $12,000 and has a scrap value of $1,500. It is expected to make 1,500,000 bottles during its useful life. Find the depreciation when 1,000,000 bottles have been produced.

21. BEST Delivery Service purchased a delivery truck for $18,500 and expected to resell it for $2,000 after driving it 150,000 miles. Find the unit depreciation for the truck.

22. Make a depreciation table similar to Table 12-2 to show the number of miles driven during the year, annual depreciation, accumulated depreciation, and end-of-year book value if the truck of Exercise 21 is driven 28,580 miles the first year, 32,140 miles the second year, 29,760 miles the third year, 31,810 miles the fourth year, and 27,710 miles the fifth year.

Year	Original Cost	Number of Miles Driven during Year	Annual Depreciation	Accumulated Depreciation	End-of-Year Book Value

23. Find the unit depreciation for an air conditioning–heating unit that cost $7,800 and has a scrap value of $600 if it is expected to operate 40,000 hours.

24. If the unit in Exercise 23 operates 2,190 hours the first year, what is the depreciation for the year?

25. If the unit in Exercise 23 operates 4,599 hours the second year, what is the depreciation for the year?

26. Wee-Kare Child Care Center purchased a van for $21,500 and expects it to be driven 75,000 miles. If the resale value of the van is projected to be $6,500, find the unit depreciation for the van.

27. Employees of Wee-Kare Child Care Center drove the van (Exercise 26) 19,740 miles the first year. Find the depreciation for the year.

Section 12.3

Find the sum of the digits (the denominator of the depreciation rate fraction) for assets depreciated for the following number of years.

28. 7 years

29. 12 years

30. 8 years

31. 2 years

32. 15 years

33. 20 years

34. 25 years

35. 40 years

36. Make a table to show the yearly depreciation of a machine that cost $4,200 and will be worth $750 at the end of 5 years.

Year	Depreciation Rate	Cost Minus Salvage Value	Depreciation Amount	Accumulated Depreciation	Book Value

37. Make a table to show the yearly depreciation of an asset that costs $21,500 and will be worth $5,000 at the end of 8 years.

Year	Depreciation Rate	Cost Minus Salvage Value	Depreciation Amount	Accumulated Depreciation	Book Value

Section 12.4

Find the decimal equivalent expressed to six decimal places for (a) the straight-line declining rate and (b) the double-declining-rate for the following times.

38. 4 years

39. 11 years

40. 16 years

41. Carneal Enterprises purchased a tractor at a cost of $8,500. If the estimated life of the tractor is 8 years and the estimated scrap value is $1,500, prepare a declining-balance depreciation schedule using a straight-line rate.

Year	Start-of-Year Book Value	Declining Rate	Depreciation Amount for Year	End-of-Year Book Value	Accumulated Depreciation

42. Concon Corp. bought office equipment for $6,000. At the end of 3 years, its scrap value is $750. Use a double-declining rate to make a depreciation schedule. Note that an asset *cannot* be depreciated below its scrap value.

Year	Start-of-Year Book Value	Declining Rate	Depreciation Amount for Year	End-of-Year Book Value	Accumulated Depreciation

43. Calculate the yearly depreciation for a computer costing $21,000 with an estimated life of 3 years and a resale value of $1,000. Make a depreciation schedule using the double-declining rate of depreciation.

Year	Start-of-Year Book Value	Declining Rate	Depreciation Amount for Year	End-of-Year Book Value	Accumulated Depreciation

Book value cannot go below $1,000.

Section 12.5

Round answers to the nearest cent in each of the following problems.

44. Find the depreciation deduction for the tenth year for a theme park structure that was purchased for $14,489 and placed in service under the ACRS method of depreciation as a 10-year property.

45. Find the depreciation deduction for the final 3 years for real property. The property was purchased for $113,984 and placed in service under the ACRS method of depreciation as a 15-year property.

46. Find the depreciation deduction for the ninth year for a property that was purchased for $302,588 and placed in service under the ACRS method of depreciation as a 10-year property.

Section 12.6

47. Find the depreciation deduction for each year for a laser printer that costs $5,800 and was placed in service at mid-year under the MACRS method of depreciation as a 5-year property.

48. Find the depreciation deduction for each year for a fork lift that costs $27,400 and was placed in service at mid-year under the MACRS method of depreciation as a 10-year property.

49. Make a depreciation table like Table 12-8 for an asset that cost $3,270 and was placed in service at mid-year under the MACRS method of depreciation as a 3-year property.

Year	Start-of-Year Book Value	MACRS Rate	Depreciation Amount for Year	End-of-Year Book Value	Accumulated Depreciation

50. Make a depreciation table like Table 12-8 for an asset that cost $16,250 and was placed in service at mid-year under the MACRS method of depreciation as a 5-year property.

Year	Start-of-Year Book Value	MACRS Rate	Depreciation Amount for Year	End-of-Year Book Value	Accumulated Depreciation

Additional Problems

1. Find the depreciable value of an asset that costs $5,323 and has a scrap value of $500.

2. Find the annual straight-line depreciation of a 486 computer system that costs $6,300 and has a scrap value of $600 after an expected life of 5 years in a college learning lab.

3. Chou's Meat Processing purchased a meat cutting machine for $7,500. Its expected life is 60,000 hours, and it will have a salvage value of $600. Find the year's depreciation on the unit if it is used 8,500 hours during the first year.

4. Find the sum-of-the-years' digits for (a) 8 years and (b) 12 years.

5. Use the ACRS table to find the eighth year's depreciation for a property that cost $45,600 and is depreciated over a 10-year period.

6. Make a depreciation schedule (table) to show the annual straight-line depreciation, accumulated depreciation, and book value for an asset that costs $7,500 and has a scrap value $1,200. The useful life of the asset is 8 years.

Year	Total Cost	Depreciation	Accumulated Depreciation	Book Value

7. Make a depreciation schedule to show the depreciation rate, yearly depreciation, accumulated depreciation, and book value for an asset that cost $9,000 and has a scrap value of $1,500 after 4 years. Use the sum-of-the-years'-digits method of depreciation.

Year	Depreciation Rate	Cost Minus Salvage Value	Depreciation Amount	Accumulated Depreciation	Book Value

8. Use the double-declining balance method to make a depreciation schedule for equipment that cost $4,500 and has a salvage value of $300. The equipment is expected to last 5 years. Show the year, beginning book value, declining rate, amount of depreciation, ending book value, and accumulated depreciation in the schedule.

Year	Start-of-Year Book Value	Declining Rate	Depreciation Amount for Year	End-of-Year Book Value	Accumulated Depreciation

9. Use the MACRS table to make a depreciation schedule for a property that cost $4,800 and was placed in service at mid-year with a 3-year recovery period.

Year	Start-of-Year Book Value	MACRS Rate	Depreciation Amount for Year	End-of-Year Book Value	Accumulated Depreciation

Challenge Problem

Are You Fully Depreciated?

Automobile manufacturers often use a special rate of depreciation to determine book value of an automobile at various times throughout the life of a car. A new station wagon was purchased for $14,400 and currently has a resale value of $10,080 after one year of operation. Find the rate of depreciation. What will be the resale value of this station wagon after two years if the rate of depreciation remains the same?

1. Find the sum-of-the-year's digits for a term of 7 years.

2. Find the depreciable value of an asset that cost $38,490 and had a scrap value of $4,800 if the straight-line method of depreciation is used.

3. The purchase price of a van was $13,500. It cost $1,350 to customize the van for special use and $50 for delivery. What is the beginning book value of the van for depreciation purposes?

4. Make a depreciation schedule (table) to show the annual straight-line depreciation, accumulated depreciation, and book value for furniture that cost $4,500 and has a scrap value of $700. The useful life of the furniture is 5 years.

Year	Original Cost	Depreciation	Accumulated Depreciation	Book Value

5. A pizza delivery car was purchased for $9,580. The car is expected to be driven 125,000 miles before being sold for $500. What is the unit depreciation on the car (depreciation per mile)?

6. A machine that cost $58,000 and will sell for $8,000 is expected to be useful for 100,000 hours. Find the depreciation per hour for the machine. If the machine is used 6,500 hours the first year, find the depreciation for the year.

7. Find the sum-of-the-years' digits for (a) 24 years and (b) 27 years.

8. Use the sum-of-the-years'-digits method to make a depreciation schedule showing the yearly depreciation for an asset that cost $7,500 and has a salvage value of $1,500. The asset is to be used for 3 years. Use the following heads on your table.

Year	Fraction	Cost Minus Salvage Value	Depreciation Amount	Accumulated Depreciation	Book Value

9. An asset has a useful life of 12 years. Find (a) the straight-line declining rate and (b) the double-declining rate of depreciation. Write the rates as decimals with six places and percents rounded to the nearest hundredth percent.

10. Use the double-declining balance method to make a depreciation schedule for a piece of equipment that cost $2,780 and has a salvage value of $300. The equipment is expected to be used 4 years. Show the year, beginning book value, declining rate, amount of depreciation, ending book value, and accumulated depreciation in the table.

Year	Start-of-Year Book Value	Declining Rate	Depreciation Amount for Year	End-of-Year Book Value	Accumulated Depreciation

11. Use the MACRS depreciation schedule to find the first year's depreciation on an asset that cost $8,580 if the asset is to be depreciated over a 3-year period.

12. Use MACRS depreciation to make a depreciation schedule for a vehicle that was placed in service at mid-year and cost $13,580. The vehicle is to be depreciated over a 3-year period.

Year	Start-of-Year Book Value	MACRS Rate	Depreciation Amount for Year	End-of-Year Book Value	Accumulated Depreciation

13. Use MACRS depreciation to find the depreciation for the fourth year for office furniture that costs $17,872. A recovery period of 7 years is used for tax purposes.

BUSINESS MATH IN ACTION

A look at statistics that shape the sports world

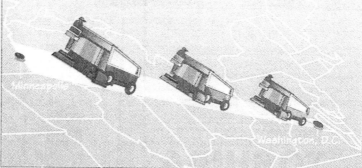

Zambonis galore

The Zamboni is the most widely used ice-resurfacing vehicle. Each of the 3,500 Zambonis travels an average of 1,100 miles each year, about the distance from Minneapolis to Washington, D.C.

Source: USA TODAY research   By Suzy Parker, USA TODAY

QUESTIONS

1. Winter Wonderland Ice Palace purchased a new Zamboni to resurface the ice. The Zamboni cost $28,452 and was set up under the MACRS depreciation schedule for 7 years. Find the first year's depreciation.

2. The expected useful life of a Zamboni is 20,000 miles. If this Zamboni travels 1,100 miles its first year, what is the depreciation using units-of-production? The salvage value is $5,000.

3. Which depreciation amount would be used for IRS reporting purposes? Which amount would be used for internal cost accounting purposes? Explain your answer.

Inventory, Turnover, and Overhead

Any business needs to know the value of materials on hand that are available for sale or for use in manufacturing items for sale. Any business also needs to know how often all merchandise is sold or used and replaced with new merchandise. The expenses incurred in operating the business are also other critical pieces of information needed to run a successful business. A knowledge of these concepts—inventory, turnover, and overhead—is important for making wise business decisions and for preparing required tax documents.

13.1
Inventory

LEARNING OBJECTIVES

1. Find the cost of goods sold using the specific identification inventory method.
2. Find the cost of goods sold using the weighted-average inventory method.
3. Find the cost of goods sold using the FIFO inventory method.
4. Find the cost of goods sold using the LIFO inventory method.
5. Use the retail method to estimate inventory.
6. Compare the methods of determining inventory.

inventory: the value of merchandise that is available for sale on a certain date.

periodic inventory: a physical count of the merchandise on hand at the end of a specified time to determine the value of merchandise available for sale.

perpetual inventory: a record of the amount and value of merchandise available for sale at any given time. Inventory records for this type of inventory are kept on computer and are adjusted with the sale of each item.

The *value* of merchandise that is available for sale on a certain date is called **inventory.** The value of inventory is important for a number of reasons. Two of the financial statements covered in Chapter 14 need inventory figures, as do various tax documents. Inventory may be checked weekly, monthly, quarterly, semiannually, annually, or at any other specific interval of time. At the end of the specified time, a physical count is made of the merchandise on hand. This type of inventory is called a **periodic inventory,** or physical inventory.

Many stores have computerized the inventory process so that the inventory is adjusted with each sale. That is, a count of merchandise on hand is available at any time. This continual inventory method is called **perpetual inventory.** Even with a perpetual inventory system, a physical count is made periodically to verify and adjust the inventory records. A discrepancy between the perpetual inventory and the actual inventory is sometimes a result of theft or loss due to damage.

Once a count of merchandise has been made, the merchandise is given a value according to various accounting methods. What makes this process time-consuming is that the cost of the goods purchased during a specific period may vary. For example, at one point in a month coffee may be purchased at $2.79 a pound. The next time coffee is ordered, the cost may be $2.93 a pound. This section discusses five methods commonly used by accountants to assign a value to an inventory: specific identification; weighted average; first-in, first-out (FIFO); last-in, first-out (LIFO); and retail.

We will use the same basic example for each of the five methods, so that you can see the different figures that each method produces. This basic example is shown in Table 13-1.

Table 13.1

Date of Purchase	Number of Units Purchased	Cost per Unit	Total Cost
Beginning inventory	29	$ 8	$232
January 15	18	7	126
February 4	9	10	90
March 3	+ 14	8	112
Goods available for sale	70		$560
Units sold	− 48		
Ending inventory	22		

Also, throughout this discussion, we will use the same formula, which shows how to find the cost of goods sold:

Cost of goods sold = cost of goods available for sale − cost of ending inventory

Table 13-1 shows that the cost of goods available for sale is $560. This figure will remain the same throughout the discussion. What will vary with each method is the cost of the ending inventory and, thus, the cost of goods sold.

Specific Identification Inventory Method

Many companies code their incoming merchandise with the purchase price or cost. Their inventory values are then based on the actual cost of each item available for sale, the **specific identification inventory method.** This method is best for low-volume, high-cost items, such as automobiles or fine jewelry, since a company must be able to identify the actual cost of the specific individual items bought. The name of this method is derived from the fact that in each case, when figuring the cost of goods available for sale and the cost of ending inventory, an *exact price per unit* is available.

specific identification inventory method: incoming merchandise that is available for sale is coded with the actual cost, so the inventory is based on the actual cost of the item.

STEP BY STEP

Using the Specific Identification Inventory Method

Step 1. Find the cost of goods available for sale by multiplying the number of units purchased by the cost per unit and then finding the total to get a total cost of goods available for sale.

Step 2. Find the cost of ending inventory by multiplying the number of units in ending inventory by the purchase price per unit.

Step 3. Find the cost of goods sold:

Cost of goods sold
= cost of goods available for sale − cost of ending inventory

EXAMPLE 1

Calculate the value of the inventory as shown in Table 13-1 using the specific identification method. Then determine the cost of goods sold.

Calculate the cost of goods available for sale from information in Table 13-1.

Find the cost of ending inventory. Use the following information.

Number of Units on Hand	Cost per Unit	Total Cost
10	$ 8	$ 80
5	7	35
3	10	30
4	8	32
Cost of ending inventory		$177

Find the cost of goods sold.

Cost of goods sold = cost of goods available for sale − cost of ending inventory

$$= \$560 - \$177$$

$$= \$383$$

Weighted-Average Inventory Method

weighted-average inventory method: the total cost of goods available for sale is divided by the total number of units available for sale to obtain the average unit cost.

Another way to place a value on the ending inventory is the **weighted-average inventory method,** in which the total cost of goods available for sale is divided by the total number of units available for sale to get the average unit cost. This method takes less time than figuring exact prices for each unit and is often used with goods that are similar in cost and whose cost is relatively stable, for example, typewriter ribbons.

STEP BY STEP

Using the Weighted-Average Inventory Method

Step 1. Find the average unit cost:

$$\text{Average unit cost} = \frac{\text{total cost of goods available for sale}}{\text{total number of units available for sale}}$$

Step 2. Find the cost of ending inventory by multiplying the number of units on hand by the average unit cost.

Step 3. Find the cost of goods sold (COGS).

$$\text{COGS} = \text{cost of goods available for sale} - \text{cost of ending inventory}$$

EXAMPLE 2

Calculate the cost of ending inventory and the COGS using the weighted-average method and the data in Table 13-1.

Find the average unit cost.

$$\text{Average unit cost} = \frac{\text{total cost of goods available for sale}}{\text{total number of units available for sale}} = \frac{\$560}{70} = \$8$$

Calculate the cost of ending inventory.

Cost of ending inventory = number of units on hand × average unit cost

$$= 22 \times \$8$$

$$= \$176$$

Calculate the cost of goods sold.

Cost of goods sold = cost of goods available for sale − cost of ending inventory

$$= \$560 - \$176$$

$$= \$384$$

FIFO (first-in, first-out) inventory method: a method of determining the cost of the ending inventory in which each sale is assumed to be from the oldest item in the inventory; that is, the most recently purchased goods are the goods remaining in the ending inventory.

FIFO: First-in, First-out Inventory Method

Many companies, especially those dealing in items that spoil or date quickly, use the **FIFO (first-in, first-out) inventory method.** In the FIFO method, the earliest items purchased (the first in) are assumed to be the first items sold (the first out). In this method, the ending inventory is made up of the most recently purchased goods. Thus cost of the goods available for sale will be relatively close to the current cost for purchasing additional items.

STEP BY STEP

Using the FIFO Inventory Method

Step 1. Determine which items (at which prices) are in ending inventory.

Step 2. Multiply price per item by the number of items and add the sums to get a total cost of ending inventory.

Step 3. Find the cost of goods sold:

Cost of goods sold
= cost of goods available for sale − cost of ending inventory

EXAMPLE 3

Use the information from Table 13-1 to find the cost of goods sold using the FIFO method.

Determine which items (at which prices) are in ending inventory.

Mar. 3	14 items	There are 22 items in ending inventory,
Feb. 4	8 items	and by this method they must be the most
	22 items	recently purchased items. Count back in
		the table from the most recently purchased
		until you have 22 items.

Multiply the price per item times the number of items. Then add the sums to get the cost of ending inventory.

Mar. 3	14 items × $ 8 = $112
Feb. 4	8 items × $10 = $ 80
	22 items $192

Find the cost of goods sold.

Cost of goods sold = cost of goods available for sale − cost of ending inventory

$$= \$560 - \$192$$

$$= \$368$$

LIFO: Last-in, First-out Inventory Method

A fourth method for determining the cost of the ending inventory and the cost of goods sold is the **LIFO (last-in, first-out) inventory method.** In this method, the oldest goods are assumed to be the goods remaining in the ending inventory. The newest goods are sold first. That is, the last item in is the first item out (LIFO). The cost of the ending inventory will be figured on the cost of the oldest stock. Thus, the difference between the cost of the goods available for sale and the replacement costs for new goods could be significant. Also, the profit on goods sold would be less since the newer, higher-priced goods were sold first.

LIFO (last-in, first-out) inventory method: a method of determining the cost of the ending inventory in which each sale is assumed to be from the goods most recently purchased; that is, the oldest goods are assumed to be the goods remaining in the ending inventory.

Even though this method does not follow natural business practices of rotating stock to maintain freshness or quality, there are some economic advantages to using this method under certain conditions. The various methods will be compared at the end of the section.

STEP BY STEP

Using the LIFO Inventory Method

Step 1. Determine which items (at which prices) are in ending inventory.

Step 2. Multiply the price per item times the number of items; then add to get the total cost of ending inventory.

Step 3. Find the cost of goods sold:

Cost of goods sold
= cost of goods available for sale − cost of ending inventory

---

EXAMPLE 4

Use the information from Table 13-1 to find the cost of goods sold using the LIFO method.

Determine which items (at which prices) are in ending inventory.

Beginning inventory: 22 items $8	You know there are 22 items in ending inventory and that with this method they were the first items purchased, so you count down from the top of the table until you have 22 items. In this case, they are all from beginning inventory.

Multiply the price per item times the number of items; then add the sums to get the total cost of ending inventory.

Beginning inventory: $8 × 22 items = $176	In this case you do not have to add since all 22 items were from beginning inventory at $8 per item.

Find the cost of goods sold.

Cost of goods sold = cost of goods available for sale − cost of ending inventory

$$= \$560 - \$176$$

$$= \$384$$

The Retail Method of Estimating Inventory

retail method: a method of determining inventory by comparing the cost of goods available for sale at cost and at retail.

Sometimes businesses do not have time to make monthly or periodic inventories. Instead, they estimate inventory cost rather than count goods individually. One method used to estimate inventory is called the **retail method.**

The retail method uses a ratio that compares the cost of goods available for sale to the retail value of those goods. That is, it compares what it costs to buy the goods with what the goods will sell for. To use this method, you need to know the value of the beginning inventory at cost and at retail, the cost and retail value of purchases and the amount of sales.

STEP BY STEP

Using the Retail Method of Estimating Inventory

Step 1. Calculate the cost of goods available for sale (using the purchase price of goods).

Step 2. Calculate the retail value of goods available for sale using cost and markup.

Step 3. Find the ratio of goods at cost price to goods at retail price and convert it to a decimal equivalent (use six decimal places if the decimal does not terminate).

$$\text{Cost ratio} = \frac{\text{cost of goods available for sale}}{\text{retail value of goods available for sale}}$$

Step 4. Find the ending inventory at retail.

Ending inventory at retail
$$= \text{retail value of goods available for sale} - \text{sales}$$

Step 5. Find ending inventory at cost and cost of goods sold.

Ending inventory at cost
$$= \text{ending inventory at retail} \times \text{cost ratio}$$

Cost of goods sold = sales × cost ratio

EXAMPLE 5

Using the following table, find the ending inventory and cost of goods sold using the retail method. You also need to know that net sales for the period are $487.

Date of Purchase	Total Cost	Total Retail Price
Beginning inventory	$232	$331
January 15	126	180
February 4	90	129
March 3	112	160
Goods available for sale	$560	$800

Steps 1 and 2 have been done for you in the table: The cost of goods available for sale at cost is $560; at retail, $800.

Find the cost ratio.

$$\text{Cost ratio} = \frac{\text{cost of goods for sale at cost}}{\text{retail price of goods available for sale}} = \frac{\$560}{\$800} = 0.7$$

Ending inventory at retail = retail price of goods available for sale − sales
$$= \$800 - \$487 = \$313$$

Find ending inventory at cost.

Ending inventory at cost = ending inventory at retail × cost ratio
$$= \$313 \times 0.7 = \$219.10$$
$$\text{Sales} \times \text{cost ratio} = \$487 \times 0.7 = \$340.90$$

Calculator Solution

The calculator can be used to:

1. Find the retail value of goods available and save in memory.

$\boxed{\text{AC}}$ 331 $\boxed{+}$ 180 $\boxed{+}$ 129 $\boxed{+}$ 160 $\boxed{=}$ $\boxed{\text{M}^+}$ ⇒ 800

2. Find the cost of goods available and leave in display.

$\boxed{\text{CE/C}}$ 232 $\boxed{+}$ 126 $\boxed{+}$ 90 $\boxed{+}$ 112 $\boxed{=}$ ⇒ 560   (Do not clear.)

3. Find the cost ratio. Display still shows 560.

$\boxed{\div}$ $\boxed{\text{MRC}}$ $\boxed{\text{MRC}}$ $\boxed{=}$ $\boxed{\text{M}^+}$ ⇒ 0.7

(The first $\boxed{\text{MRC}}$ recalls 800 from memory; the second $\boxed{\text{MRC}}$ clears 800 from memory so that a new number can be stored there.) Now the cost ratio is in memory.

4. Find the ending inventory at retail.
Clear display but do not clear memory.

$\boxed{\text{CE/C}}$ 800 − 487 $\boxed{=}$ ⇒ 313   (Do not clear.)

5. Find ending inventory at cost. Display still shows 313.

$\boxed{\times}$ $\boxed{\text{MRC}}$ $\boxed{=}$ ⇒ 219.10

Find the cost of goods sold.

$\boxed{\text{CE/C}}$ 487 $\boxed{\times}$ $\boxed{\text{MRC}}$ $\boxed{=}$ ⇒ 340.90

Table 13-2   Comparison of the Five Methods of Figuring Inventory

Method	Cost of Ending Inventory	Cost of Goods Sold	Comment
Specific identification	$177	$383	This method is the most accurate but most time consuming.
Weighted	$176	$383	This method is less accurate than specific identification but takes less time. This method is perhaps the easiest to use when the economy is relatively stable. Radical changes in prices may result in a distorted inventory value.
FIFO	$192	$368	In this method the value of the remaining inventory is closely related to the current market price of the goods. During high inflation, this method produces the highest income.
LIFO	$176	$384	In this method the value of the remaining inventory may vary significantly from the current market price of the goods. During high inflation, this method produces lower income.
Retail	$313	$340.90	This method estimates the ending inventory based on the retail prices and the net sales. Since the information needed for using this method is easily accessible, this is one of the most efficient methods.

Comparing Methods for Determining Inventory

Each of the different methods of figuring the value of inventory has advantages and disadvantages, depending on current economic conditions, tax regulations, and so on. However, it is important to know that once a business has selected a method, it must obtain permission from the Internal Revenue Service to change methods.

This section has shown the results of figuring the value of the same inventory by each of the five different methods. Table 13-2 compares the five methods and the results obtained with each.

 Self-Check 13.1

The following problems all pertain to the same business.

1. Find the cost of the ending inventory from the following information.

Number of Units on Hand	Cost per Unit	Total Cost
43	$12	_____
11	9	_____
7	11	_____
28	15	_____

2. Find the average unit cost for the information shown in the table.

Date of Purchase	Number of Units purchased	Cost per Unit	Total Cost
Beginning inventory	96	$12	_____
April 12	23	9	_____
May 8	15	11	_____
June 2	37	15	_____

3. Calculate the cost of the ending inventory and the cost of goods sold in Exercises 1 and 2 by using the weighted-average method.

4. Find the cost of goods sold and the cost of the ending inventory using the LIFO method if 22 items are on hand.

Date of Purchase	Number of Units Purchased	Cost per Unit	Total Cost
Beginning inventory	96	$12	___
April 12	23	9	___
May 8	15	11	___
June	37	15	___

Assume the items on hand are the oldest items.

13.2

 ## Inventory Turnover

LEARNING OBJECTIVE

1. Calculate inventory turnover.

Most businesses must keep a careful watch over their **inventory turnover,** which is how often the inventory of merchandise is sold and replaced. The

inventory turnover: the frequency with which the inventory is sold and replaced.

rate of inventory turnover varies greatly according to the type of business. A restaurant, for example, should have a high turnover but probably carries a small inventory of goods. A furniture company, on the other hand, would normally keep a large inventory but have a low turnover.

Knowing the turnover of a business can be useful in making future decisions and in analyzing business practices.

A low turnover rate may indicate the following:

1. Too much capital tied up in inventory.
2. Customer dissatisfaction with choice of merchandise, quality, or price.
3. Product obsolete or not properly marketed.

A high turnover rate may indicate the following:

1. Insufficient inventory that could result in a loss in sales because product is "out of stock."
2. Product is highly desirable.
3. Price may be significantly lower than the competition's price.

There are two ways to figure turnover rate: at cost or at retail. Cost means the price at which the company bought the merchandise. Retail means the price at which the company sells the merchandise.

Calculating Inventory Turnover

To figure the turnover rate at *cost,* you divide the cost of goods sold by the average inventory at cost:

$$\text{Inventory turnover rate at cost} = \frac{\text{cost of goods sold}}{\text{average inventory at cost}}$$

To figure the turnover rate at retail, you divide the net sales by the average inventory at retail:

$$\text{Inventory turnover rate at retail} = \frac{\text{sales}}{\text{average inventory at retail}}$$

Turnover can cover any period of time but is usually figured monthly, semiannually (twice a year), or yearly.

STEP BY STEP

Calculating Inventory Turnover Rate

Step 1. Find the average inventory:

$$\text{Average inventory} = \frac{\text{beginning inventory} + \text{ending inventory}}{2}$$

Step 2. Find the turnover rate:

$$\text{Turnover rate at cost} = \frac{\text{cost of goods sold}}{\text{average inventory at cost}}$$

$$\text{Turnover rate at retail} = \frac{\text{sales}}{\text{average inventory at retail}}$$

EXAMPLE 6

A local Hungarian restaurant had net sales of $32,000 for the month of June. The inventory at the beginning of June was $7,000; the ending inventory was $9,000. Find the average inventory and turnover rate at retail for June.

First find the average inventory:	To find average inventory, add beginning inventory and ending inventory and divide by 2.

Average inventory

$$= \frac{\text{beginning inventory} + \text{ending inventory}}{2}$$

$$= \frac{\$7,000 + \$9,000}{2} = \frac{\$16,000}{2} = \$8,000$$

Then find turnover rate:	To find turnover rate at retail, divide net sales by average inventory.

$$\text{Turnover rate at retail} = \frac{\text{net sales}}{\text{average inventory}}$$

$$= \frac{\$32,000}{\$8,000} = 4 \text{ times}$$

The turnover rate at retail is 4 in the month of June.	The answer is 4; note that the rate is *not* a percent.

 Self-Check 13.2

5. Rutledge Equipment Company had net sales of $335,000. The beginning inventory based on retail price was $122,000 and the ending retail price inventory was $155,000. Find the turnover rate at retail.

6. The 7th Inning Baseball Card Shop had a beginning inventory of $59,800 which was based on cost. The ending inventory, also based on cost, was $48,500. If the cost of the merchandise sold during the year was $117,500, find the turnover rate at cost.

13.3

Overhead

LEARNING OBJECTIVES

1. Calculate overhead using total department sales.
2. Calculate overhead using unit floor space.

A business encounters many expenses other than buying stock and equipment. It must pay salaries, rent, taxes, and insurance fees. It must buy office supplies and keep up equipment. These expenses, along with depreciation, are called **overhead.** The ratio between overhead and sales can say much about a firm's efficiency or inefficiency.

In addition, sometimes a company needs to know not only how much its total overhead expenses are, but also the overhead expense of each department so that it can reduce excessive overhead expenses of certain depart-

overhead: expenses required for the operation of a business, such as salaries, rent, office supplies, taxes, insurance, and upkeep of equipment.

ments to increase profits. There are many methods of figuring overhead by department. Two of the most widely used methods are according to total sales and according to total floor space. Other ways of figuring overhead are similar to these two and apply the same type of problem-solving approach.

Overhead by Total Sales

Some companies divide their total overhead expenses on the basis of *sales* for each department. To use this method, find a fraction for each department showing what part of the total sales was made by that department. Then multiply the total sales times each fraction to find the amount of overhead for each department.

STEP BY STEP

Finding Overhead Based on Total Sales

Step 1. Add the sales amounts of individual departments to find the total sales amount.

Step 2. Find the sales fraction for each department and convert it to a decimal equivalent with six decimal places if the decimal does not terminate.

$$\text{Sales fraction} = \frac{\text{sales of each department}}{\text{total sales}}$$

Step 3. Figure the amount of overhead to be assigned to each department by multiplying each department sales fraction times the total overhead.

$$\text{Overhead} = \text{department sales fraction} \times \text{total overhead}$$

EXAMPLE 7

Just For Fun's overhead expenses totaled $8,000 during one month. Find the amount of overhead for each department, based on total sales, if the store had the following monthly sales by department: cameras, $5,000; jewelry, $8,200; sporting goods, $6,700; silver, $9,200; and toys, $12,000.

Department	Monthly Sales Amount	Sales Fraction and Decimal Equivalent	Amount of Overhead for Each Department
Cameras	$ 5,000	$\frac{\$5,000}{\$41,100} = 0.121655$	$0.121655 \times \$8,000 = \$\ \ \ 973.24$
Jewelry	$ 8,200	$\frac{\$8,200}{\$41,100} = 0.199513$	$0.199513 \times \$8,000 = \$1,596.10$
Sporting goods	$ 6,700	$\frac{\$6,700}{\$41,100} = 0.163017$	$0.163017 \times \$8,000 = \$1,304.14$
Silver	$ 9,200	$\frac{\$9,200}{\$41,100} = 0.223844$	$0.223844 \times \$8,000 = \$1,790.75$
Toys	$12,000	$\frac{\$12,000}{\$41,100} = 0.291971$	$0.291971 \times \$8,000 = \$2,335.77$
Total	$41,100	1.000000	$8,000.00

Setting up and completing a table like the one shown on page 406 helps organize the information and calculations. List the sales of each department in the second column, and then find the total sales amount. In the third column, write the sales fraction for each department and its decimal equivalent. In the fourth column, multiply the decimal equivalent times the total overhead amount to find each department's overhead amount.

Overhead by Unit Floor Space

Another way of distributing overhead is by unit floor space. Each department's overhead is determined by the number of square feet the department occupies. Basically, this method is similar to the sales per department method. The floor space of each department is the numerator and the total floor space is the denominator of the floor-space fraction, which is converted to its decimal equivalent. To find the overhead for the department, multiply the decimal equivalent of the floor-space fraction times the total overhead.

STEP BY STEP

Finding Overhead Based on Floor Space

Step 1. Add the square feet of floor space in each department to find the total number of square feet of floor space.

Step 2. Find the floor-space fraction for each department and convert it to a decimal equivalent with six decimal places if the decimal does not terminate.

Floor-space fraction

$$= \frac{\text{square feet of floor space in each department}}{\text{total square feet of floor space}}$$

Step 3. Figure the amount of overhead to be assigned to each department by multiplying each floor-space fraction times the total overhead.

EXAMPLE 8

The Super Store assigns overhead to its various departments according to the amount of floor space used by each department. The store's total overhead is $25,000. Find the amount of overhead for each department using the following number of square feet: junior department, 3,000; women's wear, 4,000; men's wear, 3,500; children's wear, 3,000; china and silver, 2,500; housewares, 2,500; linens, 2,000; toys, 1,500; carpets, 3,500; and cosmetics, 500. Round the *final* answers to the nearest cent if necessary.

Setting up and completing a table like the one shown on page 408 helps organize our information and calculations. List the square feet of floor space in each department in the second column, and then find the total number of square feet of floor space. In the third column, write the floor-space fraction for each department and its decimal equivalent. In the fourth column, multiply the decimal equivalent times the total overhead amount to find each department's overhead amount.

Department	Department's Floor Space	Floor-space Fraction and Decimal Equivalent	Amount of Overhead for Each Department
Junior department	3,000	$\dfrac{3,000}{26,000} = 0.115385$	$0.115385 \times \$25,000 = \$\ 2,884.63$
Women's wear	4,000	$\dfrac{4,000}{26,000} = 0.153846$	$0.153846 \times \$25,000 = \$\ 3,846.15$
Men's wear	3,500	$\dfrac{3,500}{26,000} = 0.134615$	$0.134615 \times \$25,000 = \$\ 3,365.38$
Children's wear	3,000	$\dfrac{3,000}{26,000} = 0.115385$	$0.115385 \times \$25,000 = \$\ 2,884.63$
China and silver	2,500	$\dfrac{2,500}{26,000} = 0.096154$	$0.096154 \times \$25,000 = \$\ 2,403.85$
Housewares	2,500	$\dfrac{2,500}{26,000} = 0.096154$	$0.096154 \times \$25,000 = \$\ 2,403.85$
Linens	2,000	$\dfrac{2,000}{26,000} = 0.076923$	$0.076923 \times \$25,000 = \$\ 1,923.08$
Toys	1,500	$\dfrac{1,500}{26,000} = 0.057692$	$0.057692 \times \$25,000 = \$\ 1,442.30$
Carpets	3,500	$\dfrac{3,500}{26,000} = 0.134615$	$0.134615 \times \$25,000 = \$\ 3,365.38$
Cosmetics	500	$\dfrac{500}{26,000} = 0.019231$	$0.019231 \times \$25,000 = \$\ \ \ \ 480.78$
Total	$26,000	1.000000	$25,000.03

TIPS & TRAPS

When a problem requires several calculations, it is helpful if you can periodically check your work rather than only checking the final answer.

Interim Check: In Example 8, the total of the decimal equivalents of the sales fraction should total (or be very close to) 1.

Final Check: The sum of the amount of overhead for each department should equal or be very close to the total overhead.

 Self-Check 13.3

7. The Allimore Department Store had overhead expenses that totaled $6,000 during one month. Find the amount of overhead for each department, based on total sales, if the store had the following monthly sales by department: toys, $4,000; appliances, $6,600; children's clothing, $6,800; books, $4,600; and furniture, $8,400.

8. Savemore Discount Clothing Store assigns overhead to its various departments according to the amount of floor space used by each department. The store's total monthly overhead is $15,800. Find the amount of overhead for each department using the following number of square feet: women's clothing, 2,000; men's clothing, 1,200; children's clothing, 2,500. Round *final* answers to the nearest cent if necessary.

Chapter 13   Inventory, Turnover, and Overhead

Summary

Topic	Page	What to Remember	Examples
Figuring the amount of inventory	394	All inventory methods provide some way of finding the value of goods available for sale, the value of the ending inventory, and the value of goods sold.	Each inventory method is illustrated in the following example.

Specific identification method — 395

Incoming merchandise is coded with the actual cost, and inventory is based on the actual cost of the item.

$$\text{Cost of goods sold} = \binom{\text{cost of goods}}{\text{available for sale}} - \binom{\text{cost of ending}}{\text{inventory}}$$

Use the specific identification method to calculate the cost of goods available for sale and the cost of the ending inventory and the cost of goods sold.

Date of Purchase	Number of Units Purchased	Cost per Unit	Total Cost
Beginning inventory	17	$10	$170
January 8	25	8	200
February 3	22	12	264
March 5	20	8	160
Cost of goods available for sale			$794

Find the cost of ending inventory from the following information.

Number of Units on Hand	Cost per Unit	Total Cost
12	$10	$120
19	8	152
11	12	132
16	8	128
Cost of ending inventory		$532

Find the cost of goods sold from the preceding information: Cost of goods sold = cost of goods available − cost of ending inventory = $794 − $532 = $262

Weighted-average method — 396

$$\text{Average unit cost} = \frac{\binom{\text{total cost of goods}}{\text{available for sale}}}{\binom{\text{total number of units}}{\text{available for sale}}}$$

$$\binom{\text{Average cost of}}{\text{ending inventory}} = \binom{\text{number of units on hand}}{} \times \binom{\text{average unit cost}}{}$$

$$\text{Cost of goods sold} = \binom{\text{number of units sold}}{} \times \binom{\text{average unit cost}}{}$$

Find the average unit cost for the information shown in the table.

Date of Purchase	Number of Units Purchased	Cost per Unit	Total Cost
Beginning inventory	18	$18	$ 324
April 6	25	19	475
May 4	26	12	312
June 9	22	8	176
Cost of goods available for sale	91		$1,287

	Number of Units on Hand	Cost per Unit	Total Cost
	12	$18	$216
	18	19	342
	7	12	84
Cost of	13	8	104
ending			
inventory	50		$746

Calculate the cost of the ending inventory and the cost of goods sold in the example by using the weighted-average method.

Average unit cost

$$= \frac{\text{total cost of goods available for sale}}{\text{total number of units available for sale}}$$

$$= \frac{\$1,287}{91} = \$14.14$$

Average cost of ending inventory
= number of units on hand × average unit cost
= 50 × $14.14 = $707

Cost of goods sold
= number of units sold × average unit cost
= (91 − 50) × $14.14 = $579.74

FIFO: first-in, first-out method

396

Each sale is assumed to be from the oldest item in the inventory, and the first item in is considered to be the first item out. The ending inventory is made up of the most recently purchased goods.

Find the cost of goods sold and the cost of the ending inventory using the FIFO method if 465 items are on hand.

Date of Purchase	Number of Units purchased	Cost per Unit	Total Cost
Beginning inventory	222	$10	$2,220
January 15	142	12	1,704
February 5	134	15	2,010
March 2	141	24	3,384
Cost of goods available for sale	639		$9,318

Date of Purchase	Number of Units on Hand	Cost per Unit	Total Cost
Beginning inventory	48	$10	$ 480
January 15	142	12	1,704
February 5	134	15	2,010
March 2	141	24	3,384
Cost of ending inventory	465		$7,578

Cost of goods sold = $9,318 − $7,578 = $1,740

Topic	Page	What to Remember	Examples
LIFO: last-in, first-out method	397	Each sale is assumed to be from the newest item in the inventory, and the last item in is considered to be the first item out. The ending inventory is made up of the oldest goods.	Use the LIFO method to find the cost of goods sold and the cost of the ending inventory if 282 items are on hand.

Date of Purchase	Number of Units Purchased	Cost per Unit	Total Cost
Beginning inventory	111	$10	$1,110
April 12	343	12	4,116
May 8	191	9	1,719
June 10	106	24	2,544
Cost of goods available for sale			$9,489

Date of Purchase	Number of Units on Hand	Cost per Unit	Total Cost
Beginning inventory	111	$10	$1,110
April 12	171	12	2,052
Cost of ending inventory			$3,162

Cost of goods sold = $9,489 − $3,162 = $6,327

Topic	Page	What to Remember	Examples
Retail method	398	Inventory is estimated using the ratio of the cost of goods available for sale at cost to the cost of goods available for sale at retail.	Use the retail method to find the cost of goods sold and the cost of the ending inventory.

Calculate the cost of goods sold and the cost of the ending inventory from the following information.

	Cost	Retail
Beginning inventory	$4,824	$6,030
Purchases	872	1,090
Cost of goods available for sale	$5,696	$7,120
Less net sales		2,464
Ending inventory at retail		$4,656

$$\text{Cost ratio} = \frac{\$5,696}{\$7,120} = 0.8$$

Ending inventory at cost = $4,656 × 0.8 = $3,724.80

Cost of goods sold = $5,696 − $3,724.80 = $1,971.20

Topic	Page	What to Remember	Examples
Calculating turnover	402	Average inventory = $$\frac{\text{beginning inventory} + \text{ending inventory}}{2}$$ a. $$\text{Turnover rate at retail} = \frac{\text{net sales}}{\text{average inventory at retail}}$$ b. $$\text{Turnover rate at cost} = \frac{\text{cost of goods sold}}{\text{average inventory at cost}}$$	A store had net sales of $10,000 ($5,000 cost) with a beginning inventory of $5,000 ($2,500 cost) and an ending inventory of $6,000 ($3,000 cost). a. Average inventory at retail $$= \frac{\$5,000 + \$6,000}{2} = \$5,500$$ $$\text{Turnover at retail} = \frac{\$10,000}{\$5,500} = 1.818182$$

Topic	Page	What to Remember	Examples

b. Average inventory at cost

$$= \frac{\$2,500 + \$3,000}{2} = \$2,750$$

$$\text{Turnover rate} \atop \text{at cost} = \frac{\$5,000}{\$2,750} = 1.818182$$

Topic	Page	What to Remember	Examples
Finding overhead based on sales	404	Find the total sales amount. Then find the sales fraction for each department and convert it to a decimal equivalent. Sales fraction $= \dfrac{\text{sales amount of each department}}{\text{total sales}}$	Make a table to show the overhead by departments if overhead is assigned based on total sales and the store had the following monthly sales by department: paint, \$5,000; lumber, \$6,200; wall coverings, \$3,200; plumbing, \$3,200; and electrical, \$1,500. Overhead expenses during the month are \$1,780.
Finding overhead based on sales	404	Multiply each department's sales fraction times the total overhead to find the amount of overhead for each department.	

Department	Monthly Sales Amount	Sales Fraction and Decimal Equivalent	Amount of Overhead for Each Department
Paint	$ 5,000	$\dfrac{\$5,000}{\$19,100} = 0.261780$	$0.261780 \times \$1,780 = \$\ \ 465.97$
Lumber	$ 6,200	$\dfrac{\$6,200}{\$19,100} = 0.324607$	$0.324607 \times \$1,780 = \$\ \ 577.80$
Wall coverings	$ 3,200	$\dfrac{\$3,200}{\$19,100} = 0.167539$	$0.167539 \times \$1,780 = \$\ \ 298.22$
Plumbing	$ 3,200	$\dfrac{\$3,200}{\$19,100} = 0.167539$	$0.167539 \times \$1,780 = \$\ \ 298.22$
Electrical	$ 1,500	$\dfrac{\$1,500}{\$19,100} = 0.078534$	$0.078534 \times \$1,780 = \$\ \ 139.79$
Total	$19,100	0.999999	$1,780.00

Topic	Page	What to Remember	Examples
Finding overhead based on floor space	405	Add the square feet of floor space in each department to find the total number of square feet of floor space. Find the floor-space fraction for each department and convert it to a decimal equivalent. Floor-space fraction $= \dfrac{\text{square feet of floor space in department}}{\text{total square feet of floor space}}$ Multiply each floor-space fraction times the total overhead to find the amount of overhead for each department.	Make a table to show the overhead for a store that had \$25,000 in overhead expenses if overhead is calculated based on number of square feet in a department.

Department	Number of Square Feet
1	5,100
2	4,120
3	1,200
4	2,500

Department	Floor Space	Floor-space Fraction and Decimal Equivalent	Amount of Overhead for Department
1	5,100	$\dfrac{5,100}{12,920} = 0.394737$	$0.394737 \times \$25,000 = \$\ 9,868.43$
2	4,120	$\dfrac{4,120}{12,920} = 0.318885$	$0.318885 \times \$25,000 = \$\ 7,972.13$
3	1,200	$\dfrac{1,200}{12,920} = 0.092879$	$0.092879 \times \$25,000 = \$\ 2,321.98$
4	2,500	$\dfrac{2,500}{12,920} = 0.193498$	$0.193498 \times \$25,000 = \$\ 4,837.45$
	12,920	0.999999	$24,999.99

Self-Check Solutions

1.

Number of Units on Hand	Cost per Unit	Total Cost
43	12	$ 516
11	9	99
7	11	77
28	15	420
		$1,112

2.

Date of Purchase	Number of Units Purchased	Cost per Unit	Total Cost
Beginning inventory	96	$12	$1,152
April 12	23	9	207
May 8	15	11	165
June 2	37	15	555
	171		$2,079

$$\text{Average unit cost} = \frac{\text{total cost of goods available for sale}}{\text{total number of units available for sale}}$$

$$= \frac{\$2,079}{171} = \$12.16$$

3. Number of units on hand (ending inventory) $= 43 + 11 + 7 + 28 = 89$
Cost of ending inventory $= 89 \times \$12.16 = \$1,082.24$
Cost of goods sold $=$ cost of goods available for sale $-$ cost of ending inventory
$$= \$2,079 - \$1,082.24 = \$996.76$$

4.

	Number of Units on Hand	Cost per Unit	Total Cost
Cost of ending inventory	22	$12	$264

Cost of goods sold $= \$2,079 - \$264 = \$1,815$

5.

$$\text{Average inventory} = \frac{\$122{,}000 + \$155{,}000}{2}$$

$$= \$138{,}500$$

$$\text{Turnover rate} = \frac{\$335{,}000}{\$138{,}500} = 2.42 \text{ times}$$

6.

$$\text{Average inventory} = \frac{\$59{,}800 + \$48{,}500}{2} = \$54{,}150$$

$$\text{Turnover rate} = \frac{\$117{,}500}{\$54{,}150} = 2.17 \text{ times}$$

7.

Department	Monthly Sales Amount	Sales Fraction and Decimal Equivalent	Amount of Overhead for Each Department
Toys	$ 4,000	$\frac{\$4{,}000}{\$30{,}400} = 0.131579$	$0.131579 \times \$6{,}000 = \$ \ 789.47$
Appliances	$ 6,600	$\frac{\$6{,}600}{\$30{,}400} = 0.217105$	$0.217105 \times \$6{,}000 = \$1{,}302.63$
Children's clothing	$ 6,800	$\frac{\$6{,}800}{\$30{,}400} = 0.223684$	$0.223684 \times \$6{,}000 = \$1{,}342.10$
Books	$ 4,600	$\frac{\$4{,}600}{\$30{,}400} = 0.151316$	$0.151316 \times \$6{,}000 = \$ \ 907.90$
Furniture	$ 8,400	$\frac{\$8{,}400}{\$30{,}400} = 0.276316$	$0.276316 \times \$6{,}000 = \$1{,}657.90$
Total	$30,400	1.000000	$6,000.00

8.

Department	Floor Space	Floor-Space Fraction and Decimal Equivalent	Amount of Overhead for Each Department
Women's clothing	2,000	$\frac{2{,}000}{5{,}700} = 0.350877$	$0.350877 \times \$15{,}800 = \$5{,}543.86$
Men's clothing	1,200	$\frac{1{,}200}{5{,}700} = 0.210526$	$0.210526 \times \$15{,}800 = \$3{,}326.31$
Children's clothing	2,500	$\frac{2{,}500}{5{,}700} = 0.438596$	$0.438596 \times \$15{,}800 = \$6{,}929.82$
Total	5,700	0.999999	$15,799.99

End of Chapter Problems

The following problems apply to Hifi Restaurant

1. Calculate the cost of goods available for sale from the following information.

Date of Purchase	Number of Units Purchased	Cost per Unit	Total Cost
Beginning inventory	182	$21	
August 20	78	27	
September 12	39	28	
October 2	52	21	
Cost of goods available for sale			

2. Find the cost of the ending inventory from the following information.

Number of Units on Hand	Cost per Unit	Total Cost
13	$21	
64	27	
29	28	
48	21	
Cost of ending inventory		

3. Find the cost of goods sold from Problems 1 and 2.

4. Find the average unit cost for the information shown in the table.

Date of Purchase	Number of Units Purchased	Cost per Unit	Total Cost
Beginning inventory	182	$21	
August 20	78	27	
September 12	39	28	
October 2	52	21	
Cost of goods available for sale			

5. Calculate the cost of the ending inventory and the cost of goods sold in Exercise 2 by using the weighted-average method.

6. Find the cost of goods sold and the cost of the ending inventory using the FIFO method if 96 items are on hand.

Date of Purchase	Number of Units Purchased	Cost per Unit	Total Cost
Beginning inventory	182	$21	
August 20	78	27	
September 12	39	28	
October 2	52	21	
Cost of goods available for sale			

7. Find the cost of goods sold and the cost of the ending inventory using the LIFO method if 200 items are on hand.

Date of Purchase	Number of Units Purchased	Cost per Unit	Total Cost
Beginning inventory	182	$21	
August 20	78	27	
September 12	39	28	
October 2	52	21	
Cost of goods available for sale			

8. Find the cost of goods sold and the cost of the ending inventory using the retail method if net sales are $5,000.

Date of Purchase	Number of Units Purchased	Cost per Unit	Total Cost	Retail Price per Unit	Total Retail
Beginning inventory	182	$21		$26	
August 20	78	27		32	
September 12	39	28		35	
October 2	52	21		26	
Cost of goods available for sale					
Less net sales					
Ending inventory at retail					
Cost ratio ($8,112 ÷ $9,945)					
Ending inventory at cost ($4,945 × 0.815686)					
Cost of goods sold ($8,112 − $4,033.57)					

Section 13.2

9. Use the following inventories to find the average inventory: $2,596; $3,872.

Find the rate of stock turnover for the following. Round to the nearest tenth.

	Opening Inventory at Retail	Closing Inventory at Retail	Net Sales	Stock Turnover
10.	$ 8,920	$ 7,460	$19,270	
11.	$51,266	$42,780	$25,000	

	Opening Inventory at Cost	Closing Inventory at Cost	Cost of Goods Sold	
12.	$ 8,000	$10,000	$36,000	
13.	$26,108	$ 5,892	$73,600	

Find the overhead for each department by total sales for the following exercises.

14. The nuts and bolts department had $1,500 in sales for the month, the electrical department had $4,000, and the paint department had $2,300. The total overhead was $3,800.

15. Department 1 had $5,200 in sales for the month, Department 2 had $4,700, Department 3 had $6,520, Department 4 had $4,870, and Department 5 had $2,010. The total overhead was $10,000.

Find the overhead for each department by units of floor space for the following problem.

16. Department A has 5,000 square feet of floor space, Department B has 2,500, Department C has 4,300, and Department D has 2,700. The total overhead is $8,200.

Additional Problems

1. Calculate the cost of goods available for sale from the following information.

Date of Purchase	Number of Units Purchased	Cost per Unit	Total Cost
Beginning inventory	25	$18	
June 8	10	19	
July 7	18	20	
August 3	22	17	
Cost of goods available for sale			

2. Calculate the cost of the ending inventory from the following information

Date of Purchase	Number of Units on Hand	Cost per Unit	Total Cost
January 12	17	$18	
February 9	12	19	
March 5	7	20	
April 7	14	17	
Cost of ending inventory			

3. Calculate the cost of goods sold from Problems 1 and 2.

4. Find the average unit cost for the information shown in the table.

Date of Purchase	Number of Units Purchased	Cost per Unit	Total Cost
Beginning inventory	21	$12	
May 12	10	10	
June 9	16	11	
July 5	20	13	
Cost of goods available for sale			

5. Calculate the cost of the ending inventory and the cost of goods sold in Problem 4 by using the weighted-average method if 21 items remain in inventory.

6. Find the cost of goods sold and the cost of the ending inventory using the FIFO method if 500 items are on hand.

Date of Purchase	Number of Units Purchased	Cost per Unit	Total Cost
Beginning inventory	221	$16	
April 15	328	15	
May 12	167	12	
June 5	201	9	
Cost of goods sold available for sale			

Date of Purchase	Number of Units Purchased	Cost per Unit	Total Cost
Beginning inventory	0	$16	
April 15	132	15	
May 12	167	12	
June 5	201	9	
Cost of ending inventory			

7. Calculate the cost of goods sold and the cost of the ending inventory for the purchases in Problem 6 using the LIFO method if 225 items are on hand.

Date of Purchase	Number of Units Purchased	Cost per Unit	Total Cost
Beginning inventory	221	$16	
April 15	4	15	
May 12	0	12	
June 5	0	9	
Cost of ending inventory			

8. Find the rate of stock turnover for a business with net sales of $75,000 and an average inventory of $15,000.

9. Tyson's Fixit Store has a monthly overhead of $9,200 divided among departments according to square feet per department. Find the monthly overhead per department using the following square feet: hardware, 800; plumbing, 600; tools, 400; supplies, 600.

10. A corner grocery store has a monthly overhead of $1,500 divided among departments according to monthly sales. Find the monthly overhead per department if department sales were as follows: meats, $1,200; groceries, $2,400; dairy, $600; and housewares, $800.

Challenge Problem

Photocopier on the Blink!

That office photocopy machine is on the blink again. You are responsible for replacing the photocopier with a more powerful model and with developing a table of use by department so the expense of the copier can be charged to each department on an equitable basis. The new copier costs $7,580 and is expected to produce 500,000 copies. The following records were accumulated by department at the end of the first year.

Department	No. of Copies	Copies Fraction	Overhead Expense
Safety	8,711		
Personnel	30,872		
Accounting/Payroll	32,521		
Secretarial Pool	52,896		
Total			

1. Calculate the cost of goods available for sale from the following information.

Date of Purchase	Number of Units Purchased	Cost per Unit	Total Cost
Beginning inventory	26	$10	
March 12	32	13	
April 3	29	9	
May 5	25	12	
Cost of goods available for sale			

2. Find the cost of the ending inventory from the following information.

	Number of Units on Hand	Cost per Unit	Total Cost
	17	$10	
	12	13	
	15	9	
	25	12	
Cost of ending inventory			

3. Find the cost of goods sold from Problems 1 and 2.

4. Find the average unit cost for the information shown in the table.

Date of Purchase	Number of Units Purchased	Cost per Unit	Total Cost
Beginning inventory	26	$10	
March 12	32	13	
April 3	29	9	
May 5	25	12	
Cost of goods available for sale			

5. Calculate the cost of ending inventory and the cost of goods sold in Problem 4 by using the weighted-average method if there are 69 units on hand.

6. Use the information in Problem 4 to construct a table to find the cost of goods sold and the cost of the ending inventory using the FIFO method if 32 items are on hand.

Date of Purchase	Number of Units on Hand	Cost per Unit	Total Cost
Beginning inventory	0	$10	
March 12	0	13	
April 3	7	9	
May 5	25	12	
Cost of ending inventory			

7. Use the information in Problem 4 to construct a table to find the cost of goods sold and the cost of the ending inventory using the LIFO method if 82 items are on hand.

Date of Purchase	Number of Units on Hand	Cost per Unit	Total Cost
Beginning inventory	26	$10	
March 12	32	13	
April 3	24	9	
May 5	0	12	
Cost of ending inventory			

8. AMX Department Store's overhead expenses totaled $12,000 during one month. The sales by department for the month were as follows: cameras, $12,000; toys, $14,000; hardware, $13,500; garden supplies, $8,400; sporting goods, $9,500; and clothing, $28,600. Find the monthly overhead for all departments.

9. Make a table to show the department overhead if overhead is assigned based on number of square feet of office space for Office Supply World. The overhead expenses for a month totaled $9,000 and each department occupies the following number of square feet: furniture, 2,000; computer supplies, 1,600; consumable office supplies, 2,500; leather goods, 1,200; and administrative services, 800.

10. A restaurant had a beginning inventory of $13,900 and an ending inventory of $10,000. If the net sales for the inventory period were $47,800, find the turnover rate.

11. A retail parts business had an average inventory of $258,968 and a net sales of $756,893 for the same period. Find the rate of turnover.

12. A plant had an average inventory of $13,000 and net sales of $26,000 for the same period. Find the rate of turnover.

A look at statistics that shape your finances

Notebook PCs gain popularity

IBM plans to introduce its first notebook-size personal computer next month. Notebook PCs' growth and expected growth as a percentage of all portable computer sales:

Source: WorkGroup Technologies Inc.

By Julie Stacy. USA TODAY

QUESTIONS

1. Acme computer store inventoried their notebook computers January 1, 1993 and determined the total cost of computers on hand to be $60,000. In checking their purchasing records, they found that $528,200 worth of computers had been sold during the year. The year-end inventory was recorded as $43,800. Find the rate of turnover.

2. If this company maintains the same inventory level and market share percentage would you expect the turnover rate for 1994 to have increased, decreased or remained about the same? Explain your answer.

3. What can be said about the turnover rate in 1996 as it relates to the 1994 turnover rate if the company maintains the same inventory level and market share?

14

Financial Statements

The financial condition of a business must be monitored all the time. The owner of a business, investors, and creditors need to know the financial condition of the business before they can make decisions and plans. Lending institutions consider the overall financial health of a business before lending money. The stockholders of incorporated businesses expect to receive periodic reports on the financial condition of the corporation. Many companies or organizations hire an auditor once a year to determine this condition. Two financial statements, the balance sheet and the income statement, are normally prepared as part of this analysis. The *balance sheet* describes the condition of a business at some exact point in time, whereas the *income statement* shows how the business did over a period of time.

14.1

The Balance Sheet

LEARNING OBJECTIVES

1. Identify assets.
2. Identify liabilities.
3. Prepare a balance sheet.
4. Prepare a vertical analysis of a balance sheet.
5. Prepare a horizontal analysis of a balance sheet.

The **balance sheet** is a type of financial statement that indicates the worth or financial condition of a business *as of a certain date*. It does not give any historical background about the company or make future projections, but rather shows the status of the company on a given date. On that date, it answers the questions:

How much does the business own? What are its assets?

How much does the business owe? What are its liabilities?

How much is the business worth? What is the value of its equity (what is its capital)?

Assets are owned by the business; *liabilities* are owed to creditors by the business; *owner's equity* is the business's worth, the difference between assets and liabilities.

balance sheet: a type of financial statement that indicates the worth or financial condition of a business as of a certain date.

Identifying Assets

Assets are properties owned by the business. They include anything of monetary value and things that could be exchanged for cash or other property. **Current assets** are assets that are normally turned into cash within a year. **Plant and equipment** are assets that are used in transacting business and are more long term in nature. These types of assets can be further subdivided as follows:

assets: properties owned by the business including anything of monetary value and things that can be exchanged for cash or other property.

current assets: cash or assets that are normally turned into cash within a year.

plant and equipment: assets used in transacting business; more long term in nature than current assets.

Current Assets	**Cash**	Money in the bank as well as cash on hand.
	Accounts receivable	Money that customers owe the business for merchandise or services they have received but not paid for.
	Notes receivable	Promissory notes owed to the business.
	Merchandise inventory	Value of merchandise on hand.
Plant and equipment	**Business equipment**	Value of equipment (tools, display cases, machinery, and so on) that the business owns.
	Office furniture and equipment	Value of office furniture (desks, chairs, filing cabinets, and so on) and equipment (typewriters, computers, printers, calculators, postage meters, and the like).

Office supplies	Value of supplies such as stationery, pens, file folders, and diskettes.
Building	Value of the building, minus depreciation.
Land	Value of the property and grounds on which the building stands.

Identifying Liabilities

liabilities: amounts that the business owes.

current liabilities: liabilities that have to be paid within a short period of time.

long-term liabilities: liabilities that are to be paid over a long period of time.

Liabilities are amounts that the business owes. **Current liabilities** are those that must be paid shortly. **Long-term liabilities** are those that will be paid over a long period of time—a year or more. These types of liabilities can be further subdivided as follows:

Current liabilities	**Accounts payable**	Accounts for merchandise or services that the business owes.
	Notes payable	Promissory notes that the business owes.
	Wages payable	Salaries that a business owes its employees.
Long-term liabilities	**Mortgage payable**	The debt owed on the purchase price of the building and land.

Owner's Equity

owner's equity: what the business is worth once liabilities have been paid off; that is, the difference in total assets and total liabilities. Also referred to as capital, proprietorship, and net worth.

In addition to its debts to creditors, a firm is considered to owe its investors. This "debt" is expressed as **owner's equity**, the amount of clear ownership or the owners' rights to the properties. It is the difference between assets and liabilities. For instance, if a business has assets of $175,000 and liabilities of $100,000, the owner's equity is $175,000 - $100,000, or $75,000. Other words used to mean the same thing as owner's equity are *capital, proprietorship,* and *net worth.*

Preparing a Balance Sheet

A balance sheet (see Figure 14-1) lists the assets, liabilities, and owner's equity of a business on a specific date, using the basic accounting equation of business:

$$\text{Assets} = \text{liabilities} + \text{owner's equity:}$$
$$A = L + OE$$

STEP BY STEP

Preparing a Balance Sheet

Step 1. At the top of the sheet, write the name of the company, the name of the statement (balance sheet), and the date. (This answers the questions who, what, and when.)

Step 2. List the assets and total them.
    a. First list and total current assets.
    b. Next list and total plant and equipment.
    c. Add the two subtotals to get total assets. Draw a double line under this figure to show that a total has been reached.

Step 3. List the liabilities and total them.

    a. First list and total current liabilities.

    b. Next list and total long-term liabilities.

    c. Add the two subtotals to get total liabilities. Do *not* draw a double line under this figure; it is only another subtotal.

Step 4. List the owner's equity figure.

Step 5. Add the figures for total liabilities and owner's equity. Draw a double line under this figure.

Step 6. Make sure that the figure for assets equals the figure for total liabilities and owner's equity.

Sander's Woodworks
Balance Sheet
December 31, 19X8

	19X8
Assets	
Current assets:	
Cash	$ 1,973
Accounts receivable	2,118
Merchandise inventory	18,476
Total current assets	$22,567
Plant and equipment:	
Equipment	
Total plant and equipment	
Total Assets	$22,567
Liabilities	
Current liabilities:	
Accounts payable	$ 2,317
Wages payable	684
Total current liabilities	3,001
Long-term liabilities:	
Mortgage note payable	
Total long-term liabilities	
Total Liabilities	$ 3,001
Owner's Equity	
J. Sanders Capital	$19,566
Total Liabilities and Owner's Equity	$22,567

Figure 14-1 A Balance Sheet

Vertical Analysis of a Balance Sheet

    A **vertical analysis** of a balance sheet shows the relationship of each item on the balance sheet to the *total assets* by using the percentage formula. In this use of the percentage formula, each item on the balance sheet is the portion, the total assets are the base, and the percent of total assets is the rate. Use this version of the formula: $R = \dfrac{P}{B}$.

vertical analysis: an analysis of a balance sheet that shows the relationship between each item on the balance sheet and the total assets.

STEP BY STEP

Preparing a Vertical Analysis of a Balance Sheet

Step 1. Divide each item listed on the balance sheet by the total assets.

Step 2. Convert the decimal to a percent and round the result to the nearest tenth percent.

EXAMPLE 1

Prepare a vertical analysis of the balance sheet for Sander's Woodworks shown in Figure 14-2.

Sander's Woodworks
Balance Sheet
December 31, 19X8

	19X8	Percent of total assets 19X8
Assets		
Current assets:		
Cash	$ 1,973	8.7
Accounts receivable	2,118	9.4
Merchandise inventory	18,476	81.9
Total current assets	$22,567	100.0
Plant and equipment:		
Equipment		
Total plant and equipment		
Total Assets	$22,567	100.0
Liabilities		
Current liabilities:		
Accounts payable	$ 2,317	10.3
Wages payable	684	3.0
Total current liabilities	3,001	13.3
Long-term liabilities:		
Mortgage note payable		
Total long-term liabilities		
Total Liabilities	$ 3,001	13.3
Owner's Equity		
J. Sanders Capital	$19,566	86.7
Total Liabilities and Owner's Equity	$22,567	100.0

Figure 14-2 Vertical Analysis of a Balance Sheet

Cash: $\dfrac{\$1,973}{\$22,567} = 0.0874285 = 8.7\%$ (nearest tenth of a percent)

Accounts receivable: $\dfrac{\$2,118}{\$22,567} = 0.0938538 = 9.4\%$

Inventory: $\dfrac{\$18,476}{\$22,567} = 0.8187175 = 81.9\%$

Total assets: $\dfrac{\$22,567}{\$22,567} = 1 = 100\%$

Accounts payable: $\dfrac{\$2,317}{\$22,567} = 0.102672 = 10.3\%$

Wages payable: $\dfrac{\$684}{\$22,567} = 0.0303097 = 3.0\%$

Total liabilities: $\dfrac{\$3,001}{\$22,567} = 0.13298 = 13.3\%$

Capital: $\dfrac{\$19,566}{\$22,567} = 0.8670182 = 86.7\%$

Total liabilities and capital: $\dfrac{\$22,567}{\$22,567} = 1 = 100\%$

Note that the entries for total assets and for total liabilities and capital equal 100%. Other percents in assets and liabilities and capital should add up to 100%.

Since each item on the balance sheet is divided by the total assets, the memory of a calculator can be used to facilitate the calculation.

$\boxed{\text{AC}}$ 22567 $\boxed{\text{M}^+}$ Enter total assets into memory.
Clear display. Do not clear memory.

Calculator Solution

Enter the first amount:

$\boxed{\text{CE/C}}$ 1973 $\boxed{\div}$ $\boxed{\text{MRC}}$ $\boxed{\%}$ $\Rightarrow$ 8.74285

Enter second first amount:

$\boxed{\text{CE/C}}$ 2118 $\boxed{\div}$ $\boxed{\text{MRC}}$ $\boxed{\%}$ $\Rightarrow$ 9.38538

Continue with each amount.

TIPS & TRAPS

Be careful to use the total assets as the base when figuring each percent. Look what happens to the percent for *Wages payable* in Figure 14-2 if the total liabilities is used for the base instead of total assets:

$R = \dfrac{P}{B}$ ~~$= \dfrac{684}{3,001} = 0.227924,\ \text{or } 22.8\%$~~ $R = \dfrac{P}{B}$ $= \dfrac{684}{22,567} = 0.0303097,\ \text{or } 3.0\%$

WRONG   CORRECT

Comparing balance sheets from two years may reveal important trends in a business's operations. Such a **comparative balance sheet** can be seen in Figure 14-3. Note that the most recent date is on the *left*.

comparative balance sheet: a report form that is used to compare information on a balance sheet for two or more periods.

Sander's Woodworks
Comparative Balance Sheet
December 31, 19X8 and 19X9

			Percent of total assets	
	19X9	19X8	19X9	19X8
Assets				
Current assets:				
Cash	$ 2,184	$ 1,973	9.2	8.7
Accounts receivable	4,308	2,118	18.1	9.4
Merchandise inventory	17,317	18,476	72.7	81.9
Total current assets	$23,809	$22,567	100.0	100.0
Plant and equipment:				
Equipment				
Total plant and equipment				
Total Assets	$23,809	$22,567	100.0	100.0
Liabilities				
Current liabilities:				
Accounts payable	$ 1,647	$ 2,317	6.9	10.3
Wages payable	894	684	3.8	3.0
Total current liabilities	2,541	3,001	10.7	13.3
Long-term liabilities:				
Mortgage note payable				
Total long-term liabilities				
Total Liabilities	$ 2,541	$ 3,001	10.7	13.3
Owner's Equity				
J. Sanders, Capital	$21,268	$19,566	89.3	86.7
Total Liabilities and Owner's Equity	$23,809	$22,567	100.0	100.0

Figure 14-3   Vertical Analysis of a Comparative Balance Sheet

Horizontal Analysis of a Balance Sheet

horizontal analysis: an analysis of a comparative financial statement for two or more periods that compares entries on a horizontal line.

Another way to analyze information on a comparative balance sheet is to compare item by item in a **horizontal analysis.** While a vertical analysis figures the relationship of each item to total assets, a horizontal analysis compares the same item for two different years, finds the amount of increase or decrease in the item, and shows that change as a percent.

STEP BY STEP

Horizontal Analysis of a Comparative Balance Sheet

Step 1. Find the amount of increase or decrease for each horizontal line by subtracting the amount in the right column from the amount in the left column.

Step 2. Find the percent of increase or decrease by using $R = \dfrac{P}{B}$, where the amount of increase is the portion, the *earlier* year's item is the base, and the percent of increase or decrease is the rate.

Step 3. Round to the nearest tenth of a percent.

Prepare a horizontal analysis of the comparative balance sheet for Sander's Woodworks shown in Figure 14-4.

Cash: $2,184 − $1,973 = $211   (increase)
$211 ÷ $1,973 = 0.106944 = 10.7%   (increase)

Accounts receivable: $4,308 − $2,118 = $2,190   (increase)
$2,190 ÷ $2,118 = 1.033994 = 103.4%   (increase)

Inventory: $17,317 − $18,476 = −$1,159   (decrease)
−$1,159 ÷ $18,476 = −0.06273 = −6.3%   (decrease)

Total Assets: $23,809 − $22,567 = $1,242   (increase)
$1,242 ÷ $22,567 = 0.055036 = 5.5%   (increase)

If the most recent year is always entered first, a decrease is indicated in the calculator display with a minus sign.

17317 ⎡−⎤ 18476 ⎡=⎤ ⇒ −1159

To find percent of decrease, do not clear calculator.

⎡÷⎤ 18476 ⎡=⎤ ⇒ −0.06273

Calculator Solution

Sander's Woodworks
Comparative Balance Sheet
December 31, 19X8, and 19X9

	19X9	19X8	Increase or (Decrease) Amount*	Percent*
Assets				
Cash	$ 2,184	$ 1,973	$ 211	10.7
Accounts receivable	4,308	2,118	2,190	103.4
Inventory	17,317	18,476	(1,159)	(6.3)
Total Assets	$23,809	$22,567	$ 1,242	5.5
Liabilities				
Accounts payable	$ 1,647	$ 2,317	$ (670)	(28.9)
Salaries payable	894	684	210	30.7
Total Liabilities	$ 2,541	$ 3,001	$ (460)	(15.3)
Owner's Equity				
J. Sanders, Capital	$21,268	$19,566	$ 1,702	8.7
Total Liabilities and Owner's Equity	$23,809	$22,567	$ 1,242	5.5

*Numbers in parentheses are decreases.

Figure 14-4 Horizontal Analysis of a Comparative Balance Sheet

Accounts payable: $1,647 − $2,317 = −$670 (decrease)

−$670 ÷ $2,317 = −0.289167 = −28.9% (decrease)

Salaries payable: $894 − $684 = $210 (increase)

$210 ÷ $684 = 0.307018 = 30.7% (increase)

Total Liabilities: $2,541 − $3,001 = −$460 (decrease)

−$460 ÷ $3,001 = −0.153282 = −15.3% (decrease)

J. Sanders, Capital: $21,268 − $19,566 = $1,702 (increase)

$1,702 ÷ $19,566 = 0.086987 = 8.7% (increase)

Total Liabilities and Owner's Equity:

$23,809 − $22,567 = $1,242 (increase)

$1,242 ÷ $22,567 = 0.055036 = 5.5% (increase)

If the horizontal analysis has been made properly, the amount of change in the Total Assets line should equal the sum of the asset increases minus any asset decreases. The amount of change in the Total Liabilities line should equal the sum of the liabilities increases minus any liabilities decreases. The amount of change in the Total Liabilities and Owner's Equity line should equal the sum of the Total Liabilities and the Capital increases (or difference if one amount is a decrease). The Total Liabilities and Owner's Equity amount of change and percent of change should equal the respective Total Assets entries.

Self-Check 14.1

1. Complete the horizontal and vertical analyses on the comparative balance sheet for Maddy's Muffins. (Use parentheses to indicate decreases.)

Maddy's Muffins Comparative Balance Sheet December 31, 19X8 and 19X9						
			Increase or (Decrease)		Percent of Total Assets	
	19X9	19X8	Amount	Percent	19X9	19X8
Assets						
Current assets:						
Cash	$1,985	$1,762				
Accounts receivable	4,219	3,785				
Merchandise inventory	2,512	2,036				
Total Assets	$8,716	$7,583				
Liabilities						
Current liabilities:						
Accounts payable	$3,483	$3,631				
Wages payable	1,696	1,421				
Total Liabilities	$5,179	$5,052				
Owner's Equity						
Maddy Engman, Capital	$3,537	$2,531				
Total Liabilities and Owner's Equity	$8,716	$7,583				

14.2

Income Statements

LEARNING OBJECTIVES

1. Prepare an income statement.
2. Prepare a vertical analysis of an income statement.
3. Prepare a comparative income statement.

Another important financial statement, the **income statement,** shows the net income of a business *over a period of time.* (Remember, the balance sheet shows the financial condition of a business at a *given* time.)

    Among the many terms on an income statement, you need to know the following:

income statement: a statement that shows the net income (or loss) of a business over a period of time.

Total sales	Earnings from the sale of goods or the performance of services.
Sales returns or allowances	Refunds or adjustments for unsatisfactory merchandise or services.
Net sales	The difference between the total sales and the sales returns or allowances.
Cost of goods sold	Cost to the business for merchandise or goods sold.
Gross profit or Gross Margin	The difference between the net sales and the cost of goods sold.
Operating expenses	The overhead or cost incurred in operating the business. Examples of operating expenses are utilities, rent, insurance, permits, taxes, and employees' salaries.
Net income, or **net profit**	The difference between the gross profit (gross margin) and the operating expenses.

Preparing the Income Statement

    Calculating the cost of goods sold is an important part of preparing an income statement. You must determine how much was paid out for the goods that were sold during the period covered by the income statement. To find this cost, start with the cost of the beginning inventory (goods on hand at the beginning of the period), add purchases of goods made within the period, and subtract the cost of the ending inventory (goods on hand at the end of the period).

    Now that you know how to calculate cost of goods sold, you can go on to the three basic formulas that are used in preparing an income statement: *net sales, gross profit,* and *net income.* Everything else on the income statement is used to make up these figures, using the following formulas.

STEP BY STEP

Formulas Used in Preparing Income Statements

Net sales = total sales − sales returns and allowances
Cost of goods sold = beginning inventory + purchases
− ending inventory
Gross profit = net sales − cost of goods sold
Net income = gross profit − operating expenses

CORNER GROCERY INCOME STATEMENT For month ending June 30, 19X5	
Net sales	$25,000
Cost of goods sold	18,750
Gross profit	$ 6,250
Operating expenses	3,750
Net income	$ 2,500

EXAMPLE 2

Complete the portion of the income statement shown for the Corner Grocery by finding the gross profit and net income.

Gross profit = net sales − cost of goods sold
= $25,000 − $18,750 = $6,250

Net income = gross profit − operating expenses
= $6,250 − $3,750 = $2,500

STEP BY STEP

Preparing the Income Statement

Step 1. The first section of the income statement is concerned with net sales. Enter gross sales and *subtract* sales returns and allowances to get net sales.

Step 2. The next section of the income statement is concerned with cost of goods sold. Enter beginning inventory, *add* purchases, and *subtract* ending inventory to get cost of goods sold.

Step 3. The next section of the income statement is concerned with gross profit. *Subtract* cost of goods sold from net sales to get gross profit.

Step 4. The next section of the income statement is concerned with operating expenses. Enter all the expenses and *add* them to get total operating expenses.

Step 5. The final section of the income statement is concerned with net income. *Subtract* total expenses from gross profit to get net income.

Preparing a Vertical Analysis of an Income Statement

Much like a vertical analysis of a balance sheet, you use the percentage formula $R = \dfrac{P}{B}$, in which R is the *percent of net sales,* P is the item of the income statement under consideration, and B is *net sales.*

EXAMPLE 3

Figure 14-6 shows the vertical analysis of Wrappe's Gift Shop's income statement. Each entry is divided by the net sales, the quotient is converted to a percent, and the percent is rounded to the nearest tenth of a percent.

Figure 14-5   An Income
Statement

Wrappe's Gift Shop
Income Statement
For the year ending December 31, 19X2

Revenue:

Gross sales	$246,891
Sales returns and allowances	$ 7,835
Net sales	$239,056

Cost of goods sold:

Beginning inventory, January 1, 19X2	$ 8,247
Purchases	148,542
Ending inventory, December 31, 19X2	9,583
Cost of goods sold	$147,206
Gross Profit from Sales	$ 91,850

Operating expenses:

Salary	$ 18,500
Insurance	5,700
Utilities	1,900
Maintenance	280
Rent	6,000
Depreciation	1,500
Total operating expenses	$ 33,880
Net Income	$ 57,970

Figure 14-6   Vertical Analysis
of an Income Statement

Wrappe's Gift Shop
Income Statement
For the year ending December 31, 19X2

		Percent of Net Sales
Revenue:		
Gross sales	$246,891	103.3%
Sales returns and allowances	7,835	3.3
Net sales	239,056	100.0
Cost of goods sold:		
Beginning inventory, January 1, 19X2	$ 8,247	3.4
Purchases	$148,542	62.1
Ending inventory, December 31, 19X2	9,583	4.0
Cost of goods sold	147,206	61.6
Gross Profit from Sales	$ 91,850	38.4
Operating Expenses:		
Salary	$ 18,500	7.7
Insurance	5,700	2.4
Utilities	1,900	0.8
Maintenance	280	0.1
Rent	6,000	2.5
Depreciation	1,500	0.6
Total operating expenses	$ 33,880	14.2
Net Income	$ 57,970	24.2

Enter the net sales into memory.

$$\boxed{AC}\ 239056\ \boxed{M^+}$$

Divide each entry by net sales.

$$\boxed{CE/C}\ 246891\ \boxed{\div}\ \boxed{MRC}\ \boxed{\%}\ \Rightarrow\ 1.0327747$$

$$\boxed{CE/C}\ 7835\ \boxed{\div}\ \boxed{MRC}\ \boxed{\%}\ \Rightarrow\ 0.0327747$$

Continue by dividing each item by the net sales, which is stored in memory.

comparative income statement: a report form that is used to compare information on two or more income statements.

Preparing a Comparative Income Statement

The information from more than one income statement can be compiled as a **comparative income statement.** As with the comparative balance sheet, we put the most recent information in the first column. Both vertical and horizontal analyses of a comparative income statement can be made, as shown in Figures 14-7 and 14-8.

Davis Company Comparative Income Statement For the years ending June 30, 19X2 and 19X3				
	19X3	**% of Net Sales**	**19X2**	**% of Net Sales**
Net sales	$242,897	100.0	$239,528	100.0
Cost of goods sold	116,582	48.0	115,351	48.2
Gross profit	$126,315	52.0	$124,177	51.8
Operating expenses	38,725	15.9	37,982	15.9
Net income	$ 87,590	36.1	$ 86,195	36.0

Figure 14-7   Vertical Analysis of a Comparative Income Statement

Davis Company Comparative Income Statement For the years ending June 30, 19X2 and 19X3				
			Increase (Decrease)	
	19X3	**19X2**	**Amount**	**Percent**
Net sales	$242,897	$239,528	3,369	1.4
Cost of goods sold	116,582	115,351	1,231	1.1
Gross profit	$126,315	$124,177	2,138	1.7
Operating expenses	38,725	37,982	743	2.0
Net income	$ 87,590	$ 86,195	1,395	1.6

Figure 14-8   Horizontal Analysis of a Comparative Income Statement

   Self-Check 14.2

2. Complete the horizontal analysis of the comparative income statement for Seoul Proprietorship Oriental Groceries. Express percents to the nearest tenth of a percent.

Seoul Proprietorship Oriental Groceries Income Statement For the years ending June 30, 19X8 and 19X9				
			Increase (Decrease)	
	19X9	19X8	Amount	Percent
Net sales	$97,384	$92,196		
Cost of goods sold	82,157	72,894		
Gross profit				
Operating expenses	$ 4,783	$ 3,951		
Net income	$	$		

Financial Statement Ratios

LEARNING OBJECTIVES

1. Calculate balance sheet ratios.
2. Calculate income statement ratios.
3. Calculate other financial ratios.

Financial statements organize and summarize information about the financial condition of a business. **Financial ratios** take the information from the financial statements and show how the parts of a business relate to one another. They give a number of ways to evaluate the condition of the business.

financial ratio: shows how the parts of a business relate to one another.

Balance Sheet Ratios

CURRENT RATIO. It is important to know whether a business has enough assets to cover its liabilities. The **working capital** of a business is its current assets minus current liabilities. But is does not tell much about the financial condition of the business, and it is difficult to compare the working capital of two businesses. Look at the information about Aaron's Air Conditioning and Zelda's Zeppelins:

working capital: current assets minus current liabilities.

	Aaron's Air Conditioning	Zelda's Zeppelins
Current assets	$12,000	$615,000
Current liabilities	− 6,000	− 609,000
Working capital	$ 6,000	$ 6,000

Working capital = current assets − current liabilities

Both companies have the same working capital, but Zelda's *owes* almost as much as it *owns*. To compare these companies, we need to use ratios. A commonly used ratio in business is the **current ratio** (also called the **working capital ratio**), which tells how the current assets relate to the current liabilities.

current ratio (working capital ratio): a ratio which tells how the current assets relate to the current liabilities.

Current Ratio

$$\text{Current ratio} = \frac{\text{current assets}}{\text{current liabilities}}$$

Many lending companies consider a current ratio of 2 to 1 (2 : 1) to be the minimum acceptable current ratio for approving a loan to a business.

EXAMPLE 4

Find the current ratios for Aaron's and Zelda's. Round to the nearest hundredth if necessary.

$$\text{Current ratio} = \frac{\text{current assets}}{\text{current liabilities}}$$

Aaron's   *Zelda's*

$$\frac{\$12,000}{\$6,000} = 2 \qquad \frac{\$615,000}{\$609,000} = 1.009852 = 1.01$$

Current ratio for Aaron's is 2, or 2 to 1 (2 : 1).	Current ratio for Zelda's is 1.01, or 1.01 to 1 (1.01 : 1).	Business ratios are normally expressed in decimal form. The decimal number is a numerator that is compared to a denominator of 1.

Another ratio used to determine the financial condition of a business is the **acid-test ratio,** sometimes called the **quick ratio.** Instead of using the current assets of a business, the acid-test ratio uses only the **quick current assets,** those assets that can be readily exchanged for cash, **marketable securities,** accounts receivable, and notes receivable. Merchandise inventory is a current asset but it is not included because a loss would probably occur if a business were to make a quick sale of all merchandise.

acid-test ratio (quick ratio): a ratio used to determine the financial condition of a business; the ratio of quick current assets to current liabilities.

quick current assets: cash assets or assets that can be readily exchanged for cash, such as marketable securities and receivables.

marketable securities: current assets such as government bonds, which can be quickly turned into cash without loss.

Acid-Test Ratio (Quick Ratio)

$$\text{Acid-test ratio} = \frac{\text{quick current assets}}{\text{current liabilities}}$$

EXAMPLE 5

Find the acid-test ratio if the balance sheet shows the following amounts:

Cash = $17,342

Marketable securities = $0

Receivables = $10,345

Current liabilities = $26,345

$$\text{Acid-test ratio} = \frac{\$17,342 + \$10,345}{\$26,345} = \frac{\$27,687}{\$26,345} = 1.05 \quad \text{(nearest hundredth)}$$

The acid-test ratio is 1.05 : 1.

If the acid-test ratio is $1:1$, the business is in a satisfactory financial condition and has the ability to meet its obligations. If the ratio is significantly *less* than $1:1$ (such as $0.85:1$), the business is in poor financial condition; and if the ratio is significantly *more* than $1:1$ (such as $1.15:1$), the business is in good financial condition.

Income Statement Ratios

On a comparative income statement, horizontal analyses indicate the rate of change for the period, while vertical analyses indicate what proportion or percent each entry is of the net sales at the beginning and at the end of the period. However, the mere statement of percentages is not enough. The analyst must use these percentages as *indicators,* interpret these indicators, and determine whether the various changes are favorable or unfavorable by using *income statement ratios*.

Several useful ratios can be determined from an income statement. These ratios make comparisons possible between the major elements of the statement and net sales. These ratios are usually expressed in percents and usually (but not necessarily) cover 1 year.

Remember, the first quantity in a ratio appears in the numerator (to the left of the colon), and the second quantity appears in the denominator (to the right of the colon). Therefore, in each of the **ratios to net sales,** the denominator is the net sales. Using $R = \dfrac{P}{B}$, the rate (R) is the ratio, the portion (P) is the item considered, and the base (B) is net sales.

ratios to net sales: ratios determined from an income statement that make comparisons possible between the major elements of the statement and new sales; these ratios (usually expressed in percents) usually cover a 1-year period.

OPERATING RATIO. The **operating ratio** indicates the amount of sales dollars that are used to pay for the cost of goods and administrative expenses. A ratio of less than $1:1$ is desirable. The lower the operating ratio, the more income there is to meet financial obligations.

operating ratio: the amount of sales dollars that are used to pay for the cost of goods and administrative expenses.

STEP BY STEP

Operating Ratio

$$\text{Operating ratio} = \frac{\text{cost of goods sold } + \text{ operating expenses}}{\text{net sales}}$$

GROSS PROFIT MARGIN RATIO. The **gross profit margin ratio** shows the average spread between cost of goods sold and the selling price. The desirable gross profit margin ratio varies with the type of business. For example, a jewelry store might expect to have a ratio of 0.6 to 1 because there is a high rate of markup in jewelry. An auto parts store may, however, have a ratio of 0.25 to 1.

gross profit margin ratio: shows the average spread between cost of goods sold and the selling price.

STEP BY STEP

Gross Profit Margin Ratio

$$\text{Gross profit margin ratio} = \frac{\text{net sales } - \text{ cost of goods sold}}{\text{net sales}}$$

To illustrate the calculation of these ratios, we will use a summary income statement for Arsella Vincent's Gift Shop.

Vincent's Gift Shop Income Statement For the year ending December 31, 19X2	
Net sales	$173,157
Cost of goods sold	
Beginning inventory	$ 37,376
Purchases	123,574
Goods available for sale	$160,950
Less: Ending inventory	34,579
Cost of goods sold	126,371
Gross profit	$ 46,786
Operating expenses	17,643
Net income	$ 29,143

EXAMPLE 6

Find the two ratios to net sales for Vincent's Gift Shop. Express each answer as a percent rounded to the nearest tenth of a percent.

$$\text{Operating ratio} = \frac{\text{cost of goods sold} + \text{operating expenses}}{\text{net sales}}$$

$$= \frac{\$126,371 + \$17,643}{\$173,157}$$

$$= 0.831696 \text{ or } 83.2\%$$

$$\text{Gross profit margin ratio} = \frac{\text{net sales} - \text{cost of goods sold}}{\text{net sales}}$$

$$= \frac{\$173,157 - \$126,371}{\$173,157}$$

$$= 0.270194 \text{ or } 27.0\%$$

Other Financial Ratios

Many other comparisons of data are found on the balance sheet, income statement, or other financial documents that are useful in analyzing various aspects of the business. For instance, the *asset turnover ratio* compares the net sales to the total assets. This comparison shows the average return in sales for each $1 invested in assets. The *total debt to total assets ratio* compares the total liabilities to the total assets. This comparison shows total indebtedness of the company for each $1 in assets.

The calculations for determining these ratios are the same as for determining any ratio. The amount in the numerator is divided by the amount in the denominator to give a decimal equivalent. This decimal equivalent can be interpreted as a comparison of the decimal equivalent to 1 or it can be interpreted as a percent.

 Self-Check 14.3

3. Find the current ratios for Aaron's and Zelda's. Round to the nearest hundredth if necessary.

	Aaron's	Zelda's
Current assets	$28,000	$840,000
Current liabilities	− 7,000	− 819,000
Working capital	$21,000	$ 21,000

4. Find the acid-test ratio if the balance sheet shows the following amounts:
Cash = $32,981 Receivables = $12,045
Marketable securites = $0 Current liabilities = $22,178

5. Find the operating ratio for Sol's Dry Goods if the income statement for the month shows net sales, $15,500; cost of goods sold, $7,500; gross profit, $8,000; operating expenses, $3,500; net income, $4,500. Express answer to the nearest tenth of a percent.

6. Find the gross profit margin ratio for Sol's Dry Goods in Problem 5 to the nearest tenth of a percent.

Summary

Topic	Page	What to Remember	Examples
The basic accounting equation	426	Assets = liabilities + owner's equity	Assets = $50,000; liabilities = $10,000 $50,000 = $10,000 + owner's equity $40,000 = owner's equity
Preparing a balance sheet	426	Identify the company, the statement, and the date. List and total the assets. List and subtotal the liabilities. List the owner's equity and add it to the liabilities subtotal. Total assets equal total liabilities plus owner's equity.	*Assets* — Cash $8,000; Accounts receivable 4,860; Inventory 19,823; Equipment 8,925; Total Assets $41,608. *Liabilities* — Accounts payable $11,281; Wages payable 11,185; Total liabilities $22,466; Owners Equity Equity 19,142; Total Liabilities and Owner's Equity $41,608.

Vertical analysis of a balance sheet — 427 — Find the total value of all assets. Divide the value of each item on the balance sheet by the total value of all assets, and change each resulting decimal number to a percent, rounded to the nearest tenth of a percent.

	Assets	Percent of Total Assets	
Cash	$18,211	12.7%	$18,211 ÷ $142,942
Accounts receivable	25,019	17.5%	$25,019 ÷ $142,942
Inventory	87,523	61.2%	$87,523 ÷ $142,942
Equipment	12,189	8.5%	$12,189 ÷ $142,942
Total Assets	$142,942	100.0%	$142,942 ÷ $142,942

Horizontal analysis of a comparative balance sheet — 430 — Find the *amount* of increase or decrease for each horizontal line and then find the *percent* of increase or decrease for each horizontal line.

$$\left(\begin{array}{c}\text{Percent increase or}\\\text{decrease}\end{array}\right) = \left(\dfrac{\begin{array}{c}\text{amount of increase}\\\text{or decrease}\end{array}}{\text{original amount}}\right) \times 100$$

Assets	19X9	19X8
Cash	$ 28,134	$ 25,021
Accounts receivable	7,896	6,821
Inventory	89,087	69,598
Total Assets	$125,117	$101,440

	Increase or Decrease	
	Amount	Percent
Cash	$ 3,113	12.4%
Accounts receivable	1,075	15.8%
Inventory	19,489	28.0%
Total Assets	$23,677	23.3%

Topic	Page	What to Remember	Examples
Net sales (on income statement)	433	Net sales = total sales − sales returns or allowances	Total sales = $85,700; sales returns = $4,892 Net sales = $85,700 − $4,892 　　　　= $80,808
Gross profit (on income statement)	433	Gross profit = net sales − cost of goods sold	Net sales = $48,831; cost of goods sold = $29,512 Gross profit = $48,831 − $29,512 　　　　= $19,319
Net income (on income statement)	433	Net income (net profit) = gross profit − operating expenses	Gross profit = $21,817; Operating expenses = $3,846 Net income = $21,817 − $3,846 　　　　= $17,971
Finding cost of goods sold	433	Goods available for sale = beginning inventory + purchases made Cost of goods sold = goods available for sale − ending inventory	Beginning inventory = $16,592; purchases = $146,983; ending inventory = $18,096. Goods available for sale = $16,592 + $146,983 　　　　= $163,575 Cost of goods sold = $163,575 − $18,096 　　　　= $145,479

Vertical analysis of an income statement — 434

Divide each amount on the income statement by the net sales amount. Express the quotient as a percent, rounded to the nearest tenth of a percent.

		Percent of Net Sales
Net sales	$38,000	100.0%
Cost of goods sold	25,000	65.8%
Gross profit	13,000	34.2%
Operating expenses	7,000	18.4%
Net income	$ 6,000	15.8%

Use the following information to calculate the indicated ratio: total assets, $108,000; current assets, $40,000; total liabilities, $57,000; current liabilities, $28,000; cash, $15,892; marketable securities, $10,000; receivables, $7,486; cost of goods sold, $146,800; net sales, $179,500; gross profit, $32,700; operating expenses, $18,500; net income, $14,200.

Topic	Page	What to Remember	Examples
Current ratio	437	$\text{Current ratio} = \dfrac{\text{current assets}}{\text{current liabilities}}$	$\dfrac{\$40,000}{\$28,000} = 1.43 \text{ to } 1$
Acid-test ratio (quick ratio)	438	$\text{Acid-test ratio} = \dfrac{\text{quick current assets}}{\text{current liabilities}}$ Quick current assets are cash, marketable securities, and receivables.	$\dfrac{\$15,892 + \$10,000 + \$7,486}{\$28,000} = 1.19 \text{ to } 1$
Operating ratio	439	$\text{Operating ratio} = \dfrac{\text{cost of goods sold} + \text{operating expenses}}{\text{net sales}}$	$\dfrac{\$146,800 + \$18,500}{\$179,500} = 0.921 \text{ or } 92.1\%$
Gross profit margin ratio	439	$\text{Gross profit margin ratio} = \dfrac{\text{net sales} - \text{cost of goods sold}}{\text{net sales}}$	$\dfrac{\$179,500 - \$146,800}{\$179,500} = 0.182 \text{ or } 18.2\%$
Asset turnover ratio	440	$\text{Asset turnover ratio} = \dfrac{\text{net sales}}{\text{total assets}}$	$\dfrac{\$179,500}{\$108,000} = 1.66$
Total debt to total assets ratio	440	$\text{Total debt to total assets ratio} = \dfrac{\text{total liabilities}}{\text{total assets}}$	$\dfrac{\$57,000}{\$108,000} = 0.53$

Self-Check Solutions

1.

Maddy's Muffins
Comparative Balance Sheet
December 31, 19X8 and 19X9

	19X9	19X8	Increase or (Decrease) Amount	Increase or (Decrease) Percent	Percent of Total Assets 19X9	Percent of Total Assets 19X8
Assets						
Current assets:						
Cash	$1,985	$1,762	$ 223	12.7	22.8	23.2
Accounts receivable	4,219	3,785	434	11.5	48.4	49.9
Merchandise inventory	2,512	2,036	476	23.4	28.8	26.8
Total Assets	8,716	7,583	1,133	14.9	100.0	99.9
Liabilities						
Current liabilities:						
Accounts payable	3,483	3,631	(148)	(4.1)	40.0	47.9
Wages payable	1,696	1,421	275	19.4	19.5	18.7
Total Liabilities	5,179	5,052	127	2.5	59.5	66.6
Owner's Equity						
Maddy Engman, Capital	3,537	2,531	1,006	39.7	40.6	33.4
Total Liabilities and Owner's Equity	$8,716	$7,583	$1,133	14.9	100.0	100.0

2.

Seoul Proprietorship Oriental Groceries
Income Statement
For the years ending June 30, 19X8 and 19X9

	19X9	19X8	Increase (Decrease) Amount	Increase (Decrease) Percent
Net sales	$97,384	$92,196	$ 5,188	5.6
Cost of goods sold	82,157	72,894	9,263	12.7
Gross profits	15,227	19,302	(4,075)	(21.1)
Operating expenses	4,783	3,951	832	21.1
Net income	$10,444	$15,351	(4,907)	(32.0)

3. Aaron's $= \dfrac{\text{current assets}}{\text{current liabilities}} = \dfrac{\$28,000}{\$7,000} = 4 \text{ or } 4:1.$

Zelda's $= \dfrac{\$840,000}{\$819,000} = 1.03 \text{ or } 1.03:1$

4. Acid-test ratio $= \dfrac{\text{quick current assets}}{\text{current liabilities}} = \dfrac{\$32,981 + \$12,045}{\$22,178} = \dfrac{\$45,026}{\$22,178}$

$= 2.03 \text{ or } 2.03 \text{ to } 1$

5. Operating ratio $= \dfrac{\text{cost of goods sold} + \text{operating expenses}}{\text{net sales}}$

$$= \frac{\$7{,}500 + \$3{,}500}{\$15{,}500} = \frac{\$11{,}000}{\$15{,}500} = 0.7096774 \text{ or } 71.0\%$$

6. Gross profit margin $= \dfrac{\text{net sales} - \text{cost of goods sold}}{\text{net sales}}$

$$= \frac{\$15{,}500 - \$7{,}500}{\$15{,}500} = \frac{\$8{,}000}{\$15{,}500}$$

$$= 0.5161290 \text{ or } 51.6\%$$

End of Chapter Problems

1. Complete the following balance sheet for Fawcett's Plumbing Supplies.

Fawcett's Plumbing Supplies
Balance Sheet
March 31, 19X5

Assets	
Current assets:	
Cash	$ 1,724.00
Office supplies	173.00
Accounts receivable	9,374.00
Total current assets	
Plant and equipment:	
Equipment	$12,187.00
Total plant and equipment	12,187.00
Total Assets	
Liabilities	
Current liabilities:	
Accounts payable	$2,174.00
Wages payable	674.00
Property taxes payable	250.00
Total current liabilities	
Total Liabilities	
Owner's Equity	
D. W. Fawett, Capital	$20,360.00
Total Liabilities and Owner's Equity	

2. Complete the following balance sheet for Rooter Company.

Rooter Company
Balance Sheet
June 30, 19X5

Assets	
Current assets:	
Cash	$ 2,350.00
Supplies	175.00
Accounts receivable	8,956.00
Total current assets	
Plant and equipment:	
Equipment	$11,375.00
Total plant and equipment	11,375.00
Total assets	
Liabilities	
Current liabilities:	
Accounts payable	$ 1,940.00
Wages payable	855.00
Rent payable	775.00
Total current liabilities	
Total liabilities	
Owner's Equity	
Wilson Rooter, Capital	$19,286.00
Total Liabilities and Owner's Equity	

3. Complete the vertical analysis and horizontal analysis of the comparative balance sheet for Seymour's Videos, Inc. Express percents to the nearest tenth of a percent.

Seymour's Videos, Inc.
Comparative Balance Sheet
December 31, 19X5 and 19X6

	19X6	19X5	Increase or (Decrease) Amount	Increase or (Decrease) Percent	Percent of total assets 19X6	Percent of total assets 19X5
Assets						
Current assets:						
Cash	$ 2,374	$ 2,184				
Accounts receivable	5,374	4,286				
Merchandise inventory	15,589	16,107				
Total Assets						
Liabilities						
Current liabilities:						
Accounts payable	$ 7,384	$ 6,118				
Wages payable	1,024	964				
Total Liabilities						
Owner's Equity						
James Seymour, Capital	$14,929	$15,495				
Total Liabilities and Owner's Equity						

4. Complete the vertical analysis and the horizontal analysis of the comparative balance sheet for Miller's Model Ships. Express percents to the nearest tenth of a percent.

Miller's Model Ships
Comparative Balance Sheet
December 31, 19X8 and 19X9

	19X9	19X8	Increase or (Decrease) Amount	Increase or (Decrease) Percent	Percent of total assets 19X9	Percent of total assets 19X8
Assets						
Current assets:						
Cash	$ 2,176	$ 1,948				
Accounts receivable	2,789	1,742				
Merchandise inventory	4,985	5,450				
Total Assets						
Liabilities						
Current liabilities:						
Accounts payable	$ 901	$ 872				
Wages payable	1,342	$ 1,224				
Insurance payable	690	680				
Total Liabilities						
Owner's Equity						
Kathy Miller, Capital	$ 7,017	$ 6,364				
Total Liabilities and Owner's Equity						

5. Complete the following income statement and vertical analysis.

Marten's Family Store Income Statement For year ending December 31, 19X4		
		Percent of Net Sales
Revenue:		
Gross Sales	$238,923	
Sales returns and allowances	13,815	
Net sales		
Cost of goods sold:		
Beginning inventory, January 1, 19X0	$ 25,814	
Purchases	109,838	
Ending inventory, December 31, 19X0	23,423	
Cost of goods sold		
Gross Profit from Sales		
Operating expenses:		
Salary	$ 42,523	
Rent	8,640	
Utilities	1,484	
Insurance	2,842	
Fees	860	
Depreciation	1,920	
Miscellaneous	3,420	
Total operating expenses	$ 61,689	
Net Income		

6. Complete the following income statement and vertical analysis. Express percents to the nearest tenth of a percent.

Serpas' Gifts Income Statement For year ending December 31, 19X3		
		Percent of Net Sales
Revenue:		
Gross sales	$148,645	
Sales returns and allowances	8,892	
Net sales		
Cost of goods sold:		
Beginning inventory, January 1, 19X3	$ 12,100	
Purchases	47,800	
Ending inventory, December 31, 19X3	11,950	
Cost of goods sold		
Gross Profit from Sales		
Operating expenses:		
Salary	$ 25,500	
Rent	4,500	
Utilities	1,445	
Insurance	2,100	
Fees	225	
Depreciation	1,240	
Miscellaneous	750	
Total operating expenses		
Net Income		

7. Complete the following horizontal analysis of a comparative income statement.

Alonzo's Auto Parts
Comparative Income Statement
For years ending June 30, 19X8 and 19X9

	19X9	19X8	Increase (Decrease) Amount	Percent
Revenue:				
Gross sales	$291,707	$275,873		
Sales returns and allowances	5,895	6,821		
Net sales				
Cost of goods sold:				
Beginning inventory, July 1	$ 35,892	$ 32,587		
Purchases	157,213	146,999		
Ending inventory, June 30	32,516	30,013		
Cost of goods sold				
Gross Profit from Sales				
Operating expenses:				
Salary	$ 42,000	$ 40,000		
Insurance	3,800	3,800		
Utilities	1,986	2,097		
Rent	3,600	3,300		
Depreciation	4,000	4,500		
Total operating expenses				
Net Income				

8. Complete the following horizontal analysis of a comparative income statement. Express percents to the nearest tenth of a percent.

Designer Crafts
Comparative Income Statement
For years ending December 31,19X3 and 19X4

	19X4	19X3	Increase (Decrease) Amount	Percent
Revenue:				
Gross sales	$239,873	$236,941		
Sales returns and allowances	12,815	13,895		
Net sales				
Cost of goods sold:				
Beginning inventory, January 1	$ 27,814	$ 25,887		
Purchases	123,213	112,604		
Ending inventory, December 31	24,482	23,838		
Cost of goods sold	$126,545	$114,653		
Gross Profit from Sales				
Operating expenses:				
Salary	$ 44,772	$ 42,640		
Insurance	3,006	2,863		
Utilities	1,597	1,521		
Rent	3,600	3,600		
Depreciation	4,100	3,400		
Total operating expenses				
Net Income				

Find the current ratio for each of the following businesses. Round answers to the nearest hundredth.

Current assets	Current liabilities
9. $1,231,704	$784,184
10. $32,194	$38,714
11. $174,316	$125,342
12. $724,987	$334,169

Find the acid-test ratio for each of these businesses. Express the answer to the nearest hundredth.

13. Stevens Gift Shop: cash, $2,345; accounts receivable, $5,450; government securities, $4,500; accounts payable, $6,748; notes payable, $7,457.

14. Central Office Supply: cash, $5,745; accounts receivable, $12,496; accounts payable, $10,475.

15. Find the acid-test ratio for Edna Nunez and Company if the balance sheet shows cash, $23,500; marketable securities, $0; receivables, $12,300; current liabilities, $,27,800.

16. Find the acid-test ratio for Jefferson's Photo if the balance sheet shows cash, $6,700; marketable securities, $0; receivables, $12,756; current liabilities, $18,345.

17. Find the operating ratio and gross profit margin ratio for the following income statement:

```
      CORNER GROCERY
      INCOME STATEMENT
  For month ending June 30, 19X5

  Net sales               $25,000
  Cost of goods sold       18,750
  Gross profit            $ 6,250
  Operating expenses        3,750
  Net income              $ 2,500
```

18. Find the operating ratio for M. Ng's Grocery if the income statement for the month shows net sales, $23,500; cost of goods sold, $16,435; gross profit, $7,065; operating expenses, $3,100; net income, $3,965. Express answer to the nearest tenth of a percent.

19. Find the operating ratio for A to Z Sales if the income statement for the month shows net sales, $173,200; cost of goods sold, $138,400; gross profit, $34,800; operating expenses, $16,300; net income, $18,500. Express answer to the nearest tenth of a percent.

20. Find the gross profit margin ratio for the business in Problem 18 to the nearest tenth of a percent.

21. Find the gross profit margin ratio for the business in Problem 19 to the nearest tenth of a percent.

Challenge Problem

Is There a Profit in the Cards?

Cedar-Crest Greeting Card Company ended the year 1991 with assets that totaled $120,000. The assets for 1992 increased to $580,000. What was the rate of growth for Cedar-Crest?

Trial Test

1. Complete the horizontal analysis of the following comparative balance sheet. Express percents to the nearest tenth of a percent.

O'Toole's Hardware Store
Comparative Balance Sheet
December 31, 19X6 and 19X7

| | | | Increase or (Decrease) | |
	19X7	19X6	Amount	Percent
Assets				
Current assets:				
Cash	$ 7,318	$ 5,283		
Accounts receivable	3,147	3,008		
Merchandise inventory	63,594	60,187		
Total current assets	74,059	68,478		
Plant and equipment:				
Building	36,561	37,531		
Equipment	8,256	4,386		
Total plant and equipment				
Total Assets				
Liabilities				
Current liabilities:				
Accounts payable	5,174	4,563		
Wages payable	780	624		
Total current liabilities				
Long-term liabilities:				
Mortgage note payable	34,917	36,510		
Total long-term liabilities				
Total Liabilities				
Owner's Equity				
James O'Toole, Capital	$ 78,005	$ 68,698		
Total Liabilities and Owner's Equity				

2. Find the current ratio to the nearest hundredth for 19X7 on O'Toole's Hardware Store.

3. Find the acid-test ratio to the nearest hundredth for 19X7 on O'Toole's Hardware Store.

4. Find the current ratio to the nearest hundredth for 19X6 on O'Toole's Hardware Store.

5. Find the acid-test ratio to the nearest hundredth for 19X6 on O'Toole's Hardware Store.

6. Complete the horizontal analysis of the following comparative income statement.

Mile Wide Woolens, Inc. Comparative Income Statement For years ending December 31, 19X6 and 19X7				
			Increase (Decrease)	
	19X7	**19X6**	**Amount**	**Percent**
Revenue:				
Gross sales	$219,827	$205,852		
Sales returns and allowances	8,512	7,983		
Net sales	$211,315			
Cost of goods sold:				
Beginning inventory, January 1	$42,816	$40,512		
Purchases	97,523	94,812		
Ending inventory, December 31	43,182	42,521		
Cost of goods sold	$97,157			
Gross Profit from Sales	$114,158			
Operating expenses:				
Salary	$28,940	$27,000		
Insurance	800	750		
Utilities	1,700	1,580		
Rent	3,600	3,000		
Depreciation	2,000	2,400		
Total operating expenses	$37,040			
Net Income	$ 77,118			

7. Find the operating ratio for Mile Wide for 19X6 and 19X7.

8. Find the gross profit margin ratio for Mile Wide for 19X7.

A look at statistics that shape your finances

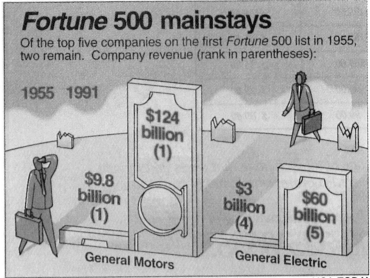

Fortune 500 mainstays

Of the top five companies on the first *Fortune* 500 list in 1955, two remain. Company revenue (rank in parentheses):

1955 1991

$124 billion (1)

$9.8 billion (1)

$3 billion (4)

$60 billion (5)

General Motors

General Electric

Source: *Fortune*

By Elys A. McLean, USA TODAY

QUESTIONS

1. Use the chart to calculate the percent of increase in income from 1955 to 1991 for General Motors.

2. Calculate the percent of increase in income for General Electric from 1955 to 1991.

3. General Motors maintained the same ranking among Fortune 500 companies while General Electric slipped from 4th to 5th. From the information found in problems 1 and 2, is company revenue a major factor in ranking Fortune 500 companies?

15

Insurance

insurance: a form of protection against unexpected financial loss.

Insurance is a form of protection against unexpected financial loss. Businesses and individuals need insurance to help bear the burden of a large financial loss. Insurance helps distribute the burden of financial loss among those who share the same type of risk. Many types of insurance are available, such as fire, life, homeowner's, health, accident, automobile, and others. Many insurance companies offer a *comprehensive policy* that protects the insured against several risks. It is common, for example, to purchase fire, flood, and earthquake insurance in one comprehensive policy. The combined rate for a comprehensive policy is usually lower than if each type of protection were purchased in a separate policy.

Before we can discuss specific types of insurance, though, you need to understand some important terms used in the insurance field:

Insured (policyholder)   The individual, organization, or business that carries the insurance or financial protection against loss.

Insurer (underwriter)   The insurance company or carrier that assures payment for a specific loss according to contract provisions.

Policy   The contract between the insurer and the insured.

Premium   The amount paid by the insured for the protection provided by the policy.

Face value   The amount of insurance provided by the policy.

| Beneficiary | The person to whom the proceeds of the policy are payable. |

15.1

Fire Insurance

LEARNING OBJECTIVES

1. Calculate fire insurance rates.
2. Calculate compensation with a coinsurance clause.

Fire insurance provides protection against fire losses or losses that may result directly from attempts to extinguish a fire, such as damage caused by water and chemical extinguishers and damage to property by firefighters.

fire insurance: insurance that covers fire losses and losses that occur in trying to extinguish a fire, such as from water, chemical extinguishers, and firefighters.

Calculating Fire Insurance Rates

Rates for fire insurance vary according to several factors, such as type of structure, location, nearness to the fire department, rating given by the fire department, water supply, and fire hazards. Most states have developed a system for classifying rates according to these factors. For example, a Class A building might be made of brick instead of wood. Or the contents of the building might be classed as resistant to fire damage, such as bags of cement, rather than fabric, which would be much more flammable (easily burned). Table 15-1 shows a sample classfication system. The area ratings in the left column are based on how close the buildings area to a fire station and how easy access is to the building and its contents.

As you can see from Table 15-1, insurance rates are expressed as an annual amount per $100 of coverage. To find the annual premium, divide the amount of coverage by $100 and multiply by the rate in the table. Do this for both building and contents.

STEP BY STEP

Calculating the Annual Insurance Premium Amount

Step 1. Find the correct rate in the table for the building being insured, and use the following formula:

$$\text{Annual premium} = \frac{\text{amount of coverage}}{\$100} \times \text{rate}$$

Step 2. Find the correct rate in the table for contents of the building, and use same formula as in step 1.

Table 15-1 Annual Fire Insurance Rates per $100

	Building Classification					
Area Rating	Class A		Class B		Class C	
	Building	Contents	Building	Contents	Building	Contents
1	$0.25	$0.32	$0.37	$0.48	$0.46	$0.51
2	$0.31	$0.45	$0.47	$0.57	$0.55	$0.76
3	$0.38	$0.48	$0.57	$0.63	$0.63	$0.80

EXAMPLE 1

The building owned and occupied by O'Toole's Hardware is insured for $85,000. Its contents are insured for $50,000. If it is a Class B building located in Area 2, find the annual premium for building and contents.

Annual premium for building

$$= \frac{\text{amount of coverage}}{\$100} \times \text{rate}$$

$$= \frac{\$85,000}{\$100} \times \$0.47 = \$399.50$$

Look up the amount of premium for a building that is classified as Class B in Area 2. The rate is $0.47. Multiply the rate times $85,000 divided by $100. The answer is $399.50.

Annual premium for contents

$$= \frac{\text{amount of coverage}}{\$100} \times \text{rate}$$

$$= \frac{\$50,000}{\$100} \times \$0.57 = \$285$$

Look up the amount of premium for contents classified as Class B in Area 2. The rate is $0.57. Multiply $0.57 times $50,000 divided by $100. The answer is $285.

The annual premium for the building is $399.50 and the premium for its contents is $285.

Coinsurance

coinsurance clause: clause added to many fire insurance policies; says that insured gets full protection up to the face value of the policy from the company only if the property is insured for 80% of its value.

Because a fire rarely destroys a whole building or all its contents, many businesses take out policies that cover only a portion of the value of the building or its contents. They thus save money on premiums by covering only 40% of their property's value, for example. To encourage businesses to take out full insurance, insurance companies offer plans that include a **coinsurance clause.** Such a clause means that the insured gets full protection (or compensation *up to* the value of the policy) from the insurance company only if the property is insured for 80% of its replacement value. If the policy covers only 40% of the value, then the insurance company pays only a portion of the loss.

The following box shows how to figure how much the insurance company will pay if your policy has a coinsurance clause in it and you do *not* have full coverage.

STEP BY STEP

Calculating Compensation with a Coinsurance Clause

Step 1. Determine how much insurance the coinsurance clause requires you to carry by multiplying 0.8 times the replacement value of your property.

Step 2. Use this formula to figure compensation:

Compensation = amount of loss up to face value of insurance

$$\times \frac{\text{amount of insurance policy}}{80\% \text{ of replacement value of property}}$$

EXAMPLE 2

Budget Construction owns a building valued at $200,000. It has a fire insurance policy with an 80% coinsurance clause, which has a face value of

$130,000. There is a fire, and the building damage is figured to be $50,000. Find what the insurance company will pay as compensation.

To find out if Budget carries as much insurance as its coinsurance clause requires, multiply $0.8 \times \$200,000 = \$160,000$. Budget has a policy worth only $130,000, so it does not get full compensation.

Use the formula to find the compensation:

$$\text{Compensation} = \$50,000 \times \frac{\$130,000}{\$160,000} = \$40,625$$

Budget receives $40,625 compensation for its loss of $50,000.

If Budget had carried a policy for 80% of the replacement value of its property, it would have gotten $50,000 \times \dfrac{\$160,000}{\$160,000} = \$50,000$ compensation for the loss.

TIPS & TRAPS

When calculating the amount of compensation an insurance company will pay, if the policy has a coinsurance clause, the compensation for the amount of loss can be *no more than the face value of the policy*, regardless of the actual dollar value of the loss.

McLean's Machine Shop is insured for 80% of the replacement value. The replacement value of the shop is $105,000. A fire causes $90,000 worth of damage to the property. How much compensation will McLean's receive from the insurance company?

$$0.8 \times \$105,000 = \$84,000 \text{ face value of policy}$$

$$\$90,000 \times \frac{\$84,000}{\$84,000} = \$90,000 \qquad \$84,000 \times \frac{\$84,000}{\$84,000} = \$84,000$$

WRONG   CORRECT

Compensation cannot exceed face value of policy.

Self-Check 15.1

1. Find the annual fire insurance premium on a Class A building located in Area 3 if the building is insured for $120,000 and its contents are insured for $75,000.

2. **a.** A Class C building and its contents are located in Area 1 and are insured for $150,000 and $68,000, respectively. Find the total annual insurance premium.
   b. If a 2% charge is added to the annual premium when payments are made semiannually, how much would semiannual payments be?

3. **a.** The market value of a building is $255,000. It has been insured for $204,000 in a fire insurance policy with an 80% coinsurance clause. What part of a loss due to fire will the insurance company pay?
   b. If a fire causes damages of $75,000, what is the amount of compensation?

4. A building valued at $295,000 is insured in a policy that contains an 80% coinsurance clause. The face value of the policy is $100,000. If the building is a total loss, what is the amount of compensation?

15.2 Motor Vehicle Insurance

motor vehicle insurance: includes liability, comprehensive, and collision insurance for the owners of motor vehicles.

liability insurance: protects the owner of a vehicle if an accident causes personal injury or property damage and is the fault of the insured or the insured's designated driver.

comprehensive insurance: covers the insured's vehicle for damage caused by fire, theft, vandalism, and other risks that do not involve another vehicle.

collision insurance: covers the insured's vehicle for damage caused by an accident that is the insured's fault.

no-fault insurance: program in a number of states that allows each person involved in an accident to submit a claim for damages to his or her own insurance company if the amount is under a certain stated maximum.

LEARNING OBJECTIVE

1. Determine the cost of automobile insurance.

Motor vehicle insurance is a major expense item for individuals and businesses because of the high risk of personal injury or death and damage to property. Insurance for motor vehicles may be purchased to protect the individual or business from several risks. These include liability for personal injury and property damage; damage or loss to the insured vehicle and its occupants caused by a collision; and damage or loss to the insured vehicle caused by theft, fire, flooding, and other incidents that may not be related to a collision. These types of insurance generally fall into three types: liability, comprehensive, and collision.

Liability insurance protects the insured from losses incurred in a vehicle accident resulting in personal injury or property damage if the accident is the fault of the insured or a designated driver.

Comprehensive insurance protects the insured's vehicle for damage caused by fire, theft, vandalism, and other risks, such as falling debris, storm damage, or road hazards such as rocks.

Collision insurance protects the insured's vehicle for damage (both personal and property) caused by an automobile accident in which the driver of the insured vehicle is *also* at fault. This type of insurance is also used when the driver of the vehicle who is at fault does not have insurance coverage.

Some states have **no-fault insurance** programs. In these states, all parties involved in an accident submit a claim for personal and property damages to their own insurance company if the amount is under a certain stated maximum. However, a person can still sue for additional compensation if the damage is above the stated maximum.

Determining the Cost of Automobile Insurance

Factors that affect the cost of automobile insurance include the location of the vehicle (large city, small town, rural area); the total distance traveled per year and the distance traveled to work each day; the types of use (such as pleasure, traveling to and from work, strictly business); the driving record and training of the insured driver(s); the academic grades of drivers who are still in school; the age, sex, and marital status of the insured driver(s); the type and age of the vehicle; and the amount of coverage desired.

Table 15-2 shows a hypothetical annual rate schedule for liability insurance. Notice that there are several columns of information. The *territory* refers to the type of area where the car is kept and driven. The *driver class* refers to such personal information about the driver as age, sex, or marital status. The 20/40 under the Bodily Injury heading means the insurance company will pay up to $20,000 for bodily injury of one individual in an accident and no more than a total of $40,000 per accident for bodily injury, regardless of the number of individuals injured in the accident. The 5, 10, 25 under the Property Damage heading indicates the premium for coverage of $5,000, $10,000, or $25,000, for damage to the property of others, including other vehicles or property such as fences and buildings that are involved in the accident.

Table 15-2 Annual Automobile Liability Insurance Premiums

Territory	Driver Class	Bodily Injury			Property Damage		
		20/40	50/100	100/300	5	10	25
1	A	$140	$155	$170	$132	$140	$143
	B	155	168	185	145	155	159
	C	163	177	198	152	163	168
2	A	167	178	189	158	167	177
	B	176	187	199	168	179	189
	C	198	210	225	196	208	218

EXAMPLE 3

Use Table 15-2 to find the annual premium for an automobile liability insurance policy in which the insured lives in Territory 1, is Class A, and wishes to have 50/100/10 coverage.

The cost of 50/100 bodily injury coverage for Territory 1 and Class A is $155. The cost of $10,000 property damage insurance in this same category is $140. Therefore, the total cost of the insurance package is $155 + $140 = $295.

Insurance tables for collision insurance are set up much the same way as Table 15-2. However, these policies usually include a *deductible clause*, which means the insured must pay a certain specified amount (the **deductible amount**) before the insurance company will begin to pay.

deductible amount: the amount that must be paid by the insured before the insurance company will begin to pay.

Self-Check 15.2

5. Find the annual premium for an automobile liability insurance policy if the insured lives in Territory 2 and is classified as a Class C driver. The policy contains 20/40/5 coverage.

6. Compare the annual premium on a 50/100/10 policy for a Class C driver in Territory 1 to a policy with the same coverage in Territory 2.

7. What are the monthly payments on an automobile liability insurance policy for a Class B driver in Territory 1 with 50/100/25 coverage?

8. How much will an automobile liability insurance policy pay an injured person with medical expenses of $8,362 if the insured has a policy with 20/40/5 coverage? How much must the insured pay the injured party?

15.3

Life Insurance

LEARNING OBJECTIVES

1. Identity types of life insurance.
2. Calculate life insurance premiums.

life insurance: a type of insurance that makes a payment to the surviving beneficiaries of insured persons in the event of their death.

Life insurance provides financial assistance to the surviving dependents of the insured person in the event of the insured person's death. Although anyone may purchase life insurance, companies often ensure the lives of their

term insurance: a type of life insurance that is purchased for a certain period of time, such as 5 or 10 years, and then must be renewed. It is the least expensive type of life insurance.

straight-life (ordinary life) insurance: a type of life insurance in which those insured agree to pay premiums for their entire lives. At the time of the insured's death, a beneficiary will receive the face value of the policy. Straight-life insurance policy builds up a cash value.

limited-payment insurance: a type of life insurance that provides permanent life protection, but the insured pays premiums for a fixed period of time, such as 20 years.

endowment insurance: a type of life insurance that is really an insured savings plan. Premiums are paid for a fixed period of time, and then the insured receives the cash value of the policy, which is equal to the face value, and the insurance expires.

employees as a fringe benefit of employment. In partnerships the beneficiary is often the surviving partner. Several types of life insurance policies are available, some of which even function as savings programs. In this section, we will look at four types of life insurance policies in common use: term, straight life, limited-payment, and endowment.

Identifying Types of Life Insurance

Term insurance is purchased for a certain period of time, such as 5, 10, or 20 years. For example, those insured under a 10-year term policy pay premiums for 10 years or until they die, whichever occurs first. If the insured dies during the 10-year period, the beneficiary of the policy would receive the face value of the policy. If the insured is still living at the end of the 10-year period, the insurance ends and the policy has no cash value. The insured can then renew the policy, but at a higher rate than paid before. Term insurance is the least expensive type of life insurance.

People who take out **straight-life (ordinary life) insurance** policies agree to pay premiums for their entire lives. At the time of the insured's death, a beneficiary will receive the face value of the policy. This type of policy also builds up a cash value. Policy holders who cancel their policy are entitled to a certain sum of money back, depending on the amount that was paid in. Thus, another difference between term and straight-life insurance is that a straight-life policy has a cash value, whereas a term policy does not.

Limited-payment life insurance is another type of policy that provides permanent life protection. The difference between straight-life and limited-payment life is that limited-payment policyholders pay premiums for a fixed period of time. After the fixed period of time (usually 20 or 30 years), policyholders no longer make payments but are insured for the rest of their lives. Naturally, this type of insurance is more expensive than straight-life insurance, since policyholders pay premiums for a shorter period of time.

The **endowment insurance** policy is the most expensive type of life insurance policy. Endowment insurance is really an insured savings plan. Premiums are paid for a fixed period of time. At the end of that time, the cash value is equal to the face value of the policy. The insured can receive the money as a lump-sum payment or in monthly payments. If the insured dies before the end of the fixed period, a beneficiary receives the face value of the policy.

Calculating Life Insurance Premiums

Table 15-3 shows typical rates for the four types of policies that have been discussed. Using this information and the following formula will allow you to find many types of premiums.

STEP BY STEP

Calculating the Annual Premium

Step 1. Look up the annual premium rate in Table 15-3.

Step 2. Multiply the rate from step 1 times the amount of coverage divided by $1,000:

$$\text{Annual premium} = \frac{\text{amount of coverage}}{\$1,000} \times \text{rate}$$

Table 15-3 Annual Premium Rates per $1,000 of Life Insurance

Age	5-year Term Male	5-year Term Female	Straight-life Male	Straight-life Female	20-year Life (Limited Payment) Male	20-year Life (Limited Payment) Female	20-year Endowment Male	20-year Endowment Female
20	4.43	4.32	10.91	10.03	18.34	17.04	20.61	20.19
30	4.88	4.68	14.97	13.53	23.82	21.96	27.68	26.98
40	7.32	6.17	21.88	19.41	31.91	29.45	41.07	39.75
50	14.03	11.57	33.68	27.44	43.97	39.78	72.24	70.15
60	29.40	23.25	54.50	46.93	63.96	56.70	—	—

EXAMPLE 4

Find the annual premium of an insurance policy with a face value of $25,000 for a 30-year-old male for (a) a 5-year term policy; (b) a straight-life policy; (c) a 20-year life policy; and (d) a 20-year endowment.

Annual premium

$= \dfrac{\text{amount of coverage}}{\$1,000} \times \text{rate}$

$= \dfrac{\$25,000}{\$1,000} \times \text{rate} = 25 \times \text{rate}$

Multiply the rate per $1,000 of coverage times 25 to find the annual premium for each policy.

Look in Table 15-3 to find the rate for each type of policy.

a. 5-year term policy: $25 \times \$4.88 = \$122$
b. Straight-life policy: $25 \times \$14.97 = \$374.25$
c. 20-year policy: $25 \times \$23.82 = \$595.50$
d. 20-year endowment: $25 \times \$27.68 = \$692$

The calculator sequence is a multiplication application. The memory function can be used to store the number 25 so that it does not have to be reentered each time.

Calculator Solution

$\boxed{\text{AC}}\ 25\ \boxed{\text{M}^+}\ \boxed{\times}\ 4.88\ \boxed{=} \Rightarrow 122$

$\boxed{\text{CE/C}}\ \boxed{\text{MRC}}\ \boxed{\times}\ 14.97\ \boxed{=} \Rightarrow 374.25$

$\boxed{\text{CE/C}}\ \boxed{\text{MRC}}\ \boxed{\times}\ 23.82\ \boxed{=} \Rightarrow 595.5$

$\boxed{\text{CE/C}}\ \boxed{\text{MRC}}\ \boxed{\times}\ 27.68\ \boxed{=} \Rightarrow 692$

Since it is often inconvenient to make large annual payments, most companies allow payments to be made semiannually (twice a year), quarterly (every three months), or monthly for slightly higher rates than would apply on an annual basis. Table 15-4 shows some typical rates for periods of less than 1 year.

EXAMPLE 5

Use Tables 15-3 and 15-4 to find the (a) semiannual, (b) quarterly, and (c) monthly premiums for a $30,000 straight-life policy on a 40-year-old female.

Annual premium

$= \dfrac{\text{amount of coverage}}{\$1,000} \times \text{rate}$

$= \dfrac{\$30,000}{\$1,000} \times \text{rate}$

$= 30 \times \$19.41 = \$582.30$

Multiply the rate per $1,000 of coverage times 30 to find the annual premium. Find the correct rate in Table 15-3.

Table 15-4 Rates for Less than 1-year Period

Semiannual, 51% of annual prem.
Quarterly, 26% of annual prem.
Monthly, 8.75% of annual prem.

a. Semiannual premium:
$582.30 × 51%
= $582.30 × 0.51 = $296.97

$$\text{Annual premium} \times \text{semiannual rate} = \text{semiannual premium}$$

b. Quarterly premium:
$582.30 × 26%
= $582.30 × 0.26 = $151.40

$$\text{Annual premium} \times \text{quarterly rate} = \text{quarterly premium}$$

REAL WORLD APPLICATION

Real Life Application

A universal life insurance policy is a relatively new type of life insurance in which the company invests the cash value of your policy and gives you a certain percent of the returns on their investments. An annual report, similar to the portion shown below, shows the amount of cash value, the face value of the policy, and the interest earned. Locate the following amounts on the report.

2. How much are the monthly premiums?

3. What is the total cash value of the policy?

4. What is the total interest credited?

5. What is the guaranteed interest rate for the cash value accumulation?

Application Questions

1. How much are the death benefits of this policy?

DEATH BENEFIT—CURRENT OPTION 1 - LEVEL

		SOC. SEC. NUMBER: 000-00-0000
BEG. OF YEAR:	60,000.00	CASH VALUE
END OF YEAR:	60,000.00	END OF PRIOR YEAR: 650.92
CURRENT SPECIFIED AMOUNT	60,000.00	IMPAIRED BY LOANS: 0.00

SUMMARY OF ACTIVITY FOR POLICY YEAR ENDING 03/04/92

MONTH BEGIN	GROSS PREMIUM	LOADING	COST OF INSURANCE	EXPENSE CHARGES	INTEREST(4) CREDITED	PARTIAL WTHDRWL	LOAN(5) ACTIVITY	CASH VALUE
03/04	35.00	2.80	8.08	0.00	4.89	0.00	0.00	679.93
04/04	35.00	2.80	8.07	0.00	5.10	0.00	0.00	709.16
05/04	35.00	2.80	8.07	0.00	5.30	0.00	0.00	738.59
06/04	35.00	2.80	8.07	0.00	5.52	0.00	0.00	768.24
07/04	35.00	2.80	8.06	0.00	5.72	0.00	0.00	798.10
08/04	35.00	2.80	8.06	0.00	5.92	0.00	0.00	828.16
09/04	35.00	2.80	8.05	0.00	6.13	0.00	0.00	858.44
10/04	35.00	2.80	8.05	0.00	6.34	0.00	0.00	888.93
11/04	35.00	2.80	8.05	0.00	6.58	0.00	0.00	919.66
12/04	35.00	2.80	8.04	0.00	6.70	0.00	0.00	950.52
01/04	35.00	2.80	8.04	0.00	7.02	0.00	0.00	981.70
02/04	35.00	2.80	8.03	0.00	7.29	0.00	0.00	1013.16
			(3)		(1)		(2)	
TOTAL	420.00	33.60	96.67	0.00	72.51		0.00	

NEGATIVE VALUES INDICATE THAT PREMIUM WAS NOT PAID PRIOR TO THE CONTRACT'S ISSUE DATE OR MONTHLY ANNIVERSARY DATE. SUBSEQUENT PREMIUM PAYMENTS INCREASE THESE VALUES.

POLICY VALUES AS OF 03/04/92:

CASH VALUE:	1,013.16	(1)INTEREST CREDITED—	
UNPAID LOANS:	0.00	GUARANTEED PORTION:	34.32
POLICY SURRENDER CHARGES:	0.00	EXCESS PORTION:	38.19
POLICY SURRENDER VALUE:	1,013.16	(2)PARTIAL WITHDRAWAL CHARGES	
(3)RIDER CHARGES INCLUDED:	0.00	INCLUDED IN ABOVE:	0.00

(4)CURRENT ANNUAL INTEREST RATE SCHEDULE APPLICABLE TO CASH VALUE ACCUMULATION:

TYPE CASH VALUE ACCUMULATED	RATE
PRIMARY, UNIMPAIRED BY LOANS	9.000
IMPAIRED BY POLICY LOANS	4.500

(5)THE CURRENT LOAN INTEREST RATE IS 8.000% PAYABLE IN ARREARS.
THE DEATH BENEFIT IS REDUCED BY ANY OUTSTANDING LOAN BALANCE.

THE GUARANTEED INTEREST RATE FOR THE LIFE OF THE POLICY IS 4.500%
YOUR PLANNED PERIODIC PREMIUM IS $35.00 PAID MONTHLY.

c. Monthly premium:
$582.30 × 8.75%
= $582.30 × 0.0875 = $50.95

Annual premium × monthly
rate = monthly premium

Again, the calculator sequence is a simple multiplication (after converting the percent to a decimal). The memory function can be used to store $582.30.

$\boxed{\text{AC}}$ 582.3 $\boxed{\text{M}^+}$ $\boxed{\times}$ .51 $\boxed{=}$ ⇒ 296.973

$\boxed{\text{CE/C}}$ $\boxed{\text{MRC}}$ $\boxed{\times}$ .26 $\boxed{=}$ ⇒ 151.398

$\boxed{\text{CE/C}}$ $\boxed{\text{MRC}}$ $\boxed{\times}$ .0875 $\boxed{=}$ ⇒ 50.95125

Self-Check 15.3

Use Tables 15-3 and 15-4 to solve each of the following.

9. Find the annual premium for an insurance policy with a face value of $45,000 for a 20-year-old female for each of the following policies:
   a. 5-year term
   b. Straight-life
   c. 20-year life
   d. 20-year endowment

10. What are the quarterly payments on a $50,000 20-year life insurance policy for a 30-year-old male?

11. What are the monthly payments on a $50,000 straight-life insurance policy for a 50-year-old male?

12. Compare a 5-year term policy for $75,000 for a 40-year-old male to the same policy for a 40-year-old female. Make the same comparison for a 60-year-old male and female.

Summary

Topic	Page	What to Remember	Examples
Fire insurance	455	Annual premium per $100 of coverage = $\dfrac{\text{amount of coverage}}{\$100} \times \text{rate}$ Annual premium per $1,000 of coverage = $\dfrac{\text{amount of coverage}}{\$1,000} \times \text{rate}$ compensation with 80% clause = amount of loss up to face value of insured $\times \dfrac{\text{amount of insurance policy}}{80\% \text{ of replacement value of property}}$	Use Table 15-1 to find the annual premium for building and contents if a building is insured for $120,000 and its contents are insured for $350,000. The building is a Class C building in Area 3. Annual premium for building: $\dfrac{\$120,000}{\$100} \times 0.63 = \$756$ Annual premium for contents: $\dfrac{\$350,000}{\$100} \times 0.80 = \$2,800$ Total premium: $\$756 + \$2,800 = \$3,556$

Topic	Page	What to Remember	Examples
Motor vehicle insurance	458	*Liability insurance:* covers the insured if responsible for an accident resulting in injury to another person or damage to another person's property. *Comprehensive insurance:* covers the insured's vehicle for damage or loss that was not caused in an accident involving another vehicle. *Collision insurance:* covers the insured for personal injury and property damage caused by an automobile accident in which other insurance does not apply.	Use Table 15-2 to find the annual premium for an automobile liability insurance policy in which the insured lives in Territory 2, is in Class C, and wishes to have 20/40/10 coverage. The cost of 20/40 bodily injury coverage for Territory 2 and Class C is $198. The cost of $10,000 property damage is $208. The total premium is $198 + $208 = $406.
Life insurance	459	In the first four examples below, find the annual premium for a 40-year-old female for a policy with a face value of $50,000:			

Topic	Page	What to Remember			Examples
Term insurance (least expensive)	460	Premium is paid for a fixed period of time or term	Coverage lasts for the term of the policy	If insured dies while premium is being paid, beneficiary receives face value of policy	No cash value A 5-year policy: $$\frac{\$50,000}{\$1,000} \times \$6.17 = \$308.50$$
Straight-life (or ordinary life)	460	Premium is paid for entire life	Coverage lasts entire life	If insured dies while premium is being paid, beneficiary receives face value of policy	Policy has some cash value if canceled. A straight life policy: $$\frac{\$50,000}{\$1,000} \times \$19.41 = \$970.50$$
Limited-payment (more expensive than straight-life)	460	Premium is paid for a fixed period	Coverage lasts entire life	If insured dies while premium is being paid, beneficiary receives face value of policy	Cash value depends on the amount paid in. A 20-year life policy: $$\frac{\$50,000}{\$1,000} \times \$29.45 = \$1,472.50$$
Endowment (most expensive)	460	Premium is paid for a fixed period	Coverage lasts for the term of the policy	If insured dies while premium is being paid, beneficiary receives face value of policy	Cash value at end of term is face value. A 20-year endowment policy: $$\frac{\$50,000}{\$1,000} \times \$39.75 = \$1,987.50$$

$$\text{Annual premium per \$1,000 coverage} = \frac{\text{amount of coverage}}{\$1,000} \times \text{rate}$$

Topic	Page	What to Remember		Examples
Premium periods of less than 1 year	461	$\left(\begin{array}{c}\text{Annual} \\ \text{premium}\end{array}\right) \times \left(\begin{array}{c}\text{rate from} \\ \text{Table 15-4}\end{array}\right) =$	$\left(\begin{array}{c}\text{monthly, quarterly,} \\ \text{or semiannual} \\ \text{premium}\end{array}\right)$	Use Tables 15-3 and 15-4 to find the quarterly premium for a $50,000 straight-life policy on a 30-year-old male.

Annual premium =
$$\frac{\$50,000}{\$1,000} \times \$14.97 = \$748.50$$

Quarterly premium =
$$\$748.50 \times 0.26 = \$194.61.$$

Self-Check Solutions

1. $\dfrac{\$120,000}{\$100} \times \$0.38 = \$456$

   $\dfrac{\$75,000}{\$100} \times 0.48 = \$360$

   $\$456 + \$360 = \$816$ total annual premium

2. **a.** $\dfrac{\$150,000}{\$100} \times 0.46 = \$690$

   $\dfrac{\$68,000}{\$100} \times 0.51 = \$346.80$

   $\$690 + \$346.80 = \$1,036.80$ total annual premium

   b. $\$1,036.80 \times 0.02 = \$20.74$ charge;
   ($\$1,036.80 + \$20.74) \div 2 = \$1,057.54 \div 2 = \$528.77$ semiannual premium

3. **a.** $0.80 \times \$255,000 = \$204,000$; since this is 80%, insurance company will pay all losses up to the face value of the policy, which is $204,000.
   b. $75,000

4. $0.8 \times \$295,000 = \$236,000$

   $100 \times \dfrac{\$100,000}{\$236,000} = \$42,372.88$ amount insurance company will pay

5. $\$198 + \$196 = \$394$

6. Class C driver in Territory 1   Class C driver in Territory 2
   $\$177 + \$163 = \$340$ $\$210 + \$208 = \$418$
   Cost for driver in Territory 2 is $78 more.

7. $\$168 + \$159 = \$327$ annual premium
   $\$327 \div 12 = \$27.25$ monthly premium

8. $8,362 for injuries; $0

9. **a.** $\dfrac{\$45,000}{\$1,000} \times \$4.32 = \$194.40$

   b. $\dfrac{\$45,000}{\$1,000} \times \$10.03 = \$451.35$

   c. $\dfrac{\$45,000}{\$1,000} \times \$17.04 = \$766.80$

   d. $\dfrac{\$45,000}{\$1,000} \times \$20.19 = \$908.55$

10. $\dfrac{\$50,000}{\$1,000} \times \$23.82 \times 0.26 = \$309.66$

11. $\dfrac{\$50,000}{\$1,000} \times \$33.68 \times 0.0875 = \$147.35$

12.

Age	Male	Female
40 years old	$\dfrac{\$75,000}{\$1,000} \times \$7.32 = \$549$	$\dfrac{\$75,000}{\$1,000} \times \$6.17 = \$462.75$
60 years old	$\dfrac{\$75,000}{\$1,000} \times \$29.40 = \$2,205$	$\dfrac{\$75,000}{\$1,000} \times \$23.25 = \$1,743.75$

End of Chapter Problems

Using Table 15–1, find the annual fire insurance premium for each of the following.

	Area Rating	Class	Building Coverage	Contents Coverage	Annual Premium Building	Contents
1.	3	A	$72,000	$26,000		
2.	1	C	$38,000	$21,000		
3.	2	B	$116,000	$41,700		
4.	2	A	$78,500	$32,300		
5.	3	C	$105,000	$63,500		

The following policies include an 80% coinsurance clause. A fire has caused the given amount of damage. Determine the amount to be paid by the insurance company.

	Value of Building	Face Value of Policy	Will the Owner Receive Full Compensation?	Amount of Damage	Amount Paid
6.	$105,600	$ 84,480		$17,000	
7.	$ 95,800	$ 72,300		$22,000	
8.	$131,300	$105,040		$65,000	
9.	$261,500	$115,500		$85,000	
10.	$ 76,400	$ 61,120		$65,000	

Use Table 15–1 when necessary to solve the following problems.

11. A sign company owns a Class A building in Area 2 valued at $95,000. The building is insured for $60,000 and the policy has an 80% coinsurance clause. How much will the owner of the sign company receive from his policy if a fire causes $38,000 in damages?

12. What part of the damages will Hampton Insurance Company pay on a building damaged by fire if the market value is $86,000 and it is insured for $68,800? The policy contains an 80% coinsurance clause.

13. Karla Jones insures her Class B building located in Area 3 for $60,000 and the contents for $35,000. Find the total annual insurance premium.

14. In Area 1, a Class C building is insured for $105,000 and its contents for $55,000. If no extra charge is added for semiannual payments, find the premium paid every 6 months.

15. The Country Store is valued at $73,500. To satisfy the 80% coinsurance clause of the policy, for how much should the owner insure the building?

16. a. John Long owns a building with a market value of $121,300. He has insured the building for $85,800. A fire has caused $52,370 in damages. How much will the insurance company pay as compensation if his policy contains an 80% coinsurance clause?

b. If he had insured the building for 80% of its value, how much compensation would he receive?

17. Find the total annual premium for full coverage of a Class A building in Area 1 if it is worth $85,000 and its contents are worth $23,200.

18. How much must the insured pay on a building worth $65,700 if it receives fire damages totaling $17,000? The building is insured for $50,000 and the fire insurance policy contains an 80% coinsurance clause.

19. a. The Greenwood Rental building is worth $86,900. The building is a Class A building in Area 3. What is the annual fire insurance premium on the building and its contents, which are valued at $32,000?

b. If the premium can be paid semiannually with a 2% annual charge added, what is the amount to be paid every 6 months?

20. Harry's Plumbing Company is in a building worth $75,000. Harry has insured the building for $50,000 with a policy containing an 80% coinsurance clause. Fire loss is found to be $37,500.

a. How much will the insurance company pay for the loss?

b. How much of the loss must he pay?

Section 15.2

Use Table 15–2 to find the total annual premium for each of the following automobile liability insurance policies.

	Territory	Driver Class	Coverage	Total Annual Premium
21.	1	B	20/40/5	
22.	2	A	50/100/10	
23.	1	C	100/300/25	
24.	2	B	50/100/25	
25.	2	C	50/100/10	

Use Table 15-2 to solve the following problems.

26. a. Explain what an insurance policy with 50/100/25 coverage means.

b. If you live in Territory 1 and are classified as a Class A driver, what would be the total cost of the annual premium for this policy?

27. If Louise Gonzales is a Class C driver and lives in Territory 1, what is her annual automobile liability insurance premium if she chooses $100,000 for bodily injury for each individual with $300,000 total bodily injury and $10,000 for property damage?

28. The company car for the Greenwood Rental Agency in Territory 2 for a Class C driver is insured with 50/100/25 coverage. What is the annual insurance premium?

29. If you have an accident that damages a fence, up to what amount would your automobile liability insurance policy pay if you have 20/40/10 coverage?

30. Larry Tremont has a collision insurance policy with a $200 deductible clause. If he hits a tree and causes $876 in damages to his car, how much must he pay and how much will the insurance company pay for his damages?

31. Sally Greenspan would like to buy a no-fault insurance policy for $20,000 and an uninsured motorist policy worth $25,000. The cost is $4.50 per $1,000 for the no-fault insurance and $3.50 per $1,000 for the uninsured motorist coverage. What is the cost of Sally's total annual premium?

32. Fred Case has an auto liability insurance policy with 20/40/10 coverage. He is responsible for an accident in which Sara Love, riding in another car, is injured. Her medical expenses totaled $36,243 and damages to her car totaled $4,756. What is the total amount Fred's insurance will pay?

33. As a Class A driver in Territory 1, Laura Jansky is buying an auto liability insurance policy with 100/300/25 coverage. She would like to pay the premium quarterly. Her insurance agent has explained that a $3.50 charge is added to the quarterly payments.
a. How much would her quarterly payments be?

b. How much has she paid at the end of the year?

34. John Malinowsky has auto liability insurance with 20/40/10 coverage. In an accident for which John is responsible, he injures a couple. The husband has medical expenses of $23,268, and his wife's expenses are $21,764. Damage to their car totaled $2,769. How much will John's insurance company pay? How much should John pay?

35. Keith Lee is a Class A driver living in Territory 1. He has auto liability insurance with 50/100/10 coverage. He is in an accident in which a woman is injured and has medical expenses of $55,452. Her car has $5,678 in damages.
a. What is Keith's annual premium?

b. How much should Keith's insurance company pay the woman for her medical expenses and the damages to her car if he is responsible?

Section 15.3

Use Table 15-3 to find the annual premium of each of the following life insurance policies.

	Sex	Age	Policy	Coverage	Annual Premium
36.	Male	20	5-year term	$30,000	
37.	Male	30	5-year term	$90,000	
38.	Female	20	Straight-life	$60,000	
39.	Male	50	Straight-life	$100,000	
40.	Female	40	20-year life	$100,000	

Use Tables 15-3 and 15-4 to find the following premiums.

	Sex	Age	Policy	Coverage	Annual Premium	Payments Monthly	Quarterly
41.	Female	60	Straight-life	$50,000			
42.	Male	20	Straight-life	$40,000			
43.	Male	30	Straight-life	$80,000			
44.	Female	50	20-Year endowment	$30,000			
45.	Male	40	20-Year life	$100,000			

Solve each of the following problems.

46. Explain the differences between term and straight-life insurance policies.

47. If Sam Molla has a 5-year term insurance policy with a value of $40,000 purchased at age 35, how much will his beneficiary receive if he dies at age 39? How much will the beneficiary receive if he dies at 41?

48. a. Find the annual premium paid by Sara Cushion, age 30, on a straight-life insurance policy for $25,000.

b. Find the quarterly premium Sara would pay on the straight-life policy.

49. Find the annual premium paid on a 20-year life insurance policy for $60,000 taken out at age 30 by a male. How much has he paid by age 45?

50. A straight-life policy purchased at age 60 by a male costs how much more per $1,000 than the same policy for a female age 60?

51. How much more would $50,000 in straight-life insurance cost in total annual premiums than $50,000 in 5-year term life insurance if both policies were purchased by a 20-year-old male?

52. How much more would be paid in monthly premiums than in annual premiums on a $50,000 straight-life term policy taken out at age 30 by a male?

53. Find the difference in monthly payments paid by a 40-year-old female on a 5-year term policy and a straight-life policy for $60,000.

54. How much are the quarterly payments paid by a husband, age 40, and his wife, age 30, if each has a 20-year life insurance policy for $70,000?

Additional Problems

Use the appropriate table to solve the following problems.

1. Find the annual fire insurance premium for Delores Garcia's Class C building and contents in Area 3 if the coverage for the building is $73,400 and the coverage for the contents is $25,000.

2. The worship house of Church of the Universe is valued at $155,000. For how much must the building be insured to satisfy the 80% coinsurance clause of the policy?

3. Jerry Roosevelt owns a building worth $75,000 that received fire damages totaling $21,500. If the building is insured for $60,000 with an 80% coinsurance clause, how much will Acme Insurance Company pay for the damages?

4. What is the total annual premium for a 50/100/10 liability insurance policy for a Class C driver who lives in Territory 2?

5. Henry Deffes is a Class B driver in Territory 1. He has liability coverage of 50/100/25. He is involved in an accident in which the other driver sustains medical expenses of $61,492 and car damages of $6,325. How much will the insurance company pay the other driver for all the damages if Henry is responsible?

6. Louisa Villa has 20/40/5 automobile liability insurance and is a Class A driver living in Territory 2. There is a $4.00 per payment fee if the premium is paid in three installments. How much is each installment and how much will Ms. Villa pay for the year?

7. Jack Moto had 50/100/10 automobile liability coverage. He is involved in an accident in which a passenger in the other car is injured and has medical expenses of $48,300. The other car was totaled at $13,500. How much will the insurance company pay for bodily injury and property damage if Mr. Moto is responsible? How much will Mr. Moto have to pay?

8. A straight-life policy purchased at age 30 by a male costs how much more per $1,000 than the same policy purchased by a female at age 30?

9. Compare the cost per year of a 20-year life insurance policy for $50,000 to a 20-year endowment policy for a 20-year-old female.

10. Penny Deutsch has a 5-year term life insurance policy with a value of $25,000 purchased at age 40. How much will her beneficiary receive should Ms. Deutsch die at age 42? At age 47?

Challenge Problem

Guess What Happens on Day 301!

Manny Bober has a fire insurance policy with a value of $120,000. His annual premium is $0.95 per $100 of coverage. If Manny cancels the policy after 300 days, what is his refund?

Trial Test

1. Find the annual premium on a $95,000 straight-life insurance policy for a 40-year-old male.

2. Find the annual premium on a 20/40/10 automobile liability insurance policy for a Class C driver in Territory 2.

3. Find the face value of a fire-protection policy on a building worth $87,500 if it is insured for 75% of its market value.

4. How much will a 50/100/10 automobile liability insurance policy pay for medical expenses of a couple injured in an accident if their total expenses were $53,768, but the expenses of each were less than $50,000?

5. Find the monthly payments on a 20-year endowment policy for $75,000 for a 30-year-old male.

6. How much are the quarterly premiums on a 50/100/25 automobile liability insurance policy for a Class B driver in Territory 1 if a 2% charge is added to annual premiums that are paid quarterly?

7. How much more are the annual premiums for a Class A driver in Territory 2 than for a Class A driver in Territory 1 if both have 20/40/5 coverage?

8. A building and its contents are insured for $78,000 and $12,760, respectively. Find the total annual premium if the building is a Class C building in area 3.

9. Find the quarterly payments on a 20-year life insurance policy for $95,000 on a 40-year-old female.

10. If you have 20/40/10 automobile liability insurance and have an accident that injures the driver of the other car, how much must you pay for the $4,562 in damages to his car and $25,760 in medical expenses?

11. Explain the differences in term and straight-life insurance policies.

12. How much insurance do you need on a $68,500 building if you wish to satisfy the 80% coinsurance clause?

13. How much more would be paid by a 30-year-old male in monthly premiums than in annual premiums for a $60,000, 20-year life insurance policy?

14. Compare the cost per year of a 20-year life insurance policy for $70,000 to a 20-year endowment policy for a 20-year-old male.

15. If you have a collision insurance policy with a $250 deductible clause, how much of $675 damage to your car will the policy cover?

16. How much will a 5-year term policy pay to the beneficiary of a 26-year-old male if he purchased the $30,000 policy at age 20?

17. The market value of a building is $72,500. It has been insured for $50,000. What percent of the damages will the policy cover? Round to the nearest whole percent.

18. A $67,200 building is insured for $40,000 by a fire insurance policy containing an 80% coinsurance clause. A fire causes $12,365 in damages. How much of the loss does the insured have to pay?

19. Find the semiannual premium for a 50/100/25 automobile liability insurance policy for a Class A driver in Territory 2 if there is no additional charge for semiannual payment.

20. Fire causes $18,700 in damages to a $98,000 building insured for $70,000. An 80% coinsurance clause is included. How much of the damages will the insurer pay?

A look at statistics that shape your finances

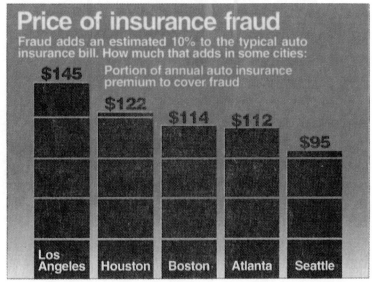

Price of insurance fraud

Fraud adds an estimated 10% to the typical auto insurance bill. How much that adds in some cities:

$145   Portion of annual auto insurance premium to cover fraud

$122 $114 $112 $95

Los Angeles   Houston   Boston   Atlanta   Seattle

Source: National Insurance Crime Bureau   By Keith Carter, USA TODAY

QUESTIONS

1. Of the five cities in the bar graph, which has the highest and the lowest annual auto insurance cost added to cover fraud?

2. Estimate the annual cost of auto insurance in Boston if there were no added charge to cover fraud?

3. The percent of the annual cost of fraud in Atlanta is what percent of that in Los Angeles? Answer to the nearest whole percent.

4. Which two cities listed may one assume are probably more nearly alike in driving safety and traffic conditions. Why could one make this assumption?

16

Taxes

tax: money collected by the government to pay for its upkeep and to provide services to tax payers.

Taxes affect everyone in one way or another. A **tax** is money collected by a government for its own support and for providing services to the populace. Governments use tax money to pay the salaries of government officials and employees. Tax monies run and staff public schools, parks, and playgrounds, and build and maintain roads and highways. Without taxes there would probably be no police and fire protection, health services, unemployment compensation, and numerous other benefits.

To meet these many needs, governments have a variety of tax types to choose from. Among the most common are sales taxes, property taxes, and income taxes.

16.1

Sales and Excise Tax

LEARNING OBJECTIVES

1. Use tables to figure sales tax.
2. Use percent method to figure sales tax.
3. Use percent method to figure excise tax.
4. Find the marked price.

The sales tax is probably the first tax that most people encounter (45 states have sales taxes). At an early age children realize that an item in the store often costs more money than the amount marked on the price tag. At the time of purchase, a store collects this extra amount, called a **sales tax,** and later pays it to the state. In some states, county or city governments charge a local sales tax in addition to the state sales tax. Many states charge no sales tax on food or medicine, and some states make other exceptions. New Jersey, for example, does not charge tax on clothing. A second type of tax, called an **excise tax,** is charged by federal, state, or local governments on such goods as alcoholic beverages, tobacco, motor vehicles, furs, and jewelry and on such services as telephone service and airline travel.

Also note that in most areas a sales tax is charged only on purchases made and delivered within the tax area. For instance, if an item is purchased in one state and delivered to another, the sales tax is not always charged. However, the state to which large purchases are delivered may impose its sales tax. For instance, if an automobile is purchased in one state and delivered to another, the state into which it is delivered may require that sales tax be paid before the automobile can be registered.

The following ways of figuring the amount of sales tax are in common use. Many businesses use computerized cash registers that automatically figure sales tax. Some states assess tax by charging a certain number of cents for each whole dollar and some number of cents on amounts less than a dollar. In other states the sales tax is a specified percent of the selling price.

sales tax: an amount of money added to the price of an item, collected by the store when the item is sold and paid to the state or local government.

excise tax: a tax charged by federal, state, or local governments on certain items, such as alcoholic beverages, tobacco, cars, furs, jewelry, telephone service, and airline tickets.

Using Tables to Figure Sales Tax

For convenience, many state and local governments distribute sales tax tables to businesses that request them. These tables allow employees to determine the proper sales tax quickly. Table 16.1 shows a small portion of a sales tax table. Note that the *state* sales tax rate in Table 16-1 is 5.5%. There is also a local sales tax of 2.25%. The result is a combined tax rate of 7.75%.

EXAMPLE 1

Find the sales tax on a purchase of $4.30 using the sales tax rate given in Table 16-1.

$4.30 falls within the interval $4.20–$4.32. The sales tax from the table is $0.33.

Table 16-1 shows the tax on purchases only up to $9.99. To find the tax on a purchase of more than $9.99, two different methods are available. You

Table 16-1 Sales Tax Table Combining local tax (2.25%) and state tax (5.5%) = total (7.75%)

Sales			Sales		
From	To	Tax	From	To	Tax
0.01 to	0.10	0.00	4.97	5.09	0.39
0.11	0.19	0.01	5.10	5.22	0.40
0.20	0.32	0.02	5.23	5.35	0.41
0.33	0.45	0.03	5.36	5.48	0.42
0.46	0.58	0.04	5.49	5.61	0.43
0.59	0.70	0.05	5.62	5.74	0.44
0.71	0.83	0.06	5.75	5.87	0.45
0.84	0.96	0.07	5.88	5.99	0.46
0.97	1.09	0.08	6.00	6.12	0.47
1.10	1.22	0.09	6.13	6.25	0.48
1.23	1.35	0.10	6.26	6.38	0.49
1.36	1.48	0.11	6.39	6.51	0.50
1.49	1.61	0.12	6.52	6.64	0.51
1.62	1.74	0.13	6.65	6.77	0.52
1.75	1.87	0.14	6.78	6.90	0.53
1.88	1.99	0.15	6.91	7.03	0.54
2.00	2.12	0.16	7.04	7.16	0.55
2.13	2.25	0.17	7.17	7.29	0.56
2.26	2.38	0.18	7.30	7.41	0.57
2.39	2.51	0.19	7.42	7.54	0.58
2.52	2.64	0.20	7.55	7.67	0.59
2.65	2.77	0.21	7.68	7.80	0.60
2.78	2.90	0.22	7.81	7.93	0.61
2.91	3.03	0.23	7.94	8.06	0.62
3.04	3.16	0.24	8.07	8.19	0.63
3.17	3.29	0.25	8.20	8.32	0.64
3.30	3.41	0.26	8.33	8.45	0.65
3.42	3.54	0.27	8.46	8.58	0.66
3.55	3.67	0.28	8.59	8.70	0.67
3.68	3.80	0.29	8.71	8.83	0.68
3.81	3.93	0.30	8.84	8.96	0.69
3.94	4.06	0.31	8.97	9.09	0.70
4.07	4.19	0.32	9.10	9.22	0.71
4.20	4.32	0.33	9.23	9.35	0.72
4.33	4.45	0.34	9.36	9.48	0.73
4.46	4.58	0.35	9.49	9.61	0.74
4.59	4.70	0.36	9.62	9.74	0.75
4.71	4.83	0.37	9.75	9.87	0.76
4.84	4.96	0.38	9.88	9.99	0.77

could use Table 16-1 by adding the taxes charged on two or more amounts that total the amount of the purchase.

EXAMPLE 2

Use Table 16-1 to find the sales tax for a purchase of $16.43.

In Table 16-1, find two amounts that add together to equal $16.43.

$9.99 + $6.44 = $16.43 $9.99 and $6.44 are both in Table 16-1.

$0.77
+ $0.50
$1.27

From Table 16-1, the tax on $9.99 is $0.77, and the tax on $6.44 is $0.50. Add the two amounts of tax to find the total tax due.

The tax on a purchase of $16.43 is $1.27.

You can also find the tax without tables, as the next section shows.

Figuring Tax Using the Percent Method

Note that, except for the first interval shown in Table 16-1, you can find the amount of tax by taking the appropriate percent of the purchase price and rounding to the nearest cent. From the table, note that tax on $0.58 is $0.04 and the tax on $0.59 is $0.05. To compare, find 7.75% of each of the amounts.

$$\$0.58 \times 0.0775 = \$0.04495 \qquad \$0.59 \times 0.0775 = \$0.045725$$
$$= \$0.04 \qquad\qquad\qquad = \$0.05$$

(rounded to the nearest cent)   (rounded to the nearest cent)

The calculated tax is the same as the amounts in the table. We can find the tax on any amount by multiplying the amount by 7.75%. With large amounts, multiplying by a percent is usually quicker than using the table, especially when a calculator is available. Remember to round the tax to the nearest cent.

EXAMPLE 3

Find the sales tax on $128.72 at 6%.

$128.72
× 0.06
$7.7232, which rounds to
$7.72

Multiply the amount of the purchase by 6%. Change the percent to a decimal (0.06). Round the answer to the nearest cent.

The sales tax is $7.72.

Since sales tax tables are not always readily available, it is convenient and practical to use percents to figure sales tax. In most states, except for the tax on purchases of less than $1, sales tax is figured by multiplying the purchase price by a percent of the purchase price. In recent years, the increasing popularity of straight percent sales tax rates has coincided with the growing availability of computerized cash registers that automatically figure such taxes.

Calculating Excise Tax

Some excise taxes are fixed amounts and are the same regardless of the cost of the goods or services. An example of such a tax is a flat-rate tax charged for arriving at or departing from an international airport on a Saturday. More typically, the excise tax is a percent of the cost of the item or service being taxed. When you buy something that carries an excise tax, you must add the sales tax *and* the excise tax to the selling price to find the total tax for the item.

EXAMPLE 4

A fashion designer bought a diamond tiara costing $8,500. The sales tax in her state is 5.5%, and the excise tax on jewelry is 10%. Find the total cost of the tiara.

$8,500 × 0.055 =	$467.50
$8,500 × 0.01 = $850.00	850.00
	$1,317.50

$8,500 + $1,317.50 = $9,817.50
total cost of tiara

Change the sales tax percent to a decimal and multiply it times the cost of the tiara. Move the decimal point one place to the left to find the amount of the 10% excise tax. Add the two taxes to find the total tax owed.

Finding the Marked Price

marked price: the price of an item before sales tax is added.

total price: marked price plus sales tax.

Sometimes a bill gives a total of purchases and sales tax. The sales tax is not itemized, but you may want to know how much the sales tax was or what the marked price of the item was. The **marked price** is the price before tax is added. The **total price** is the marked price plus the sales tax.

STEP BY STEP

Finding Marked Price

Step 1. Divide the total price by 1 + the sales tax rate written as a decimal.

$$\text{Marked price} = \frac{\text{total price}}{1 + \text{sales tax rate (as a decimal)}}$$

Step 2. Round the result to the nearest cent.

EXAMPLE 5

Find the marked price of a $23.83 total bill if there is a 5% sales tax charged.

Sales tax rate = 5% = 0.05   Convert the sales tax rate to a decimal.

$$\frac{\$23.83}{1 + .05} = \frac{23.83}{1.05} = \$22.70$$

Divide the total price by 1 + the decimal. Round to the nearest cent.

 Self-Check 16.1

1. Use Table 16-1 to find the sales tax for a purchase of $5.86.
2. Find the sales tax on a purchase of $12.36 using the sales tax rate given in Table 16-1.
3. Find the sales tax on an appliance costing $288.63 if the tax rate is 5.5%.
4. Figure the total tax on a ring that costs $2,860 in a state with a 6.5% sales tax and a 9% excise tax on jewelry.
5. What is the marked price if a total bill is $182.38 and the sales tax is 6%?

REAL WORLD APPLICATION

If you spend a night at a hotel in a small town in South Carolina, you will pay a 7% accommodations tax on the amount you pay for the room rental. You will also pay a 5% sales and use tax on the night's dinner at the restaurant.

You spent two nights at a hotel in South Carolina. The charge for the room was $52 per night. Your dinner cost $18.55 for the first night and $23.75 for the second night. Find the total bill, including all appropriate taxes.

He charges the following meals to his account: $13.75, $24.50, $21.95. Find the appropriate taxes and the amount of his total bill.

$$\$52 \times 2 = \$104$$
for 2 nights

$$\$104 \times 0.07 = \$7.28$$
accommodations tax

$$\$104 + 7.28 = \$111.28$$
for the room

$$\$18.55 \times 0.05 = \$0.93$$
sales and use tax

$$\$18.55 + \$0.93 = \$19.48$$
for the first meal

$$\$23.75 \times 0.05 = \$1.19$$
sales and use tax

$$\$23.75 + \$1.19 = \$24.94$$
for the second meal

$$\$111.28 + \$19.48 + \$24.94 = \$155.70 \text{ total bill}$$

Application Question

While on vacation in South Carolina, Russell spent 3 nights at an inn that charges $52 per night for a room.

16.2

Property Tax

LEARNING OBJECTIVES

1. Calculate property tax.
2. Determine the tax rate.

property tax: a tax collected by cities and counties on land, houses, buildings, and improvements.

market value: the expected selling price of a piece of property.

assessed value: a percentage of the estimated market value of a property. The percent is set by the city or county that charges the tax.

Most states allow cities and counties to collect money by charging a **property tax** on land, houses, buildings, and improvements and on such personal property as automobiles, jewelry, and furniture. Property tax is usually not paid on the **market value** (the expected selling price of the property), but on the **assessed value** of the property. The assessed value is a specified percent of the estimated market value of the property. This percent, which may vary according to the type of property, is set by the city or county that charges the tax. For example, your city or county may assess farm property and single-family dwellings at 25% of the market value, businesses and multifamily dwellings (duplexes, apartments) at 40% of the market value, and utilities (power companies, telephone companies) at 50% of the market value.

EXAMPLE 6

Find the assessed value of a farm with a market value of $175,000 if the assessed valuation is 25% of the market value.

$175,000 × 0.25 = $43,750   Find 25% of $175,000

Calculating Property Tax

property tax rate: the rate of tax that must be paid on a piece of property; set by the city or county collecting the tax.

mill: one thousandth of a dollar ($0.001).

The city or county government, which imposes a property tax, might express the **property tax rate,** or the amount of tax that must be paid on a piece of property, in one of several different ways. The rate could be stated as a percent of the assessed value, as an amount of tax per $100 of assessed value, as an amount of tax per $1,000 of assessed value, or in mills. A **mill** is one thousandth ($\frac{1}{1000}$, or 0.001) of a dollar. Examples 7 through 10 show how to calculate the property tax when the same tax is expressed in each of four different ways.

EXAMPLE 7

Find the tax on a home with an assessed valuation of $90,000 if the tax rate is 11.08% of the assessed value.

$90,000 × 0.1108 = $9,972   Change the rate to a decimal number and multiply it times the assessed value.

EXAMPLE 8

Find the tax on a home with an assessed value of $90,000 if the tax rate is $11.08 per $100 of assessed valuation.

$\frac{\$90,000}{\$100} = 900$ Divide the assessed value by $100 to find how many $100s are in the assessed value.

900 × $11.08 = $9,972   Multiply the number of $100s times the amount of tax owed per $100.

EXAMPLE 9

Find the tax on a home with an assessed valuation of $90,000 if the tax rate is $110.80 per $1,000 of assessed valuation.

$\frac{\$90,000}{\$1,000} = 90$ Divide the assessed value by $1,000 to find how many $1,000s are in the assessed value.

90 × $110.80 = $9,972   Multiply the number of $1,000s times the amount of tax owed per $1,000.

EXAMPLE 10

Find the tax on a home with an assessed valuation of $90,000 if the tax rate is 110.8 mills. Since *mills* means *thousandths* of a dollar, to change mills to a decimal, divide by 1,000, or move the decimal point *three* places to the left.

110.8 mills = 0.1108   Change the mills to a decimal number by moving the decimal point three places to the left.

0.1108 × $90,000 = $9,972   Multiply the decimal form of the number of mills times the assessed value to find the amount of tax owed.

TIPS & TRAPS

Be sure to use the *assessed value* in calculating the amount of property tax. Let's look at what happens if you use the market value instead of the assessed value to calculate property tax.

Sue Billing's law office has a market value of $110,000 and an assessed value of $44,280. Her town has a tax rate of $173.60 per $1,000 of assessed valuation. Find the tax owed.

Tax on market value:	Tax on assessed value:
$\dfrac{\$110,000}{\$1,000} \times \$173.60 = \$19,096$	$\dfrac{\$44,280}{\$1,000} \times \$173.60 = \$7,687.01$
WRONG	**CORRECT**

Determining the Tax Rate

How does the city or county decide what the tax rate should be? The local government uses its estimated budget to determine how much money it will need in the year ahead. The government then divides that amount by the *total* assessed value of *all* the property in its area. This calculation tells how much tax must be collected for each dollar of assessed property value. The tax rate can be written as an amount per $100 or $1,000 of assessed value by multiplying the tax rate by 100 or 1,000. Whenever you calculate the tax rate, if the division does not come out even, you round the decimal *up* to the next ten-thousandth.

REAL WORLD APPLICATION

Before purchasing investment property, an interested buyer can go to the tax assessor's office to find the amount of taxes to be paid on the property. Using a computer provided for this purpose, the assessor can find the assessed value of the property, the tax rate, and the tax. If the property is purchased before the end of the year, the seller will pay the taxes only for the number of days the seller owns the land. This amount is called the seller's *pro rata* share of the taxes and can be found by dividing the total taxes by 365 days to get the taxes due per day and then multiplying by the number of days the land is owned during that year by the seller. The buyer also pays a *pro rata* share.

Dan is interested in buying a piece of investment property. The market value is $30,500 and the assessment rate is 18% of the market value. Dan found the city tax rate to be 92.7 mills and the county rate to be 138.4 mills. Dan buys the land on April 13. What is Dan's pro rata share of the property taxes?

$30,500 \times 0.18 = \$5,490$	assessed value
$5,490 \times 0.0927 = \$508.92$	city taxes per year
$5,490 \times 0.1384 = \$759.82$	county taxes per year
$508.92 + \$759.82 = \$1,268.74$	total taxes per year

The seller owns the land for 102 days from January 1 though April 12.

$$\$1,268.74 \div 365 \times 102 = \$354.55$$
seller's *pro rata* share of the taxes

$$\$1,268.74 - \$354.55 = \$914.19$$
Dan's *pro rata* share of the taxes

Application Question

Find the seller's *pro rata* share of the city and county taxes on property with a market value of $55,600. The property is assessed at 35% of the market value; city taxes are 107.6 mills, and county taxes are 95.8 mills. The closing date is June 23, the 174th day of the year.

Self-Check 16.2

6. Find the assessed value of a store with a market value of $150,000 if the rate for assessed value is 35%.

7. What is the tax on a property with an assessed value of $88,500 if the tax is 4.5% of the assessed value?

8. Find the property tax on a vacant lot with an assessed value of $32,350 and a tax rate of $4.37 per $100 of assessed value.

9. Find the property tax on a home with an assessed value of $75,000 in a community with a tax rate of $12.75 per $1,000 of assessed value.

10. Calculate the property tax on a store with an assessed value of $150,250 if the tax rate is 58 mills.

11. Find the tax rate per $100 of assessed value of a town that anticipates expenses of $55,800 and has property assessed at $9,830,000.

16.3

Income Taxes

LEARNING OBJECTIVES

1. Find taxable income.
2. Use the tax tables to figure taxes.
3. Use the tax rate schedules to figure taxes.

income tax: tax paid on individual and business income to the federal government and some state governments.

Many state governments and the federal government collect much of their revenues through individual **income taxes.** Federal income tax regulations are enacted by the Congress of the United States, and the tax laws frequently change.

While the laws and forms change from year to year, the *procedures* for computing income tax remain basically the same. Each year an instruction booklet accompanies the current income tax forms. This booklet explains any recent changes in the tax laws, provides instructions for computing tax and filling out the forms, and contains various tax tables that are needed for filing an income tax return.

gross income: income from various sources, such as salary, investments, etc., before exemptions and deductions are subtracted.

To figure the amount of income tax owed, you begin with a business's or individual's **gross income,** which is the money, goods, and property received during the year. From this you subtract any adjustments allowed, such as credit for employee expenses that are not reimbursed by the employer; this gives you the **adjusted gross income.** Next you arrive at the **taxable income,** which is the adjusted gross income minus exemptions and deductions. The taxable income is the amount that is used to figure the taxes owed.

Exemptions provide one of the ways of reducing taxable income. One personal **exemption** is allowed for the taxpayer, and additional exemptions are allowed for the taxpayer's spouse and other dependents. Other exemptions are allowed if the taxpayer or the spouse is over 65 or blind. The Tax Reform Act of 1986 increased the amount of money that can be subtracted for each personal exemption. The deduction for personal exemptions was generally $2,150 for 1991.

A taxpayer is allowed to take **deductions,** or to deduct certain expenses such as charitable contributions, interest paid on certain loans, certain taxes, certain losses, excessive medical expenses, and certain miscellaneous expenses, to name a few. Rather than listing these expenses (called **itemized deductions**), the taxpayer may choose to take the **standard deduction.** The amount that can be subtracted for a standard deduction changes from year to year, but in a recent year it was $5,700 for married taxpayers filing jointly (if both were under 65) or a qualifying widow (widower) with a dependent child; $2,850 for married taxpayers filing separately; $3,400 for single taxpayers; and $5,000 for taxpayers who were the head of a household. This standard deduction is automatically included in the tax tables and tax rate schedules used to compute income tax liability.

The amount of tax due on taxable personal income depends also on the **filing status** of the taxpayer. The individual taxpayer must select the filing status from four categories. The *single* category is for a person who has never married or who is legally separated or who is divorced. A husband and wife filing a return together, even if only one had an income, are classified as *married filing jointly*. This filing status sometimes results in married persons paying a different tax than single persons with a comparable income. When a husband and wife each file a separate return, they are classified as *married filing separately,* and this status may result in a higher tax liability than the married filing jointly status. The filing status *head of household* should be selected by individuals who provide a home for certain other persons.

Finding Taxable Income

Whether you choose to itemize deductions or use the standard deduction, you must determine your *taxable income* before you can compute the tax.

STEP BY STEP

Finding Taxable Income

Taxable income = adjusted gross income − deductions − exemptions

EXAMPLE 11

Find the taxable income for a family of four (husband, wife, two children) if their adjusted gross income is $27,754 and itemized deductions are $5,345. Use $2,150 as the amount of each personal exemption.

Taxable income = adjusted gross income − deductions − exemptions

$$= \$27{,}754 - \$5{,}345 - (\$2{,}150 \times 4)$$

$$= \$27{,}754 - \$5{,}345 - \$8{,}600 = \$13{,}809$$

adjusted gross income: gross income minus any allowable credits.

taxable income: gross income minus exemptions and deductions.

exemptions: an amount of money that each taxpayer is allowed to subtract from gross income. Each taxpayer is allowed one exemption for him- or herself and additional exemptions for the taxpayer's spouse and other dependents.

deductions: certain expenses that the taxpayer is allowed to subtract from his or her adjusted gross income. Includes such items as charitable contributions, excessive medical expenses, interest paid on certain loans, and certain other taxes.

itemized deductions: complete listing of all deductions claimed by the taxpayer when filing the regular 1040 form; used instead of standard deduction.

standard deduction: a taxpayer may choose to subtract a standard deduction from the adjusted gross income rather than itemize his or her deductions. The amount of a standard deduction varies from year to year.

filing status: category of taxpayer; either single, married filing jointly, married filing separately, or head of household.

Table 16-2 Portion of Tax Table

1991 Tax Table—Continued

If line 37 (taxable income) is—		And you are—			
At least	But less than	Single	Married filing jointly *	Married filing separately	Head of a household
		Your tax is—			

14,000

At least	But less than	Single	MFJ *	MFS	HoH
14,000	14,050	2,104	2,104	2,104	2,104
14,050	14,100	2,111	2,111	2,111	2,111
14,100	14,150	2,119	2,119	2,119	2,119
14,150	14,200	2,126	2,126	2,126	2,126
14,200	14,250	2,134	2,134	2,134	2,134
14,250	14,300	2,141	2,141	2,141	2,141
14,300	14,350	2,149	2,149	2,149	2,149
14,350	14,400	2,156	2,156	2,156	2,156
14,400	14,450	2,164	2,164	2,164	2,164
14,450	14,500	2,171	2,171	2,171	2,171
14,500	14,550	2,179	2,179	2,179	2,179
14,550	14,600	2,186	2,186	2,186	2,186
14,600	14,650	2,194	2,194	2,194	2,194
14,650	14,700	2,201	2,201	2,201	2,201
14,700	14,750	2,209	2,209	2,209	2,209
14,750	14,800	2,216	2,216	2,216	2,216
14,800	14,850	2,224	2,224	2,224	2,224
14,850	14,900	2,231	2,231	2,231	2,231
14,900	14,950	2,239	2,239	2,239	2,239
14,950	15,000	2,246	2,246	2,246	2,246

15,000

At least	But less than	Single	MFJ *	MFS	HoH
15,000	15,050	2,254	2,254	2,254	2,254
15,050	15,100	2,261	2,261	2,261	2,261
15,100	15,150	2,269	2,269	2,269	2,269
15,150	15,200	2,276	2,276	2,276	2,276
15,200	15,250	2,284	2,284	2,284	2,284
15,250	15,300	2,291	2,291	2,291	2,291
15,300	15,350	2,299	2,299	2,299	2,299
15,350	15,400	2,306	2,306	2,306	2,306
15,400	15,450	2,314	2,314	2,314	2,314
15,450	15,500	2,321	2,321	2,321	2,321
15,500	15,550	2,329	2,329	2,329	2,329
15,550	15,600	2,336	2,336	2,336	2,336
15,600	15,650	2,344	2,344	2,344	2,344
15,650	15,700	2,351	2,351	2,351	2,351
15,700	15,750	2,359	2,359	2,359	2,359
15,750	15,800	2,366	2,366	2,366	2,366
15,800	15,850	2,374	2,374	2,374	2,374
15,850	15,900	2,381	2,381	2,381	2,381
15,900	15,950	2,389	2,389	2,389	2,389
15,950	16,000	2,396	2,396	2,396	2,396

16,000

At least	But less than	Single	MFJ *	MFS	HoH
16,000	16,050	2,404	2,404	2,404	2,404
16,050	16,100	2,411	2,411	2,411	2,411
16,100	16,150	2,419	2,419	2,419	2,419
16,150	16,200	2,426	2,426	2,426	2,426
16,200	16,250	2,434	2,434	2,434	2,434
16,250	16,300	2,441	2,441	2,441	2,441
16,300	16,350	2,449	2,449	2,449	2,449
16,350	16,400	2,456	2,456	2,456	2,456
16,400	16,450	2,464	2,464	2,464	2,464
16,450	16,500	2,471	2,471	2,471	2,471
16,500	16,550	2,479	2,479	2,479	2,479
16,550	16,600	2,486	2,486	2,486	2,486
16,600	16,650	2,494	2,494	2,494	2,494
16,650	16,700	2,501	2,501	2,501	2,501
16,700	16,750	2,509	2,509	2,509	2,509
16,750	16,800	2,516	2,516	2,516	2,516
16,800	16,850	2,524	2,524	2,524	2,524
16,850	16,900	2,531	2,531	2,531	2,531
16,900	16,950	2,539	2,539	2,539	2,539
16,950	17,000	2,546	2,546	2,546	2,546

17,000

At least	But less than	Single	MFJ *	MFS	HoH
17,000	17,050	2,554	2,554	2,557	2,554
17,050	17,100	2,561	2,561	2,571	2,561
17,100	17,150	2,569	2,569	2,585	2,569
17,150	17,200	2,576	2,576	2,599	2,576
17,200	17,250	2,584	2,584	2,613	2,584
17,250	17,300	2,591	2,591	2,627	2,591
17,300	17,350	2,599	2,599	2,641	2,599
17,350	17,400	2,606	2,606	2,655	2,606
17,400	17,450	2,614	2,614	2,669	2,614
17,450	17,500	2,621	2,621	2,683	2,621
17,500	17,550	2,629	2,629	2,697	2,629
17,550	17,600	2,636	2,636	2,711	2,636
17,600	17,650	2,644	2,644	2,725	2,644
17,650	17,700	2,651	2,651	2,739	2,651
17,700	17,750	2,659	2,659	2,753	2,659
17,750	17,800	2,666	2,666	2,767	2,666
17,800	17,850	2,674	2,674	2,781	2,674
17,850	17,900	2,681	2,681	2,795	2,681
17,900	17,950	2,689	2,689	2,809	2,689
17,950	18,000	2,696	2,696	2,823	2,696

18,000

At least	But less than	Single	MFJ *	MFS	HoH
18,000	18,050	2,704	2,704	2,837	2,704
18,050	18,100	2,711	2,711	2,851	2,711
18,100	18,150	2,719	2,719	2,865	2,719
18,150	18,200	2,726	2,726	2,879	2,726
18,200	18,250	2,734	2,734	2,893	2,734
18,250	18,300	2,741	2,741	2,907	2,741
18,300	18,350	2,749	2,749	2,921	2,749
18,350	18,400	2,756	2,756	2,935	2,756
18,400	18,450	2,764	2,764	2,949	2,764
18,450	18,500	2,771	2,771	2,963	2,771
18,500	18,550	2,779	2,779	2,977	2,779
18,550	18,600	2,786	2,786	2,991	2,786
18,600	18,650	2,794	2,794	3,005	2,794
18,650	18,700	2,801	2,801	3,019	2,801
18,700	18,750	2,809	2,809	3,033	2,809
18,750	18,800	2,816	2,816	3,047	2,816
18,800	18,850	2,824	2,824	3,061	2,824
18,850	18,900	2,831	2,831	3,075	2,831
18,900	18,950	2,839	2,839	3,089	2,839
18,950	19,000	2,846	2,846	3,103	2,846

19,000

At least	But less than	Single	MFJ *	MFS	HoH
19,000	19,050	2,854	2,854	3,117	2,854
19,050	19,100	2,861	2,861	3,131	2,861
19,100	19,150	2,869	2,869	3,145	2,869
19,150	19,200	2,876	2,876	3,159	2,876
19,200	19,250	2,884	2,884	3,173	2,884
19,250	19,300	2,891	2,891	3,187	2,891
19,300	19,350	2,899	2,899	3,201	2,899
19,350	19,400	2,906	2,906	3,215	2,906
19,400	19,450	2,914	2,914	3,229	2,914
19,450	19,500	2,921	2,921	3,243	2,921
19,500	19,550	2,929	2,929	3,257	2,929
19,550	19,600	2,936	2,936	3,271	2,936
19,600	19,650	2,944	2,944	3,285	2,944
19,650	19,700	2,951	2,951	3,299	2,951
19,700	19,750	2,959	2,959	3,313	2,959
19,750	19,800	2,966	2,966	3,327	2,966
19,800	19,850	2,974	2,974	3,341	2,974
19,850	19,900	2,981	2,981	3,355	2,981
19,900	19,950	2,989	2,989	3,369	2,989
19,950	20,000	2,996	2,996	3,383	2,996

20,000

At least	But less than	Single	MFJ *	MFS	HoH
20,000	20,050	3,004	3,004	3,397	3,004
20,050	20,100	3,011	3,011	3,411	3,011
20,100	20,150	3,019	3,019	3,425	3,019
20,150	20,200	3,026	3,026	3,439	3,026
20,200	20,250	3,034	3,034	3,453	3,034
20,250	20,300	3,041	3,041	3,467	3,041
20,300	20,350	3,049	3,049	3,481	3,049
20,350	20,400	3,060	3,056	3,495	3,056
20,400	20,450	3,074	3,064	3,509	3,064
20,450	20,500	3,088	3,071	3,523	3,071
20,500	20,550	3,102	3,079	3,537	3,079
20,550	20,600	3,116	3,086	3,551	3,086
20,600	20,650	3,130	3,094	3,565	3,094
20,650	20,700	3,144	3,101	3,579	3,101
20,700	20,750	3,158	3,109	3,593	3,109
20,750	20,800	3,172	3,116	3,607	3,116
20,800	20,850	3,186	3,124	3,621	3,124
20,850	20,900	3,200	3,131	3,635	3,131
20,900	20,950	3,214	3,139	3,649	3,139
20,950	21,000	3,228	3,146	3,663	3,146

21,000

At least	But less than	Single	MFJ *	MFS	HoH
21,000	21,050	3,242	3,154	3,677	3,154
21,050	21,100	3,256	3,161	3,691	3,161
21,100	21,150	3,270	3,169	3,705	3,169
21,150	21,200	3,284	3,176	3,719	3,176
21,200	21,250	3,298	3,184	3,733	3,184
21,250	21,300	3,312	3,191	3,747	3,191
21,300	21,350	3,326	3,199	3,761	3,199
21,350	21,400	3,340	3,206	3,775	3,206
21,400	21,450	3,354	3,214	3,789	3,214
21,450	21,500	3,368	3,221	3,803	3,221
21,500	21,550	3,382	3,229	3,817	3,229
21,550	21,600	3,396	3,236	3,831	3,236
21,600	21,650	3,410	3,244	3,845	3,244
21,650	21,700	3,424	3,251	3,859	3,251
21,700	21,750	3,438	3,259	3,873	3,259
21,750	21,800	3,452	3,266	3,887	3,266
21,800	21,850	3,466	3,274	3,901	3,274
21,850	21,900	3,480	3,281	3,915	3,281
21,900	21,950	3,494	3,289	3,929	3,289
21,950	22,000	3,508	3,296	3,943	3,296

22,000

At least	But less than	Single	MFJ *	MFS	HoH
22,000	22,050	3,522	3,304	3,957	3,304
22,050	22,100	3,536	3,311	3,971	3,311
22,100	22,150	3,550	3,319	3,985	3,319
22,150	22,200	3,564	3,326	3,999	3,326
22,200	22,250	3,578	3,334	4,013	3,334
22,250	22,300	3,592	3,341	4,027	3,341
22,300	22,350	3,606	3,349	4,041	3,349
22,350	22,400	3,620	3,356	4,055	3,356
22,400	22,450	3,634	3,364	4,069	3,364
22,450	22,500	3,648	3,371	4,083	3,371
22,500	22,550	3,662	3,379	4,097	3,379
22,550	22,600	3,676	3,386	4,111	3,386
22,600	22,650	3,690	3,394	4,125	3,394
22,650	22,700	3,704	3,401	4,139	3,401
22,700	22,750	3,718	3,409	4,153	3,409
22,750	22,800	3,732	3,416	4,167	3,416
22,800	22,850	3,746	3,424	4,181	3,424
22,850	22,900	3,760	3,431	4,195	3,431
22,900	22,950	3,774	3,439	4,209	3,439
22,950	23,000	3,788	3,446	4,223	3,446

* This column must also be used by a qualifying widow(er).

Continued on next page

Table 16-2 (continued)

1991 Tax Table—Continued

*This column must also be used by a qualifying widow(er).

23,000 – 25,999

At least	But less than	Single	Married filing jointly *	Married filing separately	Head of a household
23,000					
23,000	23,050	3,802	3,454	4,237	3,454
23,050	23,100	3,816	3,461	4,251	3,461
23,100	23,150	3,830	3,469	4,265	3,469
23,150	23,200	3,844	3,476	4,279	3,476
23,200	23,250	3,858	3,484	4,293	3,484
23,250	23,300	3,872	3,491	4,307	3,491
23,300	23,350	3,886	3,499	4,321	3,499
23,350	23,400	3,900	3,506	4,335	3,506
23,400	23,450	3,914	3,514	4,349	3,514
23,450	23,500	3,928	3,521	4,363	3,521
23,500	23,550	3,942	3,529	4,377	3,529
23,550	23,600	3,956	3,536	4,391	3,536
23,600	23,650	3,970	3,544	4,405	3,544
23,650	23,700	3,984	3,551	4,419	3,551
23,700	23,750	3,998	3,559	4,433	3,559
23,750	23,800	4,012	3,566	4,447	3,566
23,800	23,850	4,026	3,574	4,461	3,574
23,850	23,900	4,040	3,581	4,475	3,581
23,900	23,950	4,054	3,589	4,489	3,589
23,950	24,000	4,068	3,596	4,503	3,596
24,000					
24,000	24,050	4,082	3,604	4,517	3,604
24,050	24,100	4,096	3,611	4,531	3,611
24,100	24,150	4,110	3,619	4,545	3,619
24,150	24,200	4,124	3,626	4,559	3,626
24,200	24,250	4,138	3,634	4,573	3,634
24,250	24,300	4,152	3,641	4,587	3,641
24,300	24,350	4,166	3,649	4,601	3,649
24,350	24,400	4,180	3,656	4,615	3,656
24,400	24,450	4,194	3,664	4,629	3,664
24,450	24,500	4,208	3,671	4,643	3,671
24,500	24,550	4,222	3,679	4,657	3,679
24,550	24,600	4,236	3,686	4,671	3,686
24,600	24,650	4,250	3,694	4,685	3,694
24,650	24,700	4,264	3,701	4,699	3,701
24,700	24,750	4,278	3,709	4,713	3,709
24,750	24,800	4,292	3,716	4,727	3,716
24,800	24,850	4,306	3,724	4,741	3,724
24,850	24,900	4,320	3,731	4,755	3,731
24,900	24,950	4,334	3,739	4,769	3,739
24,950	25,000	4,348	3,746	4,783	3,746
25,000					
25,000	25,050	4,362	3,754	4,797	3,754
25,050	25,100	4,376	3,761	4,811	3,761
25,100	25,150	4,390	3,769	4,825	3,769
25,150	25,200	4,404	3,776	4,839	3,776
25,200	25,250	4,418	3,784	4,853	3,784
25,250	25,300	4,432	3,791	4,867	3,791
25,300	25,350	4,446	3,799	4,881	3,799
25,350	25,400	4,460	3,806	4,895	3,806
25,400	25,450	4,474	3,814	4,909	3,814
25,450	25,500	4,488	3,821	4,923	3,821
25,500	25,550	4,502	3,829	4,937	3,829
25,550	25,600	4,516	3,836	4,951	3,836
25,600	25,650	4,530	3,844	4,965	3,844
25,650	25,700	4,544	3,851	4,979	3,851
25,700	25,750	4,558	3,859	4,993	3,859
25,750	25,800	4,572	3,866	5,007	3,866
25,800	25,850	4,586	3,874	5,021	3,874
25,850	25,900	4,600	3,881	5,035	3,881
25,900	25,950	4,614	3,889	5,049	3,889
25,950	26,000	4,628	3,896	5,063	3,896

26,000 – 28,999

At least	But less than	Single	Married filing jointly *	Married filing separately	Head of a household
26,000					
26,000	26,050	4,642	3,904	5,077	3,904
26,050	26,100	4,656	3,911	5,091	3,911
26,100	26,150	4,670	3,919	5,105	3,919
26,150	26,200	4,684	3,926	5,119	3,926
26,200	26,250	4,698	3,934	5,133	3,934
26,250	26,300	4,712	3,941	5,147	3,941
26,300	26,350	4,726	3,949	5,161	3,949
26,350	26,400	4,740	3,956	5,175	3,956
26,400	26,450	4,754	3,964	5,189	3,964
26,450	26,500	4,768	3,971	5,203	3,971
26,500	26,550	4,782	3,979	5,217	3,979
26,550	26,600	4,796	3,986	5,231	3,986
26,600	26,650	4,810	3,994	5,245	3,994
26,650	26,700	4,824	4,001	5,259	4,001
26,700	26,750	4,838	4,009	5,273	4,009
26,750	26,800	4,852	4,016	5,287	4,016
26,800	26,850	4,866	4,024	5,301	4,024
26,850	26,900	4,880	4,031	5,315	4,031
26,900	26,950	4,894	4,039	5,329	4,039
26,950	27,000	4,908	4,046	5,343	4,046
27,000					
27,000	27,050	4,922	4,054	5,357	4,054
27,050	27,100	4,936	4,061	5,371	4,061
27,100	27,150	4,950	4,069	5,385	4,069
27,150	27,200	4,964	4,076	5,399	4,076
27,200	27,250	4,978	4,084	5,413	4,084
27,250	27,300	4,992	4,091	5,427	4,091
27,300	27,350	5,006	4,099	5,441	4,102
27,350	27,400	5,020	4,106	5,455	4,116
27,400	27,450	5,034	4,114	5,469	4,130
27,450	27,500	5,048	4,121	5,483	4,144
27,500	27,550	5,062	4,129	5,497	4,158
27,550	27,600	5,076	4,136	5,511	4,172
27,600	27,650	5,090	4,144	5,525	4,186
27,650	27,700	5,104	4,151	5,539	4,200
27,700	27,750	5,118	4,159	5,553	4,214
27,750	27,800	5,132	4,166	5,567	4,228
27,800	27,850	5,146	4,174	5,581	4,242
27,850	27,900	5,160	4,181	5,595	4,256
27,900	27,950	5,174	4,189	5,609	4,270
27,950	28,000	5,188	4,196	5,623	4,284
28,000					
28,000	28,050	5,202	4,204	5,637	4,298
28,050	28,100	5,216	4,211	5,651	4,312
28,100	28,150	5,230	4,219	5,665	4,326
28,150	28,200	5,244	4,226	5,679	4,340
28,200	28,250	5,258	4,234	5,693	4,354
28,250	28,300	5,272	4,241	5,707	4,368
28,300	28,350	5,286	4,249	5,721	4,382
28,350	28,400	5,300	4,256	5,735	4,396
28,400	28,450	5,314	4,264	5,749	4,410
28,450	28,500	5,328	4,271	5,763	4,424
28,500	28,550	5,342	4,279	5,777	4,438
28,550	28,600	5,356	4,286	5,791	4,452
28,600	28,650	5,370	4,294	5,805	4,466
28,650	28,700	5,384	4,301	5,819	4,480
28,700	28,750	5,398	4,309	5,833	4,494
28,750	28,800	5,412	4,316	5,847	4,508
28,800	28,850	5,426	4,324	5,861	4,522
28,850	28,900	5,440	4,331	5,875	4,536
28,900	28,950	5,454	4,339	5,889	4,550
28,950	29,000	5,468	4,346	5,903	4,564

29,000 – 31,999

At least	But less than	Single	Married filing jointly *	Married filing separately	Head of a household
29,000					
29,000	29,050	5,482	4,354	5,917	4,578
29,050	29,100	5,496	4,361	5,931	4,592
29,100	29,150	5,510	4,369	5,945	4,606
29,150	29,200	5,524	4,376	5,959	4,620
29,200	29,250	5,538	4,384	5,973	4,634
29,250	29,300	5,552	4,391	5,987	4,648
29,300	29,350	5,566	4,399	6,001	4,662
29,350	29,400	5,580	4,406	6,015	4,676
29,400	29,450	5,594	4,414	6,029	4,690
29,450	29,500	5,608	4,421	6,043	4,704
29,500	29,550	5,622	4,429	6,057	4,718
29,550	29,600	5,636	4,436	6,071	4,732
29,600	29,650	5,650	4,444	6,085	4,746
29,650	29,700	5,664	4,451	6,099	4,760
29,700	29,750	5,678	4,459	6,113	4,774
29,750	29,800	5,692	4,466	6,127	4,788
29,800	29,850	5,706	4,474	6,141	4,802
29,850	29,900	5,720	4,481	6,155	4,816
29,900	29,950	5,734	4,489	6,169	4,830
29,950	30,000	5,748	4,496	6,183	4,844
30,000					
30,000	30,050	5,762	4,504	6,197	4,858
30,050	30,100	5,776	4,511	6,211	4,872
30,100	30,150	5,790	4,519	6,225	4,886
30,150	30,200	5,804	4,526	6,239	4,900
30,200	30,250	5,818	4,534	6,253	4,914
30,250	30,300	5,832	4,541	6,267	4,928
30,300	30,350	5,846	4,549	6,281	4,942
30,350	30,400	5,860	4,556	6,295	4,956
30,400	30,450	5,874	4,564	6,309	4,970
30,450	30,500	5,888	4,571	6,323	4,984
30,500	30,550	5,902	4,579	6,337	4,998
30,550	30,600	5,916	4,586	6,351	5,012
30,600	30,650	5,930	4,594	6,365	5,026
30,650	30,700	5,944	4,601	6,379	5,040
30,700	30,750	5,958	4,609	6,393	5,054
30,750	30,800	5,972	4,616	6,407	5,068
30,800	30,850	5,986	4,624	6,421	5,082
30,850	30,900	6,000	4,631	6,435	5,096
30,900	30,950	6,014	4,639	6,449	5,110
30,950	31,000	6,028	4,646	6,463	5,124
31,000					
31,000	31,050	6,042	4,654	6,477	5,138
31,050	31,100	6,056	4,661	6,491	5,152
31,100	31,150	6,070	4,669	6,505	5,166
31,150	31,200	6,084	4,676	6,519	5,180
31,200	31,250	6,098	4,684	6,533	5,194
31,250	31,300	6,112	4,691	6,547	5,208
31,300	31,350	6,126	4,699	6,561	5,222
31,350	31,400	6,140	4,706	6,575	5,236
31,400	31,450	6,154	4,714	6,589	5,250
31,450	31,500	6,168	4,721	6,603	5,264
31,500	31,550	6,182	4,729	6,617	5,278
31,550	31,600	6,196	4,736	6,631	5,292
31,600	31,650	6,210	4,744	6,645	5,306
31,650	31,700	6,224	4,751	6,659	5,320
31,700	31,750	6,238	4,759	6,673	5,334
31,750	31,800	6,252	4,766	6,687	5,348
31,800	31,850	6,266	4,774	6,701	5,362
31,850	31,900	6,280	4,781	6,715	5,376
31,900	31,950	6,294	4,789	6,729	5,390
31,950	32,000	6,308	4,796	6,743	5,404

Continued on next page

Once you know your taxable income and filing status, you need to match it to the taxes for that income level. Tax tables like those in Table 16-2 are used to find the tax liability for taxable incomes of *less than* $50,000.

STEP BY STEP

Using the Tax Table to Figure Taxes

Step 1. Locate your taxable income under the column headed, "If line 37 (taxable income) is—".

Step 2. Move across to the column headed, "And you are—," which has the four categories of filing status listed under it. The tax you owe will appear under the appropriate category.

EXAMPLE 12

Find the tax owed by a married taxpayer filing separately on a taxable income of $19,478.

First, locate the income range in which $19,478 falls. Because $19,478 is at *least* $19,450 *but less than* $19,500, it falls within the range $19,450–$19,500.

Next, locate the tax for this taxable income range to the right in the column headed *married filing separately*. The tax is $3,243.

EXAMPLE 13

Find the tax owed by the same taxpayer in Example 12 if the taxpayer files jointly with a spouse.

For the taxable income range $19,450–$19,500, the tax for a taxpayer *married filing jointly* is $2,921.

From Examples 12 and 13 and from an inspection of Table 16-2, it is clear that a taxpayer's filing status (single, married filing jointly, married filing separately, head of household) significantly affects the amount of tax owed.

Using the Tax Rate Schedules

tax rate schedules: used to figure tax on taxable incomes of $50,000 or more.

The **tax rate schedules** are used to compute tax on taxable incomes of $50,000 *or more*. There are separate tax rate schedules for single taxpayers, heads of households, and married taxpayers (and certain qualifying widows and widowers).

The Tax Reform Act of 1986 changed the tax rate structure that had existed in the years before that. An individual's income is taxed at different rates depending on how much of his or her income falls into each of various income brackets. Table 16-3 shows the tax rates for 1991.

STEP BY STEP

Using Tax Rate Schedules to Figure Tax Owed

Locate the correct schedule according to filing status.

Find the range in which the taxable income falls.

Subtract the lower end of the range from the taxable income.

Multiply the result from step 3 by the indicated rate.

Add the dollar amount indicated for the range to the result from step 4.

Table 16-3

1991 Tax Rate Schedules

*Caution: Use **only** if your taxable income (Form 1040, line 37) is $50,000 or more. If less, use the **Tax Table**. (Even though you cannot use the tax rate schedules below if your taxable income is less than $50,000, all levels of taxable income are shown so taxpayers can see the tax rate that applies to each level.)*

Schedule X—Use if your filing status is **Single**

If the amount on Form 1040, line 37, is: Over—	But not over—	Enter on Form 1040, line 38	of the amount over—
$0	$20,350	.... 15%	$0
20,350	49,300	$3,052.50 + 28%	20,350
49,300	....	11,158.50 + 31%	49,300

Schedule Y-1—Use if your filing status is **Married filing jointly or Qualifying widow(er)**

If the amount on Form 1040, line 37, is: Over—	But not over—	Enter on Form 1040, line 38	of the amount over—
$0	$34,000	.... 15%	$0
34,000	82,150	$5,100.00 + 28%	34,000
82,150	....	18,582.00 + 31%	82,150

Schedule Y-2—Use if your filing status is **Married filing separately**

If the amount on Form 1040, line 37, is: Over—	But not over—	Enter on Form 1040, line 38	of the amount over—
$0	$17,000	.... 15%	$0
17,000	41,075	$2,550.00 + 28%	17,000
41,075	....	9,291.00 + 31%	41,075

Schedule Z—Use if your filing status is **Head of household**

If the amount on Form 1040, line 37, is: Over—	But not over—	Enter on Form 1040, line 38	of the amount over—
$0	$27,300	.... 15%	$0
27,300	70,450	$4,095.00 + 28%	27,300
70,450	....	16,177.00 + 31%	70,450

EXAMPLE 14

Find the tax on a taxable income of $58,743 for a married taxpayer filing jointly using Table 16-3.

The taxpayer would use Schedule Y-1.

Schedule Y-1 shows that the taxable income falls in the range $34,000–$82,150.

$58,743 − $34,000 = $24,473

$24,473 × 0.28 = $6,928.04

$6,928.04 + $5,100.00 = $12,039.04

The tax is $12,039.04.

EXAMPLE 15

Find the tax owed on a taxable income of $67,587 for a married taxpayer filing separately. Use Table 16-3.

The taxpayer is married filing separately, so use Schedule Y-2.

The taxable income, $67,587, falls in the range over $41,075.

$67,587 − $41,075 = $26,512

$26,512 × 0.31 = $8,218.72

$8,218.72 + $9,291.00 = $17,509.72

The tax is $17,509.72.

 Self-Check 16.3

12. Find the taxable income for a family of 6 (husband, wife, four children) whose adjusted gross income is $43,873 and itemized deductions are $9,582. (1 Exemption = $2,150.)

13. Find the taxable income for a single person whose adjusted gross income is $28,932 and itemized deductions are $4,915. (1 Exemption = $2,150.)

14. Charles Lee is single and calculates his taxable income to be $30,175. How much tax does he owe? Use Table 16-2.

15. Tommy and Michelle Fernandez have a combined taxable income of $23,300. How much tax should they pay? Use Table 16-2.

16. Bradley Bishop is married and filing his tax jointly with his wife, Margaret. Their combined taxable income is $67,983. Use the tax rate schedules (Table 16-3) to calculate the tax they must pay.

17. Dr. Steven Katz is single and has a taxable income of $60,842. Use the tax rate schedules (Table 16-3) to calculate his income tax liability.

Summary

Topic	Page	What to Remember	Examples
Sales tax	479	Sales tax can be looked up in a table or computed by hand or on a calculator if given the percent.	Use the percentage method to find the sales tax on a $1,685 fax machine at 6.6%. $1,685 × 0.066 = $111.21

Topic	Page	What to Remember	Examples
Excise tax	481	An additional tax, usually a percentage of the purchase price, may be charged on certain goods and services.	Find the total cost of a $1,436 diamond necklace if the sales tax is 7% and the excise tax is 11%. $1,436 \times 7\% = \$1,436 \times 0.07 = \$100.52$ 11% excise tax: $\$1,436 \times 11\% = \$1,436 \times 0.11 = \$157.96$ Total cost: $\$1,436 + \$100.52 + \$157.96 = \$1,694.48$
Property tax and assessed valuation	483	Property tax is based on the *assessed value,* not the *market value,* of property. Assessed value = a percent of market value	Find the assessed value of a home with a market value of $106,000 if the assessed value is 30% of the market value. $\$106,000 \times 30\% = \$106,000 \times 0.3 = \$31,800$
Four ways of expressing tax rate and figuring tax due	484	The tax rate is the number used to find how much tax is owed on property. The tax rate can be expressed in four different ways:	Find the tax on a farm with an assessed valuation of $430,000 in each case.
		As a percent of the assessed valuation	The tax rate is 8.05% of the assessed value: $\$430,000 \times 8.05\% = \$430,000 \times 0.0805$ $\qquad\qquad\qquad\qquad\quad = \$34,615$
		As an amount due for each $100 of assessed valuation	The tax rate is $8.05 per $100 of assessed value: $\dfrac{\$430,000}{\$100} \times \$8.05 = \$34,615$
		As an amount due for each $1,000 of assessed valuation	The tax rate is $80.50 per $1,000 of assessed value: $\dfrac{\$430,000}{\$1,000} \times \$80.50 = \$34,615$
		As a number of mills times the assessed valuation	The tax rate is $80\frac{1}{2}$ mills: $80\frac{1}{2}$ mills $\rightarrow 0.0805$ $\$430,000 \times 0.0805 = \$34,615$
Finding taxable income	487	$\left(\begin{array}{c}\text{Taxable} \\ \text{income}\end{array}\right) = \left(\begin{array}{c}\text{adjusted} \\ \text{gross} \\ \text{income}\end{array}\right)$ $\quad - \text{ deductions}$	Toni Wilson and her spouse earned $33,200 gross income and had itemized deductions of $8,700. They have a 7-year-old daughter. Find the taxable income, using $2,150 for each exemption. Taxable income $= \$33,200 - (3 \times \$2150)$ $\qquad\qquad\qquad\qquad\quad - \$8,700$ $\qquad\qquad = 33,200 - \$6,450 - \$8,700$ $\qquad\qquad\qquad\qquad\quad = \$18,050$
Computing tax with the tax tables	490	Find the amount of taxable income; then locate the bracket in Table 16-2 that includes this amount. Move across to the appropriate filing status column to find the tax due.	Use Table 16-2 to find Toni's tax if she and her husband file jointly. Find the range $18,800 − $18,850. Move across to the tax in the column "Married, filing jointly," which is $2,824.

Topic	Page	What to Remember	Examples
Computing tax with tax rate schedules	490	Select the appropriate schedule in Table 16-3 as determined by taxpayer filing status. Find the range that includes the taxable income. Subtract the lower end of the tax range from the taxable income and multiply this result by the indicated rate. Add the dollar amount given plus the calculated amount for total tax.	Susan Wilson has a taxable income of $53,897. Her filing status is single. Find the amount of tax she owes. Use Schedule X. The range is over $49,300. $53,897 − $49,300 = $4,597 $4,597 × 0.31 = $1425.07 Tax = $1,425.07 + $11,158.50 = $12,583.57

Self-Check Solutions

	From	To	Tax

1. $5.86   5.75   5.87   0.45

2. $12.36 $12.36 − $9.99 = $2.37; Tax on $9.99 is $0.77;
Tax on $2.37 is $0.18; Tax on $12.36 is $0.95.

3. $288.63 × 0.055 = $15.87465 = $15.87   (rounded)

4. $2,860 × 0.065 = $185.90   Sales tax
     $2,860 × 0.09 = $257.40   Excise tax
$185.90 + $257.40 = $443.30   Total tax

5. $182.38 ÷ 1.06 = $172.0566 = $172.06   (rounded)

6. $150,000 × 0.35 = $52,500

7. $88,500 × 0.045 = $3,982.50

8. $32,350 ÷ $100 × $4.37 = $1,413.695 = $1,413.70   (rounded)

9. $75,000 ÷ $1,000 × $12.75 = $956.25

10. $150,250 × 0.058 = $8,714.50

11. $55,800 ÷ $9,830,000 × $100 = $0.56765 = 0.57 (rounded)

12. Exemptions = $2,150 × 6 = $12,900
Taxable income = $43,873 − $9,582 − $12,900 = $21,391

13. Exemption = $2,150 × 1 = $2,150
Taxable income = $28,932 − $4,915 − $2,150 = $21,867

14. Locate the range that includes $30,175. $30,175 is in the range $30,150–$30,200. Look under the "single" column. The tax owed is $5,804.

15. Locate the range $23,300–$23,350. Look under the column "Married filing jointly." The tax owed is $3,499.

16. Use Schedule Y-1 since Bradley is filing jointly with his wife. The taxable income is in the range $34,000–$82,150.
$67,983 − $34,000 = $33,983
$33,983 × 0.28 = $9,515.24
$9,515.24 + $5,100.00 = $14,615.24 (taxed owed)

17. Use Schedule X, since Dr. Katz's filing status is "single."
Taxable income is in the range over $49,300.
$60,842 − $49,300 = $11,542
$11,542 × 0.31 = $3,578.02
$3,578.02 + $11,158.50 = $14,736.52

End of Chapter Problems

Section 16.1

Use Table 16-1 to find the sales tax on the following purchases.

1. $2.37   **2.** $3.72   **3.** $8.10   **4.** $2.93   **5.** $4.74

6. $11.04   **7.** $9.98

8. $29.95   **9.** $6.52   **10.** $5.47

Without using the table, calculate the sales tax or excise tax on the following purchases.
(Solutions for Exercises 11-21 are rounded to the nearest cent.)

11. $237.42 at 6% sales tax

12. $523.85 at 5% sales tax

13. $1,294.26 at 4.5% excise tax

14. $482.12 at 6% sales tax

15. $675.93 at 5% sales tax

16. $2,998.97 at 4.5% sales tax

Find the marked price if each of the following represents a total bill at the indicated sales tax rate.

17. $27.45 at 5%   *11.04*

18. $139.53 at 6%   *9.9 9*

19. $347.28 at 4.5%

20. $53.92 at 5%

21. $87.26 at 3.5%

Section 16.2

Find the assessed value of each property using the following rates:
Farm property or single-family dwellings: 25%
Commercial property or multi-unit family dwellings: 40%   *7 nov 95*
Utilities: 50%

22. Single-family dwelling with market value of $55,000   *13,750*

23. Apartment with market value of $235,000

24. Grocery store with market value of $115,000   *46,000*

25. Farmland with market value of $150,000

26. Power company with market value of $5,175,000   *2,587.00*

Find the tax on each assessed value at the indicated rate.

27. $37,000 at $1\frac{1}{2}\%$

28. $45,000 at $1\frac{3}{4}\%$

29. $12,500 at 2%

30. $575,000 at 1.8%

31. $85,000 at 2.5%

32. If the county tax rate is $3.74 per $100 of assessed value, find the tax on a property that is assessed at $35,000.

33. If the county tax rate is increased to $4.25 from $3.74 per $100 of assessed value, how much tax would have to be paid on the same $35,000? What is the amount of increase?

34. The tax rate for a city is $3.25 per $100 of assessed value. Find the tax on a property that is assessed at $125,000.

35. A home has a market value of $50,000 (assessed value = 25% of market value). Find the amount of county taxes to be paid on the home if the county tax rate is $4.00 per $100 of assessed value.

36. What is the city property tax on the house in Problem 35 if the city tax rate is $3.06 per $100 of assessed valuation?

37. Find the combined city and county tax for the property in Problems 35 and 36.

38. Find the combined city and county property tax on a business whose market value is $200,000 (assessed value = 40% of market value). The business is within the city and county whose tax rates are given in Problems 35 and 36.

Find the tax on each assessed value at the indicated rate.

39. $37,000 at $14.25 per $1,000 of assessed valuation

40. $150,000 at $15.50 per $1,000 of assessed valuation

41. $172,500 at $16.23 per $1,000 of assessed valuation

42. $32,250 at $13.78 per $1,000 of assessed valuation

43. $87,500 at $12.67 per $1,000 of assessed valuation

Change the following mill rates to decimals.

44. 34 mills

45. 63 mills

46. 51 mills

Find the tax on each property at the given assessed valuation and the indicated tax rate.

47. $12,500 at 65 mills

48. $23,275 at 55 mills

49. $52,575 at 71 mills

50. $28,750 at 64 mills

51. $32,500 at 67 mills

Complete the following table. (Express the tax levied on $1 of assessed valuation to the ten-thousandths place. Round up *any* remainder.)

Total Assessed Value	Total Expenses	Tax Rate Charged on:		
		$1	$100	$1,000
52. $11,370,000	$ 386,450			
53. $87,460,000	$4,348,800			
54. $ 5,718,000	$ 374,740			

Section 16.3

Use $2,150 for each allowed personal exemption in Problems 55 to 60.

55. Find the taxable income for Sam and Delois Johns, a husband and wife whose adjusted gross income is $18,378 and itemized deductions are $4,023.

56. Find the taxable income for the Zuckmans, a family of four (husband, wife, two children), if the wife is blind, the adjusted gross income is $34,728, and the itemized deductions are $7,246.

$$34,728 - 7,246 - 8,600. = \boxed{18,882}$$

$$(7,246 + 8,600 + 18,882 = 34,728)$$

$$\begin{array}{r} \overset{2}{2,150} \\ \times \quad 4 \\ \hline 8,600 \end{array}$$

57. Find the taxable income for the Shotwells, a family of three (husband, wife, one child), if their adjusted gross income is $22,376 and itemized deductions are $4,375.

58. Find the taxable income for Mario Gravez, a single person whose adjusted gross income is $14,312 and itemized deductions are $3,412.

$$14,312 - 3,412 - 2,149 = \boxed{8,751}$$
$$(3,412 + 2,149 + 8,751 = 14,312)$$

59. Find the taxable income for the Thungs, a family of three (husband, wife, one child), if their adjusted gross income is $66,833 and itemized deductions are $12,583.

7 Nov 95

60. Find the taxable income for Lorenda and James Atlas, a husband and wife, who have an adjusted gross income of $26,000 and are filing jointly. Their total itemized deductions are $3,589.

$$26,000 - 3,589 - 3,904 = \boxed{18,507}$$
$$3,589 + 3,904 + 18,507 = 26,000$$

Use Table 16-2 to find the tax owed by taxpayers with the following taxable incomes:

61. $19,730 (single person)

62. $19,312 (single person)

63. $14,069 (single person)

64. $26,500 (single person)

65. $16,980 (married, filing jointly)

66. $31,500 (married, filing jointly)

67. $28,450 (married, filing jointly)

68. $24,059 (married, filing jointly)

Use Table 16-3 to find the tax on the following taxable incomes.

69. $54,456 (married, filing jointly)

70. $72,478 (married, filing separately)

71. $51,200 (head of household)

72. $88,342 (single)

Additional Problems

1. Susie Chung purchased a tennis bracelet for $3,100. If she paid state sales tax of 2%, city sales tax of $5\frac{1}{4}$%, and excise tax of 8%, what was her total bill?

2. Max Jacobsen ordered a set of recordings for $21.20, including $6\frac{1}{4}$% sales tax. What was the price of the record set before tax was added?

3. What is the marked price of a box of self-stick floor tiles if the total price of $66.20 includes $3.45 sales tax?

4. Find the tax rate per $1,000 of assessed value that a local government should set if the total assessed property value is $28,500,000 and the total projected budget is $925,000.

5. A residence in Eurika Falls is taxed at $2.15 per $100 of assessed value. How much is the property tax if the residence is assessed at $32,800?

6. If the selling price of 40 acres of land includes one year's property tax of 32 mills, find the selling price of the property assessed at $11,500.

7. Using Table 16-3, calculate the income tax of a married couple filing jointly whose taxable incomes are $28,400 and $23,500.

8. Walter Bernstein has an adjusted gross income of $67,450. He is married and has two young children. If his itemized deductions are $11,736, find his taxable income and the tax. (Use $2,150 as the amount of each personal exemption.)

9. Martha Fernandez files her income tax return as head of a household with a taxable income of $23,076. If the total income tax withheld is $4,421, how much should her refund be?

10. Tim Ono is a single taxpayer with an adjusted gross income of $19,683. Find the amount of income tax due if he has itemized deductions of $3,656. (Use $2,150 as the amount of his personal exemption.)

Challenge Problem

Borrowing for an IRA

Sometimes it might pay for an individual to borrow money in order to invest in an IRA (Individual Retirement Account). Assume Jill Jones is single and has a taxable income of $23,250. Jill borrows $2000 from her Uncle Fred so that she can start an IRA that yields 9% interest per year. Uncle Fred is charging Jill 8% simple interest. Taking into account her IRA deduction on her federal income tax and her payments to Uncle Fred (over 3 years), is this a good idea?

Use the following charts to compare the tax Jill owes with or without an IRA.

Chart for People Covered by a Retirement Plan*

If you (or your spouse if you file a joint return) **were covered by a retirement plan** and:

Your filing status is:	And Form 1040A, line 14, is:	You can take:
Single, head of household, or married filing separately and did **not** live with your spouse in 1991	$25,000 or less	Full IRA deducation (use Worksheet 1 on page 35)
	Over $25,000 but less than $35,000	Partial IRA deduction (use Worksheet 2 on pages 35–36)
	$35,000 or more	No IRA deduction (but see **Nondeductible contributions** on page 34)
Married filing jointly, or qualifying widow(er) with dependent child	$40,000 or less	Full IRA deduction (use Worksheet 1 on page 35)
	Over $40,000 but less than $50,000	Partial IRA deduction (use Worksheet 2 on pages 35–36)
	$50,000 or more	No IRA deduction (but see **Nondeductible contributions** on page 34)
Married filing separately and lived with your spouse in 1991	Over -0- but less than $10,000	Partial IRA deduction (use Worksheet 2 on pages 35–36)
	$10,000 or more	No IRA deduction (but see **Nondeductible contributions** on page 34)

* If married filing separately and you were not covered by a plan but your spouse was, **you** are considered covered by a plan if you lived with your spouse at any time in 1991.

If Form 1040A, line 22, is—		And you are—				If Form 1040A, line 22, is—		And you are—			
At least	But less than	Single	Married filing jointly	Married filing separately	Head of a household	At least	But less than	Single	Married filing jointly	Married filing separately	Head of a household
				Your tax is—						Your tax is—	
20,000						**23,000**					
20,000	20,050	3,004	3,004	3,397	3,004	23,000	23,050	3,802	3,454	4,237	3,454
20,050	20,100	3,011	3,011	3,411	3,011	23,050	23,100	3,816	3,461	4,251	3,461
20,100	20,150	3,019	3,019	3,425	3,019	23,100	23,150	3,830	3,469	4,265	3,469
20,150	20,200	3,026	3,026	3,439	3,026	23,150	23,200	3,844	3,476	4,279	3,476
20,200	20,250	3,034	3,034	3,453	3,034	23,200	23,250	3,858	3,484	4,293	3,484
20,250	20,300	3,041	3,041	3,467	3,041	23,250	23,300	3,872	3,491	4,307	3,491
20,300	20,350	3,049	3,049	3,481	3,049	23,300	23,350	3,886	3,499	4,321	3,499
20,350	20,400	3,060	3,056	3,495	3,056	23,350	23,400	3,900	3,506	4,335	3,506
20,400	20,450	3,074	3,064	3,509	3,064	23,400	23,450	3,914	3,514	4,349	3,514
20,450	20,500	3,088	3,071	3,523	3,071	23,450	23,500	3,928	3,521	4,363	3,521
20,500	20,550	3,102	3,079	3,537	3,079	23,500	23,550	3,942	3,529	4,337	3,529
20,500	20,600	3,116	3,086	3,551	3,086	23,550	23,600	3,956	3,536	4,391	3,536
20,600	20,650	3,130	3,094	3,565	3,094	23,600	23,650	3,970	3,544	4,405	3,544
20,650	20,700	3,144	3,101	3,579	3,101	23,650	23,700	3,984	3,551	4,419	3,551
20,700	20,750	3,158	3,109	3,593	3,109	23,700	23,750	3,998	3,559	4,433	3,559
20,750	20,800	3,172	3,116	3,607	3,116	23,750	23,800	4,012	3,566	4,447	3,566
20,800	20,850	3,186	3,124	3,621	3,124	23,800	23,850	4,026	3,574	4,461	3,574
20,850	20,900	3,200	3,131	3,635	3,131	23,850	23,900	4,040	3,581	4,475	3.581
20,900	20,950	3,214	3,139	3,649	3,139	23,900	23,950	4,054	3,589	4,489	3,589
20,950	21,000	3,228	3,146	3,663	3,146	23,950	24,000	4,068	3,596	4,503	3,596

Source: 1991 Instructions for 1040A

Find the sales tax on purchases that have the following marked prices and sales tax rates.

1. $15.17 at 5%

2. $18.26 at $6\frac{1}{4}$%

3. $287.52 at $7\frac{3}{4}$%

4. $2.98 at 6.5%

What is the total price on items that have the following marked prices and sales tax rates?

5. $187.21 at 6%

6. $4.25 at 5.25%

Find the marked price on items that have the indicated total prices and tax rates.

7. $18.84 at 7%

8. $7.87 at 6.5%

9. $52.63 at 5.25%

10. A telephone bill of $84.15 is assessed state sales tax at the rate of 6% and excise tax at the rate of 10%. Find the total tax on the telephone bill.

11. Find the total telephone bill in Problem 10.

12. Find the assessed value of an apartment building (assessed at 40% of the market value) if the market value is $485,298.

13. Find the tax on a utility property if the assessed value of the property is $385,842 and the tax rate is 10.23%

14. Find the tax on a business property if the assessed value of the property is $176,297 and the tax rate is $7.56 per $100 of assessed value.

15. Find the tax on a home if the assessed value is $24,375 and the tax rate is $43.97 per $1,000.

16. Convert 36 mills to a decimal.

17. Find the tax on a property with an assessed value of $46,820 if the property tax rate is 87 mills.

18. A property has an assessed value of $72,000. The city tax rate for this property is $4.12 per $100 of assessed valuation. Find the city tax on the property.

19. The property in Problem 18 is located in a county that has set a property tax rate of $2.57 per $100. What is the county tax on the property?

20. Find the tax rate per $100 of assessed value that a county should set if the total assessed property value in the county is $31,800,000 and the total expenses are $957,300.

21. Use Table 16-3 to calculate the amount of tax owed by Sue Cowan if her taxable income is $52,817 and her filing status is single.
Use Schedule X.

22. Charles Wossum and his wife, Ruby, are filing their income tax jointly. Their combined taxable income is $29,872. How much tax must they pay? Use Table 16-2.

23. Juanita and Robert Gray have a gross income of $68,521, all of which is subject to income tax. They have two children and plan to file a joint income tax return. If each exemption is $2,150 and they have itemized deductions of $14,521, what is their taxable income?

BUSINESS MATH IN ACTION

A look at statistics that shape the nation

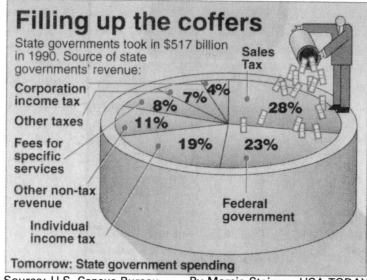

Filling up the coffers

State governments took in $517 billion in 1990. Source of state governments' revenue:

Corporation income tax

Other taxes

Fees for specific services

Other non-tax revenue

Individual income tax

Sales Tax

8% 7% 4%

11%

19% 23%

28%

Federal government

Tomorrow: State government spending

Source: U.S. Census Bureau   By Marcia Staimer, USA TODAY

QUESTIONS

1. How many billions of dollars of revenue do the states obtain from individual income tax?

2. What percent of the states' revenue comes from sales tax and the federal government?

3. How many billions of dollars of revenue come from sales tax and the federal government?

4. What percent of the states' revenue is generated by non-taxes and fees for specific services?

5. How many billions of dollars of revenue come from non-taxes and fees for specific services?

Stocks and Bonds

"Dow Plunges 300 Points," "Big Day on Wall Street," "Small Investors Hit It Big in Computer Stocks." These and other headlines in your daily paper underscore the important role of stocks and bonds. Without stocks and bonds, U.S. businesses—indeed the whole economy—would come to a grinding halt.

But just what are stocks and bonds? How are stocks different from bonds? Both stocks and bonds are sold by companies to raise money and bought by investors in the hopes of realizing a profit. But these financial instruments work in quite different ways, as you will see in this chapter.

17.1 Stocks

LEARNING OBJECTIVES

1. Read stock listings.
2. Calculate and distribute dividends.
3. Calculate current stock yield.
4. Compare price to earnings.
5. Find the cost of buying and selling stocks.
6. Calculate return on investment.

stock: a part ownership of a corporation; can be bought and sold.

share: one unit of stock.

preferred stock: a type of stock with preferential rights such as a fixed dividend (compare with common stock).

common stock: a share of ownership in a company, with voting rights (compare to preferred stock).

face value (par value): for stocks, the value at the time of issue; for bonds, usually $1,000.

stock certificate: the documents showing information of ownership.

dividend: an amount of money paid per share of stock from profits.

stock market: the buying or selling of stocks to the public; the location where such trades are made.

trade: a purchase or sale of stocks or bonds.

stock broker: a specialist in stock market trading and investments.

Any incorporated business can issue **stock.** Each **share** of stock represents partial ownership of the corporation. Thus, if a company issues 100 shares of stock and you own 50 of them, you would own half the company. (In real life, however, many corporations issue millions of shares of stock and have thousands or tens of thousands of owners.)

At the time the company issues (first sells) the stock, each share has a specific value, called the **face value (par value).** A person buying shares of stock receives a certificate of ownership, called a **stock certificate.** If the business is good, stockholders may receive a portion of the profits in the form of a **dividend** for each share they hold. Some stockholders also have voting rights in corporate affairs.

There are two basic types of stock: **preferred stock** and **common stock.** Holders of preferred stock receive certain preferential financial benefits over common stockholders. But common stockholders have voting rights in the company—one vote per share—that preferred stockholders do not have.

After the stock is issued, people buy and sell their shares in the **stock market** for prices that vary from day to day and within a day. The price of a given company's shares is affected by supply and demand: When more people want to buy than want to sell, the price tends to rise; when more people want to sell than want to buy, the price tends to fall. Keep in mind that for each sale (called a **trade**) there is both a buyer and seller at a given price, but supply and demand exert a pressure on the price to go up or down. Factors that affect demand include good news about a company's product, bad news of higher-than-expected business expenses, international events, or what people think the trend of the national economy or of the business will be.

The actual buying and selling of shares is done by a person called a **stock broker,** who specializes in work in the stock market. Usually a person who wishes to buy or sell stock contacts a broker, and the broker's representative at the actual trading location (such as at the New York Stock Exchange on Wall Street in New York or at the American Stock Exchange in Chicago) performs the transaction. The broker receives a *commission* for the services of both buying and selling stocks.

The daily prices of stocks, along with other information about the companies, are reported in newspapers. Here we look at listings from the *New York Times* to see how to read stock listings. Stock prices are listed in dollars and fractions of a dollar such as eighths, fourths, and halves. Thus $\frac{1}{8}$ means $0.125 (12$\frac{1}{2}$ cents), $\frac{1}{4}$ means $0.25 (25 cents), $\frac{1}{2}$ means $0.50, $\frac{3}{8}$ means $0.375, and so forth. Positive and negative signs show the direction of change. Thus $+\frac{1}{8}$ is read "up one-eighth" and means the price of each share has increased by one-eighth of a dollar, or $\frac{1}{8}$ **point.** A point is $1. Similarly, $-1\frac{3}{4}$ means the price of one share of stock has gone down by one and three-fourths points, or $1.75.

point: in stock listings, a number representing $1.

TIPS & TRAPS

Calculations are generally made using a calculator; therefore, you may want to memorize the decimal equivalents for eighths.

$\frac{1}{8} = 0.125$ $\frac{2}{8} = \frac{1}{4} = 0.25$ $\frac{3}{8} = 0.375$ $\frac{4}{8} = \frac{1}{2} = 0.5$

$\frac{5}{8} = 0.625$ $\frac{6}{8} = \frac{3}{4} = 0.75$ $\frac{7}{8} = 0.875$

Reading Stock Listings

Figure 17-1 shows a sample of the type of stock listings reported in the *New York Times*.

EXAMPLE 1

Referring to Figure 17-1, answer the following questions:

How many shares of Atlantic Richfield (Atl Rich) were traded today?

11,668 hundred or 1,166,800 shares

What was the difference between the high price and low price of the day?

$$\begin{array}{lll} \text{High} & 104\frac{3}{8} = & 103\frac{11}{8} \\ -\text{Low} & 101\frac{3}{4} = & 101\frac{6}{8} \\ \hline & & 1\frac{5}{8} \end{array}$$

point difference, or $\$1.62\frac{1}{2}$ per share

What was the closing price yesterday?

Today's closing price is $103\frac{1}{8}$, which is up $\frac{5}{8}$ from yesterday's close.

$103\frac{1}{8} - \frac{5}{8} = 102\frac{1}{2}$, yesterday's closing price

①	②	③	④	⑤	⑥	⑦	⑧	⑨	⑩	⑪
52 Weeks High	Low	Stock	Div	Yld %	PE Ratio	Sales 100s	High	Low	Last	Chg
37⅝	29¾	AtlGas	2.04	6.4	17	1724	32⅝	31⅜	32	− ⅝
41⅞	33¾	AtlEnrg	3.00	7.3	12	1047	41¾	40¾	41⅛	...
134¼	99⅛	AtlRich	5.50	5.3	23	11668	104⅜	101¾	103⅛	+ ⅝
888	679½	AtlRc prf	3.00	.4	...	1	693¾	693¾	693¾	−27⅞
320	240	AtlRc prf	2.80	1.1	...	1	247	247	247	+ 1½
8⅜	5⅝	Atlas		...	...	522	6½	6¼	6⅜	...
23	16¼	ATMOS	1.24	6.1	16	521	20⅞	20¼	20⅜	− ⅛
24¼	9⅛	Atwod	.57e	4.3	13	6948	13⅜	12⅜	13⅛	+ ⅜
10¼	4½	AudVd		...	19	346	8½	8⅛	8⅜	− ⅛
14⅛	7⅞	Augat		...	...	827	10⅛	9¾	9⅞	...
12¼	7⅞	Austr	.13e	1.3	...	1911	10⅝	9⅞	10¼	+ ⅛
11¼	9⅞	AustStk		...	...	333	11⅛	10⅞	11	+ ⅛
49	29½	AutoDt	.40	.9	26	12158	46⅞	44⅛	44¼	− 1⅜
42	13⅛	AutoZn		...	51	6227	40	36¾	38⅝	− ⅜
6⅛	3⅛	Avalon		...	...	84	3⅜d	3⅛	3⅛	− ⅜
28	18½	AVMCO	.40	1.6	18	322	27	24½	24½	− 2¾
27⅞	20	AveryD	.80	2.9	27x	13223u	27⅞	26⅛	27⅜	+ 1½
30	23¼	Avnet	.60	2.3	18	4524	26½	25¼	26⅜	+ ⅞
51⅛	37⅛	Avon	1.40a	2.9	26	9405	49	47	48½	+ ⅞
28⅞	15¼	Aydin	.50e	2.1	12	1860	27	24	24⅜	− 2
43¼	34⅜	BCE g	2.56	6.3	...	3346	40¾	39⅛	40⅜	+ ⅞
16¼	10½	BET	1.50e	13.6	9	228	12	11	11	− ¾
29⅝	12⅝	BJS		...	9	6273	13⅝	12⅞	13½	...
12⅛	4⅛	BMC		...	8	3017u	12⅛	11¼	11½	− ¼

Figure 17-1
(Source: *New York Times*)

Columns 1 and 2 tell you the highest and lowest prices at which the stock has sold in the last year (52 weeks).

Column 3 tells you the name of the company (in abbreviated form).

Column 4 tells you the amount of dividend paid out on the stock last year.

Column 5 tells you what percent of the current price of the stock last year's dividend represents; if no dividend was paid last year, this column will read "...".

Column 6 tells you the stock's price earnings ratio, a measure we will discuss later in this section.

Column 7 tells you the volume (number) of shares traded that day; it is expressed in 100s, so a figure of 105 means 105,000 shares were traded.

Columns 8, 9, and 10 tell you the high price, low price, and last price at which the stock sold that day.

Column 11 tells you how much today's closing price differs from yesterday's closing price for that stock.

Calculating and Distributing Dividends

Now let's take a closer look at some of the more complex information in each stock listing, starting with column 4, "Dividends."

A corporation's board of directors can vote to reinvest any profits into the business or can declare a *dividend* with some or all of the profits. The dividend can be expressed either as a percentage of the par value or as a dollar amount. It is usually declared quarterly (every 3 months), but if a business is poor or if the directors so decide, there may be no dividends at all.

Sometimes dividends vary, depending on whether the stock is preferred stock or common stock. Holders of preferred stock (which has the symbol "pf" after its name in stock listings) are entitled to first claim on the corporation's profits and assets. Thus, if a company has limited profits, it must pay all its preferred shareholders dividends before it can pay any of its common stock shareholders. Similarly, in case of bankruptcy, preferred stockholders must be paid before common stockholders. However, only holders of common stock are entitled to a vote in corporate affairs (one vote per share).

Dividends on various kinds of preferred stock are usually fixed, though with *participating preferred stock,* the stockholder can receive additional dividends if the company does well. *Convertible preferred stock* allows the stock to be exchanged for a certain number of shares of common stock later. And with **cumulative preferred stock,** dividends are earned every year. If no dividends are paid one year, the amounts not paid are recorded. These **dividends in arrears** must be paid when money becomes available before other preferred or common stock dividends are paid.

cumulative preferred stock: a type of stock in which dividends are earned each year even if the company does not pay a dividend.

dividends in arrears: dividends on cumulative preferred stock that have not been paid previously but that have priority when dividends are paid.

STEP BY STEP

Distributing Dividends from an Amount of Available Money

Step 1. First pay dividends in arrears. (Multiply the number of shares held by preferred stockholders by the rate.)

Step 2. Subtract the amount of dividends in arrears from the total amount. This is the subtotal.

Step 3. From this subtotal, pay the present year's preferred stockholders. (Multiply the number of preferred shares held by stockholders by the rate.)

Step 4. Subtract this payment from the subtotal.

Step 5. Divide the remaining amount by the number of common shares held by stockholders. This is the dividend per share for common stockholders.

EXAMPLE 2

Your company has issued 20,000 shares of cumulative preferred stock that will earn dividends at $0.60 per share and 100,000 shares of common stock. Last year you paid no dividends; this year there is $250,000 available for dividends. How are the dividends to be distributed to the preferred and common stockholders?

Preferred stockholders received no dividends last year so this year's dividends in arrears must be paid:

$$20,000 \times \$0.60 = \$12,000$$

The remaining money ($250,000 − $12,000 = $238,000) is distributed to the preferred and common stockholders for this year as follows:

To preferred stockholders: $20,000 \times \$0.60 = \$12,000$

Amount left for common stockholders ($238,000 − $12,000 = $226,000) is divided among all the common stockholders.

To common stockholders: $\dfrac{\$226,000}{100,000} = \$2.26$ per share

Notice that the $0.60 dividend per share for the preferred stock is a guaranteed but fixed rate, whereas the dividend per share of common stock has the *potential* to be higher (or lower) than that, but with no guarantee. Last year's common stock owners received no dividends, but this year they received more than did the preferred stockholders for 2 years. Since dividends are income to the stockholder, they are one measure of the desirability of owning a particular stock.

Calculating Current Stock Yield

The fifth column in Figure 17-1, "Yield %," is sometimes called the current **yield** for the stock. It is a comparative measure of the dividend. It tells (as a percent) how large the dividend is compared to today's closing price for the stock.

yield: for stocks, current yield is annual earnings per share (dividends) divided by today's closing price; for bonds, current yield is annual earnings per bond (interest) divided by today's closing price.

STEP BY STEP

Calculating Current Stock Yield

Step 1. Divide the annual dividend per share by today's closing price (expressed as a decimal):

$$\text{Current stock yield} = \frac{\text{annual dividend per share}}{\text{today's closing price}}$$

Step 2. Express the answer as a percent, rounded to the nearest tenth.

EXAMPLE 3

For Figure 17-1, ATMOS has a $1.24 dividend. Today's closing price is $20\frac{3}{8}$. Calculate the current stock yield.

$$\text{Current stock yield} = \frac{1.24}{20.375} = 0.0608588$$

$$= 6.1\%$$

This matches the figure for ATMOS in the "Yield %" column.

Notice that because the numerator of the fraction is the amount of the dividend, if no dividend has been declared, there can be no yield. This situation is indicated by three dots in the yield column.

It might seem as if a large yield would always be more desirable than a small one, but if a company is putting its profits into redevelopment instead of dividends, there may be a small yield now. However, if the company becomes a stronger business, the stock price itself might rise. If an investor sold the stock at that later time, the return on the investment then could be high, even though the yield figure now is low.

Comparing Price to Earnings

price–earnings (PE) ratio: closing price per share of stock divided by the annual net income per share.

The sixth column in Figure 17-1; "PE ratio," gives the **price–earnings (PE) ratio.** It is a measure of how much the stock is selling for compared with its per share earnings. The figures used in the calculation are the current price per share (at the close of the business day) and the annual net income per share for the last four quarters. (The last figure is reported by the company and is found by dividing the company's total earnings by the number of shares outstanding.)

STEP BY STEP

Calculating the PE Ratio

Step 1. Divide the closing price per share by the annual dividend per share:

$$\text{PE ratio} = \frac{\text{closing price per share}}{\text{annual dividend per share}}$$

Step 2. Round to the nearest whole number.

EXAMPLE 4

ATMOS (Figure 17-1) has a closing price of $20\frac{3}{8}$ and annual net income per share of $1.24. What is the PE ratio?

$$\text{PE ratio} = \frac{20\frac{3}{8}}{1.24} = \frac{20.375}{1.24}$$

$$= 16.43145$$

$$= 16$$

which matches the figure for ATMOS in the "PE ratio" column.

The PE ratio can vary, usually between 3 and 50. A high value indicates a high price relative to a stock's earnings. This situation occurs if the price is too high (the stock is overpriced) or if earnings have been low, either as a result of poor business or if the company is not yet earning to its potential. A low value for the PE ratio shows a lower price compared to earnings usually because the price is too low (the stock is undervalued) or people feel the business' potential is poor. If a PE ratio is not given in the stock listings, the company probably has lost money during the past year.

Stocks cannot be judged on any one aspect, though. One stock may have a high dividend, a high yield, and yet a high PE ratio. A cautious investor "follows the stock market" and seeks advice from knowledgeable persons in order to tell whether a particular company meets his or her investment needs.

Finding the Cost of Buying and Selling Stocks

For each purchase or sale of stock, the commission, an added cost of trading stock, must be considered in addition to the purchase or sale price. Brokers' commissions can vary; for example, *discount brokers* usually charge less because they do not give advice or provide background research about stocks but only handle buy–sell transactions. Also, the number of shares traded affects the cost of the sale. A group of 100 shares or a multiple of 100 shares is called a *round lot;* a group of less than 100 is called an *odd lot,* and there is an extra charge for trading it.

EXAMPLE 5

Your broker charges 2% of the stock price for trading round lots and an additional 1%, on the odd-lot portion. You buy 250 shares of Avon Products (Figure 17-1) at 47. What is your total cost for the purchase?

Cost for 250 shares	$250 \times \$47 = \$11,750.00$
Commission on round lot	$0.02 \times 200 \times \$47 = \$\ \ \ \ 188.00$
Commission on odd-lot portion	$0.03 \times 50 \times \$47 = \$\ \ \ \ \ \ 70.50$

The cost of purchase of stock:

$$\$11,750.00 + \$188.00 + \$70.50 = \$12,008.50$$

EXAMPLE 6

After a year you sell the 250 shares of Avon Products for $54 per share. Your broker charges the same commission percentages for selling the stock. What are your total receipts from the sale?

Proceeds from 250 shares	$250 \times \$54 = \$13,500.00$
Commission on round lot	$0.02 \times 200 \times \$54 = \$\ \ \ \ 216.00$
Commission on odd-lot portion	$0.03 \times 50 \times \$54 = \$\ \ \ \ \ \ 81.00$

Total receipt from sale of stock:

$$\$13,500.00 - \$216.00 - \$81.00 = \$13,203.00$$

TIPS & TRAPS

> Commission increases the cost of a purchase and decreases the profit from a sale. (Add the commission when figuring cost; subtract the commission when figuring profit.)

return on investment (ROI): total gain on a purchase divided by the total cost of the purchase.

Subtracting all commissions and adding in all dividends allows you to get a truer picture of the stock's contribution to your finances. This contribution, called **return on investment (ROI),** is expressed in relation to the cost of purchase as a percent to the nearest hundredth.

STEP BY STEP

Calculating ROI (a gain is assumed)

Step 1. Find the net gain by subtracting the total cost of purchase from the total receipts of sale.

Step 2. Add the amount of annual dividends to the net gain to find the total gain.

Step 3. Divide total gain by cost of purchase:

$$\text{ROI} = \frac{\text{total gain}}{\text{cost of purchase}}$$

Step 4. Express the answer as a percent, rounded to the nearest hundredth.

EXAMPLE 7

What is the return on your investment in Avon Products stock? (See Examples 5 and 6.) Assume your dividends during the past year were $1 per share.

Total receipt from sale ($13,203) minus total cost of purchase of stock ($12,008.50) gives the net gain, $1,194.50.

Adding dividends ($250 for all the shares) gives a total gain of $1,444.50.

$$\text{ROI} = \frac{\text{total gain}}{\text{cost of purchase}}$$

$$= \frac{\$1,444.50}{\$12,008.50}$$

$$= 0.120289$$

$$0.1202897 = 12.03\%$$

 Self-Check 17.1

Use information about the common stock for Audio Video (Aud Vd) (Figure 17-1).

1. What was the closing price in dollars and cents?

2. During the last year, what was its high price? Its low price?

3. What is the difference between today's high price and low price?

4. What was yesterday's closing price?

Your company has $200,000 to distribute in dividends. There are 20,000 shares of preferred stock, which earn dividends at $0.50 per share, and 80,000 shares of common stock.

5. How much money goes to preferred stockholders?

6. How much goes to common stockholders?

7. How much per share does a common stockholder receive in dividends?

8. The stock of a new company is selling for $24\frac{1}{2}$ and the company has annual income of $1.75 per share. What is its PE ratio?

You buy 250 shares of Intrepidation stock at $4 per share. Your broker charges 2% of the stock price for round lots and an additional 1% for odd lots.

9. What was the commission on the round lot? On the odd lot?

10. What was your total cost for purchasing the stock?

11. If you sell these shares through the same broker for $5 per share, what will be the commission on the round lot? On the odd lot?

12. What are your total receipts from the sale?

13. Do you have a gain or a loss? How much?

14. You purchased 100 shares of stock at $5 per share and sold them for $7 per share. During that time you received $0.50 per share in dividends. What is your return on this investment? (Disregard commissions.)

17.2 Bonds

LEARNING OBJECTIVES

1. Read bond listings.
2. Find the cost of buying and selling bonds.
3. Calculate current bond yield.
4. Compare investments.

After time passes, a corporation may need to raise more money than its initial offering of stock produced. It can then issue more stock, thereby creating more shares or ownership. However, the company management may be reluctant to do so because additional shares lessen the ownership power (dilute the rights) of the existing stockholders. To raise the needed money, the company may decide to borrow it for a short term from a bank, or for a longer term (5 years or more) from the public, by selling bonds. In exchange for money from the sale, the company issues a **bond,** a promise to repay the money at a specific later date and in the meantime to pay interest annually.

A bond has a **face value (par value),** usually $1,000, a date of repayment **(maturity date),** and a fixed *rate of interest* per year. Since a bond obligates the company to future repayment, the public's judgment of the company's future will affect sales of a bond. Investors also look closely at the amount of interest to be paid.

Since bonds are a legal debt of the corporation, if the company goes bankrupt, the bondholders' claims have priority over those of the stockholders. Bonds of businesses that are bankrupt or in financial difficulty, called *junk bonds,* can thus yield a high return—or be next to worthless—making them a risky and speculative investment.

In addition to these **corporate bonds** issued by businesses, state and local governments sell *municipal bonds* and the federal government sells *treasury bonds.* Government bonds may be often attractive to investors be-

bond: a legal promise to repay an amount of money at a fixed time, with annual interest, given by a corporation, municipality, or the federal government.

face value (par value): for stocks, the amount at the time of issue; for bonds, usually $1,000.

maturity date: the date on which a corporation will repay the face value of a bond.

corporate bond: a bond issued by a corporation, as distinguished from a minicipal or treasury bond.

cause the interest payments on them may be exempt from federal income tax. In this text, however, we will deal only with corporate bonds, which come in various types. There are *coupon bonds* in which the investor sends in a coupon at a specified time to receive interest. There are *registered bonds* in which the investor receives interest automatically by being listed with the corporation. *Convertible bonds* have a provision that allows them to be converted to stock. *Recallable bonds* allow the corporation to repurchase the bonds before the maturity date.

Once bonds are issued, people buy and sell them at varying prices in the **bond market.** Here, as in the stock market, "market conditions" prevail: A bond with high interest payments may be attractive to investors, so its price may rise, causing the bond to *sell at a premium* (a **premium bond**). Or, if interest payments are low, a bond price may tend to drop in order to attract investors, causing the bond to *sell at a discount* (a **discount bond**).

bond market: the buying or selling of bonds to the public; the location where such trades are made.

premium bond: a bond selling for more than its face value.

discount bond: a bond selling for less than its face value.

TIPS & TRAPS

Keep in mind that, no matter what the market price of a bond, the corporation pays interest on the face value of $1,000 per bond.

Reading Bond Listings

Figure 17-2 shows how bonds are listed in the *New York Times*. Let's look at the nature of each column briefly.

Column 1 tells you the name of the issuing company, the interest rate, and the last two digits of the year of maturity.

Column 2 tells you the current yield, which is the ratio of the interest being paid per bond versus the current price of the bond.

Column 3 tells you the volume (number) of bonds traded; note that, unlike stock listings, this figure does not represent hundreds of bonds traded, so if the figure reads "10" it means that 10, not 1,000 bonds, have been traded that day. Each bond has a face value of $1,000.

Column 4 tells you the percent of the face value for which the bond was selling at the close of the selling day; a figure of $97\frac{3}{4}$ in this column would mean the bond sold for 0.9775 times $1,000, or $977.50 per bond.

Column 5 tells you the change in percent of face value for which the bond sold today versus yesterday.

Note that, because there is less activity in the bond market than in the stock market, daily prices vary less, so the day's high, low, and closing prices tend to be the same and only closing prices are shown. A quick look at the closing price column in Figure 17-2 reveals only two bonds selling at exactly par value (100%). The discount bonds have a listing less than 100; the premium bonds have a listing greater than 100. ArizP is selling at a discount, whereas four of the Amoco bonds are selling bonds are selling at a premium. Some of the symbols used in the listing are explained in Figure 17-3.

STEP BY STEP

Reading and Calculating the Price of a Bond from a Bond Listing

Step 1. Find the price listed (Last). It is expressed as a percent of $1,000.

Step 2. Change the percent to a decimal.

	①	②	③	④	⑤
Bonds		Cur Yld	Vol	Last	Net Chg.
AMAX 8⅝01		9.0	1	96¼	+ ¼
AMAX 14½94		12.6	257	115	− ¼
ABrnd 8½03		8.3	29	102½	+ ⅝
AmGenl 9⅜08		9.3	82	101	− ¾
AmStor 01		cv	105	103½	− 1½
ATT 5⅝95		5.7	153	99	+ ⅞
ATT 5½97		5.9	138	93⅞	− 1⅜
ATT 6s00		6.6	1423	90½	+ ½
ATT 5⅛01		6.1	390	83⅞	+ ¾
ATT 7s01		7.3	2141	95⅞	+ ⅞
ATT 7⅛03		7.4	1620	96⅛	+ 1¼
ATT 8⅝26		8.6	2741	100⅞	+ ¼
ATT 8⅝31		8.5	2168	101	+ 1⅛
ATT 7⅛02		7.3	1590	97⅛	+ ⅞
ATT 8⅛22		8.4	9048	97	+ 1
viAmes 10s95f		...	19	17¼	+ ¼
viAmes 7½14f		cv	1024	4⅞	+ ⅛
Amoco 6s98		6.2	28	96⅞	+ ⅞
Amoco 8⅜05		8.2	46	102	...
Amoco 7⅞07		7.9	19	100	− ½
Amoco 7⅛96		7.6	20	103½	− ⅜
Amoco 8⅝16		8.3	162	103⅞	− ⅛
AmocoCda 7⅜13		6.8	207	108	− 1
Ancp 13⅞02f		cv	31	104¾	...
Andarko 6¼14		7.2	291	86¾	− ¼
Anhr 8s96		7.8	39	102¾	− ¼
Anhr 8⅝16		8.5	177	101½	+ 1
Apache 7½00		cv	720	99¼	− ¾
ArizP 7.45s02		7.8	55	95	− ½
Arml 5.9s92		6.0	21	99	...
Arml 8.7s95		9.5	33	92	+ 1
Arml 9.2s00		10.8	605	85½	+ 1⅛
Arml 8½01		10.5	358	81	+ 4⅞
Arml 13½94		12.9	279	105	+ ½
AshO 8.2s02		8.2	137	100	− ⅛
AshO 11.1s04		10.7	3	104	+ 1
AshO 6¾14		cv	245	88	− 2
ARich 8⅝00		8.4	18	103	+ 2
ARich 7.7s00		7.8	5	99¼	

Figure 17-2
(Source: *New York Times*)

Step 3. Multiply this by $1,000.

Step 4. Express the answer in dollars and cents. This is the dollar price of one bond.

EXAMPLE 8

To calculate yesterday's bond price from today's listing of ABrnd (Figure 17-2), notice that the bond closed at $102\frac{1}{2}\%$ of its face value, which was up $\frac{5}{8}\%$ from yesterday's close. So yesterday's listing must have been $\frac{5}{8}\%$ less:

$101\frac{4}{8}\% - \frac{5}{8}\% = 100\frac{7}{8}\%$ (or a listing of $100\frac{4}{8}\%$)

$101\frac{7}{8}\% = 1.01875$; $1.01875 \times \$1,000 = \$1,018.75$, yesterday's bond price

Finding the Cost of Buying and Selling Bonds

Broker's fees for trading bonds vary, but for purposes of our discussion, let us consider the commission to be $5 for each bond traded.

STEP BY STEP

Calculating the Net Receipt from a Sale of Bonds

Step 1. Multiply the price of one bond (in dollars) times the number of bonds. This gives you the gross receipt from the sale of bonds, before commission.

Step 2. Calculate the commission:

Commission = number of bonds × commission charge per bond

Step 3. Subtract the commission from the gross receipts:

Net receipts = gross receipts − commission

EXAMPLE 9

You sell three AmStor bonds at the day's closing price (see Figure 17-2). What will be your net receipt from the sale of the bonds (after deducting broker's fees)?

The price of one bond, as listed, is $103\frac{1}{2}\%$ of face value. The price, in dollars, is $1035.00 per bond.

For three bonds, your receipts will be $3,105.00, before commission.

For three bonds, commission is 3 × $5 = $15.

Subtract $15 commission for the three bonds to get $3090.00 as your net receipts from the sale.

Calculating Current Bond Yield

Investors in bonds, like investors in stocks, want to know the **yield** of their investments. In Figure 17-2 the "Cur Yld" (current yield) column gives a measure of how profitable the investment is. *Current bond yield*, sometimes called *average annual yield*, compares annual earnings (interest) with the closing price of a bond. It is expressed as a percentage of face value.

yield: for stocks current yield is annual earnings per share (dividends) divided by today's closing price; for bonds, current yield is annual earnings per bond (interest) divided by today's closing price.

Bond Tables Explained

Bonds, interest-bearing debt certificates, are quoted in percentage of the par or face value of the bond, represented as 100. The name of the issuing company is followed by the original coupon or interest rate and the last two digits of the year of maturity.

Current yield represents the annual percentage return to the purchaser at the current price. The **Last** column refers to the bond's closing price and **Net Chg.** is the difference between the week's closing price and the previous week's closing price. The majority of bonds and all municipal or tax excempt bonds are not listed on exchanges; rather, they are traded over the counter.

Other footnotes: **cv**–Bonds is convertible into stock under specified conditions. **cf**–Certificates. **dc**–Deep discount issue. **f**–Dealt in flat–traded without accrued interest. **m**–Matured bonds. **st**–Stamped. **ww**–With warrants. **x**–Ex interest. **xw**–Without warrants. **vi**–in bankruptcy or receivership or being reorganized under the Bankruptcy Act, or securities assumed by such companies. **zr**–Zero coupon issue.

Figure 17-3
(Source: *New York Times*)

STEP BY STEP

Calculating Current Bond Yield

Step 1. Divide the annual interest per bond in dollars by the current price per bond in dollars:

$$\text{Current bond yield} = \frac{\text{annual interest per bond}}{\text{current price per bond}}$$

Step 2. Express the answer as a percent.

EXAMPLE 10

What is the current bond yield for the first AMAX bond (Figure 17-2)?

$8\frac{5}{8}\%$ interest gives $0.08625 \times \$1,000$, or 86.25, interest per bond. The current price is $96\frac{1}{4}\%$ of face value, which is $962.50 per bond. The current bond yield is

$$\frac{\$86.25}{\$962.50} = 0.0896$$

$0.0896 = 9\%$, which matches the figure listed under "Cur Yld." (If commission were to be included in this calculation, the yield would decrease.)

Interest is paid on the $1,000 face value of the bond. Although the stated interest rate for the AMAX bond is $8\frac{5}{8}\%$, the current bond yield is higher, at 9%. A discounted bond always has a higher yield than its stated interest rate, while a premium bond always has a lower yield than its stated interest rate.

Comparing Investments

Many times an investor wants to know which of two investments is performing better. The investor could compare the amount in dollars that would be received by each as of today if the stock or bonds in question were to be sold. But since there may be quite different amounts invested in each, a better measure of comparative performance is the yield of each.

STEP BY STEP

Comparing the Current Yield of Two Investments

Step 1. Find the current yield, as a percent, of the first stock or bond.

Step 2. Find the current yield, as a percent, of the second stock or bond.

Step 3. Compare the answers in steps 1 and 2 to determine which is greater.

EXAMPLE 11

Which of the two Anhr bonds (Figure 17-2) is producing the greater yield?

Anhr 8s96 yield is $\dfrac{\$80}{\$1027.50} = 7.8\%$. The "s" is used to separate the whole numbers.

Anhr $8\frac{5}{8}$16 yield is $\dfrac{\$86.25}{\$1015.00} = 8.5\%$.

The second bond has the higher yield.

Self-Check 17.2

15. What is the dollar price of a bond that is listed as $98\frac{1}{2}$?

16. From Figure 17-2, what was yesterday's closing bond price for Apache?

17. A bond pays 8% annual interest and is selling for 102% of face value. What is its current yield?

18. Which of the two AMAX bonds (Figure 17-2) is producing the greater yield?

Summary

Topic	Page	What to Remember	Examples
Reading stock prices	507	Stock prices are listed in dollars and fractions of a dollar (eighths, fourths, halves).	A stock is listed as having a closing price of $21\frac{3}{4}$, up $\frac{1}{4}$ from yesterday's close. What is the price today? What was it yesterday? $21.75 today; $21.50 yesterday
Distribution of dividends	508	When dividends are distributed, dividends in arrears have first priority, then current dividends on preferred stock, then common stock dividends.	$500,000 is available for dividends, including $20,000 for dividends in arrears and $20,000 for current preferred stock dividends. How much will be given for common stock dividends? $500,000 - $40,000 = $460,000
Amount of common stock dividend (dividend per share)	508	To find the amount of a common stock dividend, divide the total amount available for common stock dividends by the total number of shares of common stocks. This is the dividend per share.	$460,000 is available for common stock dividends. There are 300,000 shares of common stock. What is the dividend per share? $\dfrac{\$460,000}{300,000} = \$1.53$ per share
Stock commission	511	Commission is charged on both buying and selling stocks. Rates vary. There is usually a higher commission for odd lots (less than 100 shares) than for round lots (multiples of 100 shares).	Taking stock commission to be 2% of the stock price for round lots and an additional 1% for the odd-lot portion (throughout this Summary), what is the commission on the purchase of 350 shares of stock selling at 13 per share? Commission on round lot: $0.02 \times 300 \times \$13 = \$78$ on odd-lot portion: $0.03 \times 50 \times \$13 = \$19.50$ Total commission: $97.50

Topic	Page	What to Remember	Examples
Cost of a stock purchase	511	Compute the cost of the stock and add commission to get the total cost of a purchase.	You purchase 350 shares of stock at $13 per share. Commission is $97.50. What is your total cost for the purchase? Cost of stock: $$350 \times \$13 = \$4,550$$ Commission $\qquad$ $\$\ \ \ 97.50$ Cost of purchase; $\qquad$ $\overline{\$4,647.50}$
Current stock yield	509	Divide annual dividends per share by today's closing price and express as a percent. This "yield %" is given in the stock listings. It is a measure of income compared to today's price.	Stock X has a $0.75 dividend and a closing price of 25. What is its current yield? $\dfrac{.75}{25} = 3\%$
Price-earnings ratio (PE ratio)	510	Divide closing price per share by the amount of annual earnings (dividends) per share, and express as a whole number. The PE ratio is a measure of the company's performance; it compares the current price to earnings. Interpretations of the PE ratio may vary.	Stock Y has a closing price of $16\frac{7}{8}$ and an annual net income per share of $1.50. What is the PE ratio? $\dfrac{16.875}{1.50} = 11.25$ PE ratio is 11. Price is "eleven times" earnings.
Receipt from a sale of stock	511	Compute receipt from stock and subtract commission to get final receipt from the sale.	You sell 350 shares of stock at $15 per share. What is your final receipt from the sale? From stock: $$350 \times \$15 = \$5,250$$ Commission: $$0.02 \times 300 \times 15 = 90$$ $$0.03 \times 50 \times 15 = 22.50$$ $$\$90 + \$22.50 = \$112.50$$ Final receipt from sale: $$\$5,250 - \$112.50 = \$5,137.50$$
Return on investment (ROI)	512	Find total gain (total receipt minus total cost plus dividends). Divide by total cost and express as a percent rounded to the nearest hundredth. The ROI figure is a measure of how much gain was "returned" to you, compared with the amount invested.	Assume your total gain from a stock is $780 (that is, $5,137.50 − $4,647.50 + dividends of $290). Assume that your total cost is $4,647.50. What is the return on your investment? $\dfrac{\$780}{\$4,647.50} = 16.8\%$
Reading bond prices	514	Bond prices are listed as a percent of face value. 100% of face value is $1,000.	A bond is listed as having a closing price of $80\frac{3}{8}$, up $\frac{1}{8}$ from yesterday's close. What is the price today? What was it yesterday? $80\frac{3}{8}\%$ of face value is $0.80375 \times \$1,000$ or $803.75 per bond today. $80\frac{3}{8}\% - \frac{1}{8}\% = 80\frac{1}{4}\%$ or $802.50 per bond yesterday.

Topic	Page	What to Remember	Examples
Reading bond volume	514	Volume figure is the actual number of bonds traded. Each bond has a face value of $1,000.	Bond A has 15 listed in the "volume" column. How many bonds were traded today? 15
Bond interest	514	Bonds pay annual interest. Interest is computed on face value, $1,000, regardless of the market price of the bond.	A bond listed as $6\frac{5}{8}91$ will pay how much interest annually? $6\frac{5}{8}\%$ of $1,000 is $66.25
Reading bond maturity date	514	The year the bond comes to maturity is given as the last two digits of the year, immediately following the annual interest rate.	What is the maturity date of a bond listed as $6\frac{5}{8}91$? The bond matured in 1991 as indicated by 91 after interest rate of $6\frac{5}{8}$.
Bond commission	515	Commission is charged on both buying and selling bonds. Rates vary.	Taking bond commission to be $5 per bond (throughout this Summary), what is the commission on the purchase of 5 bonds at $98\frac{1}{2}$ per bond? $5 \times \$5 = \$25$
Cost of a bond purchase	515	Compute cost of bonds and add commission to get the total cost of a purchase.	You purchase five bonds listed at $98\frac{1}{2}$. What is the total cost of the purchase? For one bond: $ 985 For five bonds: $4,925 Commission: $ 25 Total cost of purchase: $4,950
Current bond yield	515	Divide the annual interest per share by the current price (in dollars) per bond and express as a percent. The yield figure is given in the bond listings. It is a measure of income compared to the current price of the bond.	Bond B has 8% annual interest and a closing price of 102. What is the current bond yield? $\dfrac{80}{1,020} = 7.8\%$

Self-Check Solutions

1. $8.38 ($8\frac{3}{8} = 8.375$)

2. $8\frac{1}{2}$ points ($8) 0.50; $8\frac{1}{8}$ points ($8.13)

3. $8\frac{1}{2} - 8\frac{1}{8} = \frac{3}{8}$ points ($0.38)

4. $8\frac{3}{8} + \frac{1}{8} = 8\frac{1}{2}$ pts ($8.50)

5. $20,000 \times \$0.50 = \$10,000$

6. $200,000 - \$10,000 = \$190,000$

7. $\dfrac{\$190,000}{80,000} = \$2.38$ ($2.375) per share

8. PE ratio $= \dfrac{\$24.50}{\$1.75} = 14$

9. $0.02 \times 200 \times \$4 = \$16$; $0.03 \times 50 \times \$4 = \$6$

10. Cost of stock: $250 \times \$4 = \$1,000$; commission: $16 + \$6 = \$22$. Total cost: $1,022

11. $0.02 \times 200 \times \$5 = \$20$; $0.03 \times 50 \times \$5 = \$7.50$

12. Received for stock: $250 \times \$5 = \$1,250$; commission: $27.50. Total receipts: $1,222.50

13. Gain: $1,222.50 - $1,022 = $200.50

14. Receipt from sale: $100 \times \$7$ $= \$700$
Dividends: $100 \times \$0.50 = \$\ 50$
Total gain: $\overline{\$750}$
Cost of purchase: $100 \times \$5$ $= \$500$
Net gain: $\$750 - \$500 = \$250$
Rate of return $= \dfrac{\$250}{\$500} = 0.5$, or 50%

15. $98\frac{1}{2}\%$ of $1,000 = 0.985 \times \$1,000 = \$985$

16. Today's closing price is $99\frac{1}{4}$, down $\frac{3}{4}$ from yesterday's closing price. So yesterday's price was $99\frac{1}{4} + \frac{3}{4}$, or 100(100% of face value or $1,000).

17. $0.08 \times \$1,000 = \$80$; $0.02 \times \$1,000 = \$20$;
Current yield $= \dfrac{\$80}{\$1,020} = 0.0784$, or 7.8%

18. AMAX $8\frac{5}{8}\%$ bond has a yield of $\dfrac{\$86.25}{\$962.50} = 0.0896$, or 9.0%.

AMAX $14\frac{1}{2}\%$ bond has a yield of $\dfrac{\$145}{\$1,150} = 0.12608$, or 12.6%.

End of Chapter Problems

Section 17.1

For Problems 1 to 4 and 10 to 14, refer to Figure 17-4.

① 52 Weeks High	② 52 Weeks Low	③ Stock	④ Div	⑤ Yld %	⑥ PE Ratio	⑦ Sales 100s	⑧ High	⑨ Low	⑩ Last	⑪ Chg
33	16⅞	Heilig s	.32	1.0	23	2854	32⅝	31	31⅝	− 1⅛
48⅝	33⅝	Heinz	1.08	2.8	16	18421	40¼	38⅞	39¼	− ⅞
43¾	26½	HeleneC	.20	.5	24	811	39¼	38¾	39	...
29¼	18	HelmP	.46	2.2	40	1801	21⅜	20½	20⅝	− ⅜
50⅝	32½	Herculs	2.24	4.5	17	6601u	50⅝	47¾	49½	− ⅛
45¼	36½	Hrshey	.98	2.3	17	8484	43⅜	41½	42¼	− ⅛
78	44½	HewlPk	.80	1.1	21	38254	76¼	72⅞	73	− 2½
16⅝	10¼	Hexcel	.44	3.5	20	901	13⅛	12⅜	12¾	− ⅜
16⅝	9⅜	HiLo		...	19	626	15¾	14⅞	15⅛	− ⅜
14¼	7½	HiShear		...	18	334	9½	8½	9¼	+ ⅛
7⅞	2	Hibern		...	...	1800	5	4½	4⅝	− ¼
5⅝	4	Hilnco	.60	10.9	...	2886	5⅝	5⅜	5½	+ ⅛
6	4⅛	Hlncll	.63	10.5	...	3981	6	5¾	6	+ ¼
6¾	5¼	Hilnlll	.72a	11.1	...	1333	6⅝	6½	6½	...
7⅞	5½	HiYld	.90	11.4	...	x1423	7⅞	7⅝	7⅞	+ ⅛
7¾	6⅛	HiYdPl	.84	11.2	...	x754	7¾	7½	7½	...
78½	41	Hillnbd	.70	.9	31	1272	77½	74½	76¾	− ¾
39½	20½	Hilnbd wi		...	...	126	39⅛	37¼	38½	− ⅝
2⅜	½	vjHillD		...	...	3016	1¾	1½	1⅝	+ ⅛
49⅞	34¼	Hilton	1.20	2.7	25	5564	45⅞	42⅜	43⅞	− ⅛
99	64½	Hitachi	.80e	1.2	15	510	66½d	64½	64⅝	− 2⅛
6	3¾	Holnm		...	...	187	4½	4⅛	4⅜	+ ⅛
71⅞	32⅛	HomeD s	.12	.2	53	46328	65½	61	64	+ 2⅜
8⅞	4¼	HomeSh		...	31	75406u	8⅞	6⅜	8¼	+ 1½
6⅜	⅛	HmeFd		...	...	8845	1½	1⅛	1¼	− ¼
10¾	4½	Hmeplx	1.70e	29.6	4	1627	6⅛	5⅝	5¾	− ⅜
18⅜	13⅞	Hmstke	.20	1.3	...	9322	15⅞	15⅜	15½	− ⅜
15/16	1/32	HmstdF		...	...	395	13/16	9/16	¾	...
15/16	1/32	HmFB		...	...	13	¾	½	¾	+ ½
25½	18½	Honda	.21e	.9	20	363	23⅛	22¾	22⅞	− ⅛
75⅞	52¼	Honwel	1.65	2.3	16	x7200	73⅝	71¾	72⅞	+ ¾
32¾	23¾	HK Tel	1.36e	4.2	19	12962	32¾	30⅝	32⅝	+ 1⅞
23¼	17⅜	HMann n	.05e	.2	13	x2447	22⅛	21⅛	21⅛	− 1
11¾	2½	HrzHlt		...	28	1253	9¾	9	9⅜	− ⅜
23⅛	18¼	Hormel	.36	1.9	17	3810	19½	18½	18⅞	...
10¼	7⅞	Horsh		...	13	2408	9⅛	8¾	9	− ⅛
2⅞	1/16	Hotllnv		...	...	443	1¼	1	1⅛	− ⅛

Figure 17-4 (Source: *New York Times*)

1. a. How many shares of Hewlett Packard (HewlPk) were traded?

b. What is the difference between the high and low prices of the last 52 weeks?

c. What is today's closing price?

d. What was yesterday's closing price?

2. a. What was the dividend for one share of HewlPk stock?

b. What is the day's closing price for one share of HewlPk stock?

c. Using the information from (a) and (b), determine the current yield on HewlPk stock. Round to the nearest hundredth percent.

3. a. How much money was received in dividends for one share of Honeywell (Honwel) stock? For 50 shares? For 100 shares?

b. What is today's closing price for one share of Honeywell stock?

c. What is the current yield on Honeywell stock? Round to the nearest hundredth percent.

4. a. Calculate the current yield for Heinz. Does your answer match the "Yield %" figure?

b. Which of the two companies, Heinz or Honeywell, has the greater dividend per share?

c. Which of the two companies, Heinz or Honeywell, has the greater yield?

5. Stock A pays $1 dividend and sells for $5 a share. Stock B pays $1 dividend and sells for $50 a share. Which stock will have the greater yield? Why?

6. You own 100 shares of cumulative preferred stock that pays dividends at $0.85 per share in a company that did not pay any dividends for the past two years. This year you expect to receive dividends in arrears.
a. How much will you receive for dividends in arrears?

b. How much will you receive for this year's dividends? $85

c. If you had owned 100 shares of common stock that will pay $1.80 per share this year, how much would you have received in dividends from that investment for three years?

7. Your company has 120,000 shares of preferred stock that pays dividends at $0.25 per share and 200,000 shares of common stock. This year $500,000 is to be distributed. The preferred stockholders are also due to receive dividends in arrears for 1 year.
a. What is the amount of the dividends in arrears?

b. How much will go to the preferred stockholders for this year?

c. How much money will be distributed in all to common stockholders?

d. What is the dividend per share for the common stockholders?

8. A new company's stock is selling for $18\frac{1}{2}$ and has annual earnings of $1.20 per share. What is its PE ratio?

9. Penny Stock Corp. stock is selling for $1\frac{1}{4}$ per share and has annual earnings of $0.10 per share. What is its PE ratio?

For Problems 10 to 14, take the rate of commission to be 2% on the round lot and an additional 1% on the odd-lot portion.

10. You wish to purchase 150 shares of Hilton $43\frac{1}{8}$.

    a. What is the broker's commission on the round lot? On the odd-lot portion?

    b. What is your cost of purchasing the stock, including commission?

11. You wish to purchase 120 shares of Hunt Mfg (HMN) at $16\frac{1}{8}$.

    a. What is the broker's commission on the entire purchase?

    b. Including commission, what is your cost of purchasing the stock?

12. Later you sell the 120 shares of Hung Mfg stock (see Problem 11) for $34 per share.

    a. What is the broker's commission on the entire sale?

    b. What are your final receipts from the sale of the stock?

13. **a.** Compare your answer in Problem 11(b) with that in Problem 12(b). Do you have a net gain or a net loss? How much?

    b. Assume that you received $0.40 per share in dividends last year. Use that information and your answer to part (a) to calculate the return on your investment in Hunt Mfg. Round to the nearest hundredth percent.

14. You own 100 shares of Hormel stock, for which you paid $18\frac{1}{2}$. You received annual dividends of $0.36 per share. You are about to sell the same shares for 20. Calculate your ROI.

For Problems 15 to 23 and 26, refer to Figure 17-2.

15. a. How many AMOCO $7\frac{7}{8}$07 bonds were traded today?
   b. What is the annual interest for this bond?
   c. What is the date of maturity of this bond?

16. a. What is the dollar price of a BakrHgh bond that is listed at $103\frac{1}{2}$?

   b. What is the dollar price of an ATT bond listed at $95\frac{7}{8}$?

   c. Which of these bonds is selling at a discount? At a premium?

17. a. Calculate yesterday's closing price for an ABrnd bond.

   b. Calculate yesterday's closing price for an ArizP bond.

18. True or false? If false, explain why: In the *New York Times* listings, bond prices are given in points (dollars) and stock prices are given as a percent of face value.

For Problems 19 to 22, take the commission to be $5 per bond.

19. What is the cost of buying three $7\frac{1}{2}$14f bonds at the closing price, including commission? Closing price: $48.75 per bond.

20. How much will it cost to purchase five ARch $10\frac{3}{8}$95 bonds at the closing price? Include commission. Closing price: $1,116.25

21. After paying commission, what will you receive from the sale of ten ARich $8\frac{5}{8}$00 bonds at 103%? From one bond: $1,030.00

22. What will be your receipts from the sale of two AmGeni $9\frac{3}{8}$08 bonds? Assume you sell at 101 and that commission is deducted.

23. Corporation X has a 9% bond.
   a. How much annual interest does one bond pay (in dollars)? 9% of

   b. If you own two bonds for 3 years, how much interest will you receive?

c. If you own two bonds for 3 years and 20 days, how much interest, including accrued interest, will you receive?

24. For a bond with annual interest of $12 and current price of 112, what is the current yield?

25. Which has the greater current yield according to Figure 17-2, an ARich $8\frac{5}{8}00$ bond or an AmGeni $9\frac{3}{8}08$ bond?

26. You have invested $1,000 in bond A with yearly interest of 10% and $1,000 in bond B with yearly interest of 8%. Today's closing price for bond A shows it is selling at a premium, 120% of face value, whereas bond B is selling at a discount, 80% of face value.

a. What is the current yield on bond A?

b. What is the current yield on bond B?

c. Which is the better investment?

27. You own bond C, which has a current price of 80 and annual interest of 6%, and bond D, which has a current price of 120 and annual interest of 10%. Which bond is the better investment? Why?

Additional Problems

Assume a 2% commission on round-lot stock sales and an additional 1% on odd-lot sales. Assume a $5 sales commission per bond.

1. Over a year ago 125 shares of HardiCo were purchased at $37\frac{3}{4}$.
   a. Calculate the commission on the purchase.

   b. What was the total cost of the purchase?

2. Antonio Lewis sold 240 shares of Kalco at $45\frac{1}{8}$.

   a. Calculate the commission on the sale.

   b. What is his receipt from the sale of the stock?

3. Assume that you sold six bonds at $78\frac{1}{2}$.

   a. What is the commission on the sale?

   b. What is your receipt from the sale?

4. Assume that you purchased three bonds at $88\frac{3}{8}$.

   a. What is the commission on the sale?

   b. What is your total cost for the purchase?

5. Kalco stock has annual earnings of $1.60 per share and a closing price of $40\frac{1}{8}$.

   a. What is the PE ratio of the stock?

   b. What would the PE ratio be if the closing price were $48\frac{1}{4}$?

   c. What would be the PE ratio if the annual earnings were $1.75 per share?

6. Korporate bonds earned 9% annual interest and closed at 98, while Capco bonds earned 8% annual interest and closed at 102. Which bonds have the greater current yield?

7. What is the difference between a premium bond and a discount bond? What is a corporate bond?

8. Calculate the return on investment (ROI) of a stock if the total receipt is $3,455; the total cost, $2,755; and the dividends, $225.

9. If a bond has a current price of 150 and annual interest of $15, what is the current yield?

10. Baker, Inc., has an 8% bond.
   a. How much annual interest does one bond pay?

   b. If a purchaser holds two bonds for 4 years, how much interest will the purchaser receive?

   c. If the purchaser holds the two bonds for 4 years and 21 days, how much interest, including accrued interest, will the purchaser receive?

Challenge Problem

Linda Wright owns some 8.75% bonds from Trumble, Inc., that will mature in 6 years. She is considering selling these and buying some Martco 10.5% bonds due in 12 years. If she can sell her Trumble at 90 1/2 and buy Martco at 104 1/4, which bonds would give her a better rate of current yield?

Trial Test

For Problems 1 to 15, consider the commission on stocks to be 2% on round lots and an additional 1% on the odd-lot portion; consider the bonds to be $1,000 and the commission on bonds to be $5 per bond.

Use the following stock listing for Problems 1 to 5.

| 52 Weeks | | Stock | Sym | Div | Yield % | PE | Vol 100s | Hi | Lo | Close | Net Chg |
Hi	Lo										
68	$50\frac{1}{8}$	MAPCO	MDA	1.00		11	763	$67\frac{1}{2}$	$66\frac{1}{2}$	$66\frac{3}{4}$	$-\frac{3}{4}$

1. **a.** What is the difference between today's high and low?

   b. What is today's closing price, in dollars?

   c. What was yesterday's closing price, in dollars?

   d. How many shares were traded today?

2. Select the appropriate information to compute the current yield (not listed).

3. Last year you bought 120 shares of MAPCO at $50\frac{1}{2}$.
   a. Calculate the commission on that purchase.

   b. What was your total cost for the purchase?

4. Today you wish to sell your 120 shares of MAPCO at $66\frac{3}{4}$.
   a. Calculate the commission on the sale.

   b. What is your receipt from the sale of the stock?

5. Use your answers to Problems 3 and 4 and the dividend listed to calculate your return on this investment.

6. Your company has $200,000 to distribute in dividends to three groups:

A: One year's dividends in arrears for 5,000 shares of cumulative preferred stock ($0.40 per share)

B: The current year's dividends for those 5,000 shares of preferred stock

C: Dividends on 75,000 shares of common stock

a. How much is distributed to group A?

b. How much is distributed to group B?

c. How much is distributed to group C?

d. What is the dividend per share of common stock?

7. Select the appropriate information and calculate the current stock yield of stock A and stock B.

52 Weeks		Stock	Div	Yield %	PE	Vol 100s	Hi	Lo	Close
Hi	Lo								
$34\frac{3}{4}$	$27\frac{3}{4}$	A	1.68		9	415	$34\frac{3}{8}$	$34\frac{1}{8}$	$34\frac{1}{4}$
$65\frac{3}{4}$	$51\frac{1}{8}$	B	2.60		13	1467	$62\frac{7}{8}$	$62\frac{3}{8}$	$62\frac{5}{8}$

8. Stock C has annual earnings of $1.20 per share and a closing price of 48.

a. What is the PE ratio of stock C?

b. If earnings go up next year, but the price stays the same, will the PE ratio increase or decrease?

c. If earnings stay the same next year, but the price goes up, will the PE ratio increase or decrease?

Use the following bond listing for Problems 9 to 12.

Bond	Cur Yield	Vol (S/s in $1,000)	Close (LAST)	Net Chg
Revlln $11\frac{3}{4}$95	13.1	91	$89\frac{7}{8}$	$+\frac{3}{8}$

9. a. What is the date of maturity of the bond?

b. What is the closing price of the bond, in dollars?

c. What was yesterday's closing price, in dollars?

d. Is the bond selling at a discount or at a premium?

10. a. How much interest was received last year on one Revln bond?

b. If the bond has accrued interest for 90 days, how much interest has accrued?

11. Assume that 3 years ago you purchased five Revln bonds at 85.
a. What was the commission on the purchase?
b. What was your total cost of purchase?

12. Assume that you sell the five Revln bonds today at $89\frac{7}{8}$.
a. What is the commission on the sale?
b. What is your receipt from the sale?

c. Disregard any accrued interest or annual interest. How much gain or loss do you have on these five bonds?

13. Compare the following two stocks.
Common stock of Enron Cp (2.48 dividend; $41\frac{1}{2}$ closing price)
Preferred stock of Enron Cp (10.50 dividend; $145\frac{1}{2}$ closing price)

Which stock of Enron Cp has the greater yield, the common stock or the preferred stock?

14. Compare the following two bonds.

Mobil $7\frac{5}{8}$ 91 (closing price $94\frac{7}{8}$)
Mobil $8\frac{5}{8}$ 94 (closing price $95\frac{1}{8}$)

Which bond has the greater yield?

15. As a stock broker, you must advise your client on a purchase. Stock A is selling for 20 now. Next year an owner can reasonably expect to sell it for 22. Dividends have been steady at $1 per year.

Stock B is selling for 50 now. Next year an owner can reasonably expect to sell it for 55. Dividends have been steady at $1 per year.

a. Calculate the ROI for each investment. (Disregard commissions; assume the owner sells the stock in 1 year.)

b. Which stock, A or B, gives the higher return on investment?

A look at statistics that shape your finances.

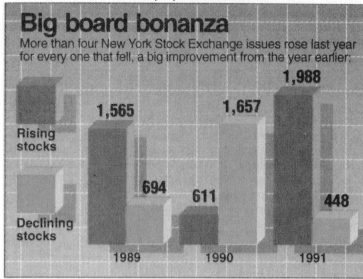

Big board bonanza
More than four New York Stock Exchange issues rose last year for every one that fell, a big improvement from the year earlier:

Rising stocks

1,565   1,657   1,988

694   611   448

Declining stocks

1989   1990   1991

Source: New York Stock Exchange

By Marty Baumann, USA TODAY

QUESTIONS

1. The ratio of stocks that rose to stocks that fell is the fraction with the stocks that rose in the numerator and the stocks that fell in the denominator.
According to the heading, what is the ratio of stocks that rose to stocks that fell?

2. Write an exact ratio and the decimal equivalent to show the relationship of stocks that rose to stocks that fell for 1991.

3. In which year was the stocks that rose less than the stocks that fell? What is the ratio of stocks that rose to stocks that fell for that year? Compare this ratio to the ratio for 1991.

Tables, Graphs, and Statistics

In today's fast-paced world business people must be able to communicate information about numbers quickly and clearly. Tables, graphs, and statistics are used in corporate reports, newspapers, professional journals, and nonfiction books and on television to present numerical information in an organized manner.

18.1 Tables

LEARNING OBJECTIVE

1. Read and interpret data.

A **table** shows one or more lists of numerical information grouped in some meaningful form. A table may be as simple as a list of entrance-test scores for students at a college over the past 5 years to show how scores have changed. It is important to give a table a title that clearly indicates its purpose and to

table: one or more lists of numerical information grouped in some meaningful form.

Table 18-1 Monthly* Membership of the Feel Good Fitness Club, 1988–1992

	1988		1989		1990		1991		1992	
	Men	Women	Men	Women	Men	Women	Men	Women	Men	Women
January	82	29	101	66	129	105	148	147	169	173
February	84	32	108	70	135	115	148	151	176	179
March	21	8	87	33	108	74	138	117	151	154
April	29	12	88	39	110	76	141	125	153	155
May	35	14	89	43	111	78	140	126	154	156
June	38	15	89	44	109	79	135	125	152	158
July	49	15	86	44	107	78	132	125	150	156
August	53	17	86	45	107	77	133	127	148	155
September	59	20	88	47	109	79	135	132	151	159
October	65	23	91	51	113	86	138	137	157	163
November	71	25	95	58	118	92	140	142	159	165
December	79	28	98	61	127	101	143	144	166	172

*Number of members at the end of each month.

define what each column of numbers represents so that the information in the table can be used effectively.

Reading and Interpreting Data

In studying Examples 1 through 3, which discuss how to use information in a table, refer to Table 18-1. The Feel Good Fitness Club has offered monthly memberships since it opened in 1988. At the end of the fifth year, the membership office prepared Table 18-1, which shows how many members the club has had at the end of each month since it opened.

You can find some information in the table with only a quick inspection: The entries for March 1988 show that during the first month 21 men and 8 women joined the club. The November 1991 entries show that between the end of October and the end of November 1991, the number of women exceeded the number of men for the first time.

You can compare information in a table by using addition, subtraction, or percents to find additional information.

EXAMPLE 1

How many men joined the health club between the end of April and the end of May 1988?

35	(number of men at the end of May, 1988)
− 29	(number of men at the end of April, 1988)
6	

Subtract the number of men club members in April 1988 from the number of men club members in May 1988.

Six men joined during May 1988.

EXAMPLE 2

Find the ratio of men to women in the club at the end of June 1991.

As you saw in Chapter 1, a ratio indicates division and can be thought of as a fraction. The *ratio* of one number to another is found by the making of a fraction that has the first number in the numerator and the second number in the denominator. Reduce the ratio if possible.

$$\frac{135}{125} \quad \text{(the number of men)} \atop \text{(the number of women)}$$

The numerator is the number of men in the club as of the end of June 1991; the denominator is the number of women.

$$\frac{135}{125} = \frac{27}{25}$$

The ratio of men to women was 27 : 25 at the end of June 1991.

| AC | 135 | ÷ | 125 | = | ⇒ 1.08   The ratio can also be written as 1.08 to 1.   **Calculator Solution**

EXAMPLE 3

What percent of increase in club members between March 1991 and March 1992 was women?

March 1992		March 1991
151 ←	(number of men) →	138
+ 154 ←	(number of women) →	+ 117
305 ←	(total members) →	255

Find the total number of club members at the end of March 1991 and March 1992 by adding the number of male and female club members.

$$\begin{array}{r} 305 \\ -255 \\ \hline 50 \end{array} \begin{array}{l} \text{(total members, March 1992)} \\ \text{(total members, March 1991)} \\ \text{(increase in members)} \end{array}$$

Subtract the total members in 1991 from the total members in 1992 to find total new members.

$$\begin{array}{r} 154 \\ -117 \\ \hline 37 \end{array} \begin{array}{l} \text{(number of women in March 1992)} \\ \text{(number of women in March 1991)} \\ \text{(increase in women members)} \end{array}$$

Subtract the number of women in 1991 from the number of women in 1992 to find increase in women members.

$$\frac{37}{50} = 0.74 = 74\%$$

74% of the additional members between March 1991 and March 1992 were women.

Divide the increase in women members by the total increase in members and multiply by 100 to find the percent of increase in women club members.

TIPS & TRAPS

It is easy to select the wrong value from a table or to use proper value in the wrong place in a problem. Plan the solution using words and labels for the table values. Then substitute the values from the table and make the calculations.

  Self-Check 18.1

Refer to Table 18-1 to answer the following questions.

1. How many more women members than men members were there in October of 1992?

2. Find the ratio of men to women in the club as of the end of December 1991.

3. What percent of increase in club members between December 1991 and December 1992 was men?

18.2

Graphs

LEARNING OBJECTIVES

1. Read and draw bar graphs.
2. Read and draw line graphs.
3. Read and draw circle graphs.

graph: a symbolic or pictorial display of numerical information.

Graphs are used in business to give a quick and easy visual interpretation of information and to emphasize changes or trends in business. Statistical information usually makes a stronger impression if it can be presented visually. Graphs, like tables, must always have a *title* so that the reader will know what the facts being illustrated represent.

Bar Graphs

bar graph: a graph made with horizontal or vertical bars and used to compare several related values.

Bar graphs are often used *to compare several related values.* Vertical or horizontal bars may be used, and the height or length of each bar corresponds to a specific value. The bars taken together show how the different values relate to one another.

Suppose you wish to graph the following data, which show that Corky's Barbecue Shack had the given sales during January through June:

January	$37,534	April	$52,175
February	$43,284	May	$56,394
March	$58,107	June	$63,784

The lowest number is $37,534 and the highest number is $63,784. Therefore, your graph must show values from $30,000 to $70,000. To avoid using very large numbers, you can indicate on the graph that the numbers represent thousands of dollars. Therefore, 65 on the graph would represent $65,000. The bars can be either horizontal or vertical, but you must be sure to label both sides of the graph clearly (use Figure 18-1). All the information needed to interpret the bars on the graph should be clearly stated. It is also important that you always title and label your graphs.

EXAMPLE 4

Draw a horizontal bar graph representing the sales from January through June for Corky's Barbecue Shack. The result should resemble Figure 18-1.

This figure shows how easy bar graphs make it to answer certain questions. For example, sales were the highest in June. Sales were the second highest in March. In April there was a decline in sales from the previous month.

Line Graphs

line graph: a graph made with a series of connected line segements used to show trends.

A **line graph** is used *to show trends.* Studying past trends shown on a line graph can help businesspeople predict future trends. A line graph of changes in some value helps you quickly determine whether the value is

536

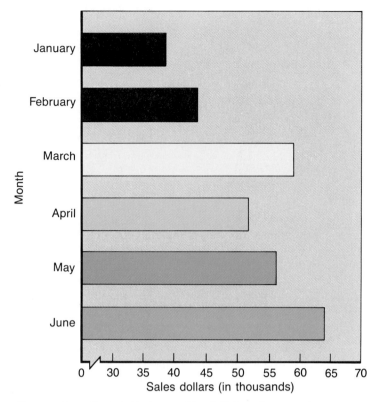

Figure 18-1   Corky's Barbecue Shack Sales, January–June

Table 18-2   Neighborhood Grocery Daily Sales for Week Beginning Monday, June 21

Monday	$1,567
Tuesday	$1,323
Wednesday	$1,237
Thursday	$1,435
Friday	$1,848
Saturday	$1,984

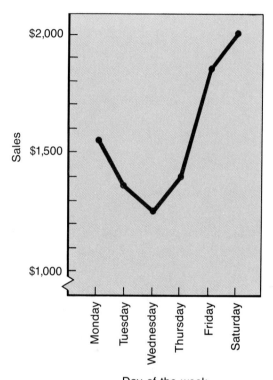

Day of the week

Figure 18-2   Neighborhood Grocery Daily Sales for Week Beginning Monday, June 21

steadily increasing, steadily decreasing, or fluctuating (sometimes increasing and sometimes decreasing). Unlike bar graphs, single line graphs do not compare several items. Instead, they show *changes* in a particular value.

EXAMPLE 5

Draw a line graph to represent the data in Table 18-2.

The smallest and greatest values in the table are $1,237 and $1,984, respectively, so the graph may go from $1,000 to $2,000 in $100 intervals. Do not label every interval. This would crowd the side of the graph and make it harder to read. Remember: the purpose of any graph is to give information that is quick and easy to understand and interpret.

The horizontal side of the graph will show the days of the week, and the vertical side will show the daily sales. Plot each day's sales by placing a dot directly above the appropriate day of the week across from the approximate value. For example, the sales for Monday totaled $1,567. Place the dot above Monday in the interval between $1,500 and $1,600. After each amount has been plotted, connect the dots with straight lines.

Figure 18-2 shows the resulting graph.

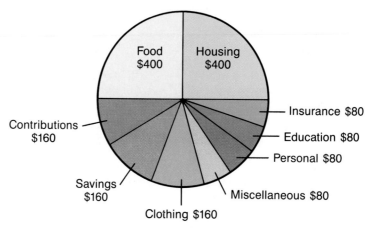

Figure 18-3   Distribution of Family Monthly Take-home Pay of $1,600 for 2-Year College Graduates

Circle Graphs

circle graph: a graph made by dividing a circle into proportionate parts to show how some whole quantity is being divided into parts.

A **circle graph** is a circle divided into two or more sections to give a visual picture of *how some whole quantity* (represented by the whole circle) *is being divided.* Each section represents a portion of the total amount being illustrated. Figure 18-3 shows a sample circle graph.

This circle graph shows visually how different portions of a family's total income are spent on nine categories of expenses: food, housing, contributions, savings, clothing, insurance, education, personal items, and miscellaneous items.

You can compute the percent of the take-home pay allowed for any of the nine categories of expenses. To do this, write a fraction with the part (category) as numerator and the whole (take-home pay) as denominator, divide to get a decimal equivalent, and then convert the decimal equivalent to a percent. Convert a decimal number to a percent by moving the decimal point two places to the right.

When the percent of each category has been calculated, the percents can be added together. The total of these percents should be 100%, except for rounding discrepancies. You can use this process to check your work.

EXAMPLE 6

Find the percent of total take-home pay spent for food in Figure 18-3.

$400 + $400 + $80 + $80
+ $80 + $80 + $160 + $160
+ $160 = $1,600

Add the amounts shown in each section of the graph to find the total take-home pay.

$$\frac{\text{Food}}{\text{Take-home pay}} = \frac{400}{1,600} = \frac{4}{16}$$

Divide the amount spent on food by the total take-home pay.

$$= \frac{1}{4}$$

$$\frac{1}{4} = 0.25 \qquad 0.25 \times 100\% = 25\%$$

Convert $\frac{1}{4}$ to a percent.

25% of the family's take-home pay is spent on food.

EXAMPLE 7

Compute the percent of take-home pay available for a vacation if the family's savings and education expenses for 1 month were used.

Savings $160
Education + 80
$240

Add savings and education costs for one month.

$(Part) \rightarrow \dfrac{240}{1,600} = \dfrac{3}{20} = 0.15 = 15\%$
$(Whole) \rightarrow$

Write a fraction with the part as the numerator and the whole as the denominator. Multiply by 100 to write the decimal as a percent.

The calculator sequence is

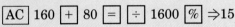

The answer is 15%.

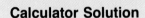

Calculator Solution

A circle graph takes longer to construct than a bar or line graph because you must perform a number of calculations before you can actually draw the graph. A circle stands for 100% of whatever quantity the graph represents, and each "slice" of the circle stands for some part of the total quantity. To divide a circle into slices for a circle graph, you need to know what fraction of the whole quantity makes up each part. Once you know the fraction for each part, you can calculate how much of the circle goes into each part. Since the whole circle has 360° **(degrees)**, you multiply the fraction for each part times 360 to find out how many degrees each slice should have.

degree: $\frac{1}{360}$ of a complete circle. There are 360° in a circle.

EXAMPLE 8

Construct a circle graph showing the following amounts, which Silver's Spa recorded as operating expenses for one month:

	Amount	Fraction for each Part of Whole	Decimal × 360 =	Number of Degrees
Salary	$25,000	$\dfrac{25,000}{53,000} = \dfrac{25}{53}$	$0.4716981 \times 360 =$	170
Rent	8,500	$\dfrac{8,500}{53,000} = \dfrac{85}{530}$	$0.1603773 \times 360 =$	58
Depreciation	2,500	$\dfrac{2,500}{53,000} = \dfrac{25}{530}$	$0.0471698 \times 360 =$	17
Miscellaneous	2,000	$\dfrac{2,000}{53,000} = \dfrac{2}{53}$	$0.0377358 \times 360 =$	14
Taxes and insurance	10,000	$\dfrac{10,000}{53,000} = \dfrac{10}{53}$	$0.1886792 \times 360 =$	68
Utilities	2,000	$\dfrac{2,000}{53,000} = \dfrac{2}{53}$	$0.0377358 \times 360 =$	14
Advertising	3,000	$\dfrac{3,000}{53,000} = \dfrac{3}{53}$	$0.0566037 \times 360 =$	20
Total	$53,000		1.00	361*

*Extra degree due to rounding

Use a compass to draw a circle. Then measure the sections of the circle with a protractor, using the calculations you just made.

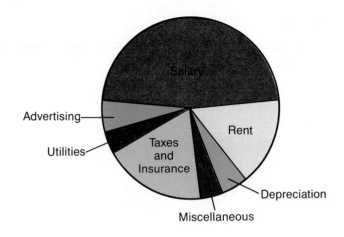

Self-Check 18.2

4. Draw a bar graph comparing the quarterly sales of the Oxford Company: January–March, $280,000; April–June, $310,000; July–September, $250,000; October–December, $400,000.

5. Use Figure 18-3 to find the percent of total take-home pay spent for contributions.

6. Use Figure 18-3 to compute the percent of take-home pay available for education if the family's education and savings funds were used.

18.3

Statistics

LEARNING OBJECTIVES

1. Find the range.
2. Find the mean.
3. Find the median.
4. Find the mode.
5. Use statistics to analyze data.

statistic: a number that describes numerical data.

A **statistic** is a number that describes numerical data. Statistics make numerical information more meaningful by helping you understand how individual pieces of information fit in with other, comparable pieces of information. Statistics may be represented in tables and graphs or used alone.

Table 18-3 shows prices of used automobiles sold on a particular weekend in Tyreville.

Range

range: result when the smallest number is subtracted from the largest number in a group of numbers.

The numbers show a **range** of used-automobile prices from a low of $1,850 to a high of $11,500. The range of a group of values (numbers) is found by subtracting the smallest number in the group from the largest number in the group. A small range indicates that the values in the group are very similar to one another, whereas a large range indicates the values are very different.

STEP BY STEP

Finding the Range of a Group of Values

Range = largest value − smallest value

Table 18-3 Prices of Used Automobiles Sold in Tyreville Over the Weekend of May 1–2

$1,850	$ 5,600
$2,300	$ 5,800
$2,750	$ 6,100
$4,600	$ 9,430
$4,800	$11,500
$5,200	

EXAMPLE 9

Find the range in the used automobile prices in Table 18-3.

Range = largest value
      − smallest value
    = $11,500 − $1,850
    = $9,650

Inspection shows that the lowest price is $1,850 and the highest price is $11,500. Subtract to obtain the range.

The range is $9,650, which is quite large. That is, the lowest and highest prices in the group are very different.

Mean

You know from the range that the used car prices vary quite a bit. In this case you might want to consider the **mean** price. Mean is the statistical term for the ordinary arithmetic average. To find the mean, or arithmetic average, add the values in a group and divide the total by the number of items added.

mean: the sum of a set of values divided by the number of values in the set.

STEP BY STEP

Finding the Mean of a Group of Values

Step 1. Add all the values.

Step 2. Divide the total by the number of values:

$$\text{Mean} = \frac{\text{sum of values}}{\text{number of values}}$$

EXAMPLE 10

Find the mean used car price for the prices in Table 18-3.

$1,850
2,300
2,750
4,600
4,800
5,200
5,600
5,800
6,100
9,430
+ 11,500
$59,930

Add the prices of the 11 cars.

$59,930 ÷ 11 = \$5,448.1818$
= \$5,448
(rounded to the nearest whole dollar)

There are 11 prices listed, so find the mean by dividing the total by 11.

The mean price is \$5,448.

On a calculator these calculations would be carried out continuously by adding all the prices and then dividing the total by 11.

Median

Another kind of average is called the **median.** The median of a group of values is found by arranging the numbers in order from the smallest to the largest (largest to the smallest) and selecting the number in the middle. If the group has an even number of values, so that no one value is exactly in the middle, find the average of the two numbers in the middle of the group.

median: the middle value in a set of values that are arranged in order from smallest to largest or largest to smallest.

STEP BY STEP

Finding the Median of a Group of Values

Step 1. Arrange the values in the group from largest to smallest.

Step 2. Find the middle value.
  a. The median is the middle value if the group has an odd number of values.
  b. The median is the average of the two middle numbers if the group has an even number of values.

EXAMPLE 11

Find the median price of used cars in Table 18-3.

$11,500
9,430
6,100
5,800
5,600
5,200 ← Median price; there are 5 values above and 5 below it
4,800
4,600
2,750
2,300
1,850

Arrange the numbers from the highest to the lowest. The median is the price in the middle of the list.

There are 11 prices. The median (middle) price is 6 from the top or 6 from the bottom. \$5,200 is the median price of the used cars.

Mode

The third average considered is the **mode.** The mode is the value or values that occur most frequently in a group of values. If no number occurs most frequently in a group, then there is no mode for that group of numbers. No used car price in Table 18-3 occurs more than once, so there is no mode for that group of used car prices.

mode: the value that occurs most frequently in a group of values.

Finding the Mode of a Group of Values

Find the value or values that occur most frequently.

EXAMPLE 12

Find the mode for this group of test grades in a mathematics class:

76, 83, 94, 76, 53, 18, 74, 76, 97, 83, 65, 77, 76, 81

The grade of 76 occurs four times. The grade of 83 occurs two times. All other grades occur once each. The grade of 76 occurs most frequently.

The mode is 76 for this group of test grades.

Putting Statistics to Work

Taken together, the mean, median, and mode describe the tendency of a group of numbers to cluster together in the center of the range of values. Sometimes it is useful to know all three of these measures, since each represents a different way of describing the numerical information. It is like looking at the same thing from three different points of view. The mean, median, and mode may each be called an *average*.

To look at just one statistic for a set of numbers often distorts the total picture. It is advisable to find the range, mean, median, and mode and then analyze the results.

EXAMPLE 13

The average cost of a home in Tyreville was $71,000 during the past 3 months. But is this "average" the mean, median, or mode? What is the range of prices? We need this kind of information to get a true picture of what a home might cost in that area. A real estate agent might provide this list of selling prices of houses over the past 3 months:

$170,000	$150,000	$50,000
$50,000	$50,000	$50,000
$49,000	$45,000	$25,000

What are the range, the mean, the median, and the mode? What do these numbers tell us about the cost of houses in this area?

Range = highest − lowest   Such a large range indicates extremes in
     = $170,000 − $25,000   prices, so a mean price does not indicate
     = $145,000   what you could realistically expect to pay
     for a home in this area.

Mean = total ÷ number of items
     = $639,000 ÷ 9   The large range, however, suggests that
     = $71,000   prices were not generally around $71,000,
     but were probably a mixture of much lower
     and much higher prices.

Median (middle amount) : $50,000
Mode (most frequent amount): $50,000

Conclusion: Because of the large range (and extreme price differences that produced the large range), the median and the mode give a more realistic picture of what a home is likely to cost in this area.

 Self-Check 18.3

7. Find the range of the following numbers: 3,850; 5,300; 8,550; 4,200; 5,350.

8. Find the mean of the following numbers: 3,850; 5,300; 8,550; 4,200; 5,350.

9. Find the median of the following numbers: 3,850; 5,300; 8,550; 4,200; 5,350.

10. Find the mode for the following numbers: 86, 94, 73, 94, 84, 86, 94.

11. Last Saturday, Autowonderland sold cars for the following prices: $15,300, $17,500, $11,400, $14,500, and $13,500. Find the range, the mean, the median, and the mode for these car prices. What do these prices tell us about the cost of cars sold last Saturday? Which statistic(s) would give the most realistic description of Autowonderland's prices on Saturday?

Summary

Topic	Page	What to Remember	Example
Tables	533	A *table* consists of one or more lists of numerical information grouped in some meaningful form.	Size of Graduating Class at Winston College, 19X5–19X9

	Men	Women	Total
19X5	130	128	258
19X6	111	149	260
19X7	125	171	296
19X8	135	168	303
19X9	141	175	316

Topic	Page	What to Remember	Example
How tables are used	534	We can compare pieces of information in a table with one another, using addition, subtraction, or percent, to find additional information.	How many more women than men graduated in 19X6? $149 - 111 = 38$ more women than men graduated in 19X6. Men made up what percent of the graduating class in 19X9? $$\frac{141}{316} = 45\%$$
Bar graphs	536	A bar graph compares several related values. Vertical or horizontal bars may be used; the height or length of each bar corresponds to a certain value.	

Topic	Page	What to Remember	Example
Line graphs	536	A line graph shows changes in some value and helps us see whether the value is increasing, decreasing, or fluctuating.	
Circle graphs	538	A circle graph shows some whole quantity, represented by a whole circle divided into smaller parts, shown by different-sized slices of the circle.	
Statistics	540	*Statistics* are numbers that describe numerical information and show how individual pieces of information fit in with other, comparable pieces of information.	We will use this information in the examples that follow: A survey of 7 computer stores in a large city showed that a certain printer was sold for the following prices: $435, $398, $429, $479, $435, $495, and $435.
Finding the range of a group of values	540	Range = largest value − smallest value	Find the range of printer prices: $$\$495 - \$398 = \$97$$
Finding the mean of a group of values	541	Mean = sum of values ÷ number of values	Find the mean price of the printer: $$\$435 + \$398 + \$429 + 479$$ $$+ \$435 + \$495 + \$435 = \$3106$$ $$\frac{\$3106}{7} = \$443.71$$
Finding the median of a group of values	541	Arrange the values in the group from largest to smallest. If the group has an odd number of values, the median is the middle value; if the group has an even number of values, the median is the average of the two middle numbers.	Find the median price of the printer: $495, $479, $435, $435, $435, $429, $398 The median price is $435.
Finding the mode of a group of values	541	The mode is the number that occurs most frequently.	$435 is the mode.

Self-Check Solutions

1. $163 - 157 = 6$

2. $\dfrac{\text{Men}}{\text{Women}} = \dfrac{143}{144}$

3. Total club members on December 31, 1991 = $143 + 144 = 287$
Total club members on December 31, 1992 = $166 + 172 = 338$

New club members between
December 1991 and 1992 $= 338 - 287 = 51$

New club members who
are men for period
December 1991 to 1992 $= 166 - 143 = 23$

Percent of new club
members that are men $= \dfrac{P}{B} = \dfrac{23}{51} = 0.45 = 45\%$

4.

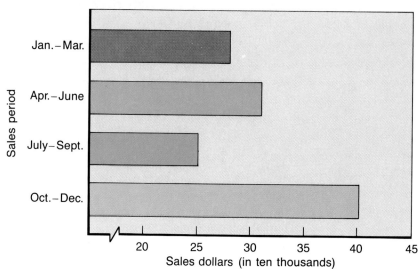

5. Percent of total take-home
pay spent for clothing $= \dfrac{P}{B} = \dfrac{160}{1600} = 0.1 = 10\%$

6. Percent of total take-home
pay spent for education
(education, savings, and
miscellaneous) $= \dfrac{P}{B} = \dfrac{320}{1600} = 0.2 = 20\%$

7. Range $= 8{,}550 - 3{,}850 = 4{,}700$

8. Mean $= (3{,}850 + 5{,}300 + 8{,}550 + 4{,}200 + 5{,}350) \div 5 = \dfrac{27{,}250}{5} = 5{,}450$

9. Arrange the numbers from smallest to greatest:

3,850   4,200   5,300   5,350   8,550

↑

middle number

Median: 5,300

10. Arrange the numbers from smallest to greatest:
73, 84, 86, 86, 94, 94, 94

Mode: 94

11. Arrange the prices in order from smallest to greatest:
$11,400 $13,500 $14,500 $15,300 $17,500
Range $= \$17{,}500 - \$11{,}400 = \$6{,}100$
Mean $= (\$11{,}400 + \$13{,}500 + \$14{,}500 + \$15{,}300 + \$17{,}500) \div 5$
$= \$72{,}200 \div 5 = \$14{,}440$
Median $= \$14{,}500$
No mode

Since the mean and median are close but the range is large, we can use
the mean and median to get a realistic picture of the cost of an automobile in this area.

End of Chapter Problems

Use Table 18-4 to solve Exercises 1 to 10. A calculator may help.

Table 18-4 Class Enrollment by Period and Days of the Week for the Second Semester

Period	Mon.	Tues.	Wed.	Thur.	Fri.	Sat.
1. 7:00– 7:50 A.M.	277	374	259	340	207	0
2. 7:55– 8:45 A.M.	653	728	593	691	453	361
3. 8:50– 9:40 A.M.	908	863	824	798	604	361
4. 9:45–10:35 A.M.	962	782	849	795	561	361
5. 10:40–11:30 A.M.	914	858	795	927	510	361
6. 11:35–12:25 P.M.	711	773	375	816	527	182
7. 12:30– 1:20 P.M.	686	734	696	733	348	161
8. 1:25– 2:15 P.M.	638	647	659	627	349	85
9. 2:20– 3:10 P.M.	341	313	325	351	136	78
10. 3:15– 4:05 P.M.	110	149	151	160	45	0
11. 4:10– 5:00 P.M.	46	72	65	67	11	0
12. 5:05– 5:55 P.M.	37	91	68	48	0	0
13. 6:00– 6:50 P.M.	809	786	796	705	373	0
14. 6:55– 7:45 P.M.	809	786	796	705	373	0
15. 7:50– 8:40 P.M.	565	586	577	531	373	0
16. 8:45– 9:35 P.M.	727	706	817	758	373	0
17. 9:40–10:30 P.M.	702	706	817	758	27	0
18. 10:35–11:25 P.M.	76	70	46	98	0	0

1. How many students were enrolled in class on Wednesday during the fifth period?

2. How many students were enrolled in classes on Monday during the eleventh period?

3. What is the total class enrollment for the third period Monday through Friday?

4. What is the total class enrollment for the ninth period Monday through Friday?

5. How many more people are enrolled in third period Monday through Friday than in ninth period?

6. Find the total class enrollment by periods Monday through Friday.

Period *Students*
1
2
3
4
5
6
7
8
9

Period	Students
10	
11	
12	
13	
14	
15	
16	
17	
18	

7. What period has the highest enrollment during the day (periods 1 to 12)?

8. What period has the highest enrollment at night (periods 13 to 18)?

9. If 1,768 day students were enrolled during the second semester, what percent of the students were enrolled in a fourth-period class on Monday? Round to the nearest tenth of a percent.

10. Complete Table 18-5, computing day enrollment (periods 1 to 12) and night enrollment (periods 13 to 18).

Table 18-5   Day and Night Class Enrollment Second Semester

	Periods	Mon.	Tues.	Wed.	Thurs.	Fri.	Sat.
Day	1–12						
Night	13–18						

Section 18.2

Use the following data for Problems 11 to 14. The Family Clothing Store recorded the following information concerning its 19X1 and 19X2 sales.

	19X1	19X2
Girls' clothing	$ 74,675	$ 81,534
Boys' clothing	$ 65,153	$ 68,324
Women's clothing	$125,115	$137,340
Men's clothing	$ 83,895	$ 96,315

11. What is the least value for 19X1 sales? For 19X2 sales?

12. What is the greatest value for 19X1 sales? For 19X2 sales?

13. If the values are given in thousands of dollars, which of the following interval sizes would be more appropriate to use in making a bar graph?
   a. $1,000 intervals ($60,000, $61,000, $62,000, . . .)
   b. $10,000 intervals ($60,000, $70,000, $80,000, . . .)

14. Draw a comparative bar graph to show both the 19X1 and 19X2 values. Be sure to include a title, explanation of the scales, and any additional information needed.

Use the following information for Problems 15 to 19. The temperatures were recorded at 2-hour intervals June 24.

12 A.M.	76°	8 A.M.	70°	2 P.M.	84°	8 P.M.	82°
2 A.M.	75°	10 A.M.	76°	4 P.M.	90°	10 P.M.	79°
4 A.M.	72°	12 P.M.	81°	6 P.M.	90°	12 A.M.	77°
6 A.M.	70°						

15. What is the smallest value?　　　**16.** What is the greatest value?

17. Which interval size is most appropriate when making a line graph? Why?

　　a. 1°　　b. 5°　　c. 50°　　d. 100°

18. Draw a line graph representing the data. Be sure to include the title, explanation of the scales, and any additional information needed.

19. Which of the following terms would describe this line graph?
a. Continually increasing   b. Continually decreasing   c. Fluctuating

Table 18-6 Automobile Dealership's New and Repeat Business

Customer	Cars Sold
New	920
Repeat	278

Answer the following questions using the information in Table 18-6.

20. What was the total number of cars sold?

21. How many degrees should be used to represent the new business on the circle (to the nearest whole degree)?

22. How many degrees should be used to represent the repeat business on the circle (to the nearest whole degree)?

23. Construct a circle graph for these data. Label the parts of the graph as "New" and "Repeat." Be sure to include a title and any additional information needed.

Section 18.3

Find the range, mean, median, and mode for the following. Round to the nearest hundredth if necessary.

24. New car mileages
17 mi/gal
16 mi/gal
25 mi/gal
22 mi/gal
30 mi/gal

25. Test scores
61
72
63
70
93
87

26. Sandwiches
   $0.95
   $1.65
   $1.27
   $1.97
   $1.65
   $1.15

27. Credit hours
   16
   12
   18
   15
   16
   12
   12

Additional Problems

Use Table 18-7 to answer the following.

Table 18-7   Happy's Gift Shoppe

| Salesperson | Sales | | | | | | |
	Mon.	Tues.	Wed.	Thurs.	Fri.	Sat.	Total
Brown	Off	$110.25	$114.52	$186.42	$126.81	$315.60	$853.60
Jackson	$121.68	Off	$118.29	Off	$125.42	Off	$365.39
Ulster	$112.26	$119.40	$122.35	$174.51	$116.78	Off	$645.30
Young	Off	$122.90	Off	$181.25	Off	$296.17	$600.32
Totals	$233.94	$352.55	$355.16	$542.18	$369.01	$611.77	$2,464.71

1. What day of the week had the highest amount in sales? What day had the lowest amount in sales?

2. What percent of the week's sales was made on Thursday? What percent was made on Monday? (Round to the nearest whole percent.)

3. Which salesperson made the most sales for the week? Which salesperson made the second highest amount in sales?

4. What percent of the day's sales for Saturday did Young make? (Round to the nearest whole percent.)

Figure 18-4 Distribution of
Costs for an $86,000 Home

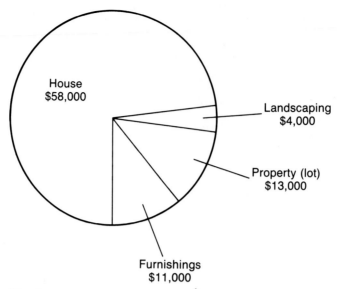

House
$58,000

Landscaping
$4,000

Property (lot)
$13,000

Furnishings
$11,000

Use Figure 18-4 to answer the following.

5. What percent of the overall cost does the lot represent? (Round to the nearest tenth.)

6. What is the cost of the lot with landscaping? What percent of the total cost does this represent? (Round to the nearest tenth.)

7. What is the cost of the house with furnishings? What percent of the total cost does this represent? (Round to the nearest tenth.)

8. Find the range, mean, median, and mode of the hourly pay rates for the following employees.

Thompson	$13.95	Cleveland	$5.25
Chang	5.80	Gandolfo	4.90
Jackson	4.68	DuBois	13.95
Smith	4.90	Serpas	13.95

9. Find the range, mean, median, and mode of the weights of the following metal castings after being milled:

Casting A	1.08 kg	Casting D	1.1 kg
Casting B	1.15 kg	Casting E	1.25 kg
Casting C	1.19 kg	Casting F	1.1 kg

10. During the past year, Piazza's Clothiers sold a certain sweater at different prices: $42.95, $36.50, $40.75, $38.25, and $43.25. Find the range, mean, median, and mode of the selling prices.

Challenge Problem

Have the computers made a mistake? You have been attending Northeastern State College (that follows a percentage grading system) for two years. You have received good grades, but after four semesters have not made the Dean's List which requires an overall average of 90% for all accumulated credits or 90% for any given semester. Below are your grade reports:

Fall			Winter			Fall			Winter		
Course	Cr Hr	Gr.	Course	Cr Hr	Gr.	Course	Cr Hr	Gr.	Course	Cr Hr	Gr.
BUS MATH	4	90	SOC.	3	92	FUNS.	4	88	CAL. I	4	89
ACC I	4	89	PSYC.	3	91	ACC II	4	89	ACC IV	4	90
ENG I	3	91	ENG II	3	90	ENG 888	3	95	ENG IV	3	96
HISTORY	3	92	ACC II	4	88	PURCH.	3	96	ADV.	3	93
ECON	5	85	ECON II	4	86	MGMT.I	5	84	MGMT.II	5	83

What is the grade point average for each semester? What is your overall grade point average for the four semesters? What is the minimum grade that would be needed in each of five courses of three credit hours each in order to raise your grade point average to 90%?

Trial Test

Use the following data for Problems 1 to 4.

42	86	92	15	32	67	48	19	87	63
15	19	21	17	53	27	21	15	82	15

1. What is the range?

2. What is the mean?

3. What is the median?

4. What is the mode?

Use the following data for Problems 5 to 8.

105	215	165	172	138
198	165	170	165	146
187	170	165	146	200

5. What is the range?

6. What is the mean?

7. What is the median?

8. What is the mode?

The following are costs of producing a piece of luggage at ACME Luggage Company: labor, $45; materials, $40; overhead, $35.

9. What is the total cost of producing a piece of luggage?

10. What percent of the total cost is attributed to labor?

11. What percent of the total cost is attributed to materials?

12. What percent of the total cost is attributed to overhead?

13. Compute the number of degrees needed for labor, materials, and overhead if a circle graph is to be constructed.

Katz Florist recorded the following sales for a 6-month period for fresh and silk flowers.

	January	February	March	April	May	June
Fresh	$11,520	$22,873	$10,380	$12,562	$23,712	$15,816
Silk	$8,460	$14,952	$5,829	$10,621	$17,892	$7,583

14. What is the greatest value of fresh flowers? Of silk flowers?

15. What is the smallest value for fresh flowers? Of silk flowers?

16. What interval size would be most appropriate when making a bar graph? Why?
    a. $100   b. $1,000   c. $5,000   d. $10,000

Use the following data to answer Problems 17 and 18. The totals of the number of daisy-wheel printers sold in the years 1987 through 1992 by Smart Brothers Computer Store are as follows:

1987	1988	1989	1990	1991	1992
983	1,052	1,117	615	250	400

17. What is the smallest value? The greatest value?

18. Draw a line graph representing the data. Use an interval of 250. Be sure to include a title, explanation of the scales, and the like.

BUSINESS MATH IN ACTION

A look at statistics that shape the nation

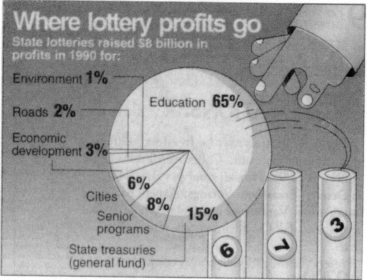

Where lottery profits go
State lotteries raised $8 billion in profits in 1990 for:

Environment **1%**

Roads **2%**

Economic development **3%**

Cities **6%**

Senior programs **8%**

State treasuries (general fund) **15%**

Education **65%**

Source: *Gaming and Wagering Business*

By Marty Baumann, USA TODAY

QUESTIONS

1. Find the amount of money allotted to each of the categories in the circle graph.

2. Verify that the percents in the graph total 100% and the dollar amounts in Problem 1 total 8 billion dollars.

ANSWERS TO ODD-NUMBERED EXERCISES

CHAPTER 1

Section 1.1

1. four thousand, two hundred nine 3. three hundred one million, nine 5. 400 7. 9,000 9. 830
11. 30,000 13. 28,000,000,000 15. 3,780,000
17. 5,180 19. 10,100,000 21. 400 23. 700,000
25. 20 27. 35 29. 28 31. 30,787 33. 1,832
35. 5,773 37. 44,014 39. 310,000 (estimate); 318,936 (exact) 41. 22,000 (estimate); 21,335 (exact) 43. 2,600 (estimate); 2,612 (exact) 45. 230 items 47. 469 dolls
49. 671 points 51. 541,679 53. 2,708,562
55. 3,988,906 57. 10,550,004 59. 200,000 (estimate); 182,902 (exact) 61. 8,000 (estimate); 7,310 (exact)
63. 75,000 (estimate); 74,385 (exact) 65. 73 tickets
67. 4,952,385 69. 782,878 71. 41,772
73. 6,938,694 75. 861,900 77. 16,500 79. 48,000
81. 30,000 83. 47,220,000 85. 162,000
87. 210,000 (estimate); 254,626 (exact) 89. 1,550,000 (estimate); 1,495,184 (exact) 91. 120 ribbons 93. 140 pieces 95. 42 R3 97. 52 R2 99. 804
101. 420 R2 103. 600 (estimate); 505 R161 (exact)
105. 119 countertops 107. 77 coins 109. 37 novels
111. 48 pages 113. 924 pencils 115. 40 plugs

Section 1.2

117. 20 R4, or $20\frac{2}{3}$ 119. 7 121. 8 R1, or $8\frac{1}{2}$
123. 12 R2, or $12\frac{2}{3}$ 125. 14 R22, or $14\frac{22}{25}$ 127. $\frac{35}{6}$
129. $\frac{13}{3}$ 131. $\frac{100}{3}$ 133. $\frac{5}{8}$ 135. $\frac{5}{6}$ 137. $\frac{7}{8}$
139. $\frac{3}{8}$ 141. $\frac{3}{4}$ 143. $\frac{2}{5}$ 145. $\frac{7}{9}$ 147. $\frac{5}{6}$ 149. $\frac{3}{5}$
151. $\frac{2}{3}$ 153. $\frac{13}{14}$ 155. $\frac{54}{72}$ 157. $\frac{10}{12}$ 159. $\frac{10}{15}$
161. $\frac{63}{77}$ 163. $\frac{117}{143}$ 165. $\frac{1}{7}$ 167. 48 169. 420
171. 1,008 173. $1\frac{3}{8}$ 175. $1\frac{5}{8}$ 177. $1\frac{29}{48}$
179. $2\frac{37}{144}$ 181. $2\frac{4}{5}$ 183. $20\frac{1}{2}$ 185. 16
187. $9\frac{5}{12}$ 189. $65\frac{1}{6}$ 191. $56\frac{1}{24}$ 193. $137\frac{59}{120}$
195. $22\frac{5}{8}$ feet 197. $\frac{1}{2}$ 199. $\frac{1}{2}$ 201. $\frac{17}{30}$ 203. $\frac{9}{14}$
205. $6\frac{1}{6}$ 207. $2\frac{1}{4}$ 209. $246\frac{13}{18}$ 211. $36\frac{7}{9}$
213. $68\frac{7}{8}$ 215. $91\frac{11}{12}$ 217. $2\frac{3}{8}$ feet 219. $\frac{7}{32}$
221. $\frac{5}{18}$ 223. $\frac{9}{20}$ 225. $3\frac{1}{3}$ 227. $2\frac{5}{8}$ 229. $\frac{5}{9}$
231. $\frac{7}{18}$ 233. $\frac{84}{125}$ 235. $\frac{8}{49}$ 237. $\frac{3}{41}$ 239. $37\frac{1}{10}$
241. $74\frac{47}{48}$ 243. $94\frac{2}{7}$ 245. $48 247. $4,110
249. $\frac{8}{5}$ 251. $\frac{4}{1}$, or 4 253. $\frac{4}{13}$ 255. $\frac{5}{8}$ 257. 3
259. $\frac{10}{21}$ 261. $\frac{1}{20}$ 263. $3\frac{3}{4}$ 265. $\frac{4}{7}$ 267. 32 pieces 269. $7\frac{3}{4}\%$ 271. $1\frac{1}{4}$ in. 273. 12 hr
275. $192 277. 4 full lengths

Section 1.3

279. five tenths 281. one hundred eight thousandths
283. two hundred seventy-five hundred-thousandths
285. seventeen and eight tenths 287. one hundred twenty-eight and twenty-three hundredths 289. five hundred and seven ten-thousandths 291. eight and one-third

hundredths 293. eight-three and one-third hundredths
295. 0.135 297. 380 299. 1,700 301. $175
303. 1.246 305. 165.8312 307. $20.93 total cost
309. 376.74 311. 57.4525 313. 135.6
315. 419.103 317. 325.74 319. 2.3068
321. 0.001474 323. $88.96 reduced 325. $92.61
327. 193.41 329. 50.076 331. 21.2352
333. 275.8 335. 198.74 337. 27,300 339. 17,454
341. 370,000 343. $12,850 345. 0.15 347. 2.187, or 2.19 349. 8.572, or 8.57 351. 33.766, or 33.77
353. 1559.789, or 1,559.79 355. 60713.235, or 60,713.24
357. 8.572 359. 0.019874 361. 0.0018
363. 37.49298 365. 0.0178 367. $0.989 (gasoline not rounded to hundreds) 369. $\frac{3}{4}$ 371. $\frac{16}{25}$ 373. $\frac{11}{2}$
375. 0.6 377. $0.12\frac{4}{8}$, or $0.12\frac{1}{2}$ 379. $0.44\frac{4}{9}$
381. 8.58 383. $21\frac{3}{5}$ 385. 0.1390, or 0.139
387. 10

Additional Problems

1. 303.28 ft 3. $0.76 5. 34.12 mi 7. 31.43 lb
9. $85.50 11. ending balance: $649.11 13. adjusted checkbook/statement balance: $6531.65 15. adjusted checkbook/statement balance: $580.13 17. adjusted checkbook/statement balance: $294.01 19. a. two deposits
b. $8.00 c. $700.81 d. seven checks e. $645.25
f. $1,100.57 g. $18.50 k. 6119

Trial Test

Section 1.1

1. 1,242 3. 44,978 5. 785 7. 62 9. five hundred three 11. 84,300 13. 80,000 15. 2,200
17. 45,000 19. 1,153 items

Section 1.2

1. $\frac{1}{6}$ 3. $\frac{7}{16}$ 5. $1\frac{19}{23}$ 7. $44\frac{13}{15}$ 9. $34\frac{1}{2}$ 11. $2\frac{7}{8}$
13. $310\frac{5}{6}$ 15. $47\frac{1}{5}$ 17. $209\frac{3}{4}$ 19. $107\frac{1}{2}$

Section 1.3

1. 30 3. 24.092 5. 224.857 7. 447.12
9. 89.82 11. 2,379.019 13. 179.24 15. 1.610, or 1.61 17. $\frac{17}{50}$ 19. 1.76 = degree drop in temperature

CHAPTER 2

Section 2.1

1. $296.83 3. deposit slip total: $894.96 5. ending balance: $4,278.24 7. ending balance: $933.71

Section 2.2

Trial Test

1. ending balance: $2,432.09 3. adjusted statement and checkbook balance: $1,589.10

CHAPTER 3

Section 3.1

1. subtraction **3.** division **5.** multiplication and subtraction **7.** $N = 17$ **9.** $N = 7$ **11.** $A = 12$ **13.** $N = 4$ **15.** $A = 24$ **17.** $X = 7$

Section 3.2

19. The number is 9. **21.** The number is 5. **23.** The amount of money spent on supplies is $96. **25.** 416 fan belts should be ordered. **27.** The amount spent on groceries is $57.50. **29.** Shaquita earns $8.75 each hour. **31.** Molly earns $272.32 for 37 hours of work. **33.** Wall paper for the kitchen will cost $116.73. **35.** The total weight of the shipment is 830 pounds. **37.** Each shirt was reduced by $3.02. **39.** There were 11 executive desks and 29 secretarial desks. **41.** There are 280 headlights purchased at a cost of $3,906. There are 720 taillights purchased at a total cost of $5,436.

Additional Problems

1. The raise is $663. **3.** Each small drum holds 18.25 gallons. **5.** Mr. Exum sold 8 autos. **7.** Mary's salary is $26,400. **9.** Art earns $5.00 per hour; Bart earns $5.50 per hour; Fargo earns $6.50 per hour.

Trial Test

1. addition **3.** multiplication **5.** $N = 11$ **7.** $A = 18$ **9.** $A = 5$ **11.** $N = 6$ **13.** The number is 26. **15.** The new salary is $285. **17.** 130 containers are needed. **19.** 116 ceramic cups and 284 plastic cups were sold. The value of the ceramic cups was $464. The value of the plastic cups was $994.

CHAPTER 4

Section 4.1

1. 23% **3.** 82% **5.** 3% **7.** 34% **9.** 60.1% **11.** 100% **13.** 300% **15.** 99% **17.** 20% **19.** 65% **21.** 304% **23.** 750% **25.** 81.1% **27.** 254% **29.** 39% **31.** 33.33% **33.** 3%

Section 4.2

35. 0.846 **37.** 0.52 **39.** 0.03 **41.** 0.0002 **43.** 0.09 **45.** $\frac{1}{5}$ **47.** $1\frac{7}{10}$ **49.** $3\frac{61}{100}$ **51.** 0.36 **53.** 0.06 **55.** 0.004 **57.** $\frac{1}{4}$ **59.** 3 **61. a.** $\frac{1}{3}$ **b.** 0.333 **63. a.** 12.5% **b.** $\frac{1}{8}$ **65. a.** 80% **b.** $\frac{4}{5}$ **67. a.** 62.5% **b.** 0.625

Section 4.3

69. $2.014 **71.** $36.25 **73.** 200% **75.** 6% **77.** 400 **79.** 5 **81.** 80% **83.** 11.52 **85.** 199% **87.** 400% **89.** 561.96 **91.** 20%

Section 4.4

93. 30 **95.** 210 **97.** 115 **99.** 800 **101.** $66\frac{2}{3}\%$ or 66.67% **103.** 33.33% **105.** 300% **107.** $1.80 tax **109.** 540 fuses were inspected. **111.** $1.60 tax paid **113.** 88.72% of the seats were filled. **115.** $37,800,000 **117.** $2,754.70 **119.** 15% **121.** $7.05

Additional Problems

1. $51.66 saved **3.** $9.71 new pay per hour **5.** $0.94 **7.** $6,373.91 original cost **9.** 890 shirts in stock

Trial Test

1. 0.24 **3.** 0.09 **5.** 0.275 **7.** 0.005 **9.** 0.00125 **11.** 24% **13.** 60% **15.** $37\frac{1}{2}\%$ or 37.5% **17.** $\frac{7}{8}$ **19.** $\frac{1}{3}$ **21.** 21% **23.** $37\frac{1}{2}\%$ or 37.5% **25.** 77.78% (rounded) **27.** $P = 0.26$ **29.** $P = 113$ **31.** $R = 250\%$ **33.** 100% of 32 is 32. **35.** $B = 2,130$ **37.** $B = 113$ **39.** $P = 2.52$ **41.** $R = 3\frac{1}{3}\%$ **43.** $R = 78\%$ **45.** $R = 10.34\%$ or 10% (rounded) **47.** $R = 60\%$ **49.** $B = \$15,333.33$ **51.** $R = 15\%$ raise

CHAPTER 5

Section 5.1

1. $425 **3.** 480 **5.** $1,076.40 **7.** Allen = $483.14 Brown = $206.26 Pick = $316.02 Sayer = $372.48 Lovet = $228.80 **9.** $200 **11.** $216.45 (gross weekly earnings) **13.** $486.15 **15.** $910 **17.** $400 **19.** $800 **21.** $7,800 **23.** $1,191.20 **25.** $334.64

Section 5.2

27. $0 **29.** $54 **31.** $22 **33.** $22.67 (tax) **35.** $132.40 **37.** FICA: 5.52; Medicare: $1.29 **39.** FICA: $22.82; Medicare: $5.34 **41.** FICA: $9.73; Medicare: $2.28 **43.** FICA: $1,488; Medicare: $348 **45.** FICA: $3,441.00; Medicare: $888.85

Employee	With-holding Tax	FICA	Medicare	Total Deduc-tions	Net Earnings
47. Abrams	$0	$ 8.99	$2.10	$33.10	$111.97
49. Mason	$0	$10.23	$2.39	$12.62	$152.38

51. $378

Additional Problems

1. $381.28 **3.** $160.27 **5.** $579 **7.** 360.00 **9.** $53.24

Trial Test

1. $354 **3.** $262.50 **5.** $126 **7.** $522 **9.** FICA: 922.40; Medicare: $5.24 **11.** $0 **13.** $221.27 **15.** net earnings: $173.90 **17.** net earnings: $255.82 **19.** net earnings: $194.05 **21.** $378 **23.** $0

CHAPTER 6

Section 6.1

1. $45 **3.** $25.50 **5.** $7.57 **7.** $102.50 **9.** $19.80 **11.** $94.50 **13.** $16.50 trade discount **15.** $18 **17.** $6.13 **19.** $336.03 **21.** $1.25; $23.75 **23.** $0.02; $.87 **25.** $357; $1,743 **27.** 95%; $399.95 **29.** 97%; $699.54

Section 6.2

31. 0.8 (0.9); 0.72; $144 **33.** 0.8 (0.85) (0.9); 0.612; $918 **35.** 0.85 (0.95); 0.8075; $323 **37.** $513 net price **39.** $2,592 net price **41.** 82%; 18% **43.** 65.02%; 34,98% **45.** 28% **47.** 16.21% **49.** 32% **51.** $595 is better deal; net price $570. **53.** table at $190 better deal; net price $169.10 **55.** $260 better deal; net price $189.54.

Section 6.3

57. No **59.** $3 **61.** $0.50 **63.** $161.70 **65. a.** $0.84 **b.** $28 **67. a.** $321.44 **b.** same as part (a). **c.** $328 **69.** $204.08 credited to account; $419.92 balance due

Additional Problems

1. 0.72675; 27.325% **3.** $1,673.25 **5.** the $25 set is the better deal **7.** $99.91 **9.** $306.12 credited to account; $438.88 outstanding balance

Trial Test

1. $110 trade discount **3.** $29.24 net price **5.** $250 chair is better deal; net price $200 **7.** 0.684 net decimal equivalent **9.** receipt of goods **11.** $1,080 net price **13.** end of month **15.** $2 cash discount **17.** $392 amount due **19.** $489.60 total net price **21.** $618.56 credited to account; $276.44 outstanding balance

CHAPTER 7

Section 7.1

1. 150%; $75 **3.** 200%; $41; $82 **5.** 58%; $52.48; $90.48 **7.** 85%; 100%; $45.33; $53.33 **9.** $6; $21 **11.** $C = \$36$; $R = 25\%$ **13.** markup = $39.80; markup % = 25.1% **15.** cost (B) = $24; $S = \$36$ **17.** $C = \$35.70$; $S = \$51$ **19.** markup % = 31.62%; markup amount = $18.50 **21.** $C = \$14$; $M = \$21$ **23.** $57; 56.14%; 35.96% **25.** $0.44; 28.21%; 22% **27.** $68.45; $95.83; 28.57% **29.** $49.60; $74.40; 60% **31.** $16.11; $2.84; 17.63% **33.** $1.89; $10.88; 17.37%

Section 7.2

35. amount of markdown = $4.48; markdown % = 15% **37.** markdown = $109.99; markdown % = 22.22% **39.** markdown = $82; sale price = $27.99 **41.** markdown = $179.20; sale price = $100.80 **43.** first reduction: markdown = $200; markdown percent = 16.68%; second reduction: markdown = $399.60; markdown percent = $599.40 **45.** $0.90

Additional Problems

1. $1.80 **3.** $15.75; $29.25 **5.** $9; $29 **7.** $14.00 **9.** $5; $30%

Trial Test

1. $7.16 **3.** $C = \$15.50$ (cost) **5.** $S = \$22.68$ **7.** $26.07 (discount) **9.** $S = \$126.75$ **11.** 25% (rounded) **13.** $S = \$160$ **15.** $48.74

CHAPTER 8

Section 8.1

1. $I = \$120$ **3.** $I = \$2,252.25$ **5.** $I = \$144$ **7.** $I = \$30,254.40$; total amount to be repaid = $45.534.40 **9.** $R = 15.5\%$ **11.** $R = 12.5\%$ **13.** $R = 15\%$ **15.** $T = 3$ years **17.** $T = 1\frac{1}{2}$ years **19.** $T = 2$ years **21.** $T = 9$ months **23.** $P = \$500$ **25.** $P = \$1,000$ **27.** $P = \$1,500$ **29.** $P = \$900$ **31.** $\frac{7}{12}$ year **33.** $\frac{4}{3}$ or 1.3333 years **35.** $\frac{1}{4}$ or 0.25 year **37.** $I = \$1,050$ **39.** $I = \$20$ **41.** $I = \$12$ **43.** $I = \$16$

Section 8.2

45. exact time **47.** 217 days **49.** 154 days **51.** 130 days **53.** 191 days **55.** 485 days **57.** ordinary: August 10; exact: August 8 **59.** ordinary: October 12; exact: 284 days **61.** ordinary: February 28: exact: February 26 **63. a.** $105 **b.** $103.56 **c.** $105 **65. a.** $51.67 **b.** $51.29 **c.** $52 **67.** Lida Jenkins **69.** $2,000 **71.** $90.50 **73.** $140.78 (discount); The proceeds at 14% are $50.28 less than the proceeds at 9%. **75.** $26.47 **77.** $10,032.77

Additional Problems

1. $220 **3.** $48 **5.** $40 **7.** $236.25 **9.** $39.59

Trial Test

1. $210 **3.** 20% **5.** 287 days **7.** 159 days **9.** $8,400 **11.** $28.14 **13.** $665 **15.** $21.25 **17.** 9 months **19.** 20% **21.** $462.50 **23.** $64 **25.** $169.01 **27.** $44.30

CHAPTER 9

Section 9.1

1. $166.40 **3.** $708.64 **5.** $189.90 difference **7.** 6.84848 **9.** $2,318.01 compound amount $318.01 compound interest **11.** $1,312.40 compound interest **13.** 12.36% **15.** $0.36 **17.** $15.01 compound interest $2,015.01 compound amount **19.** The 2-year investment yields the most interest ($339.72).

Section 9.2

21. $1,126.97 **23.** $574.37 **25.** $3,157.64 **27.** $154.16 **29.** $1,592.55 **31.** $2,913.80 **33.** $11,000 in 18 months is better.

Additional Problems

1. $2,375.10 **3.** $41.22 **5.** $17.32 **7.** $3,731.10 **9.** $4,781.07

Trial Test

1. $450.09 compound interest **3.** $3,979.45 compound interest **5.** $3,579.12 compound amount $579.12 compound interest **7.** 12.55% effective rate **9.** $30 compounded monthly, $29.73 compounded daily. **11.** $2,669.55 **13.** $2,951.58 **15.** $680 in 1 year is slightly better. **17.** Option 2 yields the greater return by $0.68. **19.** $1,006.60

CHAPTER 10

Section 10.1

1. $37,618 **3.** $2,730.13 **5.** $21,510.40 **7.** $4,917.15 **9. a.** $41,039.10 **b.** yes **11.** $109.336.50

Section 10.2

13. $37,240 **15.** $51,178.50 **17.** $663.43 **19.** $22.759.80 **21.** $490,900

Section 10.3

23. $10,311.07 **25.** $7,870.49 **27.** $17,708.46 **29.** $14,424.85 **31.** $7,500

Trial Test

1. $19,350.00 **3.** $41,739.13 **5.** $5,727.50 **7.** $60,819.20 **9.** $28,269.88 **11.** $104.74 **13.** $34,724.80

CHAPTER 11

Section 11.1

1. $5.81 **3.** 2.1% **5.** $85 monthly payment; $729 to be financed **7.** $577 **9.** $462.60

Section 11.2

11. $132.14 **13.** $91.54 **15.** $571.87 **17.** $358.63 **19.** $56.88 **21.** $26.94 **23.** $50.11

Section 11.3

25. $5.19 **27.** $187.50 finance charge; $1,687.50 total price; $140.63 monthly payment **29.** $8.75 finance charge; $611.61 unpaid balance

Section 11.4

31. 26.7% **33.** 26.6% **35.** 21.50% **37.** 20.50% **39.** 14.25%

Section 11.5

41. $77,600 **43.** $882.31 **45.** $188,630.80 **47.** $711.33 interest; $170.98 principal

49.

Payment Number	Interest	Portion to: Principal	Balance Owed
1	$711.33	$28.20	$77.571.80
2	$711.07	$28.46	$77,543.34
3	$710.81	$28.72	$77,514.62

51. $64,175.20

Additional Problems

1. $60.50　**3.** $19.21　**5.** $276.53　**7.** 39.8%
9. 21.5%

Trial Test

1. $34　**3.** $36　**5.** 22.2%　**7.** $2.89　**9.** $12.60
11. 22.5%　**13.** $236.58　**15.** $158.33　**17.** $\frac{23}{98}$
19. $427.84

21.

Payment	Principal	Interest	Balance
$1,045.00	$253.33	$711.67	$99,746.67
$1,045.00	$255.34	$789.66	$99,491.33

CHAPTER 12

Section 12.1

1. $12,000　**3.** $2,300　**5.** $1,900　**7.** $4,500
9. $1,000　**11.** $800

Section 12.2

13. $0.084　**15.** $0.25; $1,750　**17.** $0.40; $3,200
19. $0.50; $2,080　**21.** $0.11　**23.** $0.18
25. $827.82　**27.** $3,948

Section 12.3

29. 78　**31.** 3　**33.** 210　**35.** 820
37. depreciation amount each year: $3,666.67; $3,208.33;
$2,750.00; $2,291.67; $1,833.33; $1,375.00; $916.67; $458.33

Section 12.4

39. a. 0.090909　**b.** 0.181818　**41.** Accumulated
Depreciation each year end: $1,062.50; $1,992.19; $2,805.67;
$3,517.46; $4,140.28; $4,685.25; $5,162.09; $5,579.33
43. Accumulated Depreciation each year end: $14,000.00;
$18,666.67; $20,000.00

Section 12.5

45. $6,839.04; $6,839.04; $6,839.04　**47.** $1,160; $1,856;
$1,113.60; $668.16; $668.16; $334.08　**49.** $1,089.89;
$2,543.41; $3,027.70; $3,270.00

Additional Problems

1. $4,823　**3.** $977.50　**5.** $4,104

7.

	Depreciation Rate	Depreciation Amount	Accumulated Depreciation	Book Value
1	$\frac{4}{10}$	$3,000	$3,000	
2	$\frac{3}{10}$	$2,250	$5,250	
3	$\frac{2}{10}$	$1,500	$6,750	
4	$\frac{1}{10}$	$ 750	$7,500	

9. $2,310

Trial Test

1. 28　**3.** $14,900　**5.** $0.07264　**7. a.** 300
b. 378　**9. a.** 8.33%　**b.** 16.67%　**11.** $2,859.71
13. $2,232.21

CHAPTER 13

Section 13.1

1. $8,112　**3.** $4,291　**5.** ending inventory: $3,558.94;
cost of goods sold: $4,553.06　**7.** ending inventory: $4,308;
cost of goods sold: $3,804

Section 13.2

9. $3,234　**11.** 0.5 times　**13.** 4.6 times

Section 13.3

15. $2,231.76; $2,017.17; $2,798.28; $2,090.13; $862.66

Trial Test

1. $1,237　**3.** $476　**5.** $761.76, ending inventory;
$475.24, cost of goods sold　**7.** $892, ending inventory;
$345, cost of goods sold　**9.** furniture: $2,222.23; computer
supplies: $1,777.78; consumable office supplies: $2,777.78;
leather goods: $1,333.33; administrative services: $888.89
11. 2.92 times

CHAPTER 14

Section 14.1

1. $11,271, total current assets; $23,458, total assets; $3,098,
total current liabilities; $3,098, total liabilities; $23,458, total
liabilities and owner's equity　**3.** Increase (decrease)
amount column: $190; $1,088; (518); $760; $1,266; $60; $1,326;
($566); $760　Increase (decrease) percent column: 8.7%; 25.4%;
(3.2)%; 3.4%; 20.7%; 6.2%; 18.7%; (3.7%); 3.4%　Percent of total
assets—19X6 column: 10.2%; 23.0%; 66.8%; 100.0%; 31.6%;
4.4%; 36.0%; 64.0%; 100.0%　Percent of total assets—19X5
column: 9.7%; 19.0%; 71.3%; 100.0%; 27.1%; 4.3%; 31.4%;
68.8%; 100.0%

Section 14.2

5. $225,108, net sales; $112,229, cost of goods sold; $112,879,
gross profit from sales; $61,689, total operating expenses;
$51,190, net income.　Percent of net sales column: 106.1%,
6.1%, 100%, 11.5%, 48.8%, 10.4%, 49.9%, 50.1%, 18.9%, 3.8%,
0.7%, 1.3%, 0.4%, 0.9%, 1.5%, 27.4%, 22.7%　**7.** Increase
(decrease) amount column: $15,834; ($926); $16,760; $3,305;
$10,214; $2,503; $11,016; $5,744; $2,000; $0; ($111); $300;
($500); $1,689; $4,055　Increase (decrease) percent column:
5.7%; (13.6%); 6.2%; 10.1%; 6.9%; 8.3%; 7.4%; 4.8%; 5.0%; 0%;
(5.3%); 9.1%; (11.1%); 3.1%; 6.2%

Section 14.3

9. 1.57 to 1　**11.** 1.39 to 1　**13.** 0.87 to 1
15. 1.29:1　**17.** operating ratio: 0.9 or 90%; gross profit
margin: 0.25 or 25%　**19.** 0.893 or 89.3%　**21.** 0.201 or
20.1%

Trial Test

1. 19X7 column: $74,059, total current assets; $44,817, total
plant and equip.; $118,876, total assets; $5,954, total current
liabilities; $34,917, total long-term liabilities; $40,871, total
liabilities; $118,876, total liabilities and owner's equity. 19X6
column:$68,478, total current assets; $41,917, total plant and
equip.; $110,395, total assets; $5,187, total current liabilities;
$36,510, total long-term liabilities; $41,697, total liabilities;
$110,395, total liabilities and owner's equity. Increase or
decrease columns: $2,035, 38.5%; $139, 4.6%; $3,407, 5.7%;
$5,581, 8.2%; (970, 2.6%); $3,870, 88.2%; $2,900, 6.9%, $8,481,
7.7%; $611, 13.4%; $156, 25.0%; $767, 14.8%; ($1,593, 4.4%);
($1,593, 4.4%); ($826, 2.0%); $9,307, 13.5%; $8,481, 7.7%.
3. 1.76 to 1　**5.** 1.60 to 1　**7.** 0.64 or 64% for both 19X6
and 19X7

CHAPTER 15

Section 15.1

1. $273.60, $124.80　**3.** $545.20, $237.69　**5.** $661.50,
$508　**7.** $20,754.18　**9.** $46,928.78　**11.** $30,000
13. $562.50　**15.** $58,800　**17.** $286.74
19. a. $483.82　**b.** $246.75　**21.** $300　**23.** $366
25. $418　**27.** $361　**29.** $10,000　**31.** $177.50
33. a. $81.75　**b.** $327　**35. a.** $295　**b.** $50,000
medical expenses; $5,678 property damage; $55,678 total

Section 15.2

21. $300　**23.** $366　**25.** $418　**27.** $361
29. $10,000　**31.** $177.50　**33. a.** $81.75　**b.** $327
35. a. $295　**b.** $50,000 medical expenses; $5,678
property damage; $55,678 total

Section 15.3

37. $2,139.20 **39.** $3,368 **41.** $2,346.50; $205.32; $610.09 **43.** $1,197.60; $104.79; $311.38 **45.** $3,191; $279.21; $829.66 **47.** $40,000; $0 **49.** $1,429.20; $21,438 **51.** $324 **53.** $69.51

Additional Problems

1. $200 **3.** 21,500 **5.** $50,000 medical; $6,325 property; $56,325 total **7.** $48,300 medical; $10,000 property; $3,500 paid by Mr. Moto **9.** $25,000; $0

Trial Test

1. $2,078.60 **3.** $65,625 **5.** $181.65 **7.** $53 more **9.** $727.42 **11.** explanations will vary **13.** $71.52 **15.** $425 **17.** 69% **19.** $177.50

CHAPTER 16

Section 16.1

1. $0.18 **3.** $0.63 **5.** $0.37 **7.** $0.77 **9.** $0.51 **11.** $14.25 **13.** $58.24 **15.** $33.80 **17.** $26.14 **19.** $332.33 **21.** $84.31

Section 16.2

23. $94,000 **25.** $37,500 **27.** $555 **29.** $250 **31.** $2,125 **33.** $1,487.50; $178.50 **35.** $500 **37.** $882.50 **39.** $527.25 **41.** $2,799.68 **43.** $1,108.63 **45.** 0.063 **47.** $812.50 **49.** $3,732.83 **51.** $2,177.50 **53.** $0.05; $4.97; $49.73

Section 16.3

55. $10,055 **57.** $11,551 **59.** $47,800 **61.** $2,959 **63.** $2,111 **65.** $2,546 **67.** $4,271 **69.** $10,827.68 **71.** $10,787

Additional Problems

1. $3,572.75 **3.** $62.75 **5.** $705.20 **7.** $10,112 **9.** $960

Trial Test

1. $0.76 (rounded) **3.** $22.28 (rounded) **5.** $198.44 **7.** $17.61 (rounded) **9.** $50 (rounded) **11.** $97.62 **13.** $39,471.64 (rounded) **15.** $1,071.77 (rounded) **17.** $4,073.34 **19.** $1,850.40 **21.** $4,142.77 **23.** $46,400

CHAPTER 17

Section 17.1

1. a. 3,825,400 **b.** $33\frac{1}{2}$ points ($33.50) **c.** 73 ($73) **d.** $75\frac{1}{2}$ ($75.50) **3. a.** $1.65; $82.50; $165 **b.** $72\frac{7}{8}$ (72.875) **c.** 2.26% **5.** A's yield 20%; B's yield 2%; A's yield is higher **7.a.** $30,000 **b.** $30,000 **c.** $440,000 **d.** $2.20 per share **9.** 12.5 or 13 **11. a.** $41.93 **b.** $1,976.93 **13. a.** Gain: $2,014.67 **b.** ROI: 104.34%

Section 17.2

15. a. 19 **b.** $78.75 **c.** 2007 **17. a.** $1,018.75 **b.** $955.00 **19.** $161.25 **21.** $10,250.00 **23. a.** $90 **b.** $540 **c.** $545 **25.** AmGeni yield is higher **27.** Yield for C: $7\frac{1}{2}$%; Yield for D: $8\frac{1}{2}$%; Bond D has the greater yield.

Additional Problems

1. a. $103.81 **b.** $4,822.56 **3. a.** $30 **b.** $4,680 **5. a.** 25 **b.** 30 **c.** 23 **7.** Premium bond sells for more than face value. Discount bond sells for less than face value. Corporate bond is issued by a corporation. **9.** 1%

Trial Test

1. a. 1 point or 1.00 **b.** $66.75 per share **c.** $67.50 per share **d.** 76,300 **3. a.** $131.30 **b.** $6,191.30 **5.** 28.5% **7.** Stock A: 4.9%; Stock B: 4.2% **9. a.** 1995 **b.** $898.75 per bond **c.** $895 **d.** discount **11. a.** $25 **b.** $4,275 **13.** preferred **15. a.** Stock A: 15%, Stock B: 12% **b.** Stock A

CHAPTER 18

Section 18.1

1. 795 **3.** 3,997 **5.** 2,531 **7.** Period 5 **9.** 54.4%

Section 18.2

11. 19X1: $65,153; 19X2: $68,324 **13.** (b) **15.** 70° **17.** (b) **19.** (c) **21.** 276° **23.** Automobile Dealership's New and Repeat Business

Section 18.3

25. Range: 32, mean: 74.33, median: 71, no mode **27.** Range: 6, mean: 14.43, median: 15, mode: 12

Additional Problems

1. Saturday; Monday **3.** Brown; Ulster **5.** 15.1% **7.** 80.2% **9.** range: 0.17 kg; mean: 1.145 kg; median: 1.125 kg; mode: 1.1 kg

Trial Test

1. 77 **3.** 29.5 **5.** 110 **7.** 165 **9.** $120 **11.** 33.3% **13.** Labor: 135°, materials: 120°, overhead: 105° **15.** $5,829 **17.** Smallest: 250, greatest: 1,117

INDEX

Glossary terms are defined on the page on which they occur. Glossary terms and their page numbers are indicated in blue in the Index.

Accelerated cost-recovery system (ACRS), 373
Accounts payable, 426
Accounts receivable, 425
Acid-test ratio (quick rqatio), 438
ACRS (accelerated cost-recovery system), 373
Addends, 4
Addition, decimals, 20
  fractions, 12–14
  key words in equations, 104
  whole numbers, 4
Adjustable-rate mortgage, 343
Adjusted bank statement balance, 74
Adjusted checkbook balance, 74
Adjusted gross income, 487
Amortization of a loan, 344
Amortize, 285
Amount of an annuity, 306
Annual percentage rate (APR), 338
Annual percentage rates, 338–43
Annuities, 306–28
  amount of an annuity, 307–11
  amount of annuity due, 308–11
  amount of ordinary annuity, 307–08
  present value, 311–12
  sinking funds, 313–14
  summary, 315–16
Annuity, 306
Annuity certain, 307
Annuity date, 307
APR (annual percentage rate), 338
Assessed value, 483
Assets, 363, 425
ATM (automatic teller machine), 73
Automatic teller machine (ATM), 73
Average daily balance, 336

Balance sheet, 425–32
  assets, 425–26
  comparative balance sheet, 429–32
  horizontal analysis, 430–32
  liabilities, 426
  owner's equity, 426
  preparation, 426–27
  ratios, 437–39
  summary, 441
  vertical analysis, 427–30
Bank discount, 261
Bank reconciliation, 73
Bank records, 66–97
  reconciling a checking account, 71–77

summary, 78–79
using checking account forms, 67–71
Bank statement, 71
  reading, 71–73
  reconciling with checkbook, 73–77
Banker's rule, 258
Bar graph, 536
Bar graphs, 536
Base, 137
Base, solving for, 138–39, 142–43
Basic calculations, 1–65
  decimals, 18–26
  fractions, 8–18
  summary, 26–31
  whole numbers, 2–8
Bill of lading, 201
Bond, 513
Bond market, 514
Bonds, 513–17
  bond listings, 514–15
  cost of buying and selling, 515
  current yield, 515–16
  summary, 518–19
Book value, 365

Carrying charge (finance charge), 330
Cash discount, 196
Cash discounts, 196–202
Cash price, 330
Catalog price, 191
Check, 67
Checking accounts, endorsing a checking, 69–70
  filling out a check stub, 68–69
  making out a check, 67–69
  making out a deposit slip, 67
  reading a bank statement, 71–73
  reconciling an account, 71–77
  using a check register, 69
Check register, 69
Check stub, 68
Circle graph, 538
Circle graphs, 538–40
Coinsurance clause, 456
Collateral, 343
Collision insurance, 458
Commission, 164
  plus salary, 164
  straight, 164
Common stock, 506
Comparative balance sheet, 429

Comparative income statement, 436
Complement, 192
Compound amount, 285
Compound interest, 248, 285, 284–305
  annuities, 306–14
  calculating, 285–86
  compounding daily, 290
  effective rate, 289
  future value, 285–91
  periods less than year, 288–89
  present value, 291–93
  summary, 294–95
  using a table, 287–88
Comprehensive insurance, 458
Constant ratio formula, 338
Consumer credit, 329–62
  annual percentage rates, 338–43
  home mortgages, 343–47
  installment loans, 330–32
  open-end credit, 334–38
  rule of 78, 332–34
  summary, 347–48
Contingent annuity, 307
Conventional mortgage, 343
Corporate bond, 513
Cost, 217
Cumulative preferred stock, 508
Current assets, 425
Current liabilities, 426
Current ratio (working capital ratio), 437

Date of maturity, 332
Decimal fraction, 18
Decimals, 18–26
  adding, 20
  converting fractions to decimals, 24
  converting fractions to percents, 133–34
  converting percents to decimals, 134–36
  converting percents to fractions, 136–37
  converting to fractions, 23–24
  converting to percents, 132–33
  dividing, 22–23
  multiplying, 20–21
  nonterminating (repeating), 24
  place-value chart, 18
  rounding, 18–19
  subtracting, 20

Decimals (*cont.*)
summary, 30–31
terminating, 24
Declining-balance depreciation, 369–72
Deductible amount, 459
Deductions, 487
Deductions (payroll), 165–75
finding employer's taxes, 173–75
finding Medicare tax, 170–73
finding Social Security tax, 170–73
finding unemployment taxes, 173–75
finding withholding tax by percentage, 168–70
finding withholding tax by table, 166–68
Degree, 539
Denominator, 9
Deposit slip, 67
Deposits in transit, 73
Depreciation, 363–92
accelerated cost-recovery system, 373–74
declining-balance method, 369–72
modified accelerated cost-recovery system, 374–76
straight-line method, 364–65
sum-of-the-years' digits method, 367–369
summary, 376–78
units-of-production method, 366–67
Difference, 5
Difference, in word problems, 105, 106
Differential piece rate, 163
Discount, 190
Discount bond, 514
Discounted note, 263
Discount rate, 191
Discounts, 190–216
cash discounts, 196–202
discounted note, 263–64
end of month (EOM), 199
freight terms, 201–2
net decimal equivalent, 194–95
ordinary dating method, 197–99
partial payments, 200–1
promissory notes, 261–65
receipt of goods (ROG), 200
simple discount note, 261–63
single discount equivalent, 195–96
single trade discounts, 190–93
summary, 203–05
trade discount series, 193–96
Discount, simple, 261–65
Dividend, 7, 506
Dividends in arrears, 508
Division, decimals, 22–23
fractions, 16–17
key words in equations, 104
whole numbers, 7–8
Divisor, 7
Double-declining-balance depreciation, 370
Down payment, 330
Due date, 256

Effective rate, 289
Employer's taxes, 173–75
End-of-month (EOM) discount, 199
Endorse, 69
Endowment insurance, 460
EOM (end-of-month) discount, 199
Equality, key words in equtions, 104
Equation, 98
proportion, 107

Equations, converting word problems into, 104–8
customary notation, 100
key words, 104
multiple use of unknown, 102
removing parentheses, 102–103
solving, 99–102
solving a simple, 99–100
solving with multiple operations, 100–1
summary, 108–10
using to solve problems, 98–130
writing, 104–8
Estimated life (useful life), 363
Exact interest, 254
Exact time, 254–58
Excise tax, 479, 481–82
summary, 493
Exemption (withholding allowance), 165
Exemptions 487

Face value (par value), 261, 506, 513, 454
FDIC (Federal Deposit Insurance Corporation), 75–76
Federal Deposit Insurance Corporation (FDIC), 75–76
Federal Insurance Contributions Act tax (FICA), 170
Federal unemployment tax (FUTA), 173
Federal withholding tax (FWT), 165
FICA (Federal Insurance Contributions Act) tax, 170
FIFO (first-in, first-out) inventory method, 396
Filing status, 487
Finance charge (carrying charge), 330
Financial ratio, 437
Financial statements, 424–53
acid-test ratio, 438–39
balance sheet, 425–32
current ratio, 437–38
gross profit margin ratio, 439–40
income statements, 433–37
operating ratio, 439
ratios, 437–41
summary, 441–42
Fire insurance, 455–57
calculating rates, 455–56
coinsurance, 456–57
insurance summary, 464–65
First-in, first-out (FIFO) inventory method, 396
Fixed-rate mortgage, 343
FOB shipping point, 201
Formula, percentage, 137–40
Formula, rearranging, 137
Fraction line, 9
Fractions, 8–18
adding, 12–14
converting decimals to fractions, 23–24
converting fractions to whole or mixed numbers, 9
converting mixed numbers to improper fractions, 10
converting to decimals, 24
converting to percents, 133–34
decimal, 18–26
dividing, 16–18
multiplying, 15–16
reducing to lowest terms, 10–11
rewriting in higher terms, 11–12

subtracting, 14–15
summary, 27–30
FUTA (federal unemployment tax), 173
Future value, 285–91
compounding interest daily, 290
compound interest for less than year, 288–89
finding effective rate, 289
using compound interest table, 287–88
using compound interest to calculate, 285–86
FWT (federal withholding tax), 165

Graph, 536
Graphs, 536–40
bar graphs, 536
circle graphs, 538–40
line graphs, 536–38
summary, 544–45
tables, and statistics, 533–56
Greatest common divisor (GCD), 11
Gross earnings (gross pay), 161
Gross income, 486
Gross loss, 218
Gross margin, 433
Gross pay (gross earnings), 161
calculating, 162–65
commission payments, 164
for piecework, 163–64
of salaried personnel, 162
of workers paid hourly, 162–63
Gross profit, 217, 433
Gross profit margin ratio, 439

Home mortgages, 343–47
Horizontal analysis, 430
Hourly rate (hourly wage), 162

Improper fraction, 9
Income statement, 433
Income statements, 433–37
Income statements, comparative income statements, 436–37
preparation, 433–37
ratios, 439–40
vertical analysis, 434–36
Income tax, 486
Income taxes, 486–92
summary, 393–94
taxable income, 487
tax rate schedules, 490–92
tax tables, 488–90
Installment loan, 329
Installment loans, 330–32
Installment or total price, 330
Insurance, 454–77
calculating rates, 455–56, 460–63
coinsurance, 456–57
fire insurance, 455–57
life insurance, 459–63
motor vehicle insurance, 458–59
summary, 463–65
Insured, 454
Insurer, 454
Interest, 248
compound, 285–90
simple, 248–61
Interest period, 285
Inventory, 393–403
Inventory, 394
FIFO (first-in, first-out) method, 396–97
LIFO (last-in, last-out) method, 397–98

overhead, 403–6
retail method, 398–400
specific-identification method, 395–96
summary, 407–9
turnover, 401–3
weighted-average method, 396
Inventory turnover, 401
Itemized deductions, 487

Last-in, last-out (LIFO) inventory
method, 397
Least common denominator (LCD),
12–15
Liabilities, 426
Liability insurance, 458
Life insurance, 459–63
calculating premiums, 460–63
summary, 463
types of insurance, 460
LIFO (last-in, last-out) inventory
method, 397
Limited-payment life insurance, 460
Line graph, 536
Line graphs, 536–38
List price, 191
Long-term liabilities, 426

MACRS (modified accelerated
cost-recovery system), 374
Maker, 261
Markdown, 218, 225–29
calculating a series, 226–27
perishable or seasonal items, 227–28
summary, 231
Marked price, 482
Market value, 483
Marketable securities, 438
Markup, 217–24, 226–29
based on cost, 218–20
based on selling price, 221–23
calculating a series, 226–27
comparisons based on cost and selling
price, 223–24
formula with selling price and cost,
218
perishable or seasonal items, 227–28
summary, 229–31
Maturity date, 513
Maturity value, 250
Mean, 541–42
Median, 542
Medicare tax, 171–73
Mill, 484
Minuend, 5
Mixed number, 9
Mode, 542–43
Modified accelerated cost-recovery
system (MACRS), 374–76
Mortgage, 343
Mortgage payable, 426
Motor vehicle insurance, 458–59
summary, 464
Multiplicand, 5
Multiplication, decimals, 20–21
fractions, 15–16
key words in equations, 104
of, 105
twice, 106
whole numbers, 5–7
Multiplier, 5

Net decimal equivalent, 194
Net earnings (net pay), 161
Net income, 433

Net loss, 218
Net pay (net earnings), 161
Net price, 191
Net profit, 218, 433
Net sales, 433
No-fault insurance, 458
Nonsufficient funds (NSF), 73
Nonterminating or repeating decimal, 24
Nonzero digit, 4
Notation, used in writing equations, 100
Notes payable, 426
Notes receivable, 425
NSF (nonsufficient funds fee), 73
Numerator, 9

Of, in word problems, 105
Open-end credit, 334–38
average daily balance method, 336–38
unpaid balance method, 335–36
Open-end loan, 329
Operating expenses, 217
Operating ratio, 439
Ordinary annuity, 307
Ordinary interest, 254
Ordinary time, 254–58
Outstanding checks, 73
Overhead, 403–6
based on floor space, 405–6
based on total sales, 404–5
summary 410–11
Overtime rate, 162
Owner's equity, 426

Par value (face value), 506, 513
Parentheses, in equations, 102–3
Partial product, 5–7
Payee, 68, 261
Payor, 68
Payroll, 161–89
calculating gross pay, 162–65
determining deductions, 165–75
finding Social Security and Medicare
taxes, 170–73
finding unemployment taxes, 173–75
finding withholding tax by percentage,
168–70
finding withholding tax by table,
166–68
gross pay based on commission, 164
gross pay for piecework, 163–64
gross pay of salaried personnel, 162
gross pay of workers paid hourly,
162–63
reading a pay stub, 174
summary, 176–77
Pay stub, reading, 174
Pay, take-home, 161
Percents, 131–60
converting decimals to percents,
132–33
converting fractions to percents,
133–34
converting to decimals, 134–36
converting to decimals and fractions,
134–37
converting to fractions, 136–37
solving formula for base, 138–39
solving formula for portion, 138
solving formula for rate, 140
solving problems, 140–45
solving problems for base, 142–43
solving problems for portion, 141–42
solving problems for rate, 143–45
summary, 145–46
using percentage formula, 137–40

Periodic inventory, 394
Perpetual inventory, 394
Piecework rate, 163
Place-value system, 2–3
Plant and equipment, 425
Policy, 454
Policyholder, 454
Portion, 137–38, 141–52
PR (price-earnings) ratio, 510
Preferred stock, 506
Premium, 454
Premium bond, 514
Present value, 291–93
annuities, 311–12
calculating, 291–92
using a table, 292–93
Present value of an annuity, 311
Price-earnings (PE) ratio, 510
Principal, 248
Problem solving, with equations, 98–130
Proceeds, 261
Product, 5
partial, 5–7
Promissory note, 261
Promissory notes, 261–65
discounted note, 263–64
simple discount note, 261–63
Proper fraction, 9
Property tax, 483–86
calculating, 484–85
determining tax rate, 485–86
rate, 484
summary, 493
Proportion, 107

Quick current assets, 438
Quick ratio (acid-test ratio), 438
Quotient, 7

Range, 540–41
Rate, 137, 248
solving for, 140, 143–45
Ratios to net sales, 439
Real property, 343
Receipt of goods (ROG) discount, 200
Reciprocals, 17
Reduced price, 218
Refund fraction, 332
Remainder, 7
Repeating or nonterminating decimal, 24
Restricted endorsement, 70
Retail method (of determining
inventory), 398
Return on investment (ROI), 512
Returned check, 73
Returned check fee, 73
Revolving charge accounts, 334
ROG (receipt of goods) discount, 200
ROI (return on investment), 512
Rule of 78, 332–34

Salary, 162
Salary plus commission, 164
Sales tax, 479–81
summary, 492
Salvage value (scrap value), 363
Scrap value (salvage value), 363
Selling price, 217
Semimonthly, 162
Service charge, 72
Share, 506
Simple discounts, 261–65
discounted note, 263–64
promissory notes, 261–65

Simple discounts (*cont.*)
  simple discount note, 261–63
  summary, 267–68
Simple interest, 248–61
  fractional parts of year, 250–51
  maturity value of loan, 250
  ordinary and exact time, 254–58
  summary, 266–67
  using formula, 249–54
  using table, 259–61
Single discount equivalent, 195
Single discount rate, 191
Single trade discounts, 190–93
Sinking fund, 313–4
Social Security tax (SS), 170–73
Specific identification inventory
  method, 395
SS (Social Security tax), 170
Standard deduction, 487
State unemployment tax (SUTA), 173
Statistic, 540
Statistics, 540–43
  mean, 541–42
  median, 542
  mode, 542–43
  range, 540–41
  summary, 545
  tables, and graphs, 533–56
Stock, 506
Stock broker, 506
Stock certificate, 506
Stock market, 506
Stocks, 506–13
  cost of buying and selling, 511
  dividends, 508–9
  price-earnings ratio, 510–11
  return on investment, 512
  stock listings, 507–8
  summary, 517–18
  yield, 509–10
Straight commission, 164

Straight-life (ordinary life)
  insurance, 460
Straight-line depreciation, 364–65
Straight-line rate, 370
Subtraction, decimals, 20
  difference, 105, 106
  fractions, 14–15
  key words in equations, 104
  whole numbers, 4–5
Subtrahend, 4–5 (5)
Suggested retail price, 191
Sum, or total, 4
Sum-of-the-years'-digits
  depreciation, 367–69
SUTA (state unemployment tax), 173

Table, 533
Tables, 533–35
  summary, 544
Tax, 478
Tax rate schedules, 490
Taxable income, 487
Taxes, 161–89, 478–504
  employer's taxes, 173–75
  excise tax, 481–82
  income taxes, 486–92
  Medicare tax, 170–73
  property tax, 483–86
  sales tax, 479–81
  Social Security tax, 170–73
  summary, 176–77, 492–94
  unemployment taxes, 173–75
  withholding tax, 166–70
Term, 261
Term insurance, 460
Terminating decimal, 24
Time, 248
Total, in word problems, 106
Total or installment price, 330
Total, or sum, 4
Total price, 482

Total sales, 433
Trade, 506
Trade discount, 191
Trade discount series, 193–96
Turnover, 401–3
  summary, 409
Twice, in word problems, 106

Underwriter, 454
Undiscounted note, 262
Unemployment taxes, finding, 173–75
Units-of-production depreciation,
  366–67
Unknown, 98
  multiple use of, 102
Unpaid balance, 335
Useful life (estimated life), 363

Vertical analysis, 427

Wages payable, 426
Weighted-average inventory method,
  396
Whole numbers, 2–8
  adding, 4
  dividing, 7–8
  multiplying, 5–7
  place-value chart, 2
  reading, 2–3
  rounding, 3
  subtracting, 4–5
  summary, 26–27
Withholding allowance (exemption),
  165
Withholding tax, 166–70
Working capital, 437
Working capital ratio (current ratio),
  437

Yield, 509, 515